Eyewitness Accounts of the American Revolution

Alexander Graydon's Memoirs of His Own Time

Edited by John Stockton Littell

The New York Times & Arno Press

GRAYDON'S

MEMOIRS OF HIS OWN TIME.

Sic ego sim ; liceatque caput canescere canis,
    Temporis et prisci facta referre senem.—TIBULLUS.

MEMOIRS

OF

HIS OWN TIME.

WITH

REMINISCENCES

OF THE

MEN AND EVENTS

OF THE

REVOLUTION.

BY

ALEXANDER GRAYDON.

EDITED BY

JOHN STOCKTON LITTELL,

MEMBER OF THE HISTORICAL SOCIETY OF PENNSYLVANIA.

PHILADELPHIA:
LINDSAY & BLAKISTON.
1846.

GRIGGS & CO., PRINTERS.

CONTENTS.

CHAPTER I.

CHAPTER II.

A*

CHAPTER III.

CHAPTER IV.

CHAPTER V.

CHAPTER VI.

CHAPTER VII.

CHAPTER VIII.

CHAPTER IX.

CHAPTER X.

CHAPTER XI.

CHAPTER XII.

CHAPTER XIII.

CHAPTER XIV.

CHAPTER XV.

CHAPTER XVI.

APPENDIX.

X   CONTENTS.

EDITOR'S INTRODUCTION.

No apology will be offered by the Editor for the republication of this volume. The candid and intelligent reader, whatever may be his political predilections, who, in the spirit of honourable inquiry, seeks only for truth, who can value manly sincerity, and appreciate the importance of the subjects truthfully and gracefully discussed by its accomplished Author, would feel his understanding insulted, and his taste and judgment questioned, by any such attempt.

Five and thirty years have elapsed since, at an obscure, provincial press, the first edition of this Work was anonymously, issued, and left to win its way, by slow degrees, and without any of the adventitious aids so abundantly characteristic of the present time, to public notice and favour. It was, moreover, at that comparatively early period of our national being, a far more serious enterprize to write and to publish a book, even of the modest dimensions of this, than can easily be conceived by those who only regard, with feelings approaching to wonder, the rapid and endless multiplications of the press at this more prosperous and more literary era. In addition to these disadvantages, although its respectable printer availed himself of such facilities for its external decoration as his, then, remote position enabled him to command, the appearance of the volume was singularly unattractive and defective. To these formidable obstacles to its success may be superadded yet another. The title,—a most important feature in the mystery of authorship,—failed to convey a just idea of its character and scope, and it dropped, unheeded, from the press.* The personal friends of the Author,—and they were numerous and warmly attached,—it is true encouraged the publication of the Work by liberal subscriptions for copies, which, to some extent, were subsequently distributed as gifts; but its sale, at the book-stores, was extremely restricted, and scantily contributed to the liquidation of expenses incurred.

This edition is presented to the public with a title somewhat modified, but, as the Editor conceives, more expressive and appropriate; and this is the only freedom, in the way of alteration, he has presumed to take.

The personal nature of these Memoirs has left but little for the Editor to add, in regard to their estimable Author; who has, with an unrestrained and a steady hand, frankly delineated his own character throughout the work. This, at all times, an extremely delicate and difficult task, is said, by those who knew him well, to have been faithfully accomplished; and although there was little beyond the limits of habitual and gentlemanly propriety for

---

* The original title was as follows:—

"Memoirs of a Life, Chiefly Passed in Pennsylvania, within the Last Sixty Years, with Occasional Remarks upon the General Occurrences, Character and Spirit of that Eventful Period. Harrisburgh: Printed by John Wyeth. 1811."

him to expose in the way of confession, that confession has been honestly and courageously made.

In the year 1785, having received, from the Executive Committee of Pennsylvania, an appointment to the Prothonotaryship of the newly organized county of Dauphin, MR. GRAYDON removed to Harrisburgh for the purpose of entering upon the duties of his office, which he continued to perform in a manner alike creditable to himself and advantageous to the public, until his sudden expulsion by Governor McKean,—to whom belongs the unenviable distinction of being the father of political proscription in the United States. He then retired to a small farm which he possessed in the vicinage of Harrisburgh, where he continued to reside until the year 1816, when he returned to Philadelphia with the intention of engaging in literary pursuits, and, with a view to the increase of a very restricted income, of entering upon the business of a Publisher.

> "There never breathed a man who, when his life
> Was closing, might not of that life relate
> Toils long and hard,"*

and MR. GRAYDON was, by no means, a fortunate exception to the general rule. Ere he could mature the plans, from which, in his life's decline, he had hoped to secure the independence he coveted, and which would have adorned, with a peculiar grace, his character, tastes, and years; or from which to repair the breach unexpectedly, cruelly, and causelessly made by arbitrary and vindictive Executive power, he yielded to the mandate which all must obey, and closed his honourable, useful, and virtuous life on the second day of May, 1818, in the sixty-seventh year of his

* WORDSWORTH.

B

age. MR. GRAYDON was twice married. His first wife, in whom he has well succeeded in engaging the interest of the reader, was MISS WOOD, from Berks country, who died at Harrisburgh early in the year 1794. His second wife was MISS THEODOSIA PETTIT, daughter of Colonel CHARLES PETTIT, of Philadelphia, who survived her husband eighteen years. He had no children by either marriage.

MR. GRAYDON was ardently attached to literature, and to literary pursuits. He was a frequent and acceptable contributor to the "PORT FOLIO" in its palmiest days of popularity and influence. These contributions, which, for the most part, were modestly denominated "NOTES OF A DESULTORY READER," contain his opinions of the authors whose works he had read, accompanied with occasional critiques upon their style, and are invariably written in the strain of candour and ease that so remarkably characterize the Memoirs; affording, moreover, indubitable evidence of the elevation and purity of his own sentiments, and of an enlarged, well disciplined and highly cultivated mind. His literature, indeed, was various, extensive, and elegant to a degree unusual at the time in which he lived; and not very common among his steam-propelling, money-seeking countrymen, at any subsequent period.

It was, at one time, the wish of the Editor to incorporate these articles into this edition of the Memoirs, but he was reluctant to swell the volume by the addition of matter having no connexion with the topics of which it treats. If, however, another edition should be called for, the original intention may be deemed worthy of reconsideration; or they may, perhaps, form a separate volume, under the title of "Remains." They were valuable contributions, and creditable to the periodical literature of the day, and are certainly deserving of publication and preservation.

The Editor of the "Port Folio" in a notice of the Memoirs, contained in his number for April, 1818, in language appropriate and strong, declares that the "performance is one of the most interesting which the loom of American authorship has produced;" and, in adverting to the unfortunate garb in which it came forth, remarks farther, that he felt no surprise that the public had failed to discover the "GEM, that was concealed beneath an unpromising. exterior." The brief critique is valuable, both on account of the justness of the writer's views, and also as evidence of a generous and candid contemporaneous appreciation of our Author. The following extract will not be unacceptable to the reader:—

"We shall not hesitate to say, in going back to a book that was published before our labours commenced, that our object is to stimulate the reading part of the community to the vindication of their taste, which deserves reproach while these *Memoirs* lie forgotten on the shelves. To those who would acquire a familiar view of the state of manners and public opinion about the time that our Revolution commenced, there is nothing which contributes so much accurate testimony; and to others, who have not forgotten this eventful period, we know of nothing more captivating. We are aware that the fastidious delicacy of some has been offended by the freedom with which the writer has spoken of individuals; but a very great distinction must be admitted between conversation and writing. Zimmerman justly remarks, that 'to entertain readers is only to deliver freely in writing that which, in the general intercourse of society, it is impossible to say with safety and politeness.' It is time thatt his mawkish delicacy

should be overcome, or we shall have nothing manly in our literature; nothing true in our history, or just in our memoirs. Our
writers, to be popular, must deal in the most ridiculous bombast
and fulsome panegyric. Our western world must be peopled by
nothing but a race of orators, like those who fulmined the thunder
of eloquence on classical grounds, and heroes who would have
rivalled a Marlborough, a Prince Eugene, or a Marshal Saxe. If
Cumberland and Marmontel had written under all the restrictions
which the fastidiousness of some of our good republicans would
impose upon the Press, where would be the witchery of their
pages? If the *optimates* of our cities—we should say, *persons in
society,* if we could accompany the observation by a fac-simile of
the customary shrug—if such people will insist on an exemption
from the jurisdiction of the Press, they must contribute their quota
to the general fund of amusement and instruction in some other
way. If they would prevent us from laughing at the ostentation
of the exterior of their houses, let them show that hospitality and
refinement dwell within the doors. If they cannot discern the
pleasures and utility of literature, let them respect the pursuits
of wiser men, and not act as if all knowledge was confined to the
conclave of a bank or a counting-room. In conclusion, we
must observe of MR. GRAYDON's book, that its veracity and its
candour are altogether beyond impeachment, and he has questioned no man's morality."

Within a few weeks after the above was written, when called
upon to record the demise of this excellent man, the same writer,
who enjoyed the pleasure and advantage of his personal friendship, thus feelingly alludes to the much regretted event:—"MR.
GRAYDON was one of the few survivors of that old school of ac-

complished gentlemen, who flourished before our Revolution ;—
at a period when the courtesy of society was not disturbed by
insubordination in systems, nor violated by laxity in sentiments.
That he has indulged himself in some harshness in these *Memoirs*
will not be denied; nor will that language be censured by those
who remember the merciless persecution by which it was pro-
voked.

> " ————— " So looks the chased lion
> Upon the daring huntsman that has galled him ;
> Then makes him nothing."

In his youth, Mr. GRAYDON was remarkable for the elegance of
his person, and he retained that advantage in an uncommon degree to his latest hour. The elements of his temper were kindness
and good will; he was frank and generous; his disposition was
sociable and equally fitted to win esteem or disarm resentment;
his conversation, chaste and pleasant, diffused the same agreeable
feelings around him which seemed to warm his own heart. His
last private communication to the writer of this memorial, derives
peculiar interest from the melancholy event by which it was
speedily followed. The letter contained a translation of a Latin
epigram; and though the muse of our friend cannot boast the
melody of the Swan, yet she breathes the same prophetic strain.
The reader will require no apology for the insertion of an extract
from Mr. GRAYDON's letter to the Editor :—

" —— In a slow convalescence from a lingering indisposition,
I have amused myself with the enclosed translation, which is at
the service of the Port Folio, if worthy of its pages. It struck
me as a pleasing trifle, and though no poet, I had a mind to try
how I could dress it in English metre. I am not unmindful of

B2

the story in Gil Blas of the Archbishop of Granada,—the old
gentleman so celebrated for his homilies.   For, though like him,
I may not be sensible of a *decadence* in my mental faculties, it
may nevertheless exist; and, whether or not, every person, I presume who has attained to my years (65) will feel a want of the
vis animæ or *animi*, that is necessary to the ready performance of
a literary undertaking, &c."

THE ORIGINAL.

Avulsa è ramo, frons ò miseranda, virenti,
Marcida quo vadis?—Quo vadam, nescio—Quercum
Maternam columenque meum stravêre procellæ.
Indé mihi illudit Zephyrus, Boreasve; vagamque
Nec contrá nitor.   Quo TENDUNT OMNIA, TENDO;
Quò fertur pariter folium lauri rosæque.

ATTEMPTED IN ENGLISH.

Torn from thy murturing branch, poor, fallen leaf,
    What hapless lot awaits thy withering form?
Alas! I know not, but I mourn in chief,
    My parent oak laid prostrate by the storm.

Hence, doomed the sport of every vagrant breeze,
    I'm hurried up the mount, then down again;
One while I mildew under shading trees,
    Now, whirl'd afield, I bleach upon the plain.

In short, I GO, WHERE ALL THINGS EARTHLY TEND.
    And, unresisting, meet my wasting foes:
For oaks and brambles have one common end—
    The foliage of the laurel and the rose.

*   *   *   *   *   *   " The Memoirs contain some things that
are bold and unpalateable, but it is a work of unexampled candour and truth; and will conduce more to a veritable history of

the times, to which it relates, than any other publication now extant." * * * "Mr. GRAYDON never lost sight of those imperishable principles for which he had contended on the field. He cherished the love of liberty, which beat in his heart until it became the impression of his conscience and the conviction of his understanding. Though a severe sufferer from political intolerance, nothing like tergiversation could be ranked among his failings. The perilous appearances in our political horizon never alarmed the soldier of the Revolution, who knew that the relations of truth and justice are immutable."

In the year 1822, Mr. JOHN GALT, well known for his many entertaining and valuable contributions to English literature, caused the re-publication of the Memoirs at Edinburgh, in a handsome volume, to which he prefixed a dedication to the American Envoy, then resident near the Court of St. James. In this dedication Mr. GALT bears the following judicious testimony to the merit and character of the work:—

"It is remarkable, that a production so rich in the various excellencies of style, description and impartiality, should not have been known to the collectors of American books in this country, especially as it is, perhaps, the best personal narrative that has yet appeared relative to the history of that great conflict which terminated in establishing the Independence of the United States. The candour with respect to public occurrences, which it displays—the views of manners in Pennsylvania, prior to the memorable era of 1776—and the incidental sketches of historical characters, with which it is enriched, cannot fail to render the volume a valuable addition to the stock of general knowledge, and will, probably, obtain for the Author no mean place among those who have added permanent lustre to the English language."

Commendations, thus unequivocal, from sources entitled to deference and weight, render it unnecessary to dwell longer upon the subject. It only remains for the Editor to allude, with becoming brevity, to his humble labours; and, while freely admitting a general and a cordial sympathy with the Author in the feelings and opinions he has so well portrayed and expressed, to disclaim responsibility for their utterance where it may not justly attach to him.

He has, indeed, on several occasions, in the notes, ventured to express dissent from the judgments of the writer; subsequent developments having placed within his reach, information which could not have been accessible to Mr. GRAYDON.

The observations appended by the Author to the last page of his private copy of the "MEMOIRS," are annexed to the original conclusion, in justice to him, and as a more befitting, present termination of the volume. But, as the Editor may not alter or mollify any of its expressions, it is but justice to himself to remark, that this is done without concurrence, on his part, in all the sentiments they contain. On the contrary, he cannot, whatever may be his own predelictions, indulge in indiscriminate censure of the acts of any party that may chance to be in the ascendant. The great mass of the native population—and any disparagement of the other, influential and gradually controlling portion, is emphatically disclaimed—who, alone, cherish an *exclusive*, or, at least, predominant attachment to the soil and institutions of their country, are, without doubt, patriotic; and, perhaps, the only serious charge that may reasonably be placed to their account, is that of a too great ductility towards mere party-leaders; adopting, without due examination or reflection— such as becomes intelligent citizens deserving of their freedom and independence—the plausible dogmas of ignorant, unprincipled demagogues, or of inexperienced and reckless experimentalists.

Whatever may have been the defects of the "Madisonian Policy," to which Mr. GRAYDON alludes—and in regard to which the knowledge of the Editor is entirely historical—it cannot, he presumes, be denied that the Government of the country, at that gloomy period, was encompassed by difficulties and menaced by dangers of no ordinary character; and, as it was a manifest and monstrous dereliction of filial duty to withhold the necessary aid in her extrication and defence, so was it little short of treason to interpose obstacles to the complete and triumphant vindication of her rights and honour. Yet, to such unnatural lengths have party antipathies, rage, and blindness, tempted men whose services and genius would otherwise have deserved and commanded unqualified admiration and gratitude. It is, assuredly, the part of wisdom to avoid warlike or angry collision and controversy with other nations, alike injurious in their tendency to prosperity and to morals;—let the people, therefore, look well to their rulers, and be duly careful in their selection;—but it is equally an obvious dictate of patriotism, whatever the "policy," by which she may become involved, at any and at every sacrifice, to shield the country from discomfiture and disgrace. Nor can the Editor permit the fears or the doubts of the Author, or of other equally thoughtful and patriotic men, to weaken his firm and abiding faith in the permanency of our institutions. Of the lasting prevalence of republican feeling, and of the rapidly progressive and widely spreading love for these institutions, no genuine son of the soil should ever encourage or entertain a doubt. It is true, that the people—fondly loved, and caressingly flattered by those who alone are capable of serving them, and who are, therefore, exclusively deserving of their smiles and offices, and honours—have made some startling mistakes, which have paled the cheek, and checked the warm current of patriotic hope. We have seen, for example, a citizen of consummate ability, of profound learning, and of unsurpassed experience, hurled from the high station which his genius and talents adorned, in the whirl of popularity achieved by a patriotic and fortunate General, whose great military talents, and brilliant exploits in the field, were deemed sufficient qualifications for the most elevated of civic trusts!

We have, also, seen a statesman who, for forty years, has been a leading public servant,—exercising, in the national councils, a commanding and conservative influence; and who, for two-thirds of this long period of toilsome, self-sacrificing devotion to his country, has been, of that country,—under the guidance of a higher Intelligence,—thrice the preserver;—an illustrious offspring of its free, equalizing, and nurturing institutions,—its greatest living name,—we have seen this wise and generous man, OSTRACISED by strangers who are called his countrymen; and another, without name, or fame, or service, elevated, by the controlling influence of the same law-created citizens, from the "thick darkness" of obscurity, to the CHAIR OF WASHINGTON! Such occurrences overshadow with temporary gloom and despondency, the prospect into futurity, and sicken the heart and depress the spirit of the enlightened patriot, whose duty it is, notwithstanding, never to despair while there is service to render or while a sacrifice is required.

After he had commenced the preparation of the Memoirs for

the press, and had made considerable progress in the division of the work into chapters for the greater convenience of reference,— a plan not adopted by the Author,—the Editor was fortunate in procuring a copy of the Edinburgh edition in which MR. GALT had performed this service in a manner somewhat different, but, on the whole, very satisfactorily; and his arrangement, in this respect, with slight modification, has been adopted. Beyond this, however, MR. GALT did not venture to proceed.

To this Edition, a TABLE OF CONTENTS, and a general INDEX have been added; and also an APPENDIX containing illustrative matter, which could not, without burdening the page, be crowded into notes.

Acknowledgements are due to MR. ANDREW GRAYDON, of Harrisburgh, for the kindness and courtesy which unreservedly placed at the disposal of the Editor, documents that have greatly facilitated his researches, and especially for the use of his Uncle's private copy of the Memoirs, to many of the pages of which the Author had appended notes with a view, unquestionably, to a future republication. These notes have been faithfully transcribed and placed where their writer evidently intended them to appear; while those of the Editor have received their appropriate designation.

The volume is thus submitted, once more, but in a befitting dress, to the candour of the intelligent and discriminating reader, as a valuable addition to the historical literature of the country for whose independence and happiness its Author perilled his fortunes and his life; and whatever may be his impressions in respect to the opinions which it contains, their manifest sincerity will command respect, and the style and temper of their expression, while deserving of general imitation, will challenge good-will and admiration.

The beautiful tribute of WORDSWORTH to the Memory of LAMB, is, with slight modification, almost equally applicable here, and may, not inappropriately, terminate the trespass of the Editor upon the patience of his reader :—

> " To a good man of most dear memory
>   This stone is sacred.   Here he lies apart
>   From the great city where he first drew breath,
>   Was reared and taught; and humbly earned his bread
>   To the strict labours of the merchants' desk,
>   By duty chained.   Not seldom did these tasks
>   Tease, and the thought of time so spent depress
>   His spirit, but the recompense was high;
>   Firm Independence, Bounty's rightful sire;
>   Affections warm as sunshine, free as air;
>   And when the precious hours of leisure came,
>   Knowledge and wisdom, gained from converse sweet
>   With books, or while he ranged the crowded streets
>   With a keen eye, and overflowing heart:
>   So genius triumphed over seeming wrong,
>   And pour'd out truth in works by thoughtful love
>   Inspired—works potent over smiles and tears.
>   And as round mountain-tops the lightning plays,
>   Thus innocently sported, breaking forth
>   As from a cloud of some grave sympathy,
>   Humour and wild instinctive wit and all
>   The vivid flashes of his spoken words."

J. S. L.

Germantown, Pennsylvania,
    April 11th, 1846.

MEMOIRS OF A LIFE,

PASSED CHIEFLY IN PENNSYLVANIA.

INTRODUCTION.

THE dealers in self-biography, ever sedulous to ward off the imputation of egotism, seldom fail to find apologies for their undertakings. Some, indeed, endeavour to persuade themselves, that they design their labours merely for their scrutoires; while others, less self-deceived, admit they have an eye to the public. The Cardinal De Retz is brought out at the request of a lady; Rousseau, by the desire of showing himself to a misjudging world, in all the verity of nature; Marmontel, writes his life for his children at the instance of their mother; and Cumberland, so far as his motives can be collected from his introduction, because he lived and was an author. If, from these, we recur to the account given of himself, by our own Franklin, we shall find, that, although addressed to his son, it is intended for the world; and that the acknowledged motives to it, are a combination of family curiosity and personal vanity, with the desire of showing the connexion between thrifty youth and respectable age—a kind of practical comment on the useful truths, contained in Poor Richard's almanac.

Next to the good fortune of having figured in some brilliant, active career; of having been the companion of a hero, or the depository of state secrets; of having seen cities and men; of having wandered "through antres vast, and deserts idle," or been

2

the subject of "moving accidents by flood and field;" the avowed inducement of Mr. Cumberland, is perhaps the most plausible.

Unfortunately, for the person, who, here presumes to appear before the public, he is without one of these claims to attention. He has no pretensions to fame or distinction in any kind, neither as soldier, nor statesmen, nor traveller, nor author. He is not wholly without hope, however, that his presumption may be palliated; and that, in his object, of giving a representation of the character, spirit and more minute occurrences of his time, it will be perceived, that there is no form, into which his work can be thrown, with so much advantage, as into that of personal memoirs. By his own story, if he is not misled by self-love, a kind of menstruum is afforded, for the incongruous mass of his materials, serving to harmonize, in some degree, the abrupt transitions and detached details, which, a delineation of the various incidents of "many coloured life" requires.

As to himself, he is fully conscious, that

it matters not,
To whom related, or by whom begot;

and, therefore, he would fain buttress his undertaking, by the opinion of an eminent poet, as vouched by Mr. Walpole, viz. "That if any man were to form a book, of what he had seen or heard himself, it must, in whatever hands, prove a most useful and entertaining one." A most seducing ignis-fatuus truly, considering the latitude with which it is laid down!

But, far from wishing to forclose the reader by an opinion, which he must own he considers a very questionable one; or to lure him on to an expectation of what he might vainly seek to find, he announces at his outset, that the pages here set before him, hold out no other inducement to his perusal, than such as may arise from the fidelity with which he will relate incidents within the scope of ordinary life; and depict some occurrences, which came under his notice, during the progress of the revolution, and since its consummation. In doing this, he will have occasion to speak as well of others as himself. He may sometimes resort to motives in accounting for men's actions; and, as these receive their qualities from the mind of the agent, he will with equal freedom and truth disclose the complexion of his own, having little, he thinks, no inclination that it should pass for better than it is. If the mould in which it has been formed, is not the most perfect, so neither, does he trust, is it absolutely the most worthless: if not calculated to produce a cast to the taste of worldly wisdom; one, that may advance experimentally the sound philosophy of thrift, and practically mark the routes to private wealth and public greatness, it will yet be found abundantly fruitful, in negative instruction on both points.

CHAPTER I.

Bristol.—The Author's account of his family, and early education.—Society of Philadelphia.—Accident.—Family history.—Quakers.—School at Bristol.— School discipline.—Mr. Dove.—Philadelphia Academy.—Mr. Kinnersley.— Anecdote.—Early Adventure.—Author's early Character.—Ballad.—Death of the Author's father.—Latin School.—Mr. Beveridge.—Anecdotes of Mr. Beveridge.—School anecdote.—Singular petition.—Beveridge's poems.—Philadelphia.—Academy.—Author's early class-mates.

My recollections of the village of Bristol, in which I was born on the 10th of April, N. S., in the year 1752, cannot be supposed to go farther back than to the year 1756 or 1757. There are few towns, perhaps, in Pennsylvania, which, in the same space of time, have been so little improved, or undergone less alteration.* Then, as now,† the great road leading from Philadelphia to New York, first skirting the inlet, at the head of which stand the mills, and then turning short to the left, along the banks of the Delaware, formed the principal and indeed only street, marked by any thing like a continuity of building. A few places for streets, were opened from this main one, on which, here and there, stood an humble, solitary dwelling. At a corner of two of these lanes, was a Quaker meeting house; and on a still more retired spot, stood a small Episcopal church, whose lonely grave yard with its

---

* Just about the time of writing these memoirs, Bristol took a start, and has since become a place of fashionable resort during the summer months, to which its baths and chalybeate waters, together with its convenience to the inhabitants of Philadelphia, by means of the then newly invented steamboats, have, no doubt, principally contributed.

† 1811.

surrounding woody scenery, might have furnished an appropriate
theme for such a muse as Gray's. These, together with an old
brick jail, (Bristol having once been the county town of Bucks,)
constituted all the public edifices in this my native town. Its
site, though flat, is not unpleasant, particularly along the bank of
the Delaware, rising to a commanding height from a fair and
gravelly margin. Hence, the eye might rove at large both up
and down the river, and after traversing a fine expanse of water
in an oblique direction, find an agreeable resting place in the town,
of Burlington on the opposite shore.*

As in this country, there is little temptation to the tracing of a
long line of ancestry, I shall content myself with deducing a very
brief genealogy. And this, not so much perhaps, from an acquiescence in the revolutionary idea of the insignificance of an
illustrious pedigree, as from real inability to produce one. I can
go no farther, at least, than to vouch, that we had a coat of arms
in the family, borne about on the body of an old-fashioned chaise,
and engraved upon our spoons, and a double-handled caudle
cup. But if instead of groping amidst the darkness of transat-
lantic heraldry, we confine ourselves to our own shores, which
seems much the most congenial to the noble spirit of independence
we are pleased to manifest on other occasions, I am warranted in
asserting, that I am descended from ancestors, respectable both
as to station and character; from a stock not ignoble, but honest
and generous: And if parental propensities are transmitted to off-

---

* Bristol, in 1846, is the largest town in Bucks county, and is distant twenty
miles from Philadelphia. "The Delaware branch of the canal from Easton ter-
minates here in a spacious basin, bringing to the place an extensive coal trade.
The Philadelphia and Trenton Railroad passes in the rear of the town. Steamboats are constantly touching at the landing." Besides the Episcopal church,
above mentioned, and Quaker meeting house, there is now a Methodist meeting
house, a bank, (the Bank of Bucks county,) an extensive flouring mill, several
hotels and stores. " The distinguishing characteristic of the place, is its quiet-
ness and rural beauty. The population in 1840 was 1,438. Scott, in his geo-
graphy published in 1806, says that Bristol, at that time, contained 90 houses.
By the census of 1800, the population was 511; in 1810, 628; in 1820, 908.
Bristol was incorporated as a borough by Sir William Keith, governor of the province of Pennsylvania, on the 14th of November, 1720."—ED.

spring in the human race, but in half the degree that they are among quadrupeds, the value we may be disposed to set on virtuous progenitors, is very far from chimerical. Several years residence on a farm, has afforded me opportunity for some observations upon the nature of domestic animals; and I have found, what I should have been disposed to laugh at, had I not proved it, that, among the ox kind especially, the vices, which seemed mere habits of the female parent, have invariably descended to her offspring. I venture this remark, though not quite in unison with the tone of the subject; and though liable to be strained into an assumption of worth on my part, to which I may in fact be wholly destitute of pretension.

My father was an Irishman, and, as it appears from some imperfect documents in my possession, came to this country in the year 1730. He was born, I think, in Longford, and was brought up under the care of his maternal grandfather in Dublin, or its neighbourhood. Being designed for the pulpit, he had received a suitable education, to which, having added many of the accomplishments at that time in fashion, he was distinguished in Philadelphia both as a scholar and a gentleman. It was not long since, that the late chief justice Shippen informed me, he was the person always appealed to, in the coffee-house controversies of the young men of the day, on points of science and literature. During his presidency of the county courts of Bucks, he had made himself, as I have understood, a very tolerable lawyer, insomuch that at the time of his death, he was, as I have been informed, in nomination for the office of a judge of the supreme court of Pennsylvania. From the copies of letters to his friends in Ireland, soon after his arrival in Philadelphia, he appears not to have taken up very favourable sentiments of its inhabitants. "Most of our trading people here," says he, "are complaisant sharpers; and that maxim in trade, to think every man a knave, until the contrary evidently appears, would do well to be observed here if any where.—In this province we have a toleration for all religions, which some have enlarged so far, as to make a neglect and indifference of all religion, their only religion." These being the opinions of a young man but of about two and twenty years of age, it is not improbable, that they were too hastily formed; but if, unfortunately for the honour of our infant metropolis, they were correct, it is some relief to hear, that mercantile integrity, joined to genuine and unaffected hospitality, was also to be found there, as appears from the following extract of a letter, dated the 18th of March, 1731. " Soon after we arrived here, it happened, and I hope providentially for us, (himself and his father-in-law, Mr. Emerson, who made one family,) that we rented a house from one Mr. Peter Baynton, adjacent to his own, who is a considerable merchant in this city. As he is a man of singular sobriety, and not well affected to the reigning humour in this town, he has admitted us into his chief confidence, and distinguished us as his principal friends and associates, insomuch that he will enter upon no project or design in trade, without admitting us to a share in it: and from the success of some we have already undertaken, we have not the least room to doubt of his sincerity and kindness." Such is my father's sketch of Philadelphia manners eighty years ago.* From the same letter it appears, that at the instance of this Mr. Baynton, he had contemplated with him a partnership in trade, to be carried on in the town of Burlington, which, he observes, " though it be now somewhat obscure, it has yet many advantages capable of improvement."

This contemplated removal, however, did not take place. He continued in business in Philadelphia, and in the war, probably, with Spain, which broke out in the year 1741, was concerned with several of the principal merchants in that city in building and fitting out the Tartar privateer.† This vessel, supposed to be the finest, as she was the largest, that had at that time, been built on the Delaware, had a singular fate. On her passage to the sea, at a fine season of the year, she was lost in the bay. To make the most of a gentle breeze that was blowing, she was

---

* 1731.

† Commanded by Capt. Macky. She was launched 24th May, 1744. More than eighty people were drowned, among whom were Mr. Legate of New Castle, Capt. McKnight of Philadelphia, and Capt. Bodeman. She was a sharp-built vessel, and out of all proportion rigged and masted, and under ballasted. She overset in a moment with but little wind, and went down instantly. Letter 31st July, 1774, from Lynford Lardner to Richard Penn.

under full sail, when either from a deficiency of ballast, a dispro-
portion in her rigging, or some other fault in her construction, she
was almost instantaneously overturned by a flaw from the shore.
The greater part of the owners, who had formed a party to see
her out of the capes, were on board, and among them my father.
So mild was the day, and so little cause was there for apprehension, that he was amusing himself on deck with one of Moliere's plays, when the disaster occurred. Finding himself pre-
cipitated among the waves, he immediately seized on a chest that
had floated from the vessel, and placing himself on the middle of it,
its extremities served to support a sailor on each side of him. In
this situation, they were driven at the mercy of the waves for a
considerable time, without any prospect of relief. They were
sometimes about to quit their hold, and at once resign themselves
to a fate, which appeared inevitable. This was peculiarly the
case with one of the sailors, whom my father exerted himself to
the utmost to encourage, since if he had abandoned the chest, it
would have lost its equilibrium, and in the weak, exhausted state
in which they were, they must all have perished. At length, a
vessel hove in sight and appeared to be making towards them :
It proved to be so, and they were taken up while yet enough of
vital power remained, to render the means used for their restoration efficacious. The captain, if I am not mistaken, and the
greater part of the Tartar's crew, were drowned, as were most of
the owners that were on board. Although I have heard my father
relate the circumstances of this misfortune, and have since heard
it spoken of in the family, my recollection of the particulars is
very imperfect.

My mother, the second wife of my father, was the eldest of
four daughters; she was born in the island of Barbadoes, and
when about seven years of age, was brought to Philadelphia by
her parents, who then came to reside in that city. Her father
was a German, born, if I mistake not, in Frankfort on the Maine.
He had been engaged in trade while in Barbadoes, and brought
with him into Pennsylvania, a pretty good property. Her mother
was from Scotland, having first drawn breath in the city of Glasgow; but by what means a pair of so little national affinity as
these my grand parents on the mother's side, were brought to-

gether, I never learned. From their conversation, however, I remember they had resided some time in London, previously to their settling in Barbadoes. Notwithstanding the apparent want of associating principles in some respects, they yet agreed very well: While the tongue of my grandfather faithfully retained the character of its original dialect, that of his spouse, though in a less degree, bore testimony also, to the country of her extraction; and while he, a determined episcopalian, had his pew in Christ's church, she, a strict presbyterian, was a constant attendant at *Buttonwood* meeting house. No feuds, however, were engendered by this want of religious conformity; and if my grandfather sometimes consented to hear a sermon at the meeting house, it might be considered as a concession on his part, for a sermon of archbishop Tillotson, which was regularly read aloud, by one of the family on Sunday evening. Though a loud talker, and somewhat rough and boisterous in his manner, the old gentleman was at bottom, highly liberal, benevolent, and good natured. The good lady, on the other hand, was rather austere; and the management of her family, strongly tinctured with the primitive discipline of her church. Her countenance, on Sunday, always assumed an unusual degree of severity, and while under her tutorage, I might truly say, in the meaning of the poet, it shone no Sabbath day to me. Then, instead of rest, my labours were augmented; then chapters were to be read, and long catechisms to be conned or repeated. The best things may be overdone; and the imposition of hard and unreasonable tasks is more apt to create disgust, than conciliation to instruction. So, at least, it was with me: I deemed my tutoress unfeeling and tyrannical, while, by her, I was considered as reprobate and incorrigible.

Although my progenitors, on neither side, appear to have possessed the talent of amassing wealth, there is a circumstance common to both, which seems unequivocally to indicate liberality and sincerity of heart. And yet it is a circumstance, which, probably, would have escaped me, had it not been noticed by my uncle, by marriage, the late judge Biddle.* Your family, said he one

---

* Edward Biddle, Esq. WILKINSON, in his "Memoirs" warmly eulogizes him. "He was a man whose public and private virtues commanded respect, and excited

day to me, has had an honour which has happened to few, that of inducing two persons wholly unconnected with you, to attach themselves to you; to make your interests their own, and without contract or pecuniary tie, to remain with you till their deaths. One of these was a Scotchman, of the name of Thomas Gordon, who came into my grandfather's service in Philadelphia, in the capacity of a clerk, continued with him after he had declined business, and remained among us long after his death, until the time of his own decease, which happened at Reading, in the year 1777. He was born in Aberdeen, and had been bred to business in a counting-house at Rotterdam. He never was married. In his latter days, he became a perfect clock in regularity; was a truly honest man, and what will be thought still better by many, he was a genuine whig of *seventy-six*, though too old or infirm to carry arms in the revolutionary contest. The other, was a maiden lady of the society of friends, who, upon occasion of my mother being in want of a female domestic, offered to assist her for a short time, came into the family soon after I was born, and never left it until taken from us by death, at an advanced age, in the year 1794. Her name was Ann Burgess; she was a woman of good understanding and reputably connected.

With the exception of the family of Doctor Denormandie, our own, and perhaps one or two more, the principal inhabitants of Bristol were Quakers. Among these, the names of Buckley, Williams, Large, Meritt, Hutchinson and Church, are familiar to me. The last, bred to the trade of a cooper, but who had put his son in the business, and employed himself more in the management

admiration from all persons: He was speaker of the last assembly of Pennsylvania under the proprietory government, and in the dawn of the Revolution devoted himself to the cause of his country, and successfully opposed the overbearing influences of Joseph Galloway: ardent, eloquent, and full of zeal, by his exertions, during several days and nights of obstinate, warm and animated discussion, in extreme sultry weather, he overheated himself, and brought on an inflammatory rheumatism, which radically destroyed his health, and ultimately deprived society of one of its greatest ornaments, and his country of a statesman, a patriot and a soldier; for he had served several campaigns in the war of 1756, and if his health had been spared, would, no doubt, have occupied the second or third place in the Revolutionary armies."—ED.

of a small farm and nursery of fruit trees, was a sincere and steady friend to our family. He was married to the sister of Ann Burgess, just mentioned, and was a very worthy man, possessing a good natural understanding, with a strong addiction to philosophical speculations. His attachment to my father went beyond friendship: it reached to admiration and veneration. He thought him, as he has often told me, one of the best and wisest men that ever lived. I never knew him do a foolish thing, said he, but once. Upon my asking him what that was; it was, said he, on occasion of some worthless fellow reporting that he had seen one or more Indians in the swamp beyond the church, assembling a body of the militia, of which he was colonel,* and marching out with drums beating, and colours flying, against the supposed enemy. But this instance is equivocal. Whether my father gave credit to the report or not, others might, and no doubt did believe it: It was also incumbent on him to be alert; to inculcate that duty upon his men, and to inure them to alarms: and although more silence, and less parade, might have been more truly military, yet something of the "pride, pomp, and circumstance of glorious war," is allowable to militia, particularly to a body which had certainly never encountered an enemy. Besides, to the calm incredulity of friend Church upon this occasion, we might perhaps safely add, a little both of the spirit of party and of quakerism. The people of his society, from principles averse from war, were charged with being too friendly to the Indians; with being too ready to palliate their enormities, and consequently, indisposed to listen to the alarming accounts, which the panic produced by Braddock's defeat, had spread throughout the country. By this event, every obstacle to their incursions being removed, in the minds of the timid they were to be looked for

---

* In Franklin and Hall's Gazette of February 9th, 1747, eight of the officers of Bucks county it is there stated—Alexander Graydon, Captain; Anthony Denormandie, Lieutenant; James Barker, Ensign. In the same paper of the 15th March, same year, it is farther stated—Superior officers of a regiment in Bucks county, Alexander Graydon, Esq., Colonel, Matthew Hughes, Esq., Lieutenant Colonel; John Denormandie, Esq., Major. He was also recommended in a nomination for a field officer in the Provincial Corps raising in 1758, but he declined the appointment. See his letter in Appendix.

every where. From the consternation that prevailed, I can still recollect, that the horrors of a discomfiture by such a foe, were among my most early and lively impressions. To the terrors of the tomahawk and the scalping knife, the imagination adds the savage yells, the gloomy woods and dismal swamps, which are their usual accompaniments; and, hence, minds that have been deeply impressed by the fatal fields of Braddock and St. Clair, are well prepared for the sombre interest imparted by Tacitus's affecting description of that of Varus, visited after an interval of six years, by Germanicus:—*Occulta saltuum, mæstos, locos, visuque ac memoria deformes. Medio campi albentia ossa, ut fugerunt, ut restiterunt disjecta vel aggerata.* "Those deep and dreary recesses, hideous both to sight and memory; with the whitening bones, scattered or heaped together, as either they belonged to those who fell in flight, or met their fate resisting."

There being no traces in my memory, of any incidents worthy of remark, during the period of my infancy, I pass on to the era of my removal to Philadelphia, for the sake of my education. This, I suppose to have been, between my sixth and seventh year. I recollect little or nothing of going to school at Bristol, farther than that there was one, and the master's name Pinkerton, a kind, good humoured Irishman, from whom I might have learned, that as one thing was *cruel* big, so another might be *cruel* little. In the city, I lived with, and was under the care of my grandfather. The school he first put me to, was that of David James Dove, an Englishman, and much celebrated in his day, as a teacher, and no less as a dealer in the minor kind of satirical poetry. To him were attributed some political effusions in this way, which were thought highly of by his party, and made a good deal of noise. He had also made some figure, it seems, in the old world, being spoken of, as I have heard, though in what way I know not, having never seen the work, in a book, entitled—The Life and Adventures of the Chevalier Taylor.* As the story went,

---

* This was Taylor the occulist, spoken of in Boswell's life of Johnson, and who, though sprightly, was, according to the doctor, an instance how far impudence could carry ignorance. He challenged me once to talk Latin with him, says the doctor. I quoted some of Horace, which he took to be my own speech. He said a few words well enough.

some one reading this performance to Mr. Dove on its first appearance, with the mischievous design of amusing himself at his
expense, as he knew what the book contained, he (Dove) bore
testimony to the truth of the contents, with which, he said, he
was perfectly acquainted, exclaiming, as the reader went along,
true, true as the gospel! but when the part was reached, in which
he himself is introduced in a situation somewhat ridiculous, he
cried out, it was a lie, a most abominable lie, and that there was
not a syllable of truth in the story. At any rate, Dove was a hu-
mourist, and a person not unlikely to be engaged in ludicrous
scenes. It was his practice in his school, to substitute disgrace
for corporal punishment. His birch was rarely used in canonical
method, but was generally stuck into the back part of the collar
of the unfortunate culprit, who, with this badge of disgrace towering from his nape like a broom at the mast-head of a vessel for
sale, was compelled to take his stand upon the top of the form,
for such a period of time, as his offence was thought to deserve.
He had another contrivance for boys who were late in their morning attendance. This was to despatch a committee of five or six
scholars for them, with a bell and lighted lantern, and in this
"odd equipage," in broad day light, the bell all the while ting-
ling, were they escorted through the streets to school. As Dove
affected a strict regard to justice in his dispensations of punishment, and always professed a willingness, to have an equal measure of it meted out to himself in case of his transgressing, the
boys took him at his word ; and one morning, when he had over-
staid his time, either through laziness, inattention, or design, he
found himself waited on in the usual form. He immediately admitted the justice of the procedure, and putting himself behind
the lantern and bell, marched with great solemnity to school, to
the no small gratification of the boys, and entertainment of the
spectators. But this incident took place before I became a scholar. It was once my lot to be attended in this manner, but what
had been sport to my tutor, was to me a serious punishment.

The school was, at this time, kept in Videll's alley, which
opened into Second, a little below Chesnut street. It counted a
number of scholars of both sexes, though chiefly boys; and the
assistant, or writing master, was John Reily, a very expert pen-

3

man and conveyancer, a man of some note, who, in his gayer
moods affected a pompous and technical phraseology, as he is
characterized under the name of Parchment, in a farce written
some forty years ago, and which, having at least the merit of novelty and personality, was a very popular drama, though never
brought upon the stage.   Some years afterwards, Dove removed
to Germantown, where he erected a large stone building, in the
view of establishing an academy upon a large scale; but I believe his success was not answerable to his expectations.   I know
not what my progress was under the auspices of Mr. Dove, but
having never in my early years, been smitten with the love of
learning, I have reason to conclude, it did not pass mediocrity.
I recollect a circumstance, however, which one afternoon took
place at my grandfather's, to the no small entertainment of the old
gentleman, who often adverted to it afterwards.   Dove was there,
and in endeavouring to correct my utterance, as I had an ill habit
of speaking with my teeth closed, as if indifferent whether I spoke
or not, he bawled out in one of his highest tones: " Why don't
you speak louder? open your mouth like a Dutchman—say
yaw."*

Being now, probably, about eight years of age, it was deemed
expedient to enter me at the academy, then, as it now continues

---

* This DOVE was a *satirical poet*, and has been described by Judge Peters, an
early pupil of his, as a "sarcastical and ill-tempered doggerelizer, who was but
ironically *Dove;* for his temper was that of a hawk, and his pen the beak of a fal-
con pouncing on innocent prey."
He became, says Watson, a teacher of languages in the Philadelphia Academy, and was chiefly conspicuous for the part he took in the politics of the day,
and by his caustic rhymes in ridicule of his opponents, he wrote poetical illustrations to accompany the caricatures which abounded in his time, and was, himself, in turn, a rich subject for the caricaturist. Watson records a characteristic
anecdote of Charles Thomson, secretary to the Congress of 1776. When young,
Thomson resided in the family of Dove, who, with his wife, was much addicted
to scandal, a propensity in the highest degree offensive to the honourable nature
of the future secretary. Wishing to leave them, but dreading their tongues, he
adopted an ingenious expedient to prevent their injurious exercise. He gravely
inquired of them one evening, if his conduct, as a boarder, had been satisfactory
to them. They promptly replied in the affirmative. Would you, then, asked
Thomson, be willing to give me a certificate to that effect? "O, certainly." A
certificate was accordingly given, and the next day he parted from them in
peace.—ED.

to be, under the name of a university, the principal seminary in Pennsylvania; and I was accordingly introduced by my father, to Mr. Kinnesley, the teacher of English and professor of oratory. He was an Anabaptist clergyman, a large, venerable looking man, of no great general erudition, though a considerable proficient in electricity; and who, whether truly or not, has been said to have had a share in certain discoveries in that science, of which Doctor Franklin received the whole credit. The task, of the younger boys, at least, consisted in learning to read and to write their mother tongue grammatically; and one day in the week (I think Friday) was set apart for the recitation of select passages in poetry and prose. For this purpose, each scholar, in his turn, ascended the stage, and said his speech, as the phrase was. This speech was carefully taught him by his master, both with respect to its pronunciation, and the action deemed suitable to its several parts. Two of these specimens of infantile oratory to the disturbance of my repose, I had been qualified to exhibit: Family partiality, no doubt, overrated their merit; and hence, my declaiming powers were in a state of such constant requisition, that my orations, like worn out ditties, became vapid and fatiguing to me; and consequently, impaired my relish for that kind of acquirement. More profit attended my reading. After Æsop's fables, and an abridgement of the Roman history, Telemachus was put into our hands; and if it be admitted that the human heart may be bettered by instruction, mine, I may aver, was benefited by this work of the virtuous Fenelon. While the mild wisdom of Mentor called forth my veneration, the noble ardour of the youthful hero excited my sympathy and emulation. I took part, like a second friend, in the vicissitudes of his fortune, I participated in his toils, I warmed with his exploits, I wept where he wept, and exulted where he triumphed.

As my lot has been cast in a turbulent period, in a season of civil war and revolution, succeeded by scenes of domestic discord and fury, in all of which I have been compelled to take a part, I deem it of consequence to myself, to bespeak toleration for the detail of a school-boy incident, that may in some degree serve to develope my character. It may equally tend to throw some light on the little world, upon whose stage I had now entered. A few days after I had been put under the care of Mr. Kinnersley, I was told by my class-mates, that it was necessary for me to fight a battle with some one, in order to establish my claim to the honour of being an academy boy: that this could not be dispensed with, and that they would select for me a suitable antagonist, *one of my match*, whom after school I must fight, or be looked upon as a coward. I must confess, that I did not at all relish the proposal. Though possessing a sufficient degree of spirit, or at least irascibility, to defend myself when assaulted, I had never been a boxer. Being of a light and slender make, I was not calculated for the business, nor had I ever been ambitious of being the cock of a school. Besides, by the laws of the institution I was now a subject of, fighting was a capital crime; a sort of felony deprived of clergy, whose punishment was not to be averted by the most scholar-like reading. For these reasons, both of which had sufficient weight with me, and the last not the least, as I had never been a wilful transgressor of rules, or callous to the consequences of an infraction of them, I absolutely declined the proposal; although I had too much of that feeling about me, which some might call false honour, to represent the case to the master, which would at once have extricated me from my difficulty, and brought down condign punishment on its imposers. Matters thus went on until school was out, when I found that the lists were appointed, and that a certain John Appowen, a lad who, though not quite so tall, yet better set and older than myself, was pitted against me. With increased pertinacity I again refused the combat, and insisted on being permitted to go home unmolested. On quickening my pace for this purpose, my persecutors, with Appowen at their head, followed close at my heels. Upon this I moved faster and faster, until my retreat became a flight too unequivocal and inglorious for a man to relate of himself, had not Homer furnished some apology for the procedure, in making the heroic Hector thrice encircle the walls of Troy, before he could find courage to encounter the implacable Achillus. To cut the story short, my spirit could no longer brook an oppression so intolerable, and stung to the quick at the term coward which was lavished upon me, I made a halt and faced my pursuers. A combat immediately ensued between Appowen and myself, which for some time, was maintained on each side, with equal vigour and determination, when unluckily, I received his fist directly in my gullet. The blow for a time depriving me of breath, and the power of resistance, victory declared for my adversary, though not without the acknowledgment of the party, that I had at last behaved well, and shown myself not unworthy the name of an academy boy. Being thus established, I had no more battles imposed upon me, and none that I can recollect of my own provoking; for I have a right to declare, that my general deportment was correct and unoffending, though extremely obstinate and unyielding under a sense of injustice.* I gave an early instance of this, in once burning the rod with which my father had corrected me; and upon his finding it out, and correcting me a second time, I declared I would drown myself, and ran towards a creek in a meadow not far off, with such an appearance of determination to execute the threat, that he thought proper to despatch a servant after me in haste; and upon my being brought back, rather to yield to the violence of my temper, than persist in the attempt to subdue it.

In saying my resistance proceeded from a sense of injustice, I would by no means have it understood, that my father had been culpable. I rather suppose, that a too ardent idea of the rights of a child, had led me to consider that conduct oppressive, which was merely the effect of a paternal concern for my welfare.

While upon the topic of those early adventures, by which we are initiated into the ways of the world, I may mention a circumstance of another nature, which happened not very long after my arrival in the city. One evening about dusk, I was amusing myself on the pavement before the door, with some marbles; for having never been very strongly incited by a spirit of gambling, I frequently played alone, and even when I had a companion I gene-

---

* The poignancy of my feelings on such occasions, has given me a degree of veneration for justice which I have rarely discovered in others. Nor has my own interest or that of my connexions or country, ever led me to espouse their cause, when unsupported by right. Hence, I can never be a patriot in the modern acceptation of the word; more especially, as in sifting the merits of a cause, I have a most unlucky propensity of referring all acts of subsequent aggression to the original wrong. A monstrous supererogation of morality this, in the eyes of orthodox patriotism.

rally preferred playing *in fun*, to speak technically, to playing *in earnest*. A little, skulking rogue, with whom I had no kind of acquaintance, came up to me, and as he joined me in play with some marbles of his own, he took occasion to observe, that his were too small for him, but as mine, on the contrary, were large and exactly suited to his hand, he proposed an exchange, offering me the odds, first, of two, and then of three for one. Having no disposition to traffic with him, being pleased with my own and satisfied with their number, I at first objected to his proposal, but he pressed me in so earnest a manner to accommodate him with but a part of mine, that after some hesitation, I consented. Without giving me time for a resumption of my first determination, he picked up six or eight of my marbles, and throwing me down three or four times the number of his own, the amount of boot being apparently wholly unworthy of calculation, he decamped in a twinkling. Upon gathering up the commodities I had received in such abundance, I found them rather light; and on closer inspection, discovered, that as they had been but clay in the hands of the potter, so I had been an equally ductile material in the hands of a swindler. These things are but puerilities, and very trifles, it is true, but can it be said that they are irrelative to the objects I set out with? And are they not prototypes of the transactions, which the more important scene of man every day exhibits? If swindling and oppression beset us in infancy, does experience warrant us in affirming that the state of manhood is exempt from them?

Might I here be pardoned a brief recognition of the qualities my childhood had unfolded, I might say, that, with a sufficient share of obstinacy and impatience of control, I had never manifested a propensity to mischief; and though I might sometimes have been a follower, I had never promoted or been a leader in those pranks which are denominated *unlucky:* Thank Heaven, I had never been guilty of a trick, and rarely, if ever, of a lie. I had no cunning, and consequently, gave no token of those talents which might qualify me, one day, to rise in a commonwealth. On a scrutiny, therefore, of my character, the possibility might have been inferred, that in an evil hour and at a riper age, my passions might have hurried me into acts of fatal rashness, as, under better stars, they might have impelled me into the path of a Hampden; but, that in no situation, I could have trod the track of a Gracchus or a Drusus.

The Gracchi fond of mischief making laws,
And Drusi popular in faction's cause.

Neither could the unshrinking determination which must enter into the composition of a Brutus, have justly been imputed to me; not even on the specious ground of public good: my stuff was not so stern.

My amusements, as I have already said, depended much upon myself. I had a passion for drawing; and my early essays were considered as indications of much genius for the art. I was in the practice also, of cutting men and horses out of cards. By separating the legs of the bipeds, I mounted them without difficulty; and by a similar process on those of the quadrupeds, I could give them a firm stand on a table. By these means I could either send them a hunting with a pack of hounds, in like manner set upon their feet, or attach unmounted horses to sleighs or wheel carriages (all of which I manufactured) at pleasure. My talent also gave me the command of regiments of cavalry, and my evenings, when there was no company, were generally employed in arranging them in order of battle. Divided into two bodies, they were disposed in hostile array, while round pieces of card representing cannon balls, were the missiles alternately thrown at the different corps; that side being held to be defeated, which was first battered down. It was truly a war of extermination, as the vanquished were always cut off to a man. Both my grandfather and grandmother, as well as my aunts, were pleased with my exhibitions; and it became a matter of doubt in the family, whether my genius most inclined me to the profession of a limner or a general.

Music, too, was an art for which I had discovered a propensity, and had already the enthusiasm of an *amateur*. From the drums and fifes of Otway's regiment, which every morning passed our door, I had, among other tunes, learned the grenadier's march; and I remember one day being on a visit to my father, who then resided in the country at a place of Doctor Denormandie's, as I was whistling it with great devotion, and marching to it in proper time, he was delighted with the truth of my ear and the correctness

of my performance: For he was much of a musical man, and
played upon the violin, though, as I have been informed by one
of his old friends, with more of science than execution.

Another circumstance of some affinity to the topic, I cannot
withhold, since it is an evidence of my coincidence in taste with
the celebrated Mr. Addison.   I have somewhere seen it mentioned,
that he was a warm admirer of the ballad of *Salley of the alley*.   I
once, when very young, heard my mother sing it over a cradle,
and was so enraptured with its simple pathos, that I was continually
importuning her to repeat it.   Whether it was the composition or
the melody which had charmed me, I know not, but to my infant
heart it appeared inimitably tender and affecting.   The only verse
I recollect of it is the following:—

> Of all the days within the week,
> I dearly love but one day,
> And that's the day that comes between
> Saturday and Monday :
>   For then I'm drest
>   All in by best,
> To walk abroad with Sally,
> She is the darling of my heart
> And lives in our alley.

Though an old ballad, it is possible that it may be yet so well
known as to render this recital unnecessary, if not to give it an
appearance of triteness.   At any rate, I should hardly have ventured to notice it had it not been dignified by the approbation of
a respectable name.*

---

* The author of the Ballad was Henry Carey, translator of Dante, and a popular English poet. " The works of Carey do not appear in any of our great col-
lections, where Walsh, Duke, and Yalden slumber on the shelf. Yet Carey was
a true son of the muses, and a most successful writer. To this ballad of ' Sally in
our alley,' he prefixed an argument so full of nature, that the song may derive
an additional interest from its simple origin. The author assures the reader that
the popular notion, that the subject of his ballad had been the noted Sally Salis-
bury, is perfectly erroneous, he being a stranger to her name at the time the song
was composed.

" As innocence and virtue were ever the boundaries of his muse, so in this little
poem he had no other view than to set forth the beauty of a chaste and disinterested passion even in the lowest class of human life. The real occasion was this:

It was some time before my entering into the Latin school, that I had the misfortune to loose my father. This was in March, 1761. He had just finished a country house on a favourite spot, sufficiently elevated to overlook the adjacent district for some miles round, and to command a view of the town of Bristol, distant not quite a mile, as well as that of Burlington, together with an extensive intervening tract of meadow ground, stretching to the shore of the Delaware, whose bright expanse was also subjected to the eye. He had long been improving the site before he began to build; had planted it with the best fruits in every kind, and given to it the style of embellishment, both with respect to the disposition of the grounds and the trees, which was at that time in fashion. But this residence, at once so cherished and delightful, he was permitted to enjoy not quite a year. The blow was desolating to my mother, " whose heart was apt to feel ;" and who, in addition to the calamity of being bereaved of one with whom her union had been happiness uninterrupted, found herself at about the age of two and thirty, solely involved in the cares of a young family of four children, of whom I, about to complete my ninth year, was the eldest. To me, who was at home when the event took place, it was rather a shock than a matter of poignant grief. It was the first death that had been brought home to me; and the deep distress of the family, together with the dismal apparatus of coffins and hearses, could not fail to overwhelm me in the general gloom. The next day I was sent to Philadelphia, whither the remains of my father, attended by his faithful and dejected friend Joseph Church, were conveyed for interment. As funeral honours upon these occasions, are the only solace of the

A shoemaker's 'prentice, making holy-day with his sweetheart, treated her with a sight of Bedlam, the puppet-shows, the flying-chairs, and all the elegancies of Moorfields; whence proceeding to the Farthing Pie-house, he gave her a collection of buns, cheese-cakes, gammon of bacon, stuffed beef, and bottled ale; through all which scenes the author dodged them (charmed with the simplicity of their courtship,) whence he drew this little sketch of nature; but, being then young and obscure, he was very much ridiculed for this performance; which, neverthless, made its way into the polite world, and amply recompensed him by the applause of the divine Addison, who was pleased, more than once, to mention it with approbation."—*D'Israeli's Calamities of Authors.*—ED.

afflicted, they were here bestowed with an unsparing hand. Much pomp was shown, and much expense incurred, both of which would have been saved had the will of the deceased, which enjoined a plain and economical burial, been previously opened. The pall, sustained by six of his old city friends, I followed as chief mourner, and saw the body deposited in the grave yard of Market street meeting-house, in or near the tomb wherein his first wife had been laid. My father, as already mentioned, came to this country a married man, and was about twenty years older than my mother. Though he died possessed of a large and valuable landed property in the neighbourhood of Bristol, consisting of an equal part of one thousand acres, purchased in conjunction with Mr. M'Ilvaine in the year 1752 of William Whitaker of London, it was encumbered; and the provision, made necessary by a settlement on his first marriage, for two children, who were the issue of it, rendered the residue inadequate to the support of his widow and her children. Hence, a removal of the family to Philadelphia became expedient, and was resolved on as soon as the requisite arrangements could be made; and it accordingly took place in the course of the year.*

* I was unwilling to enlarge on the topic of my family, or I might have said a great deal more of my father. From the enthusiasm with which I have heard him spoken of by some who knew him, I have reason to infer, that he was not only a man of unquestionable probity, but that there was, also, much of attraction in his character. Among his qualities, was that of a singularly clear and harmonious voice, which he frequently exercised in reading aloud. His choice of books for this purpose, often fell upon Telemaches, Don Quixote, and Shakspeare, passages from all of which, I remember to have heard him read; particularly the opening of the first, which introduces the disconsolate Calypso with her attendant nymphs, and the two strangers just shipwrecked on her isle, and to which he gave all the romantic melancholy and pathos that belong to it. From Don Quixote, the mad attack on the wind-mills and the sheep, by his elevated voice and theatrical manner, for he really acted the passages, lost nothing of the animation originally impressed upon them by their inimitable author. Nor was Shakspeare more a sufferer in his hands. Parts of his Henry IV. I have heard him read, and also of his Julius Cæsar, in which the speech of Marcellus the Tribune, beginning

" Wherefore rejoice, what conquests brings he home?
What tributaries follow him to Rome, &c."

from the uncommon energy of his manner of reciting it, is particularly impressed on my mind. I have understood from my mother that he had been a member of

I have said that I was about to enter the Latin school. The person whose pupil I was consequently to become, was Mr. John Beveridge, a native of Scotland, who retained the smack of his vernacular tongue in its primitive purity. His acquaintance with the language he taught, was, I believe, justly deemed to be very accurate and profound. But as to his other acquirements, after excepting the game of backgammon, in which he was said to excel, truth will not warrant me in saying a great deal. He was, however, diligent and laborious in his attention to his school; and had he possessed the faculty of making himself beloved by the scholars, and of exciting their emulation and exertion, nothing would have been wanting in him to an entire qualification for his office. But, unfortunately, he had no dignity of character, and was no less destitute of the art of making himself respected than beloved. Though not perhaps to be complained of as intolerably severe, he yet made a pretty free use of the ratan and the ferule, but to very little purpose. He was in short no disciplinarian, and consequently very unequal to the management of seventy or eighty boys, many of whom were superlatively pickle and unruly. He was assisted, indeed, by two ushers, who eased him in the burden of teaching, but who, in matters of discipline, seemed disinclined to interfere, and disposed to consider themselves rather as subjects than rulers. I have seen them slily slip out of the way when the principal was entering upon the job of capitally punishing a boy, who from his size, would be likely to make resistance. For this had become nearly a matter of course; and poor Beveridge, who was diminutive in his stature, and neither young nor vigorous, after exhausting himself in the vain attempt to denude the delinquent, was generally glad to compound for a few strokes over his clothes, on any part that was accessible. He had, indeed, so frequently been foiled, that his birch at length was rarely brought forth, and might truly be said to have lost its terrors—it was *tanquam gladium in vagina repositum.* He indemnified himself, however, by a redoubled use of his ratan.

a conversation and reading club in Philadelphia, in which the task of reading a new book was always devolved on him when present, and that, in this capacity, Young's Night Thoughts, on their coming out, were read by him to the company.

So entire was the want of respect towards him, and so liable
was he to be imposed upon, that one of the larger boys, for a
wager, once pulled off his wig, which he effected by suddenly
twitching it from his head under pretence of brushing from it a
spider; and the unequivocal insult was only resented by the
peevish exclamation of *hoot mon!*

Various were the rogueries that were played upon him; but
the most audacious of all was the following. At the hour of con-
vening in the afternoon, that being found the most convenient,
from the circumstance of Mr. Beveridge being usually a little beyond the time; the bell having rung, the ushers being at their
posts, and the scholars arranged in their classes, three or four of
the conspirators conceal themselves without, for the purpose of
observing the motions of their victim. He arrives, enters the
school, and is permitted to proceed until he is supposed to have
nearly reached his chair at the upper end of the room, when instantly the door and every window-shutter is closed. Now,
shrouded in utter darkness, the most hideous yells that can be
conceived, are sent forth from at least three score of throats; and
Ovids, and Virgils, and Horaces, together with the more heavy
metal of dictionaries, whether of Cole, of Young, or of Ainsworth,
are hurled without remorse at the head of the astonished preceptor, who, on his side, groping and crawling under cover of
the forms, makes the best of his way to the door. When attained,
and light restored, a death-like silence ensues. Every boy is at
his lesson; no one has had a hand or a voice in the recent atro-
city: what then is to be done, and who shall be chastised.

> *Sævit atrox Volscens, nec teli conspicit usquam*
> *Auctorem, nec quo se ardens immittere possit.*

> Fierce Volscens foams with rage, and gazing round
> Descries not him who aim'd the fatal wound;
> Nor knows to fix revenge.—

This most intolerable outrage, from its succeeding beyond expectation, and being entirely to the taste of the school, had a run
of several days; and was only then put a stop to by the interference of the *faculty,* who decreed the most exemplary punish-

ment on those who should be found offending in the premises, and by taking measures to prevent a farther repetition of the enormity.

I have said, and with truth, that I was no promoter of mischief; but I will not take upon me to assert, that I was proof against the irresistible contagion of such a scene, or that I did not raise my voice in the discordant concert of the screamers: though I can safely declare, that I never threw at the master, and that I was wholly ignorant of the contrivers and ringleaders of this shameful proceeding.

In the year 1765, Mr. Beveridge published by subscription a small collection of Latin poems. Of their general merit I presume not to judge, but I think I have heard they were not much commended by the British reviewers. The latinity probably is pure, the prosody correct, the versification sufficiently easy and sounding, and such as might serve to evince an intimate acquaintance with the classics of ancient Rome: But I should doubt their possessing much of the soul of poetry. One of them is neither more nor less than an humble petition in hexamaters, and certainly a very curious specimen of pedantic mendicity. It is addressed to Thomas Penn, the proprietary of Pennsylvania; and the poet very modestly proposes, that he should bestow upon him a few of his acres, innumerable, he observes, as the sands of the Delaware; in return for which, his verse shall do its best to confer immortal fame upon the donor. By way of farther inducement to the gift, he sets before his excellency the usual ingratitude of an enriched and unknown posterity, on the one hand; and on the other, the advantage which Ajax, Æneas and Mæcenas derived from the muses of Homer, of Virgil and Horace. But lest I might be suspected of misrepresentation, let my good quondam preceptor speak for himself.

Jugera quum tibi sint quot habet DELAVARUS arenas,
Quid magnum minimo tribuas si propria parvœ.
Fundamenta casœ, Boreæ quâ frigora pellam.
Non dabis ingrato dederis licet œris egeno,
Quodque tibi minimum, magnum esset pauca roganti.
Sin renuas, tanti nec sint commercia nostra,
Hoc quoque ne pigeat cito spem prœcidere vanam.

4

Nec periisse puta, dederis quod vivus amico ;
Credere fas sit enim, si quid mea carmina possint,
Sera licet, majora feras quam MEXICO nobis,
Seu Tagus auriferis exundans mittit arenis ;
Auguror et si quid vives post fata superstes.

Quid juvat ignotis, ingratis forsitan, auri
Pondera, frugiferis vel millia jugera campis
Linquere post natis ?   Nequeunt nam prodere famam
Divitiæ, nequeunt titulis monumenta superbis.

Quid foret Æneas, et magni nominis Ajax,
Atque alii quorum sunt nomina multa virorum ;
Ni foret et vates divini carminis auctor
Mæonides, sacro qui primus vertice Pindi
Deduxit faciles Phœbo plaudente, Camœnas ?

Vel quid Mæcenas animi mentisque benignæ
Ni benefacta sui celebrasset carmen Horati,
Et Maro munificum cecinisset gratus amicum ? &c. &c.

Might not one here be tempted to exclaim in the spirit of Prior
to Boileau!

Pindar, that eagle mounts the skies,
While virtue leads the noble way :
Too like a vulture *Bev'ridge* flies
Where sordid int'rest lures the prey.

I never heard, however, that the poet was the better for his application: I rather think that the proprietor was of opinion, there
was a want of reciprocity in the proposal, and that, whatever the
carmen Horati vel Maronis might have been worth, that of Mr.
Beveridge did not amount to a very valuable consideration.

Another of the principal poems in this collection is a pastoral,
which, if Mr. Beveridge had had the salutary fear of Boileau before his eyes, he certainly would not have written; since, never
was production more completely under the lash of the following
satirical lines.

Viendrai-je, en une Eglogue entouré de troupeaux
Au milieu de Paris enfler mes chalumeaux,
Et dans mon cabinet assis au pied des hêtres,
Faire dire aux echos des sottises champêtres ?

The complainant in this pastoral is an Edinburgh cit, whom he appropriately calls Urbanus: nevertheless he is, without the smallest difficulty, transformed into a shepherd, surrounded with sheep, and proclaiming to the echoes his *sottises champetres*, in strains like these—

> Audiit et planctus gemebunda remurmurat Echo.
> Echo sola meos miserata est, inquit amores;
> Tristia nam mæstis ex saxis assonat imis,
> Flebile luctisonis responsat et usque cicutis.
> Me miserum quoties exclamo, lugubris illa
> Me miserum ingeminat gelidis e vallibus: Eheu,
> Clamanti exclamat, repetitis vocibus, Eheu!

But after all, it is perhaps too much to expect from a modern, good Latin, good poetry, and good sense, all at the same time.

As it frequently happens in human affairs, that men are misplaced, and that those found in a subordinate station are better fitted for the supreme authority than those who are invested with it, so it generally was in the Latin school of the academy. The ushers, during the term of my pupilage, a period of four years, or more, were often changed; and some of them, it must be admitted, were insignificant enough: but others, were men of sense and respectability, to whom, on a comparison with the principal, the management of the school might have been committed with much advantage. Among these was Mr. Patrick Allison, afterwards officiating as a Presbyterian clergyman in Baltimore; Mr. James Wilson, late one of the associate justices of the supreme court of the United States; and Mr. John Andrews, afterwards Doctor Andrews of the University of Pennsylvania. It is true, they were much younger men than Mr. Beveridge, and probably unequal adepts in the language that was taught; but even on the supposition of this comparative deficiency on their part, it would have been amply compensated on the score of judicious discipline and instruction.

With respect to my progress and that of the class to which I belonged, it was reputable and perhaps laudable for the first two years. From a pretty close application, we were well grounded in grammar, and had passed through the elementary books, much to the approbation of our teachers; but at length, with a single exception, we became possessed of the demons of liberty and idleness. We were, to a great degree, impatient of the restraints of a school; and if we yet retained any latent sparks of the emulation of improvement, we were, unfortunately, never favoured with the collision that could draw them forth. We could feelingly have exclaimed with Louis the fourteenth, *mais a quoi sert de lire!* but where's the use of all this pouring over books! One boy thought he had Latin enough, as he was not designed for a learned profession; his father thought so too, and was about taking him from school. Another was of opinion that he might be much better employed in a counting-house, and was also about ridding himself of his scholastic shackles. As this was a consummation devoutly wished by us all, we cheerfully renounced the learned professions for the sake of the supposed liberty that would be the consequence. We were all, therefore, to be merchants, as to be mechanics was too humiliating; and accordingly, when the question was proposed, which of us would enter upon the study of Greek, the grammar of which tongue was about to be put into our hands, there were but two or three who declared for it. As to myself, it was my mother's desire, from her knowing it to have been my father's intention to give me the best education the country afforded, that I should go on, and acquire every language and science that was taught in the institution; but, as my evil star would have it, I was thoroughly tired of books and confinement, and her advice and even entreaties were overruled by my extreme repugnance to a longer continuance in the college, which, to my lasting regret, I bid adieu to when a little turned of fourteen, at the very season when the minds of the studious begin to profit by instruction. We were at this time reading Horace and Cicero, having passed through Ovid, Virgil, Cæsar, and Sallust. From my own experience on this occasion, I am inclined to think it of much consequence, that a boy designed to complete his college studies, should be classed with those of a similar destination.

Of a dozen or more class-mates, the lapse of more than forty years, puts it out of my power to recognise more than three of them, who are yet alive; though there may be others; settled at a distance. One of those, who was the exception to the idle propensity I have mentioned, has lately filled an important office in the state; another of them, though a boy of good parts and much vivacity, early betook himself to a very retired walk of life, from which he never emerged; and the third, with whom I have ever continued in the closest intimacy and friendship, leads, in ease and affluence on his paternal estate, the happy life of a country gentleman, within a convenient distance of the metropolis.

In making this enumeration, there occurs to me a member who joined us perhaps about a year before I left the college. I cannot call him a boy, since he was married, and for ought I know, between thirty and forty years of age. His puckered cheeks, at least, would have justified the latter part of this conjecture. He was preparing himself for the pulpit of an anabaptist meeting-house, and although the acquisition of his Latin was sufficiently arduous in all conscience, he was yet courageous enough to be looking forward to the attainment also of the Greek and the Hebrew. With a rueful length of visage and features of the coursest mould, his figure was tall, raw-boned and ungainly, and certainly a very heterogeneous ingredient in the mass in which he had chosen to compound it. But he was not more distinguished by the uncouth-ness of his appearance than by the meekness of his deportment. It was of the back of this overgrown school-boy that Beveridge usually strove to avail himself, in those abortive, flagellant efforts I have mentioned; and the function, however unpleasing to the Brobdingnagian, he had too strong a sense of duty to decline. Such was the personage, who, from a clerical ardour, had been tempted to transform himself into this scholastic phenomenon. His name, I think, was Stevens; and though I have amused my self with the recollection of his ludicrous attributes, it is with still more satisfaction I bear testimony to those, that, from their simple benevolence, were truly respectable.

4*

CHAPTER II.

Retrospective events in the Author's history.—Philadelphia.—Yellow fever.—
Lodging house.—Foot races.—Paxton boys.—They threaten the city.—Ogle
and Friend.—Author's early amusements.—School anecdotes.—Sailing excursion.—Swimming and Skating.—Abbé Raynal.—Lodging-house guests.—
Baron De Kalb.—Lady Moore.—Lady Susan O'Brien.—Woodward.—Sir William Draper.—Frank Richardson.—Anecdote.—Major Etherington.—Anecdote.—Majors Small and Fell.—General Reid.—Captain Wallace.—Anecdote
of Joseph Church.—Rivington the printer.

ALTHOUGH it was in my fifteenth year, as already mentioned,
that I took my leave of the academy, yet the circumstances I am
now about to avert to were antecedent to that event, and are to
be considered · as having taken place within the five years preceding it.

Among the persons who were acquainted and visited at my
grandfather's, were Doctor Laughlin M'Lean* and his lady.
The latter rarely missed a day, when the weather was favourable,
of calling upon our countrywoman, my grandmother; and I well
remember, she was always attended or rather preceded by a small
white dog, enormously fat, in which quality he even exceeded his
mistress, who yielded to few of her species and sex, in the possession of an enviable *embonpoint*.   The doctor was considered
to have great skill in his profession, as well as to be a man of wit
and general information, but I have never known a person who
had a more distressing impediment in his speech.   Yet, notwithstanding this misfortune, he some years after, on his return to
Europe, had the address to recommend himself to a seat in the
British House of Commons.   He is understood to be the same
Lauchlan Macleane, who at Edinburgh evinced a generous benevolence in administering to the relief of the celebrated Oliver

---

* Dr. LAUCHLAN MACLEANE.   See Appendix B.—ED.

Goldsmith, as related in the life of that poet; and it is this circumstance which has principally induced me to notice him here.

About the year 1760 or 1761, to the best of my recollection, the city was alarmed by a visitation of the yellow fever. I can say nothing of the extent of its ravages, having been, happily, too young to be infected with the panic it produced, or to have been at all interested in the inquiry, whether it had an adequate cause. My impression rather was, that it was an occurrence by no means to be deprecated, since the schools were shut up, and a vacation of five or six weeks, its fortunate consequence. As the city was deserted by such as could leave it without too much inconvenience, my grandfather took refuge at his country house near Germantown, whither, as one of his family I accompanied him, and remained there until the danger was supposed to be over.

It was in the fall, probably of this very year, that my mother removed to Philadelphia, in the view of keeping a lodging house, an employment, which in Pennsylvania, has been the usual resource of persons in her situation, that is, of widows, reputably brought up, left in circumstances too slender for the support of their families. She began with taking boys who went to the academy, of which there were generally a number from the southern provinces and the West India islands. Being thus established, I left my grandfather's for her house, and by this change of residence, bid adieu to the old route, which for about two years I had traversed in going to and returning from school, in the winter four times, and in the summer six times a day. I had my choice, indeed, of different streets, and sometimes varied my course; but it generally led me through what is now called Dock street, then a filthy uncovered sewer, bordered on either side by shabby stables and tan-yards. To these, succeeded the more agreeable object of Israel Pemberton's* garden (now covered in part by the

---

* This property, together with the mansion erected thereon, was originally in possession of William Clarke, Esq. For several years, says Watson, the premises were occupied by some of the earlier governors. It was purchased by Andrew Hamilton, Esq., Attorney General. Its next owner was Israel Pemberton, and subsequently became celebrated as " Pemberton's House and gardens." The building was large, containing many parlours and chambers, and stood on

bank of the United States)* laid out in the old fashioned style of
uniformity, with walks and allies nodding to their brothers, and
decorated with a number of evergreens carefully clipped into py-
ramidal and conical forms.　Here the amenity of the view usually
detained me for a few minutes: Thence, turning Chestnut street
corner to the left, and passing a row of dingy two-story houses,
I came to the Whale bones, which gave name to the alley, at the
corner of which they stood.　These never ceased to be occasionally an object of some curiosity, and might be called my
second stage, beyond which there was but one more general object of attention, and this was to get a peep at the race horses,
which in sporting seasons were kept in the widow Nichols's
stables, which from her house, (the *Indian Queen* at the corner of
Market street,) extended perhaps two-thirds or more of the way
to Chestnut street.　In fact, throughout the whole of my route,
the intervals took up as much ground as the buildings; and with
the exception of here and there a straggling house, Fifth street
might have been called the western extremity of the city.

My course was much shortened by the removal to my mother's,
who had taken a house in Arch street, facing the Friends burying
ground.　The first lads that were placed with her, were two
brothers, the sons of a colonel Lewis of Virginia.　The younger,
named Samuel, about a year older than myself, had the attractions of a pleasing countenance and great gentleness of manners.
Though he belonged to a younger class than mine, the living and
sleeping together were sufficient to cement a warm attachment

the south side of Chestnut street, a short distance west of Third.　After the decease
of Mr. Pemberton, it was occupied by ALEXANDER HAMILTON, as Secretary of
the Treasury of the United States.　The building was razed about the year 1800,
and the grounds divided into building lots upon which were soon erected more
convenient structures, many of which have already given place, in their turn, to
the loftier and more commodious edifices of still more recent time.—ED.

* Purchased by the late Mr. Stephen Girard, and occupied for many years by
him as a successful banker.　His bank was in high credit at the time of his
decease, and, under his able and judicious management, had always, and frequently during periods of depression and trial, sustained its high reputation.　At
his death, the building was occupied and known as "the Girard Bank,"—a new
institution under far different auspices, which, in due time, met with a violent end.
The *building* remains, however,—a lucky circumstance!—ED.

between us, and there was not a boy in the school in whose welfare and competitions I took so decided an interest; the ardour of which was in almost perpetual requisition, from the circumstance of his being a champion in the gymnastic exercise of running, which was then the rage. The enthusiasm of the turf had pervaded the academy, and the most extravagant transports of that theatre on the triumph of a favourite horse, were not more zealous and impassioned, than were the acclamations which followed the victor in a foot-race round a square. Stripped to the shirt, and accoutred for the heat by a handkerchief bound round the head, another round the middle, with loosened knee-bands, without shoes, or with mocasons instead of them, the racers were started; and turning to the left round the corner of Arch street, they encompassed the square in which the academy stands, while the most eager spectators, in imitation of those who scour across the course at a horse-race, scampered over the church burying ground to Fifth street, in order to see the state of the runners as they passed, and to ascertain which was likely to be foremost, on turning Market street corner. The four sides of this square cannot be much less than three-quarters of a mile;* wherefore, bottom in the coursers, was no less essential than swiftness, and in both, Lewis bore away the palm from every one that dared enter against him. After having in a great number of matches completely triumphed over the academy, other schools were resorted to for racers; but all in vain: Lewis was the Eclipse that distanced every competitor, the swift-footed Achilles, against the vigorous agility of whose straight and well-proportioned form, the long legged stride of the overgrown, and the nimble step of the dapper, were equally unavailing. I was scarcely less elated with his triumphs, than if I myself had been the victor: I was even supremely happy in the circumstance, which gave me a claim to a more than common degree of interest in him, and from my experience of the force of these associations, in which, by a kind of metonymy, we take the place of the real agent, I can fully enter into the feelings of the butcher, who ecstacied at the good be-

* Overrated, as from the description of the city in Proud's History of Pennsylvania, it appears that the distance is not half a mile, being only a little more than 700 yards.

haviour of his dog at a bull baiting, exclaimed to Charles the Second, "Damme, sir, if that is'nt my dog!" Since the time of those exploits, in which I was too young to enter the lists, I have valued myself upon my own agility in running and jumping; but I have never had the vanity to suppose, that at my best, I could have contended with any chance of success, in so long a race against Lewis.

At what time I was separated from this friend of my youth I cannot remember; but have to regret, that I lost the opportunity of seeing him, when several years afterwards, having I know not what business in Philadelphia which required despatch, he called upon me one evening when I chanced to be out, and as he was obliged to leave the city very early in the morning, staid in the hope of meeting me till a very late hour. But my engagements unfortunately detained me too long, and he had been obliged to depart before I returned. This could not have been long before the war, probably between the year 1770 and 1772, when we had both attained to years of manhood; but whatever may have been his destiny, I have never since heard of him.*

Of all the cities in the world, Philadelphia was for its size, perhaps, one of the most peaceable and unwarlike; and Grant was not wholly without data for supposing, that with an inconsiderable force he could make his way, at least, through Pennsylvania. So much had the manners of the Quakers, and its long exemption from hostile alarm, nourished this disposition, that a mere handful of lawless frontier men, was found sufficient to throw the capital into consternation. The unpunished, and even applauded massacre of certain Indians at Lancaster,† who in the jail of that town had vainly flattered themselves that they possessed an asylum, had so encouraged their murderers, who called themselves *Paxton boys*, that they threatened to perpetrate the like enormity upon a

---

* It is not only possible but probable, that he might have been one of the Lewis's who defeated the Indians in the great battle of Point Pleasant in the year 1774. There was a General and a Colonel Lewis, brothers, the latter of whom fell in the action.—*See Cuming's Tour*, p. 123.

† This was in December, 1763; six Indians were killed at Conestoga Manor on the 14th of this month; and the remainder of the tribe being fourteen in number were killed at Lancaster on the 27th.—*2d Proud*, p. 326.

number of other Indians under the protection of government in
the metropolis;* and for this purpose, they at length put themselves in arms, and actually began their march. Their force,
though known to be small in the beginning, continually increased
as it went along, the *vires acquirit eunde* being no less the attribute of terror than of fame. Between the two, the invaders were
augmented to some thousands by the time they had approached
within a day or two's journey of their object. To the credit,
however, of the Philadelphians, every possible effort was made
to frustrate the inhuman design of the banditi; and the Quakers
as well as others, who had proper feelings on the occasion, exerted themselves for the protection of the terrified Indians, who
were shut up in the barracks, and for whose immediate defence,
part of a British regiment of foot was stationed there. But the
citadel or place of arms was in the very heart of the city, all
around and within the old court-house and Friend's meeting-
house. Here stood the artillery, under the command of captain
Loxley,† a very honest, though little, dingy-looking man, with
regimentals, considerably war-worn or tarnished; a very sala-
mander or *fire drake* in the public estimation, whose vital air was
deemed the fume of sulphureous explosion, and who, by whatever means he had acquired his science, was always put foremost
when great guns were in question. Here it was that the grand
stand was to be made against the approaching invaders, who, if
rumour might be credited, had now extended their murderous
purposes, beyond the savages, to their patrons and abettors.
Hence, the cause had materially changed its complexion, and
instead of resting on a basis of mere humanity and plighted faith,
it had emphathically become the cause of self-preservation; little
doubt being entertained that the capital would be sacked, in case
of the predominance of the barbarous foe. In this state of consternation and dismay, all business was laid aside for the more
important occupation of arms. Drums, colours, rusty halberts
and bayonets, were brought forth from their lurking places; and,

* About 140 in number.—*2d Proud*, p. 326.

† This doughty gentleman was a Lieutenant under Braddock in 1756, and
was certainly a man of considerable influence and repute, notwithstanding the
humorous description of the text.—ED.

as every good citizen who had a sword had girded it to his thigh, so every one who had a gun had placed it on his shoulder. In short, *bella, horrida bella,* war, destructive war, was about to desolate the hitherto peaceful streets of Philadelphia.

But with all this, the old proverb was not belied; and the benign influence of this *ill wind* was sensibly felt by us school-boys. The dreaded event was overbalanced in our minds by the holydays which were the effect of it; and so far as I can recall my feelings on the occasion, they very much preponderated on the side of hilarity.

As the defensive army was without eyes, it had, of course, no better information than such as common bruit could supply; and hence, many untoward consequences ensued: One was the near extinction of a troop of mounted butchers from Germantown, who, scampering down Market street with the best intentions in the world, were announced as the Paxton boys, and by this mistake, very narrowly escaped a greeting from the rude throats of captain Loxley's artillery. The word FIRE was already quivering on his lips, but Pallas came in shape of something, and suppressed it. Another emanation from this unmilitary defect of vision, was the curious order, that every house-holder in Market street should affix one or more candles at his door before daylight, on the morning of the day on which, from some sufficient reason no doubt, it had been elicited that the enemy would full surely make his attack, and by no other than this identical route, on the citadel. Whether this illumination was merely intended to prevent surprise, or whether it was that the commander who enjoined it was determined, like Ajax, that if perish he must, he would perish in the face of day, I do not know, but certain it is, that such a decree went forth and was religiously complied with. This I can affirm from the circumstance of having resided in Market street at the time. The sage precaution, however, proved superfluous, although with respect merely to the nearness of the redoubted invaders, there was colour for it. It was soon ascertained that they had reached Germantown, and a deputation of the least obnoxious citizens with the olive branch, was sent out to meet them. After a parley of some days, an armistice was agreed upon, and peace at length so effectually restored, that the formidable stragglers who had excited so much terror, were permitted, as friends, to enter the city.

Party spirit, at this time, ran very high, and the Paxton* men

---

* Generally known as "the Paxton boys,"—from the township of *Paxton*, in Lancaster county, associated to avenge alleged barbarities of the Indians. Among their leaders were Stewart, Calhoun, Smith and Dickey. They created much excitement at the time, (1764.) "In this year,"—says Watson—"under an alarm of intended massacre, fourteen being previously killed on the Conestoga, the Indians sought shelter in Lancaster, and, for better security, were placed under bolts and bars in the county prison; but, at noon, a party on horseback, from the country, rode through the streets to the prison, and there forcibly entered and killed unresisting men and women on the spot. The citizens of Lancaster were loudly blamed for their apathy. They suffered the perpetrators of this cruel outrage to depart unpunished. Meanwhile other friendly Indians who had received information of this massacre, sought refuge in Philadelphia, the news of which exasperated the "Paxton boys," who at once resolved to march to the city, for the purpose of completing the destruction they had commenced, and also to take summary vengeance upon the friends, residing there, of their intended victims.

"The news of their approach, which outran them, was greatly magnified; the utmost excitement prevailed, and a fearful struggle was anticipated. Among the citizens of Philadelphia were many who entertained feelings of bitter hostility towards the unfortunate race, for their conduct during the Indian war. The 'Paxton boys,' to the number of several hundred, armed with rifles, and clad in hunting shirts, affecting the rudest manners, approached the city in two divisions as far as Germantown, and the opposite bank of the Schuylkill, where they finally entered into affected negotiations with the citizens, at the head of whom was Dr. Franklin, and returned to their homes, to the terror of the country through which they passed.

"In the meantime, the Indians sought refuge in Philadelphia, having with them their Moravian minister. They were at first conducted, by order of the governor, to the barracks in the Northern Liberties; but the highlanders there refused them shelter, although it was cold December weather, and for several hours they were exposed to the unrestrained insults of the rabble. They were subsequently sent to New York. They were guarded by a company of seventy highlanders as far as Amboy, where they were stopped by order of General Gage. They next returned to Philadelphia. All these removals were measures of security, as fears were still entertained from many of the excited citizens, who were favourable to the movements which threatened their destruction. In the midst of the panic caused, at night, by the reported proximity of the 'Paxton boys,' the town was illuminated, alarm bells were sounded, and the citizens hastened for arms to the barracks. Many young Quakers joined the defenders there, where they speedily threw up intrenchments. Dr. Franklin and others, who went forth to meet the leaders, conducted them into the city, that they might point out, if possible, those who had been guilty of alleged excesses. But they failed to make the necessary recognition, and fearing that the

5

were not without a number of clamorous advocates, who entirely
justified them on the score of their sufferings from the savages,
who, during the war, had made incursions upon them, and murdered their kindred and friends.   It was even alleged, that the
pretended friendly Indians had been treacherous, having always
maintained an understanding with the hostile ones, and frequently
conducted them into our settlements: But this rested on mere
suspicion, without a shadow of proof that ever I heard of.   It
was enough, however, to throw it out to obtain partisans to the
opinion ; and, whether the Paxton men were "more sinned
against than sinning," was a question which was agitated with so
much ardor and acrimony, that even the school-boys became
warmly engaged in the contest.   For my own part, though of the
religious sect which had been long warring with the Quakers, I
was entirely on the side of humanity and public duty, (or in this,
do I beg the question?) and perfectly recollect my indignation at
the sentiments of one of the ushers who was on the opposite side.
His name was Davis, and he was really a kind, good natured
man ; yet from the dominion of his religious or political prejudices, he had been led to apologize for, if not to approve of, an
outrage, which was a disgrace to a civilized people.   He had
been among the riflemen on their coming into the city, and talking with them upon the subject of the Lancaster massacre, and
particularly of the killing of Will Sock, the most distinguished
of the victims, related with an air of approbation, this rodomontade of the real or pretended murderer.   " I," said he, " am the
man who killed Will Sock—this is the arm that stabbed him to
the heart, and I glory in it."   Notwithstanding the fine colouring
of Mr. Davis, young as I was, I am happy in being able to say,
that I felt a just contempt for the inglorious boaster, who appeared
to me in the light of a cowardly ruffian, instead of a hero.   There
was much political scribbling on this occasion; and among the

citizens were well prepared to make good their defence, they professed to be
satisfied and soon returned to their homes."
    The Indians remained in the city for several months, where their numbers
were speedily thinned by the ravages of the small-pox. Fifty-six were buried in
the Potter's Field, now known as Washington *Square*, the good people of Philadelphia preferring this to the more euphonous designation of PARK !—ED.

pamphleteers of the day, Doctor Franklin, drew his pen in behalf of the Indians, giving a very affecting narrative of the transaction at Lancaster, which, no doubt, had its effect in regulating public opinion, and thereby putting a stop to the farther violence that was meditated.

But it was not alone by hostile alarms, that the good people of Philadelphia were annoyed. Their tranquillity had been likewise disturbed by the uncitizenlike conduct of a pair of British officers, who, for want of something better to do, had plunged themselves into an excess of intemperance; and in the plentitude of wine and hilarity, paraded the streets at all hours,

A la clartě de cieux dans l'ombre de la nuit,

to the no small terror of the sober and the timid. The firm of this duumvirate was Ogle and Friend, names always coupled together, like those of Castor and Pollux, or of Pylades and Orestes. But the cement which connected them, was scarcely so pure as that which had united those heroes of antiquity. It could hardly be called friendship, but was rather a confederacy in debauchery and riot, exemplified in a never ending round of frolic and fun. It was related of Ogle, that upon hiring a servant, he had stipulated with him that he should never get drunk but when his master was sober. But the fellow some time after requested his discharge, giving for his reason, that he had in truth no dislike to a social glass himself, but it had so happened, that the terms of the agreement had absolutely cut him off from any chance of ever indulging his propensity.

Many are the pranks I have heard ascribed, either conjointly or separately, to this *par nobile fratrum*. That of Ogle's first appearance in Philadelphia, has been thus related to me by Mr. Will Richards, the apothecary, who, it is well known, was, from his size and manner, as fine a figure for Falstaff as the imagination can conceive. "One afternoon," said he, "an officer in full regimentals, booted and spurred with a whip in his hand, spattered with mud from top to toe, and reeling under the effects of an overdose of liquor, made his entrance into the coffee-house, in a box of which I was sitting, perusing a newspaper. He was

probably under the impression, that every man he was to meet
would be a Quaker, and that a Quaker was no other than a
licensed Simon Pure for his amusement: for no sooner had he
entered, than throwing his arms about the neck of Mr. Joshua
Fisher with the exclamation of—"Ah, my dear Broadbrim give
me a kiss," he began to slaver him most lovingly. As Joshua
was a good deal embarrassed by the salutation, and wholly unable
to parry the assault or shake off the fond intruder, I interfered
in his behalf and effected a separation, when Ogle, turning to me,
cried out, 'Hah! my jolly fellow, give me a smack of your fat
chops,' and immediately fell to hugging and kissing me, as he
had done Fisher. But instead of the coyness he had shown, I
hugged and kissed in my turn as hard as I was able, until my
weight at length brought Ogle to the floor and myself on top of
him: Nevertheless, I kept kissing away, until nearly mashed and
suffocated, he exclaimed, 'for Heaven's sake let me up, let me
up, or you will smother me!'   Having sufficiently tormented him
and avenged Joshua Fisher, I permitted him to rise, when he
seemed a good deal sobered, and finding that I was neither a
Quaker nor wholly ignorant of the world, he evinced some respect
for me, took a seat with me in a box, and entering into conversation, soon discovered, that however he might be disguised by intoxication, he well knew what belonged to the character of a gentleman.   This," said Richards, " was the commencement of an
acquaintance between us ; and captain Ogle sometimes called to
see me, upon which occasions he always behaved with the utmost
propriety and decorum."

   This same coffee-house, the only one indeed in the city, was
also the scene of another affray by Ogle and Friend in conjunction.   I know not what particular acts of mischief they had been
guilty of, but they were very drunk, and their conduct so extremely disquieting and insulting to the peaceable citizens there
assembled, that being no longer able to endure it, it was judged
expedient to commit them ; and Mr. Chew happening to be there,
undertook, in virtue probably of his office of recorder, to write
their commitment: But Ogle, facetiously jogging his elbow, and
interrupting him with a repetition of the pitiful interjection of
"*Ah, now, Mr. Chew !*" he was driven from his gravity, and

obliged to throw away the pen. It was then taken up by Alderman M———n with a determination to go through with the business, when the culprits reeling round him, and Ogle in particular, hanging over his shoulder and reading after him as he wrote, at length, with irresistible effect, hit upon an unfortunate oversight of the alderman. "Ay," says he, "my father was a justice of peace too, but he did not spell that word as you do. I remember perfectly well, that instead of an S he always used to spell CIRCUMSTANCE with a C." This sarcastic thrust at the scribe, entirely turned the tide in favour of the rioters; and the company being disarmed of their resentment, the alderman had no disposition to provoke farther criticism by going on with the *mittimus*.

The irregularities of these gay rakes were not more eccentric than diversified; and the more extravagant they could render them, the better. At one time, they would drive full tilt through the streets in a chair; and upon one of these occasions, on approaching a boom which had been thrown across the street, in a part that was undergoing the operation of paving, they lashed forward their steed, and sousing against the spar with great violence, they were consequently hurled from their seats, like Don Quixote in his temerarious assault of the windmills. At another time, at Doctor Orme's, the apothecary, where Ogle lodged, they, in emulation of the same mad hero at the puppet show, laid about them with their canes upon the defenceless bottles and phials, at the same time assaulting a diminutive Maryland parson, whom, in their frolic, they kicked from the street-door to the kitchen. He was a fellow lodger of Ogle's; and, to make him some amends for the roughness of this usage, they shortly after took him drunk to the dancing assembly, where, through the instrumentality of this unworthy son of the church, they contrived to excite a notable hubbub. Though they had escaped, as already mentioned, at the coffee-house, yet their repeated malfeasances had brought them within the notice of the civil authority; and they had more than once been in the clutches of the mayor of the city. This was Mr. S———, a small man of a squat, bandy-legged figure; and hence, by way of being revenged on him, they bribed a negro with a precisely similar pair of legs, to carry him a billet, which

5*

imported, that as the bearer had in vain searched the town for a
pair of hose that might fit him, he now applied to his honour to
be informed where he purchased HIS stockings.

I have been told that General Lee, when a captain in the
British service, had got involved in this vortex of dissipation; and
although afterwards so strenuous an advocate for the civil rights
of the Americans, had been made to smart severely for their vio-
lation, by the mayor's court of Philadelphia.

The common observation, that when men become soldiers they
lose the character and feelings of citizens, was amply illustrated
by the general conduct of the British officers in America. Their
studied contempt of the *mohairs*, by which term all those who
were not in uniform were distinguished, was manifest on all occasions: and it is by no means improbable, that the disgust
then excited, might have more easily ripened into that harvest
of discontent, which subsequent injuries called forth, and
which terminated in a subduction of allegiance from the parent
land.

At the era of these various intestine commotions, I could not
have more than completed my twelfth year. My attention to my
school exercises, as already observed, was not at this time to be
complained of; and a part of my evenings was either employed
in writing them or committing them to memory. In relation to
the latter, I will mention a circumstance which to me appeared
remarkable, though perhaps it was not peculiar. After labouring
in vain to master my task, I have gone to bed, scarcely able to
repeat a line of it, but in the morning when I awoke, it has been
perfect in my memory. The same thing has often occurred in
respect to tunes I have been desirous of acquiring: and indeed I
have ever found, that the morning was the propitious season for
the exertion of my mental faculties. But though not materially
deficient in attention, it had not the smallest reference to future
utility ; and something less than

> A wizard might have said,
> I ne'er shall rise by benefice or trade.

A scramble was ever my aversion, and the unthriftiness of my
character might also have been inferred, from my indifference to

those games which have gain for their object. I never could boast my winning at marbles or chuckers; and as I chiefly played them for pastime, I never attained to that degree of perfection in them, which the keener stimulus of profit is calculated to produce, and which alone perhaps can lead to the fame of a *dabster*. When in possession of any of these implements that were reckoned handsome or good, I never felt the inclination I have observed in those of better trading parts, of turning them into pence: with me they were hobby horses, not articles of commerce; and though I had no dislike to money, it never impressed me as a primary good, a circumstance more essential than may be imagined, to what is called success in life. I do not speak of this as a virtue; and if it were one, I have certainly little reason to rejoice in it. It is not one of those, at least, which leads to riches and advancement; or which, under the world's law, has a right to look for other than its own reward. In gymnastic exercises, however, my relish was keen and altogether orthodox. For those of running, leaping, swimming and skating, no one had more appetite; and for the enjoyment of these, fatigue and hunger were disregarded. To these succeeded a passion for fowling and boating; fishing being too sedentary and inactive for my taste. If furnished on Saturday afternoon or other holyday, with cash enough for the purchase of powder and shot, or the hire of a batteau or skiff, as the propensity of the day might incline, I had nothing more to wish for. In my land rambles, the environs of Philadelphia for several miles round, were thoroughly traversed, from the uplands of Springetsbury, Bushhill and Centre-wood, to the low grounds and meadows of Passyunk and Moyamensing; while, in my water excursions, the sedgy shores of the Delaware, as well as the reedy cover of Petty's, League and Mud Islands, were pervaded and explored in pursuit of ducks, reed-bird and rail. No pestilent vapours then arose from these marshes; and instead of the deadly fevers which have since proceeded from, or been fostered by them, their effluvia gave a zest to the cold morsel in the locker.

But notwithstanding the ardour with which these sports were

pursued, I not unfrequently surrendered myself to the reveries of a pleasing melancholy, to which I have ever been occasionally inclined. For hours together have I sat alone, listening to the church bells, which it was the custom to ring on the evening before market day, and which, from the back part of a house wherein we some time resided on the south side of Arch street, were heard to much advantage. Rousseau, who takes great pains to represent himself as different from all others, and who seems to suppose that the mould in which he was cast has been broken, informs us, that the chime of bells always singularly affected him. But the lively testimony of my own feelings assures me, that never, not even on the day when he took a ramble in the suburbs of Annecy while Madam de Warrens was at vespers, and gave himself up to those delightful illusions, of which he has given so enchanting a description, was he more under the influence of their transporting sounds than I have been. How often has the simple melody of *Turn again Wittington*, " resounding through the empty-vaulted night," completely lifted me from the earth; absorbed me in etherial visions, and sublimed me into such abstraction from this low world and its concerns, as to identify my conceptions with those of the poet, when he exclaims,

> How vain the ardour of the crowd,
> How low, how little are the proud,
> How indigent the great !

The amusements I have been speaking of, were of no advantage to me as a student; but what was lost to the mind by my strong addiction to active recreations, was gained to the body; and tended to invigorate a constitution naturally tender. My exercises were often carried to toil. I was extremely fond of rowing, and took great delight in feathering my oar, sometimes skimming it along the surface of the water in the manner of a wherry man, sometimes resting it horizontally between the thole pins in the fashion of a bargeman. I had also made some proficiency in sculling, which appeared to me a highly enviable qualification: but the trimming of sails, laying a boat to the wind, with the management of the helm and the application of the proper terms,

were, in my eyes, acquisitions more truly honourable than the best
of those which are attained in a college. The subject recalls a
memorable expedition I engaged in, when perhaps about the age
of thirteen. Returning from morning school at eight o'clock, a
boy, a brother of the late Mr. Robert Morris, proposed an excursion to Chester, for the purpose of seeing the Coventry frigate
which there rode at anchor. From an over greediness of gratification, his plan was to have two boats, whereas one would have
been very ample for four of us, the number of the company.
But then the projector of the voyage might have found competitors for the helm, which he wished to engross; and had, accordingly, secured an unambitious ship-mate, in a son of captain
Loxley, of Paxton war memory, already mentioned. A skiff he
had already prepared for himself and his comrade, and suggested
where a batteau might be obtained for the other two of the party,
one Corbett from the island of Montserrat, and myself. Each
boat had a sail, and he observed, that as the wind and tide would
be favourable, we could run down in a few hours. I objected,
that I had not breakfasted. Neither had he, he said, nor indeed
any of us ; but this was of little consequence, as we could furnish ourselves with cakes.   My mind fluctuated awhile between
the charms of the adventure and the impropriety of going without permission, and consequently subjecting my mother to a
most distressing state of anxiety on my account : For I was neither an habitual truant-player, nor a contemner of the feelings of
a most affectionate parent, though I should have been ashamed
to have said so. But such was the eagerness for the frolic with
my associates, that it would not admit of a moment's delay ; and
the allurements of pleasure proving too potent for principle, I
yielded to persuasion, and we embarked. It was a fine morning ;
a gentle breeze propelled us in our course, and in a few hours
we were delightfully wafted to the place of destination. We
saw the frigate, had the pleasure of sailing round her, the satisfaction of counting her guns, of contemplating her bright sides,
(for she appeared to be new,) of admiring her rigging, and the
duck-like beauty with which she sat upon the water. But here
fruition ended. Water excursions are keen whetters of the appetite, and the calls of hunger began to be importunate. I forget

whether we had taken any cakes with us, but if we had, the supply had been very insufficient for the day's provision. Hereupon,
a canvass took place of the state of our pockets: they were found
empty and pennyless: We were, in short, a miserable crew of
Gautiers sans argent, and being too proud to beg for victuals,
we had no resource but unripe fruit. As the wind was unfavourable to our return, we were obliged to wait for the turning of the
tide, and in the mean time, employed ourselves in sauntering
about the village, the orchards, and the shore. We found, too,
that we were very much out in our reckoning, the tide of flood
not making for above an hour later than our calculation. At
length, however, we had the satisfaction to find, that the marks
we had made in the sand were unequivocally encroached upon
by the water, and that floating substances were at a stand, if not
really changed in their direction. We hailed the event, and immediately embarked. But now our toils began. It was already
late in the afternoon: The wind, still ahead, had considerably increased, and the lowering aspect of the sky indicated approaching
rain. It came on about dusk, and in this situation we had to tug
at our oars like galley slaves, for the whole distance of from sixteen to eighteen miles. Then it was, we perceived the folly of
our two boats. It was between ten and eleven at night when we
reached the city, wet, almost starved, and exhausted with labour.
As I well knew what must be my mother's cruel situation, I
hastened to show myself, and found her a prey to the most afflicting uncertainty. She had not been able to obtain any satisfactory tidings of me, and knew not what to conclude. My trespass, however, being readily forgiven, I appeased my hunger and
went to bed. Extreme fatigue, especially when it has been mingled with anxiety, is unfavourable to repose, and I slept but ill.
I was tormented with distressing dreams, contending, as it
seemed, with tasks above my strength, and buffeting with waves
"in night and tempest wrapt."

> Borne by th' outrageous flood
> To distance down, I ride the ridgy wave,
> Or whelm'd beneath the boiling eddy sink.

The exercises of swimming and skating were so much within

the reach of the boys of Philadelphia, that it would have been surprising, had they neglected them, or even had they not excelled in them. Both Delaware and Schuylkill present the most convenient and delightful shores for the former, whilst the heat and the length of the summers invite to the luxury of bathing; and the same rivers seldom fail in winter, to offer the means of enjoying the latter; and when they do, the ponds always afford them. Since the art of swimming has been, in some degree, dignified by Dr. Franklin's having been a teacher of it, and having made it the subject of a dissertation, I may, perhaps, be warranted in bringing forward my remark. When in practice, I never felt myself spent with it; and though I never undertook to swim farther than across Schuylkill, at or near the middle ferry where the bridge now stands, it appeared to me that I could have continued the exercise for hours, and consequently have swum some miles. To recover breath, I only found it necessary to turn upon my back, in which position with my arms across my body or pressed to my sides, since moving them as many do, answers no other purpose than to retard and fatigue the swimmer; my lungs had free play, and I felt myself as perfectly at ease, as if reclined on a sofa. In short, no man can be an able swimmer, who only swims with his face downward: The pressure of the water on the breast, is an impediment to respiration in that attitude, which, for that reason cannot be long continued; whereas, the only inconvenience in the supine posture, is, that the head sinks so low, that the ears are liable to receive water, a consequence which might be prevented by stopping them with wool or cotton, or covering them with a bathing cap.

With respect to skating, though the Philadelphians have never reduced it to rules like the Londoners, nor connected it with their business like Dutchmen, I will yet hazard the opinion, that they were the best and most elegant skaters in the world. I have seen New England skaters, Old England skaters, and Holland skaters, but the best of them could but " make the judicious grieve." I was once slightly acquainted with a worthy gentleman, the quondam member of a skating club in London, and it must be admitted that he performed very well for an Englishman. His *High*

Dutch, or as he better termed it, his *outer edge* skating, might, for aught I know, have been exactly conformable to the statutes of this institution : To these, he would often appeal ; and I recollect the principal one was, that each stroke should describe an exact semicircle. Nevertheless, his style was what we should deem a very bad one. An utter stranger to the beauty of bringing forward the suspended foot towards the middle of the stroke, and boldly advancing it before the other, at the conclusion of it, thus to preserve throughout his course, a continuity of movement, to rise like an ascending wave to its acme, then, gracefully like a descending one, to glide into the succeeding stroke without effort either real or apparent—every change of foot with this gentleman, seemed a beginning of motion, and required a most unseemly jerk of the body ; and unequivocal evidence of the want of that power, which depends upon a just balance, and should never be lost—which carries the skater forward with energy without exertion ; and is as essential to his swift and graceful career, as is a good head of water to the velocity of a mill wheel. Those who have seen good skating will comprehend what I mean, still better those who are adepts themselves ; but excellence in the art can never be gained by geometrical rules. The two reputed best skaters of my day, were General Cadwallader and Massey the biscuit baker ; but I could name many others, both of the academy and Quaker school who were in no degree inferior to them ; whose action and attitudes were equally graceful, and like theirs, no less worthy of the chisel than those, which in other exercises, have been selected to display the skill of the eminent sculptors of antiquity.* I here speak, be it observed, of what the

---

* Watson also informs us that "during the old fashioned winters, when, about New Year's day, every one expected to see or hear of an 'Ox Roast' on the Delaware, upon the thick ribbed ice, the river's surface was covered with skaters. Of the many varieties of skaters of all colours and sizes mingled together, and darting about here and there, 'upward and downward, mingled and convolved ;' a few were at all times distinguished above the rest for dexterity, power and grace, and among these were William Tharpe, Dr. Foulke, Governor Mifflin, C. W. Peale, George Heyl, and Joe Claypoole, not to omit a black Othello who, from his apparent muscle and powerful movement, might have sprung, as did the Moor from 'men of royal siege.' In swiftness he had no competitor ; he outstripped the wind ; the play of his elbows in alternate movement with his ' low

Philadelphians *were*, not what they *are*, since I am unacquainted with the present state of the art; and as from my lately meeting with young men, who, though bred in the city had not learned to swim, I infer the probability, that skating may be equally on the decline.

The Abbé Raynal,* when speaking of Philadelphia, in his Philosophical History of the East and West Indies, observes that the

gutter' skates, while darting forward and uttering occasionally a wild scream peculiar to his race while in active exertion of body, was very imposing in appearance and effect. Of the gentlemen before enumerated, George Heyl took the lead in graceful skating, and in superior dexterity in cutting figures and 'High Dutch' within a limited space of smooth ice. On a larger field of glass, among others he might be seen moving about elegantly and at perfect ease, in curve lines, with folded arms, being dressed in red coat (as was the fashion) and buckskin 'tights,' his bright broad skates in an occasional round flashing upon the eye; then again to be pursued by others he might be seen suddenly changing to the back and *heel forward* movement, offering them his hand, and at the same time eluding their grasp by his dexterous and sudden deviations to the right and left, leaving them to the toil of 'striking out' after him with all their strength.

"The next best skater, was Dr. Foulke. Skating 'High Dutch,' and being able to cut the letters of his own name at one flourish constituted his fame as a skater.

"C. W. Peale, (founder of the Museum) was only distinguished for using a remarkable pair of 'gutter skates,' with a singular prong, capped and curved backwards, with which he moved leisurely about in curve lines. They looked as if they had been brought to him from afar, as a contribution to the curiosities of his Museum."—ED.

* This celebrated person was born in 1712: educated among the Jesuits, and had even become a member of their Order: but was expelled for denying the supreme authority of the church. He afterwards associated with Voltaire, D'Alembert, and Diderot, and was, by them, employed to furnish the theological articles for the Encyclopedia. In this, however, he received the assistance of the Abbé Yvon, to whom he did not give above a sixth of what he received; which, being afterwards discovered, he was obliged to pay Yvon the balance. His most celebrated work is his Political and Philosophical History of the European settlements in the East and West Indies; which has been translated into all the languages of Europe and much admired. This work was followed in 1780 by another entitled the Revolution of America, in which the Abbé pleads the cause of the Americans with zeal. The chief trait in Raynal's character was his love of liberty; but when he saw the length to which the French Revolutionists were proceeding, he made one effort to stop them in their career. In May, 1791, he addressed a letter to the Constituent National Assembly, in which, after complimenting them upon the great things they had done, he cautioned them against the dangers of going farther. He lived not only to see his forebodings of public

6

houses are covered with slate, a material amply supplied from quarries in the neighbourhood. But, unfortunately, for the source from which the Abbé derived his information, there were no such quarries near the city that ever I heard of, and certainly but a single house in it with this kind of roof, which, from that circumstance, was distinguished by the name of *The Slate House.* It stood in Second street, at the corner of Norris's alley, and was a singular old fashioned structure, laid out in the style of a fortification, with abundance of angles both salient and re-entering. Its two wings projected to the street in the manner of bastions, to which, the main building retreating from sixteen to eighteen feet, served for a curtain. Within, it was cut up into a number of apartments, and on that account, was exceedingly well adapted to the purpose of a lodging house, to which use it had been long appropriated. An additional convenience, was a spacious yard on the back of it, extending half way to Front street, enclosed by a high wall, and ornamented with a double row of venerable, lofty pines, which afforded a very agreeable *rus in urbe,* or rural scene in the heart of the city. The lady who had resided here and given some celebrity to the stand by the style of her accommodations, either dying or declining business, my mother was persuaded by her friends to become her successor; and, accordingly obtained a lease of the premises, and took possession of them to the best of my recollection, in the year 1764 or 1765.*

calamity realized, but to suffer his share of it. After being stripped of all his property, which was considerable, by the robbers of the Revolution, he died in poverty, March, 1796, in the eighty-fourth year of his age.—*Lond. Ency.*—ED.

* The slate-roof house is still standing, in 1846, a creditable monument to the forbearance of its lady-owner, in the midst of the general war which, for years, has been steadily waged against every relic of the olden-time. How much longer it will be suffered to remain it were vain to conjecture. Its origin, its uses, and the historical characters who, from time to time, have dwelt within its walls, should create a feeling of interest, for its preservation on the part of Philadelphians; and prompt the adoption of immediate measures for that patriotic purpose. In this age of "Constitutional scruples," the city councils might not feel at liberty to appropriate the sum necessary for its purchase and restoration ; but the citizens themselves by limiting the sum to a trifle, might readily fill a subscription for a few thousand dollars, and, by placing it under the guardianship of the city, insure for it the necessary care.

We are informed by the zealous chronicler, Watson, that this house was erected

While in this residence, and in a still more commodious one in the upper part of Front street, to which she some years afterwards removed, she had the honour, if so it might be called, of entertaining strangers of the first rank who visited the city. Those who have seen better days, but have been compelled by hard necessity, to submit to a way of life, which to a feeling mind, whoever may be the guests, is sufficiently humiliating, are much indebted to Mr. Gibbon, for the handsome manner in which he speaks of the hostess of a boarding house at Lausanne. With the delicacy of a gentleman and the discernment of a man of the world, the historian dares to recognise that worth and refinement are not confined to opulence or station; and that although, in the keeper of a house of public entertainment, these qualities are not much to be looked for, yet, when they do occur, the paying for the comforts and attentions we receive does not exempt us from the courtesy of an apparent equality and obligation. An equally liberal way of thinking, is adopted by Mr. Cumberland, who tells us in his Memoirs, that the British coffee-house was kept by a Mrs. Anderson, a person of great respectability. If, then, an education and situation in early life, which enabled my mother to maintain an intercourse in the best families in the city, pretentions, in no degree impaired by her matrimonial connexion, or an industrious, irreproachable conduct in her succeeding years of widowhood, can give a claim to respect, I have a right to say with Mr. Cumberland, that the principal lodging house in Philadelphia, was kept by a person of great respectability.

A biographical sketch of the various personages, who, in the course of eight or nine years, became inmates of this house,

for Samuel Carpenter whom he eulogizes for his early public spirit, and that it was occupied by William Penn, on his second visit in the year 1700. One month after Penn's arrival, John Penn, called the "American," was born in this house. In 1703, the property was purchased by William Trent, the founder of Trenton—the capitol of New Jersey, for £850. Watson quotes a letter from James Logan in 1700 to Penn as follows: "William Trent designing for England is about selling his house, (that he bought of Samuel Carpenter,) which thou lived in, with the improvement of a beautiful garden. I wish it could be made thine, as nothing in this town is so well fitting a Governor. His price is £900 of our money, which it is hard thou can'st not spare."

He could not spare it, however, and it became the property of a Mr. Norris, in whose family it still continues.—ED.

might, from the hand of a good delineator, be both curious and amusing. Among these, were persons of distinction, and some of no distinction: many real gentlemen, and some, no doubt, who were merely pretenders to the appellation. Some attended by servants in gay liveries; some, with servants in plain coats, and some with no servants at all. It was rarely without officers of the British army. It was at different times, nearly filled by those of the Forty-second or Highland regiment, as also by those of the Royal Irish. Besides these, it sometimes accommodated officers of other armies, and other uniforms. Of this description, was the Baron de Kalb, who visited this country probably about the year 1768 or 1769; and who fell a major-general in the army of the United States at the battle of Camden. Though a German by birth, he had belonged to the French service, and had returned to France, after the visit just mentioned. During our revolutionary contest, he came to tender us his services, and returned no more. The steady and composed demeanour of the Baron, bespoke the soldier and philosopher; the man who had calmly estimated life and death, and who, though not prodigal of the one, had no unmanly dread of the other. He was not indeed a young man; and his behaviour at the time of his death, as I have heard it described by Mons. Dubuisson, his aid-de-camp, was exactly conformable to what might have been supposed from his character.*

* "The representation of the Baron,"—says the author in a MS. note—"as an enthusiast for liberty, whose sacred cause he crossed the Atlantic to espouse, is one of the 'lame and impotent conclusions' of our republican fanatics. He cared just as much for our liberty, probably, as did the other French subjects who assisted us under the standard of the Count de Rochambeau. He, no doubt, thought the occasion favourable for crippling the power of Britain, and of avenging the loss of Canada. At the same time, he was politic enough to take the tone of the people he was acting with, and might, therefore, have talked of liberty with the rest, but he would have deemed it quite sufficient to his fame, to be considered as at once faithful to France and her allies, and of having acquitted himself as a brave and accomplished soldier; and this was all we had to require of him."

The Baron was born in Germany, about the year 1717. When young, he entered into the service of France, in which he continued for forty-two years, and obtained the rank of brigadier-general. In 1757, during the war between England and France, he was sent, by the French government, to the American

Another of our foreign guests, was one Badourin, who wore a white cockade, and gave himself out for a general in the Austrian service; but whether general or not, he, one night, very unexpectedly left his quarters, making a masterly retreat with the loss of no other baggage than that of an old trunk, which, when opened, was found to contain only a few old Latin and German books. Among the former, was a folio, bound in parchment, which I have now before me; it is a ponderous tract of the mystical Robert Fludd, alias de Fluctibus, printed at Oppenheim in the year 1618, and in part dedicated to the duke de Guise, whom the author informs us he had instructed in the art of war. It is to this writer probably, that Butler thus alludes in his Hudibras:

> He, Anthroposophus and *Floud*,
> And Jacob Behman understood.

From this work of Mr. Fludd, which among a fund of other important matter, treats of astrology and divination, it is not improbable that its quondam possessor Mr. Badourin, might have been a mountebank-conjuror, instead of a general.

Among those of rank from Great Britain with whose residence we were honoured, I recollect Lady Moore and her daughter, a

colonies, in order to learn the points in which they were most vulnerable, and how far the seeds of discontent might be sown in them towards the mother country. He was seized, while in the performance of his commission, as a suspected person, but escaped detection. He then went to Canada, where he remained until its conquest by the British, after which he returned to France. In 1777, during the war of the revolution, he came a second time to the United States, and offered his services to Congress. They were accepted, and he was soon after made a major-general. At first he was placed in the northern army, but, when the danger which threatened Charleston from the formidable expedition under Sir Henry Clinton, in 1778, rendered it necessary to reinforce the American troops in the South, a detachment was sent to them, consisting of the Maryland and Delaware lines, which were put under his command. Before he could arrive, however, at the scene of action, General Lincoln had been made prisoner, and the direction of the whole southern army devolved upon the Baron, until the appointment of General Gates. On the 15th of August, Gates was defeated near Camden by Lord Rawdon, and, in the battle, De Kalb, who commanded the right wing, fell, covered with wounds, while gallantly fighting on foot. A tomb was erected to his memory, by order of Congress, in the cemetery of Camden.—*Ency. Amer.*—ED.

sprightly Miss, not far advanced in her teens, and who having apparently no dislike to be seen, had more than once attracted my attention.* For I was just touching that age when such objects begin to be interesting and excite feelings, which disdain the invidious barriers, with which the pride of condition would surround itself. Not that the young lady was stately; my vanity rather hinted, she was condescendingly courteous; and I had no doubt, read of women of quality falling in love with their inferiors: Nevertheless, the extent of my presumption was a look or a bow, as she now and then tripped along through the entry. Another was Lady Susan O'Brien, not more distinguished by her title, than by her husband, who accompanied her, and had figured as a comedian on the London stage, in the time of Garrick, Mossop and Barry. Although Churchill charges him with being an imitator of Woodward,† he yet admits him to be a man of parts;

* Sir Henry Moore, the last British governor of New York, that I remember, (says Mrs. Grant,) came up this summer to see Albany and the ornament of Albany, Aunt Schuyler; he brought Lady Moore and his daughter with him. This is the same family alluded to in the text, but I was not aware (says the author in a MS. note) that Sir Henry was governor of New York. Mrs. Grant and myself, probably not differing much in age, appear nearly at the same time to have been looking back on the scenes of our youth, and to have brought to remembrance not only some of the characters, but to have coincided in our remarks on several subjects. The Miss Moore alluded to, I remember to have heard, was, some years after the time of this our joint recognition of her, considered as an elegant woman in England, where, it was said, she led the fashions.

      † Woodward, endowed with various powers of face,
        Great master in the science of grimace,
        From Ireland ventures, favourite of the town,
        Lur'd by the pleasing prospect of renown;
        A squeaking Harlequin made up of whim,
        He twists, he twines, he tortures every limb,
        Plays to the eye with a mere monkey's art
        And leaves to sense the conquest of the heart.
        We laugh, indeed, but on reflection's birth,
        We wonder at ourselves, and curse our mirth,
        His walk of parts he fatally misplaced,
        And inclination fondly took for taste;
        Hence hath the Town so often seen displayed
        Beau in burlesque, high life in masquerade,
        But when bold wits, not such as patch up plays,
        Cold and correct in these insipid days,

and he has been said to have surpassed all his cotemporaries in the character of the fine gentleman; in his easy manner of treading the stage, and particularly of drawing the sword, to which action he communicated a swiftness and a grace which Garrick imitated, but could not equal.* O'Brien is presented to my recollection as a man of the middle height, with a symmetrical form, rather light than athletic. Employed by the father to instruct Lady Susan in elocution, he taught her, it seems, that it was no sin to love; for she became his wife, and, as I have seen it mentioned in the Theatrical Mirror, obtained for him,.through the interest of her family, a post in America. But what this post was, or where it located him, I never heard.

A third person of celebrity and title was sir William Draper,†

> Some comic character, strong-featured, urge
> To probability's extremest verge,
> Where modest judgment her decree suspends,
> And for a time, nor censures, nor commends,
> Where critics can't determine on the spot,
> Whether it is in Nature found or not,
> There Woodward safely shall his powers exert,
> Nor fail of favour where he shows desert.
> Hence he in Bobadil such praises bore,
> Such worthy praises, Kitely scarce had more.
>   *Churchill's Rosciad.*—Ed.

* Shadows behind of Foote and Woodward came;
Wilkinson this, O'Brien was that name.
Strange to relate, but wonderfully true,
That even shadows have their shadows too!
With not a single comic power endued
The first a mere mere mimic's mimic stood.
The last, by nature formed to please, who shows,
In Johnson's Stephen, which way Genius grows;
Self quite put off, affects, with too much art,
To put on Woodward in each mangled part;
Adopt his shrug, his wink, his stare: nay, more,
His voice and croaks; for Woodward croak'd before.
When the dull copier simple grace neglects,
And rests his Imitation in defects,
We readily forgive; but such vile arts
Are double guilt in men of real parts.
                  Churchill's Rosciad.—Ed.

† *Vide* correspondence in the "Letters of Junius." In his celebrated controversy with the "great unknown," sir William displayed a degree of ability and

who made a tour to this country, a short time after his newspaper encounter with Junius. It has even been suggested that this very incident sent the knight on his travels. Whether or not, it had so important a consequence, it cannot be denied, that sir William *caught a tartar* in Junius; and that when he commenced his attack, he had evidently underrated his adversary.

During his stay in Philadelphia, no one was so assiduous in his attentions to him as Mr. Richardson, better known at that time by the name of Frank Richardson, then from England on a visit to his friends. This gentleman was one of the most singular and successful of American adventurers. The son of one of our plainest Quakers, he gave early indications of that cast of character which has raised him to his present station, that of a colonel in the British guards. At a time, when such attainments formed no part of education in Pennsylvania, he sedulously employed himself, in acquiring skill in the use of the small sword and the pistol, as if to shine as a duellist, had been the first object of his ambition. Either for a contempt for the dull pursuits of the " home

---

skill that challenged the admiration even of his relentless adversary. He attained the rank of General in the British army. He was born at Bristol, (England) where his father held the post of collector of the customs. He was thoroughly educated at Eton and at Cambridge. In 1763, he was " conquerer of Manilla." He arrived at Charleston, South Carolina, in January, 1770, and during the summer of that year visited Maryland where he was received with much hospitality. From Maryland he passed into New-York, and while there, was married to Miss De Lancey, who died in 1778, leaving him a daughter. In 1779, he was appointed Lieutenant-Governor of Minorca. He died at Bath, January, 1787.

WRAXALL says he was " a man hardly better known to posterity by his capture of Manilla, than by his correspondence with JUNIUS. He was endowed with talents which, whether excited in the field or in the closet, entitled him to great consideration. His vanity, which led him to call his house at Clifton, near Bristol, " Manilla Hall," and there to erect a cenotaph to his fellow-soldiers, who fell before that city during the siege exposed him to invidious comments. * * JUNIUS's obligations to his officious friendship for the Marquis of Granby was indelible: for, however admirably written may be his letter of the 21st of January, 1769, which opened the series of those celebrated compositions, it was Draper's answer, with his signature annexed to it, that drew all eyes towards the two literary combatants. Great as were JUNIUS's talents, yet, if he had been left to exhale his resentment without notice or reply, he might have found it difficult to concenter on himself the attention of all England.—But, the instant that Sir William avowedly entered the lists as Lord Granby's champion, a new interest was awakened in the public mind."—ED.

keeping youth " of his day, or from the singularity of his propensities repelling association, he was solitary and rarely with companions. Fair and delicate to effeminacy, he paid great attention
to his person, which he had the courage to invest in scarlet, in
defiance of the society to which he belonged, in whose mind's
eye, perhaps as to that of the blind man of Locke, this colour from
their marked aversion to it, resembles the sound of a trumpet;
and no less in defiance of the plain manners of a city, in which
except on the back of a soldier, a red coat was a phenomenon,
and always indicated a Creole, a Carolinian, or a dancing master.
With these qualifications, and these alone, perhaps, Mr. Richardson, at an early age, shipped himself for England, where soon,
having the good fortune to establish a reputation for courage by
drawing his sword in behalf of a young man of rank, in a broil at
the theatre, he was received into the best company, and thence
laid the foundation of his preferment. Such, at least was the
generally received account of his rise. But whether accurate or
not, his intimate footing with sir William, is an evidence of the
style of his company whilst abroad, as well as of the propriety of
his conclusion, that his native land was not his sphere.*

As the story went: on Mr. Richardson's first going to England,
he happened to be in the same lodgings with Foote, the comedian, with whom he became intimate. One day upon his coming
out of his chamber, "Richardson," says Foote to him, "a person
has just been asking for you, who expressed a strong desire to
see you, and pretended to be an old Philadelphia acquaintance.
But I knew better, for he was a d——d ill-looking fellow, and I
have no doubt the rascal was a bailiff; so I told him you were
not at home." But here either Foote's sagacity had been at fault,
or he had been playing off a stroke of his humour, the visiter
having really been no other than Mr. ————, a respectable

* He is the same Richardson alluded to in the following extract of a letter from
General Washington to Mr. Reed, dated 14th January, 1776: "Mr. Sayre has
been committed to the tower, upon the information of a certain Lieutenant or
Adjutant Richardson (formerly of your city,) for treasonable practices; an intention of seizing his majesty, and possessing himself of the Tower, it is said in
"The Crisis." But he is admitted to bail himself in five hundred pounds, and
two sureties in two hundred and fifty pounds each."—*Sparks' Writings of Washington*, Vol. iii. p. 242.—ED.

merchant of Philadelphia, though not a figure the most debonair to be sure.

From Philadelphia, sir William passed on to New-York, where, if I mistake not, he married. During his residence in that city, he frequently amused himself with a game of rackets, which he played with some address; and he set no small value on the talent. There was a mechanic in the place, the hero of the tennis court, who was so astonishingly superior to other men, that there were few whom he could not beat with one hand attached to the handle of a wheelbarrow. Sir William wished to play with him, and was gratified; the New-Yorker having urbanity enough to cede the splendid stranger some advantages, and even in conquering, to put on the appearance of doing it with difficulty: Yet, apart, he declared that he could have done the same with the incumbrance of the wheel-barrow. These are heresay facts: they come, however, from persons of credit, in the way of being acquainted with them.

But what imports it the reader to know, that sir William Draper was a racket-player? Nothing, certainly, unless we reflect, that he was a conspicuous character, the conqueror of Manilla, and still more, the literary opponent of Junius. Without granting something to celebrity of this latter sort, what possible interest could we take in learning that doctor Johnson liked a leg of pork, or that he could swallow twelve or more cups of tea at a sitting?*

Major George Etherington, of the Royal Americans, was an occasional inmate of our house, from its first establishment on the large scale, until the time of its being laid down, about the year 1774. He seemed to be always employed in the recruiting service, in the performance of which, he had a snug, economical

* Much attention was paid to sir William, in Philadelphia, and among others who waited on him was a Mr. Wharton, an old Quaker who, from his pride and affected dignity of manner, received the title of *Duke*. Sir William observing that he entered the room and remained with his hat off, begged that as it was contrary to the custom of his society to do so, he would dispense with this unnecessary mark of respect. But the "*Duke*" feeling his pride piqued at the supposition that he should uncover to Sir William Draper or to any other man, promptly corrected the mistake, into which Sir William's considerate politeness had betrayed him, by bluntly giving him to understand that his being uncovered, was not intended as a compliment to him, but was for his own convenience and comfort—the day being warm.—ED.

method of his own. He generally dispensed with the noisy ceremony of a recruiting coterie; for having, as it was said, and I
believe truly, passed through the principal grades in its composition, namely, those of drummer and sergeant, he was a perfect
master of the inveigling arts which are practised on the occasion,
and could fulfil, at a pinch, all the duties himself. The major's
forte was a knowledge of mankind, of low life especially; and he
seldom scented a subject that he did not, in the end, make his
prey. He knew his man, and could immediately discover a fish
that would bite: Hence, he wasted no time in angling in wrong
waters. His superior height, expansive frame, and muscular
limbs, gave him a commanding air among the vulgar; and, while
enforcing his suit with all the flippancy of halbert elocution, he
familiarly held his booby by the button, his small, black, piercing
eyes, which derived additional animation from the intervention of
a sarcastic, upturned nose, penetrated to the fellow's soul, and
gave him distinct intelligence of what was passing there. In fact,
I have never seen a man with a cast of countenance so extremely
subtile and investigating. I have myself, more than once,
undergone its scrutiny; for he took a very friendly interest in my
welfare, evinced by an occasional superintendance of my education, in so far at least, as respects the exterior accomplishments.
Above all things, he enjoined upon me the cultivation of the
French language, of which he had himself acquired a smattering
from a temporary residence in Canada; and he gave me a pretty
sharp lecture upon a resolution I had absurdly taken up, not to
learn dancing, from an idea of its being an effeminate and unmanly recreation. He combated my folly with arguments, of
which I have since felt the full force; but which, as they turned
upon interests, I was then too young to form conceptions of, they
produced neither conviction nor effect. Fortunately for me, I
had to deal with a man who was not thus to be baffled. He
very properly assumed the rights of mature age and experience,
and accordingly, one day, on my return from school, he accosted
me with, " Come here young man, I have something to say to
you," and with a mysterious air conducted me to his chamber.
Here I found myself entrapped. Godwin, the assistant of Tioli,
the dancing master, was prepared to give me a lesson. Ether-

ington introduced me to him as the pupil he had been speaking of, and saying, he would leave us to ourselves, he politely retired. The arrangement with Tioli was, that I should be attended in the major's room until I was sufficiently drilled for the public school; and the ice thus broken, I went on, and instead of standing in a corner, like a goose on one leg (the major's comparison) "while music softens and while dancing fires," I became qualified for the enjoyment of female society, in one of its most captivating forms.

Major Etherington had a brother in the rank of a captain, so like himself, as to realize the story of the two Socias, and to remove half the improbability of the plot of Shakspeare's Comedy of Errors. Any one, at a first sight, might have mistaken the one for the other, at least I did, for a moment; but on a close inspection it would be discovered, that the captain was more scant in his proportions, as well as several years younger than his brother. Tom, for so the captain was familiarly called by the major, had taken his turn to recruit in Philadelphia, while his superior was employed elsewhere. From a comparatively weaker discernment of human character, he had enlisted a lad and converted him into his waiting man, whom George, on a junction which soon after took place, pronounced to be a fool, and wholly unfit for a soldier. This the captain denied strenuously, and the question became the frequent topic of good humoured altercation between them, until an incident occurred, which gave the major an unequivocal triumph. One morning very early, the brothers lodging in the same apartment, this recruit, and for the first time, common servant of the two, softly approached the bed of the major, and gently tapping him on the shoulder to awaken him, very sapiently inquired, if he might clean his shoes. George, with infinite presence of mind, replied, that it was not material, but "go," says he, "and ask my brother Tom if you may clean his." The poor fellow did as he was bid, and probably as he would have done if he had not been bidden; and Tom's slumbers became victims also, to the same momentous investigation. The major took care to relate the circumstance at the breakfast table, and, of course, obtained a unanimous suffrage to his opinion, that the captain's recruit was not exceeding wise.

Although Etherington was extremely deficient in literature, few persons possessed more acuteness of intellect, or a happier talent for prompt replication. A warm dispute having one day taken place at the coffee-house, between Mr. Bradford, who kept it, and Mr. Delancey of New York, in which the parties appeared to be proceeding to blows, major Etherington stepped between them and separated them. The next day, on a supposition of partiality to Delancey, he was roundly taken to task by Bradford. He observed, that he had merely interfered as a common friend to both. " No sir," said Bradford, " you were the decided champion of Delancey, you laid your hands upon me, and kept your face to me, while your back was turned to him." " Very well then, sir," said Etherington, with quickness, "I treated you politely, and Mr. Delancey with a rudeness for which I owe him an apology." A ready, unexpected turn of this kind, has always a good effect on the bystanders, and they accordingly lent their aid in restoring good humour.*

As I have said that the major commenced his military career in the humblest walks of his profession, the reader may expect to hear of the exploits which produced his extraordinary promotion.

---

* There is another instance of his mental readiness, I had introduced into my manuscript, but which I was advised to suppress, as it was supposed to offer matter for malignant interpretation. But as I find my mother's character is well understood and remembered, I see no objection to introducing it now; nor for my own part, did I before. The major, one day, in passing the kitchen door, received upon his clothes a little dirty water which Miss Ann Burgess, the elderly Quaker lady, already mentioned as one of the family, had, without seeing him, cast out of a bowl. The major was more disturbed at the accident than might have been expected from one of his character, and was not quite appeased by the evident concern and all the excuses the culprit could make, when she thought proper to set before him the conduct of Major Small, when a precisely similar accident which some time before had happened to him from the hands of my mother, aggravated, too, by the circumstance of his having been full dressed for an assembly, a toilet labour no less arduous with him, than the five hours work of the haughty Celia of Swift. Instead, said she, of Major Small's refusing to be satisfied with her apologies, he made her a low bow, begged that she would be under no concern about the matter, and, very respectfully, walked up to her and kissed her. Then I am to kiss you, I suppose, Eh! said Etherington. This lucky hit, while it alarmed and completely embarrassed the maidenly preciseness of the old lady, not aware that she had given an opening for it, put Etherington into a good humour and amicably terminated the affair.

7

But it was not to martial prowess that he owed it. The world gave out, that a certain wealthy widow of the county of New Castle, became enamoured of him, and first purchased him a commission. His saving knowledge soon enabled him to purchase a better one, and from a captaincy, the station in which I first knew him, he had risen to that of a colonel, when I last saw him in Philadelphia, just at the approach of the war. What then brought him there is uncertain. He was, however, taken notice of by the committee of safety; required to hasten his departure, and in the mean time, put under his parole. He endeavoured to make a jest of the matter, by assuring them, that they need not be under the least apprehension of his going an inch nearer to the scene where fighting was to be looked for. He several times called to see us while in town, and observing me in the light infantry uniform, he undertook to recommend to me, between banter and earnest, that if I inclined to a military life, at once to get a commission in the British service, which he would charge himself to procure for me: That as to our idle parade of war, it would vanish in smoke, or, if seriously persisted in, would infallibly terminate in our disgrace, if not ruin. I asked him if he had been to see us exercise. "Oh no," said he, "that would be highly improper; we make it a point in the army never to look at awkward men; we hold it unpolite." The colonel was no doubt correct in his opinion of our tactics; though I was nettled a little at his contemptuous manner of treating us. But I here dismiss him with the observation, that he was a singular man, who knew the world and turned that knowledge to his advantage. He had certainly much mental ability, and of a cast, which he himself conceived would have well qualified him for the bar; a profession, for which, he has told me, nature intended him. In this estimate of his talents, however, it is not improbable, that he might have attributed too much to management and chicane, which had essentially availed him in the business of recruiting: For he valued himself upon them here; and I well remember that upon my mother's telling him of captain Anstruther, who had recruited in his absence, sending a drum about before he left the city, to proclaim, that if any one had been aggrieved by him or his party, to call upon him and he should be redressed, he re-

plied—" And was'nt he a d——d fool for his pains?" In mentioning captain Anstruther it occurs to me, that he may be the
same who is stated to have fallen as a general officer in the battle
of Corunna.

There were two other majors, with whose company we were a
long time favoured. These were Majors Small and Fell; and if
names had any appropriation to the persons of those who bear
them, these might very well have been interchanged; for Small
was a stout, athletic man, who might be supposed to possess a
capacity for *felling*, while the other was one of the smallest men
I have seen. Some one asking, one day, if major Small was at
home? "No," says Fell, " but the *small major* is." Small is a
principal figure in Trumbull's print of the death of Warren. He
is represented in the humane attitude of putting aside with his
sword, a British bayonet, aimed at the breast of the dying patriot.[*]

Another officer of the British army, who was some time our inmate, is suggested by a notice of his death in the Monthly Magazine of March, 1807. This was General John Reid, who is stated
to have died in his 87th year, the oldest officer in the service. In
this account of him, it is said, that in the meredian of his life,
he was esteemed the best gentleman German flute performer in
England: that he was also particularly famed for his taste in the
composition of military music, and that his marches are still admired. This gentleman was a colonel at the time I speak of him.
His fame as a performer on the flute I recollect, as also to have
heard him play: but probably I was too little of a connoiseur to
duly appreciate his talents. I cannot say that my expectations were
fully answered; his tones were low and sweet, but the tunes he
played were so disguised and overloaded with variations, as with
me to lose much of their melody.

From these gentlemen of the army, I pass to one of the navy,
rude and boisterous as the element to which he belonged. His
name I think was Wallace, the commander of a ship of war on
the American station, and full fraught, perhaps, with the ill humour
of the mother country towards her colonies, which she was already

* See Appendix C, for an interesting account of the battle of Bunker's
Hill.—Ed.

beginning to goad to independence. His character upon the coast, was that of being insolent and brutal beyond his peers; and his deportment as a lodger, was altogether of a piece with it. Being asked by my mother, who, by the desire of the gentlemen, was in the custom of taking the head of her table, if he would be helped to a dish that was near her, "Damme, madam," replied the ruffian, "it is to be supposed that at a public table every man has a right to help himself, and this I mean to do." With a tear in her eye she besought him to pardon her, assuring him that in future he should not be offended by her officiousness.

At another time, when Joseph Church of Bristol, who has already been mentioned as a friend of the family, was in town and at our house, which, in his visits to the city, he always made his home, my mother mentioned to the gentlemen, who were about sitting down to supper, but three or four in number, of whom captain Wallace was one, that there was a friend of hers in the house, a very honest, plain man of the society of Friends, and begged to know if it would be agreeable to them that he should be brought in to supper. They all readily assented, and none with more alacrity than Wallace. Accordingly Mr. Church was introduced, and sat down. During supper, the captain directed his chief discourse to him, interlarded with a deal of very course and insolent raillery on his broad brim, &c. Church bore it all very patiently until after supper, when he at length ventured to say—"Captain, thou has made very free with me, and asked me a great many questions, which I have endeavoured to answer to thy satisfaction: Wilt thou now permit me to ask thee one in my turn?" "Oh, by all means," exclaimed the captain, "any thing that you please, friend—what is it?" "Why, then, I wish to be informed, what makes thee drink so often; art thou really dry every time thou carriest the liquor to thy mouth?" This was a home thrust at the seaman, whose frequent potations had already produced a degree of intoxication. At once, forgetting the liberties he had taken, and the promise he had given of equal freedom in return, he broke out into a violent rage, venting himself in the most indecent and illiberal language, and vociferating, with an unlucky logic which recoiled upon himself—"What! do you think I am like a hog, only to drink when I am dry?" But matters had gone too far for a reply; and the object of his wrath very prudently left the table and the room as expeditiously as possible. It cannot be denied, that there was some provocation in the question proposed: but he knows little of the Quaker character, who does not know, that the non-resisting tenent does not prohibit the use of dry sarcasm, which here was unquestionably in its place.

It would be easy to extend these biographical details; but my materials, at best, are too deficient in interest to warrant much presumption on the patience of the reader: I shall therefore only add to the list, the names of Hancock* and Washington, each of whom had at different times sojourned at our caravansary.

Yet another, of some eminence, though not exactly in the same kind, whom I ought not to omit, was Rivington, the printer, of New York. This gentleman's manners and appearance were sufficiently dignified; and he kept the best company. He was an everlasting dabbler in theatrical heroics. Othello, was the character in which he liked best to appear; and converting his auditory into the "most potent, grave and reverend signiors" of Venice, he would deliver his unvarnished tale :

"Her father lov'd me, oft invited me," &c.

With the same magic by which the listening gentlemen were turned into senators, my mother was transformed into Desdemona; and from the frequent spoutings of Rivington, the officers of the 42d regiment, and others, who were then in the house, became familiarized to the appellation, and appropriated it. Thus, Desdemona, or rather Desdy, for shortness, was the name she generally afterwards went by among that set of lodgers; and I recollect the concluding line of a poetical effusion of Lieutenant Rumsey of the 42d, on occasion of some trifling *fracas*, to have been—

"For Desdy, believe me, you don't become airs !"

In the daily intercourse with her boarders, which my mother's custom of sitting at the head of her table induced, such familiarities might be excused. They were only to be repelled, at

* For a Sketch of the Life and Character of Hancock, see Appendix D.—Ed.

7*

least, by a formal austerity of manner, which was neither natural to her, nor for her interest to assume. The cause of umbrage was a midnight riot, perpetrated by Rumsey, Rivington and Doctor Kearsley, in which the doctor, mounted on horseback, rode into the back parlour, and even up stairs, to the great disturbance and terror of the family; for, as it may well be supposed, there was a direful clatter. *Quadrupedante sonitu quatit ungula domum.*

CHAPTER III.

The Author mixes in new Society.—Is destined for the Law.—His characteristic Indolence.—American players.—Anecdotes.—Dramatic Poetry.—Author's pursuits.—Debating Society.—Metaphysical subtleties.—Causes of youthful follies.—Letters of Junius.—Tamoc Caspipina.—Mr. Duché.

ABOUT the year 1769 or 1770, my grandfather died. My inattention to dates disqualifies me for fixing the year, nor is it material. His disorder was a complication of dropsy and asthma. I well remember being with him a few evenings before his death, and seldom saw him in better spirits. He was anticipating my future consequence in life; and, as like too many others, I was destined in vain,

> *D'une robe a longs plis balayer le barreau—*
> To sweep, with full-sleev'd robe, the dusty bar.*

He was making himself merry with the fancy of my strutting with my full-bottomed periwig and small sword, the costume he attached to a *bannister* of law, as he was pleased to term what in England is called a barrister. But it will be recollected, that I have already said that the old gentleman was a German, no great adept in English, and let me add, no great scholar in any language; although his manners were those of a man of the world, and a frequenter of good company, somewhat blunt, however, and occasionally facetious. The story of the toper and flies, worked up into an ode by Peter Pindar, I have more than once heard related of him. The scene was laid in Philadelphia, where, being at a friend's house to dine,

---

* This quotation would apply better, or at least more literally, if gowns had been worn at our bar.

and asked to take some punch before dinner, he found several flies in the bowl. He removed them with a spoon, took his drink, and with great deliberation was proceeding to replace them, "Why, what are you doing, Mr. Marks,"* exclaimed the entertainer, "putting flies into the bowl?" "Why, *I* don't like them," said he, "but I did not know but you might,"—his mode of suggesting that the bowl should have been covered; for decanters and tumblers, be it observed, are a modern refinement in the apparatus of punch drinking. Whether the story really originated with my grandfather, and travelled from the continent to the islands, where Doctor Wolcott picked it up; or whether the humour was of insular origin, and merely borrowed and vamped up by my grandfather, I pretend not to decide, but certain it is, that he had the credit of it in Philadelphia, many years before the works of Peter Pindar appeared.

If want of occupation, as we are told, is the root of all evil, my youth was exposed to very great dangers. The interval between my leaving the academy, and being put to the study of the law at about the age of sixteen, was not less than eighteen months; an invaluable period, lost in idleness and unprofitable amusement. It had the effect to estrange me for a time from my school-companions, and, in their stead, to bring me acquainted with a set of young men, whose education and habits had been wholly different from my own. They were chiefly designed for the sea, or engaged in the less humiliating mechanical employments; and were but the more to my taste for affecting a sort of rough independence of manners, which appeared to me manly. They were not, however, worthless; and such of them as were destined to become men and citizens, have, with few exceptions, filled their parts in society with reputation and respectability. As I had now attained that stage in the progress of the mind, in which

> Neglected Tray and Pointer lie
> And covies unmolested fly,

the void was supplied by an introduction into the fair society, with which these young men were in the habit of associating. It

---

* Joseph Marks; the name might have been mentioned before.

consisted generally of Quakers; and there was a witching one
among them, with whom, at a first interview in a party on the
water, I became so violently enamoured, as to have been up,
perhaps, to the part of a Romeo or a Pyramus, had the requisite
train of untoward circumstances ensued. But as there were no
feuds between our houses, nor unnatural parents to "forbid what
they could not prohibit," the matter in due time, passed off without any dolorous catastrophe. Nor was it long before I was
translated into a new set of female acquaintance, in which I found
new objects to sigh for. Such, indeed, I was seldom, if ever,
without, during the rest of my nonage; and with as little reason,
perhaps, as any one, to complain of adverse stars. Nevertheless,
I should hesitate in pronouncing this season of life happy. If its
enjoyments are great, so are its solicitudes; and although it
should escape the pangs of "slighted vows and cold disdain," it
yet is racked by a host of inquietudes, doubt, distrust, jealousy,
hope deferred by the frustration of promised interviews, and
wishes sickening under the weight of obstacles too mighty to be
surmounted. In the language of the medical poet,

> " The wholesome appetites and powers of life
> Dissolve in languor. Your cheerful days are gone ;
> The generous bloom that flush'd your cheeks, is fled.
> To sighs devoted and to tender pains,
> Pensive you sit, or solitary stray,
> And waste your youth in musing."

But the peril of fine eyes, was not the only one which beset
me. During my residence in the State-house, I had contracted
an intimacy with the second son of Doctor Thomas Bond, who
lived next door; a connexion which continued for several years.
He was perhaps a year older than myself, and had, in like manner, abandoned his studies, and prematurely bidden adieu to the
college of Princeton. Handsome in his person, in his manner,
confident and assured, he had the most lordly contempt for the
opinion of the world, that is, the sober world, of any young man
I have known ; as well as a precocity in fashionable vices, equalled
by few, and certainly exceeded by none. Admiring his talents

and accomplishments, I willingly yielded him the lead in our amusements, happy in emulating his *degagee* air and rakish appearance. He it was who first introduced me to the fascination of a billiard-table, and initiated me into the other seductive arcana of city dissipation. He also showed me where beardless youth might find a Lethe for its timidity, in the form of an execrable potion called wine, on the very moderate terms of two and six pence a quart. At an obscure inn in Race street, dropping in about dark, we were led by a steep and narrow stair-case to a chamber in the third story, so lumbered with beds as scarcely to leave room for a table and one chair, the beds superseding the necessity of more. Here we poured down the fiery beverage; and valiant in the novel feeling of intoxication, sallied forth in quest of adventures. Under the auspices of such a leader, I could not fail to improve; nor was his progress less promoted by so able a second. In a word, we aspired to be rakes, and were gratified. Mr. Richard Bond, was the favourite of his father, studied physic under him, and notwithstanding his addiction to pleasure, would probably have made a respectable figure in his profession: for he had genius, no fondness for liquor, no unusual want of application to business, and vanity, perhaps, more than real propensity, had prompted his juvenile excesses. But he was destined to finish his career at an early age, by that fatal disease to youth, a pulmonary consumption. He had a presentiment of this, and frequently said when in health, it would be his mortal distemper. Yet his frame seemed not to indicate it: he had a prominent chest, with a habit inclined to fulness. Our intimacy had ceased for some time before his death. I know not why, unless he had been alienated by a latent spark of jealousy, in relation to a young lady, for whom we both had a partiality; mine, indeed, slight and evanescent; his, deep and more lasting, and which, I have understood, only ended with his life.

As it was necessary I should be employed, the choice of a vocation for me, had for some time engaged the attention of my near connexions. The question was, whether I should be a merchant, a physician, or a lawyer. My inclinations were duly consulted. I had no predilection for either, though I liked the law the least of the three, being sensible that my talents were not of the cast which would enable me to succeed in that profession. I searched my composition in vain, for the materials that would be required. If they were there, the want of fortitude to bring them forth, would be the same as if they were not; and this seemed a deficiency I could never supply. To rise at the bar with due gravity and recollection; to challenge the attention of the court, the jury, and the by-standers; to confide in my ability to do justice to a good cause; to colour a bad one by the requisite artifice and stimulation; and to undertake to entertain by my rhetoric, where I must necessarily fail to convince by my logic, I felt to be a task far beyond my strength; and I shuddered at it, in idea only, even in my most sanguine, self-complacent moments. To what this infirmity, inaccurately termed diffidence, is owing, or whether it be a defect in the mental or bodily powers, is not, I believe, ascertained; yet it exists to a degree scarcely superable in some, while in others, it is a sensation almost unknown. It appears, however, to be considerably under the influence of education, since, if felt at all, it never shows itself in a thorough bred Quaker: neither do we suppose it to exist in a Frenchman, though the phrase *mauvaise honte*, is a proof that the imbecility has been recognised by the nation; a circumstance we might be led to doubt, too, from the account given by Doctor Moore of the National Assembly.* He tells us, that of the great number of members of which it was composed, there appeared to be none who could not express themselves with perfect freedom and ease; and that there seemed to be a continual competition for the possession of the tribune. How different, he observes, from an assembly of Englishmen! I might add, of Americans! But that the feeling is natural, if indeed there could be a doubt of it; that it was known to the ancients, and that it is not merely an effect of modern manners, is evinced from the following lines of Petronius on *Dreams*, in which the trepidation is not only recognised, but very strongly depicted.

---

* There is a striking coincidence between these observations and the following, in Miss Edgeworth's novel of "Patronage." "Strange that France should give a name to that malady of mind which she never knew, or of which she knows less than any other nation, upon the surface of the civilized globe!"

"Qui causas orare solent, legesque forumque
Et pavido cernunt inclusum corde tribunal."

I have said it is inaccurately termed diffidence: it rather appears to me, to proceed from too much pride and self-attention, a kind of morbid sensibility, ever making *self* the principal figure in the scene, and overweeningly solicitous for the respect of the audience: dreading, in equal degree, its contempt and the humiliation of a failure. Hence, as one that is too fearful of falling will never excel in the hazardous exercises, such as riding and skating, so the destined public speaker who will not risk a fall, can never expect to succeed. If he is too fastidious to submit to occasional humiliation, he must undergo the perpetual one of being really, as well as reputedly unqualified for his profession. Some diffidence or distrust of our powers, does, no doubt, attend the species of *mauvaise honte* we are speaking of; but it is more often, I believe, the distrust of being able to display the talents we possess, or at least ascribe to ourselves, than an underrating of them; and appears to have its primary cause, as already said, in a temperament of too much susceptibility to shame,—and if so, the French have given it a very proper appellation.

But notwithstanding my conviction of an inaptitude for the bar, it was, however, the profession assigned me. I had declared for the study of physic, and overtures had accordingly been made to a practitioner of eminence, but he happening at the time to have as many students as he wanted, declined taking another. Failing here, it was deemed inexpedient any longer to defer placing me somewhere. I had certainly been already too long unemployed; and my uncle, (the executor of my father's will, in conjunction with my mother) who had all along been desirous that I should go to the bar, his own profession, again recommended it; and proposed taking me into his own family, where, by his assistance, the use of his library, which was a very ample one, and an occasional attention to the business of his office, that of Prothonotary of the Common Pleas, which he held as deputy of the late Governor Hamilton, then residing at Bushhill, I had the means of acquiring a knowledge of the law, both as to principle and practice; and the proposal being in many respects eligible and agreeable, was embraced. I was sensible that it was no less to my advantage than reputation, that I should be doing something: there was no one, with whom, in the character of a master, I could expect to be more pleasantly situated than with my uncle, who was a man of unbounded benevolence and liberality; and my imagination went to castle-building in the remote prospect of a trip to England, for the purpose of completing my education at the temple; for whatever may be the case now, this was the grand desideratum or *summum bonum* with the aspiring law-youth of my day. As to the sober part of the calculation, whether the occupation I was about to embrace was adapted to my talents, would command my application, and be likely to afford me the means of future subsistence, it was put aside for the more immediately grateful considerations already mentioned. I cannot venture to pronounce, however, that the medical profession would have suited me much better. In truth, I was indolent to a great degree; and with respect to that heroic fortitude which subdues the mind to its purposes, withdraws it at will from the flowery paths of pleasure, and forces it into the thorny road of utility, the distinguishing trait in the character of Cæsar, and which justifies the poet in designating him as "the world's great master, and *his own*," I have very little to boast of. I was ever too easily seduced by the charm of present gratification, and my general mood in youth, was an entire apathy to gainful views. With the strongest inclination to be respectable in life, and even with ambition to aspire to the first rank in my professsion, I yet felt an invincible incapacity for mingling in the world of business, the only means by which my desire could be gratified. imagination, almost ever in a state of listless, amorous delirium,

> Where honour still,
> And great design, against the oppressive load,
> By fits, impatient heaved,

could rarely be brought down to the key of sober occupation, or attuned to the flat *fasque nefasque* of the sages of the law;* and

---

* This state of mind is admirably represented by this short passage in Waverley: "all that was common-place, all that belonged to the every-day world, was melted away, and obliterated in these dreams of imagination."

8

my acquaintance with them, was of course, a very slight one. Were we justified in laying our unthriftiness on nature, I might say, that she never intended me for a man of business. If she has denied me the qualifications of an advocate, she has not certainly been more liberal to me of those of a trafficker; for whether it be owing to pride, to dulness, to laziness, or to impatience, I could never excel in driving a bargain: And as to that spirit of commercial enterprise or speculation, which only asks the use of money to increase it, I never possessed a spark of it; and consequently, though I have sometimes had cash to spare, it rarely, if ever, was employed; for the very good reason, that commodities in my hands, always turned out to be drugs. In thus characterizing myself, I affect not singularity: for the discomfort of my declining age, I but depict myself too truly.

A short time before the epoch of my becoming a student of law, the city was visited by the company of players, since styling themselves, The old American company. They had for several years been exhibiting in the islands, and now returned to the continent in the view of dividing their time and labours between Philadelphia and New-York. At Boston,

> they did not appear,
> So peevish was the edict of the may'r,

or at least of those authorities which were charged with the custody of the public morals. The manager was Douglas, rather a decent than shining actor, a man of sense and discretion, married to the widow Hallam, whose son Lewis, then in full culmination, was the Roscius of the theatre. As the dramatic heroes were all *his* without a competitor, so the heroines were the exclusive property of Miss Cheer, who was deemed an admirable performer. The singing department was supplied and supported by the voices of Wools and Miss Wainwright, said to have been pupils of doctor Arne; while in the tremulous drawl of the old man, in low jest and buffoonery, Morris, thence the minion of the gallery, stood first and unrivalled. As for the Tomlinsons, the Walls, the Allens, &c., they were your bonifaces, your Jessamys, your Mock Doctors, and what not. On the female side, Mrs. Douglas was a respectable, matron-like dame, stately or querulous as occasion required, a very good Gertrude, a truly appropriate lady Randolph with her white handkerchief and her weeds; but then, to applaud, it was absolutely necessary to forget, that to touch the heart of the spectator had any relation to her function: Mrs. Harman bore away the palm as a duenna, and Miss Wainwright as a chambermaid. Although these were among the principal performers at first, the company was from time to time essentially improved by additions: Among these, the Miss Storers, Miss Hallam and Mr. Henry, were valuable acquisitions; as was also a Mr. Goodman, who had read law in Philadelphia with Mr. Ross. This topic may be disgusting to persons of gravity; but human manners are my theme, as well in youth as in age. Each period has its play things; and if the strollers of Thespis have not been thought beneath the dignity of Grecian history, this notice of the old American stagers may be granted to the levity of memoirs.

Whether there may be any room for comparison between these, the old American company, and the performers of the present day, I venture not to say. Nothing is more subject to fashion than the style of public exhibitions; and as the excellence of the Lacedemonian black broth, essentially depended, we are told, on the appetite of the feeder, so, no doubt, does the merit of theatrical entertainments: I cannot but say, however, that in my opinion, the old company acquitted themselves with most animation and glee—they were a passable set of comedians. Hallam had merit in a number of characters and was always a pleasing performer. No one could tread the stage with more ease: Upon it, indeed, he might be said to have been cradled, and wheeled in his go-cart. In tragedy, it cannot be denied, that his declamation was either mouthing or ranting; yet a thorough master of all the tricks and finesse of his trade, his manner was both graceful and impressive, "tears in his eyes, distraction in his aspect, a broken voice, and his whole function suiting with forms to his conceit." He once ventured to appear in Hamlet either at Drury lane or Covent Garden, and was endured. In the account given of his performance, he is said not to have been to the taste of a London audience, though he is admitted to be a man of a pleasing and interesting address. He was, however, at Philadelphia, as much the soul of the Southwark theatre, as ever Garrick was of Drury lane; and if, as doctor Johnson allows, popularity in matters of taste is unquestionable evidence of merit, we cannot withhold a considerable portion of it from Mr. Hallam, notwithstanding his faults.

The subject of this old company, opens the door to a trifling anecdote of a very early origin. Over their stage, in imitation of the sons of *Drury*, they have fixed the motto of *Totus mundus agit histrionem*—The whole world act the player. Some young ladies, one evening, among whom was one of my aunts, applied to the gentleman who attended them for the meaning of the words. Willing to pass himself off for a scholar, and taking for his clew, probably, the word *mundus*, he boldly interpreted them into— " We act Mondays, Wednesdays and Fridays," and the ladies were satisfied. But, to the lasting disquiet of the unlucky beau, they were not long after undeceived by some of their more learned acquaintance.

Although the theatre must be admitted to be a stimulus to those vices, which something inherent in our nature renders essential to the favoured hero of the comic drama and the novel, it was yet useful to me in one respect. It induced me to open books which had hitherto lain neglected on the shelf. A little Latin, and but a little, was the chief fruit of my education. I was tolerably instructed in the rudiments of grammar, but in nothing else. I wrote a very indifferent hand, and spelled still worse than I wrote. I knew little or nothing of arithmetic; that, as a branch of the mathematics, being taught in the academy after the languages. But now I became a reader of plays, and particularly of those of Shakspeare, of which I was an ardent and unaffected admirer. From these I passed to those of Otway and Rowe, and the other writers of tragedy, and thence to the English poets of every description. Poetry, indeed, has continued to be my favourite reading; and when I feel disposed to read aloud, it is always my choice. From being wholly unapprised of the structure of the sentences, and the place of the pauses in prose, the reading of it requires much greater attention to the management of the breath; and is therefore to me, much the most difficult and laborious. Nor has my bias for metrical compositions been confined to the English authors. A small knowledge of French has enabled me to make acquaintance with the HENRIADE of Voltaire, the poems of Boileau, and those of some other writers; and that it has not been more general, has principally been owing to want of books. Nevertheless, I cannot but subscribe to the decree of the English critics, that the French is not the language of the Muses, at least in their sublimer moods. What, for instance, can be more completely unharmonious and halting, than these lines in the Henriade, which appear to have been considerably laboured to the end of producing a grand effect?

"On entendoit gronder ces bombes effroyables,
De troubles de la Flandre enfants abominables,
Le salt pêtre enfoncé dans ces globes d'arain,
Part, s'echauffe, s'embrase, et s'ecarte soudain:"

"Cannons and kettle drums—sweet numbers these." The term *salt pêtre*, though no doubt susceptible of elegance in French poetry, since it is used by one of its greatest masters, would in ours, set all collocation at defiance; and could appear in no other metre than doggerel. Observations, however, of this kind should not be dogmatically urged, since how far our taste for melody may be natural or artificial, is not easy to ascertain. But certainly the music of French numbers is extremely flat and monotonous to an English ear, though, to a French one, our best-sounding measure may be sing song no less vapid.

In the Latin classics too, I have been a dipper; and the best of my progress in that language is to be ascribed to my fondness for its poetry. Why was I not, when at school, imbued with the same relish! I might then have been a scholar, and the whole body of Roman poetry, the *Corpus omnium veterum poetarum latinorum*, (a huge, unwieldy tome, which had belonged to my father) in a chronological series from Andronicus and Ennius to Maurus Terentianus, might have been at my finger ends; whereas now, only scraps of it are occasionally elicited with difficulty, either when disposed to learn, upon what subjects it was that Lucretius, Catullus, Tibullus, Propertius, Lucanus, Statius, &c. &c. had respectively employed their pens; or when I would follow Mr. Gibbon in his references to the poets of later times, the Cal-

8 *

phurnius's, the Nemesianus's, the Claudianus's, the Prudentius's
and Sidonius's. Still, according to my manner, this was but a
species of amusement, the *dulce* without a particle of the *utile*, to
me who had no manner of concern with the decline of the Roman
empire or the songsters which belonged to it. It was not however
Latin, but English poetry, which first led me astray: I did not, it
is true, *pen stanzas*, but I often read them when I should have
engrossed; I had, as Junius says of sir William Draper, "the
melancholy madness of poetry without the inspiration."

The only project I embraced which promised advantage to me
in my profession, or indicated a serious design to pursue it, was
my joining a society of young men, instituted for the purpose of
disputing on given subjects, as well as of reciting passages from
the English classics. It chiefly consisted of law students, though
there were some among us who were designed for the pulpit; and
the members were generally such as had obtained degrees in the
seminaries either of Princeton or Philadelphia. The first question
in which I was appointed to take a part, was that very hackneyed
one, "Whether a public or a private education is to be preferred." There were two on each side ; and our reasonings were
reduced to writing and read in full assembly, where the president
pro tempore made his decision. I soon discovered that the arguments I had to reply to, though proceeding from one of high
reputation for scholarship, had been borrowed almost word for
word from Rollins's belles-lettres. .Restrained by delicacy from
exposing the plagiarism, I answered them as well as I could from
my own resources, and had some allowances made me, since it
had become pretty well known, that Rollin was my real antagonist. In fact, my opponent would hardly have ventured to put
himself so much in my power by stealing from so common a
book, had he not calculated pretty largely on my unacquaintance
with any books. It next fell to me to propound a question ; and
having not long before met with one in a magazine which was
suggested as a curious subject of investigation, I submitted it to
the assembly. It was, "Whether there be most pleasure in the
reception, or communication of knowledge." As proposer of the
question I had the choice of my side, as well as the conclusion
of the argument; and I declared for the "communication." As

this was a subject on which school books gave no light, the disputants had to draw solely from their own funds; and in some, there was a considerable falling off. To me the topic was as new as to any of them; but my production had the good fortune to be approved, and to aid in obtaining the decision of the president. But I soon became weary of this scholastic employment. It appeared to me both puerile and pedantic; and the formality of addressing the chair with the feigned gravity of a pleader, required a kind of grimace I felt myself awkward at. Indeed, the two orations I had written, like that of Cicero for Milo, were not delivered by their author, who did not appear; but they were read for me by my friend and fellow-student, Andrew Robeson. I once, however, with this same gentleman, risked my declaiming powers, in a scene of *Venice Preserved ;* but in what character I appeared I do not remember.

I also involved myself about this period, in metaphysical subtleties; and with Mr. James Hutchinson, the late Doctor Hutchinson, who then lived with Bartram, the apothecary, and with whom I had become intimate, I frequently reasoned upon fate, "fixed fate, free-will, fore-knowledge absolute," &c. Our acquaintance found cement in the circumstances of our both being Bucks county men and exactly of an age. The doctor's father, Randal Hutchinson, a Quaker, did the mason-work of my father's house at Fairview;* and agreeably to the custom in the country, resided with him while employed in it. From family tradition, for I do not remember old Randal, he was what might be called a *queer put.* Being once called upon for his song on occasion of a little merriment, he declined it with the dry remark that he could do his own singing: and so indeed it appeared, as he was in the habit every evening after work, of singing out in rustic drone to his hands assembled round him, a celebrated political poem of that time, entitled *The washing of the Blackmoor white.* It was levelled, if I do not mistake, at the aristocracy of the day; and if so, the doctor had a sort of hereditary right to that zeal against the WELL BORN of his own, which has rendered his name a favourite signature with democratic essayists. But for all this, he

---

* Part of this farm was subsequently converted into an occasional race-ground.

was a friendly man, and no foe to good company; and as to political propensities, they seem in some men to be inherent instincts, wholly independent of the reasoning faculty, and no more
to be resisted than a constitutional tendency to be fat or lean: A
sort of restless spirits these, prone to act, to confederate and intrigue; and who, though not absolutely bad at heart, have yet a
lamentable itch for mischief.   If there are such men, my quondam
friend was one of them.

    The old and the austere may declaim as they will against the
follies and vices of youth, the natural propensities will still prevail; and for one student of law that is restrained by the solid
eloquence of Professor Blackstone from " whiling away the awkward interval from childhood to twenty-one," two or three perhaps are lead astray by the seducing rake of Doctor Hoadley.
Ranger, returning to the temple in a disordered dress, after a
night of riot and debauchery, has unfortunately, more allurements
for a young man of metal, and still more unfortunately for the
generality of young ladies, to whom it is his first desire to be
agreeable, than the sober, orderly student, pale with the incipient
lucubrations of twenty years.   I will not undertake to say, that
authors are right in exhibiting such characters as a Dorimant, a
Jones, a Pickle, a Ranger, or a Charles Surface, but in so doing
they draw from nature, and address themselves to the taste of
their readers.   Has ever novel or comedy been popular, whose
hero is a man of strict morality and virtue?   The Grandison of
Richardson, the Bevil of Steel, and Henry of Cumberland, are
but insipid characters in the eyes of those who are customers for
the productions of the novelist and dramatist.   Happy indeed,
are they, who, without being lost to the feelings of youth, can yet
indulge them with discretion and moderation; and who do not
forget, that although the fashionable gaieties may for a time recommend them to the thoughtless of both sexes, it is application
to business that must provide the means of ease, contentment and
respectability in life.   Such was not my case.   I wanted strength
of mind for the judgment of Hercules, and was for seizing the
present moment with Horace.   I might not live to be old, and if
I did, what were its dull satisfactions in comparison of the vivid,
enthusiastic enjoyments of youth! In this temper, I plunged deep

into dissipation, with the exception of gaming, having never found much attraction in the fortuitous evolutions of a shuffled pack of cards, or a shaken dice box. But the pleasures of the table, the independence of tavern revelry, and its high-minded contempt of the plodding and industrious, were irresistibly fascinating to me. Though without the slightest addiction to liquor, nothing was more delightful to me than to find myself a member of a large bottle association sat in for serious drinking; the table officers appointed, the demi-johns filled, the bottles arranged, with the other necessary dispositions for such engagements; and I put no inconsiderable value upon myself for my supposed, "potency in potting," or, in modern phrase, my being able to carry off a respectable quantity of wine. Although a grievous headach was the usual penalty of my debauch, the admonition vanished with the indisposition, while a play or some other frivolous reading, beguiled the hours of penance. I blush to think of the many excesses I was guilty of while involved in this vortex of intemperance. Wine rarely deprived me of my feet, but it sometimes inflamed me to madness; and, in the true spirit of chivalry, the more extravagant an enterprize the greater was the temptation to achieve it. Every occupation requires its peculiar talents, and where mischief is the object, the spirit of noble daring is certainly an accomplishment. Hence, my energy on these occasions was duly appreciated by my companions. As to those convivial qualifications, which are *wont to set the table in a roar*, I had never any pretentions to them, though few enjoyed them with more relish. But these talents are often fatal to the possessor and they hastened, if they did not induce, the catastrophe of poor Kinnersley, a son of the already mentioned teacher at the academy. As he was several years older than myself, he belonged to an elder class in the school of riot; yet I have sometimes fallen in with him. He had not indeed the gibes and flashes of merriment, which are attributed to *the jester of Horwendillus's court;* but of all men I have seen, he had the happiest knack of being gross without being disgusting, and consequently, of entertaining a company sunk below the point of attic refinement. Modest by nature, and unobtrusive, probably from a conviction that he thereby gave zest to his talents, he always suffered himself to be called upon for his song, which he then generally accompanied with his violin, to the exquisite delight of his hearers. He possessed humour without grimace or buffoonery; and in the character of the drunken man, which he put on in some of his songs, and which may be endured as an imitation, he was pronounced by Hallam to be unequalled. But unfortunately, the character became at length too much a real one; and it is to be lamented, that one whose exterior indicated a most ingenious disposition, should prematurely close his career by habitual intemperance.

The study of the law, as may be supposed, went on heavily during this round of dissipation. I occasionally looked into Blackstone, but carefully kept aloof from the courts, where my attendance as a future candidate for the bar, was not to be dispensed with. Light reading was the day's amusement; and, as already said, it chiefly consisted of poetry and plays. The novels of Fielding and Smollet I had read; but as for those of Richardson, I had some how taken up the idea, that they were formal stuff, consisting chiefly of the dull ceremonials relating to courtship and marriage, with which, superannuated aunts and grandmothers torment the young misses subjected to their control. But taking up one evening the last volume of Clarissa, I accidentally opened it at a letter relating to the duel between Lovelace and Morden. This arrested my attention, and I soon found that the concerns of men, not less than those of the other sex, were both understood and spiritedly represented by the author. I immediately procured the work, and read it with more interest than any tale had ever excited in me before. The cruel, unmerited misfortunes of Clarissa, often steeped me in tears: yet the unrelenting villany of her betrayer, was so relieved by great qualities, so entirely was he the gentleman when he chose to put it on, that the feeling of destestation was intermingled with admiration and respect; and had figure, rank, fortune, borne me out in the resemblance, his, of all the characters I had met with, would in the vanity of my heart, have most prompted me to an imitation; though abhorring as much as any one his vile plotting and obduracy. Like the young man mentioned in the letters of Lord Chesterfield, I almost aspired to the catastrophe, as well as the accomplishments of this *libertine destroyed*. Nor was I singular

in this ambition: Lovelace has formed libertines, as MacHeath
has formed highwaymen. A young American, when at the
temple, between forty and fifty years ago, played the part of the
former with too fatal success, of which, I have been told, he preserved, and sometimes showed the story, written by himself: and
that this character was the model which the young Lord Lyttleton
prescribed to himself, appears to me evident from the cast of
some of his letters. Rowe's Lothario, which Doctor Johnson
tells us is the outline of Lovelace, is ever more favoured by an
audience than the virtuous and injured Altamont whom, even the
circumspect Mr. Cumberland brands with the epithet of *wittol:*
And is there a young and giddy female heart, that does not beat
in unison with Calista's when she exclaims:

> " I swear I could not see the dear betrayer
> Kneel at my feet, and sigh to be forgiven,
> But my relenting heart would pardon all,
> And quite forget 'twas he that had undone me."

Richardson, it is true, could not have made his story either
natural or interesting without ascribing great qualities to Lovelace.
So refined and all accomplished a woman as Clarissa, was not to
be taken with an ordinary man; yet what shall we say of the instruction intended to be conveyed by the exhibition of such a
character! Villain as he is, I very much fear, that to the youth
of both sexes, he is, upon the whole, more admired than detested.
The probability therefore is, that after all our attempts at advice
and reformation, the world will proceed according to its original
impulse, and that each season of life will retain the propensities
adapted to its destination.

He who presumes to face the world in the character of his own
biographer, ought to be armed with resolution for the encounter
of great difficulties. To expose his follies, though but his very
early ones, is far from a pleasant task; and yet it is in some degree, imposed upon him by the obligation he is under to represent himself truly. To do it lightly, as I have done, may argue
with some, too much indulgence for vice; and to treat the matter as a subject for deep humiliation and contrition, would be to
assume an austerity, I must confess I do not harbour. Still I can

say with truth, that the delineation is painful; and that I feel it to require an apology on the score of decorum.

It was about this time that the letters of Junius appeared, and from the English gazettes found their way into ours. The celebrity of these philippics excited general attention, and, of course, mine; but the mere fashion of admiring them, would never have prevailed over my indifference to their subject matter, to induce me to read them, had they not possessed a charm unusual in such performances. I sought them with avidity, and read them with delight. Some diversity of opinion still exists with respect to their style. Cumberland gives us to understand, that he sees little to admire in them; Johnson, however, seems to have thought differently; and their continued popularity must be considered as something more than equivocal evidence of their merit.* Mr. Heron conceives their author, whoever he was, to have formed his style in a great measure, on Chillingworth, Swift, Bolingbroke and Shebbeare. I am unacquainted with the writings of Chillingworth, nor do I discern in Junius any great likeness to Swift; but there is certainly a striking resemblance in his manner to *The dedication to a noble lord*, prefixed to the remarks on the History of England by Bolingbroke, and also to Angeloni's Letters by Doctor Shebbeare, which, when I read them many years ago, appeared to me to be written with uncommon spirit, elegance and force. But if Junius formed his style upon these distinguished writers, he sometimes drew his observations from those who are nearly obsolete. In his fifteenth letter, which is addressed to the Duke of Grafton, there is an allusion to a sentiment in *Bacon's Advancement of Learning*, of which Mr. Heron does not seem to have been aware. "Yet, for the benefit of the succeeding age," says Junius in his concluding sentence, "I could wish that your retreat might be deferred until your morals shall happily be ripened to that maturity of corruption, at which the worst examples cease to be contagious." Bacon has it, that "men o'erspread with vice, do not so much corrupt public manners, as those that are

---

* Their "merit" it were folly to deny. This is great, beyond dispute; but certainly much of their long continued popularity must be attributed to the still unrevealed mystery of their authorship.—ED.

half evil, and in part only." *Putredo serpens magis contagiosa est quam matura.* I think in some of the early editions of this letter, the words "as philosophers tell us," were inserted between the words "which" and "the," reading thus—"at which, as philosophers tell us, the worst examples cease to be contagious."

Were it warrantable to infer an imitation from a similitude in a single point, Mr. Heron might go back to the Latin classics, and add the names of Horace, Juvenal and Petronius to those of the English writers, whom Junius is supposed to have studied and to have had in his eye. That abrupt and indignant use of the imperative mood, so frequent in him, is also to be met with in each of these Latin authors. "Content yourself, my lord, with the many advantages," &c.—"Avail yourself of all the unforgiving piety," &c.—"Return, my lord, before it be too late," &c.— "Take back your mistress"—"Indulge the people. Attend New Market," &c.—"Now let him go back to his cloister," &c. Thus Horace—*I nunc, argentum et marmor vetus*, &c.—*I nunc et versus tecum meditare canoros;* and Juvenal, speaking of Hannibal, *I demens, et sævos curre per Alpes;*—and in the eloquent reflections over the body of Lycas in Petronius, the speaker exclaims, "*Ite nunc mortales, et magni cogitationibus pectora implete. Ite cauti, et opes fraudibus captas per mille annos, disponite.*" But whether Junius had models or not, he probably surpassed all who went before him in the graces of diction. He appears to have imparted an unknown music to English prose, and to have given it a fascination, in no wise inferior to the language of Rousseau. The beginning of his sentences are no less harmonious than his cadences at their close; nor, to my ear, can any lines in poetry, taking the preceding passage along with them, flow with more sweetness and ease, than do the following, in one of the letters to the Duke of Grafton. "You had already taken your degrees with credit in those schools, in which the English nobility are formed to virtue," &c., as do also the four concluding periods of the letter containing the remarked sentiment from Lord Bacon. I am aware it may be thought, that too much stress is here laid on mere sound; but if we analyze the sources from which our relish of good composition is derived, we shall be compelled to acknowledge the great importance of the ear in the discernment

9

of literary excellence. Cicero, as we are told by Lord Kames, I think, has even employed redundant words for the improvement of his harmony; and Rousseau informs us, that he has spent whole nights in constructing and rounding a period; hence may be inferred the importance these great writers attached to this part of their art.

As it was highly fashionable at this time to speak of Junius, he is descanted upon in the letters of Tamoc Caspipina, which came out in Philadelphia in the year 1771. In these, he is *prettily* denominated *The knight of the polished armour*, a fancy, with which the writer seems not a little pleased, since he has taken care that the idea shall not be lost for want of repeating.* These letters proceeded from the pen of the Rev. Mr. Duché, a very popular preacher of the Episcopal denomination. He had a fine voice and graceful delivery, but was never rated high in point of ability. His sermons were deemed flowery and flimsy, like the letters of Caspipina.

Mr. Duché was a whig *before*, and, I believe, *after* the Declaration of Independence; but being in Philadelphia when the British army took possession of it, and thinking, probably, that his country was in a fair way of being subdued, he changed sides, and wrote a very arrogant, ill-judged letter to General Washington, in which he advises him to renounce a cause which had very much degenerated, and to "negotiate for America at the head of his army." Mr. Duché was weak and vain, yet probably not a bad man: His habits, at least, were pious; and, with the exception of this political tergiversation, his conduct exemplary. His whimsical signature of Tamoc Caspipina, is an acrostic on his designation, as, The Assistant Minister Of Christ's Church And St. Peters, In Philadelphia, In North America.†

---

* "I find C— grows more and more dissatisfied with Junius. He entreated Sir William Draper, who was at New York in October last, once more to enter the lists with this *Knight of the polished armour*. Sir William, however, very politely replied, that he had engagements on his hands at present of a more agreeable nature. Your Lordship has doubtless seen Lady Draper before this time, so that you may guess what these engagements were."—*Caspipina's Lett. to Rt. Hon. Viscount P.*, 4th July, 1771.—Ed.

† A gentleman well acquainted with Mr. Duché in England, after the transactions alluded to, conceiving that his conduct was mistaken here, and particu-

larly as to his being a Whig *after* the Declaration of Independence, expressed his wish that in the event of a second edition of these Memoirs, I would correct and alter the passage. But though willing to gratify this gentleman, I cannot do so at the expense of truth; and I have no reason to suppose I have mis-stated any fact. As to my comments, they may not, perhaps, be warranted, but that must much depend on the political opinions of the time. Such a letter as the one alluded to might not, under some circumstances, have been arrogant, but from my impression of the character of Mr. Duche, and the part he acted, I am not induced to alter or suppress the epithet. Although pious and exemplary in his deportment, as I have admitted, he was much of a courtier, and, in my view, a person of so light a character as to be carried away by the prevailing fashion of thinking among what are called the better sort, by whom, at this time, the Whig cause was considered vulgar and rapidly on the decline. If the justness of the American claims warranted the blood which had already been spilt for them, the battles of Lexington and Bunker's Hill, with the invasion of Canada and assault on Quebec, the Declaration of Independence was not a moral but simply a political question; and whether the measure was judicious or not, it could not convert a cause, originally good, into a seditious and criminal rebellion. For this reason it certainly savoured of arrogance in Mr. Duché, to say the least of it, merely for this difference in opinion, to reproach his late associates with *sinister views*, and to advise GENERAL WASHINGTON to desert and betray them.

See Appendix E, for this celebrated Letter, and others relating to the subject above referred to by Mr. Graydon.—ED.

CHAPTER IV.

My irregular course of life had much impaired my health, for the re-establishment of which, and to enable me to pursue my studies without interruption from my free-living companions, my uncle advised my spending the approaching summer in Yorktown. Mr. Samuel Johnson, the Prothonotary of that county, was his particular friend, a respectable man who had been in the practice of the law, and had a very good library. Having been apprised of the project, he kindly offered me the use of his books, as well as his countenance and assistance in my reading. Accordingly, I submitted to become an exile from Philadelphia, with nearly the same objects and feelings of Propertius, when he left Rome for Athens.

> " Magnum iter ad doctas proficisci cogor Athenas—
> Romanæ turres, et vos valeatis amici
> Qualiscunque mihi, tuque puella vale."

Not that York* was an Athens; but I was sent thither for improve-

---

* York, the seat of justice for York county, is interesting on account of the revolutionary associations here adverted to. It is situated on the banks of Co-dorus creek. It is a rich and thriving borough, with a spirited and intelligent population of over five thousand. Among the public buildings of the place, the new court-house, finished in 1842, at a cost of about $150,000, will at once attract attention. Congress retired to York from Philadelphia, immediately after

ment, and there were various attractions in the city from which it was, no doubt, prudent to withdraw me. It was in the spring of 1773, that I was transferred to this pleasant and flourishing village, situated about twelve miles beyond the Susquehanna. It was this circumstance which rendered it an eligible retreat for Congress in the year 1778, when General Howe was in possession of the Capitol and eastern parts of Pennsylvania.* I was

the battle of Brandywine, in September, 1777, and for nine months occupied the old court-house, which stood, until 1841, in the centre of the public square. Its population, at the period of Mr. Graydon's residence, could hardly have exceeded 1500. In the year 1800 the number of its inhabitants was 2500.— Rail roads afford convenient and daily access to Philadelphia, a distance of 83 miles—and to Baltimore, distant 56 miles. The society of York is excellent, and the citizens of the borough are influential throughout the county and state.— ED.

* Or rather when the Capitol held possession of Sir William Howe. We learn from the "Memoirs" of LEE, that, "while Washington was engaged, without cessation, in perfecting his army in the art of war, and in placing it out of the reach of that contagious malady so fatal to man, Sir William was indulging, with his brave troops, in all the sweets of luxury and pleasure to be drawn from the wealthy and populous city of Philadelphia; nor did he once attempt to disturb that repose, now so essential to the American general. Thus passed the winter; and the approaching spring brought with it the recall of the commander of the British army; who was succeeded by Sir Henry Clinton, heretofore his second."

WRAXALL, indeed, says that the "Howes appear to have been either lukewarm, or remiss, or negligent, or incapable. Lord North's selection of those two commanders excited, at the time, just condemnation; however brave, able, or meritorious, they might individually be esteemed as professional men. Their ardour in the cause itself was doubted; and still more questionable was their attachment to the administration. Never, perhaps, in the history of modern war, has an army, or a fleet, been more profusely supplied with every requisite for brilliant and efficient service, than were the troops and ships sent out by Lord North's Cabinet in 1776, across the Atlantic. But, the efforts abroad, did not correspond with the exertions made at home. The energy and activity of a Wellington, never animated that torpid mass. Neither vigilance, enterprise, nor co-operation characterized the campaigns of 1776 and 1777. Dissipation, play, and relaxation of discipline, found their way into the British camp."

LEE, with a just and generous regard for the reputation, even of an enemy, says, in his Memoirs, in reference to the earlier movements of Sir William in America, "it would be absurd to impute to him a want of courage, for he eminently possessed that quality. To explain, as some have attempted to do, his apparent supineness, by supposing him friendly to the Revolution, and, therefore, disposed to connive at its success, would be equally stupid and unjust, for no part

9*

well received by Mr. Johnson, but with that formal, theoretical kind of politeness, which distinguishes the manners of those who constitute the *better sort*, in small secluded towns: and if, in these days, the Prothonotary of a county of German population, was not confessedly the most considerable personage in it, he must have been egregiously wanting to himself. This could with no propriety be imputed to my patron. Although apparently a mild and modest man, he evidently knew his consequence, and never lost sight of it, though to say the truth, I received full as much of his attention as either I desired or had a right to expect: He repeated the tender of his books and services, complimented me with a dinner, suggested that business and pleasure could not be well prosecuted together, and consigned me to my meditations.

I established myself at a boarding-house, at whose table I found a practising attorney, a student of law, another of physic, and a young Episcopal clergyman, who had lately arrived from Dublin. The first was a striking instance of what mere determination and perseverance will do, even in a learned profession. He was an Irishman, a man of middle age—the extent of whose attainments was certainly nothing more, than in a coarse, vulgar hand, to draw a declaration; and in equally vulgar arithmetic, to sum up the interest due upon a bond. His figure was as awkward as can well be imagined, and his elocution exactly corresponded with it. From the humble post of under-sheriff, he had lately emerged to his present station at the bar, and was already in good practice. By industry and economy, his acquisitions soon exceeded his expenses; and he died not long since, in pretty affluent circumstances. Justice, however, requires it should be added, that his want of brilliant qualities, was compensated by an adequate portion of common sense, by unblemished integrity, and liberality in his dealings with the poor. Nor should it be forgotten, that after having taken part with his adopted country in the struggle for her rights, he did not, like too many of his countrymen, by a blind obedience to vindictive passions, much more than

of Sir William's life is stained with a single departure from the line of honour." It must be confessed, however, that at this time Sir William had not become acquainted with the allurements of Philadelphia society, where, "*snug as a flea*," as facetiously sung by the poet, he revelled long and luxuriously.—ED.

efface the merit of his services.—The law-student was from Wilmington; an easy, good-natured young man, whose talents appeared to be misplaced in their present direction. They were, probably, better adapted to the army, into which he entered on the breaking out of the war, and was killed at the battle of Brandywine, holding the rank of a Major in the Pennsylvania line.— The student of physic, though with some rusticity to rub off, was yet a pretty good scholar; nor was he deficient in natural endowments. To these, he added a manly and honourable way of thinking, which made him respectable in the army, (which he also afterwards joined,) as well as in the path of civil life, in which he possesses an honourable station in the western country.

The clergyman was only an occasional lodger, his pastoral duties often calling him to Maryland and elsewhere, which produced absences of several weeks at a time. He had probably the propensities of that species of gownman, which I have heard Whitfield call a *downy doctor;* as, whatever might have been his deportment on solemn occasions, in his intercourse with me, he did not seem to be one who considered the enjoyment of the present sublunary scene, by any means unworthy of regard. One day, as I was strumming a tune from the Beggar's opera, upon a fiddle I had purchased, with a view of becoming a performer upon it, he entered my apartment. "What," says he, "you play upon the violin, and are at the airs of the Beggar's opera!" He immediately began to hum the tune I had before me, from which, turning over the leaves of the note-book, he passed on to others, which he sung as he went along, and evinced an acquaintance with the piece, much too intimate to have been acquired, by any thing short of an assiduous attendance on the theatre. After amusing himself and me for some time with his theatrical recollections, "I am," said he, "to give you a sermon next Sunday, and here it is," pulling from his pocket a manuscript. Perusing the title page, he read, it was preached at such a time in such a place, and at another time in such a place, giving me to understand from the dates, that it was not of his own composition, and that he made no difficulty of appropriating the productions of others. In a word, Mr. L—— seemed in all respects to be what was then called in Pennsylvania a Maryland Parson; that is, one who could accommodate himself to his company, and pass, from grave to gay, from lively to severe," as occasion might require. Among his other accomplishments, he was no incompetent jockey; at least I have a right to infer so, from the results of an exchange of horses between us, a short time before my return to the city: I do not, however, insinuate that he took me in, but merely that he had the best of the bargain.

Besides my fellow boarders there were several young men in the town, whose company served to relieve the dreariness of my solitude; for such it was, compared with the scene from which I had removed. These, for the most part are yet living, generally known and respected. There was also in the place an oddity, who, though not to be classed with its young men, I sometimes fell in with. This was Mr. James Smith,* the lawyer, then in considerable practice. He was probably between forty and fifty years of age, fond of his bottle and young company, and possessed of an original species of drollery. This, as may perhaps be said of all persons in this way, consisted more in the manner than the matter; for which reason, it is scarcely possible to convey a just notion of it to the reader. In him it much depended on an uncouthness of gesture, a certain ludicrous cast of countenance, and a drawling mode of utterance, which taken in conjunction with his eccentric ideas, produced an effect irresistibly comical; though on an analysis it would be difficult to decide, whether the man or the saying most constituted the jest. The most trivial incident from his mouth was stamped with his originality, and in relating one evening how he had been disturbed in his office by a cow, he gave inconceivable zest to his narration,

---

* Mr. Smith, was a signer of the Declaration of Independence. He was a native of Ireland, whence his father emigrated, it is supposed, between 1715 and 1720. James Smith received his education at the College of Philadelphia. After his admission to the bar, he removed to the vicinity of Shippensburgh, and there established himself as a lawyer and surveyor, but soon after removed to York, where he continued to reside, during the remainder of his life. He held high rank at the bar and, was greatly distinguished for his wit and good humour. He was a member of several important conventions. In 1775, he was elected to Congress, and retained his seat in that body, until November, 1778, when he resumed his professional business, from which he withdrew in 1800. He died in 1806.—ED.

by his manner of telling how she thrust her nose into the door, and *there roared like a Numidian lion*. Like the picture of Garrick between tragedy and comedy, his phiz exhibited a struggle between tragedy and farce, in which the latter seemed on the eve of predominating. With a sufficiency of various reading to furnish him with materials for ridiculous allusions and incongruous combinations, he was never so successful as when he could find a learned pedant to play upon : and of all men, Judge Stedman, when mellow, was best calculated for his butt. The judge was a Scotchman, a man of reading and erudition, though extremely magisterial and dogmatical in his cups. This it was which gave point to the humour of Smith, who, as if desirous of coming in for his share of the glory, while Stedman was in full display of his historical knowledge, never failed to set him raving by some monstrous anachronism, such for instance, as " don't you remember, Mr. Stedman, that terrible bloody battle which Alexander the Great fought with the Russians near the Straits of Babelmandel?" " What, sir!" said Stedman, repeating with the most ineffable contempt, " which Alexander the Great fought with the Russians! Where, mon, did you get your chronology?" "I think you will find it recorded, Mr. Stedman, in Thucidydes or Herodotus." On another occasion, being asked for his authority for some enormous assertion, in which both space and time were fairly annihilated, with unshaken gravity he replied, " I am pretty sure I have seen an account of it, Mr. Stedman, in a High Dutch almanac printed at *Aleepo*," his drawling way of pronouncing Aleppo. While every one at table was holding his sides at the expense of the judge, he, on his part, had no doubt that Smith was the object of laughter, as he was of his own unutterable disdain. Thus every thing was as it should be, all parties were pleased ; the laughers were highly tickled, the self-complacency of the real dupe was flattered, and the sarcastic vein of the pretended one gratified ; and this, without the smallest suspicion on the part of Stedman, who, residing in Philadelphia, was ignorant of Smith's character, and destitute of penetration to develope it.

York, I must say, was somewhat obnoxious to the general charge of unsociableness, under which Pennsylvania had always laboured: or if I wrong her, I was not the kind of guest that was calculated to profit of her hospitality. Perhaps I approached her under unfavourable auspices, those of a young man debauched by evil communications; or perhaps there was a want of congeniality between her manners and mine. Be it as it may, there was but a single house in which I found that sort of reception which invited me to repeat my visit; and this was the house of a Jew. In this, I could conceive myself at home, being always received with ease, with cheerfulness and cordiality. Those who have known York, at the period I am speaking of, cannot fail to recollect the sprightly and engaging Mrs. E., the life of all the gaiety that could be mustered in the village: always in spirits, full of frolic and glee, and possessing the talent of singing agreeably, she was an indispensable ingredient in the little parties of pleasure which sometimes took place, and usually consisted in excursions to the Susquehanna, where the company dined, and, when successful in angling, upon fish of their own catching. It was upon one of these occasions, the summer before I saw her, that she had attracted the notice of Mr. John Dickinson, the celebrated author of the *Farmer's Letters*. He had been lavish in her praise in the company of a lady of my acquaintance, who told me of it, and thence inferred, how much I should be pleased with her when I got to York. I paid little attention to the information, having no conception that I could take any interest in the company of a married woman, considerably older than myself and the mother of several children. The sequel proved how much I was mistaken, and how essential to my satisfaction was female society; the access to a house in which I could domesticate myself, and receive attentions, not the less grateful from apparently being blended with somewhat maternal. The master of the house, though much less brilliant than the mistress, was always good-humoured and kind; and as they kept a small store, I repaid as well as I could the hospitality of a frequent dish of tea, by purchasing there what articles I wanted.

After whiling away about six months, the allotted time of my exile, reading a little law in the morning, and either fowling, riding or strolling along the banks of the Codorus, a beautiful stream which passes through the town, in the afternoon, I at length set out on my return to Philadelphia. For the sake of company and yet more for the satisfaction of seeing the country, I took a circuitous route, crossing the Susquehanna at M'Call's ferry, at the *Narrows*. This place is rude and romantic to a great degree. The water is extremely deep, above ———— fathoms,* as it is stated in Scull's map, and the current much obstructed by rocks, which rise above the surface in huge and shapeless craggs. Leaving the river, we crossed the Octararo, which discharges itself into it; and thence, shaping our course through a pleasant country to Newark and Wilmington, we reached Philadelphia after a journey of three or four days, in the latter part of October.

I cannot take my final leave of York before mentioning, that I visited it again when Congress held their session there, in the year 1778. Mr. Johnson, who had been a widower, was then married to a lady from Maryland. The laws having been silenced by arms, he was no longer Prothonotary; and what was still more unfortunate for him, he had no chance of ever becoming so again, being much disaffected to the American cause. I found him extremely soured by the state of affairs: He was at no pains to conceal his disgust at it, and shook his head in fearful anticipation of future calamities. Five years had produced a considerable change in respect to the inhabitants of the town. The young men I had been acquainted with had been generally in the army, and were consequently dispersed. The E——'s were not there; or at least, I did not see them; and if my memory does not mislead me, the family had removed to Baltimore.

Although I had not made myself a lawyer, I returned to the city somewhat improved in health, as well as in my habits of living. My disposition, however, was unaltered. I still affected the man of pleasure and dissipation; had a sovereign contempt for matrimony, and was even puppy enough, with shame I yet think of it, to ape the style of Lovelace, in some of my epistolary

---

* From the account of Theodore Burr, who threw the immense arch of 360 feet, 4 inches, over the river at this place, in the winter of 1814–15, the depth of the water is 150 feet.

This noble bridge was, in part, carried away by the flood of March, 1846—the greatest known within fifty years.—ED.

correspondencies.   As my uncle was still bent on qualifying me
for the practice of my profession, he proposed my pursuing my
studies, for the winter, under the direction of Mr. James Allen.
As this gentleman was without a clerk, my being there was considered as a matter of mutual convenience.   In return for the use
of his books, I did the business of his office, which was not very
burdensome, and left me sufficient time for reading.   Mr. Allen,
the second son of old Mr. William Allen,* the chief justice, and
perhaps the richest and most influential person in the province,
was a man of wit and pleasantry, who, for the gratification of his
ambition, was determined also to be a man of business, the only
road in Pennsylvania, to honours and distinction.   For this purpose, he engaged in the practice of the law, in which, at this
time, he was very assiduous and attentive.   As he was very
gentlemanly in his manners, good-humoured and affable, I passed
my time with him altogether to my mind.   His good sense and
good breeding, suggested the true line of behaviour to one beyond the age of apprenticeship, and who, though doing the business of a clerk, did not perform it for hire.   He also took a
friendly interest in my improvement, submitting the cases in
which he was consulted to my previous examination and opinion,
and treating the timidity which many feel on first speaking in
public, as a weakness very easily overcome.   In relation to the

* The same gentleman alluded to by Howe in his " *Narrative*," quoted b;
Sparks, in the Appendix, to the 4th vol. of the writings of Washington, a
Mr. WILLIAM ALLEN, a gentleman who was supposed to have great family in
fluence in the province of Pennsylvania; Mr. Chalmers, much respected in the
three lower counties on the Delaware and in Maryland; and Mr. Clifton, the
Chief of the Roman Catholic persuasion, of whom there was said to be many in
Philadelphia, as well as in the rebel army, serving against their inclinations:
these gentlemen were appointed commandants of corps, to receive and form fo
service all the well-affected that could be obtained, (meaning loyalists, of course,
and what was the success of these efforts ?"—To the honour of the American
name, and with native pride—I answer in Howe's own language,—" In May.
1778, when I left America, Colonel Allen had raised only 152 rank and file:
Colonel Chalmers, 336, (a goodly proportion, however, for the three patriotic counties on the Delaware!) and Colonel Clifton, 180; which, together with three
troops of Light Dragoons, consisting of 132 troopers, and 174 *real volunteers* from
Jersey, under Colonel Vandyke, amounting in the whole to 974 men, constitute
all the force that could be collected in Pennsylvania, after the most indefatigabl
exertions during eight months."—ED.

subject, he gave me, I remember, a very laughable account of his own *coup d'essai* in conjunction with the facetious Harry Elwes, at Easton.

To have been regular in the history of my education I should have mentioned, that I had already acquired sufficient knowledge of French to be able to read it with tolerable facility. I now undertook to learn the use of the small sword of a Mr. Pike, who had lately arrived in Philadelphia, and was much celebrated for his ability both as a dancing and fencing master. Amusement and exercise were my inducements to the undertaking, little thinking that I was acquiring professional skill, and that a sword, in a year or two, would be a badge of my calling. From what I have since seen, I do not think that Mr. Pike, although, like Rousseau's master, sufficiently *fier de l'art de tuer un homme,* was an accomplished swordsman. He nevertheless probably taught the science very well, and had certainly a knack of close pushing, which I have never met with in any other; that is, in the exercise of *quarte* and *tierce,* by placing the point of his foil near the guard of his adversary's, he could disengage and thrust with such quickness, as with certainty to hit the arm of the assailed. I laboured in vain, for six or eight months to acquire this dexterity: from continued practice, however, the slight of hand came at last, upon which I valued myself not a little, and was equally valued by others. There was but one other pupil in the school who had been equally successful, and this was my particular friend the reverend Mr. Clay, of New-Castle, who was then a merchant, and who, in respect of his present clerical function, might say, *non hos quæsitum munus in usus.* This accomplishment had nearly brought me, when in the army, into perilous contact with a Doctor Skinner,* who had the fame of a duellist, and having

---

* ALEXANDER SKINNER.—He is depicted at large, by General Henry Lee, in his "Memoirs of the War in the Southern Department of the United States." "He was a native of Maryland. He was virtuous and sensible; full of original humour of a peculiar cast; and eccentric in mind and manners. In person and in love of good cheer, as well as in dire objection to the field of battle, he resembled, with wonderful similitude, Shakspeare's Falstaff. Yet Skinner had no hesitation in fighting duels, and had killed his man. When urged by his friends to explain why he, who would, when called upon by feelings of honour to risk his life in single combat, advance to the arena with alacrity, should abhor so

already killed his man.   A Mr. Hanson of Maryland, who had
been a scholar of Pike, and knew what I could do, had made a
considerable bet with the doctor, that he would find a person in
the army, who in spite of him, would hit him in thrusting *tierce,* or
rather *quarte over the arm.*   He called upon me, when the army

dreadfully, the field of battle,—he uniformly, in substance, answered, that he
considered it very arrogant in a surgeon (whose province it was to take care of
the sick and wounded) to be aping the demeanour and duty of a commissioned
officer, whose business it was to fight: an arrogance which he cordially contemned, and of which he should never be guilty.   Moreover,—he would add,—
he was not more disposed to die than other gentlemen; but that he had an utter
aversion to the noise and turmoil of battle.   It stunned and stupified him.   However, when Congress should think proper to honour him with a commission, he
would convince all doubters that he was not afraid to push the bayonet."   General
Lee, in describing an action near a stream over which his dragoons could not
pass—being too wide for their horses to leap, and too deep in mud for them to
attempt to ford—it was impossible to pursue the advantage his troops had gallantly gained, and "having only sabres to oppose to the enemy's fire, and those
sabres withheld from contact by the interposing chasm, he was forced to draw
off from the vain contest, after several of his dragoons had been wounded,
among whom was Dr. Irvin, surgeon of the legion cavalry," states, that such
was Dr. Skinner's unvarying objection to Irvin's custom of risking his life,
whenever he was with the corps going into action, that, kind and amiable
as he was, he saw with pleasure, that his prediction, often communicated to
Irvin to stop his practice, (which, contrasted with his own, Skinner felt as a bitter
reproach) was at length realized, when Irvin was brought in wounded; and he
would not dress his wound, although from his station he had a right of preference,
until he had attended upon all the privates—reprehending with asperity Irvin's
custom, and sarcastically complimenting him, occasionally, with the honourable
scar he might hereafter show.

Surely he was the Dr. Sitgreaves of Cooper!

When he first appeared in the lower country, he wore a long beard and huge
fur cap, the latter through necessity, the first through some superstitious notion,
the meaning of which it was impossible to penetrate.   An officer who really
esteemed him, asking him "why he suffered his beard to grow to such an unusual
length," he tartly replied, "It is a secret, sir, betwixt my God and myself, that
human impertinence shall never penetrate."   On a night alarm at Ninety-Six, as
Colonel Lee was hastening forward to ascertain the cause, he met Skinner in
full retreat, and stopping him, said, "what is the matter Doctor, whither so fast
—not frightened I hope?"   "No, Colonel, no," replied Skinner, "not absolutely
frightened, but, I candidly confess, most damnably alarmed."

Being once asked which of the ladies of South Carolina possessed in his estimation, the greatest attractions? he replied, "The widow Izard beyond all comparison.   I never pass her magnificent sideboard, but the plate seems ready to
tumble into my pocket."—ED.

lay at Haerlem heights, to know if I would push: With some reluctance I consented, but before the time appointed arrived, some movement took place, which separated me from Mr. Skinner, and the question was not decided. The instruction I received from Pike, I considerably improved by practice, and began to grow vain of my skill, until I met with Major Clow (or Clough) of Colonel Baylor's dragoons, who had been a pupil of Angelo and others of the best masters in Europe. He soon convinced me that I had still much room for improvement; though he was pleased to assure me, that I was by far the best fencer he had met with in America, and much superior to Benson, a fencing master in New York.

During the time of my being with Pike, Mentges, who was afterwards a Colonel in our service, had opened a fencing school. Among his scholars were Messrs. Robeson* and Bradford;† then

---

* Perhaps the son of him—mentioned as *Robinson*, by Watson, whose orthography in names, like the style of his inimitable "Annals" is *sui generis!*

The gentleman, referred to by Watson, "was Clerk of the Provincial Council, and owner of the first hired prison. In 1685 he gave offence to the council, and they resolved 'that the words spoken by him, concerning the impeachment against Judge Moore, was drawn *hab nab*, which expression of his we do unanimously declare to be undecent, unallowable, and to be disowned.' " Soon after, it was farther resolved, that Patrick Robinson could not be removed from his Clerk's office until he was legally convicted of the offence. They, however, determine " that he shall be readily dismissed from any public office of trust in this government."—ED.

† Bradford commenced his professional career at a very early age, and his instructive history is deserving of the attention of those, especially, upon whom adverse fortune has laid her depressing hand. His circumstances were exceedingly restricted, and he was several years at the Bar with few or no clients; and so discouraging appeared his prospects, that at one time he seriously contemplated the abandonment of his professional hopes, and the adoption of the sea as his new and perilous home.

Mr. Bradford was buried in the grave-yard of St. Mary's, in the ancient, rural city of Burlington, New-Jersey; and his monument bears the following beautiful and comprehensive inscription, which supersedes the necessity of farther biographical details:

" Here lies the remains of WILLIAM BRADFORD, Attorney-General of the United States, under the Presidency of WASHINGTON; and previously Attorney-General of Pennsylvania, and a Judge of the Supreme Court of that State. In private life he had acquired the esteem of all his fellow-citizens. In professional attainments he was learned as a lawyer, and eloquent as an advocate. In the execu-

students of law, the former already spoken of, and the latter of whom became a Judge of the Supreme Court of the State, and afterwards Attorney-General of the United States. Coming into the school I was asked to take a foil, and in succession contended with each of these gentlemen; but the result was unlucky for Mentges,* as it too plainly evinced his incapacity for the business he had undertaken, and of course, soon deprived him of his pupils.

At the city tavern, which had been recently established, and was in great vogue, I often spent my evenings. It was at this time much frequented by Mr. William Hockley, a gentleman of fortune, who was liable to fits of mental derangement; and while these prevailed was a prominent figure at all public places: for as he was perfectly harmless, it was not thought necessary to restrain him from going abroad. The effects of this misfortune

tion of his public offices, he was vigilant, dignified and impartial. Yet, in the bloom of life; in the maturity of every faculty that could invigorate or embellish the human mind; in the prosecution of the most important services that a citizen could render to his country; in the perfect enjoyment of the highest honours that public confidence could bestow upon an individual; blessed in all the pleasures which a virtuous reflection could furnish from the past, and animated by all the incitements which an honourable ambition could depict in the future— he ceased to be mortal. A fever, produced by a fatal assiduity in performing his official trust at a crisis interesting to the nation, suddenly terminated his public career, extinguished the splendour of his private prosperity, and on the 23d day of August, 1795, in the 40th year of his age, consigned him to the grave—Lamented, Honoured and Beloved."—Ed.

* The COLONEL MENZIES, of Garden; who relates the following amusing anecdote: "Sometime previous to the evacuation of Charleston, Colonel Menzies, of the Pennsylvania line, received a letter from a Hessian officer within the garrison, who had once been a prisoner, and treated by him with great kindness, express. ing an earnest desire to show his gratitude, by executing any commission with which he would please to honour him. Colonel Menzies replied to it, requesting him to send twelve dozen *Cigars;* but, being a German, and little accustomed to express himself in English, he was not very accurate in his orthography, and wrote *Sizars.* Twelve dozen pairs of *Scissors* were accordingly sent him, which, for a time, occasioned much mirth in the camp, at the Colonel's expense; but no man knew better how to profit from the mistake. Money was not, at the period, in circulation; and by the aid of his runner, distributing his scissors over the country, in exchange for poultry, Colonel Menzies lived luxuriously, while the fare of his brother officers was a scanty pittance of famished beef, bull-frogs from ponds, and cray-fish from the neighbouring ditches."—Ed.

appeal too forcibly to humanity, to be considered as the subject of merriment, otherwise the flights of this gentleman might, for a short time, have been truly amusing. His fancies were the most lively and brilliant that can be imagined. He had full persuasion that he excelled in every thing that was worthy of attention, though the turf and the theatre were the chief scenes of his glory. Sometimes he achieved the exploits himself; at others, he only witnessed their performance, and, like Horace's *haud ignobilis Argis*, conceived he had been the hearer of the most wonderful actors.

"Se credebat miros audire trajedos."

Whatever he chose to do, that he chose to do best: Hallam was but a fool to him when he chose to be a player; he had more than once, when a fencer, disarmed Pike with a pipe shank; and had taken, when a sportsman, all the purses at all the race-grounds between Savannah and New York. His vivid conceptions supplied him with a stud; and he would run over the names of his horses and their pedigrees, descanting, as he went along, on the respective merits of his riders with astonishing volubility, and with a gaiety and sprightliness of manner, that even Garrick, if he could have equalled, could not have excelled: And this rodomontade was occasionally accompanied by so peculiarly agreeable and animated a laugh, as might have served for a model, to a performer of genteel comedy. Yet, notwithstanding these wild coruscations of genius, Mr. Hockley, when himself, was remarkably dull and phlegmatic; one, who never perhaps had had a foil in his hand, and who had little or no relish for races or plays. His case would almost induce a belief, that there was really "a pleasure in being mad, which none but madmen know;" and that however deplorable the condition of the melancholy or raving maniac, there is a malady of the mind, which, in its paroxysms, is nothing more than a delightful illusion, *Mentis gratissimus error*.

I suppose the time I have now arrived at, to be the winter of 1774–5. From this era, although I could not look back upon my conduct with approbation, I could yet do it without anguish or remorse. I had spent much time unprofitably, but had been guilty of no baseness: I had been rather dissolute in my habits

10*

—too indulgent to gay profligacy, and had even sometimes associated with it to the disadvantage of my character, but had happily preserved myself free from its contagion. I neither liked liquor
nor gaming; I had contracted no debts—used no unwarrantable
means to obtain money or credit; nor, among my vanities and
follies, had I ever committed an action, which might tend to deprive me of that self-respect, which is the best security for a future
course of honourable and moral conduct. I was open, however,
to a galling, self-reproach, in that at the age of nearly twenty-
three, instead of being in a situation to maintain myself, I was
still dependant upon my mother, not only for necessaries, but my
pocket-expenses, which though not extremely profuse, were less
limited than they ought to have been.*

But a period was now approaching which tended equally to
interrupt the pursuits of pleasure and of business; and, inasmuch
as it did the latter, to lessen my chagrin at being disqualified for
engaging in it. Pennsylvania, hitherto so tranquil and so happy,
was in common with her sister provinces, about to experience the
calamities, which sooner or later, seem the inevitable destiny of
every region inhabited by man. Her golden age was at its
close; and that iron era which was to sever the ties of friendship
and of blood; to set father against son, and brother against
brother, with many other frightful evils in its train, was about to
supervene. The ministry seemed resolved upon enforcing their
assumed right of taxing the colonies, and there was an equal determination on the part of America, to resist the pretension. The
supremacy of the mother country, it was held, on the one hand,
necessarily involved the right of legislating over, and consequently
of imposing taxes on, every part of her dominions;† while it was

---

* Even this reproach I might have spared myself, had I reflected that there
was exclusively due to me from my father's estate about 170*l.* the proceeds
of a prize drawn in the Academy lottery, by a ticket presented to me by my
grandfather, and for which he, as trustee for me, took a bond from my father, receiving the money, dated Sept. 14th, 1756, and which money I never demanded.
But what is this to the world? Not much to be sure. Still it is something to a
proscribed man, interested in mitigating as much as possible his atrocities.

† My doctrine has ever been, that legislation involves in it every possible
power and exercise of civil government.—*Lord Lyttelton's Letters.*

The same doctrine is maintained by General Burgoyne in his Letters to General Lee, and elsewhere.

contended on the other, to be a fundamental principle of the constitution, that no money could be drawn from the people without their consent, signified through the medium of a representation in parliament; and that as the colonists had no such representation, they were not subject to parliamentary taxation. An exception was, however, made with respect to the regulation of trade, and a distinction was taken between internal and external taxes; the latter of which only, not having revenue for their object, it was said, could be constitutionally laid. The discussion of the points in controversy, only served to put the parties farther asunder. To the Americans, it disclosed the disadvantages of a dependance on a power so remote as that of Britain, and so oppressed by a weight of debt. .It was also perceived, that as we were not, so neither could we be, efficiently represented in her parliament; and that, in any shape, therefore, to admit her right to tax us, would be to throw ourselves entirely on the generosity of a nation, tempted to large exactions from the consideration that she would be relieved in proportion to what she could draw from us,* and prompted to invigorate the arm of coërcion from her observation of our rapidly increasing strength, which, if not speedily repressed and held in subjection, might soon defy control.† A similar view of the subject, no doubt, led the ministry

* The American war, said Mr. Windham, he was afraid had been undertaken for no better reason, than the hope of saving ourselves, by taxing America.— Speech in 1792.

"*May 1st*, 1774."

† "There is a great business in agitation, and has been for some time; but, without the thorough-bass of opposition, it makes no echo out of Parliament. Its Parliamentary name is—REGULATIONS FOR BOSTON. Its essence, the question of *sovereignty over America*. Shall I tell you in one word, my opinion? If the Bostonians resist, the dispute will possibly be determined in favour of the crown by force. If they temporize or submit, waiting for a more favourable moment, and preparing for it, the wound, skinned over, will break out hereafter with more violence, not that I lay any stress on my conjectures. People collect their guesses from what they have read, heard, or seen, but times are unlike; and a single man can sometimes give a new colour to an age."

"*November 24th* 1774."

"Don't tell me I am grown old and peevish and supercilious—name the geniusses of 1774, and I submit. The next Augustan age will dawn on the other side of the Atlantic. There will, perhaps, be a Thucydides at Boston, a Xeno-

to appreciate the importance of retaining in due dependance so fruitful a field of exaction; and to conceive, that if the application of force should be necessary for the purpose, the sooner it should be applied the better. All things considered, they had certainly some grounds to calculate upon success: And as to the proposal, of raising by our own legislatures, the supplies that might be asked for, besides, that an acquiescence in it, would very strongly resemble a renunciation of sovereignty, it is scarcely in the nature of power to condescend to petition for that which it supposes itself able to compel; and pride is ever more gratified in the exercise of generosity, than in the performance of justice. The ministry had the support of a great majority of the nation at home. Interest, which made resistance popular with us, made compulsory measures popular with them. It was this collision, that at this time, severed the two countries; though nature, which had placed the Atlantic ocean between them, had thereby interposed an insurmountable bar to a much longer colonial connexion on constitutional principles.* In another view, when the nurturing season is past, the young of all kinds are left to act for themselves. Even man, by a law of his own, pursuing that of nature, has appointed a time for the enfranchisement of youth; and America had perhaps completed her years of minority. But waving analogies, that may be fitter for illustrations than arguments, the merits of the question, were, I think, on the side of the

phon at New York, and, in time, a Virgil at Mexico, and a Newton at Peru. At last, some curious traveller from Lima will visit England and give a description of the ruins of St. Paul's, like the editions of Balbec and Palmyra; but am I not prophesying, contrary to my consummate prudence, and casting horoscopes of empire like Rousseau? Yes; well, I will go and dream of my visions." —Walpole's Letters to Horace Mann.—ED.

* Dr. Franklin, writing in his journal on the 14th December, 1774, says, "In the course of conversation, more than sixteen years ago, long before any dispute with America, the present Lord Camden, then Mr. Pratt, said to him: 'For all what you Americans say of your loyalty, and all that, I know you will one day throw off your dependence on this country; and, notwithstanding your boasted affection for it, you will set up for independence.'" Dr. Franklin said that he answered him, "No such idea was ever entertained by the Americans, nor will any such ever enter their heads, unless you grossly abuse them." "Very true," replied Mr. Pratt, that is one of the main causes I see will happen, and will produce the event."—ED.

colonies; and the inference, that the authority contended for by Britain, would ultimately reduce them to vassalage, was by no means chimerical. This being generally perceived and assented to, a great proportion, and perhaps a great majority of the most wealthy and respectable in each of the provinces, was arrayed in opposition to the ministerial claim. I speak of the early stages of the contest. In Pennsylvania, this was certainly the case, though as to the extent to which the opposition should be carried, there was doubtless a great diversity of opinion; many sincere whigs considering a separation from the mother country as the greatest evil that could befal us. The merchants were on the whig side, with few exceptions; and the lawyers, who, from the bent of their studies, as well as their habit of speaking in public, were best qualified to take a lead in the various assemblies that became necessary, were little less unanimous in the same cause.

A few, indeed, of the oldest and most conspicuous practitioners in Philadelphia were either disaffected or lukewarm. Among these, Mr. Joseph Galloway,* though a member of the first Congress, was known to be a disapprover of the measures pursuing. By obtaining a seat in Congress, therefore, his design undoubtedly was, to impede, if he could not divert the current of affairs; but finding no matter to work upon, and taking the hint, probably, from a halter coiled up in a box, that was said to be sent to him, he gave up the contest, and went off to the invading army, as soon as an opportunity offered. From Mr. Chew,† Mr. Tilghman,‡

---

* See Appendix F, for a biographical notice of Mr. Galloway.—ED.

† MR. CHEW was prominent in early times. In 1772 he was preferred to the Bench. Perhaps no one exceeded him in an accurate knowledge of Common law, or in the sound exposition of Statutes; his solid judgment, tenacious memory, and persevering industry, rendered him a safe and steady guide. At the bar his language was pertinent and correct, but seldom characterized by effusions of eloquence; his arguments were close, and frequently methodized on the strict rules of logic; his object always seemed to be to produce conviction, not to obtain applause."—*Watson's Annals.*

The name will be remembered from its association with "Chew's House," and the Battle of Germantown. He was the owner of the property, which still (1846) remains in the family.—ED.

‡ Mr. I. Tilghman, father of Mr. Edward Tilghman and of Mr. William Tilghman, late Chief Justice of Pennsylvania.—ED.

and Mr. Shippen,* no activity was expected or claimed, as they were what was called *Proprietary* men, and in the enjoyment, under that interest, of offices of trust and importance. Their favourable disposition to the American cause, was, however inferred, from the sons of the first two having joined the military associations. Mr. John Ross, who loved ease and Madeira, much better than liberty and strife, declared for neutrality, saying, that *let who would be king, he well knew that he should be subject.* An observation, which, judging only from events, may be thought by some, to contain as much intrinsic wisdom as the whole of the *Farmer's Letters*, with all the legal, political, and constitutional knowledge they display. But the abuse of liberty, ought not to induce apathy to oppression, however it may dispose us to deliberate before we plunge into a new order of things. Mr. James Allen was also suspected of having no very cordial affection for the cause, although he shouldered a musket in the ranks of the militia. What chiefly led to the suspicion, was, that he had laboured to organize a committee of privates, which, however accordant such a measure might be, with the republican spirit, that was coming in fashion, it was, to say the least of it, a very questionable experiment on military subordination and discipline. As business had, for some time, been entirely laid aside, I no longer attended his office, and consequently had less opportunity of knowing his real sentiments. His brother, Mr. Andrew Allen, the attorney-general, was more ardent, and considered also to be more sincere. He had attached himself to the corps of city Cavalry, commanded by Mr. Markoe; but not long after, recognising his error, he withdrew, giving out that he would hang up his cap and regimentals as monuments of his folly, and upon the declaration of independence, he sought an asylum with General Howe. These were the principal gentlemen of standing in the profession who may be considered as exceptions to the temper of the Pennsylvania bar.

On the whig side of the question, Mr. John Dickinson, always in the political antipodes of Mr. Galloway, was, at this time,

---

* Edward Shippen, Chief Justice of Pennsylvania, born 1729, died April 15, 1806. He was a cousin of Dr. Wm. Shippen of the University, and father of Mrs. General Arnold.—ED.

most prominent and distinguished. By his Farmer's Letters, he had acquired a high reputation, both for patriotism and ability; though he was, if I mistake not, among the disapprovers of independence, and thence fell under a cloud, which obscured him all the war, and even involved him in the suspicion of disaffection and toryism.* Next in conspicuousness to Mr. Dickinson, among the members of the city bar, were Mr. Reed† and Mr.

---

* For a Sketch of the Life and Character of Mr. Dickinson, see Appendix G.— ED.

† Mr. Reed was the son of Mr. Andrew Reed, from Ireland, "engaged in trade in the town of Trenton," and was born there in 1742.

In 1775, at the age of 33 years, he was elected President of the Provincial Convention. In the same year he was appointed Military Secretary to WASHINGTON, who appears to have entertained a high opinion of his talents and patriotism. In June, 1776, he was, at the suggestion of WASHINGTON, appointed by Congress Adjutant-General of the Continental Army. The Appendix to the fourth volume of Sparks' "Life and Writings of WASHINGTON" contains a correspondence between General WASHINGTON and Mr. Reed, upon the subject of a misunderstanding between them, to which the reader, who may feel an interest in the matter, is referred.

On the 12th of May, 1777, Reed was elected a brigadier by Congress, and in September in the same year, he was elected to the Continental Congress. "Such, however, was the active interest which he took, in the operations of the campaign in Pennsylvania, that he did not join the delegation in Congress at all under this election. But just at the close of the campaign, a new election took place on the 10th of December when he was again chosen, Franklin and Robert Morris being in the same delegation." The attempt to bribe General Reed by Governor Johnstone, one of the British Commissioners, who arrived in 1778, is detailed at length in the modest and appropriate "Life of Joseph Reed" by his grandson Mr. Henry Reed, of Philadelphia. Associated as Commissioners with Mr. Johnstone, were the Earl of Carlisle, and Mr. William Eden, afterwards Lord Aukland. They left England in April, 1778. Walpole alludes to them on the 5th of March, in his letter to Horace Mann. "You will have been impatient for the consequences of Lord North's Conciliatory Plan. The substantial consequences cannot, you are sensible, be known till the Commissioners arrive in America and return the answer of the Congress." It is to the son of the Earl of Carlisle, who fell at Waterloo, that Byron beautifully and penitentially alludes in the third Canto of Childe Harold:

> " Their praise is hymn'd by loftier harps than mine ;
> Yet one I would select from that proud throng,
> Partly because they blend me with his line,
> *And partly that I did his Sire some wrong.*"

In October 1778, Walpole again writes, "Governor Johnstone is returned, the other two Commissioners remain to make peace, to which we are told the Ameri-

M'Kean,* each of whom was distinguished both during and after
the revolution.   The young gentlemen of the profession with a

cans are disposed ; a proof of which is our sending another army thither." The
reason for Johnstone's return is thus accounted for by the Editor of Walpole's
Letters : " Governor Johnstone had been charged by the Congress with an attempt
to corrupt and bribe General Reed with the sum of ten thousand pounds and a
public situation in the Colonies; to which offer the General is said to have
answered, 'that he was not worth purchasing, but, such as he was, the King of
England was not rich enough to do it.'   In consequence of this, the Congress in-
terdicted all intercourse and correspondence with the Commissioners while
Governor Johnstone continued one of them.   He therefore resigned and returned
to England."

In a letter to George Selwyn, of the 6th of November, Mr. Charles Townshend
says, " Governor Johnstone is as mad as a bull.   He foams at the mouth, and
swears that he will impeach Lord Howe and Sir William, for not reducing
America.   Wedderburn says, he talks in a very manly style; and he is much
caressed by ministers whom he has abused in so coarse a style to the Americans :
You may be sure he caresses them in his turn.   He puts me in mind of a character of King James I., given by an old Scotch Lord at his accession : ' Ken you
an ape! If I'se hold him he will bite you; if you hold him, he will bite
me.'   General Reed, by the unanimous vote of both branches of the state government was, in 1778, elected " President " of Pennsylvania.   He was subsequently
re-elected to Congress, and died, at Philadelphia, in March 1785, in his forty-third
year.

His career,—his public career especially, was short but truly brilliant.   Like
his illustrious friend, William Bradford, of whom mention has already been made,
and whose pre-eminent abilities he was among the first to discover and appreciate,
he lived at a stirring period, fruitful in great events, many of which were crowded
into the brief time allotted to him here, and with which his name is honourably
and permanently associated.—ED.

* THOMAS McKEAN—afterwards Chief Justice and also Governor of Pennsylvania—an able and ardent politician of the ultra democratic school, although his
training and associations in early life were of a character to influence to the
adoption of an opposite political creed.   He was a zealous revolutionary patriot
and, in his earlier political career especially, is entitled to warm commendation.
He was born at Chester, in Pennsylvania, in 1734, and commenced the practice
of his profession at the age of twenty-one.   In October, 1762, he was elected a
member of the Assembly for the county of New Castle, and was annually
returned for seventeen successive years, although he resided in Philadelphia for
the last six years of that period.   He was a delegate to the General Congress,
which met at New York in 1765.   In the same year he was appointed Judge of
the Court of Common Pleas and of the Orphan's Court for the county of New
Castle.   In November term, 1765, and February term, 1766, he was one of the
bench that ordered the officers of the court to proceed in their duties, as usual,
on unstamped paper.   In 1771 he was appointed Collector of the port of New
Castle.   He was appointed a delegate to the General Congress of 1774, from the

few exceptions, were also in whig politics; and accordingly fell into some of the associations which were forming for the purpose of acquiring a knowledge of tactics. In the country the same spirit was prevalent at the bar, the members of which, some of whom were of the first eminence, distinguished themselves by their zeal in opposition to the ministerial claims; and as these

lower counties of Delaware, and he continued to serve in that body until 1783. He was President of Congress in 1781, and, although a member of that body, he held and executed the office of Chief Justice of Pennsylvania, from the year 1777. He was exceedingly active in promoting the Declaration of Independence, which he signed, and soon after that event marched with a battalion, of which he was Colonel, into New Jersey, to support General WASHINGTON, and acquitted himself gallantly in several dangerous skirmishes, while he remained with the army. Upon his return to Delaware, he drew up, in a single night, a Constitution for that State, which, on the following day, was unanimously adopted by the Assembly. In 1777 he acted as "President" of the state of Delaware. "At that period," as he relates, " he was hunted like a fox by the enemy ; and was compelled to remove his family five times in the course of a few months, and at length placed them in a little log house on the banks of the Susquehanna." While here he was treated with great deference by the country people, and the straggling Indians, who had their village in that vicinity. The Chief Justice, when on the Bench, wore an immense cocked-hat, and was dressed in a scarlet gown. He discharged the office of Chief Justice for twenty-two years, and "gave striking proofs of ability, impartiality and courage."

" He was a member of the Convention of Pennsylvania that ratified the Constitution of the United States, and made a masterly speech in its support." He was also a member of the Convention that formed the first Constitution of Pennsylvania ; a body composed of some of the purest and ablest men of any age or nation, but whose wise and patriotic labours became unpalatable to the "*progressive democracy*" of recent and more enlightened times ; and Pennsylvanians have now the privilege and the honour of living under a Constitution, the work of men, previously "unknown to fame," and whose magnificent labours will, it is believed, prove satisfactory to the " democracy," however " progressive," for several years to come !

In 1779, Judge McKean was elected Governor of Pennsylvania, and held the office during the constitutional period of nine years, having been twice re-elected. In 1803 it was proposed to him to become a candidate for the Vice-Presidency— a post of honour *then*, as it had previously, been filled by men who had earned the respect of their country—but he declined. " In 1808 he retired from public life, in which he had been engaged for fifty years, and died in June, 1817, in his 84th year. He was one of the fathers of the Republic, and in this quality will be honoured, aside from the resentments which his proceedings as a *party-politician* engendered."—ED.

11

very forcibly appealed to the pocket, the great body of German farmers, extremely tenacious of property, were readily gained. Exceptions however were to be found: The Menonists and some other sects were generally disaffected. As to the genuine sons of Hibernia, it was enough for them to know that England was the antagonist. Stimulants here, were wholly superfluous; and the sequel has constantly shown, that in a contest with Englishmen, Irishmen, like the mettlesome coursers of Phaeton, only require reining in. *Labor est inhibere volentes.* The spirit of liberty and resistance being so generally diffused, it seems scarcely necessary to mention, that it drew into its vortex the mechanical interest, as well as that numerous portion of the community in republics, styled *The People;* in monarchies, *The Populace;* or still more irreverently, *The Rabble or Canaille.* But notwithstanding this almost unanimous agreement in favour of liberty, neither were all disposed to go the same lengths for it, nor were they perfectly in unison in the idea annexed to it. Wilkes had just rendered the term popular in America; and, though perhaps there is not any one in our language more indefinite, yet the sense in which it was doubtless most generally received, was that which brings it nearest to licentiousness and anarchy, since hallowed by the phrases of *Equality, and the Rights of Man.*

The Quakers, as a society, were charged with disaffection, and probably with truth. They were desirous, however, of screening themselves under their non-resisting principles and known aversion to war; and in this, although they might not have been sincere, they at least were consistent. But notwithstanding their endeavour to keep aloof from the contest, a good number of their young men swerved from their tenets; and affecting cockades and uniforms, openly avowed themselves fighting men. They went so far as to form a company of light infantry, under the command of Mr. Copperthwaite,* which was called *The Quaker Blues*, and instituted in a spirit of competition with *The Greens*, or, as they were sneeringly styled, *The silk stocking company*, commanded by

---

* JOSEPH COWPERTHWAIT.—He was Sheriff of Philadelphia County, and subsequently a Justice of the Peace. A gentleman of intelligence and influence.—
ED

Mr. John Cadwalader,* and which having early associated, had already acquired celebrity. This nickname evinced, that the canker worm, jealousy, already tainted the infantile purity of our patriotism. The command of this company, consisting of the flower of the city, was too fine a feather in the cap of its leader to be passed by unenvied: it was, therefore, branded as an aristocratic assemblage, and Mr. (since general) Mifflin, had the credit of inventing the invidious appellation. To this association I belonged. There were about seventy of us. We met morning and evening, and from the earnest and even enthusiastic devotion of most of us to learn the duty of soldiers, the company, in the course of a summer's training, became a truly respectable militia corps. When it had attained some adroitness in the exercises, we met but once a day. This was in the afternoon, and the place of rendezvous the house of the captain, where capacious demi-johns of Madeira, were constantly set out in the yard where we formed, for our refreshment before marching out to exercise. The ample fortune of Mr. Cadwalader had enabled him to fill his cellars with the choicest liquors; and it must be admitted, that he dealt them out with the most gentlemanly liberality. He probably meant it, in part, as an indemnification for our voluntary submission while under arms, to all the essential points, as well as the little etiquette of subordination, required of privates under the most regular discipline.

On taking a retrospect of the company, and looking round for

---

* John Cadwalader was, subsequently to this period, appointed Colonel of one of the City Battalions, from which rank he rose to that of Brigadier-General, and was entrusted with the command of the Pennsylvania troops in the Winter campaign of '76 and '77. He acted in this command, and as a volunteer, in the Battles of Princeton, Brandywine, Germantown, Monmouth, and on other occasions, and received the thanks of Washington, whose confidence and esteem he always possessed. He was appointed to command one of the divisions into which the army was separated when Washington determined to attack the enemy at Trenton; but in consequence of the ice in the river, neither he nor General Irvine, the commander of another division, could cross the river in time. But, the day after Washington's return, he effected the passage, supposing him still on the Jersey side, and pursued the vanquished enemy to Burlington. In 1778, he was appointed by Congress, General of Cavalry—an appointment which he declined on the score of being more useful in the station which he occupied. He died Feb. 10, 1786, in the 44th year of his age.—*Ency. Amer.*—ED.

those who remain of it, I see a few who are yet alive and in respectable situations. Much the greater number, however, have resigned their places to that posterity, for whose interests it was the fashion of seventy-six to be extremely concerned. It is to be hoped, therefore, that posterity will continue to pay the easy recompence of an annual toast to the memory of those *departed* friends, who no longer stand in their way. But I am chiefly struck with the strong tendency to evaporation, which inheres in a fiery zeal; as well as with the utter insignificance of that dull quality, consistency, on the versatile scale of republican virtue. I have a gentleman in my eye who was ever among the foremost in patriotism, and for volunteering our services on every occasion. Was there an enterprise in view, replete with difficulty and danger! *The Greens*, in his opinion, should monopolize, or at least partake of the glory. Was there a sacrifice to be made to economy! They should be the first to set an example of frugality to their countrymen. In short, were it "to fight, to fast, to drink up Elsil, eat a crocodile, he'd do't." Yet this gentleman, so full of zeal in seventy-five, was so thoroughly emptied of it in seventy-six, as to translate himself to the royal standard in New York; for which, however, he found a salvo in the Declaration of Independence. On the conclusion of the war, he was, in consideration of his youth and inexperience when he committed the *faux pas*, permitted to return to the bosom of his country, and adroitly falling in with the views of the prevailing party, he obtained a subordinate appointment in the Treasury Department, during the Presidencies of Washington and Adams: when again wheeling about with the public sentiment, which ushered into office first M'Kean and then Jefferson, he obtained, upon the principle probably of a *quid pro quo*, an office from each of them, the latter of which he yet retains, and, like the French revolution, returning to the point from which it set out, he is now as pure a patriot as he was at the commencement of his career. It must be confessed, that the gentleman has had a serpentine course: Yet, without arraigning his motives, which may have been good, though diversified, I shall content myself with observing, that he has had the singular fortune to behold with equal eye, the carting of the tories in Philadelphia in the year 1775; the sad havoc of the whigs in

New York, in the year 1776; the discomfiture of the anti-federalists, in the years 1790 and 1794; then the overthrow and persecution of the federalists in the year 1800: In each and every of
these turmoils, he has contrived to be uppermost, and still rides
triumphant on the surface of the *tempestuous sea*, an unequivocal
proof of his fitness for the times in which he has been destined to
appear.   This instance would not have been adverted to, were it
not that in an illustration of the times, it was too remarkable to be
omitted.

In preparing for the scene of war that was approaching, no
martial employment was neglected.   It was even deemed of consequence to be a marksman with a pistol; and connected with
this object, I recollect an unpleasant incident, which might also
have proved a serious one.   Captain Biddle and myself having
gone out to take a shot, and posted ourselves in a situation,
thought convenient and safe, we marked our target on a board
fence, in a cross street, between Arch and Race streets.   We had
fired several times, and were loading again, when a man suddenly
coming upon us, out of breath, pale as ashes, without his hat
and his hair standing on end, exclaimed, that we had killed his
child.   This information, as may be supposed, put a stop to our
amusement; and we immediately accompanied him to his house,
with feelings not to be envied.   When we arrived, however, we
found matters not so bad as had been anticipated.   The child was
crying in its mother's arms : it had been struck upon the body ; but
the force of the blow had been broken by a loose, linsey petticoat.
The ball had passed through a pane of glass; and from the appearance of the hole exactly corresponding to its size without di-
verging cracks, it must have had considerable force, though discharged at a distance which we thought greater than our pistols
would carry.   By expressions of concern for the accident and the
accompaniment of a few dollars, our transgression was overlooked,
and all perturbation composed.

The daily unremitted course of exercise which my military
duties and my fencing, at this time composed, had thoroughly
established my health.   The serious aspect of the times, had also
brought temperance into fashion; and instead of tavern suppers,
I generally passed my evenings with my female acquaintance,

11*

among whom there was one to whom my affections were deeply and permanently engaged. The attachment was reciprocal; and the din of arms which threatened us with a separation, involving a cruel uncertainty in respect to the destiny of our love, but served to render it more ardent and more tender.* Vows of constancy were mutually plighted; and we gave so much of our time to each other, that I had little to spare to my quondam companions, whom I was really desirous of shaking off, and who, on their part, complained that I had turned dangler, and become good for nothing. There was a time when their raillery might have had some effect, but now it was entirely thrown away, and, like a true knight, I wholly devoted myself to my mistress and my country.

Among the disaffected in Philadelphia, Doctor Kearsley was pre-eminently ardent and rash.† An extremely zealous loyalist, and impetuous in his temper, he had given much umbrage to the whigs; and if I am not mistaken, he had been detected in some hostile machinations. Hence he was deemed a proper subject for the fashionable punishment of tarring, feathering and carting. He was seized at his own door by a party of the militia, and, in the attempt to resist them, received a wound in his hand from a bayonet. Being overpowered, he was placed in a cart provided for the purpose, and amidst a multitude of boys and idlers, paraded through the streets to the tune of the rogue's march. I happened to be at the coffee-house when the concourse arrived there. They made a halt, while the Doctor foaming with rage and indignation, without his hat, his wig dishevelled and bloody from his wounded hand, stood up in the cart and called for a bowl of punch. It was quickly handed to him; when, so vehement was his thirst, that he drained it of its contents before he took it from his lips. What were the feelings of others on this lawless proceeding, I know not, but mine, I must confess,

---

* "And flinty is her heart can view,
To battle march a lover true,
Can hear, perchance, his last adieu,
Nor own her share of pain."

† Nephew of the celebrated Dr. John Kearsley—founder of "Christ Church Hospital for Poor Widows." A gentleman much distinguished for his public spirit, and architectural taste."—Ed.

revolted at the spectacle. I was shocked at seeing a lately respected citizen so cruelly vilified, and was imprudent enough to say, that had I been a magistrate, I would, at every hazard, have interposed my authority in suppression of the outrage. But this was not the only instance which convinced me, that I wanted nerves for a revolutionist. It must be admitted, however, that the conduct of the populace was marked by a lenity which peculiarly distinguished the cradle of our republicanism. Tar and feathers had been dispensed with, and excepting the injury he had received in his hand, no sort of violence was offered by the mob to their victim. But to a man of high spirit, as the Doctor was, the indignity in its lightest form was sufficient to madden him: it probably had this effect, since his conduct became so extremely outrageous, that it was thought necessary to confine him. From the city he was soon after removed to Carlisle, where he died during the war.

A few days after the carting of Mr. Kearsley, Mr. Isaac Hunt, the attorney, was treated in the same manner, but he managed the matter much better than his precursor. Instead of braving his conductors like the Doctor, Mr. Hunt was a pattern of meekness and humility; and at every halt that was made, he rose and expressed his acknowledgments to the crowd for their forbearance and civility. After a parade of an hour or two, he was set down at his own door, as uninjured in body as in mind. He soon after removed to one of the islands, if I mistake not, to Barbadoes, where, it was understood, he took orders.*

Not long after these occurrences, Major Skene of the British army, ventured to show himself in Philadelphia.† Whatever

---

* He *did* take orders, and upon his return to England, became a tutor in the family of the Duke of Chandos. He was the father of Mr. Leigh Hunt, celebrated for his poetic genius, and for many valuable contributions to English literature.—ED.

† We are glad not to lose sight of this truly loyal and facetious gentleman. In the Appendix to the 3d volume of *Sparks' Life and Writings of Washington*, is the following notice of him:

" Major Skene had been appointed Governor of Ticonderoga and Crown Point, and empowered to raise a regiment in America. On this ground he was taken into custody, when he arrived in Philadelphia, June, 1775; his papers were examined by order of Congress, and he was retained as a prisoner. He had been

might have been his inducement to the measure, it was deemed expedient by the newly constituted authorities, to have him arrested and secured. A guard was accordingly placed over him at his lodgings, at the city tavern. The officer to whose charge he was especially committed, was Mr. Francis Wade, the brewer, an Irishman of distinguished zeal in the cause, and one who was supposed to possess talents peculiarly befitting him for the task of curbing the spirit of a haughty Briton, which Skene undoubtedly was. I well recollect the day that the guard was paraded to escort him out of the city on his way to some other station. An immense crowd of spectators stood before the door of his quarters, and lined the street through which he was to pass. The weather being warm, the window sashes of his apartment were raised, and Skene, with his bottle of wine upon the table, having just finished his dinner, roared out in the voice of a Stentor, " *God save great George our king!*" Had the spirit of seventy-five in any degree resembled the spirit of Jacobinism, to which it has been unjustly compared, this bravado would unquestionably have brought the Major to the *lamp-post*, and set his head upon a pike; but as, fortunately for him, it did not, he was suffered to proceed with his song, and the auditory seemed more generally amused than offended.

many years in the army; was an ensign at Carthagena and Porto Bello, under General Wentworth; he served in Flanders; was a Lieutenant at the battle of Culloden; served under Sir Jeffrey Amherst in Canada; was first Major of Brigade at the conquest of Martinique and Havana, at which latter place he entered the breach when it was stormed; was often wounded; was appointed to run a line between Canada and the British Colonies, and to superintend the settlement of the border country, then uninhabited; and, in 1773, he applied to Lord Dartmouth to recommend him to the King for the appointment of Governor of Ticonderoga, Crown Point, and their dependencies, where he, at that time, commanded a corps of militia, having lands and a residence at the southern extremity of Lake Champlain."—ED.

CHAPTER V.

In the spring of 1775, Congress assembled in Philadelphia. It was in every respect a venerable assembly; and although Pennsylvania had delegated to it some of her most distinguished characters, they were supposed to be eclipsed by the superior talents which came from the southward and eastward. New England had sent her Adams's, and Virginia her Lee's and Henry's; all of whom were spoken of as men of the first rate abilities. Not long after the organization of this body, their president, Peyton Randolph of Virginia, died, and John Hancock, of Boston, was selected to supply his place. Towards the close of the year, they passed a resolution for levying some continental battalions, four of which were to be raised in Pennsylvania. One had already been raised and officered by the province; but as the applicants for commissions in this, were not of my set of acquaintance, I did not apply. Upon the promulgation, however, of this resolution of Congress, I signified to the committee of safety, in whom the power of appointment was lodged, and of which body my uncle was a member, my wish to be employed. The appointments were made, and in a list of thirty-two captains, I ranked the sixteenth, and accordingly received my commission from Congress, dated January the 6th, 1776. Upon this nomination of the committee of safety, which also extended to all the inferior commissioned officers, the field officers, who had already been assigned to particular battalions, had a meeting for the purpose of selecting their captains and subalterns. In this arrangement, it fell to my lot to be attached to the third battalion, under the command of Colonel John Shee, and of which Mr. Lambert Cadwalader, the younger brother of Mr. John Cadwalader, already mentioned, was Lieutenant-Colonel. It appeared to have been the primary object of these gentlemen, to select as much as possible their officers from the city and its neighbourhood, of whom they had a greater proportion than was to be found in either of the other regiments, respectively commanded by St. Clair, Wayne and Magaw. But this circumstance, though it might have a propitious influence on the discipline of the regiment when raised, was certainly unfavourable to the business of recruiting, since, as the country was chiefly to be depended upon for men, country officers would of course, have the best chance of obtaining them.

But two gentlemen of what might be called our principal families, had come forward on this occasion. These were Mr. Cadwalader, and Mr. William Allen, who was appointed Lieutenant-Colonel of the regiment of St. Clair: so that of four sons, the eldest alone, Mr. John Allen, was an acknowledged disapprover of our proceedings. The father, too old to be active, was yet supposed to lean to the whig side. It would appear, however, from the sequel, that this family were either never cordial in the cause, or that they had inconsiderately imagined that its object might be obtained by a resolute show of resistance, merely; since upon the adoption of the measure of independence, all the sons, excepting James, joined General Howe in New York. He remained at home, and took his chance with his native country, though wholly inactive. I remember once seeing him on New York island, towards the close of the summer of 1776, where he probably came to see how the land lay. But he was then in declining health, and in somewhat more than a year after, was relieved from all sublunary solicitudes; as was his father also, before the close of the war. The revolution was fatal to this family, precipitating it from the very pinnacle of importance in Pennsylvania, down to the lowest depth of insignificance with both parties. Its early whigism had perhaps as much disgusted the tories, as its final defection had exasperated the whigs; and the British army, though it yielded it protection, afforded it little of respect. Mr. William Allen endeavoured to recover his consequence by raising, or endeavouring to raise, a regiment on the royal side in Philadelphia in the year 1778, very pompously heading his recruiting advertisement with the words, *nil desperandum Teucro duce, et auspice Teucro.* It is to be presumed, however, that this swaggering motto referred to General Howe, and not to himself.

Nor, in adverting to the mutability of human affairs, can we overlook the unfavourable tendency of the contest to the proprietary family. Both the brothers, John and Richard Penn, had been governors of Pennsylvania; the former being in office at the beginning of hostilities. By yielding to the torrent, which it would have been impossible to withstand, he gave no offence, and avoided reproach; though it was deemed expedient to have him secured and removed from Philadelphia, on the approach of the royal army in the year 1777. Mr. Richard Penn, having no official motives for reserve, was even upon terms of familiarity with some of the most thorough-going whigs, such as General Lee and others: An evidence of this was the pleasantry ascribed to him, on occasion of a member of Congress, one day observing to his compatriots, that at all events "they must hang together:" "If you do not, gentlemen," said Mr. Penn, "I can tell you that you will be very apt to hang separately."*

Of all the governors of Pennsylvania under the old *regime*, he was probably the most popular, though his popularity might not have been precisely of the kind which irradiates a favourite of the present day. It was, it must be confessed, a good deal confined to the city; and perhaps rather much to that description of persons, who are not the chosen people of Virginian republicanism.

---

* This witticism is claimed for Franklin by Sparks, who thus relates it in his Life of Franklin, page 408. It was at the signing of the Declaration of Independence.

"We must be unanimous," said Hancock; "there must be no pulling different ways; we must all hang together." "Yes," replied Franklin, "we must, indeed, all hang together, or most assuredly we shall all hang separately."

It has been ascribed also to Mr. John Penn, one of the signers of the Declaration of Independence, and a member of Congress from North Carolina. Who shall settle the knotty point!—ED.

But it was such as was then in fashion, and good and substantial enough for those who knew no better. It required, however, fewer sacrifices; and might yield possibly as much pleasure on retrospection, as that enjoyed by the most idolized of our democratic worthies.*

Against the expected hostilities, Pennsylvania had made immense exertions. Prior to the four regiments of St. Clair, Shee, Wayne and Magaw, that of De Haas, and Hand's rifle regiment, were already raised and equipped; and afterwards, Irvine's, and two provincial battalions, respectively commanded by Miles and Atlee, in the whole, nine regiments, complete and very reputably officered. Had all the other provinces done as much in proportion to their ability, and the men been enlisted for the war, we might have avoided the hair-breadth 'scapes which ensued.

To return to smaller concerns. An anxiety little inferior to that of the colonels, in procuring what they thought good officers for their regiments, at this time, agitated the commanders of companies, in respect to the subalterns that should be assigned them. My second lieutenant, Mr. Forrest,† who had served his apprenticeship to an apothecary in Philadelphia, I well knew to be active, capable, and more than commonly adroit in the military exercises; but my first lieutenant, I had not yet seen. I was not, however, long in the dark, and when he appeared, I cannot say that his exterior was the most prepossessing; or that it announced those qualities we at first look for in the soldier. He was tall, extremely thin, and somewhat lounging in his appearance; and to add to its uncouthness, he wore an enormous fur cap. Colonel Shee used

---

* Richard Penn was the brother of John Penn, Governor of Pennsylvania, at the commencement of hostilities. He is described in Watson's Annals, as "a fine portly looking man,—a *bon vivant*, very popular. He died in England in 1811, at the age of 77 years.—ED.

† Subsequently known as Colonel Forrest, and distinguished for zeal and activity during the revolution. He was in several engagements, and had the character of being a brave and skilful officer. After the war he resided at Germantown, where his opinions underwent a remarkable change. He attached himself to the society of Quakers, adopting their language and garb. He was a man of considerable humour, and of manners agreeable to the "sovereign people," who, in 1815, elected him to Congress. He died in the year 1826, at the age of eighty-three years.—ED.

to describe somewhat humourously, his first impression upon *him*; and when he was first seen by a little Scotch servant boy of my mother's, who afterwards became my drummer, he emphatically exclaimed: *Well, sic an a spindle!* Yet for all this, any man might have thought himself honoured in having Mr. Edwards for his lieutenant. Though born in Pennsylvania, he was recent from a college in Rhode Island. Possessing good sense, a remarkable aptitude to take a polish, and talents to recommend himself to his superiors in command, he soon obtained the favour of the colonels of the regiment, with whom he was upon a very familiar footing. He was, besides, a man of courage; and in the course of the war, became the aid-de-camp and particular friend of General Lee; so much so, that he was one of the principal devisees in the will of that officer. Of my ensign, it will be enough to say, that he was a plain and unaspiring man, who, in the walk of humble duty, "kept the noiseless tenor of his way."

The object now was to raise my company, and as the streets of the city had been pretty well swept by the preceding and contemporary levies, it was necessary to have recourse to the country. My recruiting party was therefore sent out in various directions; and each of my officers as well as myself, exerted himself in the business. Among the many unpleasant peculiarities of the American service, it was not the least that the drudgery, which in old military establishments belong to sergeants and corporals, here devolved on the commissioned officers; and that the whole business of recruiting, drilling, &c., required their unremitted personal attention. This was more emphatically the case in recruiting; since the common opinion was, that the men and the officers were never to be separated, and hence, to see the persons who were to command them, and above all, the captain, was deemed of vast importance by those inclining·to enlist: for this reason I found it necessary, in common with my brother officers, to put my feelings most cruelly to the rack; and in an excursion I once made to Frankford, they were tried to the utmost. A number of fellows at the tavern, at which my party rendezvoused, indicated a desire to enlist, but although they drank freely of our liquor, they still held off. I soon perceived that the object was to amuse themselves at our expense, and that if there might be one or two among

12

them really disposed to engage, the others would prevent them. One fellow in particular, who had made the greatest show of taking the bounty, presuming on the weakness of our party, consisting only of a drummer, corporal, my second lieutenant and myself, began to grow insolent, and manifested an intention to begin a quarrel, in the issue of which, he no doubt calculated on giving us a drubbing. The disgrace of such a circumstance, presented itself to my mind in colours the most dismal, and I resolved, that if a scuffle should be unavoidable, it should, at least, be as serious as the hangers which my lieutenant and myself carried by our sides, could make it. Our endeavour, however, was to guard against a contest; but the moderation we testified, was attributed to fear. At length the arrogance of the principal ruffian, rose to such a height, that he squared himself for battle and advanced towards me in an attitude of defiance. I put him by, with an admonition to be quiet, though with a secret determination, that, if he repeated the insult to begin the war, whatever might be the consequence. The occasion was soon presented; when taking excellent aim, I struck him with my utmost force between the eyes and sent him staggering to the other end of the room. Then instantly drawing our hangers, and receiving the manful co-operation of the corporal and drummer, we were fortunate enough to put a stop to any farther hostilities. It was some time before the fellow I had struck, recovered from the blow, but when he did, he was quite an altered man. He was as submissive as could be wished, begging my pardon for what he had done, and although he would not enlist, he hired himself to me for a few weeks as a fifer, in which capacity he had acted in the militia; and during the time he was in this employ, he bore about the effects of his insolence, in a pair of black eyes. This incident would be little worthy of relating, did it not serve in some degree to correct the error of those who seem to conceive the year 1776 to have been a season of almost universal patriotic enthusiasm. It was far from prevalent in my opinion, among the lower ranks of the people, at least in Pennsylvania. At all times, indeed, licentious, levelling principles are much to the general taste, and were of course popular with us; but the true merits of the contest, were little understood or regarded. The opposition to the claims of Britain origi-

nated with the better sort: it was truly aristocratic in its commencement; and as the oppression to be apprehended, had not
been felt, no grounds existed for general enthusiasm.   The cause
of liberty, it is true, was fashionable, and there were great preparations to fight for it; but a zeal proportioned to the magnitude of
the question, was only to be looked for in the minds of those
sagacious politicians, who inferred effects from causes, and who,
as Mr. Burke expresses it, "snuffed the approach of tyranny in
every tainted breeze."*

Certain it was, at least, that recruiting went on but heavily.
Some officers had been more successful than others, but none of
the companies were complete; mine perhaps contained about
half its complement of men, and these had been obtained by
dint of great exertion.   In this situation, Captain Lenox of Shee's
regiment also, suggested the trying our luck on the eastern shore
of Maryland, particularly at Chester, situated on the river of that
name.   It having been a place of some trade, it was supposed
there might be seamen or *long shore* men there, out of employ.
We accordingly set out on the expedition, making our first effort
at Warwick, an inconsiderable village, a few miles within the
boundaries of Maryland.   Here we remained a day or two, our
stay having been prolonged by bad weather.   At the tavern we
put up at, we made acquaintance with a gentleman of note, who
resided in the neighbourhood, and pretty generally known by the
familiar name of Dan Heath.   He seemed to like our company,
as he was continually with us while we staid.   Mr. Heath was a
sportsman, and apparently too little interested in political concerns, to be either much of a whig or a tory, though from the indifference he evinced, we rather concluded him the latter.   He
helped us, however, to recruit, a fellow, he said, who would do
to stop a bullet as well as a better man, and as he was a truly worth-

---

* "The American Revolution is, universally, admitted to have begun in the
upper circles of society.   It turned on principles too remote and abstruse for vulgar apprehension or consideration.   Had it depended on the unenlightened mass
of the community, no doubt can be entertained, that the tax imposed by parliament, would have been paid without a question.   Since, then, the upper circle of
society did not take its impulse from the people, the only remaining inquiry is
who gave the Revolutionary impulse to that circle itself?   It was unquestionably
PATRICK HENRY."— *Wirt's Life of Henry.*—ED.

less dog, he held, that the neighbourhood would be much indebted to us for taking him away. When we left Warwick, he fulfilled his promise of accompanying us some miles under pretence of aiding us in getting men, but as he showed us none, we were convinced that he attended us more for his own sake than ours, and that having nothing to do, probably, he had availed himself the opportunity to kill a little time. He gave the tone to the conversation on the road, which generally turned on the sports of the turf and the cockpit; but he never spoke with so much animation, as when expatiating on those feats of human prowess, wherein victory is achieved by *tooth and nail*, in modern phrase, by biting and gouging: and pointing out to us one of the heroes of these direful conflicts: " There," says he, " is a fellow that has not his match in the country: see what a set of teeth he has, a man's thumb would be nothing to them."

On bidding good morning to Mr. Heath, with whose vivacity we were amused, we pursued our course to Chester, and as soon as we arrived there, delivered our letters of introduction. The gentlemen to whom they were addressed, received us with the utmost politeness, and declared their warmest wishes for the success of our errand, though accompanied with expressions of regret, that they could not give us encouragement to beat up in their town, as well because there were few, if any, in it, that were likely to enlist, as that their own province was about raising troops; and as that was the case, it would not be taken well should they assist in transferring any of their men to the line of Pennsylvania. With such unfavourable prospects in Maryland, it would have been folly to have proceeded farther: we therefore, set off on our way home the next morning, declining several invitations to dinner. We found this country well deserving of its reputation for hospitality. Between Warwick and Georgetown, we were taken home to lodge by a gentleman of the name of Wilmer, whom we had never seen before: We were warmly pressed by Mr. Harry Pierce, with whom we met by accident on the road, to spend some time with him at his residence in the neighbourhood, and met with no less cordiality, from Mr. Thomas Ringold, of Chester, who had once when very young, lodged at my mother's. Returning by Warwick, we sent forward our solitary recruit, for whom we tossed up; and in winning, I was, in fact, but a very small gainer, since his merits had been set at their full value by Mr. Heath ; and he was never fit for any thing better than the inglorious post of camp colour man.

After this unsuccessful jaunt, I bent my course to the Four-lane ends, Newtown, and Corryell's ferry ; thence passing into Jersey, I proceeded to the Hickory tavern, to Pittstown, Baptisttown, Flemmingtown, and other towns, whose names I do not remember.   As Captain Stewart (the late General Walter Stewart) of our regiment, had recently reapt this field, I was only a gleaner: In the whole of my tour, therefore, I picked up but three or four men: and could most sincerely have said,

> That the recruiting trade, with all its train,
> Of endless care, fatigue, and endless pain,

I could most gladly have renounced, even without the very preferable alternative of Captain Plume.   My number of privates might now have amounted to about forty, but these were soon augmented by the noble addition of one and twenty stout native Americans, brought by Lieutenants Edwards and Forrest from Egg Harbour.

Towards spring, our battalion was complete; and already, from the unremitted attention that had been paid to it by the officers of every grade, it had made, for so short a time, a very laudable progress in discipline.   Besides partial drillings it was exercised every morning and evening; and what was of still more importance, habits of obedience and subordination were strictly inculcated and maintained.   We were comparatively well armed, uniformed and equipped ; and it is but justice to say, that in point of all the exteriors, by which military corps are tested, ours was on a footing with the most promising on the continent.   We were quartered in the barracks, together with the other battalions that were raising; and by way of counteracting the general gloom, not diminished by the practice of fast-days and sermons, borrowed from New England, we promoted balls and other amusement.   Had the contest been a religious one, and our people been inflamed by a zeal on points of faith like

12*

the Crusaders or the army of Cromwell, this might have been
the proper method of exciting them to acts of heroism; but they
were to be taken as they were, and as this was not the case, it
was certainly not the mode to make soldiers in Pennsylvania.
The puritanical spirit was unknown among us; and the endeavour to promote it, did but conflict with other propensities on
which a military ardour might be engrafted. It might, however, have been wholly different in New England; but whether
so or not, General Lee, with his usual profaneness, treated their
solemnities with ridicule, telling them, in the spirit of the ancient
fable of Hercules and the wagoner, that *Heaven was ever found
favourable to strong battalions.*

About the close of the month of May, I was appointed to carry
a sum of money in specie to General Schuyler at Lake George,
for the purpose of promoting the operations in Canada; and I
owed my nomination to this service to the friendly intentions of
President Hancock, who had particularly designated me. Ensign
Stout was the officer assigned by Colonel Shee to accompany me.[*]
We accordingly set out in a chair, that being thought the most
convenient mode of carrying the money, which was enclosed in
two or three sealed bags. One soldier mounted and armed in
addition, constituted the escort; and we were furnished with
credentials for obtaining fresh horses as often as they might be
necessary. To see the country between New York and the Lake,
which was entirely new both to my companion and myself, was
highly agreeable; but we did not so well like the responsibility
of our charge. It is obvious that it might have been wrested from
us, without great difficulty, even though each one of the triumvirate had possessed the bravery of Cæsar. Hence, policy dictated

---

[*] Colonel John Shee. He was, I think, from Lancaster county. He had the
confidence of Washington, who, in a letter to the President of Congress, of 10th
June, 1776, says, "to Congress I submit the propriety of keeping the two Continental
battalions, under Colonels Shee and Magaw, at Philadelphia, where there is the
greatest probability of a speedy attack upon this place from the King's troops."

It will be seen, hereafter, that, having obtained leave of absence to visit his
family, he "converted that leave into an entire abdication of his command." An
extraordinary procedure, certainly, on the part of an officer who had proved his
capacity and zeal, and who had enjoyed, in a high degree, the confidence and
esteem of his superiors.—Ed.

the concealment of the treasure, so far as might consist with the requisite vigilance. At Princeton, where we dined on the second day of our journey, we thought proper to have our bags brought into our room. The inn-keeper, like the generality of his profession, was loquacious and inquisitive; and being an extremely good whig into the bargain, took the liberty of sounding us respecting the contents of our bags, of which he had formed a very shrewd guess. We did not think it necessary to deny that they contained money, or to conceal from him the object of our mission, which he was equally desirous of knowing. Upon learning that the destination was Canada, he entered into a dissertation upon our affairs in that quarter, telling us among other things, that the Prussian General, the Baron Woedkie, had been a few days before at his house, on his way to that country. But he reprobated the Baron in very hard terms, repeatedly exclaiming with a most significant emphasis, that *he was no general;* and in the sequel, favouring us with his reasons for this opinion, gave us to understand, that he (the Baron) had made his servant grease with a feather a certain part, to which he gave its very coarsest appellation, that had suffered from the friction of riding. Whether our host had become acquainted with this circumstance by looking through a key-hole, or by what other means, we were not informed, but its unlucky effect upon him, convinced me of the justness of the observation, that *no man is a hero to his valet de chambre.* This same Baron it was, who, finding liberty, one day, the impassioned theme of some members of Congress and others, exclaimed—*Ah, liberdy is a fine ding; I likes liberdy; der koenig von Prusse is a great man for liberdy!* and so no doubt he was, for his own liberty or importance as a member of the Germanic body; and it might puzzle many a flaming demagogue to show a better title to the character.*

* The honest Baron, however, was not more absurd than was the sticklers for Bonaparte, who always connected liberty with his name and views, as the same men did those of Robespierre, when riding at the top of the revolutionary wheel. With them liberty appeared to mean hostility to all regular, legitimate government; which, in the same vocabulary signifies tyranny. New power creates new men, *ergo*, the devotion to it of all ambitious insignificants.

Brigadier-General the Baron de Woedtke.—Wilkinson in his *Memoirs* gives some account of this Prussian officer; but it is, by no means, flattering.

But notwithstanding this requisite for our service, evinced by the Baron's love of liberty, I believe he did not very well suit us; and that although *The Prussian General* made a great noise upon his first appearance, the public mind in respect to him, whether correct or not, pretty well accorded with that of our host, who, at parting with us, expressed much anxiety for our safety and that of our charge, recommending to us in future, not to take our bags out of the chair, where we breakfasted and dined. The propriety of this advice we were aware of, and observed it where practicable; that is, where the treasure was sufficiently under our eyes without removal.

At New York, we spent about an hour in a slight survey of the barricades, which General Lee had caused to be thrown across some of the streets; and on our way out of town, fell in with a New England regiment at exercise. Its commander was extremely busy, in instructing his troops in street firing, at that day, our most favourite manœuvre; as we simply supposed that all our great battles were to be fought in our cities. We surveyed these men with all the respect that was due to the great military reputation of their country; but, we were obliged to confess, that they did not entirely come up to the ideas we had formed of the heroes of Lexington and Bunker's hill. This, we took to be a militia corps, from the circumstance of its not being a

He had been sent with instructions to the Baron, to detach 500 men, to cover General Arnold's retreat from Montreal. In his search for the Baron, he encountered difficulties and hardships, which are graphically described: "After a night's rest in a filthy cabin, I resumed my march, and the first officer of my acquaintance whom I met, was Lieutenant-Colonel William Allen, of the second Pennsylvania regiment, who, to my inquiry for De Woedtke, replied, he had '*no doubt the beast was drunk, and in front of the army.*' I then informed him of my orders for a detachment. His reply was remarkable: 'This army, Wilkinson, is conquered by its fears, and I doubt whether you can draw any assistance from it; but Colonel Wayne is in the rear, and if any one can do it, he is the man.' On this I quickened my pace, and half an hour after met that gallant soldier, as much at his ease as if he was marching to a parade of exercise; he confirmed Allen's report respecting De Woedtke, and without hesitation determined to execute the order."

"The Baron," says Sparks, "had been for many years an officer in the army of the King of Prussia, and had risen to the rank of Major. Coming to Philadelphia with strong letters of recommendation to Dr. Franklin from persons of eminence in Paris, he was appointed by Congress a Brigadier-General. He died at Lake George in the summer of 1776."—ED.

whit superior, in any visible respect, to the worst of ours.   However, thought we, these men may nevertheless have some knack
at fighting, which only discloses itself in the moment of action.

After leaving New York, we passed through a number of
villages between that city and Albany; but these, of which the
almanacs will give a much more accurate account than I can, I
shall neither undertake to name or locate.   Poughkeepsie, however, must be excepted ; as here we quartered for a night, under
the hospitable roof of *old* Doctor Baird, so called to distinguish
him from his son of the same profession.   The doctor was a relation of Mr. Stout's, and on my being made known to him, I had
the satisfaction to find that he had formerly been acquainted with
both my father and mother, of whom he spoke in the warmest
and most friendly terms.   My mother, he was pleased to say, he
remembered, the finest girl in Philadelphia ; and that she had the
manners of a lady bred at a court.   The old gentleman was one
of those who went under the denomination of tories; but if it
was justly applied, he possessed too much liberality to permit his
politics, in any degree, to interfere with the duties of hospitality.
He considered us probably as young men, deluded but not seditious; as accessary to, but not responsible for, the calamities
which were about to befal the country; and in addition to a good
supper, entertained us with the military exploits of the Duke of
Marlborough, who appeared to be his favourite hero.

In the morning betimes we pursued our journey, and in the
course of it, reached Albany about noon.   Here we dined with a
gentleman in regimentals bearing the title of major; though I do
not either recollect his name, or the corps to which he belonged,
if indeed he belonged to any, for majors and captains had by this
time, become very good travelling appellations.   He had just returned from Canada, and drew a most lamentable picture of our
affairs in that country, descanting upon men and things with equal
freedom and satire.   He delivered himself with unusual flippancy; and wound up a very animated philippic upon our military operations in that quarter, with an, " in short, gentlemen, we
have commissaries there without provisions ; quarter-masters without stores; generals without troops; and troops without discipline,
by G—d."

Leaving Albany, we passed by Stillwater, Saratoga, and other places, which have since acquired interest from the defeat and surrender of General Burgoyne and his army. Near to Fort Edward we met Doctor Franklin, Mr. Carroll, and (I think) Mr. Chase, returning from Canada, to which they had been deputed commissioners from Congress.* We delivered them a letter from that body, as we had been enjoined to do in case of meeting them, as also to take their orders in respect to our ulterior proceedings : As they made no change in our destination, we went on. Immediately beyond Fort Edward, the country assumed a dreary, cheerless aspect. Between this and lake George, a distance of about twelve miles, it was almost an entire wood, acquiring a deeper gloom, as well from the general prevalence of pines, as from its dark, extended covert being presented to the imagination as an appropriate scene for the "treasons, stratagems and spoils" of savage hostility ; to which purpose, it had been devoted in former days of deadly dissension. It was in this tract of country that several actions had been fought ; that Baron Dieskau had been defeated ; and that American blood had flowed, as well as English and French ; in commemoration of which, the

---

* The commissioners were Dr. Franklin, Samuel Chase, and Charles Carroll of Carrollton, all signers of the Declaration of Independence ; and the Reverend John Carroll, afterwards Romish Archbishop of Baltimore, whose religious profession and character, and French education peculiarly fitted him, it was supposed, "to exercise a salutary influence with the priests in Canada, who were known to control the people." Mr. Chase was greatly distinguished by his eloquence, abilities, and zeal in the revolutionary cause. In 1791, he was appointed Chief Justice of the general Court of Maryland ; and five years afterwards was promoted by WASHINGTON, to the office of an associate judge of the Supreme Court of the United States. Having, in his official conduct, given much offence to the Democratic party, he was impeached by the House of Representatives. His trial before the Senate "is memorable on account of the excitement which it produced, the ability with which he was defended, and the nature of his acquittal."

He continued the exercise of his judicial functions, with signal ability, until his decease, on the 19th of June, 1811.

Charles Carroll of Carrollton, the last of the signers of the Declaration, was born in 1737. He was a member of Congress for several years. He served in the United States from 1788 to 1791, from which time until 1801, he was an active member of the Senate of Maryland—his native state. He died on the 14th of November, 1832.—ED.

terror we attach to the adventitious circumstances which seem to accelerate man's doom, had given to a piece of standing water near the road, the name *bloody pond*. The descending sun had shed a browner horror on the wilderness; and as we passed the dismal pool, we experienced that transient emotion of commisseration, which is natural to the mind when contemplating past events, involving the fall of friends, the fortune of war, and the sad lot of human kind. *Denique ob casus bellorum, et sortem hominum.*

At length, after a journey of three hundred and thirty miles, arriving at the quarters of General Schuyler, on the border of the Lake, we acquitted ourselves of our charge. He proposed to me, if agreeable, to go on with it; but in addition to attractions of a private nature, which drew me to Philadelphia, the wish to be there in order to make provision for our march to New York, orders for which had been daily expected before we set out, induced me to decline the opportunity of seeing the country beyond the Lake, as well as my friends in the northern army. We therefore only staid at this post, until the return despatches to Congress were prepared, which was the third day after our arrival.

Though General Schuyler has been charged with such haughtiness of demeanour, as to have induced the troops of New England to decline serving under his command, as stated in Marshall's Life of Washington, the reception we met with, was not merely courteous but kind. His quarters being contracted, a bed was prepared for us in his own apartment, and we experienced civilities that were flattering from an officer of his high rank. Though thoroughly the man of business, he was also a gentleman and man of the world; and well calculated to sustain the reputation of our army in the eyes of the British officers, (disposed to depreciate it,) as is evidenced by the account given by General Burgoyne of the manner in which he was entertained by him at Albany. But that he should have been displeasing to the *Yankees*, I am not at all surprised: he certainly was at no pains to conceal the extreme contempt he felt for a set of officers, who were both a disgrace to their stations and the cause in which they acted!*

---

* Peabody, in his Life of Sullivan, speaks of General Schuyler "as a brave and indefatigable officer, whose unpopularity through a large portion of the

Being yet a stranger to the character of these men, and the constitution of that part of our military force which in Pennsylvania was considered as the bulwark of the nation, I must confess my surprise at an incident which took place while at dinner. Besides the General, the members of his family and ourselves, there were at table a lady and gentleman from Montreal. A New England Captain came in upon some business, with that abject servility of manner, which belongs to persons of the meanest rank: he was neither asked to sit or take a glass of wine, and after announcing his wants, was dismissed with that peevishness of tone we apply to a low and vexatious intruder. This man, in his proper sphere, might have been entitled to better treatment; but when presuming to thrust himself into a situation, in which, far other qualifications than his were required, and upon an occasion too which involved some of the most important of human interests, I am scarcely prepared to say, it was unmerited.*

The day we spent at this station was employed in taking a view of the remains of Fort William Henry, and in sauntering

---

country it is not easy to explain." Mr. Graydon has briefly solved the mystery. Of the justice of the above observations, respecting New England officers, we have no means of judging. It cannot, however, fail to excite a feeling of regret that such severity of expression was considered necessary in regard to them, whatever may have been their demerits. Our New England brethren nobly performed their *whole* duty throughout the entire war, and well have they since sustained their republican institutions and character.

General Schuyler had the reputation of being cold and reserved in his intercourse with officers and men. Such was his natural disposition. But he was a brave, accomplished and devoted patriot, and his name and reputation will ever be dear to his country.

General Wilkinson's impressions, however, appear to have been of a different and more favourable character. He says, " Schuyler was an *eléve* of Major-General Bradstreet in the seven years' war, possessed a strong, fertile and cultivated mind ; with polished manners he united the most amiable disposition and insinuating address, and his convivial pleasantry never failed to interest and enliven his society ; in the discharge of his military duties, he was able, prompt, and decisive, and his conduct in every branch of service marked by active industry and rapid execution."—ED.

* See in Appendix H, a letter from GENERAL WASHINGTON to President Reed, dated " Head Quarters, Passaic Falls, 18th Oct., 1780," on the subject of General Schuyler and General Arnold, also showing that he never had any particular consideration for, or confidence in, the latter.—ED.

along the margin of the immense fountain of pure water which constitutes Lake George. We were much indebted upon this occasion to the polite attentions of Mr. Brockolst Livingston,* who was at this time one of the Aids-de-camp of Gen. Schuyler, and who so far dispensed with his avocations as to show us what was worthy of being seen. We lost no time in setting off, as soon as the despatches were ready for us; and returned with all possible expedition, in order to prepare ourselves for the expected march of our regiment to join the main army under the Commander-in-chief. Orders for that purpose had already been received, and were complied with in about a week after our return. The troops were transported by water to Trenton; from whence marching to Elizabethtown, they were again embarked in vessels which carried them to New York.

---

* Son of the celebrated William Livingston—Governor of New Jersey. He was entered as a student at Nassau Hall, Princeton, but left the College, in 1776, for the field, and became one of the family of Gen. Schuyler. He was afterwards attached to the suite of Gen. Arnold, with the rank of Major, and shared in the honour of the conquest of Burgoyne.

In 1779 he accompanied Mr. Jay to Spain, as private Secretary. In 1802 he was called to the Bench of the Supreme Court of New York, and in 1806, was transferred to that of the Supreme Court of the United States, which station he held, with distinguished ability, until his decease in March, 1823, in the 66th year of his age.—Ed.

13

CHAPTER VI.

The Author leaves Philadelphia.—Appearance of the Army.—Character of the Soldiers.—Erection of Fort Washington.—Fort Lee.—Character of General Mifflin.—An odd Character.—Connecticut Light Horse.—Character of the Army.—Declaration of Independence.—Statue of George III.—British land on Long Island.—Action with the Enemy.—New York.—Privations of Soldiers.— Long Island.—Entrenchments.—Skirmishing.—Midnight Scene in Camp.— Retreat to New York.—Reflections.—Washington vindicated.—General Howe. —Conduct of the British.

THE much deprecated event of marching from Philadelphia, was not the less afflicting for having been foreseen. The reader is acquainted with the attraction which existed there; and it is for those alone who have felt the effervescence of the passions, to form a just conception of the pangs, attendant on this separation from it. To say it was a disruption of my heart strings, would be a language neither too forcible nor figurative for the occasion. The other absences imposed by the demands of imperious duty, were not without disquietude; but they were cheered by the prospect of a speedy termination. This, before me, was a toiling sea without a shore; a dreary, illimitable void; and in subjecting myself to the stern mandate which now forced me away, I recognise a sacrifice which imparts some merit to my poor exertions in behalf of my country. If equal deprivations were sustained by others, I venture confidently to affirm, that estimated by the measure of suffering, none were greater than my own. On account of my late service interfering with the necessary preparations for the march, I had been permitted for about a week, to defer the moment of exile. When no longer to be postponed, I took my passage in the stage, where, indifferent to all around me, I sat ruminating on scenes of happiness departed, cheerless and lost to every hope of their return. Dreams of glory, it is true, sometimes crossed my imagination, but discordant to the tone of the predominant passion, the images were painful, and deeply tinged with despair. In so desolating a frame of mind, I perceived the necessity of active duty, which should leave me no time for reflection; and under this impression, as I approached my place of destination, became as impatient for its attainment as I had been reluctant in setting out for it; eager to immerse myself in martial occupations,

> "As in the hardy camp and toilsome march,
> Forget all softer and less manly cares."

A considerable portion of our motley army had already assembled in New York and its vicinity. The troops were chiefly from the eastern provinces; those from the southern, with the exception of Hand's, Magaw's, and our regiment, had not yet come on. The appearance of things was not much calculated to excite sanguine expectations in the mind of a sober observer. Great numbers of people were indeed to be seen, and those who are not accustomed to the sight of bodies under arms, are always prone to exaggerate them. But this propensity to swell the mass, had not an equal tendency to convert it into soldiery; and the irregularity, want of discipline, bad arms, and defective equipment in all respects, of this multitudinous assemblage, gave no favourable impression of its prowess. The materials of which the eastern battalions were composed, were apparently the same as those of which I had seen so unpromising a specimen at Lake George. I speak particularly of the officers, who were in no single respect distinguishable from their men, other than in the coloured cockades, which, for this very purpose, had been prescribed in general orders; a different colour being assigned to the officers of each grade. So far from aiming at a deportment which might raise them above their privates, and thence prompt them to due respect and obedience to their commands, the object was, by humility, to preserve the existing blessing of equality: an illustrious instance of which was given by Colonel Putnam, the chief engineer of the army, and no less a personage than the nephew of the Major-General of that name. " What," says a person meeting him one day with a piece of meat in his hand, " carrying home your rations yourself, Colonel!" " Yes," says he, " and I do it to set the officers a good example." But if any aristocratic tendencies had been really discovered by the Colonel among his countrymen, requiring this wholesome example, they must have been of recent origin, and the effect of southern contamination, since I have been credibly informed, that it was no unusual thing in the army before Boston, for a Colonel to make drummers and fifers of his sons, thereby, not only being enabled to form a very snug, economical mess, but to aid also considerably the revenue of the family chest. In short, it appeared, that the sordid spirit of gain was the vital principle of this greater part of the army.* The only exception I recollect to have seen, to these miserably constituted bands from New England, was the regiment of Glover from Marblehead.† There was an ap-

* This sentiment is supported by a passage in a letter from General Washington to General Reed, dated Cambridge, 10th February, 1776.

"Notwithstanding all the public virtue which is ascribed to these people, there is no nation under the sun that pays more adoration to money than they do."

I am aware that these references to General Washington's sentiments will be strongly repulsive to the feelings of many worthy men, from the consideration that the General's character stands particularly high in New England, and that in that quarter of the Union are found not only the greatest number of his admirers, but also many of the ablest defenders of his policy and fame. But can these confidential declarations of his opinions, emanating from an ardent love of his country and zeal in her cause, justly lessen him in the estimation of a single man of liberality and understanding? Is truth to be eternally muffled up and the materials of faithful history suppressed, lest her exposure in certain instances may be displeasing to some good men and grateful to a malignant faction? for useful it cannot be. To the promulgation indeed of these truths, the retribution is certain. His book, " the unkindest cut of all," to an author, will not sell. It will be shunned like a pestilence in those places, where the truths it holds out, are unwelcome. For this reason I have been given to understand that my publication will not do at all for a New England market. Some repugnance of the same kind would seem to exist against it in New York, as not long since a book-seller of that city informed me he could not dispose of a single copy. Even in its birth-place, Pennsylvania, it is very illy calculated for popularity; and as for Virginia and her dependencies sweeping the whole Southern States to Louisiana inclusive, it must then be, if not too contemptible for notice, a subject of the bitterest execration. Nevertheless, I am consoled by the invincible pride of conscious honesty and the *major amica veritas*, in a collision with all other friendships.

† John Glover, a native of Marblehead, in Massachusetts, a Brigadier-General in the army of the United States. With his command he formed the advance of the army in its passage of the Delaware, and was, of course, at the Battle of Trenton. He conducted Burgoyne's army, after its surrender, through the New Eng-

pearance of discipline in this corps; the officers seemed to have mixed with the world, and to understand what belonged to their stations. Though deficient, perhaps, in polish, it possessed an apparent aptitude for the purpose of its institution, and gave a confidence that myriads of its meek and lowly brethren were incompetent to inspire. But even in this regiment there were a number of negroes, which, to persons unaccustomed to such associations, had a disagreeable, degrading effect.

If there were any troops here, at this time, from Jersey, I do not recollect seeing them; and those of New York, appeared not to be very numerous. They, however, afforded officers, who might have been distinguished without a badge; and who were sufficiently men of the world, to know that the levelling principle was of all others, the most incompatible with good soldiership. Colonel Hamilton* had been furnished by this province, making his *debut* in the new career as a captain of artillery; but I never saw him in this capacity, and I believe he was soon taken into the family of the Commander-in-chief. Reinforcements were yet expected from the southward. Among these were Miles's† and

land States. He enjoyed, in a very high degree, the confidence and esteem of the Commander-in-chief, whose commendation was warmly bestowed. He served throughout the war with high reputation.—ED.

* ALEXANDER HAMILTON, a name not very dear to the "progressive democracy" of our party-ridden country, but nevertheless, one of the brightest and greatest that ever adorned the annals of any nation. His personal appearance is graphically described by Sullivan in his " Familiar Letters," already quoted : " He was under middle size, thin in person, but remarkably erect and dignified in his deportment. His hair was turned back from his forehead, powdered, and collected in a club behind. His complexion was exceedingly fair, and varying from this only by the almost feminine rosiness of his cheeks. His might be considered, as to figure and colour, an uncommonly handsome face. When at rest, it had rather a severe and thoughtful expression; but when engaged in conversation, it easily assumed an attractive smile. When he entered a room it was apparent, from the respectful attention of the company, that he was a distinguished person.

His appearance and deportment accorded with the dignified distinction to which he had attained in public estimation." At the period of his death, in July, 1804, he was in his 48th year.—ED.

† MILES is mentioned by WASHINGTON in his letter to the President of Congress, dated New York, August 12th, 1776:

" The enemy have made no movements of consequence, nor have we any farther intelligence of their designs. Colonel Smallwood and his battalion got in on

Atlee's provincial regiments from Pennsylvania; Hazlet's* from Delaware, and Smallwood's† from Maryland, both, I think, on the continental establishment; and in addition, large drafts from the militia of Pennsylvania.   All these were assembled in time for the opening of the campaign : but although the multitude, of which they were a part, contained some excellent raw materials, and was not without officers of spirit, possessing feelings suitable to their situation, yet diffused throughout the mass, they were certainly extremely rare.   The eye looked round in vain for the leading gentry of the country; those, most emphatically pledged to the cause, " by life, by fortune, and by sacred honour ;"‡ and taking the army in the aggregate, with its equipments along with it, he must have been a novice or a sanguine calculator, who could suppose it capable of sustaining the lofty tone and verbal energy of Congress.   In point of numbers merely, it was deficient; though a fact then little known or suspected.   Newspapers and common report, indeed, made it immensely numerous ; and it was represented that General Washington had so many men, that he wanted

Friday; and Colonel Miles is also here with two battalions more of Pennsylvania riflemen."

* Colonel John Haslet : He distinguished himself at the Battle of Long Island. In 1776, with seven hundred and fifty men, he attacked the enemy's outposts at the Village of Mamaronec, and forced their guards, taking thirty-six prisoners, a pair of colours, and sixty stand of arms.   He was killed at the Battle of Princeton.

† Colonel William Smallwood was at the action of White Plains.   He was promoted to the rank of general, and, in 1777, was despatched to take command of the Maryland Militia on the Western Shore.   He joined the main army in September of the same year, and was at the Battle of Germantown.   In 1785, he was elected to Congress, and the same year, Governor of Maryland.   He died, February, 1792.—Ed.

‡ Congress, to be sure, were privileged; and there must be civil functions as well as military.   But these were a good deal a matter of choice ; and as the war was a common cause, the very creature of association, its rubs should have been somewhat equalized.   Thoughts of this kind, however, would sometimes intrude into minds soured by hard duty.   Another thing which also tended to lessen the number of young men of figure was, that many prudent men thought the time extremely convenient for sending their sons to Europe for education.   There they could be better taught and were out of harm's way; and upon the whole, one is justified in saying as Cornelius Nepos does of the Athenians, in his Life of Thrasybulus, *nam jam illis temporibus fortius boni pro libertate loquebantur, quam pugnabunt.*

no more, and had actually sent many home, as superfluous.   It is true, there were men enough coming and going; yet his letters of that day demonstrate how truly weak he was in steady, permanent soldiers.

It was probably between the twentieth and twenty-fifth of June, that I arrived in this busy scene; in a few days after which, our regiment and Magaw's* were marched towards Kingsbridge, and encamped upon the ground on which Fort Washington was erected.   We were here under the command of General Mifflin, and immediately employed in the construction of that fortress, under the direction of Colonel Putnam, who, as already mentioned, was our principal engineer, and, considering his want of experience, not destitute, perhaps, of merit in his profession.   As a man may be a rhetorician or a logician though unacquainted with the terms of the art, so might Mr. Putnam have been a good practical artist, though misterming the *Gorge* the *George*.   But this was merely a mistake in pronunciation; and I will not permit myself to question, that he had real science enough to have smelt out Moliere's jest about a *demi-lune* and a *lune toute entiere*.†

---

* Colonel ROBERT MAGAW.—He was appointed to the command of Fort Washington.   When General Howe demanded the surrender of the garrison, Colonel Magaw returned the following gallant answer to the British Adutant-General:—

"*15th November*, 1776."

" Sir, if I rightly understand the purport of your message from General Howe, communicated to Colonel Swoope, this post is to be immediately surrendered, or put to the sword.   I think it rather a mistake, than a settled purpose of General Howe, to act a part so unworthy of himself, and of the British nation.   But give me leave to assure his Excellency, that, actuated by the most glorious cause that mankind ever fought in, I am determined to defend this post to the very last extremity.—Robert Magaw."—ED.

† Colonel RUFUS PUTNAM.—In regard to his qualifications as an engineer, General WASHINGTON, in his letter to Congress of 20th December, 1776, says, "I have also to mention, that, for want of some establishment in the department of engineers; agreeably to the plan laid before Congress, in October last, Colonel Putnam, who was at the head of it, has quitted, and taken a regiment in Massachusetts.   I know of no other man tolerably well qualified, for the conducting of that business.   None of the French gentlemen, whom I have seen, with appointments in that way, appear to me, to know any thing of the matter." And again in his letter to Congress, from Pompton Plains, in July, 1777, he remarks,

In the course of some weeks, our labours had produced immense mounds of earth, assuming a pentagonal form, and finally
issuing in a fort of five bastions. As Cæsar, in his operations,
has been said to have made great use of the spade, I shall not
insist upon the *improbus labor* being beneath the dignity of a
soldier; but certain it is, that we then thought it so, and that the
continual fatigue-duty we were subjected to, was not only extremely
irksome, but unfavourable also to our improvement in tactics,
which, nevertheless, was assiduously attended to. The perpetual clouds of dust which the dry weather of the season occasioned, gave us the appearance of scavengers; a circumstance
sadly at variance with the neatness of person inculcated by
Colonel Shee, and of which he was an enthusiastic admirer: it
made our duty also extremely severe, and gave me an inflamma-
tion in my eyes, which was the only indisposition I experienced
during the campaign. Sickness, however, on the approach of
fall, prevailed among our men to a great degreee; and little
more than half our number, was at any time fit for duty. Thus,
without fighting, are armies " sluggishly melted away."

One of the chief objects in building Fort Washington is understood to have been, to prevent the enemy passing up the Hudson,
on whose eastern bank it stood, on very commanding ground.
On the opposite side of the river, Fort Lee, in the same view,
was afterwards erected: and these, with the sinking of some
hulks in the channel, were expected, or at least hoped, to be
sufficient for the purpose. But the inefficacy of these impedi-
ments was soon evinced by two frigates, that taking advantage
of a favourable wind, sailed by us with great gallantry, in English
phrase, returning our fire *in great style*. We were too high for
their guns to be brought to bear upon us with any certainty;
though one ball was thrown into the fort. Our elevated situation
was nearly as unfavourable to the success of our fire upon them;

"Colonel Putnam, I imagine, will be with him (General Schuyler) before this, as
his regiment is part of Nixon's brigade, who will answer every purpose he can
possibly have for an engineer at this crisis."

Colonel Putnam served well and faithfully, throughout the war; at its close he
held the rank of Brigadier-General, and was, subsequently, one of the first settlers in the North Western territory.—ED.

to remedy which in future, a battery was constructed below, in a very advantageous position. But this was attended with no better effect; as two other frigates, not long after, passed in defiance of the guns of both batteries, and apparently without having sustained the slighest injury. I afterwards learned, however, when prisoner in New York, that upon one of these occasions, one of the frigates had been hulled, and some men killed and wounded; among the latter, a midshipman, a son of Mr. Courtland Skinner, of Amboy, lost his arm.

To have been regular, I should have mentioned the arrival of the hostile forces, and their occupancy of Staten Island as a preparatory station. From the uncertainty in what quarter they might invade us, the utmost vigilance was inculcated every where, and observed at our post. The lines were manned every morning an hour before day-light; we were several times formed for action; and once marched to Bloomingdale in full expectation of meeting the enemy, who it was confidently asserted, had made good a landing there, or in the neighbourhood. The intelligence proved untrue, if such indeed had been received. But it is not improbable, that it was merely a contrivance of General Mifflin, to inure us to alarms and render us alert, objects, that to a certain extent, were not without utility; but the General was a bustler, who harassed us unnecessarily; and, considering the unavoidable severity of our duty, to the real injury of the health of the troops. His manners were better adapted to attract popularity than to preserve it. Highly animated in his appearance, and possessing in an eminent degree the talent of harranguing a multitude, his services in giving motion to the militia, were several times, in the course of the war, felt and acknowledged; but that he was equally calculated to keep alive military ardour and confidence, cannot be affirmed. He was full of activity and apparently of fire; but it rather resembled the transient blaze of light combustibles, than the constant, steady flame of substantial fuel: though in saying this it should be mentioned, that I have no ground to insinuate that his fortitude was not equal to any demand that might have been made upon it. He assumed a little of the veteran from having lain before Boston; was very fond of telling us that he would bring us into a scrape; and it must be confessed, that he was considerably happy in the display of that apathy to human carnage, which is affected by great commanders, in the spirit of which the great Frederick tells us, that "When sovereigns play for provinces, the lives of men are but as counters." So much 'tis better to direct the game, than be a component part of its machinery! But whatever might have been Mifflin's deficiencies, he had many qualifications for his station that too many others, placed in higher ones, wanted. He was a man of education, ready apprehension and brilliancy; had spent some time in Europe, particularly in France, and was very easy of access with the manners of genteel life, though occasionally evolving those of the Quaker. In delineating both men and events, my object is truth; otherwise the friendly attention I never fail to receive from this gentleman, might have led me into a strain of less qualified encomium.*

The first frigates that passed us, took their station in Tappan sea, where an attempt was made to set them on fire. It failed as to the larger vessels, but a tender was destroyed. One of the persons who embarked in this service as a volunteer, was the surgeon's mate of our regiment, a singular character and degenerate son of Mordecai Yarnall, a Quaker preacher. I was amused

---

* General THOMAS MIFFLIN.—He was appointed Quarter-master-General by WASHINGTON, in 1775. Richard Henry Lee, in his reply to WASHINGTON's letter informing him of this, says:—" I think you could not possibly have appointed a better man, to his present office than Mr. Mifflin. He is a singular man, and you certainly will meet with the applause and support of all good men, by promoting and countenancing real merit and public virtue, in opposition to all private interests and partial affection." He distinguished himself at the siege of Boston by his coolness and intrepidity, and, at the age of 32, was appointed by Congress, a Brigadier. In 1777 he was promoted to the rank of Major-General. In 1783, he was elected to Congress from Pennsylvania, his native state, and presided, with ability and dignity, over the deliberations of that body. In 1785, he was speaker of the Legislative Assembly, and subsequently, president of the Supreme Executive Council. He had been a member of the convention which framed the Constitution of the United States, and, in 1799, assisted as president of the convention, in forming the new Constitution of the State. He was the first Governor under this Constitution, and held the office for nine years, having been thrice elected. As president of Congress, he received, at Annapolis, the resignation of General WASHINGTON, as Commander-in-chief, delivering on the occasion, a brief, but eloquent address in reply to the speech of WASHINGTON. He died, at Lancaster, on the 21st of January, 1800, aged 56.—ED.

with his oddities, and sometimes listened to his imitations of his father's manner of preaching, as well as that of many others of the public friends. Though a temporary apostate from the principles of his forefathers, in which he had been strictly brought up, I never doubted that they had taken root in him; and that if he was not prematurely cut off, they would vegetate and fructify in due season: nor was I mistaken. Many years after, I saw him zealously sustaining his paternal vocation, surrounded by a circle of friends. He had come to preach in the town in which I resided: I went to hear him, and had the pleasure of taking him home with me to dinner with several of his attendants, where every thing passed with as much gravity and decorum, as if I had never seen him in any other character. Mr. Yarnall's former profaneness could not but have occurred to him on this occasion; but whatever might have been his recollections, he dissembled them admirably.

Among the military phenomena of this campaign, the Connecticut light horse ought not to be forgotten. These consisted of a considerable number of old fashioned men, probably farmers and heads of families, as they were generally middle aged, and many of them apparently beyond the meridian of life. They were truly irregulars; and whether their clothing, their equipments or caparisons were regarded, it would have been difficult to have discovered any circumstance of uniformity; though in the features derived from "local habitation," they were one and the same. Instead of carbines and sabres, they generally carried fowling pieces; some of them very long, and such as in Pennsylvania, are used for shooting ducks. Here and there, one, "his youthful garments, well saved," appeared in a dingy regimental of scarlet, with a triangular, tarnished, laced hat. In short, so little were they like modern soldiers, in air or costume, that, dropping the necessary number of years, they might have been supposed the identical men who had in part composed Pepperil's army at the taking of Louisbourg. Their order of march corresponded with their other irregularities. It "spindled into longitude immense," presenting so extended and ill-compacted a flank, as though they had disdained the adventitious prowess derived from concentration. These singular dragoons were volunteers, who came to make a tender of their services to the Commander-in-chief. But they staid not long at New York. As such a body of cavalry had not been counted upon, there was in all probability a want of forage for their *jades,* which, in the spirit of ancient knighthood, they absolutely refused to descend from; and as the general had no use for cavaliers in his insular operations, they were forthwith dismissed with suitable acknowledgments for their truly chivalrous ardour.* An unlucky trooper of this school had by some means or other, found his way to Long Island, and was taken by the enemy in the battle of the 27th of August. The British officers made themselves very merry at his expense, and obliged him to amble about for their entertainment. On being asked, what had been his duty in the rebel army, he answered, that it was *to flank a little and carry tidings.* Such at least was the story at New York among the prisoners.

But notwithstanding the unwarlike guise of the troops from New England, there was no part of the continent perhaps, in which so little impression could be made, or in which the enemy was so cautious of advancing. Their numbers and zeal rendered them formidable when fighting on their own ground *pro aris et focis;* and pitiful as was the figure the eastern men made this campaign, the defence of Bunker's hill was worthy of the bravest veterans.† I attempt not to assign a cause for the falling

---

* It appears from a letter of GENERAL WASHINGTON, that they refused fatigue duty, because it was beneath the dignity of troopers.

† GENERAL WASHINGTON writes under date of 10th February, 1776, to Joseph Reed: "The party sent to Bunker's Hill had some good and some bad men engaged in it. One or two courts have been held on the conduct of part of them. To be plain, these people are not to be depended upon if exposed; and any man will fight well if he thinks himself in no danger. I do not apply this only to these people. I suppose it to be the case with all raw and undisciplined troops."— *Sparks,* Vol. iii. p. 285.

With no other motive than a love of justice, a protest must here be entered against a judgment so severe as that expressed by our author in the text. Whatever may have been the deficiencies of a portion of the New England troops in equipment and discipline—deficiencies by no means peculiar to them—the courage, fortitude, and self sacrificing zeal with which the trials and difficulties of the Revolution were met, endured, and finally overcome, ought not to be questioned. All this is matter of history. The country that could furnish such "exigent

off; and should even be fearful of recognising it, were there not documents in existence, and hundreds yet alive to attest the truth of my representations. I have in vain, endeavoured to account for the very few gentlemen and men of the world, that at this time appeared in arms from this country, which might be considered as the cradle of the revolution. There were some, indeed, in the higher ranks; and here and there a young man of decent breeding, in the capacity of an aid-de-camp or brigade major; but any thing above the condition of a clown, in the regiments we came in contact with, was truly a rarity. Was it, that the cause was only popular among the yeomanry? Was it, that men of fortune and condition there, as in other parts of the continent, though evidently most interested in a contest, whose object was to rescue American property from the grasp of British avidity, were willing to devolve the fighting business on the poorer and humbler classes? Was it, in short, that they held the language of the world, and said,

> "Let the gull'd fools the toils of war subdue,
> Where bleed the many to enrich the few?"

Or was it, that that simple way of thinking and ill appreciation of military talent, which had made a drivelling deacon,* second

men" as PRESCOTT, WARREN, GREENE, KNOX, PUTNAM, LINCOLN, STARK, and SULLI-VAN; an ADAMS, a HANCOCK, an OTIS and a QUINCY, cannot be supposed to be deficient in enlightened patriotic zeal, or in men with "hearts to do and dare," all that brave and patriotic men *may* do and dare, in defence of their liberties and rights; and the page of History glows with the story of their services, sufferings and worth.—ED.

* This was General Ward,* with whose resignation and that of Brigadier Frye, GENERAL WASHINGTON makes himself merry in a letter to General Lee, published in the Memoirs of the latter. So little does the character of the time appear to be known at present, that I deem it necessary to fortify my remarks.

---

* GENERAL ARTEMAS WARD.—He had been appointed, by the Provincial Congress of Massachusetts, commander of all the forces raised by that Colony. He was the first Major-General in the American army. He graduated at Harvard, in 1748. "For several years he was an active and useful member of the General Court, and, in 1774, one of the Provincial Congress. He served in the war previous to the peace of Paris, and when the Revolutionary struggle commenced, was appointed Major-General, and was even thought of as Generalissimo.

14

in command, was then prevalent among them? Whatever was the reason, New England was far behind the other provinces in the display of an ardent, unequivocal zeal for the cause, in the quality of her officers; and notwithstanding that she has since shown herself more prolific of liberal, well-informed, exigent men, than any other part of the union, her soldiery, at the time I am speaking of, was contemptible in the extreme.

Neither did the fighting department appear to be fashionable among the gentry of Virginia. It must be admitted that she furnished some gentlemen aids-de-camp and volunteers, and afterwards, corps of cavalry, respectably officered; but the serious, drudging business of war, devolves on the infantry; and in this description of force, she evinced but little brilliancy. One of her regiments, I recollect, did duty with us when we were encamped on Haerlem heights. Its commander had the appearance of a reputable planter, and might for any thing I know to the contrary, have been both patriotic and brave; but neither himself nor his officers, were of the kind that bespoke the *elite* of their country : they were not in the style of their vocation; in a word, they were not Baylors, nor Griffins, nor Lees, nor Monroes. But allowing every possible merit to these gentlemen, it does not lessen the force of my observation in respect to their State, of whose subsequent exertions, I am ignorant.

He commanded the troops at Cambridge until the arrival of WASHINGTON, when he was placed at the head of the right wing at Roxbury. His firmness and intrepidity were strikingly displayed on various trying occasions. He resigned his commission in April, 1776, though at the request of WASHINGTON he continued for some time longer in command. He was afterwards chosen one of the Council of Massachusetts, where he was distinguished for his integrity and independence of spirit. He was elected to Congress on the organization of the General Government, and died late in the year 1800, at the age of seventy-three."—*Enc. Amer.*—ED.

BRIGADIER-GENERAL JOSEPH FRYE.—WASHINGTON writes concerning him to Congress, 31st August, 1775 :—" He entered into the service as early as 1745, and rose through the different military ranks, in the two succeeding wars, to that of Colonel. From these circumstances, together with the favourable report made to me of him, I presume he sustained the character of a good officer, though I do not find it distinguished by any peculiar service." Colonel Frye received from Congress the appointment of Brigadier-General in the Continental army, upon the recommendation of the Commander-in-chief.

He resigned his commission in April, 1776.—ED.

Among the mistakes of my life, in a view to advancement, I may justly reckon my not essaying the aid-de-camp career. To the rank and pay of major, which followed the appointment, an exemption from hard duty immediately took place, and the fortunate incumbents had cause to hug themselves in a world of other pleasant consequences. They, comparatively, fed well and slept well; used horses legs instead of their own, upon a march; and were, besides, in the true road to preferment. The late General Walter Stewart,* was a younger Captain than myself, in the same regiment. But he chose the better path I allude to: in doing so he escaped captivity, was warmly recommended to Congress by his General, and complimented with a regiment, while his elder officers were languishing in captivity, neglected, superseded and forgotten. Captain Scull, also, of our regiment, had attached himself to General Thomson; and the Colonels fearing they should lose more of us, were assiduous in representing the employment of an aid, as not only unworthy of a man of spirit, but as being out of the line of promotion: In the latter, at least, they were egregiously mistaken.

The Declaration of Independence,† whose date will never be

---

* Honourable mention is made of Colonel Walter Stewart by GENERAL WASHINGTON in his letter of 13th January, 1780, to Lord Sterling. Colonel Stewart rendered valuable services at the time of the revolt in the Pennsylvania line, which were recognised by WASHINGTON and Wayne.—ED.

† The Declaration of Independence was read, in public, by Commodore Hopkins, from "the platform of an Observatory which had been erected by Rittenhouse, at the rear of the State House. But few people assembled to hear it, and among these there were no manifestations of enthusiasm. They quietly retired at its conclusion. It was above the comprehension of the mass. The principles upon which it was based, and the language of the Declaration itself, were not immediately appreciated and understood. Another proof of what has been elsewhere asserted in these 'Memoirs'—that the 'Revolution is universally admitted to have begun in the upper circles of society.' The apathy, timidity, or ignorance, thus manifested at its birth-place was not imitated elsewhere, and whatever may have been the reception of the great intelligence by the army—among the people, and nowhere more warmly than at Boston, the news was received, according to BOTTA, 'with transports of joy.' Nor were any of those public demonstrations omitted which governments are accustomed to employ, on similar occasions, to conciliate the favour of the people. The artillery was fired, bonfires were kindled, the people seemed actually delirious with exultation. On the 11th of July, the manifesto of Congress was published in New York, and was read to each brigade of the American army, which, at that time, was assembled in the

forgotten so long as Liberty remains the fashion, and demagogues continue to thrive upon it, was, with the utmost speed, transmitted to the armies; and when received, read to the respective regiments. If it was not embraced with all the enthusiasm that has been ascribed to the event, it was at least hailed with acclamations, as no doubt any other act of Congress, not flagrantly improper, would at that time have been. The propriety of the measure had been little canvassed among us; and perhaps it was to our honour, considered merely as soldiers, that we were so little of politicians. A predilection for republicanism, it is true, had not reached the army, at least the Pennsylvania line; but as an attempt to negotiate in our unorganized situation, would probably have divided and ruined us, the step was considered wise, although a passage of the Rubicon, and calculated to close the door to accommodation. Being looked upon as unavoidable, if resistance was to be persisted in, it was approved; and produced

vicinity of the city: it was received with universal acclamation. The same evening the statue of George III., which had been erected in 1770, was taken down and dragged through the streets. It was decided that the lead of which it was composed, should be converted into musket balls. These excesses, however blameable in themselves, were not without utility if considered politically; they excited the people and hurried them on to the object that was desired. At Baltimore, Independence having been proclaimed in the presence of cannoniers and militia, the people could not contain their enthusiasm. The air resounded with salutes of artillery, and the shouts that hailed the freedom and happiness of the United States of America. The effigy of the King became the sport of the populace, and was afterwards burnt in the public square. The rejoicings at Boston were the greatest of all. Independence was there proclaimed from the balcony of the State House, in the presence of all the authorities, civil and military, and of an immense concourse of people, as well from the city itself as from the country. The garrison was drawn up in order of battle in King street, which from that moment took the name of State street; the troops formed in thirteen detachments, to denote the thirteen United States. At a given signal, a salute of thirteen cannon was fired upon Fort Hill, which was immediately answered by an equal number from the batteries of the Castle, of the Neck, of Nantasket, and of Point Alderton. The garrison, in their turn, fired thirteen salutes of musketry, each detachment firing in succession. The authorities and most considerable inhabitants then convened at a banquet prepared in the Council Chamber. All the bells rung in token of felicitation; the joy was universal, and its demonstrations were incessantly renewed. In the evening all the ensigns of royalty, lions, sceptres or crowns, whether sculptured or painted, were torn in pieces and burned."—ED.

no resignations among the officers that I am aware of, except that of Lieutenant-Colonel William Allen, already mentioned, who was with his regiment in Canada. He called at our camp on his way to Philadelphia, where he appeared somewhat surprised and mortified that his example had no followers.

Being now independent, we had no farther use for a king, or even the semblance of one; for which reason the equestrian statue of George the Third, in New York, was thrown down and demolished. The head of the King was cut off by way of inflaming the public valour: but so little was the spirit of seventy-six like the spirit of subsequent eras, that the act was received with extreme coldness and indifference. Had even George himself been among us, he would have been in no great danger of personal injury, at least from the army. We were, indeed, beginning to grow angry with him; and were not displeased with Paine for calling him a *royal brute*, but we had not yet acquired the true taste for cutting throats.

The suspense in which we had for many weeks been held, in respect to the meditated operations of the enemy, was at length removed by the landing of a considerable force on the 22d of August, on Long Island. Among the measures taken to counteract him, hand-bills, addressed to the German troops, inviting desertion by a promise of land, were prepared by Congress, and endeavoured to be circulated among them. For this business, Christopher Ludwig, a baker of Philadelphia, was, among others, selected. As he was a German, and had been a soldier in his younger days, he was supposed to be peculiarly fitted for the purpose. Full of zeal for the cause, he was already at his post, and was bold enough to undertake the perilous employment; but whether he ventured himself in the enemy's camp, I never learned. I rather suspect he was shy, as he well knew the penalty of detection in such an enterprize. At any rate, the overtures had no effect: no deserters came over to us. This Ludwig, though far advanced in years, could yet play the old soldier with much address, and thence contrived to make himself conspicuous. Being employed some time after to manage the ovens, he assumed the title of *Bakermaster-General of the army*, and made a vow never to shave his beard until a fortunate conclusion of the contest.* It is a little remarkable, that the patriotism of the Baker-General should have displayed itself in the same manner as that of Cato did, during the civil war of Rome, who, as we are informed by Lucan, neither shaved, nor cut his hair.

> " Ut primum tolli feralia viderat arma,
>   Intonsos rigidam in frontem descendere canos
>   Passus erat, mœstamque genis increscere barbam..

> For when he saw the fatal faction's arm,
>   The coming war, and Rome's impending harm ;
>   Regardless quite of every other care,
>   Unshorn he left his loose neglected hair,
>   Rude hung the hoary honours of his head,
>   And a foul growth his mournful cheeks o'erspread."

The forces of the enemy, which had been landed on Long Island, had extended themselves as far as Flatbush and New Lots, between which places and our works at Brooklyn, runs a ridge of pretty lofty hills. Here it was, that being met by our troops under the command of Generals Sullivan and Stirling, the action of the 27th of August commenced; of which, as I was not pre-

* Mr. Graydon, on a leaf of his private copy of the Memoirs, wrote, " a gentleman corrects me, and says, it was not until a conclusion of the war, but until we regained possession of Philadelphia. Be it so."

CHRISTOPHER LUDWICK—the " Baker-General "—lies conspicuously buried in the grave-yard of St. Michael's (Lutheran) Church, at the upper end of Germantown. From his monument we learn that he was born in Germany, where he learned his "trade and business of Baker. In early life he was a soldier and a sailor, and visited the East and West Indies. He came to Philadelphia in 1755, and by industry and integrity accumulated a handsome property, part of which he devoted to the service of his adopted country, in the contest for Independence. Was appointed Baker-General to the Army, and, for faithful services, received a written testimony from the Commander-in-chief. On every occasion his zeal for the relief of the oppressed was manifest, and by his last will he bequeathed the greater part of his estate for the education of the poor, of all denominations, *gratis*. He lived and died respected for his integrity and public spirit. Reader, such was LUDWICK. Art thou poor? venerate his Character. Art thou rich? imitate his Example."

MR. LUDWICK died in 1801, aged nearly 81 years.—In his humble sphere he rendered faithful service in the cause of Independence; services which entitle him to grateful remembrance, and more than justify a passing tribute to his patriotism and worth.—ED.

sent, I know nothing more than is given in the historical accounts of this affair. The manifest superiority of the enemy on this occasion, owing more to mismanagement, perhaps, on our side, than want of bravery in the troops engaged, rendered it expedient to draw our forces to the point that had been chosen for the contest; and an express was accordingly sent off, requiring the immediate march of Shee's and Magaw's regiments to New York. Being forthwith put in motion, we proceeded with the utmost speed, and reached the city in the afternoon; but by this time the conflict was over, and the firing had ceased. Here, therefore, we were quartered for the night, under orders to be in readiness to cross the East river by break of day in the morning. Glover's regiment was also moved to this place, and was under similar orders for Long Island. Few particulars of the day's combat were yet known, though it was pretty well ascertained that we had been handled severely, and lost a considerable number of officers and men; but what proportion had been killed, or were prisoners, was merely conjecture. New York was, at this time, a scene of tumult and confusion, and, it might be added, of dismay.

The circumstances, however, did not deprive me of my appetite, and the inclination for a good supper, which I had not for some months enjoyed; and therefore, as soon as our men were dismissed to their quarters, which was not until dark, Mr. Forrest and myself, set out in pursuit of this object. But some of the public houses were full, others had no eatables in them, and we began to fear, that this little enjoyment we had promised ourselves, was not to be obtained; and that we should be obliged to go to bed supperless. After trying the best looking inns to no purpose, we essayed those of more humble appearance, and at length entered one, that was kept by a middle-aged, matronly lady. We asked if she could give us supper; she gave us the common answer, that there was nothing in the house. We were now about to give the matter up, and had retired beyond the door, with somewhat of a disconsolate air, perhaps, when the good woman seemed touched with compassion for us. She had probably sons of her own; or if not, she was of that sex which, Ledyard tells us, is ever prone to acts of kindness and humanity.

She called us back and told us, that she believed she could make
out to give us a lobster. At this we brightened up, assuring her,
as we really thought, that nothing could be better: and being
shown into a small, snug apartment, we called for a pint of
wine. We now thought ourselves, instead of outcasts, favourites
of fortune, as upon comparing notes with our brother officers,
next day, we found we had reason, since scarcely one of them
had been able to procure a mouthful. Our lobster being quickly
served up, we fell to with most excellent appetites, and between
it and our wine entirely forgot our toils, most fervently realizing
the sentiment of the song, that "*a bottle and kind landlady cure
all again.*"

On the next day, early in the forenoon, we were transported to
Long Island; marched down to the entrenchments at Brooklyn,
and posted on their left extremity, extending to the Wallabout.
The arrival of our two battalions, (Shee's and Magaw's, which
always acted together,) with that of Glover, had the effect, I have
always found to be produced, by a body of men under arms,
having the appearance of discipline. Although, owing to the
dysentery which had prevailed in our camp, our number was so
reduced, that the two regiments could not have amounted to
more than eight hundred men, making in the whole, when joined
with Glover's, about twelve or thirteen hundred; yet it was evident
that this small reinforcement, inspired no inconsiderable degree of
confidence. The faces that had been saddened by the disasters
of yesterday, assumed a gleam of animation, on our approach;
accompanied with a murmur of approbation in the spectators occasionally greeting each other with the remark, that "*these were
the lads that might do something.*" Why it should be so, I know
not, but the mind instinctively attaches an idea of prowess, to
the silence, steadiness, and regularity of a military assemblage;
and a hundred well dressed, well armed, and well disciplined
grenadiers, are more formidable in appearance, than a disjointed,
disorderly multitude of a thousand. Our regiments, to be sure,
could not arrogate such perfection; but that they were distinguished in our young army, may be inferred, from an official letter from General WASHINGTON, wherein he states, that "they had
been trained with more than common attention." To sustain

the duty now imposed upon us, required both strength of body
and of mind. The spot at which we were posted, was low
and unfavourable for defence. There was a *fraised* ditch in its
front, but it gave little promise of security, as it was evidently
commanded by the ground occupied by the enemy, who entirely
enclosed the whole of our position, at the distance of but a few
hundred paces. It was evident, also, that they were constructed
batteries, which would have rendered our particular situation extremely ineligible, to say the least of it. In addition to this discomfort, we were annoyed by a continual rain, which, though
never very heavy, was never less than a searching drizzle, and
often what might, with propriety, be called a smart shower. We
had no tents to screen us from its pitiless pelting; nor, if we had
had them, would it have comported with the incessant vigilance
required, to have availed ourselves of them, as, in fact, it might
be said, that we lay upon our arms during the whole of our stay
upon the island.* In the article of food, we were little better off.
We had indeed, drawn provisions, whose quality was not to be
complained of. Our pickled pork, at least, was good; but how
were we to cook it. As this could not be done, it was either to
be eaten as it was, or not eaten at all; and we found upon trial,
that boiling it, although desirable, was not absolutely necessary;
and that the article was esculent without culinary preparation. I
remember, however, on one of the days we were in this joyless
place, getting a slice of a barbacued pig, which some of our
soldiers had dressed at a deserted house which bounded our lines.

There was an incessant skirmishing kept up in the day-time
between our riflemen and the enemy's irregulars; and the firing

---

* Had not this work been written a few years too early, I might have scienti-
fically talked of our *bivouacking;* but like the man who had been all his life
talking prose without knowing it, we, poor ignorants!—had been *bivouacking*
here two nights without being sensible that we were in the performance of a
grand operation, become grand at least, from the raking up, and applying to it
of an old obsolete French word, by the great Napoleon; and which all military men
since, are ambitious of being engaged in, for the sake of employing in despatches
and private letters, this new and fascinating phrase. Even Sir Walter Scott resolved not to be behind them in fashionable graces,—tells us in his Waterloo.

"That line so black
And trampled, marks the bivouack."

was sometimes so brisk, as to indicate an approaching general engagement. This was judiciously encouraged by General WASHINGTON, as it tended to restore confidence to our men, and was, besides, showing a good countenance to the foe.

On the morning after our first night's watch, Colonel Shee took me aside, and asked me what I thought of our situation. I could not but say, I thought it a very discouraging one. He viewed it in the same light, he said, and added, that if we were not soon withdrawn from it, we should inevitably be cut to pieces. So impressed was he with this conviction, that he desired me to go to the quarters of General Reed, and to request him to ride down to the lines, that he might urge him to propose a retreat without loss of time. I went, but could not find him at his quarters, or at any of the other places where it was likely he might be. It was not long, however, before he came to our station, and gave the Colonel an opportunity of conferring with him. This day passed off like the last, in unabating skirmishing and rain. After dark, orders were received and communicated to us regimentally, to hold ourselves in readiness for an attack upon the enemy; to take place in the course of the night. This excited much speculation among the officers, by whom it was considered a truly daring undertaking, rendered doubly so from the bad condition of our arms, so long exposed to the rain: and although we had bayonets, this was not the case with the whole of our force, upon whom we must depend for support. It was not for us, however, to object to the measure: we were soldiers, and bound to obey. Several nuncupative wills were made upon the occasion, uncertain as it was, whether the persons to whom they were communicated would survive, either to prove or to execute them. I was for a while under the impression that we were to fight; and, in the language of the poet, was " stiffening my sinews and summoning up my blood," for what, with the rest, I deemed a desperate encounter. But when I came to consider the extreme rashness of such an attempt, it suddenly flashed upon my mind, that a retreat was the object; and that the order for assailing the enemy, was but a cover to the real design. The more I reflected upon it, the more I was convinced that I was right; and what had passed in the morning with Colonel Shee, served to confirm me in my opinion. I communicated my conjecture to some of the officers, but they dared not suffer themselves to believe it well founded, though they gradually came over to my opinion ; and by midnight, they were, for the most part, converts to it. There was a deep murmur in the camp which indicated some movement; and the direction of the decaying sounds, was evidently towards the river. About two o'clock, a cannon went off, apparently from one of our redoubts, "piercing the night's dull ear," with a tremendous roar. If the explosion was within our lines, the gun was probably discharged in the act of spiking it; and it could have been no less a matter of speculation to the enemy, than to ourselves. I never heard the cause of it ; but whatever it was, the effect was at once alarming and sublime ; and what with the greatness of the stake, the darkness of the night, the uncertainty of the design, and extreme hazard of the issue whatever might be the object, it would be difficult to conceive a more deeply solemn and interesting scene. It never recurs to my mind, but in the strong imagery of the chorus of Shakspeare's Henry the Vth, in which is arrayed, in appropriate gloom, a similar interval of dread suspense and awful expectation.

As our regiment was one of those appointed to cover the retreat, we were, of course, among the last to be drawn off, and it was near day-break before we received orders to retire. We were formed without delay, and had marched near half way to the river, when it was announced that the British light horse were at our heels. Improbable as was the circumstance, it was yet so strenuously insisted upon, that we were halted and formed, the front rank kneeling with presented pikes, which we had with us, to receive the charge of the supposed assailants. None, however, appeared ; and the alarm must have proceeded from the fear of those who gave it, magnifying the noise of a few of our own horsemen into that of squadrons of the enemy. We again took up the line of march, and had proceeded but a short distance, when the head of the battalion was halted a second time. The orders we had received were erroneous: We were informed that we had come off too soon, and were commanded with all expedition to return to our post.*   This was a trying business to young soldiers; it was, nevertheless strictly complied with, and we remained not less than an hour in the lines before we received the second order to abandon them.†   It may be supposed we did not linger; but though we moved with celerity, we guarded against confusion, and under the friendly cover of a thick fog, reached the place of embarkation without annoyance from the enemy, who, had the morning been clear, would have seen what was going on, and been enabled to cut off the greater part of the rear.   One of my soldiers being too feeble to carry his musket, which was too precious to be thrown away, I took it from him, and found myself able to carry it, together with my own fusee.   On attaining the water, I found a boat prepared for my company, which immediately embarked, and taking the helm myself, I so luckily directed the prow, no object being discernible in the fog, that we touched near the centre of the city.   It was between six and seven o'clock, perhaps later, when we landed at New York; and in less than an hour after, the fog having dispersed, the enemy was visible on the shore we had left.

Next to the merit of avoiding a scrape in war, is that of a dexterous extrication from it; and in this view, the removal of so

* This is stated in Gordon's history, vol. 2, page 103, to have been owing to a mistake of Colonel Scammell, who delivered the orders to General Mifflin to bring off the whole covering party, instead of a particular regiment.

† This circumstance is noted by General HEATH in his Memoirs:—"In this retreat from the Island, and which was well conducted, an instance of discipline and of true fortitude was exhibited by the American guards and pickets. In order that the British should not get knowledge of the withdrawal of the Americans, until their main body had embarked in the boats and pushed off from the shore, (a matter of the highest importance to their safety,) the guards were ordered to continue at their respective posts, with sentinels alert, as if nothing extraordinary was taking place, until the troops had embarked: they were then to come off, march briskly to the ferry, and embark themselves.   But the guard came off, and had nearly reached the landing-place, when they were ordered to face about, march back, and re-occupy their former posts; which they instantly obeyed, and continued at them, until called off to cross the ferry.   Whoever has seen troops in a similar situation, or duly contemplates the human heart in such trials, well know how to appreciate the conduct of these brave men, on this occasion."—ED.

great a number of men, stated I think at nine thousand, with cannon and stores, in one night, was, no doubt, a masterly movement, though not classible perhaps with the great retreats. The Memoirs of the Duke of Sully relate an operation very similar to it, and to which much applause is given. This was achieved by the Prince of Parma, whose army, lying between Rouen and Caudebec, was in the night transported across the Seine, and thus preserved from the destruction that impended from the forces of Henry the IVth, ready to fall upon it in the morning. " Could it appear otherwise," observes the writer, "than a fable or an illusion? Scarce could the king and his army trust the evidence of their own eyes."

After a comfortable breakfast, which I got at the coffee-house, I met with Colonel Melchior of the commissary department. Being one of my old and particular Philadelphia acquaintances, he offered me his bed to repair my want of rest. I had not slept for two nights; and as my brother, a lad of about nineteen and an ensign in the regiment, had undergone the same fatigue, I took him along with me, and locking the door of the apartment to exclude intruders, we snatched a refreshing nap of five or six hours: after which, we felt ourselves alert and ready for the farther tasks which duty might impose.

General WASHINGTON has been censured for risking his army upon Long Island, and General Howe for permitting it to escape with impunity.* Reasoning from the facts which have evolved, the blame in both cases, seems to be well founded. But this is not the mode of judging contingent events. In conducting the war on our side, a great variety of interests was to be consulted. Our

---

* SPARKS ascribes the unfortunate issue of the Battle of Long Island, " to the illness of General GREENE. He had superintended the erection of the military works, and become thoroughly acquainted with the grounds. In the hope of his recovery, WASHINGTON deferred sending over a successor, till the urgency of affairs made it absolutely necessary ; and then General PUTNAM took the command, without any previous knowledge of the posts which had been fortified beyond the lines, or of the places by which the enemy would make their approach; nor had he time to acquire this knowledge before the action. The consequence was, that, although he was the commander on the day of the battle, he never went beyond the lines at Brooklyn, and could give no other orders than for sending out troops to meet the enemy at different points."—ED.

cities, were, if possible to be maintained, and no property to be sacrificed without the most manifest necessity, lest it might create disgust and disaffection.   Congress, also, was to be obeyed; in which body, no doubt, there was enough of local feeling.   Hence, New York must be defended; and if so, there was nothing wrong in risking an action on Long Island; it was even better than awaiting it in the city.   Add to this, that the combatants had not yet measured arms with each other; and General WASHINGTON was not without ground for hope, that his troops would prove equal to the invaders.   He knew the British were not invincible.   He had even seen them panic struck under Braddock and Dunbar, and was aware of their having been staggered by a handful of irregulars at Bunker's hill.   But it is sufficient for his exculpation, that the necessity of attempting the defence of New York, was too imperious to be dispensed with.   Otherwise, there can be no question, that with the unpromising army he commanded, he should have been extremely cautious of committing himself in insular posts.   No General will, of choice, convert his army into a garrison, and invite a siege.   Had this been done at New York, General Howe, by blockading it, would soon have reduced us to the necessity of starving, surrendering, or fighting our way out again; a few batteries and redoubts do not render a place capable of sustaining a siege, or had he preferred an assault, what fortifications were there to justify the assertion, that it was tenable for a single day?

As to General Howe, I have scarce a doubt that he might have carried the entrenchments at Brooklyn, and cut off the troops posted there.   Even without intercepting with his ships of war, the passage of East river, the retreat across it would have been sufficiently difficult and tardy, to have rendered the loss of much the greater portion of our army inevitable.   That the works would have been well defended and cost him a great many men, can neither be affirmed nor denied.   The feelings of raw troops are too uncertain to be calculated upon; and considering what had recently happened, it is rather to be presumed, that the defence would not have been obstinate.   But General Howe, it should be remembered, was yet a stranger to our circumstances and the character of our force.   Though he had just vanquished a part of it in the open field, the remainder was behind entrenchments, supported by redoubts; and he had cause for being cautious from what had happened at Bunker's hill. Besides, he probably reasoned as we at first did, that our losses might be more easily supplied than his own; and, from the boldness of Congress in declaring independence in defiance of the concentrated power of Britain, he had certainly grounds to conclude, that their resources were great and their army extremely numerous. In addition to these considerations, he had no reason to calculate on our precipitate retreat. He was preparing to attack us under the cover of batteries; and, in that case, might have been enabled to destroy the rear of our force with little loss to himself. It must, however, be admitted, that the character of Sir William's Generalship rather savoured of caution than enterprise.

CHAPTER VII.

Americans abandon New York.—Take post at Fort Washington.—Character of Officers.—Fire in New York.—Putnam.—Greene.—Promotions.—Fort Washington threatened.—Summoned by General Howe.—Americans attacked and retire.—Account of the Engagement.

On the thirty-first of August, the day after the retreat from Long Island, we marched beyond King's-bridge towards the Sound, and crossing the Brunx, encamped about eighteen or or twenty miles from the city of New York. I say encamped, though, in fact we had no canopy but the sky, and nothing between our bodies and the earth, but the clothes we had on, and the blanket which each of us carried along with him. We might, however, have lodged comfortably on the green sward, had not the imaginations of some of our party been still haunted by light horse; an alarm having been given in the night, whether in jest or earnest, I cannot say, that they had assailed us again. But it turned out to be nothing more than the scampering of a few colts, that were probably equally alarmed at seeing so many two-legged intruders extended on their feeding grounds.

My memory does not enable me to say how long we remained at this place; but I recollect we were soon joined by a portion of the army, among which was the regiment of Hazlet from Delaware. When the post was sufficiently strengthened to observe the motions of the enemy hovering in the Sound, and threatening the country about Frogs-point, we retook our old ground at Fort Washington. While here, we acted in detachment at Morrisania, then menaced by a body of the British, which had been thrown into Buchanan's and Montresors islands, lying in the mouth of Haerlem river, within two hundred or a hundred and fifty yards of the main land. I recollect, at least, that their sentinels appeared to be within gun-shot,* and that, one day, I had considerable difficulty in restraining Captain Miller of Magaw's regiment, who carried a rifle, from shooting one of them, which he had no doubt he could do. This was a kind of warfare which appeared to me both cruel and useless; and I reprobated it so earnestly, that for this time, I turned Miller from his purpose. But the carrying a rifle, is too apt to create an appetite for the savage mode of warfare which does its work in concealment; and makes a merit of destroying the enemy whenever and where-ever he may be found.

At the time of these movements, the main army very impro-perly still lingered at New York. There cannot remain a doubt, that this city should have been evacuated, as soon as possible, after the quitting of Long Island. This was as obvious to me then as it is now, and I had backed my opinion with the bet of a beaver hat, that there would be no attempt to defend it. It

---

* GENERAL HEATH states that "the chain of sentinels within half gun-shot of each other, were planted from one side of the shore to the other, and near the water passage between Morrisania and Montresors Island, which in some places is very narrow. The sentinels on the American side were ordered not to fire at those of the British, unless the latter began; but the British were so fond of beginning, that there was frequently a firing between them. This having been the case one day, and a British officer walking along the bank on the Montresors side, an American sentinel, who had been exchanging some shots with a British sentinel, seeing the officer, and concluding him to be better game, gave him a shot and wounded him. He was carried up to the house on the island. An officer with a flag soon came down to the creek, and called for the American officer of the picket, and informed him, that if the American sentinels fired any more, the commanding officer on the island would cannonade Colonel MORRIS' house in which the officers of the picket were quartered. The American officer immedi-ately sent to our General to inquire what answer should be returned. He was directed to inform the British officer, that the American sentinels had always been instructed not to fire on *sentinels*, unless they were first fired upon, and then to return the fire; that such would be their conduct: as to the cannonading of Colonel MORRIS' house, they might act their pleasure. The firing ceased for some time, but a raw Scotch sentinel, having been planted one day, he very soon after discharged his piece at an American sentinel, nearest to him, which was immediately returned. This brought down a British officer, who, calling to the American officers, observed, that 'he thought there was to be no firing between sentinels.' He was answered that their own began. 'He shall then pay for it.' The sentinel was directly after relieved, and the firing ceased, the sentinels be-coming so civil to each other, as to supply each other with tobacco by throwing it across the stream."—ED.

15*

appears from documents since published, that it was the opinion of the Commander-in-chief, that it should be abandoned, as well as of other officers in whom he principally confided, though not of the majority of the council of war. Not long after, however, the propriety of the measure became so apparent, that it was universally concurred in, and the place was given up, though not without a considerable loss of stores. Previously to this operation, our numbers had been much reduced by the desertion of great bodies of the militia, and some of the other troops that had been infected by their bad example, as appears from the letters of the General. A greater loss than themselves, was that of the arms and ammunition they took away with them. I very well recollect, that it was found necessary to post a guard at King's-bridge to stop the fugitives ; and that upon one of them being arrested with a number of *notions* in a bag, there was found among them, a cannon ball, which, he said, he was taking home to his mother for the purpose of pounding mustard. Such was the story; and though I was not a witness of the fact, I can vouch for its being entirely in character. An instance of shameful cowardice was also given by Parson's and Fellow's brigades (in which, their Generals, however, were not implicated) as mentioned in an official letter of the 16th of September : on this occasion I have understood that the General lost all patience, throwing his hat upon the ground in a transport of rage and indignation.* A day or two after this dastardly affair, better conduct was shown by some companies of Colonel Weedon's regiment from Virginia, and some rangers composed of volunteers from different New England regiments under the command of Major Leitch and Colonel Knolton, both of whom were mortally wounded.

The army now took a position upon the high grounds surrounding Fort Washington, comprehending the heights of Haer-

* According to General HEATH, this was on the 15th of September. He says, " Here the Americans, we are sorry to say, did not behave well ; and here it was as fame hath said; that GENERAL WASHINGTON threw his hat on the ground, exclaiming 'are these the men with which I am to defend America !' But several things may have weight here ;—the wounds received on Long Island were yet bleeding ; and the officers, if not the men, knew that the city was not to be defended."—ED.

lem and the difficult pass towards King's-bridge. A double row of lines was thrown up, nearly extending from Haerlem river to the Hudson, on the south, looking towards New York, of which General Howe was now in possession. General WASHINGTON appears to have had a good opinion of this post: but though certainly strong by nature and improved by entrenchments in its most accessible parts, its eligibility, for any other purpose, than that of a temporary encampment, was very questionable. It was liable to the same objection, as the posts of Brooklyn and New York. It was only open to the country on the side of King's-bridge; and consequently, the slightest demonstrations of the adversary, in that quarter, must have induced its abandonment, unless we should have been disposed for an encounter of similar difficulties to those, from which we were just extricated, and again trying the fortune of an escape across a river under the very paws of the enemy. But the idea, about this time, seems to have been taken up of making our resistance, *a war of posts;* or of disputing inch by inch, our ground. This sort of war, however, when referring to the operations of a weaker army, in a country without regular fortresses, appears to be scarcely practicable, unless it should have the good fortune to be protected by a succession of Thermopyles. There are few posts which may not be turned and blockaded by a superior force; and the experience of a campaign is sufficient to evince the fallacy of supposing a position to be good merely because its approaches are difficult.* The impropriety of remaining in the present one, was immediately perceived by Lee, who joined us about the middle of October. He declared at once against the policy of having any thing to do with the islands, about which we had been clinging so pertinaciously; and with a figure somewhat too bold for the genius of our patriotism, exclaimed, that "he would give Mr. Howe a *fee-simple* in them."

---

* This opinion is corroborated by General Sarrazin's observations in his His-tory of the War in Russia and Germany, on the post of Borodino, tending to show the facility of manœuvring Kutusoff out of it, and, of course, the impropriety of attacking such posts, if strong, since the holders of them may always be forced to abandon. To prove the justice of his assertion, he quotes Kutusoff's letter to the Emperor Alexander.

But before we permit ourselves to arraign the conduct of the Commander-in-chief, we ought to obtain a clear idea, of what his operations should have been.   Because, inferior to the foe, was he, therefore, to have kept at an awful distance from him? Would this have satisfied the country, or promoted the cause it had in' hand?   It had been buoyed up into an exalted opinion of its prowess; and thence expected fighting, if not victories. To have wholly shunned the conflict then, would have been a confession of a weakness, which, as the people were not prepared for, it was dangerous to expose: It would have been too sudden a descent from the high ground of independence.*

* Congress, in October, had *resolved*, "that Fort Washington be retained as long as possible." "This decision," says Sparks, "appears to have been partly in consequence of a resolve of Congress, passed five days before, desiring General Washington 'by every art, and at whatever expense, to obstruct effectually the navigation of the river between Fort Washington and Mount Constitution, as well to prevent the regress of the enemy's frigates lately gone up, as to hinder them from receiving succour.' On the following November, Washington wrote to Greene, then at Fort Lee, expressing his conviction, that the enemy would invest Fort Washington, and adding, 'I must recommend to you to give every attention in your power, and all the assistance you can, to that garrison.' In a letter to General Greene, dated 8th November, 1776, General Washington writes, 'If we cannot prevent vessels from passing up, and the enemy are possessed of the surrounding country, what valuable purpose can it answer to attempt to hold a post, from which the expected benefit cannot be had? I am, therefore, inclined to think, that it will not be prudent to hazard the men and stores at Fort Washington; but, as you are on the spot, I leave it to you to give such orders as to its evacuation, as you may judge best, and so far revoking the order given to Colonel Magaw to defend it to the last.'"

On the 16th of the same month, in a letter to General Lee, he announces, that Colonel Magaw "finding there was no prospect of retreating across the North River, surrendered the post." The loss of killed and wounded was not then known, but Washington believed it to have been considerable, from the length and severity of the engagement. In a subsequent letter he says, "Colonel Magaw could not get the men to man the lines, otherwise he would not have given up the Fort." The garrison at Fort Washington consisted of four Colonels, four Lieutenant-Colonels, five Majors, forty-six Captains, one hundred and seven Lieutenants, thirty-one Ensigns, one Chaplain, two Adjutants, two Quarter-masters, five Surgeons, two Commissaries, one Engineer, one Wagon-master, and 2607 privates. The censure that has been cast upon the Commander-in-chief in connexion with this surrender, prompts the extension of this note beyond what, under other circumstances, might be considered its proper limit. Like every other action of his life, the lapse of time, and the collection and concentration of authentic know-

About the middle of October, General Howe having drawn his main body to Frog's-point, the immediate necessity of a removal of our army from its present post became apparent; and was resolved on accordingly. It is not to be supposed, without ascribing an extreme want of discernment to our counsels, but that the danger of remaining on a strip of land embarrassed by the Hudson and the Sound, must have been perceived and duly estimated, before the arrival of General Lee. Nevertheless it seems to have been considered, that by hovering about New York, restricting the limits of the enemy, and thereby obliging him to have recourse to counteracting movements, the campaign might be consumed in fruitless operations. This mode of proceeding, extremely perilous, and only harassing to ourselves, may probably be referred in part to a proud military spirit, which

ledge, exhibits still more conspicuously, the wisdom and ability which always characterized his proceedings. In a letter to President REED, dated 22d August, 1779, caused, says Sparks, "by the tenour of Mr. Reed's letter, and by General LEE's *Queries* respecting the capture of Fort Washington, which were designed to cast blame and disparagement upon the Commander-in-chief"—General WASH-INGTON thus wrote: "When I came to Fort Lee, and found no measures taken towards an evacuation, in consequence of the order before mentioned; when I found General GREENE, of whose judgment and candour I entertained a good opinion, decidedly opposed to it; when I found other opinions so coincident with his; when the wishes of Congress to obstruct the navigation of the North River, which were delivered in such forcible terms, recurred; when I knew that the easy communication between the different parts of the army, then separated by the river, depended upon it; and, lastly, when I considered that our policy led us to waste the campaign without coming to a general action on the one hand, or suffering the enemy to overrun the country on the other, I conceived that every impediment, that stood in their way, was a means to answer these purposes;—these, when thrown into the scale with those opinions, which were opposed to an evacuation, caused that warfare in my mind, and hesitation, which ended in the loss of the garrison; and, being repugnant to my own judgment of the advisableness of attempting to hold the post, filled me with the greater regret. The two great causes which led to this misfortune, and which I have before recited, as well, perhaps as my reasoning upon it, which occasioned the delay, were concealed from public view, and of course left the field of censure quite open for any and every labourer, who inclined to work in it; and afforded a fine theme for the pen of a malignant writer who is less regardful of facts than of the point he wants to establish, where he has the field wholly to himself, where concealment of a few circumstances answers his purposes, or where a small transposition of them will give a very different complexion to the same thing."—ED.

could not brook the supposed disgrace of flying before the foe, and in part to that prime source of our disasters, short enlistments and the militia system.   For want of a permanent established force, which would have placed our cause above the reach of vulgar opinion, the public mind was perpetually to be consulted.   The popularity of the measure declaratory of independence was suspended on our chance of success; and this would principally be estimated by the ground we maintained or lost.   Hence, as every acre had its political value, the defensive warfare on the large scale, could not safely be adopted; nor for that reason, can the Fabian fame, of "never having yielded the public safety to clamour," be fully ascribed to General WASHINGTON.

While the main army remained at the heights of Haerlem, a period of five weeks, from about the middle of September to the middle of October, we (Shee's and Magaw's regiments) constituted a part of it, and did duty accordingly.   It was my chance to be on guard on the night of the fire at New York,* on the picket, advanced about a mile in front of our lines.   For a considerable extent, the heavens appeared in flames, and from the direction of the light, I could not doubt there was a conflagration in the city.   I might have been distant from it about nine miles; and had not my situation been overlooked by a hill directly in front, the cause might perhaps have been distinctly developed.   Whether this fire was produced by accident or design, has never, I believe, been ascertained.   By the British it was considered as proceeding from us.   A few weeks after, having, for some purpose which I do not recollect, been sent, together with Captain Beatty, with a flag, we talked with the officer who met us, about the extent of the fire and its cause.   He said he was unacquainted with the cause, but presumed Mr. WASHINGTON's people knew more about it than they did.†

The antipathy prevailing between the southern and eastern troops, had been the cause of a court martial, of which I was a

---

* This it appears from General HEATH's "Memoirs," was on the night between the 20th and 21st of September.

† This officer was right according to Judge Henry. See his account of this fire, page 185, of his "Campaign against Quebec."

member, upon the conduct of Lieutenant Stewart, of Smallwood's regiment, better known by his subsequent title of Major Jack Stewart. He had been arrested by General Silliman, on account of some alleged disrepect or disobedience to that officer. As the majority of the court were southern men, it was not at all wonderful that Stewart was soon acquitted with honour. In so contemptible a light were the New England men regarded, that it was scarcely held possible to conceive a case, which could be construed into a reprehensible disrespect of them. Thinking so highly as I now do of the gentlemen of this country, the recollection is painful, but the fact must not be dissembled: Even the celebrated General Putnam, riding with a hanger belted across his brawny shoulders, over a waistcoat without sleeves (his summer costume) was deemed much fitter to head a band of sicklemen or ditchers, than musketeers. He might be brave, and had certainly an honest manliness about him; but it was thought, and perhaps with reason, that he was not what the time required. We had a regular army to oppose, and this could only be done by discipline and regular soldiership.* Neither did General

---

* Mr. Graydon in a note, writes: "That General Putnam was deficient in these points, may be inferred from the following passage in a letter dated 15th January, 1777, from General Washington to General Reed: 'Many days ago I wrote to General Putnam, supposing him to be at Princeton. What he can be doing at Crosswicks, I know not, after my repeated wishes to hear of him at Princeton. Surely he is there by this time!'"

The quotation from General Washington's letter certainly authorizes no such inference; and the sneer of our author is unjust. General Putnam, always distinguished, proved himself equal to every emergency, and this, notwithstanding his defective education, which, in truth, was extremely restricted. He was bred, from his earliest boyhood, to agricultural pursuits. If wanting in polish, which, from the nature of his occupations, may be admitted, the deficiency was more than counterbalanced by his noble and disinterested zeal in the cause which he defended with unwavering fidelity, and of which, he was at once an ornament and a support. In 1755, at the commencement of the war between England and France, at the age of thirty-seven, he was appointed commander of a company and joined the army near Crown Point. In 1757, he was promoted to the rank of Major. During the entire war he was distinguished for his bravery and ability, and in 1764, retired to his country-home. He was soon called to fill several offices in Salem, Massachusetts, his native-town, and to represent it in the General Assembly. When hostilities commenced between England and the Colonies, "Putnam received the intelligence while ploughing in the middle of a field; he

Greene himself, shine with all the *eclat* that his character has since deservedly acquired.*

There were none, by whom an unofficer-like appearance and deportment could be less tolerated than by a city-bred Mary-lander, who, at this time, was distinguished by the most fashion-ably cut coat, the most *macaroni* cocked hat, and hottest blood in the union; if there was any exception, it was to be found among the children of the sun of a still more southern location. Among all these, the point of honour was maintained, as it still seems to be, with considerable punctilio ; and the dashing man-ner of Stewart, and indignant tone of Captain Smith (now Gene-ral Smith,) who testified in his behalf, impressed the court, I remember, with a high idea of their military qualities: and brave men they certainly were—a praise, indeed, due to the officers from Maryland generally; as well as to those of Small-wood's battalion, which behaved well and suffered severely on

left his plough there, unyoked his team, and, without changing his clothes, set off for the scene of action. He levied a regiment under Colonial authority in Con-necticut, and marched to Cambridge. His Colony appointed him a Major-General, and Congress soon after confirmed to him the same rank in the Continental army. About this time the British offered him the rank of Major-General in His Majesty's service, with a pecuniary remuneration for his treason; but the temptation could not influence him." He served throughout the war, and died May 29th, 1790, aged seventy-three years.—Ed.

* In what respect GENERAL GREENE was deficient, we are not informed. We may infer, however, that the author has reference to his deportment, also. His father was an artizan, and a Quaker preacher, near the town of Warwick in Rhode Island. An ignorant and illiterate man, unable properly to estimate the value and advantages of education, but who is said to have been very careful of the moral and religious instruction of his children. GREENE was a self-educated man. In 1770, he was elected to the State Legislature, and in 1774, enrolled himself as a private in a company called the Kentish guards. "After the battle of Lexington, the State of Rhode Island raised what was termed an army of observation, and chose GREENE its commander, with the title of Major-General. His elevation from the ranks may give some idea of the estimation in which his military talents were held." His services were of the most brilliant character, and it has been said that WASHINGTON was anxious, in the event of his decease, that GREENE should be his successor. It is very generally admitted, that of all the officers engaged in the revolutionary contest, GREENE was most eminently qualified to succeed to the high command, if death had deprived the country of the services of WASHINGTON.

GENERAL GREENE, died, within three years after the termination of the war, at the age of forty-four years.—Ed.

Long Island and at White Plains. Its officers exhibited a martial appearance by a uniform of scarlet and buff; which, by the by, savoured somewhat of a servility if imitation, not fully according with the independence we had assumed. The common soldiers from the east and south, did not much better assimilate than the officers; but a traffic was soon established between the former and the Pennsylvanians. This consisted in a barter of the ration of rum for that of molasses. The Yankees did not care for the first, and our Irishmen could very well dispense with the latter. It has been supposed that the Pennsylvania line consisted chiefly of Irish, but this would by no means appear from my company. Out of seventy-three men, I find there were twenty from Ireland, four from England, two from Scotland, two from Germany, and the remaining forty-five were Americans. To these, adding four American officers, the proportion of Irish is but little more than a fourth.

The official letters of General Washington ascertain the movement of the army towards White Plains to have commenced on the twentieth of October. We were very desirous of being attached to it, both for the sake of variety, and the better opportunity of seeing service and acquiring distinction; but to our extreme chagrin, found that we were to remain in our prison. It was perhaps supposed, we had an affection for the work of our hands; but if so, nothing could be more erroneous. We were weary of the sameness of garrison duty, which, from the great extent of ground we had to guard, became very severe. It was not unusual for a captain to be on guard twice a week, and a subaltern oftener.

Our battalion was now commanded by Lieutenant-Colonel Cadwalader;* Colonel Shee, having before the march of the army, obtained leave of absence to visit his family, and converted that leave into an entire abdication of his command. This was certainly an extraordinary incident, and one I have never heard accounted for. Whatever cause he might have had for disgust, or

---

* COLONEL LAMBERT CADWALADER.—He was made prisoner on the surrender of Fort Washington, but, at the request of General Prescott, who, when himself a prisoner, at Philadelphia, had received attentions from Colonel Cadwalader's father—he was immediately released without parole by Sir William Howe.—ED.

for conceiving that our affairs were tending to ruin, his duty seemed too imperious to be relinquished; and when Colonel Cadwalader acquainted some of us with his suspicion and indeed conviction, that he would not return, we were truly astonished. But though I attempt not to apologize for his conduct, I must say, that he had some useful talents for the command of a regiment. He was remarkably attentive to the necessary accomodations of every kind, whether of food, clothing, tents, arms or accoutrements; indefatigable in his endeavours to promote discipline, and even enthusiastic in what regarded the neatness and soldier-like appearance of the corps. He was, moreover, gentlemanly and agreeable in his manners. Whether his promptness in discerning difficulties overmatched his fortitude in sustaining them, I venture not to say; but he left us in the manner stated. Mr. Shee is no longer in a situation to be hurt by a recognition of his delinquency, if such it was; nor is it mentioned from a disrespect to his memory. Such a motive I disclaim. With me, he was ever friendly, and free from party rancour: personally, I liked the man, and accepted his civilities, which I never failed to receive on meeting him in Philadelphia.

An event that took place a few weeks after the retirement of the Colonel, had almost tempted some of us to follow his illaudable example. The committee, or council of safety, as it was now called, had undergone a regeneration; and consisted, with perhaps an exception or two, of a new set of members. Persons acquainted with the genius of liberty, will not be surprised at this. To borrow the language of French paradox, there is nothing permanent in a revolution, but change. In the auction of popularity, the bid is ever more attended to than the inclination or ability to pay; and the most boldly-dashing patriot is ever the most successful one. So it proved in the council. New men, inflated with a little brief authority, are always glad of an occasion for displaying their consequence; and partial to the source from whence they derive their importance, they are ever ready to recognise aristocratic oppression. In this spirit, they lent an ear to all the idle, ill-founded reports of the cowardly, skulking soldiers, who, under pretence of sickness, or otherwise, had found their way to Philadelphia. These fellows told the council that

their Captains had cheated them, and the Council, without inquiry, seemed to take the matter as proved. They accordingly
wrote an illiberal letter to Colonel Cadwalader on the subject,
which he thought it his duty to lay before us, though despising
the low spirit that had dictated it. In addition to this affront,
this same body, who still retained the power of appointment to
military command, went on in the manufacture of Majors and
Colonels, in utter disregard of the claims of the officers in service,
and sometimes, from the coursest materials. An hour's visit to
the camp, seemed to have more merit in their eyes, than daily
and nightly duty in it; and a little self-puffing, with due incense,
could hardly fail to propitiate these great dispensers of commissions.* One instance of their propensity to make promotions,
occurred in the case of an Adjutant, who had been enclosed
by the Hessians in the battle of Long Island. He contrived
to conceal himself in the woods 'till dark, when, from his
understanding and speaking German, he was enabled to answer
and elude their sentries; and by so doing to get back to our lines.
For this piece of address, which consisted merely in good hiding

* Similar practices and treatment of the officers doing duty on the Canada
frontier in the war of the Madison Administration, in aid of their Imperial ally,
have excited a similar remark. In the spirited address to the public, dated
Buffalo, June 12th, 1815, and signed by Col. Robert Purdy and William Thomas,
in behalf of the officers of the Line, and of the Hospital and Medical Staff, is this
passage:

" They regret, too, that a winter's campaign at Washington should often avail
more than seven in the field; and that those who remain at their posts on a
frozen frontier, in the performance of their duty, should thereby lose their grade,
to give place to some who have been basking in the sunshine of favouritism,
and feasting on the delicacies of the metropolis." The just inference from such
facts as these, is, that parasites are as much at home at democratic, as at royal
courts, the eternal babble about intrigue and corruption in the latter notwithstanding. By observations of this kind, I would, forasmuch as in me lies, prevent the deception which popular forms of government impose on benevolent
minds. Whatever other excellencies they may possess, Justice, Honour and Generosity are not among their attributes, and whatever of patriotism and virtue
they may boast, 'tis certainly not the man of probity who succeed the best in
them. Displease whom I may by such avowals of the truth, my mite shall be
contributed to undeceiving the world; and I should hold myself a traitor to my
fellow men, if, undertaking to promulgate the results of my experience, I should
conceal or misrepresent facts on which the happiness of future generations may
essentially depend.

and speaking his mother tongue, the council invested him with a *majority*, at once jumping him over the heads of all the Captains and subalterns in the line. This Adjutant was Menzies, already spoken of as a fencing-master in Philadelphia; and who first appeared there in the less dignified character of a dancer on the stage, a circumstance which rendered his preferment still more galling. I should be unjust, however, if I did not say, that Menzies, though at this time little known, turned out to be an honest, worthy man, attentive to duty, correct in his demeanour, and generally esteemed, though certainly not for talents that could throw others into shade, or justify his irregular advancement.

Conscious of integrity, soured by hard duty, and smarting under the reflection, that while we were sustaining the severest privations, the very men who imputed fraud to us, were snug and secure at their fire-sides, we declared that we would not remain a day longer in a service, at once so thankless and preposterous. Colonel Cadwalader, to whom we made the declaration, remonstrated against its rashness, while he admitted the enormity of the provocation. He observed to us, that nothing could justify such a step in the heat of a campaign; that it would ruin us in the public opinion, and embitter our future lives; that it would recoil upon ourselves, and be an everlasting blister to our sensibility. In short, he said every thing which a sensible, prudent man, acquainted with the world, could say upon the occasion. We felt the full force of his reasoning and acquiesced in it; though I have not an idea that one of us would have put the threat in execution, had we been left entirely to ourselves. Our vapouring was the effect of sudden passion, which at length vented itself in the following letter, written and sent off with nearly as little consideration, as we had used in taking up our first resolution.

"GENTLEMEN,

"Were it not that some expressions of resentment are natural to the human mind when it feels itself injured, we should disdain the meanness of telling you, how much we were mortified on seeing your letter to Colonel Cadwalader, containing your illiberal charge against the Captains of his battalion, of withholding the pay due to their men.

"For the same reason, we cannot forbear mentioning our dissatisfaction at the late appointments and promotions, wherein some that have never been in service, are preferred to those who have undergone the toils and dangers of a severe campaign, and others of an inferior rank to those of a superior, without any proof, or, as we presume, suggestion of misbehaviour in the latter.

"As to the accusation of fraud! we are above it. We mean not a vindication: to attempt it, would betray a meanness which might almost justify the base suspicion. In a word, we deny the charge, and rest perfectly easy under a consciousness that it cannot be supported.

"As to the promotions, we shall only say, that the man who feels no indignity upon such occasions, wants an essential qualification for a soldier, and is, in our opinion, unworthy to bear a commission.

"But do not imagine, gentlemen, by this, that we are envious of superior merit. For our parts, we pretend to very little; and in any other service, for merit is rated by comparison, we should think ourselves inadequate to our present appointments. We entered into the army not for pay or preferment, but to serve our country to the best of our poor abilities: 'Tis this alone which keeps us in at this hour, as we conceive, and in so doing, we hope we may not incur the imputation of vanity, that notwithstanding the insignificance of our services, the cause as well as our honour, might suffer from our resignations. However, we mean not to continue in the army, nor do we intend to accept of commissions on the new establishment; and it is a matter of the utmost indifference to us, how soon the council of safety may take it into their heads to appoint others more to their satisfaction in the room of, gentlemen,

"Your most obedient servants."

This angry epistle was signed, I think, by five of us. We heard no more of it; but in the sequel, we had reason to wish that it never had been written; and were convinced, that silence under suffering, is generally, if not always, wise.

The *denouement* of the drama, in which we were acting a part, was now rapidly approaching. After the action of White Plains, of which, as I was not there, I shall say nothing, General Howe

16*

with his army, was falling down upon our post; and we had little doubt, that his object was to invest it without delay. On receipt of this intelligence, Colonel Cadwalader proposed to me to walk with him to the Fort, (for we were now stationed in the lines of Haerlem heights,) that we might endeavour, by an examination of its means of defence, to collect, whether it could be the design to hold it. We went and reconnoitered it, and the result was, that it was absolutely untenable, and must be abandoned; though still, all the measures taking, seemed to point to a defence. I will not undertake minutely to describe the situation of the Fort, as my memory might not enable me to do it truly. But I recollect, as it has been observed by General Lee, that there were no barracks, or casemates, or fuel, or water within the body of the place. It was an open, earthern construction, with ground at a short distance on the back of it, equally high if not higher; without a ditch of any consequence, if there was a ditch at all; no outworks, an incipient one on the north, not deserving the appellation, or any of those exterior, multiplied obstacles and defences, that, so far as I can judge, could entitle it to the name of a fortress, in any degree capable of sustaining a siege. It required no parallels to approach it: the citadel was at once within reach of the assailants. In addition to this, there were no magazines of any kind prepared; and it is stated in the *Annual Register*, which carried on the history of the war, that with its other deficiencies, there was not found in it ammunition adequate to the shortest defence. Yet, it was to be defended, as will soon appear: and Gordon, in his history, gives a letter from Colonel Magaw, stating that he could hold out until the latter part of December, an opinion which shows him to have been more miserably deficient in judgment than ever we supposed him to be. He had heard of sieges being protracted for months and even years; he had a good opinion of the spirit of his garrison; and, as the place he had to defend was called a Fort, and had cannon it, he thought the deuce was in it if he could not hold out a few weeks. Such, probably, were the *data* of his calculation; nor, though friendly to the memory of a sincere and gallant man, can I suppose them a jot better.

While we remained in this incertitude in respect to our destination, and the main armies were manœuvering above us about the Brunx, Lord Percy, who commanded the British troops on York Island, thought proper, one day, to appear in force in the plains of Haerlem, lying between his and our advanced posts. It was on Sunday, the day his lordship was supposed to prefer for his military operations.* As we were both too insignificant and too distant to admit the supposition that it was intended as a diversion, in favour of General Howe, his object probably was to put our countenance to the test; to feel our pulse, and if he found it tremulous, to push us into the Fort. But, on the other hand, if he found it full and regular, it was only to bluster awhile with his artillery; skirmish a little with his small arms, and retire. This was all, at least, that came of a very pompous display. We had one field piece with which we answered his fire; and from the carcass of a white horse, which was left to bleaching on the ground he occupied, we had satifactory evidence that our balls had reached him. It was not our business to quit the high ground in force, although some of our men were permitted to skirmish with the light parties which approached us. The firing was pretty warm, and a few men killed and wounded on either side. An Irish lad of about eighteen, who belonged to my company, killed a British soldier and brought off his arms; which on the evening parade, were formally presented to him by Colonel Cadwalader, in reward of his bravery. History has preserved no record of this affair, which, trifling as it was, is as well deserving of memorial, as many others that have been preserved in the transactions of our *petite guere.* Had it passed between the grand armies, it would without doubt have been taken notice of; but as it did not, we are reduced to the unfortunate situation of Sir John Falstaff at the battle of Shrewsbury, in being obliged, though late, to attend to its booking ourselves. The celebrated Thomas Paine,† how-

---

* It was probably, on the 27th of October, as it is noted in General HEATH's Memoirs, that in the forenoon of that day, a heavy cannonade was heard towards Fort Washington, and as this was the day of the action at White Plains, it is probable there was a concert between Generals HOWE and PERCY.

† When this man's pamphlet, "Common Sense," first appeared, Dr. FRANKLIN was generally considered as the real author. Paine but the ostensible one. It made considerable noise, and certainly put things in a new and strong light, but,

ever, happened to witness the proceeding from Fort Lee, and gave us a handsome puff in one of the Philadelphia papers of the day.

Another affair, which never got beyond the precincts of our secluded position, was the carrying a Hessian picket on the side of King's-bridge. This was achieved by one of our sergeants and a few men, but three or four days before we were taken. The officer of the guard was killed; and the sergeant, with the savage exultation of one of Homer's heroes, appeared in his uniform on the parade.

It was now November, and the nights becoming cold. It was the season, too, for north-easterly storms, one of which is rendered memorable to me, from a circumstance of some interest which accompanied it. I was upon guard with Lieutenant Davidson, of our battalion, at a place distinguished by the appellation of *The point of rocks*, which skirted the road leading to King's-bridge. This was our most advanced picket towards New York, and only separated from that of the enemy by a valley a few hundred yards over. The night, as already mentioned, was extremely raw, rainy and tempestuous; and the only shelter the spot afforded was an old caboose, which had been placed here by way of guard-

---

to a sober mind, unheated by controversy, there seems but little in it, to enforce the conclusions it aims at. It made the author, however, conspicuous, and introduced him to the notice of the principal Whigs of the day. Hence, his good reception at Head Quarters, and acquaintance with the Commander-in-chief, whom he seems to have considered from that time, as embarked with him in the general cause of reforming, republicanizing, and democritizing the world; than which nothing was more foreign to the views of the General, or those of the others, who took a lead in the early stage of the contest. One of the most untoward consequences of a successful resistance of government, is the unavoidable association in the undertaking, of the worst men with the best, of fools, fanatics, system-mongers, reformers and *philosophers*, with men of sense, moderation and virtue, who, wishing to stop when the true object of the controversy is attained, are seldom suffered to do it, or, if fortunate enough to prevail, they are, thenceforth viewed with suspicion and charged with apostacy. Thus General WASHINGTON is accused by this incendiary, of having deserted his principles, because of his not aiding and comforting him in his design of first revolutionizing England, and then France; and that sincere friend of the General, Mr. JEFFERSON, does his best to give colour to the charge, by fostering Paine, as a persecuted patriot, and formally escorting him in a public vessel to this country from France.

house. A kind of chimney had been built at the mouth of it, and a fire here in calm weather, rendered it tolerably comfortable; but at this time, the smoke produced and driven into the cabin by the storm, could not be endured; neither was the shelter from the driving rain by any means sufficient: we were dripping wet. In this miserable situation, Davidson proposed our going to a deserted house on the low ground directly across the road, where we could have a fire, and be dry and comfortable. But this I refused to do, since, though not more than thirty or forty yards from our post, and though rather an extension than a dereliction of it, yet it varied the station as to ourselves. The non-commissioned officers and the rest of the guard were, indeed, to remain there, but in case of disaster there would be blame, and the responsibility was upon us, and particularly upon myself. In this resolution, I for a long time persisted against the repeated importunities of my companion, who ingeniously obviated my objections, until at length, the storm rather increasing than abating, I consented about midnight to go to the house, first taking the precaution to continue the line of sentinels from the point of rocks across the road and round the building at some distance from it, so that it was impossible it should be approached by the enemy unperceived, should he endeavour to grope his way into unknown hostile ground, in one of the darkest and most dismal nights that can be conceived. We had located ourselves in an outer room, where we had a good fire, and had already pretty well dried ourselves. Davidson was stretched along a bench fixed to the wall, half asleep, if not wholly so, and I was sitting before the fire, when a sudden noise of feet and voices reached the door. The latch was lifted, and as I rose up, not without considerable alarm, the first object that presented itself was a British soldier, with his musket and fixed bayonet in his hand. Who are you? said I, a deserter! "No deserter," was the answer. My emotion did not prevent my preserving a pretty good countenance, though my first impression was, that we were surprised, and should be bayonetted out of hand. But this idea was scarcely formed, when the appearance of one of my own men behind the British soldier, changed it to a more pleasing one, and justified, if it did not induce, the addition of the term *deserter*, to the question of *who are you*? In fact, he was a deserter; but though in the very act of committing the crime he revolted against its opprobrium. I understood him, and softened down the ungraciousness of my salutation, by asking him if he had come over to us. He answered, yes. Our sentinel had done his duty, but awkwardly, in not having disarmed the soldier, and introduced him in a less questionable shape.

The bustle of the incident having completely roused Davidson, and set him upon his legs, we fell to questioning our refugee. He called himself Broderick, was an intelligent fellow, and brought with him the last newspaper from New York. He had for some time, he said, projected coming over to us, and had availed himself of this stormy night to put his design in execution. By means of the darkness, he had been enabled to separate himself from his comrades without their perceiving it, and had probably got to our sentries before they discovered him to be gone. He informed us that we might expect to be attacked in six or eight days at farthest, as some time had been employed in transporting heavy artillery to the other side of the Haerlem, and as the preparations for the assault were nearly completed. Among other things, he told us, that our situation at this house was a very unsafe one, as their patroles, still speaking as a Briton, passed very near it, and might easily sweep us off; and indeed he appeared uneasy at the idea while he staid with us. This was not long. I put him under the care of a trusty sergeant, with orders to guard him vigilantly, and to take him to head quarters, as soon as it should be light enough to find the way there. The hint we had received in regard to the enemy's proximity, and still more our own knowledge of the comparative insecurity of our present station with the one we had left, induced us to return to the latter, *maugre* the comforts of a snug room and good fire. We accordingly drew in our sentinels, and repaired to the caboose, where we weathered out the remainder of the night, by this time pretty well advanced.

The deserter's information turned out to be correct, as in not more than eight or ten days, I think, Colonel Magaw, the commandant of the fort, was summoned by General Howe to surrender it. He returned the usual answer, that he would defend it to the last extremity. This was announced to us at evening parade by Colonel Cadwalader, who in a few words put us in mind of what

our country and our honour demanded of us, and enjoined it both
on officers and men to see that their arms and ammunition were
in order, and to hold themselves in readiness to take their posts
before day-light the next morning.   The plan of defence adopted
by Colonel Magaw, was, instead of cooping up his garrison in the
fort, to draw it out into the post which had been occupied by the
main army.   This consisted of the strong grounds towards King's-
bridge on the north, the elevated, steep and rocky bank of Haerlem river on the east, and the entrenchments on the south; the
western limit or rear of the position, being the Hudson river, commanded to a certain extent by Forts Washington and Lee on
either side.   Although I have always supposed that this post would
require at least ten thousand men for its support, perhaps in that
number I am much below the mark, as I find it stated by the
King of Prussia in his history of the seven years war, that sixteen
thousand men were very inadequate to the defence of Berlin, three
miles in circumference, say nine or ten of our miles.*   Now the
circuit to be defended by Magaw was scarcely less, if I have not
much forgotten its dimensions, than four or five miles: the scale
in the map of Chief-Justice Marshall's Life of Washington, would
make it not less than seven: And to do this, he had *nominally*
something more than two thousand soldiers, *really* little more than
half their number: For I cannot set any great value upon the
militia poured in upon us, on the evening before, and on the
morning of the engagement.   My complaisance to the sovereign
people will not carry me so far as to compliment them with being
soldiers without an iota of discipline or ever having seen an enemy,

---

* A case perhaps still more in point occurred during the same war, when General Fonquet with ten thousand six hundred and eighty men, undertook to defend
the post of Landshut, at which there were redoubts, against General Laudohn with
an army of thirty-four thousand men.   A particular account of this is to be found
in the 13th volume of the King of Prussia's works.   The force of Fonquet was
deemed wholly insufficient, as there were intervals of ground of two thousand
paces or more left undefended.—We had intervals perhaps proportionably large,
that we were unable to man; hence, if General Fonquet received the warmest
approbation of the king his master for his unsuccessful attempt, (for he was beaten
and made prisoner,) it is surely unnecessary for the American historian to seek
an apology for the loss of Fort Washington in the rawness of some of the troops,
to whom its defence was committed.

even though every tenth man among them were a Cæsar in valour, or a Cato in patriotism.* Several individuals, however, of this description of force behaved bravely.

I cannot give a stronger proof of my ill opinion of the Fort, than when I say, that of the alternatives presented to Colonel Magaw of confining his defence to it, or of extending his operations to so large a circuit, he adopted the right one in choosing the latter. It might indeed be made a question whether the defence should not have been restricted to the oblong hill on which the Fort was erected: But this ground being considerably weaker than that of the banks of the Haerlem, (taking the river into consideration,) the temptation to prefer the latter both for this reason, and because it had somewhat of the advantage of an outwork in keeping the assailants at a distance, always a *desideratum* with the besieged, might have prevailed with a more experienced commander than Magaw. I have no doubt, however, that the works and defences of the fortress should have comprehended the whole of this hill, called Mount Washington, in which case, with adequate preparation and magazines, it might have stood a siege.† There was yet another mode which would, in some degree, have contracted the position: and this was, instead of manning the outer entrenchments towards New York to have placed the men in the inner one, and upon the high grounds about Colonel Roger Morris's house. This would have shortened the front on Haerlem river, and by more compacting the force, have put its several parts into a better condition of mutual succour and support. But, besides, that this disposition would not have very considerably abridged the circuit to be defended,

---

* So much is risked in speaking thus of militia, that too many accessories cannot be brought to sustain the assertion. General WASHINGTON thus wrote to General REED after the affairs of Trenton and Princeton: "If the militia cannot be prevailed upon to restrain the foraging parties, and to annoy and harass the enemy in their excursions and upon a march, they will be of very little use to us, as I am sure they never can be brought fairly up to an attack in any serious affair."

† Mr. Stedman, in his History of the War, blames Colonel Magaw for suffering his men, upon being driven from their outposts to crowd into the Fort instead of forming upon this hill: But, improperly, I presume, as the Hessians must have been in possession of the north end of the hill, as soon as Rawlings was driven from it.

and that it might have been liable to some positive objections I am not aware of, the *desideratum* already adverted to, would naturally induce a preference of the farther lines; and no doubt the calculation was, that after fighting to the utmost in the first, we might fight again in the second.   In fact, the idea of taking an extensive range, and equally resisting in every part the compression to the centre, the effect and advantage of regular fortifications sufficiently manned, is extremely plausible and seducing; insomuch, that none but an old General who has been taught by long experience to know the importance of adhering to rules of proportion, as well in the management of animate as inanimate machinery, will have the boldness to disregard it.   Whether these last two schemes of defence or either of them, occurred to our Commander, I do not know; but if they did occur, they were probably contemplated as dernier resorts, or efforts in reserve, which, it would be time enough to employ, when our first exertions should have been overpowered.   The same reasoning might have induced General Greene to suppose, that after slaughtering a host of the enemy, we might methodically withdraw into the citadel of Fort Washington: and then, provided each of us had killed his man, and thus fulfilled the object of the operation, if any object it had, we might have been snugly slipped over the Hudson, as erst we had been over the East river.   But *in bello non licet bis errare*, we should beware of repeating a mistake in war; and how this fine project was marred and the garrison put *hors de combat* will now be seen.   I repeat, however, that the error was in attempting to defend the place, not in the disposition of the troops, which, all things considered, was perhaps, as advantageous as possible.

But supposing Fort Washington tenable, "what single purpose," as it has been observed by General Lee, "did it answer to keep it?   Did it cover, did it protect a valuable country?   Did it prevent the enemy's ships from passing and repassing with impunity?"   No; but we had been too much in the habit of evacuating posts, and it was high time to correct the procedure.   This garrison must stand, because it had been hitherto too fashionable to run away; and Pennsylvania and Maryland must

17

pay for the retreating alacrity of New England.* If any thing
better can be made of General Greene's motives for retaining
the post, as mentioned in General WASHINGTON's official letter
to Congress, I am willing to take to myself the discredit of .per-
version. If what I say should be thought to implicate the Commander-in-chief, and to impugn his decision, I cannot help it.
A good man he undoubtedly was, nor will party malignity be
ever able to deprive him of the fame of a truly great one. But
my veneration for truth, is even greater than that for his character; nor will my admiration of his virtues induce me to say, that
his military career was without a blemish.†

On the sixteenth of November, before day-break, we were at
our post in the lower lines of Haerlem heights; that is, our regiment and Magaw's, and some broken companies of Miles's and
other battalions, principally from Pennsylvania. This might be
called our right wing, and was under the command of Colonel
Cadwalader; our left, extending to the Hudson above, and on
the north side of the fort towards King's-bridge, was commanded
by Colonel Rawlings‡ of Maryland, who had there his own regiment of riflemen, and probably some other troops; though as the
position was narrow, numbers were not so essential to it, as to
other parts of the general post. The front or centre extending
a considerable distance along Haerlem river,§ was committed to

* Once for all let me be understood as only alluding in these remarks to the
bad constitution of the New England troops; and by no means to the people
generally, who have no doubt the means of furnishing as good officers as any
other part of the Union. But from their shameful inattention to it, this campaign,
the southern officers were warranted in their indignation.

† Subsequent developments prove, as we have shown, that the opinion of General WASHINGTON was adverse to the course which circumstances beyond his control, compelled him to adopt. If the information, since so faithfully collected and
concentrated by the indefatigable SPARKS, had been within reach of our author,
we have too high an opinion of his candour to suppose that he would have indulged in a strain of remark as unjust as it is painful to peruse.—ED.

‡ COLONEL MOSES RAWLINGS.—General WASHINGTON speaks of him in his letter
to John Augustine Washington, 19th November, 1776: "By General Greene's
account the enemy have suffered greatly on the north side of Fort Washington.
Colonel Rawlings' regiment was posted there, and behaved with great spirit."—
ED.

§ In calling this the front, I conform to Judge Marshall's description of the

the militia of the Flying Camp, and Colonel Magaw placed himself in the most convenient station for attending to the whole,
having selected one or two officers to assist him as aids-de-camp.
I think it was between seven and eight o'clock, when they gave
us the first shot from one of their batteries on the other side of
Haerlem river. It was well directed, at a cluster of us that
were standing together observing their movements; but it fell
short by about ten or fifteen yards, and bounded over the spot
we had precipitately abandoned. In correcting this error they
afterwards shot too high, and did us no harm; at least, while I
remained in this part of the field, which though enfiladed or
rather exposed in the rear, was too distant to be very seriously
annoyed. They had better success in front, killing a man with
a cannon ball, belonging to our pickets, which they drove in.
Soon after, they approached the lines in great force under cover
of a wood, in the verge of which they halted, and slowly began
to form, giving us an occasional discharge from their artillery.
Tired of the state of suspense in which we had remained for several hours, I proposed to Colonel Cadwalader, to throw myself
with my company into a small work or ravelin about two hundred yards in advance, for the purpose of annoying them as they
came up. To this he assented, and I took possession of it; but
found it was a work that had been little more than marked out,
not knee high, and of course affording no cover. For this reason, after remaining in it a few minutes, with a view to impress
my men with the idea that a breastwork was not absolutely necessary, I abandoned it, and returned into the intrenchment.
This unimportant movement was treated with some respect: Not
knowing its meaning, it induced the troops that were in column,
immediately to display; and the irregulars to open upon us a

action. As the longest line of the position, it was the front, but seems improperly
so called when it is considered that, except at its upper extremity, no troops were
posted on it. It would be more correct, therefore, to consider the posts, the one
crossing the island on the north under Colonels Rawlings and Baxter, and the
other on the south, under Colonel Cadwalader, as two distinct and unconnected
positions, separated as they were by a space of about three miles. This interval
for above half its extent, lying along the banks of the Haerlem, was to depend for
defence on casual supplies of troops, as they could be spared from other places.

scattering fire. Soon after my return to the lines, it being observed that the enemy was extending himself towards the Hudson
on our right, Colonel Cadwalader detached me thither with my
company, with orders to post myself to the best advantage for
the protection of that flank. I accordingly marched, and took
my station at the extremity of the trench, just where the high
grounds begin to decline towards the river. This situation, from
the intervention of higher land, concealed from my view the
other parts of the field; and thence, disqualifies me from speaking of what passed there, as an eye-witness: But that the
action had begun in earnest, I was some time after informed
by my sense of hearing. It was assailed by a most tremendous roar of artillery, quickly succeeded by incessant vollies of small arms, which seemed to proceed from the east and
north; and it was to these points, that General Howe chiefly directed his efforts. The direct and cross fire from his batteries on
the east side of the Haerlem, effectually covered the landing of
his troops, and protected them also in gaining the steep ascents
on our side. It was no disgrace to the militia, that they shrunk
from this fire; such of them at least as were exposed to it without cover. I question whether the bravest veterans could have
stood it, unless I am deceived as to the advantage of the ground
on which the batteries were erected. When the heights were
gained, the enemy planted there must maintain themselves by
their small arms, since the artillery from their batteries would
be equally fatal to them as to us. On receiving intelligence
that embarkations of British troops were about to be thrown
across Haerlem river in his rear, Colonel Cadwalader made detachments from his position (already much too weakly manned)
to meet this body of the enemy, as yet unopposed by any part
of our force. The first detachment arrived in time to open a fire
upon the assailants before they reached the shore, and it was
well directed and deadly. Nevertheless their great superiority
of force, adequately aided by artillery, enabled them to land, and
by extending themselves, to gain the heights. On this ground
it was that a sharp contest ensued; speaking of which in his
official account of the action, General Howe says, " it was well defended by a body of the rebels:" and so it undoubtedly was, when

it is considered that but about one hundred and fifty of our men, with a single eighteen pounder, were opposed by eight hundred British troops, under cover of a battery. But overpowered by numbers, the resistance was ineffectual; and the detachments engaged in it, retired towards the fort. Rawlings, on his part, made a gallant stand against the Hessians under the command of General Knyphausen, to whom had been assigned the perilous glory, of gaining this strong piece of ground, differing essentially from that on the borders of Haerlem river, in the want of opposite heights for batteries. The Germans here lost a great many men; but as they had been bought by his Britannic majesty, he had an unquestionable right to make a free use of them; and this seemed to be the conviction of General Howe. Rawlings also suffered a good deal in proportion to his numbers. He had I think two officers killed; and himself, Major Williams, and some others, were wounded; one of whom, a Mr. Hanson, died in New York. The attainment of the post of Rawlings, put the Hessians in possession of the ground which commanded the fort; as that, possessed by the British, commanded the open field. Hence, the contest might be said to be at an end.

Colonel Cadwalader, aware that he was placed between two fires; and that the victorious enemy in his rear, would soon extend themselves across the island, ordered a retreat just in time to prevent his interception.

But I here suspend my own relation for the purpose of introducing a more ample statement of unquestionable authenticity, obligingly furnished by a friend; and which, embracing more detail, and mentioning some interesting particulars but little known, will occupy a few pages, much to the advantage of these Memoirs.

"Fort Washington stood on an eminence, situated on the margin of the Hudson, or North river, about two miles and a-half below King's-bridge. The access to the level on the top of it, is steep and difficult on every side, except on the south, where the ground is open, and the ascent gradual, to the fort. The hill extends along the North river about half a mile from the fort; and at the termination of it were some small works,

17*

which, with the natural strength of the place, were deemed a sufficient protection against the enemy, in that quarter.

" Nearly opposite to the fort, on the west side of Haerlem river, a body of men was posted to watch the motions of the enemy, who had erected works on the high and commanding ground east of that river, apparently with the design of covering a landing of troops in that part of the island of New York. From this post, along the west side of Haerlem river, to Colonel Roger Morris's house, a distance of not less than a mile and a-half, there were no troops posted either for observation or defence.

" About a mile below Morris's house, two lines, nearly parallel to each other, were constructed by General WASHINGTON, when the army retired to the upper part of the island, after the evacuation of New York. These lines extended from the vicinity of Haerlem river, across the island, to the North river, and were in length, each about a mile. The first line, towards New York, intersected the great road leading to King's-bridge, after the height is ascended from Haerlem plains: It was a slight intrenchment, with a few weak bastions, without platforms for cannon, and furnished with no other ordnance than a few old iron pieces of small caliber, scarcely fit for use, and an iron six pounder mounted on trucks. The second line was stronger, both from the nature of the ground, which afforded small eminences for bastions closed in the rear, and from having the intervals between the bastions strongly picketed. These lines were defensive works for the whole American army. The first line seemed calculated, rather for retarding the approach of the enemy, than as a seriously defensive work; it being nothing more (with the exception of the bastions) than a shallow ditch, with the earth thrown outwards. The second line was formed at a proper distance from the first, so as to protect the latter by musketry as well as cannon, and to drive out the enemy, should he get possession of it: but this second line, on the day of the attack of Fort Washington, was from necessity, wholly without defence, either of troops, or artillery of any description.

" A summons having been sent by General Howe, on the day preceding the attack, to Colonel Magaw, to surrender the fort;

and having met with a spirited refusal, the attack on the fort, and the posts connected with it, was expected, and actually took place on the following day. Colonel Magaw, who commanded on the island, remained in the fort; Colonel Rawlings, with his regiment of riflemen, was posted on the rear of Mount Washington; Colonel Baxter, with his regiment of militia, on Haerlem river, opposite Fort Washington; and Colonel Lambert Cadwalader, at the first line, about two and a half miles from the fort, with about eight hundred men, including a reinforcement of a hundred militia sent him, about ten or eleven o'clock in the morning.

" The operations of the enemy were announced early in the morning, by a cannonade on Colonel Rawlings' position, and a distant one, from the heights of Morrisania, on the line occupied by Colonel Cadwalader; the former with the view of facilitating the attack on that point, by three thousand Hessians; the latter, to favour the approach of Lord Percy, with one thousand six hundred men.

"At ten o'clock in the morning, a large body of the enemy appeared on Haerlem plains, preceded by their field pieces, and advanced with their whole body, towards a rocky point of the height, which skirted the plains in a southern direction from the first line, and at a considerable distance from it—and, commencing a brisk fire on the small work constructed there, drove out the party which held it, consisting of twenty men, and took possession of it: the men retiring with the picket guard to the first line. The enemy, having gained the heights, advanced in column, on open ground, towards the first line; whilst a party of their troops pushed forward, and took possession of a small unoccupied work in front of the first line; from whence they opened their fire with some field pieces and a howitzer, upon the line, but without effect. When the column came within proper distance, a fire from the six-pounder was directed against it; on which, the whole column inclined to their left, and took post behind a piece of woods, where they remained. As it was suspected that they would make an attempt on the right of the line, under cover of the wood, that part was strengthened.

" Things remained in this position for about an hour and a

half, during which interval, General WASHINGTON, with Generals
Putnam, Greene, Mercer, and other principal officers, came over
the North River from Fort Lee, and crossed the island to Morris's
house; whence they viewed the position of our troops, and the
operations of the enemy in that quarter. Having remained there
a sufficient time to observe the arrangement that had been made
for the defence of that part of the island, they retired by. the way
they came, and returned to Fort Lee, without making any change
in the disposition of the troops, or communicating any new
orders. It is a fact, not generally known, that the British troops
took possession of the very spot on which the Commander-in-
chief, and the general officers with him, had stood, in fifteen
minutes after they left it.

" Colonel Rawlings was some time late in the morning attacked
by the Hessians, whom he fought with great gallantry and effect,
as they were climbing the heights; until the arms of the riflemen
became useless from the foulness they contracted from the frequent repetition of their fire. From this incident, and the great
superiority of the enemy, Colonel Rawlings was obliged to retire
into the fort. The enemy having gained the heights, immediately pushed forward towards the fort, and took post behind a
large store-house, within a small distance of it.

"But to return to what passed at the first line towards New
York. Intelligence having been received by Colonel Cadwalader, that the enemy were coming down Haerlem river in boats,
to land in his rear, he detached Captain Lenox with fifty men, to
oppose them, and, on farther information, a hundred more, with
Captains Edwards and Tudor.* This force, with the addition of
about the same number from Fort Washington, arrived on the
heights near Morris's house, early enough to fire on the enemy in
their boats,† which was done with such effect, that about ninety
were killed and wounded. The great superiority, however, of the

* The subalterns under Captain LENOX, were Lieutenants LAWRENCE and
TILTON, and Ensign M'INTIRE—the others are unknown.

† This body from the Fort, from the testimony of an eye witness, and by permission of the gentleman who furnishes the account, I am authorized to state,
did not arrive so early; neither was it engaged. It consisted of the Flying
Camp, and could not be brought into action.

enemy, (their numbers amounting to about eight hundred men,) prevailed over the bravery and good conduct of our troops, who, with some loss retired to Fort Washington.

" This body of the enemy immediately advanced, and took possession of the grounds in advance of, and a little below Morris's house, where some soldiers' huts had been left standing, not far from the second line. This position of the enemy being observed, it was expected they would march down and take possession of the second line, (which from the want of men, was entirely without defence,) and thereby place the troops in the first line, between two fires. This important movement did not, however, take place; owing, as was afterwards learned, to the apprehension they entertained, that the enclosed bastions concealed therein a number of men, whose fire would greatly annoy them. They hesitated;—and this being perceived, from the delay that took place, Colonel Cadwalader, to avoid the fatal consequences that must have resulted from the expected movement, immediately resolved to retire to the fort, with the troops under his command; and as the measure required promptness and activity, he sent orders to the right and left of the line, to move off towards Fort Washington, on the signal being given; which, after a proper interval of time, being made, the whole was put in motion, (those on the left retiring obliquely towards the centre of the second line,) passed the second line and when they came opposite to the body of the enemy posted at the huts, received their fire, which was returned in an irregular manner; and, pursuing the road which led to the fort, under the heights by the North river, arrived there with little or no loss.

" The militia under Colonel Baxter, posted on Haerlem river, were attacked by the British guards and light infantry, who landed on the island of New York, protected by the fire from the work on the heights on the opposite side of the river. A short contest ensued; but our troops, overpowered by numbers, and leaving behind them Colonel Baxter, who was killed by a British officer as he was bravely encouraging his men, retired to the fort. The guards and light infantry, then crossed the island to the heights on the North river, a little below the fort, under which Colonel Cadwalader with his party, but a few minutes before, had passed, in his way to the fort."*

* General WILKINSON says, "I conversed with General GREENE, respecting the affair at Fort Washington, who was chiefly blamed for attempting to hold the place, and I recollect well, he observed, 'I would to God we had had ten thousand men there.' He was of opinion the ground was tenable, and that it was lost by the insufficiency of our force, and I am inclined to the same opinion."—*Mems.*, *vol.* 1.—ED.

CHAPTER VIII.

The Author a Prisoner.—Conduct of British Officers and Soldiers.—The Author's Treatment.—State of Prisoners.—Visits to Prisoners.—Treatment.—Major Maitland.—Reflections.—Americans and English contrasted.—Character of General Howe.—Killed and Wounded.—Character of Mr. Becket.—Humanity of British Officers.—March of Prisoners to New York.—Occurrences on the Road.—Generosity of a Highlander.—Disposal of Prisoners.—Officers' Quarters.—Baggage Restored.—Author appears in Regimentals.—Reflections.

THESE things, or the greater part of them, had probably passed before I had abandoned my station, taken as already mentioned, in pursuance of orders for strnegthening the right. The line of entrenchment was too extensive to be manned without leaving intervals. Some of these were large, and intervening hillocks cut off the communication in some parts; otherwise, the whole of us under the command of Colonel Cadwalader must have retreated at the same time. The first notice that I had of the entrenchment being given up, was from an officer I did not know, posted at some distance from me, going off with his men. I called to him to know what he meant. He answered, that he was making the best of his way to the fort, as the rest of the troops had retreated long since. As I had no reason to doubt his veracity, I imme- diately formed my company, and began to retire in good order, which is more than I can say of my neighbour or his corps; and amidst all the chagrin, I afterwards felt, that the events of the day had been so unpropitious to our glory, I had the satisfaction to reflect, that the men were always obedient, and ready to par- take of any danger their officers would share with them. This, however, was but matter of inference; since I never was at- tacked, though continually fronted by a strong force, and incom- moded by their ordnance, though without being injured by it. After proceeding some hundred paces I reflected that I had no

orders for what I was doing; and that, although I had no right
to expect exactness, in a moment of such pressure, it was yet
possible my movement might be premature. I knew nothing of
what had passed in the centre, or of the enemy being master of
the high grounds in my rear about Colonel Morris's house, from
which, no doubt, had proceeded the cannon balls that whizzed
by us; and for which, coming in that direction, I could not account. To be entirely correct in my conduct, I here halted my
men, and went myself to a rising ground at some distance, from
which I might have a view of the lines where Colonel Cadwalader had been posted. They seemed thoroughly manned; and
at the instant, I beckoned to the officers to march back the company, which they immediately put in motion; but looking more
attentively, I perceived that the people I saw, were British and
Hessian troops that were eagerly pressing forward. Upon this,
I hastened back to my party, and as there was no time to be
lost, being in a situation to be cut to pieces by a corps of cavalry, I ordered them under the command of my ensign, to make
the best of their way and join the body of men, which none
doubted being our own, on the heights beyond the inner lines;
and that I would follow them as fast as I could, for I was a good
deal out of breath with the expedition, I had used in going to
and returning from the ground, which gave me a view of the
outer lines. I accordingly walked on, accompanied by Forrest
who did not choose to leave me alone. Edwards was not with
me, having been promoted to the command of a company and
employed as already mentioned. The body I had pointed to and
directed my company to join, under the idea of their being our
own men, turned out to be the British, consisting of Colonel
Stirling's divisions of Highlanders, a circumstance that was not
at first perceived on account of the distance; nor, owing to the
smoke of an irregular fire which they kept up, and the entrenchment in which they were posted, covering them to the breast,
was it manifest until we got pretty near them. Upon this discovery, we held a moment's consultation, and the result was,
that hemmed in as we were on every side, there was no chance
of escaping; and that there was nothing left but to give ourselves up to them. Had we been aware, at first, of their being

the enemy, we might have eluded them by shaping our way along the shore of the Hudson, as my men, soon discovering who they were, had done; but in full confidence that they were our people, I bent my course in the opposite direction to the main body, in the view of meeting Colonel Cadwalader there, and taking his farther orders. Thus circumstanced, we clubbed our fusees in token of surrender, and continued to advance towards them. They either did not or would not take the signal; and though there were but two of us, from whom they could not possibly expect a design to attack, they did not cease firing at us. I may venture to say, that not less than ten guns were discharged with their muzzles towards us, within the distance of forty or fifty yards; and I might be nearer the truth in saying, that some were let off within twenty. Luckily for us, it was not our riflemen to whom we were targets; and it is astonishing how even these *blunt* shooters could have missed us. But as we were ascending a considerable hill, they shot over us. I observed they took no aim, and that the moment of presenting and firing, was the same. As I had full leisure for reflection, and was perfectly collected, though fearful that their design was to give no quarter, I took off my hat with such a sweep of the arm as could not but be observed, without ceasing however to advance. This had the intended effect: A loud voice proceeded from the breast-work, and the firing immediately ceased. An officer of the forty-second regiment advanced towards us; and as I was foremost, he civilly accosted me by asking me my rank. Being informed of this, as also of Forrest's, he inquired where the fort lay and where Colonel Magaw was. I pointed in the direction of the fort, and told him I had not seen Colonel Magaw during the day. Upon this, he put us under the care of a sergeant and a few men, and left us. The sergeant was a decent looking man, who, on taking us into custody, bestowed upon us in broad Scotch the friendly admonition, of *Young men, ye should never fight against your king.* The little bustle produced by our surrender, was scarcely over, when a British officer on horseback, apparently of high rank, rode up at full gallop, exclaiming, *What! taking prisoners! Kill them, kill every man of them.* My back was towards him when he spoke; and although by this

18

time, there was none of that appearance of ferocity in the guard, which would induce much fear, that they would execute his command, I yet thought it well enough to parry it, and turning to him, I took off my hat, saying, *Sir I put myself under your protection.* No man was ever more effectually rebuked. His manner was instantly softened: He met my salutation with an inclination of his body, and after a civil question or two, as if to make amends for his sanguinary mandate, he rode off towards the fort, to which he had inquired the way.

Though I had delivered up my arms, I had not adverted to a cartouch box which I wore about my waist, and which, having once belonged to his Britannic Majesty, presented in front, the gilded letters G. R. Exasperated at this trophy on the body of a rebel, one of the soldiers seized the belt with great violence, and in the attempt to unbuckle it, had nearly jerked me off my legs. To appease the offended loyalty of the honest Scot, I submissively took it off and delivered it to him, being conscious that I had no longer any right to it. At this time a Hessian came up. He was not a private, neither did he look like a regular officer: He was some retainer, however, to the German troops; and was as much of a brute as any one I have ever seen in the human form. The wretch came near enough to elbow us; and half unsheathing his sword, with a countenance that bespoke a most vehement desire to use it upon us, he grinned out in broken English, *Eh, you rebel, you dam rebel!* I had by this time entire confidence in our Scotchmen; and therefore regarded the caitiff with the same indifference, that I should have viewed a caged wild beast, though with much greater abhorrence.

These transactions which occupied about ten minutes, passed upon the spot on which we were taken, whence we were marched to an old stable or out house, where we found about forty or fifty prisoners already collected, principally officers, of whom I only particularly recollect Lieutenant Brodhead of our battalion. We remained on the outside of the building; and for nearly an hour, sustained a series of most intolerable abuse. This chiefly proceeded from the officers of the light infantry; for the most part, young and insolent puppies, whose worthlessness was apparently their recommendation to a service, which placed them in the post of danger, and in the way of becoming food for powder, their most appropriate destination next to that of the gallows. The term rebel, with the ephithet *damned* before it, was the mildest we received. We were twenty times told, sometimes with a taunting affectation of concern, that we should every man of us be hanged; and were nearly as many times paraded with the most inconceivable insolence, for the purpose of ascertaining whether there were not some deserters among us; and these were always sought for among the officers, as if the lowest fellow in their army was fit for any post in ours. "There's a fellow," an upstart Cockney would exclaim, "that I could swear was a deserter." "What countrymen, are you sir? Did you not belong to such a regiment?"—I was not indeed challenged for a deserter; but the indignity of being ordered about by such contemptible whipsters, for a moment unmanned me, and I was obliged to apply my handkerchief to my eyes. This was the first time in my life, that I had been the victim of brutal, cowardly oppression; and I was unequal to the shock; but my elasticity of mind was soon restored, and I viewed it with the indignant contempt it deserved.

For the greater convenience of guarding us, we were removed from this place, to the barn of Colonel Morris's house, already mentioned, which had been the head quarters of our army, as it now was of the royal one. This was the great bank of *deposit* for prisoners taken out of the fort; and already pretty well filled. It was a good new building and we were ushered into it among the rest, the whole body consisting of from a hundred and fifty, to two hundred, composing a motley group to be sure. Here were men and officers of all descriptions, regulars and militia, troops continental and state, some in uniforms, some without them, and some in hunting shirts, the mortal aversion of a red coat. Some of the officers had been plundered of their hats and some of their coats; and upon the new society into which we were introduced, with whom a showy exterior was all in all, we were certainly not calculated to make a very favourable impression. I found Captain Tudor here, of our regiment, who, if I mistake not, had lost his hat. It was here also that not long after I saw Ensign Steddiford of our regiment at a little distance, at large, and in close conference with Major Skene. So friendly an intercourse be-

tween a British officer and a rebel was so strikingly in contrast
to the general insolence I had received and was still treated with,
that it baffled every hypothesis I could frame to account for it.
But it was afterwards explained by Steddiford. The garrison
had capitulated; and Skene being desirous to walk to this part
of the field, had proposed to Steddiford to accompany him, observing with the frankness and circumspection of an old soldier,
that each would be a safeguard to the other. "I," says he,
"shall protect you from our men, and you will protect me from
yours, should there be any of either lurking in the woods, and
disposed to hostility." Shortly after, it was announced by an
huzza, that the fort had surrendered. This, I think, was about
two o'clock.

The officer who commanded the guard in whose custody we
now were, was an ill-looking, low-bred fellow of this dashing
corps of light infantry. Had dates accorded, he might have been
supposed the identical scoundrel that had sat for the portrait of
Northerton, in Fielding's Tom Jones. As I stood as near as
possible to the door for the sake of air, the enclosure in which
we were being extremely crowded and unpleasant, I was particu·
larly exposed to his brutality; and repelling with some severity,
one of his attacks, for I was becoming desperate and careless of
safety, the ruffian exclaimed, *Not a word, sir, or damme I'll give
you my butt*, at the same time clubbing his fusee and drawing it
back as if to give the blow. I fully expected it, but he contented himself with the threat. I observed to him that I was in
his power, and disposed to submit to it, though not proof against
every provocation.

As to see the prisoners was a matter of some curiosity, we
were complimented with a continual succession of visitants,
consisting of officers of the British army. There were several of
these present, when a Serjeant-Major came to take an account of
us; and particularly, a list of such of us as were officers. This
sergeant, though not uncivil, had all that animated, degagè impudence of air, which belongs to a self-complacent non-commissioned officer of the most arrogant army in the world; and with
his pen in his hand and his paper on his knee, applied to each of
us, in turn, for his rank. He had just set mine down, when he

came to a little squat, militia officer from York county, who, somewhat to the deterioration of his appearance, had substituted the dirty crown of an old hat, for a plunder-worthy beaver that had been taken from him by a Hessian. He was known to be an officer from having been assembled among us, for the purpose of enumeration. *You are an officer, sir!* said the sergeant; *Yes*, was the answer. *Your rank, sir!* with a significant smile. I am *a keppun*, replied the little man in a chuff, firm tone. Upon this, there was an immoderate roar of laughter among the officers about the door, who were attending to the process; and I am not sure, I did not laugh myself. When it had subsided, one of them addressing himself to me, observed with a compliment that had much more of sour than sweet in it, that he was really astonished I should have taken any thing less than a regiment. To remove as much as possible the sting of this sarcastic thrust at our service, for I must confess I was not sufficiently republican, to be insensible of its force, I told him, that the person who had produced their merriment, belonged to the militia, and that in his line as a farmer, he was no doubt honest and respectable.

Although the day was seasonably cool, yet from the number crowded in the barn, the air within was oppressive and suffocating, which, in additon to the agitations of the day, had produced an excessive thirst; and there was a continual cry for water. I cannot say that this want was unattended to: the soldiers were continually administering to it by bringing water in a bucket. But though we, who were about the door, did well enough, the supply was very inadequate to such a number of mouths; and many must have suffered much. Our situation brought to my recollection that of Captain Holwell and his party, in the black hole at Calcutta; and had the weather been equally hot, we should not have been much better off. The fellow who had menaced me with his butt, stood with his fusee across the door, and kept us closely immured. I did not choose to ask favours of him; but addressing myself to the officers without the door, who had been put in good humour by their laugh at our poor militia captain, I asked them, if they made no distinction between officers and privates. Most certainly we do, said one of them. I then observed, that it would be very agreeable to us to be

somewhat separated from them now, and to receive a little fresh
air. Upon this, the sentinels were withdrawn to the distance of
about ten or twelve feet from the building; and we were told,
that such of us as were officers might walk before the door.
This was a great relief to us, as well as to the men in giving
them more room.

As I was walking here, a gentleman, who I was afterwards
informed was Major Maitland, of the 71st, I think, came up and
entered into conversation with me. He had one arm in a sling,
and it appeared to me, he had lost a hand. He regretted the
extremes to which matters had been carried, and touched upon
our infatuation, as he termed it, in attempting resistance to the
power of Britain. He assumed the unqualified justness of her
cause, and the consequent unjustness of ours; and adverting to
the day's business, he observed, that I must be aware, that as
we were taken by storm (speaking of myself and the other
prisoners here collected) our lives were forfeited by the laws of
war, and that we might have been put to the sword, without
any just impeachment of their humanity; but such, added he, is
the clemency of the British nation, that we have not availed
ourselves of the right, but shall, on the contrary, treat you with
every indulgence. This was delivered in the tone of a lecture
which precludes the necessity of a reply. Accordingly, I gave
it none; and as the manner was mild and well intended withal,
I received it in good part: as civility was a rarity, the value of
this attention was proportionably enhanced and duly appreciated.
The Major confirmed to me the surrender of the fort, which I
had at first doubted, though I can hardly tell why. I certainly
never had the expectation that it could have held out long: and
I cannot here forbear remarking, that its incapacity for defence,
is unequivocally recognised by General WASHINGTON in his
official letter to Congress. " I sent," says he, "a billet to
Colonel Magaw, directing him to hold out, and I would endeavour in the evening to bring off the garrison if the fortress
could not be maintained, as I did not expect it could, *the enemy
being possessed of the adjacent ground.*" Now, had the attempt
been to defend the fort alone, instead of its environs, which had
constituted the post of the main army, this effect of the enemy's

possessing the adjacent ground, would at once have taken place; and the fort have been untenable. The fort then, was not calculated upon as the point to be defended; but it was the position in the open field. Hence, we were improperly termed a garrison; and two thousand men, of which half were militia, were pitted against the whole of the British army. For seven thousand troops were actually employed in the attack, and the rest ready to support them. It was certainly enough then, that we fought them and withstood their efforts until noon. Because posts had been evacuated; because Long Island, New York, King's-bridge and White Plains had successively been found untenable by the concentred force of the continent, this handful was to apologize to the country, for the supposed disgrace of our arms, and the defective constitution of our military system. As "the troops were in high spirits and would make a good defence,* why e'en let these southern men," says Generals Putnam and Greene, "take the glory of it to themselves: Whatever be their fate, they will kill a good number of the enemy; and desperate expedients are adapted to the declining state of our cause." These, it is true, were dashing counsels: nevertheless, to those acquainted with the unfriendly, repulsive temper which prevailed between the southern and eastern troops, and the selfish clannish spirit, testified on all occasions by the latter,† there would be nothing very revolting in the imputation of such motives; in which also, the historian in the Annual Register, might find a clew to the solution of the enigma, why an operation on so large a scale, should have been committed to but a Colonel. It was, at any rate, a current opinion among us who were taken, that we had been sacrificed to selfish feeling; nor upon a cool consideration of all the circumstances, after a lapse of four and thirty years, can I see full cause to renounce that opinion. I do not believe, at least, that if we had been New England men, we should have been left there. If Greene really knew no better at this era, he was deeply instructed by his error;

* See General WASHINGTON's letter, above alluded to, which shows that the defence or evacuation of the post, rested on the discretion of General GREENE.

† One instance of it, was a partial exchange of prisoners, continually carried on in favour of the eastern officers, to the cruel discouragement of the southern.

since, whatever were the characters of his subsequent generalship, it never disclosed symptoms of rash audacity.*

But I must not forget I am a captive. Among the events
of the afternoon was the meeting with a captain Wilson, of the
light infantry, who called to inquire, whether there were any
gentlemen among us from Philadelphia. Upon telling him that
I was, he asked me if I knew Mr. Philip Wilson, a merchant
of that city. I told him I had a slight acquaintance with him,
as also with his brother Edward. " They are both," says he,
" brothers of mine, and though I detest their principles," he was
obliged perhaps to go farther on this point than a refined politeness might warrant, on account of his brother officers and soldiers
standing by, " I shall be happy to render you every service in
my power." He then minuted my name and rank on his tablets,
as he did Tudor's, for the same reason of knowing his brothers;
and told us, he would do himself the pleasure of calling upon
us in New York. He informed us, also, that he had seen Major
West, Captain Lenox, I think, and some others of our friends at
the fort, who had been inquiring for us. During the remainder of

---

* Our author, again alludes with considerable bitterness, to General GREENE,
apparently entertaining an opinion derogatory to his ability, and character as
a military man. Posterity has already assigned to this truly great man, his
just position, by the side of WASHINGTON. In 1786, ALEXANDER HAMILTON, pronounced a *Eulogium* on General GREENE, before the society of the Cincinnati,
at New York. It is but just, that the deliberate opinion of so competent a
judge, should accompany that of the respectable and estimable author of the
" MEMOIRS·"

"So long as the measures, which conducted us safely through the first, and
most critical stages of the war, shall be remembered with approbation; so long
as the enterprises of Trenton and Princeton, shall be regarded as the dawnings
of that bright day, which, afterwards broke forth with such resplendent lustre;
so long, as the almost magic operations of the remainder of that remarkable
winter, distinguished, not more by these events, than by the extraordinary spectacle of a powerful army, straightened within narrow limits, by the phantom of
a military force, and never permitted to transgress those limits with impunity,
in which skill supplied the place of means, and disposition was the substitute for
an army;—so long, I say, as these operations shall continue to be the object of
wonder, so long ought the name of GREENE, to be revered by a grateful country.
To attribute to him a portion of the praise, which is due as well to the formation
as to the execution of the plans, that effected these important ends, can be no
derogation from that wisdom and magnanimity, which knew how to select, and
embrace counsels worthy of being pursued."—ED.

the day, if I except a sight of General Howe, who was pointed out to me at a little distance, and the burning of a pretty large brick house hard by, which happened, as the soldiers told us, through the carelessness of some grenadiers in cooking beef steaks, nothing occurred of any consequence: but in the evening a most advantageous change took place, and from the custody of a low ruffian, we were transferred to that of a gentleman.

This was Lieutenant Becket, to the best of my recollection of the 27th or 37th regiment. Upon taking the guard in the evening, he expressed concern about our lodging, and proposed to us to accompany him into the barn-loft to see whether that would do. He was also attended by some of his brother officers. We ascended by a very good step ladder, and found a spacious room, well roofed and floored and clear of lumber. "This, gentlemen, I think may do," said he; "I dare say, you have sometimes lodged in a worse place." That we had, we told him, and that this was as comfortable as we could desire. "I will send you, if I can," said he, at going away, "a bottle of wine: but at any rate, a bottle of spirits," and as to the latter, he was as good as his word; a soldier, in about a quarter of an hour brought it to us, and this was our substitute for supper as well as dinner. In the morning, a little after sunrise, a soldier brought me Mr. Becket's compliments with a request that I would come down and breakfast with him, bringing two of my friends with me, as he had not the means of entertaining more. I thankfully accepted his invitation, and took with me Forrest and Tudor. He was seated on a bench before the door with a good fire before him, and the soldiers of the guard in a semicircle about him. Besides the bench we were accommodated with a chair or two, and he gave us a dish of very good coffee with plenty of excellent toast, which was the only morsel we had eaten for the last twenty-four hours; more fortunate in this than our fellow sufferers, who got nothing until the next morning, when the first provisions were drawn. The soldiers were chatting and cracking their jokes on each other while we breakfasted; and I was surprised at the easy familiarity which seemed to prevail between them and their officer. But it appeared to be perfectly understood between them, that their coteries, though so near each other, as that every word from either might be heard by both, were yet entirely distinct, and that each had an exclusive right to its own conversation: still they did not interrupt ours, being silent when we talked. The fact was, that Mr. Becket was the darling of his soldiers; and one of them told us, that we should find few men like him. I had here an opportunity to observe, the striking difference between their appointments and ours. While our poor fellows, were some of them already ragged, and even the best of them, clad in flimsy, threadbare clothes, with worse stockings and shoes, these were tight and comfortable in body and limbs; and every soldier was accommodated with a woollen night cap, which most of them had yet on. A sad contrast for the contemplation of the American soldier! Wisdom is no less attributable to nations than to individuals; and the British army, if I may so express myself, is a sensible establishment, in which every possible regard is had to both comfort and safety. Though, in extremities, it may be the business of the soldier to die, it is not forgotten, that he is to live if he can, consistent with his duty; and to this consideration, it appears to me, much attention was paid by General Howe in his operations against our post. He could not have had a doubt that his attack would be successful, yet this was not enough: it must be conducted with an eye to the saving of men, and the purchasing it as cheap as possible. Had he immediately advanced against our lines on the south, the loss of the British troops, would, in all probability, have been heavy; whereas, in making his principal effort by Haerlem river under cover of his batteries, it was comparatively small: and when he had gained the high grounds in this quarter, he was at once master of the field.

It has been said, that we could not have chosen a better adversary than General Howe;* and it is not improbable that one

---

* Such, at least, was the opinion generally entertained in England. WALPOLE, who certainly

> "knew not how to spare,
> Yet seldom judged unjustly,"

is not sparing of *his* opinions. He writes to Horace Mann, 7th July, 1778, "General Howe is returned, richer in money than laurels."

WRAXALL's opinion of the HOWES has already been quoted.—ED.

more enterprising and less methodical, might have pushed us harder: Yet, though he was indolent, often treated us with unnecessary respect; and, in a too great security of his prey, might have meant to play us, as an angler plays a fish upon his hook, I am still inclined to think, that when he acted, he fought his army to advantage; that his dispositions were good, and planned with much discretion. General Burgoyne bears testimony to the faultless propriety of his disposition at Bunker's Hill, and General Lee says, that "in the capacity of an executive soldier, he was all fire and activity, brave and cool as Julius Cæsar." In the affair of Fort Washington, he must have had a perfect knowledge of the ground we occupied. This he might have acquired from hundreds in New York; but he might have been more thoroughly informed of every thing desirable to be known, from one Dement,* an officer of Magaw's battalion, who was intelligent in points of duty, and deserted to the enemy, about a week before the assault. This man was probably an emissary from them; he was an European, I recollect, and not originally an officer of the corps; his name, at least, is not among those appointed by the committee of safety.

Our situation under Mr. Beckett was as agreeable as it could be made. The term rebel was entirely banished from our hearing. When speaking of the belligerents, it was your people and our people, and the manners of all about him, took the tone he gave. His acquaintance too, seemed of an order wholly different from the rakehells we had seen yesterday; nor do I recollect a single instance of incivility to any one of us, while under his care. But notwithstanding this, my heart was ill at ease. It was

---

* This man's name once helped me to a tolerable pun, and as this species of wit is often detailed by Mr. Boswell in his Life of Johnson, it is hoped that this single instance may be tolerated here. He was a coarse, ill-looking fellow; and it being reported in New York, after we were taken, that a Miss A——, a very pretty, delicate girl, who had resided at Morrisania, countenanced him as her lover, Doctor McHenry was expressing his astonishment at it, when I repeated to him the adage—Quos deus vult perdere, prius *dementat.*"—*Note by Mr. Graydon.*

The reader will pardon this, in consideration of the classic character and propensities of our learned *pun*-dit; but it must be the last trial, at least in this manner, of his forbearance!—Ed.

the prey of chagrin and a most afflicting uncertainty. I was deeply mortified at the idea that we were disgraced in the eyes of our countrymen, with whom the belief was current, that Fort Washington was impregnable; and the events of the action had been, moreover, peculiarly unpropitious to the fame of the continental battalions from Pennsylvania. All the glory that was going, had, in my idea of what had passed, been engrossed by the regiment of Rawlings, which had been actively engaged, killed a number of the enemy, and lost many themselves; and although it seldom, if ever, happens, that there is close fighting in every part of a field, yet it is this alone which obtains *eclat*, or, that in the view of the world, escapes contempt. As to the merit of preserving a good countenance; being firm in a post; and only relinquishing it when no longer tenable, or expedient to be retained; it can only be appreciated by persons of military experience: It is at best, but of a negative kind, and has nothing in it of brilliancy.* How many did they kill? How many did they lose? are the questions which produce the data on which martial fame is calculated; and these were much against us. The number of British killed, by General Howe's account, was not large; and the whole loss is fixed by Mr. Stedman at eight hundred, by much the greater part of which was sustained by the Hessians, who attacked Rawlings, in a post extremely difficult of access, naturally, and rendered still more so by works and abbatis. In the two battalions of Cadwalader and Magaw, there were but two or three officers wounded, and one killed, or rather reputed killed, as I have recently understood that he survived his wounds, though very grievous, and was some years after living at Germantown. This was Captain Miller, who, as already mentioned, was going to shoot a sentinel on Montezores island. Among the wounded, was Captain Lenox, very slightly, and Ensign M'Intire, badly. As to myself, I was conscious I had done my duty, but this must

---

* I was not aware at this time, that detachments from our regiments had maintained a contest which entitled them to the praise of the enemy; for by the concurrent testimony of General Howe, and the historian, Mr. Stedman, the ground on which they fought was obstinately defended: and I have still so much of the *esprit du corps* and pride of a soldier about me, as to be gratified by the circumstance.

remain unknown; and I was unable to put aside the reflection, that we were both sacrificed and disgraced; captive to an enemy, whose system it was to treat us with contempt; to stigmatize us as rebels and load us with opprobrium; and that all this was, probably, but a prelude to the impending ruin and subjugation of my country. In addition to these dismaying considerations, I thought my brother killed. I had intelligence from the fort, that he was not there; neither had any one seen him after he had left the intrenchments; though it was suggested, that a boat-load of the garrison that had been hard pressed, had got over to Fort Lee, and that he might have been in it. There was also room to hope, that if not among these, (admitting the circumstance of the boats having gone over to be true,) he might be at the village of Haerlem, in which, it was said, there was a small collection of prisoners. Being impatient to satisfy myself, and know the worst, I applied to Mr. Becket, for permission, if not improper, to go to Haerlem; and if not successful there, to traverse the field of action. He granted my request without hesitation; but observed, it was proper I should have a soldier with me, to protect me and account for my being at large; and had he not been too polite, he might have added, to guard me, which, it would have been a neglect of duty in him, not to have attended to. I went to Haerlem, but received no satisfaction. There were, indeed, some prisoners there, in the custody of the German troops; but they had neither seen my brother, nor heard any thing of him. I then returned, and took my course, with my attendant, along the banks of Haerlem river, where the action had been warm. Within a few hundred yards of the barn in which we were quartered, I met with the bodies of three or four soldiers of our battalion, who had fallen by musket-balls; but obtained nothing in regard to the object of my pursuit. Weary of the melancholy errand, and reflecting that the day would be insufficient to complete the search, I gave it up with a determination to look as much as pos- sible on the favourable side of things, and wait in patience for the event. Some time after, Mr. Becket, who took a friendly interest in the cause of my distress, applied to a gentleman on horseback, who had superintended the interment of the dead, to know whether he had met with the body of an officer in the

19

uniform I wore, as I was anxious for the fate of a brother, who was missing. With much delicacy, addressing himself to me, he replied: "No sir, we buried no one with linen fine enough to have been your brother." This information, though not conclusive, was encouraging: and the liberality of our present treatment, added to the fineness of the morning, though pretty sharp, gave a fillip to my spirits, and a more pleasing turn to my thoughts. The sun looked vastly brighter to my eyes than it had done an hour before, and I began to flatter myself that matters might not be so bad, as in a desponding moment I had supposed; that ere long we should be exchanged, and have an opportunity of retrieving the disgrace of our recent discomfiture. In this frame of mind, conversation took a more cheerful course, and I satisfied some of Mr. Becket's inquiries respecting our affairs. He was particularly inquisitive as to the character of General WASHINGTON, of whom, from misrepresentations, no doubt propagated for political purposes, he had received some very erroneous impressions. Appearing to think favourably of him as a soldier, and as to the exterior qualifications of a gentleman, he had yet understood, that he was a man of desperate fortune, who, having wasted his own property, had also dissipated that of his wife by play, and had now no resource but in war and confusion. I assured him that nothing could be farther from the truth than this idea; and left him, I believe, convinced of his error. Though he spoke with much moderation of the contest, the merits of which were but glanced at, he seemed to entertain no doubts of the justice of the side on which his profession had placed him, as well as our inability to withstand the power of the mother country. He was forcibly struck with the ill condition of our troops, the badness of their arms, and insufficiency, in every respect, of our appointments; and observed, that a gentleman of our army required more than an ordinary degree of fortitude to take the field under such disadvantages.

The distinguished liberality of Mr. Becket's deportment, requires of me something more than a mere passing remembrance. If my memory does not much deceive me, he told us he was an Irishman, and a married man. His figure was pleasing, rather manly than elegant; tall, and though not corpulent, indicative of a temperament inclining to fulness. His face was fine and beamed with candour and benevolence. He might have passed for a man of twenty-eight or thirty, though he could not well have been less than thirty-five, having served, as he informed us, in the war of *fifty-six*, probably in the latter part of it, and it lasted until sixty-three. He mentioned this circumstance in adverting to the cannonade of the preceding day, which he said had far exceeded in heaviness, any he had ever heard in Germany, or in his life. He had been long in service, and appeared to be generally known and respected in the army; being, indeed, eminently calculated to be beloved and admired; and so far as I could judge of him from the acquaintance of a day, he possessed the qualities, which, with equal power would have made him a Titus, and have given him a legitimate claim to the designation of *deliciæ humani generis*. The command of the guard, in his mode of exercising the function, resembled a trust committed to him for our benefit; and his conduct bespoke the guardian rather than the jailer.

About noon, a young officer, smartly dressed and well mounted, rode up with his horse in a foam, and pulling out his watch, observed, that he had scarcely been an hour in coming from New York. He was a genuine, smooth-faced, fresh-coloured Englishman, and from the elegance of his horse, and self-importance of his manner, I supposed him to be a person of family and consideration. " Becket," said he, looking round him, " this is a damn'd strong piece of ground—ten thousand of our men would defend it against the world." " I don't know that," returned Becket; " the ground, to be sure is strong, in some parts, but you go too far: I would not undertake its defence against the world, I assure you." The conversation then passed to other topics, and the cavalier, after a few minutes, rode off to exhibit himself elsewhere. Several other incidents, equally unimportant, occurred in the course of the day; but one, that from the substantial good which attended it at the time, I cannot omit: And this was, that from the table of General Jones, the officer of the day, with whom Mr. Becket dined, there came to me about two o'clock, a plate or small dish of victuals amply supplied. The contents consisted of two or three slices of corned beef with cabbage, the leg and wing of a turkey, with bread, &c. in proportion. In the language of Lord Kaimes, " could peace afford a sweeter scene," than was exhibited in the conduct of this kind, generous, noble-hearted gentleman! To be admired, it only needs to be faithfully depicted, and this is all my feeble pencil aims at. It consisted of a series of attentions, as delicate as they were friendly, of which, the following is an additional instance. In the evening we were drawn up for the purpose of being marched a part of the way towards New York. Being formed in the usual manner, in two ranks, with the officers on the right, in order to be foremost when faced for the march, our commander took his station in front, and gaily flourishing a switch which he held in his hand, with a kind of apologetic smile for the liberty he was taking with us, " Come, gentlemen," said he, " we are all soldiers," (combining us with his own men, enclosing us in two lines; and who, at the same time received the word of command,) *To the right face;* then giving the word *March,* he good-humouredly walked along with us, without losing sight, however, of the decorum which actual duty required. When we had proceeded about half a mile, we were halted, for the purpose, as I afterwards found, of relieving the guard. As we stood here, an officer wrapped up in a camblet cloak, young and of a very pleasing address, who had been talking with Becket, came up to me, observing, that the evening was very cool, and asked if such weather was usual with us at this season of the year. I told him it was not unusual in the latter part of November. After an observation or two on this topic, he expressed his hope that I had been well treated. As well as possible, I replied, by some, and as ill by others. " I am extremely sorry for it," said he, " but there are rascals in all services." Soon after, Mr. Becket* informed us, that he was about to leave us, telling me that he would make it a point to obtain information respecting my brother, and that he would not fail to acquaint me with the result in New York; then bringing up Captain Manuel,

---

* His name was, probably, Beckwith, not Becket. In a list of the British officers there is a Mr. Onslow Beckwith, a second lieutenant in the 23d regiment on the 24th of April, 1762, who is presumed to be the gentleman here alluded to. There is no one of the name of Becket on the list.

the person who was to succeed him, he introduced me to him, with a particular recommendation of me to his care, and wished us a good evening.

Under the command of Captain Manuel we continued our march until within six or seven miles of New York. We were here quartered very comfortably for the night, in the back part of a vacant house, of which Mr. Manuel took to himself the front. Although he had not the amenity and ease of manners so eminently possessed by his predecessor, he far outwent him in ceremonious civility; and in one or two interviews I had with him, he almost overwhelmed me with bows. It would be unjust, however, not to say, that his usage of us was unexceptionable, though we were not much favoured with his company. Here, for the first time, we drew provisions for the almost famished prisoners, in which number, the reader knows, I have no right to include myself, and one or two of my friends; and it was politely referred to me, as the eldest officer in the company, to put my name to the provision return, made out also by ourselves. In the morning, early, the rest of the prisoners from the fort and Haerlem village, had come on; and being all assembled, we took up the line of march, preparatory to our untriumphal entry into the city of New York. From the circumstance of our being most advanced, we had the honour of forming the van of the procession, strung out to a great length, between a line of British infantry on either side. Captain Manuel, from an effect of the arrangements, had now ceased to accompany us; instead of whom, we, in front, were escorted by a Captain Warren, a young Irishman of the Inniskillen regiment. He was not uncourteous or disobliging; and was extremely prompt in attending to the want of drink, which sometimes occurred upon the road, on these occasions, offering the contents of his canteen to mix with the water that was brought us. But he was somewhat too lavish of the term *rebel*, extremely offensive to my ear, I must confess, however appropriate it might be. In the English language, it is too much interwoven with the idea of state criminality, to be other than highly opprobrious. It might be doubted, nevertheless, whether in the mouth of Captain Warren, it had its full malignity; and whether its adoption was not less owing to a design to stigmatize, than to the insufficiency of his vocabulary.

19*

He was fond of chatting, and, I might add, of boasting of the prowess of the British troops, whom he took occasion to compare with ours. I told him that I had often seen them before, and admitted that they were well dressed and well armed, to which circumstances, might perhaps be owing, their apparent advantage over ours. He took what I said in good part; and what is a proof, that he ought to be excepted from the real scoundrels in the British service, is, that some time afterwards, meeting him in the street at New York, he stopped me, and behaved with an entirely correct civility.

On the road, as we approached the city, we were beset by a parcel of soldier's trulls and others, who came out to meet us. It was obvious, that in the calculation of this assemblage of female loyalty, the war was at an end; and that the whole of the rebel army, WASHINGTON and all, were safe in durance. Which is WASHINGTON? Which is WASHINGTON? proceeded from half a dozen mouths at once; and the guard was obliged to exert itself to keep them off. Some of them assailed us with vollies of Billingsgate; and Colonel Maxwell, who rode along side of us, and whom I immediately recognised for a Captain Maxwell, who had once lodged at my mother's, had enough to do to silence one of them, calling out repeatedly: "Away with that woman! Take her way! Knock her down, the bitch! Knock her down!"

Previously to entering the city, we were drawn up for about an hour, on the high ground near the East river. Here, the officers being separated from the men, we were conducted into a church, where, if I mistake not, we signed a parole. While in this building, which, with the addition of those spectators who pressed in along with us, was pretty much crowded, a portly, well looking, middle-aged non-commissioned officer of the forty-second regiment, approached me, observing in a low voice, that he was sure he had seen me before: "Was not my name ——?" I answered in the affirmative. "I thought so," said he, "I have often seen you at your mother's in Philadelphia; and though you were then but a boy, I clearly retrace your features. As you are probably in want of money, may I beg you to accept of this?" slipping into my hand a dollar. I objected to taking it, as I might never have an opportunity of repaying him. "No matter if you have not," said he; "it is but a trifle, but such as it is, you cannot oblige me more than by accepting it." I accordingly put it in my pocket, the confusion and bustle of the scene preventing my taking measures for ascertaining the means of seeing him again; and having never afterwards met with him, I am still indebted to this amount, together with the gratitude that is inseparable from it, to this worthy, generous man, whose memory, it seems, was better than that of Colonel Stirling, Captain Grant, and many others, who had better means of recollection, than this sergeant. They did not see me, it is true; and if they had, they were doubtless too much in the Bute system of politics, to have any charity for our rebellion, or one engaged in it. But Mr. Stirling, when a Captain, I always thought a haughty, self-important man, too intent on things above him to cast a glance at those beneath; and, whether correct or not in this opinion, having, in truth, no right to expect any thing from him or his clan, I was not disappointed; nor should I have thought of taking notice of them, had not the disloyal officiousness of their sergeant, somehow prompted my pencil to give them a nook in the back ground.

I ought before to have mentioned a visit from a Mr. Johnson, of Georgia, who had been my fellow pupil at Pike's fencing school. Whether it was on the day, or the day after we were taken, I do not remember, but Johnson, whose politics I had not before known, was, I found, a staunch government man, and invested with a commission in the royal army. He appeared not displeased at seeing me well, but was at no pains to conceal his exultation at our misfortune, and the prospect he thence derived, of our being speedily subdued. Thus called upon, I bragged a little in my turn, though with a heart much less assured than his.

Our men were confined in churches and sugar-houses, and quarters were assigned for us who were officers, in the upper part of the town, in what was called *the holy ground*. But, besides, that it was not *tout-à-fait honnête* or entirely correct, to become a charge to his Britannic Majesty, after having presumed to resist his royal authority, I was somewhat apprehensive that his fare might not be the most sumptuous; and therefore, though but with the single dollar in my pocket, which I owed to the bounty of the benevolent Highlander, I yet ventured to take boarding at four dollars per week. I knew that I had an excellent banker in Philadelphia, and that if specie was to be procured, my good mother would take care to get it, and send it to me. The person with whom I boarded was a Mrs. Carroll, who, under the protection of General Robertson, commandant of the town, was hardy enough to entertain rebels. She passed for the particular favourite of this gentleman; and was sufficiently young and buxom, to give probability to the imputation. She played her cards with much address, and bent her politics, if she had any, to her interest. She was, no doubt, tory or whig, as best suited the company she happened to be in; and, of course, with us, was always the latter—shaping accordingly her news and her anecdotes, of which she picked up abundance when she went abroad, and detailed to us on the opening of the budget on her return. With due allowance for her influences and motives, we were flattered, and sometimes instructed by her communications. What led me to these quarters, was the circumstance, of some of the Pennsylvania officers taken on Long Island, being already in them, viz. Colonels Atlee and Miles; Major Burd, Captain Herbet, &c. There was also there a Mr. Coursey or De Courcey, of Smallwood's regiment; and they now, besides myself, received the addition of Colonel Magaw, Major West, Captains Lenox and Edwards, and Doctor McHenry, who afterwards became a member of General Washington's family and Secretary of War. Colonel Cadwalader, (through the interest of General Prescott, who, when a prisoner with us, had been liberally treated by Doctor Cadwalader, the father of the Colonel,) was immediately released, and went home on parole.

From the number of her boarders, Mrs Carroll might be supposed to have a very large house, but this was not the fact. It was but an humble tenement in Queen's street, of two stories, with two or three chambers: but adjoining it, was a building, which, having been abandoned, we, at her instance, under the auspices of General Robertson, took possession of, and furnished with our own mattresses and blankets. Nothing was scarcer in New York, this winter, than fuel; but, clubbing our weekly allowance of coal, we were enabled to supply for our hostess, the parlor and kitchen fire.

The next object of our cares, was our baggage at Fort Washington. The security of that, belonging to those taken in the fort, was stipulated for on its surrender; and although I could not claim the benefit of the capitulation, I did not doubt, that mine, as a part of the mass, would fare as well as the rest. It chiefly consisted of a mattress and trunk, in which, was a bundle of letters, the fruits of an interesting correspondence, which had never been intermitted, from the time of my leaving Philadelphia, to that of my captivity; and which, I valued far beyond all my other possessions. They were now more precious than ever; since all letters, to or from us, being subjected to inspection, the intercourse must cease; and the reperusal of these must console me for the privation of recent communications. My anxiety, however, was soon removed, by the safe arrival by water, two or three days after our reaching New York, of my trunk and mattress. I lost, indeed, a fowling-piece, small-sword and some other articles: but these were of little consequence; and I thought myself supremely fortunate in losing no more. The advantage of a change of clothes, being by this time very desirable, I gladly availed myself of the contents of my trunk, which, besides linen, stockings, &c., afforded me a better suit of regimentals, and a newer hat than those I had on. As I saw no reason why I should not wear them, I put them on for the purpose of taking a walk through the city. My fellow-lodgers, who had been taken on Long Island, being older and more prudent than myself, evinced some surprise at my temerity. To them I appeared much better dressed than *rebel beseemed;* and they predicted the probability of insult and abuse, should I exhibit myself in a trim so remote from the garb of humility; for as to themselves, they had, with the exception of Colonel Atlee, and one or two more, exchanged their martial habiliments for plain clothes; and even in these, they rarely went out. Without regarding their suggestions, however, I sallied forth alone, and walked past the coffee-house, down to the battery. Finding the gate-way open, I entered it, and after traversing it to its extremity, I strolled back again; almost every sentinel, to my great surprise, I must confess, handling his arms to me as I passed. Leaving the battery, I took a turn into another part of the town, and after a considerable round, regained my lodgings, without having met with the smallest molestation. But I afterwards learned from Mr. Theophilact Bache, (of whom I shall have occasion to speak in the sequel) that he well recollected, once seeing me pass the coffee-house, probably at this very time; and that he and some other gentlemen, had been obliged to exert themselves to prevent some blackguards insulting me. This conduct of mine would seem to indicate an arrogance, or an apathy, that I can aver was not in my character. It was not a want of feeling, but an excess of it, which prompted me to the proceeding. Revolting against the design to treat us as state criminals, and to overwhelm us with the odium attached to that condition ; smarting, too, from the personal insults I had received, and in a state of cruel suspense respecting my brother, the prevailing colour of which was, that he had been killed, my mind was slightly tinctured with that sombre enthusiasm, which exults in the opportunity of setting persecution at defiance ; and which in its excess, can subdue the strongest instincts of nature, as was evinced in the ferocious heroism of Charlotte Corday.

CHAPTER IX.

ONE of the first measures of the Howes, in consequence of
their late success, was to issue a proclamation, tendering pardon
to such as should renounce the cause of rebellion. I only recollect its general tenor, and that the proffered grace might have
been spared. Not more than one or two, and indeed not one
to my certain knowledge, embraced the invitation, although
warmly recommended to us by Mr. Commissary Loring. This
was, no doubt, a matter both of surprise and mortification; and
one, which in no degree tended to mitigate the contemptuous
rigour of our treatment.

Mr. Beckwith, it may be recollected, had promised to call
upon me. He kept his word, and sought me at our allotted
quarters on the holy ground. Not finding me there, or meeting
with any one who could tell him where I lodged, he left a message for me, importing that after the most diligent inquiry, he
had not been able to learn any thing respecting my brother.
Some time after, meeting in the street, a sergeant who had belonged to his guard, I inquired for him, and was informed, that,
very shortly after I had seen him, he had embarked for Rhode
Island.

Among the rare exceptions to the haughty demeanour of our
lordly masters, might be mentioned, the occasional civility of

Major Skene, who seemed, for himself, to have adopted the conciliatory mode of conduct, and sometimes called to see us. Besides a slight acquaintance he had made with Colonels Atlee and Miles, he had, while in durance among us, contracted a sort of general acquaintance with the *rebel character* of America; and he appeared not to think very ill of it, notwithstanding its collision with the high pretensions of British supremacy, of which, he was an unqualified votary. He was a portly man, about forty, or forty-five, apparently frank and good-humoured; and so far was he from resenting the usage he had received from us, that he acknowledged he had been treated full as well as he had a right to expect, since he had made it a point to be as troublesome and vexatious as possible.

Between two and three weeks had elapsed, when I received a letter from my mother. It was brought by a Captain Hesketh, of the British army, who had been a prisoner with us. It acquainted me he had money for me; but a piece of intelligence of still greater consequence, was, that my brother was safe and at home. A boat had got over the Hudson, as I had heard, and to avoid falling into the hands of the enemy, by whom he had been closely pressed, he had put himself on board. Nothing now was wanting to make me as happy as my situation would admit. I waited upon Captain Hesketh, found him at home, and was very politely treated both by him and his lady, to whose notice I had been particularly recommended by Miss Amiel, of Philadelphia, a mutual acquaintance. Among other things, Mrs. Hesketh, who was the most communicative, informed me, that they had met General WASHINGTON on their road, at the head of his army, which must indeed have been a small one; though this unwelcome truth being spared, I had not the courage to elict it by any questions. And this account agrees with a letter of the General, to the Board of War, dated Brunswick, the 30th of November, wherein he speaks of having met with Captain Hesketh and his family. Of the same date, from the same person, and in his own hand, I shall now present the reader with a letter, which, considering the pressing situation of affairs, displays a mind at once superior to adversity, and alive to the impressions of humanity, and the feelings of private distress. It appears to be in answer to a letter from my mother, on hearing of my captivity.

"*Brunswick*, 30*th Nov*. 1776.

"MADAM,

" Your letter to your son (enclosed to me) went in the day after it came to my hands, by a flag which happened to be going to New York.

" I am very sorry for the misfortune of your son's captivity, but these are accidents which must be experienced and felt in war. Colonel Cadwalader, who has been suffered to return to Philadelphia, would be able to inform you of your son's health. Any hard money, which you may be able to forward to me, or Mr. Tilghman, (who is of my family) shall be contrived to him by some means or other.

" I am, Madam,

" Your very humble servant,

"Go: WASHINGTON."

This letter is given *verbatim* as it is written, without presuming to supply what may be supposed an omission in the last line. The words *to be sent*, after the word *contrived*, appear to be wanting. Whether they were left out through inadvertence, or in compliance with an American mode of speaking, taken notice of by Doctor Witherspoon, in an essay under the signature of " A Druid," I shall not undertake to decide. I can only say, that if it is an Americanism, I never heard it before,* and that it is not common in Pennsylvania. It is, however, perfectly intelligible, and analogous to other contractions in the language of business.

The letter spoken of by the General, as having been enclosed to him, and sent in by a flag, I did not receive until some time after that by Captain Hesketh. It had, probably, wandered out of its road, into the hands of a British officer of the same Christian and surname, as well as rank, as this gentleman told a lady of my acquaintance in Philadelphia, when General Howe after-

* An *Americanism*, certainly, but it was seldom, indeed, that General WASH-INGTON thus transgressed. The expression is common among a portion of our Western countrymen—and is not unusual, it is believed, in New-England.—ED.

wards got possession of it, that he had been fortunate enough to find a mother in this country, from whom he had received some very affectionate letters.

It was about this time, that I received a billet from Captain Wilson already mentioned. It was equally addressed to Major West, Captain Tudor and myself; and stated that a tour of duty into Jersey, had been the cause of his not attending to us before; and after apologizing for not waiting on us, for some cause or other, it requested our company to dine with him on the day but one after its date, in which case, he would send his servant to show us the way to his quarters. We understood from his note, that he was fearful of paying his respects personally, in the usual manner. It was obviously the system of the British army to treat us as persons, with whom to maintain an intercourse, would, on their part, be both criminal and degrading; and Wilson, from whatever cause, appeared more than ordinarily solicitous to avoid any ground for suspicion of too much attention to us. West was indisposed, but Tudor and myself, for the sake of a little variety, waiving etiquette agreed to dine with him ; and when the day came, were conducted to his house, or rather to his chamber, by a soldier. The dinner party was small, consisting, besides ourselves, only of our entertainer and a Lieutenant, whose name I have forgotten. He was a tall, and stout young Irishman, who, by way of high recommendation, Wilson took an opportunity to inform me, was very brave; and had killed with his own hand, a Captain of ours at White Plains. This, I was, no doubt, to take as a compliment to myself, being as much as to say, I consider you as a brave man too, sir, by supposing you capable of appreciating the quality in another, though even at the expense of your own side. This young Ajax, however, was modest and unassuming; and both he and the Captain, acted in exact conformity to that creed of a professional soldier, which, according to Lucan, is as old as the civil war of the first triumvirate, and contained in the declaration of Pompey's Generals Afranius and Petreius to Cæsar, that

> " War with its own occasions came unsought,
> And found them on the side for which they fought."

The bottle was briskly circulated, and in the course of the afternoon, there were several droppers in; among others, a curious
little creature, who bore the commission of either a Captain or a
Lieutenant. He had the appearance of a youth not exceeding
twenty, and was one of the smallest and lightest men I ever beheld; a genuine *master Slender*, that might have been "made
out of a cheese-paring after supper:" If he weighed a hundred, it was much. From the conversation, in which he took
his full proportion, it appeared that he had either a wife or a
mistress; for he complained that his lady, whom he called Bet-
sey or Kitty, had grown vastly too fond of the pleasures of the
town, and by inference, somewhat too indifferent to himself.
The circumstance, however, did not seem likely to break his
heart; and the less so, from not being thought necessary to be
locked up in that repository. He evinced, in another instance,
not necessary to detail, that he was an utter stranger to the nicer
feelings; and from such a graceless compend of premature debauchery being treated with some attention, I was induced to
consider him as the degenerate offspring of some great sire.
Another person, who joined us in the evening, appeared to belong to the navy. He was probably a surgeon, Captain of a
transport, or something in that way, as, though he wore a cockade, he had no uniform. He was called upon for his toast.
"What have you been drinking?" said he: "Peace, reconciliation,
and so forth," replied Wilson. But the fellow, either stupid or
perversely malignant, gave, Confusion to the rebels. This produced at least confusion in the company, which was extremely
disconcerted and hurt, our host in particular. Perceiving this
I determined to give the circumstance the go by with the best
possible grace; and therefore, with a silent contempt for the
toast, I drank to Captain Wilson. He returned the compliment,
and the other gentlemen bowing around the table without repeating the sentiment, it was only swallowed by the giver, who
not long after, took his leave. The general hilarity was soon restored in the true national style, which, without the "feast of
reason," has certainly much of the "flow of soul;" and whatever a rigid policy might dictate elsewhere, it was wholly laid
aside at this table. Tory or whig, loyal or disloyal, was out of

the question; and about eight or nine o'clock, Captain Wilson, putting us under the care of a soldier with a lantern in his hand, permitted us to depart, with full as much wine on board, as in conscience was due to our slight acquaintance with his brothers in Philadelphia: and thus by a single act of Irish hospitality, he cancelled the obligation he had voluntarily imposed upon himself, of rendering us every service in his power. Something, however, was due to this gentleman for a treatment of us, altogether liberal and obliging.

But, while from the advantage of bearing commissions, we had the benefit of free air and the use of our limbs, our poor devoted soldiers were enclosed within walls, scantily supplied with provisions of bad quality, wretchedly clothed, and destitute of sufficient fuel, if indeed they had any. Disease was the inevitable consequence of such a situation; and their prisons of course, soon became hospitals. A fatal malady was generated; and the mortality, to every heart not steeled by the spirit of party, was truly deplorable. I once, and once only, ventured to penetrate into these abodes of human misery and despair. But, to what purpose repeat my visit, when I had neither relief to administer, nor comfort to bestow! What could I say to the unhappy victims who appealed to me for assistance, or sought my advice as to the alternative of death or apostacy? For until rendered worthless and unfit for military duty by disease, they might enlist, and thus rescue themselves from the sufferings that awaited them. I endeavoured to encourage them with the hope of an exchange, but humanity forbade my counselling them to rush on sure destruction: I rather chose to turn my eye from a scene I could not meliorate; to put from me a calamity which mocked my power of alleviation.

Our own condition, too, though a paradise to theirs, was becoming hopeless. To say nothing of the danger of legal punishment, it indicated a captivity without end, or at least commensurate with the war. To other existing obstacles, a new one was added by the capture of General Lee,* considered by General Howe as a deserter from the British army, and therefore, not

---

* For an account of this capture, see Appendix I.—Ed.

entitled to exchange. Meanwhile the sternness of power was displayed with unabating rigour and systematic perseverance. In this scene of military despotism, I sometimes indulged my melancholy in an evening walk, when, imagination taking its flight to the shores of the Delaware, insensibly led my steps to the western part of the city. Having been the theatre of the late fire, it was marked by devastation; and as nothing is more congenial to the soul in gloom, than to wander among ruins,

> "What time the moon, in solemn splendour pours
> Long threads of silver through the gaping towers,"

it was the time I chose, to take my solitary ramble through the deserted and dilapidated edifices of Broadway. Here, amid the irregularly indented battlements which frowned in desolation, I meditated on the horrors of this guilty city, where "poor misfortune felt the lash of vice," and thousands of my unhappy countrymen were perishing under the hand of proud, unfeeling authority: Not poniarded, it is true, before the faces of their oppressors, nor murdered by the impious mockery of judicial investigation, but remorselessly consigned to slow consuming tortures, equally fatal and potent to destruction. In this, I admit, I speak the language of indignant feeling; but unless the suffering of the American prisoners was the effect of dire necessity, the British nation should be less clamourous about the massacre of Jaffa, since the quality of her humanity, when compared with that of France, would be precisely that of Nero, when contrasted with Domitian's; and hence, the whitest, it must be granted, by a very few gradations. The former, as we are told by Tacitus, had the grace to avert his eyes from the enormities he ordained; while those of the latter, feasted on human agony, and noted down the sighs of those who dared to sympathize with the victims. *Nero tamen subtraxit oculos; jussitque scelera, non spectavit: præcipua sub Domitiano miseriarum pars erat, videre et aspici; cum suspiria nostra subscriberentur.*

It is no grateful office to apologize for obduracy; nor is it for the sufferers to seek excuses for the conduct of their oppressors. Justice, nevertheless demands, that due consideration should be had for the situation of the invading army; the scantiness of

20*

its limits; its ability to guard its prisoners, and means of subsisting them; nor would the bandaged Deity, on a scrutiny, I fear, entirely hold guiltless the assertors of liberty and declared protectors of the rights of man. By her own pitiable policy, the balance in an exchange of prisoners, was miserably against Congress; and her annual enlistments opposed a formidable bar to the most sacred duties both of honour and humanity. But the heroic epoch of seventy-six, had its full leaven of selfishness; and whether we appealed to our own or the French revolution, no two things will be found less alike than *patriotism* and *philanthrophy*, however it may be the fashion to speak of them as the same. When the great business is to raise an empire or to save one, what care we for the welfare of a minute inconsiderable part; and a part too, not having the slightest relation to ourselves? In the scale of public utility, what comparison can there be between an ignorant, mercenary soldier, and an enlightened member of the grand National Council, whose precious neck might, peradventure, be " destined to the cord,"* in case of an unprosperous issue to the contest! It is for your Howards to " plunge into the infection of hospitals, to take guage and dimensions of misery, depression and contempt;" it is for them, " to survey the mansions of sorrow and pain, *to remember the forgotten, to attend to the neglected;*" Congress had far higher concerns. Possibly, I go too far; yet there were certainly prisoners in our hands, who, if not equal in amount to those in the hands of the enemy, would at least have obtained a partial exchange; perhaps, with proper management, the release of the whole of the men; and the obstacle arising from the situation of Lee, might have been restricted to the officers. But this would not have done; there was an ugly rub in the affair: the time of enlistment having expired, our men were no longer soldiers, while those of the enemy were still subject to command, and in a condition, immediately to take the field. Is it not probable, therefore, that we ourselves may owe a little to the manes of our devoted countrymen? But should I still be deemed censurable for the freedom of my observations, perhaps some of the letters of General WASH-

* An expression of General GAGE's in some of his publications.

INGTON, whose discretion will not be questioned, might be brought to my aid: from these it might appear, that the army was not always cherished with the most paternal care. Revolutions, however, are not the soil for any but the stoical virtues; and, counting every life that was lost, all the vile plebeian carcasses which have served to dress the hot bed, so rankly teeming with political *fungi*, is there a statesman of nerve, a hopeful pupil of the Monticello school, who would not say, that, upon every principle of political economy, our independence was cheaply purchased?*

But the situation of the suffering soldiery, was not unattended to by their more fortunate officers; and the means of relieving them were the subject of our daily consideration. The most obvious, was, to present an address to Sir William Howe; but it was suggested, that, as the condition of the men could not but be known to him, it was to be considered as designed; and that, therefore, to state it, might be deemed impertinent, and be, in effect, injurious rather than beneficial to the end in view. This consideration, for awhile, restrained any interference in their behalf; but at length, it was resolved that a representation should be made. A memorial was prepared and signed by Colonels Magaw, Miles and Atlee, and they appointed me to deliver it. I accordingly repaired to head quarters; and meeting with some gentlemen of the family at the door, I presented it to them, with a request that it might be submitted as soon as convenient, to the Commander-in-chief. They promised it should be laid before him without delay, and inquired my name and rank, as the contents of the paper, not being known, it might be supposed to relate to myself, and at any rate, as on the deliverer of a paper, there rests a certain degree of responsibility for its contents.

As soon as we had obtained a supply of cash, we equipped ourselves generally in plain clothes, in which we were less conspicuous, and consequently, more at ease. There was a very

* A revolution in the aggregate, is a no less glorious thing than a battle, but they both lose many of their charms on an analysis; and this must account for the puny features of my narrative, when compared with the noble countenance of general history. It ought also to plead for me, with those, who may charge me with, *Etalant au public notre misanthropie.*

large store kept by one Coffin, in which, it was confidently said, Sir William Howe had a concern. From its containing the best assortment of goods, we gave it our custom; and I accordingly called there one day, to buy some cloth and other articles, but as my gold had been clipped, it could not be taken, and I left the store with an apprehension that my coin would be useless to me. Very soon after, however, Mr. Coffin contrived to let me know, that he had waived his objection, and that my money would be received; and after this, I found myself a welcome customer for all of it I could spare.

Although there must have been in New York a number of refugees from Philadelphia, I presume they did not go much abroad, as I do not remember ever meeting one of them in the street; and the only one who ventured to call upon us, was Colonel William Allen, already mentioned. He came to our lodging once or twice, in the evening. His situation was an extremely awkward one. In civil contests, there seems no medium; and neither side will tolerate neutrals. Having borne arms with us, he had not the merit of an orthodox tory with the British; neither had he any claim to the whiggism of the day, having renounced the cause of independence, and associated his fortunes with those of the enemy. In this predicament, however exempt from personal animosity we might be, there could be nothing cordial or free in our intercourse: it admitted only of a constrained and formal civility. I have little doubt, however, that Mr. Allen's personal feelings were, at this time, more with us than his new friends. As I have infinitely more satisfaction in recollecting and recording acts of generosity than of intolerance, I cannot omit to note the attention I received from Mr. Heathcote Johnson, of Amboy. This gentleman used to spend a good deal of his time in Philadelphia, had lodged at my mother's, and consequently, remembered me, though much younger than himself. Meeting him one day in the street, he stopped me, and in a very friendly manner invited me to spend a few weeks with him at Amboy. This, I could on no account have consented to, had I been at liberty to leave New York; but that not being the case, I availed myself of this restriction in declining his invitation. He replied that it might be got over; and that if I would favour him with my

company, he had no doubt, but that he had sufficient influence
to obtain an extension of my limits.   I was now obliged to decline his civility in more positive terms, though with a due impression of the liberality and kindness which had prompted it.

Other attentions, of a character not wholly dissimilar, as coming
from the royal side, we could well have dispensed with.   These
were from Captain Davenport and Colonel Houssacker, quondam
whigs and officers of our army.   The first, originally appointed a
lieutenant in our regiment, had, by the promotion of two of our
captains to the station of *aids-de-camp*, and of our major to the
lieutenant-colonelcy of a new battalion, risen to the command of
a company, as had also Tudor and Edwards, the latter already
spoken of as my first lieutenant.   This Davenport was an Irishman, who had been but a short time in Philadelphia; but by
means of good connexion there, an air of the world, and a consummate degree of effrontery, he had obtained not only a commission, but much consequence.   He dressed well, and had a
plausible exterior, but was found wholly destitute of honour and
principle.   After our retreat from Long Island, he remained in
New York, either sick or pretending to be so, and though repeatedly urged and commanded to join the regiment, he staid
there until the British took possession of it.   He was certainly a
voluntary captive, if not a deserter; and there can be little doubt
that he had renounced our cause and made his peace with the
enemy.   He notwithstanding came to see us, and wished to
be sociable as formerly, affecting to consider himself as a prisoner,
and alledging in proof of it, his confinement in the provost prison,
where I believe he had been a short time.   We understood him,
but, as we had no absolute certainty of his baseness, we did not
think it necessary to discard him; for as he frequented the coffee-
house, mixed with the British army and tories, we often received
intelligence through him, that we could not otherwise have obtained; and as he cared as little for one side as the other, his only
objects being whole bones and an adherence to the prevailing one,
he had no temptation to deceive us.   As to Houssacker, he had
been originally commissioned a Major of Wayne's battalion.   He
had, if I mistake not, been an Adjutant of the Royal Americans;
and was considered a capable disciplinarian.   He was a German,

or rather a man of no country or any country; a citizen of the world, a soldier of fortune, and a true mercenary. Thinking that our cause was going down rapidly, he saw no reason for adhering any longer to it; but came over to the enemy in the season of our extreme adversity, though he did not reach us until after the affairs of Trenton and Princeton. Not liking the name of a deserter, he called himself a prisoner, but certainly, if he was one, he had made much better terms than we had. He told us, however, that all was over; and that General WASHINGTON was reduced to the necessity of giving enormous bounties for only two or three weeks service; that by means of these, and harranguing his troops, he contrived to keep a few in the field, but that there was not the smallest doubt, that the business was up, and America subdued. His inference was, that we ought immediately to make our peace. " What do you shut yourselves up here for ?" said he, in his rattling manner, to Miles, Atlee and Magaw, with whom he was acquainted. " Why don't you go to the coffee-house and mix with the British army, as I do? They will use you well you may depend upon it. And, to be sure, the thing was easy enough; it was only to change sides, to cry *peccavi*, and receive forgiveness." Nevertheless, Colonel Houssacker made no proselytes to his opinion, or rather to his principles. Our affairs, it must be confessed, were at a very low ebb; in so far, at least, as success was dependant on sheer fighting. The immense multitude which had taken the field in the beginning of the summer, was no longer to be found: it had vanished; three short months from the opening of the campaign, had melted it away. Perhaps, not less than two-thirds of it, had gone home; no inconsiderable part had been put *hors de combat* by the enemy; and the feeble remnant yet in arms, was not calculated to inspire confidence.

Still we flattered ourselves that things were better than they appeared; and notwithstanding the dire bodings of Houssacker, our spirits were not a little raised by the handsome *coups de main* of Trenton* and Princeton; both of which came to our knowledge,

* See, in Appendix I, a letter from General WASHINGTON to Colonel REED or Colonel CADWALADER. SPARKS says he did not find this letter among WASHING-TON'S papers; WILKINSON gives it in his Memoirs, but he does not mention

though imperfectly. The mere circumstance of showing the country that the enemy was not invincible, we deemed of incalculable importance. It was in vain that the truth was disguised in the papers: enough was learned from other channels, to convince us that some signal advantages had been obtained, and to induce a belief that the spirit of America was rising with the crisis. We were always anxious to see the newspapers, though, to be disgusted and mortified, was the never failing result of a sight of them. But mercilessly as they *be-rebelled* us, the refugees, to our great delight, were not always spared; as may be collected from the following superlatively stupid paragraph, which appeared in the paper of Hugh Gaines. It was substantially, if not precisely, in these words:—" One of the rebels who had lately taken the benefit of the commissioners proclamation, complaining to a British officer, that he was not treated as a gentleman, the officer replied:— ' I take a gentleman to be a man of honour, and as it is plain no rebel can be such, you, having been one, cannot expect to be treated better than you are.' " I felt a strong itch to cast a squib at this Bœotian attempt at a sarcasm; but the difficulty was to give it publicity. There was no getting it into a newspaper, and detection would infallibly have obtained the author a lodging in the provost prison. Upon consulting with Edwards, it was agreed to endeavour to have it placed in a conspicuous part of the coffee-house; and accordingly, in the evening, we procured a black boy, who, for the small fee of a quarter of a dollar or half a crown, undertook to lay, unobserved, the following production, sealed and addressed, " To the officers of the British army," in one of the boxes of the coffee-room:

" A friend to government, presents his warmest and most submissive acknowledgments to his ' very worthy and approved good masters,' the gallant officers of the British army, *ever pre-eminent in mercy,*[*] for their manly and immortal triumph over the rebel, who had lately the unparalelled audacity to appear in the company

whence he obtained it. Its publication by WILKINSON, who, doubtless, considered it genuine,—and SPARKS agrees with him,—is no proof of its authenticity. On the contrary, from *internal evidence*, we should pronounce it to be a forgery.—ED.

[*] Words in a letter or proclamation of General Gage, while at Boston.

of gentlemen—I say, *gentlemen ;* for from that witty and ingenious sarcasm, which appeared in Mr. Gaines' last paper, it is incontestably proved that no rebel can be such; and it is therein no less clearly demonstrated, that every man who wears a red coat, and has the magnanimity to insult a person in his power, has every claim to that respectable character, which humanity, politeness and true heroism can confer. But, while I applaud the glory, I cannot but condemn the policy of the deed; for who knows, but that some of these poor, shabby rascals, may have the arrogance to call thenselves gentlemen on their own dunghill, and even to venture upon retaliation? It is true, their cowardice and meanness of spirit, have hitherto induced them to treat their prisoners with the utmost lenity and civility; but, from the spirit of enterprize, they have lately discovered, it is much to be feared, that they may, one day, pluck up courage enough to look a British officer in the face, or even to insult a captive.

"But I wander from my point, which was merely to celebrate this illustrious exploit, which far transcends the most heroic achievements of your ancestors. How shall I express my satisfaction of your conduct? In a word, I am dumb with admiration, and ' in silence muse your praise.' "

We remained in ignorance of the issue of our machination, until the following evening, when, Davenport calling upon us, immediately testified by his countenance (for he was not an unpleasant rogue) that some amusing mischief had occurred. "You are a couple of pretty fellows," said he to Edwards and myself; " you have made a devil of an uproar at the coffee-house !" We affected not to know what he meant, but he insisted upon it, that it was by us, and us alone, that a letter had been addressed to the British officers, which had set some of them raving mad. We found he had seen it, as he mentioned its contents. Some of the officers, he told us, only laughed at it, and said it was very well done, while others were so outrageous, as to put up a notice in the coffee-room, importing, that " no *white-washed rebel* should presume to set his foot there again, under pain of being turned or kicked out;" for they supposed it to proceed from a refugee. Davenport judged better; and was persuaded that we were its authors; though we dissembled so well, that he appeared at length to doubt. We were highly tickled at the success of the contrivance, but knew better than to put ourselves into the power of a man so unprincipled. He several times afterwards returned to the charge, persisting in his assertion that the letter was ours; but we were so guarded, that he was never able to extort from us an admission that we knew any thing of the matter: To have gotten into the clutches of Conyngham, would have been paying too dearly for our joke.

This Conyngham was the provost marshal, and by the concurrence of all who had been under his dominion, he was a fellow that would not have disgraced the imperial throne of the Cæsars, in the darkest days of Roman tyranny; nor the republic of France, at the most refulgent era of Jacobinism. A just respect for the enlightened and moral policy of our rulers, forbids my carrying the adaptation farther. Davenport himself bore testimony to his villany; one of whose traits, was, that in the evening, he would traverse his domain with a whip in his hand, sending his prisoners to bed, with the ruffian like *Tattoo* of, *Kennel ye sons of bitches! Kennel, G—d damn ye!* Colonel Ethan Allen too, in the *narrative of his captivity*, says, that "he was as great a rascal as the army could boast of," with the single exception of Joshua Loring, the commissary of prisoners; and he winds up a most violent, and possibly, not ill deserved invective against the commissary, in the following energetic and characteristic strain of eloquence. "He (meaning Loring) is the most mean spirited, cowardly, deceitful and destructive animal in God's creation below; and legions of infernal devils, with all their tremendous horrors, are impatiently ready to receive Howe and him, with all their detestable accomplices, into the most exquisite agonies of the hottest regions of hell-fire."*

---

* ETHAN ALLEN was a Brigadier-General in the Revolutionary army. He was a native of Connecticut, but received his very limited education in Vermont; his parents having emigrated to that State while he was very young. "At the request of the Legislature of Connecticut, Allen collected a body'of about 230 *Green Mountain boys*—as the settlers of Vermont were then designated—and marched against the Fortresses of Ticonderoga and Crown Point. At Castleton he was joined by Colonel ARNOLD. They arrived at the lake opposite to Ticonderoga on the evening of May 9th, and having, with great difficulty procured boats,

21

Should this language be thought too highly wrought, it should be remembered, that few have ever more severely felt the hand of arbitrary power than Allen ; and that he had but recently emerged from the provost guard, to which, for some alleged infringement of parole, he and Major Otho H. Williams, afterwards General Williams, a very gallant and already distinguished officer, had been committed.* Allen had been brought from Halifax to

landed 83 men on the other shore during the night. The day, however, beginning to dawn, Allen was obliged to attack the Fort before his rear could cross the lake, having previously animated his soldiers, by a harangue, which he concluded with saying, ' I now propose to advance before you, and in person to conduct you through the wicket-gate; but, inasmuch as it is a desperate attempt, I do not urge on any one contrary to his will. You that will undertake voluntarily, poise your firelocks.' They all immediately poised their firelocks. He then advanced at the head of the centre file to the wicket-gate, where a sentry snapped his fusee at him, and retreated, followed by Allen, who formed his men upon the parade. The apartments of the commanding officer having been pointed out to him by a sentry who asked for quarters, he instantly repaired thither, and, holding his sword over Captain de Laplace, whom he found undressed, demanded the surrender of the Fort. The latter asking him by what authority, ' I demand it,' said Allen, ' In the name of the Great Jehovah, and of the Continental Congress.' De Laplace was constrained to comply, and the Fort with its stores and garrison, was given up. General Allen was a man of strong mind and of an enterprizing spirit. He was taken prisoner in Canada. He was kept in irons and treated with much severity. His Narrative of his captivity is curiously written, but, is evidently, a faithful account. He died suddenly in 1789. Allen was an infidel. He adopted sundry wild and absurd notions, among others, believing with Pythagoras that the soul of man, after death, would live again in beasts, birds and fishes. He often said that he would live again under the appearance of a large white horse. These opinions, however, he was supposed to profess, more from an affectation of singularity than conviction. While sitting in his library conversing with a physician, Dr. Elliot, Allen was informed that his daughter was dying, and desired to speak with him. He and Elliot immediately repaired to her chamber. His wife was distinguished for her piety, and had instructed her daughter in the principles of Christianity. As soon as her father stood at her bedside, she said to him, ' I am about to die ; shall I believe in the principles you have taught me, or shall I believe in what my mother has taught me ?' He became greatly agitated; his chin quivered; his whole frame shook ; and, after waiting a few moments, he replied, ' Believe what your mother has taught you.' "—*Ency. Amer.*

————" Hear the voice within,
The small, still voice of conscience, hear it cry,
AN ATHEIST THOU MAY'ST LIVE, *but* CAN'ST NOT DIE !"—*Gifford.*—ED.

* OTHO HOLLAND WILLIAMS : He rose to the rank of Adjutant-General, in which station he remained until the close of the revolutionary war. He greatly distin-

New York, a short time before the taking of Fort Washington, and was admitted to parole when we were. His figure was that of a robust, large-framed man, worn down by confinement and hard fare; but he was now recovering his flesh and spirits; and a suit of blue clothes, with a gold laced hat that had been presented to him by the gentlemen of Cork, enabled him to make a very passable appearance for a rebel colonel. He used to show a fracture in one of his teeth, occasioned by his twisting off with it, in a fit of anger, the nail which fastened the bar of his hand-cuffs; and which drew from one of the astonished spectators, the exclamation of " damn him, can he eat iron?" I had become well acquainted with him, and have more than once heard him relate his adventures while a prisoner before being brought to New York, exactly corresponding both in substance and language, with the. narrative he gave the public in the year 1779. I have seldom met with a man, possessing, in my opinion, a stronger mind, or whose mode of expression was more vehement and oratorical. His style was a singular compound of local barbarisms, scriptural phrases, and oriental wildness; and though unclassic and sometimes ungrammatical, it was highly animated and forcible. In the following sentence of his narrative, though it is not perhaps strictly correct in its construction, there is to me, a flash of moral pathos not unworthy of a Robertson. " When the fleet," says he, " consisting of about forty-five sail, including five men of war, sailed from the cove (of Cork) with a fresh breeze, the appearance was beautiful, abstracted from the unjust and bloody designs they had in view." Notwithstanding that Allen might have had something of the insubordinate, lawless frontier spirit† in his composition, having been in a state of hostility with the government of New York before the war of the revolution, he appeared to me to be a man of generosity and honour; several instances of which occur in his publication, and one, not equivocal, came under my own

guished himself in the disastrous battle of Camden. Previous to the disbandment of the army, Congress made him a Brigadier-General. He died in 1794. —Ed.

   † A spirit resembling that given by Scott to his Borderers, and which perhaps is common to men residing on the verge of policed communities, when the law is feeble and inefficient, and consequently contemned.

observation.   General WASHINGTON, speaking of him in an official letter of May the 12th, 1788, observes, with a just discrimination, that there was an original something in him which commanded admiration.

The representation which had been submitted to Gen. Howe, in behalf of the suffering prisoners, was more successful than had been expected.   About a week, I think, after its delivery, the memorialists were given to understand, that their statement and propositions had been considered by Sir William Howe; and that he was disposed to accede to them.   These were, if I mistake not, that the men should be sent within our lines, where they should be receipted for, and an equal number of the prisoners in our hands returned in exchange.   Policy, no less than humanity, recommended the measure; since our men, no longer soldiers and too debilitated for service, even should they incline to re-en-list, gave a claim to sound men, immediately fit to take the field; and there was, moreover, great danger that, if they remained in New York, the disease with which they were infected, might be spread throughout the city.   That these considerations had their weight in the favourable result of the application cannot be doubted.   At any rate, hope was admitted into the mansions of despair : the prison doors were thrown open, and the soldiers who were yet alive and capable of being moved, were conveyed to our nearest posts, under the care of our regimental surgeons, to them a fortunate circumstance, since it enabled them to exchange the land of bondage for that of liberty, and to return to the bosom of their families and friends.   Among these was Doctor M'Henry, with whom, from a residence in the same house, I was becoming intimate, though I had been but little acquainted with him before.   The mention of this gentleman, brings along with it the recollection of my obligation to him, for his kindness and medical care of me, under the attack of a quinsy, but a very few days before he left us.*

Immediately after the release of our men, a new location was

---

* JAMES MCHENRY. He was appointed Secretary of War by WASHINGTON, early in 1796, and was dismissed, with Colonel PICKERING, Secretary of State, by the elder President ADAMS.—ED.

assigned to us; and on the 22d of January, (1777,) as I find from Ethan Allen's narrative, though my recollection would have placed it in the middle of February, we were removed to Long Island, and by our parole, restricted to a district, consisting of Flat-bush, New-lots, Flat-lands and Gravesend, at each of which places, a part of us, were billetted on the inhabitants by Commissary Loring, for the stipulated sum of two dollars a head per week. What induced our removal from New York, I never learned: but without any inclination to assign undue importance to a trifle, it is not improbable, that the squib thrown into the coffee-house, as already mentioned, might have had its influence in bringing about the measure. Whatever some of the British officers might have thought, the refugees and tories could have had no doubt of the quarter whence it came. Its tenor, and still more, its consequences could not but have been both offensive and mortifying to them; and their feelings were entitled to the attention of Sir William Howe, whose protection they had sought. In addition to this, it is probable, that in other respects we did not sufficiently conform to the state of humiliation, in which it was the policy to place us. We took the full latitude of our parole, traversing the streets in all directions, with a good deal of assurance; and once, when the Tea-water pond was frozen over and covered with British officers, who thought themselves skaters, a few of us were audacious enough to mingle in the exercise, from the malicious pleasure more than any thing else, of showing them what arrant bunglers they were. But, to whatever cause it might be owing, it was, to the generality of us, a most unwelcome step. It was placing another river between us and our homes and though, in fact, we should be as visible to the eyes of Congress on Long Island, as at New York, we could not but consider the measure as unpropitious to an exchange; and we regarded our transportation across the East river as a consignation to "dumb forgetfulness," where, no longer thought of by friends or foes, we were destined to waste the best of our days in a state of hopeless captivity.

21*

CHAPTER X.

FLAT-BUSH was the place assigned for the officers of our regiment, as well as those of Magaw's. Here also, were stationed
Colonels Miles, Atlee, Rawlings and Major Williams, the indulgence of arranging ourselves agreeably to our respective circles
of acquaintance, having been granted by Mr. Loring, of whom,
for my own part, I have nothing hard to say. It is true, he
laboured under that " curse of great ones," in having the " forked
plague " fixed on him by Sir William: Yet as there is little doubt,
that he considered himself amply indemnified by his office, he
was not " robbed at all."   Mr. Forrest and myself were billetted
on a Mr. Jacob Suydam.   His house was pretty large, consisting of
buildings which appeared to have been erected at different times,
the front and better part of which, was in the occupation of Mr.
Theophilact Bache and his family, from New York.   Though we
were in general, civilly enough received, it cannot be supposed,
that we were very welcome to our Low Dutch hosts, whose habits of
living were extremely parsimonious, and whose winter provision was
barely sufficient for themselves.   Had they been sure of receiving
the two dollars a-week, it might have reconciled them to the
measure; but payment appeared to them to depend on the success
of our cause, (Congress, or ourselves, being looked upon as the
pay-masters,) and its failure, in their eyes, would in both cases

induce a stoppage of payment. They were, however, a people who seemed thoroughly disposed to submit to any power, which might be set over them; and whatever might have been their propensities or demonstrations at an earlier stage of the contest, they were now the dutiful and loyal subjects of His Majesty George the Third; and entirely obedient to the behests of their military masters in New York. As it was at the instance of these, that we were saddled upon them, they received us with the best grace they could put on. Their houses and beds we found clean; but their living extremely poor, and well calculated to teach the luxurious, how infinitely less than their pampered appetites require, is essential to the sustentation of life. In the apostrophe of Lucan,

> " O prodiga rerum
> Luxuries, nunquam parvo contenta paratu,
> Et quæsitorum terra pelagoque ciborum
> Ambitiosa fames, et lautæ gloria mensæ!
> Discite quam parvo liceat producere vitam."

Thus translated by Rowe:

> " Behold! ye sons of luxury, behold!
> Who scatter in excess your lavish gold;
> You who the wealth of frugal ages waste,
> T' indulge a wanton supercilious taste;
> For whom all earth, all ocean are explor'd
> To spread the various proud voluptuous board,
> Behold! how little thrifty nature craves."

A sorry wash made up of a sprinkling of bohea, and the darkest sugar on the verge of fluidity, with half-baked bread, fuel being among the scarcest articles at Flat-bush, and a little stale butter, constituted our breakfast. At our first coming, a small piece of pickled beef was occasionally boiled for dinner, but, to the beef which was soon consumed, succeeded *clippers* or clams, and our unvaried supper was *supon* or mush, sometimes with skimmed milk, but more generally with buttermilk blended with molasses, which was kept for weeks in a churn, as swill is saved for hogs. I found it, however, after a little use, very eatable; and supper soon became my best meal. The table company con-

sisted of the master of the house, Mr. Jacob Suydam, an old
bachelor, a young man, a shoemaker of the name of Rem Hagerman, married to Jacob's niece, who, with a mewling infant in her
arms, never failed to appear. A black boy, too, was generally in
the room; not as a waiter, but as a kind of *enfant de maison*,
who walked about, or took post in the chimney corner with his
hat on, and occasionally joined in the conversation. It is probable, that but for us, he would have been placed at the table;
and that it had been the custom before we came. Certain it is,
that the idea of equality, was more fully and fairly acted upon in
this house of a British subject than ever I have seen it practised
by the most vehement declaimers for the rights of man among
ourselves. It is but fair, however, to mention, that I have never
been among our transcendent republicans of Virginia, and her
dependencies. But notwithstanding some unpleasant circumstances in our establishment, every member of the family, the
black fellow, to whom we had been the cause of some privations,
excepted, was exceedingly courteous and accommodating. Rem
Hagerman, and *Yonichy*, his wife, gave themselves no airs; nor
was our harmony with uncle Jacob ever interrupted, but on a
single occasion, when, soured a little by I know not what provocation, he made a show of knocking down Forrest with a pair of
yarn stockings he had just drawn from his legs, as he sat in the
chimney-corner one evening preparing for bed. It was, indeed,
but an offer, though it might, for aught I know, have amounted
to an assault in law, as Jacob was not so far from the person
menaced, but that the feet of the stockings, if held by the other
extremity, and projected from an extended arm, might possibly
have reached him; and a pair of long-worn yarn stockings, might,
from daily alluvion, have acquired somewhat of the properties of
a cudgel. But moments of peevishness were allowable to our
host; since, though we had for some time been consuming his
provisions, he had never seen a penny of our money and it was
somewhat doubtful, to say the truth, whether he ever would; for,
considering the contractors for our boarding liable for it, we never
thought of paying it ourselves. As the Low Dutch are a people
little known in Pennsylvania, and more especially, as it is my
avowed intention to advert to the character of the time, this

sketch of their domestic economy and manners, may not be
thought impertinent. In a word, from what I saw of them on
Long Island, I was led to consider them as a people, quiet and
inoffensive beyond any I had seen; such, from whom no enthusiastic efforts, either of good or evil tendency, were to be looked
for; who were neither prolific of Catos nor Catilines; and who,
had they been the sole occupants of this great continent of ours,
would still have been colonists, and never known what it was to
be independent republicans.   Their religious, like their other
habits, were unostentatious and plain; and a silent grace* before
meat, prevailed at the table of Jacob Suydam.   When we were
all seated, he suddenly clasped his hands together, threw his head
on one side, closed his eyes, and remained mute and. motionless
for about a minute.   His niece and nephew followed his example;
but with such an eager solicitude that the copied attitude should
be prompt and simultaneous, as to give an air of absurdity, to
what might otherwise have been very decent.   Although little of
the vernacular accent remained on the tongues of these people,
they had some peculiarities in their phraseology.   Among these,
instead of asking you to sit, or sit down to table, they invited you
to *sit by;* and this I even observed in General Schuyler, when I
was at Lake George.   It might be asked by a stickling New
Yorker, if "sit by" is not as proper, and even more so, than
"sit down," which, in strictness, is a redundancy.   A Philadelphian might admit it: but it would be no evidence of his want of
candour, should he add, that it was, nevertheless, extremely awkward English.

* Mrs. GRANT, in her " Memoirs of an American Lady," speaking of the state
of religion among the settlers about Albany, says, "Their religion, like their
original national character, had in it little of fervor or enthusiasm; their manner of
performing religious duties, was regular and decent, but calm, and to more
ardent imaginations, might appear mechanical.   None ever doubted of the great
truths of revelation, yet few seemed to dwell on the result with that lively delight
which devotion produces in minds of keener sensibility.   If their piety, however, was without enthusiam, it was also without bigotry; they wished others to
think as they did, without showing rancor or contempt towards those who did
not.   In many individuals, whose lives seemed governed by the principles of
religion, the spirit of devotion seemed to be quiescent in the heart, and to break
forth in exigencies; yet that monster in nature, an impious woman, was never
heard of among them."—*Mem., chap.* v.—ED.

The morning after our arrival at this place, we encountered Mr. Bache in the piazza, which extended the whole length of the building on the south side. His being an Englishman and a determined royalist, did not prevent him from accosting us very civilly, and manifesting a disposition to maintain a friendly intercourse with us, notwithstanding the difference in our political sentiments. Having long resided in New York, he was acquainted with the grounds of the contest; and well knew, that the opposition to the mother country, was not confined to a low and desperate faction, as it was the fashion among the loyalists to represent it. He was aware, that his brother in Philadelphia,* (married to the daughter of Doctor Franklin) had embraced the Whig side of the question, as well as others of the first respectability in America; and was, therefore, perfectly sensible, that we were not the insignificant rebels, which policy depicted us. But whatever was the motive, the behaviour of Mr. Bache was altogether free from intolerance and party rancour: it was more, it was hospitable and kind. In addition to frequent invitations to tea, and to partake of his Madeira, to help us along a little, as he expressed it, in allusion to the mean fare of Jacob's table, I was indebted to him for the offer of his purse, although he neither knew me nor my connexions. As I stood in no need of it, I declined it, but with a due sense of the obligation the mere offer imposed. I availed myself, however, of the tender of his services in executing small commissions for me when he went to New York, which was almost every day; and among these, he once negociated a bill of exchange in my favour, on Major

* Mr. RICHARD BACHE.—He was married to SARAH FRANKLIN, on the 29th of October, 1767. It was of this patriotic lady, that M. DE MARBOIS thus wrote to Dr. FRANKLIN, from Philadelphia, on the 4th January, 1781 :

"If there are in Europe any women, who need a model of attachment to domestic duties, and love for their country, Mrs. BACHE may be pointed out to them as such. She passed a part of the last year in exertions to rouse the zeal of the Pennsylvania ladies, and she made on this occasion such a happy use of the eloquence which you know she possesses, that a large part of the American army was provided with shirts, bought with their money, or made by their hands. In her applications for this purpose, she showed the most indefatigable zeal, and the most unwearied perseverance, and a courage in asking, which surpassed even the obstinate reluctance of the Quakers in refusing."—ED.

Small. It might have been this circumstance which led the Major to a knowledge that my mother, (at whose house he had long, and at different times, been a lodger, as already mentioned,) had sons in the American army. For, on conversing once with Captain Hutchins, in London, on the subject of the war, he said to him, "would you have believed it, Hutchins, that *Desdy* had two of her sons in arms against us?" But this fact could not have appeared quite so unnatural to the Captain, as it did to the Major, since, not very long after, for his attachment to the American cause, he was obliged to relinquish the British service, having first been arrested on a charge of treasonable practices. Captain Hutchins, I think, was a native of New Jersey.* On his coming over to us, he was appointed to the post of Geographer-General, which had probably been created for him. From his long and frequent residence in our house, he was domesticated in it: He was a worthy and a pious man; but one, who, in his continued complaints of the injustice of the British government, in not fully remunerating his services, betrayed but little knowledge of the world. Cæsar, it is true, sent Labienus his pay and baggage, when that officer thought proper to join the standard of Pompey; but this was an instance of singular generosity. If Captain Hutchins, after spending the greater part of his life in the British army, chose to renounce it for that of America, he should at least have granted to his old employers, the privilege of some ill humour, and not have been too outrageous, even though some pecuniary deficiency had been its consequence: what was patriotism in his eyes—in theirs, was ingratitude; and the right of thinking was mutual. But if these vile monarchists were unjust to a relinquisher of their cause, what shall we say of the conduct of our own republican rulers, to old officers, who have always been faithful? Com-

---

* Thomas Hutchins, to whom General Washington wrote, 20th August, 1786, upon the subject of "authentic documents wanted by the Empress of Russia, respecting the language of the natives of this country, for the purpose of compiling a universal Dictionary." Washington farther writes:—"Persuaded that a gentleman of your taste for science in general, and particularly of your capacity of acquiring the information in question, will enter upon the task with pleasure, I make no apology for troubling you with it."—Ed.

paring the destiny of many of these with that of the adherents to
the British government, I fear we shall not all be able to say
with Rousseau : *Heureux, toutes les fois que je medité sur les
governemens, de trouver toujours dans mes recherches, de nouvelles
raisons d'aimer celui de mon pays.*[*]

Besides Mr. Bache, there were at this time, several New
Yorkers, with their families, residing at Flat-bush.   Of these,
Mr. Axtle, was apparently the first in point of wealth and importance.   I think he had been of the Governor's council.   He
was neatly seated at a country-house at the entrance of the
village from New York ; and I had once the honour of supping
with him, together with eight or ten of my fellow-prisoners, that
had been selected on the occasion.   What the object of this
single attention was, could not be divined ; but after partaking
of the hospitality, it would be wrong to ascribe it to other than
a liberal motive, and after having obtained a footing in his
house, it was our own fault that it was not improved.   In the
family of Mr. Axtle, there was a Mr. Frederick Depeyster, a
young man better known in the village by the fondling appellation of Feady ; and two young ladies, all of whom, were the
relations of Mrs. Axtle.   One of these, a Miss Shipton, had so
much toleration for our cause, as some time after, to marry a
Major Giles of our army.   Next in consequence to Mr. Axtle,
might be placed Mr. Matthews, the mayor of New York, who
divided his time between the village and the city, in each of
which he had a house.   There were also here a Mr. Sherbroke,
and a Mr. Jauncey ; and Major Moncrief, of the British army, a
relation by marriage to Mr. Bache, spent much of his time here,
where he had a daughter.   But the principal personage in a low
Dutch village appears to be the *Domine,* or Minister; and Flat-
bush, at this time, revered her Domine Reubell, a rotund, jolly
looking man, a follower of Luther and a tory, on whom were
billetted Colonels Atlee and Miles.   At Flatlands, an adjacent
hamlet, there was also a Domine Van Zinder, a disciple of Cal-
vin, and a Whig.   He was in person as well as principles, a

---

[*] Happy, so often as I contemplate other governments, to find, in my researches, as I always do, new reasons for loving that of my own country !

perfect contrast to Mr. Reubell, being a lean and shrivelled little man, with silver flowing locks, "which streamed like a meteor to the troubled air," as he whisked along with great velocity in his chair through Flat-bush.   Recalling his figure and triangular sharp-pointed hat, I have before me, the express image of the learned Knickerbocker's William the Testy. This latter Domine was distinguished by a species of pulpit eloquence, which might be truly said, to "bring matters home to mens' business and bosoms."   Mr. Bache assured me, that, in once descanting on the wily arts of the devil, in seducing and ensnaring sinners, he likened him to my landlord, Jacob Suydam, sneaking and skulking about to get a shot at a flock of snipes; small birds of the plover kind, which, at certain seasons are very numerous on the beach; and in shooting of which, old Jacob, it seems, was eminently skilful and successful.   I was indebted to Mr. Bache for much other local information; and was gratified to find, that our defence of Fort Washington, was considered by the British officers, as far from pusillanimous or disgraceful.*

There was a fatiguing sameness in our occupations, for which we had no cure.   During a residence of about five months upon Long Island, I was but once beyond the limits to which we were restricted, and this was to dine with Mr. Wallace, one of the principal merchants of New York, who now resided at Jamaica.   Together with Major West and Captain Lenox, I had been recommended to him by the house of the Nesbits, or of Conyngham and Nesbit (I am not sure of the firm) in Philadelphia, to whose friendship I was also indebted, as it was unsolicited, for a letter of credit on him, which, however, I had no occasion to use.   An instance, by the by, of the liberal uses of that commerce, which, in the enlarged and enlightened mind of Mr. Jefferson, only tends to corrupt and narrow the heart; and to sink those employed in it, into the most worthless part of the community.   It was this circumstance, which procured us an invitation to dine with him; to enable us to do which, he had obtained for us a temporary dispensation from our parole, from

* Even General HOWE declared that the place had been well defended by the "Rebels."—ED.

22

Mr. Loring. We cheerfully availed ourselves of the little variety this visit would afford us, and waited upon Mr. Wallace, who entertained us with much hospitality. But there was one incident, I must confess, I did not altogether relish: perhaps it was designed as a delicate mode of assuring us, that the civility we received, was not to be considered, in any degree as a toleration of our principles. After dinner, the son of our entertainer, a boy of about seven or eight years of age, came into the room, and his father putting a glass of wine into his hand, asked him what he drank. "Church and King," pronounced the little fellow, in an audible voice. I did not know until now, that I had made so much progress in republicanism. Although loyalty to the king, had but lately been an ardent feeling in America, and had certainly been mine; and although I had recently contemplated becoming an Episcopalian, from an idea that it was the duty of all men to conform to the established religion of their country, where, to their minds, there were no essential objections to its tenets—yet the sentiment appeared to me degrading and slavish in the extreme. This is an instance how much our opinions are swayed by our passions and habits, and a corroboration of the remark of Lord Chatham, "that the first blood drawn in the contest, would prove an *irritabile vulnus*, a wound that could not be healed, but which would fester and mortify the whole body."

Upon our first arrival at Jamaica, after putting up our horses at an inn, we concluded to take a ramble through the town before we went to Mr. Wallace's. We had accordingly strolled to nearly the end of the main street, when we observed a soldier, or non-commissioned officer, coming after us. We suspected his business to be with us, when approaching with due military etiquette, he gave us to understand, that he came by order of Colonel Fanning, who desired to speak with us at his quarters. We immediately returned with him, and were conducted to the colonel, who informed us, that he presumed we were prisoners; and if so, as we were without our limits, he conceived it his duty to inquire into the cause of it. We told him that we came to dine with Mr. Wallace, who, we understood, had obtained permission for us so to do, from the commissary of prisoners.

Had we any certificate or evidence of this? he asked. We replied, we had not, as we had entirely referred the matter to Mr. Wallace, and relied upon his assurance that we were privileged. Finding that he still seemed to consider it a dubious point, whether we ought to be detained or set at liberty, we thought it time to assert ourselves, a little, and told him that it was a matter of the utmost indifference to us, what part he might adopt. After a moment's consideration, however, he thought proper to dismiss us. This Mr. Fanning had been secretary to Governor Tryon, and now commanded a regiment of new levies, stationed at this place. Though we assumed some cavalier airs on the occasion, it cannot be said, that the colonel had exceeded his duty, or betrayed any wantonness of authority.

As Mr. Wallace was from Ireland, it probably, would not have comported with the hospitality of his table, to have suffered us to leave it, unexhilarated. He pushed the bottle, therefore; and detained us, anti-church and king-men, as we were, until we had received as much of his Madeira, as we could carry home with any tolerable convenience.

Among the very few incidents which occurred to vary the wearisome sameness of Flat-bush, was the arrival, one day, of two or three officers of the British guards, to pay their respects to Captain Richardson of Magaw's regiment, who, they had but lately learned, was the brother of Colonel Francis Richardson, already mentioned in the early part of these Memoirs. I did not see them, but the circumstance was related to me by Edwards, who was cruelly mortified in the reflection, that a worse specimen in outward appearance of the officers of our army, could hardly have been found, than in the person of Captain Richardson. In addition to a mean slouching figure, he was disgustingly slovenly, and wretchedly calculated to support either the dignity of his brother or our army. Whether he was unlucky enough to be found by his visiters, I do not recollect; but it was unquestionably the interest of those who were piqued for the reputation of the American service, to keep him out of sight, or at least, to have him furbished up before appearing. As it was the policy of the enemy to vilify us, and depreciate our cause by representing its supporters as vulgar and contemptible, it consequently stimulated us to appear to as much advantage as possible. Those who may think we attached too much importance to a good exterior, in the situation in which we were, know nothing of the qualifications respected among military men; and they would betray no less ignorance of the common feelings of mankind, should they doubt that the respectability of our army was not of vast importance to our undertaking: as much, if not more, I will venture to affirm, than even the respectability of Congress, a small, invisible body, not possessing the means of sensible impression on the mass of the people. In civil contests, it is highly requisite for the party in opposition to government, to counteract the advantage of recognised authority, by an appearance that may raise them above contempt, than which nothing can be more unfavourable to them.* This was strikingly exemplified at least, in our revolution; and is another instance of its dissimilarity to that of the French, whose object being the subversion of society, found its early strength to consist in the vaunted baseness of its partisans.

We had now been captive nearly seven months, and the obstacle to an exchange, seemed in no likelihood to be removed. We had seen the letters which had passed upon the subject, between the commanders of the two armies; and although we were satisfied with the reasoning on our side, and consoled in some degree, by the feeling manner, in which our situation was adverted to by General WASHINGTON, we were far from being reconciled to our fate. Notwithstanding that Lee's being considered as a deserter by Sir William Howe, was the ostensible bar, it occurred to me, that the reluctance felt by Congress to restoring without an equivalent, the British soldiers in their possession, was their principal motive for disagreeing to any cartel that should be attended with that consequence. The rash, though not undeserved letter to the Council of safety too, stared full in the face, the unlucky wights, who had been indiscreet enough

---

* "The habits and prejudices of the English people," says Mr. Fox, in his History of the Reign of James II., "are in a great degree aristocratical; nor had he (the Duke of Monmouth) before him, nor indeed have we since his time, had one single example of an insurrection that was successful, unaided by the ancient families and great landed proprietors."

to put our names to it: and, as the council might be supposed
to have some influence in the general concerns of the Confederation, we sometimes, in our desponding fits, conceived ourselves
no less the victims of resentment than of policy.　Before our
removal to Long Island, Colonel Miles had been permitted to
visit his family in Pennsylvania; and as he had been charged
with some proposals relative to an exchange of prisoners, he had
an interview with General Howe, either upon his going in, or
his return.　On this occasion, he received no very favourable
impression of the literary talents or critical acumen of his Excellency, who, in commenting on the communications of General
WASHINGTON, among other shrewd remarks, observed, that they
were very *badly compiled*.　For the General himself, he expressed
much respect; but lamented that he was surrounded by a set of
lawyers, who led him astray, and who contributed to, if they
did not solely cause, this bad *compilation* of his letters.　Who
compiled for Sir William, is not ascertained, that I know of, but
I believe it was generally admitted, that in this particular, he
was not better served than General WASHINGTON.　General Lee
tells us, that "McKensey, Balfour, and Galloway were his
scribes; and that all the damned stuff which was issued to the
astonished world, was theirs."

Captivity is justly comprehended in the catalogue of human
woes; its poignancy is recognised by Shakspeare in his play of
Othello, and it is among the calamities, which are particularly
adverted to, in the excellent liturgy of the Church of England.
What peculiar sickness of the heart it is, may be collected from
Rowe's beautiful allusion to it, in the wailings of Calista.

> " So the poor captive in a foreign realm,
> 　Stands on the shore and sends his wishes back,
> 　To the dear, native land from whence he came."

How often have I done this from the summit of the commanding heights which bounded our district towards Brooklyn,
and afforded an extensive view of East Jersey.　Here, like Tom
Jones, from the top of Mazard hill, and for a similar cause, have
I frequently reflected with a sigh upon the vast tract of land,
which lay between me and my home.　For although the par-

ticular object of my contemplation, was not within my sight, I had, as was observed of Jones, by his discerning companion, a pleasure in looking that way. In my melancholy hours, I had made this spot, the scene of an elegiac essay, where, having located my forlorn captive, about sunset, I say,—

> Here on the lofty summit as he stood,
>   His wistful eyes still sought the western shore;
> There, ting'd with gold, the distant hills he view'd
>   Where yet her sons fair freedom's ensign bore.

My unaffected conviction of the poverty of my poetic talent, forbids a recital of more than a few stanzas of my fragmentary production, which are selected, as well because they serve to show my impressions at the time, in regard to the cruelty of the enemy, as that they confer attributes on General WASHINGTON, which seem precisely, those which are the award of the present day, and will be that of all posterity. After a bitter apostrophe to Howe for the imputed murder of our soldiery, the doom-denouncing bard proceeds,

> For Heaven is just, and though the dazz'ling rays
>   Of royal favour, dignify thy name,
> Yet dire remorse shall tear thy future days,
>   And hist'ry damn thee to eternal fame.
>
> Then too, shall truth impartially record,
>   The gen'rous efforts of the patriot few,
> Rous'd by their wrongs to draw th' the avenging sword,
>   And crush fell tyranny's destructive crew.
>
> First in the deathless animating page,
>   Thy fame, great WASHINGTON! illustrious shines;
> Unsullied by the breath of party rage,
>   More brilliant than Golconda's glitt'ring mines:
>
> For conduct, dignity and valour fam'd,
>   'Midst dark adversity serenely great,
> Thy dauntless soul with godlike ardour flam'd
>   And soar'd above the scowling blasts of fate.
>
> 'Twas then, majestic Delaware! thy wave,
>   Became immortal from the splendid deed, &c.

When the attempt to settle a cartel had proved abortive, it was rumored that we were to be shipped for England; and this we should generally have preferred to remaining where we were. We figured to ourselves something of the nature of an adventure in the measure ; and from what Ethan Allen had told us, we did not doubt that we should find in it, some sources of gratification. The step, however, was not rationally to be looked for; there could be no inducement to it, though there might be for the threat, upon the supposition that we had connexions powerful enough to prevail with Congress for an exchange. The most sanguine among us, had now given up the hope of deliverance; and, in addition to the pining tediousness of our situation, that engine for breaking hearts, the provost-prison, was ever open to receive the victims of brutal insolence and malignity. That this was no chimera, the following incident will prove. Some fellows, one morning, on the road to New York market with fish, were stopped by Captain Lenox and two other officers, Lieutenant Wright of Maryland, and Lieutenant Stewart of Delaware, I think, who wished to buy some ; but they were told by the fishmongers, that they would not sell to rebels. This produced reproachful language on both sides, when the officers laying hold of the fish, began to bandy them about the jaws of the ragamuffins that had insulted them. A complaint was immediately lodged with General Robertson ; the accused were escorted by a guard to New York, and on the statement of the complainants, being found in aggression, they were required to make acknowledgements to the injured ; which, refusing to do, they were forthwith consigned to the custody of the provost-marshal. With him they remained for two or three weeks ; but, at length, were released, without being held to the concessions at first demanded. Conyngham, it seems, had used them well; partly owing, probably, to instructions from General Robertson, and partly to Mr. Lenox's being well supplied with money and appearing of consequence, which better than any thing else, is calculated to mollify the heart of a genuine caitiff in power.

It was a generally received opinion among us, that a close confinement would be a virtual cancelling of our parole ; and hence, when these gentlemen were returned to their district, without the exaction of a new one, they submitted it to a board of officers, whether or not they would be justified in going away. I forget what officers composed the board; I only recollect that Colonel Ethan Allen was one, and that his opinion, was that of a man of honour and sound casuist. He admitted, that they had a right to escape from their actual confinement, but that now the case was altered; and that, although no new parole had been given, yet the obligation of the former one, should be considered as returning on their enlargement; and that they were under the same restraint, in point of honour, that they had been before their commitment to the provost. This was also the opinion of the board, and unanimously approved, as well by the gentlemen immediately interested, as by others. I have mentioned this circumstance, principally to show, that Allen, however turbulent a citizen under the old *regime*, was not the vulgar ruffian, that the New York royalists represented him.

While in this state of dejection, from the unavailing negotiation to establish a cartel, an incident, as little expected, as any other within the compass of possibility, took place. —————— It was, to the best of my recollection, early in the month of June, that, one day, meeting with Mr. Christian Huck,* the lawyer, a refugee from Philadelphia, at Flat-bush, informed me, that my mother was in New York. The astonishment and even incredulity, I expressed by my manner, induced him to repeat his assurance that such was the fact, that he had seen her and conversed with her, and that I might expect to see her at this place, either on the

---

* Afterwards Captain Huck, of Tarleton's Dragoons, I think, and the same who was killed in South Carolina in 1780–1. "This Mr. Huck" says Mr. Graydon, "had read law in Philadelphia, with Mr. Isaac Hunt, before mentioned, and had received the early part of his education at the Charity School of the Academy, when I was a pupil there. He is spoken of in our accounts of him, as a monster of profaneness and cruelty. But this ferocity must have been acquired by the fury with which the war was waged in the Southern quarter, as I remember nothing of these tiger-qualities in him, and I knew him from his boyish years up to those of manhood. If he was distinguished for any thing, it was for an affected sapience and a pretension to more knowledge than he possessed. A waggish fellow-student of his, the late Mr. Edward Tilghman, aware of this trait in his character, once asked him if a *Felo-de-se* could inherit an estate, when Huck, applying his finger to his nose, in an attitude of profound thought, replied, that, in some cases, he believed he could."

present or succeeding day.   Although aware that she yielded to
none in the ardour of maternal affection, yet nothing could be
more unlooked for than this event; and even the pleasure I promised myself in seeing her, did not compensate for the disapprobation I felt at the imprudence of the undertaking; improper, in
every point of view, in which I could contemplate it.   When I
reflected upon the difficulties she had to encounter, and her
timidity in every mode of travelling, and particularly by water,
which would be occasionally necessary in her journey, I could not
but conclude, that there must be some very extraordinary motive
for it; and my desire to meet her, was mixed with a painful
anxiety.

She arrived the day after she had been announced, having hired
a person at Brooklyn, to bring her from thence in a chair.   Her
only object, I found, was to see me, and to endeavour to procure
my release on parole; as she had heard, that we were harshly
treated, and on the point of being sent to England.   The fatigue
and anxiety of her journey, had so far overcome her, that on
reaching New York, she had been ill for a few days, and had put
herself under the care of a Doctor Carlton or Charlton, who, though
he appeared to have acquitted himself well enough as a physician,
had extremely shocked and disgusted her by his intolerant toryism.   Upon finding what her errand was, he seemed to take
pleasure in confirming to her, that the prisoners were to be sent
to England, and hanged there, he added, for aught that he knew:
but that, at any rate, it was what they richly deserved.   She had
been visited, I learned, by the Allens, or some of them, Huck,*
as already mentioned, and some others from Philadelphia, who
were anxious to hear what was going on in that quarter.   Upon

---

* General HENRY LEE disposes of HUCK in a very summary manner. "Captain HUCK, of Tarleton's legion, had been detached by Lieutenant-Colonel TURN-
BULL, commanding at Hanging Rock to disperse some of the exiles of South
Carolina, who had lately returned to the State and were collecting in the neighbourhood of that place to assist in protecting their country. The captain, with
forty dragoons, twenty mounted infantry, and sixty militia, ventured thirty miles
up the country where the very exiles he was sent to disperse, attacked and destroyed his detachment. The captain, notorious for his cruelties and violence,
was killed, as were several others, and the rest dispersed."—ED.

mentioning her business to Mr. John Allen, he advised her not to
be scrupulous as to the terms of my release, since the business
would very soon be over, and a pardon be all that could be obtained by any who had borne arms.   But before stating what took
place on this side of the lines, let us go back a little to what occurred on the other.

The projected undertaking had been long in contemplation;
and the friends as well as members of the family had been consulted on the occasion.   Some advised it, but the greater part
disapproved of it.   Having acquaintances on both sides, my
mother indiscriminately took their opinions; and so far as party
feeling appeared to enter into the question, it was observable, that
the tories were for the measure, the whigs against it.   The former
were, of course, advocates for the benignity of General Howe;
and as they were incredulous, or affected incredulity, as to the ill
treatment of prisoners, they would have rejoiced in her success,
as an instance to the contrary.   The latter, did not, in the first
place, think the application would be of any avail; and, as upon
this particular occasion, they were in the predicament, which
Rochefoucault tells us, all men are in at all times, viz., that of
" discovering something in the misfortunes of their best friends,
which does not entirely displease them," they would, probably,
have been better satisfied, that we should all have grown old
in captivity, than have become vouchers for British clemency by
an immediate release: As it was inconvenient for Congress to
exchange us, it appeared to them much better that we should remain prisoners until the conclusion of the war, if peradventure we
should so long live, than, by coming out on parole, furnish the
tories with a circumstance they might turn to the advantage of
their side.   So stern a thing is patriotism, when the comfort of
third persons only is concerned!   As my mother, however, possessed too little of the Roman spirit to be duly moved by such
magnanimous considerations, the feelings of nature prevailed;
and she resolved on the enterprize.   She purchased a horse and
chair for the occasion, and set out for Philadelphia, her residence
being at this time at Reading, to which place, she had removed,
with several other families of her acquaintance, in the preceding
winter, when the enemy had penetrated through Jersey to the

Delaware. On her arrival in the city, one Fisher, a Scotchman, and relation of my grandmother, was officious in tendering his service to drive her to New York. As he was a retailer of dry goods, his object, no doubt, was traffic; and to bring home with him some scarce light articles, in the chair box. The offer was accepted; they set off, and had nearly reached Princeton, when, to their great astonishment, they were overtaken by a detachment of cavalry, which had been sent in pursuit of them, with orders to arrest their progress. The cause was this. Fisher, it seems, was a tory either real or putative; and the fact having been made known to General Mifflin, who was then in the city, it had set him a fidgeting, and, as no one could exactly foresee the consequences that might result to the infant nation, should a suspected Scotch shop-keeper get out of Philadelphia into New York; the hue and cry on the occasion, was proportionably eager and vehement. It cannot be denied, however, that the proceeding was quite in rule. The culprits were immediately taken into custody; but my mother's guilt being merely that of bad neighbourhood, (*nimium vicina Cremonæ*,) having been wholly ignorant of the political tenets of her companion, she was conducted to the quarters of General Sullivan, who commanded at this post. Here she remained until due order was taken in the premises, when, she found, that, instead of proceeding on her journey, she was under the necessity of retracing her steps towards Philadelphia, under an escort of horse. When they had got back as far as Bristol, means were found for Mr. Fisher, the only prisoner, to pursue his way, without the chair, with which he had been accommodated so far; and Colonel M'Ilvaine, an old and particular friend, and indeed connexion of the family, kindly offering to accompany my mother to the Head Quarters of our army, from whence, the proper measures might be taken for her proceeding into the British lines; her horse's head was once more turned towards New York. They reached the hospitable mansion of Mr. Vanhorne, of Bound-brook, on the evening of the day they set out. It fortunately turned out, that he had been acquainted with my father, and having connexions in Brunswick, he furnished my mother with a letter of introduction extremely useful to her, on her arrival there. Passing over unimportant particulars, she was conducted with her horse and chair to the enemy's lines, by Major Scull, who was then obliged to leave her, and commit her to the courtesy of some Hessian officers, who were on duty there. It happened, during the ceremony of the flag, that a gun was somewhere discharged on our side of the lines. This infringement of military etiquette, was furiously resented by the German officers, who expressed themselves with a vehemence of gesture extremely alarming to my mother, who discovered what it related to, from the frequent repetition of the words *flag of truce;* the only ones she understood. She supported herself as well as she could, under this inauspicious introduction into the hostile territory; and remaining in her chair, her horse was led by a soldier to the quarters of General Matthew or Matthews, who commanded in Brunswick.* Here, she alighted, and was shown into a parlour, where, in a few minutes, were set before her a decanter of wine and some biscuits. Being faint, and much in need of refreshment, she helped herself to a biscuit, and drank two glasses of wine; the first having proved so cordial and restorative to her dejected spirits, as to induce her to take a second. General Matthews did not keep her very long in waiting; and, on his appearing, being made acquainted with her object, and desire of being passed on to New York, as soon as might be convenient, he promised it should be attended to: his manner was that of a man of humanity and perfect good breeding. Upon leaving the General's quarters, her first care was to deliver the letter of Mr. Vanhorne. She readily found the house of the person to whom it was addressed, (I think Mr. Clarkson) was invited in, and seated alone in a parlour. There soon after came in two or three British officers, who, entering into conversation with the ease of men of fashion, gave her to understand that there had been a ball the preceding evening, at which had been the Miss Vanhorne's, the ladies whom they now called to see. These gentlemen, one of whom was Sir John Wrottesley,

---

* There is a General MATTHEW spoken of by Mr. Cumberland near the close of his Memoirs. A son of Mr. Cumberland had married the General's daughter, and he is called " a truly noble and benevolent gentleman." In all probability he is the same who commanded at Brunswick.

were such frequent visiters at this house, that my mother, during her stay in it, became pretty well acquainted with them, as I found, upon her once meeting Sir John, with Miss Susan Vanhorne, in the street of Flat-bush. Accosting her in a very sociable manner, he adverted to the circumstance of her finding me, who had then the *honour* of being introduced to him; and less, I cannot say, British baronet though he was, since his demeanour was truly gentlemanly and worthy of his rank. By the same means, she had the opportunity of often seeing Colonel Donop,* a Major Hendricks and a Major Pauli, all of the German troops; the latter of whom, was polite enough to take charge of her horse and chair; to promise to send them to Mr. Vanhorne's, at Bound-brook, and in the mean time, to supply the necessary forage.

There were five of the Misses Vanhorne, all handsome and well bred, who, not long after, with their mother, a widow lady, removed from this place to Flat-bush. A Mr. Clarkson, who was a connexion of theirs; if I mistake not, their uncle by marriage, and the very gentleman, at whose house they staid at Brunswick, and at which, my mother was so hospitably entertained, had a house also at Flat-bush. Being a whig, he had left it on the approach of the enemy; and it had been a good deal injured by the Germans. He was now permitted to return to it; and Mrs. Vanhorne and her daughters came along with him. Perhaps the way to this measure, was smoothed by the interest of the officers already mentioned; and ladies often are the means of mitigating the ferocities of war.

After being detained a week or more at Brunswick, my mother, with a number of other passengers, embarked in a sloop or shallop, for New York. The vessel in her passage, was fired upon by some of our people from the shore, but without injury

---

* Count DONOP; He was made a prisoner at Red-Bank, and WASHINGTON, in his letter to CHRISTOPHER GREENE, October 24th, 1777, says, "Count Donop in particular, is a man of importance, and ought by all means to be taken care of!"

"He died of his wounds," says Sparks, "three days after the action, at a house near the fort. A short time before his death, he said to Monsieur Duplessis, a French officer, who constantly attended him in his illness. 'It is finishing a noble career early; I die the victim of my ambition and of the avarice of my sovereign.'"—ED.

23

to any one, and the destined port was at length attained without
farther difficulty. Among the many unexpectedly agreeable
circumstances of her situation at Brunswick, there were some
unpleasant ones she had no means of avoiding. Although the
political conversation of the British officers ought to have been
restrained in the presence of the Misses Vanhorne, who had some
relations in our Service, it was sometimes such as to be extremely offensive to an American ear. An instance of this kind
arose from the following circumstance. A young man of our
army had been recently killed by the British cavalry, and his
body so cruelly hacked and mangled by their sabres, that General
WASHINGTON thought proper to send it in for their inspection.
It was brought to the post of Sir George Osborne, who with much
admired *sang froid*, simply returned for answer, that *he was no
coroner.* This circumstance was a theme of considerable merriment, and the *bon mot* of Sir George not a little applauded.

As Mr. Bache with his family, had been latterly a good deal
in New York, and, consequently, his part of Mr. Suydam's
house, become less necessary to him, he permitted my mother
to occupy it during her stay at Flat-bush. This was highly convenient to her, and she became, in some degree, naturalized to
her new situation. Her accustomed flow of good spirits returned; and as she came pretty well supplied with cash, she
contrived to get something better than *clippers* and *supon;* and
to give one or two tea-drinkings, at which the *rebel clan* that
attended them, was honoured with the company of some of the
Misses Vanhorne, avowed whigs, notwithstanding their civility
to the British officers. She also availed herself of the opportunity
of learning from Major Williams, the art of making Johnny
cakes, in the true Maryland fashion; and good part of an afternoon, I remember, was spent in the notable cookery. But these
recreations did not interfere with the object of her expedition,
and her design of getting me home. I, in vain, endeavoured
to dissuade her from her purpose. She was resolved to prove
the result of an application; and, in this view, in one of her first
visits to New York, called upon Mr. Galloway, who was supposed to have much influence at Head Quarters. He spoke en-
couragingly of the attempt, and said, he had little doubt, but it

would succeed.   What would be the proper mode of applying to Sir William Howe? she asked.   By memorial, said Mr. Galloway; at the same time, kindly offering to sketch one out for her, if she chose it.   As she could do no less than accept his offer, and thank him for it, he went to work, and in a few minutes produced, what he said, accorded with his ideas on the subject. He then read to her, what he had written, purporting, that, "Whereas Mrs ——, had always been a true and faithful subject of his Majesty George the Third; and whereas, her son, an inexperienced youth, had been deluded by the arts of designing men,"——"O, sir," said she, "that will never do; my son cannot obtain his release on these terms."   "Then, madam," said he, somewhat peevishly, "I can do nothing for you."   She endeavoured to soften as well as she could, the refusal to comply with what he had recommended, and left him, a good deal depressed in her expectations.   Fearful, that, in her ardour to obtain her object she might be tempted to go too far, I had cautioned her against yielding to any improper concessions; and had solemnly declared, that I would accept of my enlargement upon no other terms than those of an exchange, or a parole. This first discomfiture, did not induce an abandonment of her pursuit: in a matter which interested her feelings, no one was more persevering; and she continued to advise with every one, she thought likely to have influence, and a disposition to assist her. Among the rest, she addressed herself to a Mr. Andrew Elliot, a person of respectability, and well known both in Philadelphia and New York.   His advice was, that she should go at once in person to General Howe.   Those you have applied to, or may apply to, said he, have little or no interest, though they may not choose to say so; but a direct, personal application to the Commander-in-chief, will, I verily believe, be propitious to your wishes.   She had been some time between Flat-bush and New York, before this was suggested to her; and she secretly resolved to take an opportunity of putting it in execution.   On one of her excursions to the city, she had been waited upon by her old acquaintance, Captain Grant, of the forty-second regiment.   From him she found, that Colonel Stirling, and most of the old officers of the regiment, were there; but upon Grant's being unable to deny, that he, and consequently, the rest of them, knew, she had a son a prisoner, she at once testified by the coldness of her manner, that she had expected something better from them than a total neglect of me. Unacquainted with the human heart, under the baneful influence of party fury, and making no allowance for the repulsive nature of misfortune, especially when coupled with imputed guilt, she had made calculations little warranted by the practice of the world, more particularly of that part of it, which is flushed with prosperity.

On account of some meditated operation of the army, no one at this time was permitted to pass the lines; and so far from getting me home with her, she was not without anxiety respecting her own return, which had been already longer protracted than she had counted upon. This interdiction of intercourse continued for several weeks; but as soon as it was removed, and it became probable, that General Howe's attention was less engrossed by great concerns, she determined to give the advice of Mr. Elliot, a trial. Accordingly, one morning she went to New York, and without acquainting me with her design, which she knew I would oppose, boldly waited upon Sir William Howe; and asking to speak with him, was shown into a parlour, where, taking a seat, and meditating upon the manner of addressing him when he should appear, he came into the room, and had got pretty near her before she perceived him. Rising, she said, "Sir William Howe, I presume!" He answered by a bow. She then made known her business, doubtless in her best style of elocution, and concluded by expressing the greatness of her obligation for his Excellency's permission for me to go home with her on parole. "And then immediately to take up arms against us again, I suppose!" said the General. "By no means, sir; I solicit his release upon parole; that will restrain him until exchanged: but on my own part, I will go farther, and say, that if I have any influence over him, he shall never take up arms again." Here, the feelings of the patriot were wholly lost in those of the "war-detesting" mother. The General seemed to hesitate, but gave no answer. On the renewal of her suit, however, he appeared by his manner, for he was sparing of words to assent, and so she construed it. But to put the matter out of doubt, she asked: "Have I your Excellency's

permission for my son to go home with me on his parole?" Bowing, he answered "yes." "May Colonel Miles and Major West,"
added she, be permitted to go also?" "Now, madam," observed
the General, "you are making two requests instead of one."
She begged his pardon for presuming to do so, as she ought certainly to be satisfied with the great favour already granted; and
inquired if she was to mention the matter to Mr. Loring. He
said it was unnecessary, as the proper measures would be taken
to effect the purpose. The reason of her mentioning Colonel
Miles, and Major West, was, that they had already obtained a
promise of being liberated on parole; and she was apprehensive,
that unless they were put upon the same footing with me, I should
suspect improper terms had been made, and mar the whole business. This caution, probably, was unnecessary; the boon was
extended to these gentlemen, as I presume it would have been,
had they not been mentioned. From the General's quarters she
immediately went to Mr. Loring, whom she had known in Philadelphia, where he had some time resided, and acquainted him
with the indulgence which had been granted her; upon which, he
was pleased to observe, that it was more than I was entitled to,
as not one of the prisoners had been more upon his high horse.

Whatever grounds there may be for ascribing cruelty to General
Howe, it must be admitted, that no obduracy appeared at this interview; and I have been careful to give it, precisely as it was
related by my mother. War, indeed, in its essence is cruelty, especially civil war: Its tendency is to make men ferocious and merciless. In conflicts, in which our lives are continually at stake, we
at length become callous even to the loss of our own party, and
have, of course, still less concern for the destruction of our adversaries, notwithstanding, that particular situations may sometimes call forth striking examples of sympathy and generosity.
When, moreover, we consider the foe as obnoxious to legal
punishment, our hearts are too apt to be steeled against all "com-
punctious visitings of nature." Such seems to be the nature of
man; and the apathy of Howe to the miseries of his prisoners,
serves to show that he was too like the bulk of his species, ever
prone to severity against the opposers of established authority,
when partaking of, or friendly to it. What was the conduct of
23*

the Duke of Alva, in the Low Countries? That of the British, which we, as liege subjects, did not then disapprove, against the rebels in the year forty-six, commemorated by Smollet, in his "Mourn, hapless Caledonia, mourn?" What were the hideous enormities of the French republicans against the people of *La Vendee*, and what mercy was evinced towards Burr, by the high-toned advocates of prerogative, under the mild sway of Mr. Jefferson? Though the abuse of power is always detestable, yet it may not be improper to look at home, before we devote others to destruction as monsters of unheard of cruelty. I neither have palliated, nor do I mean to palliate the sufferings of the prisoners at New York: they were shocking to humanity, and no one witnessed them with more anguish than myself; but this is no reason that we should not ask ourselves whether it was to be expected, that they were at once to be set at liberty, and if not, what other mode or place of confinement was within the power of the enemy? or if the want of good and sufficient food, and other accommodations was the cause of the mortality, are we perfectly sure they had better to administer? If, in an entirely new state of the world, we are, on account of former injuries, to reject the aid of the only nation upon earth which has power to rescue us from impending perdition, it certainly behoves us, to inquire calmly into the extent of her aggressions, and for our own sakes, if not for hers, or the sake of justice, to admit the effect of any alleviating circumstances which may be found. But few of us, I trust, are in the unhappy predicament, to have been so hysterically alarmed during the war, as to be unable to forgive; or to have incurred disgraces which can only be washed out and avenged by the common destruction of our old enemy and ourselves.

CHAPTER XI.

The Author leaves Long Island for New York and Elizabethtown.—Author arrives at New York.—Travelling Companions.—Tench Coxe.—Arrival at the American Camp. — General Washington. — Colonel Hamilton. — American Army.—General Wayne.—Occurrences on the Road.—Author arrives at Philadelphia.—Arrival at Reading.—Political Feelings.—Declaration of Independence.—Character of Franklin.—Leading Men.—Mr. Canon.

It was not long before the welcome summons arrived for our repairing to New York, for the purpose of being transported from thence in a flag vessel to Elizabethtown; and upon this occasion, we were escorted to the end of the village, by a no small troop of our less lucky fellow-prisoners. It was made a condition by Loring, that our boarding should be paid before we left Flat-bush; and the heart of old Jacob, was accordingly gladdened by the sight of a sum of money he had despaired of receiving. He and I parted very good friends; and it was but justice to say, that the treatment I received from him and his family, Mr. and Mrs. Hagerman, was both civil and obliging. As there was no subject upon which we, prisoners, had been so much in the dark, and were at the same time, so anxious to be informed of, as that of the state of our army and public affairs in general, Tudor, on my coming away, furnished me with a kind of cypher, by which, as soon as I had time to inform myself, I was to satisfy him by letter on certain points he particularly wished to know. The disguise was not in the character, but in the substitution of one piece of information for another,—for instance, a lady who was to be named, was to signify the army, and if that was strong and in a prosperous train, it was to be indicated by announcing the health and charming looks of the lady. There was a scale in the key, by which the intelligence might be graduated; and

it was so contrived, as to admit of the transmission of pretty
satisfactory information in a few important particulars. Knowing the deep interest that was taken in the expected communication, it was among my first cares on getting home, to perform
this duty. But I must admit, that my statements, though correct
in the main, were rather more flattering, than rigid truth would
warrant. I could not endure the thought of reducing my companions in misfortune to despair. It was certainly admissible on
this occasion, to adopt the practice of painters; and in preserving the lineaments and character of the countenance, to render the portrait as pleasing as possible. It had the effect, as I
afterwards learned, to put them in good heart: for, although I
had not said every thing which might have been wished, it was
ascribed to a propensity I was supposed to have, of looking
rather on the unfavourable side of things; and as I, so little sanguine, had ventured to say so much, it was inferred, that I
might, with truth have said a great deal more.

The particulars of this pleasing trip to New York, have entirely escaped my memory; as, how we travelled, though I presume it was in a wagon for the convenience of carrying our
baggage; whether it was in the forenoon or afternoon; whether
we left the city on the day we reached it, &c., though as to this,
it is more than probable, that it was not until the day after, as I
well recollect breakfasting with my mother at the house of Mr.
Matthews, the Mayor, and that his daughter, who entertained us,
was so much to my taste, that, for the moment I quite forgot the
politics of her father, and might even have swerved, perhaps,
from my loyalty to an allegiance, a thousand times sworn elsewhere. But it must not be imagined from the circumstance of
this breakfast, that I had apostatized from my principles. I have,
fortunately, an excuse for accepting civilities from the offspring
of an inveterate, and reputedly persecuting tory, which, I am
not without hope, will obtain my pardon from the most determined and least compounding republican of the present hour.
A Miss Seymour, a cousin of Miss Matthews, had long been desirous of getting to Philadelphia to see her father who lay sick
there; and as it was known to Mr. Matthews that my mother
was soon to go thither, he had made himself acquainted with

her, and recommended his niece to her protection in the meditated journey. This it was, that procured me the honour of
breakfasting with Miss Matthews, with whom her cousin stayed.
But who, pray, was this sick Mr. Seymour? methinks I hear
some high-toned, fastidious *seventy-six* man exclaim. He was,
you may rest assured, sir, no "anti-revolutionary adherent of
the enemy." He was no less a personage than Commodore
Seymour, who, at this time, had the command of the Delaware
gun-boats.—Yes, Commodore of the gun-boats! Another pecca-
dillo, if haply they may be so called, of a similar complexion, I
must confess myself guilty of; though, from an exuberance of
good fortune, not always attending my imputed apostacies, I
have, if I would avail myself of it, an equally good come off
here. To make a *profert* then of my offence with its ablution
along with it, I undertook to bring out, and actually did bring
out with me, at the request of Mr. Tench Coxe, now in the full
tide of republican orthodoxy, a letter to a lady in Philadelphia,
to be delivered by my own hand to another lady in that city;
which commission I faithfully executed. I cheerfully did that
for him, which shortly before, would have been the greatest
favour to myself:

Haud ignarus mali, miseris succurere disco.

Having alluded to this gentleman before, and in a manner, that
may not be pleasing to him, although I have said nothing which
does not arise from facts, of which he will not deny the correctness, I here sincerely avow, that I am much more disposed to do
him a good than evil office. Notwithstanding the contrasted vicissitudes of our fortune, and that the great eras of his political
ascension, have been those of my depression, I have not forgotten
our boyish days, of which he, not long since put me in mind;
my early acquaintance in his family; the pleasant hours I have
passed with himself and his brother (nearer my own age) as well
at his father's house in town, as at his seat on the Schuylkill;
and that his mother was always spoken of by mine, as the nearest friend of her youth. Such recollections are far more grateful
to the heart, than the bitter collisions of interested manhood, or
the "fury passions" of political dissension.

But not to linger in New York at a moment so precious, I

have to state, that after the signing of a new parole by Miles,
West and myself, at the office of Mr. Loring, our little party with
the addition of Miss Seymour, embarked in a small sloop for
Elizabethtown-point, then held by us. The officer commanding
on this occasion, was a son of Doctor Auchmuty, among the
most distinguished in New York, for his zeal in the royal cause.
The behaviour of this gentleman was perfectly agreeable to us;
and we parted on the most civil terms. It is not impossible,
though such rapid promotions are hardly to be looked for in the
British army, that he may be the General Auchmuty, who not
long since, acquitted himself so well at Montevideo; as he was
stated in the newspapers to be a son of the Doctor.* The weather being fine, but with very little wind, our passage was a
pleasant one ; and in the course of the day, we had once more
the happiness of treading our own ground. I should in vain endeavour to describe my feelings on this occasion; for although
they were chastised by the recollection, that my present liberty
was held on sufferance, they were yet light, joyous and tumultu-
ary. I had been about eight months captive ; and it was more
than a year since I had seen Philadelphia. It must now have
been from my best data for ascertaining it, about the middle of
July. Our army lay at Morristown ; and after casting about for
the means of being conveyed thither, we, at length, found them
in a coal-wagon, little inferior to a coach and six, in a journey,
which too much crowded the mind with pleasing ideas, to admit
of much concern about the choice of a vehicle. When within a
few miles of our destination, we met the General, on horseback,
with three or four attendants. He recognised us, and stopping
a few minutes congratulated my mother on the success of her
errand; and at going on, informed us, that he should return to
camp in a few hours, where he expected to see us. By his ap-

---

* LIEUTENANT-GENERAL SIR SAMUEL AUCHMUTY.—He was the youngest son of
the Reverend Dr. Auchmuty, Rector of Trinity Church, New York; was born
June 22d, 1758, and received his education at King's (now Columbia) College.
He joined the Royal army under Sir Wm. Howe, as an ensign in the 45th
regiment, in 1776. Mr. Graydon in a note, says, "He was, I remember, rather a serious young man, modest and unassuming in his manners, though I
should have supposed him one or two and twenty, instead of nineteen, which the
date of his birth made him at the time referred to."—ED.

pointment, on his return, Colonel Miles, Major West and myself
waited upon him at his marquee in the evening. In the course
of conversation, he asked what we conceived to be the objects
of General Howe, provided the question did not, in our opinion,
interfere with our parole. Colonel Miles taking the word, replied, that in his opinion, he meditated a co-operation with the
northern army by means of the Hudson.   The General heard
him out, and then observed, that indications and probabilities
both tended to that conclusion ; but, that nevertheless, he had
little doubt, that his object was Philadelphia.   I mention this, as
it is stated by Mr. Marshall, that he was a good deal embarrassed
on this occasion, and rather inclined to believe, that the movements of General Howe would be up the Hudson.   Whatever
might have happened afterwards to alter or unsettle his opinion,
it was certainly at this time, as I have mentioned ; and he spoke
as if his conviction was strong. He had unquestionably good
intelligence ; and a person who had communicated with him,
had, not long before, been executed as a spy at Brunswick.
This man, who generally resided at New York, under the disguise of a zealous royalist, had been indiscreet enough to unbo-
som himself to Major Williams, who, in the spring of this year,
on the prospect of an exchange, which however proved abortive,
had been summoned to that city. He gave him much information as to what was passing there ; and among other things
which regarded us, told him, that interest had been made for my
going out on parole, but I was considered not sufficiently *well
disposed*, (the fashionable phrase for yielding whiggism,) to be
entitled to the indulgence.   It was but a few weeks after this
interview with Williams, that, in attempting to induce two British soldiers to desert to our army with intelligence, he was detected and suffered.

   The day of our arrival and the succeeding one, we spent at
Morristown; and here, for the first time, I had the pleasure of
knowing Colonel Hamilton. He presided at the General's table,
where we dined ; and in a large company in which there were
several ladies, among whom I recollect one or two of the Miss
Livingstons and a Miss Brown, he acquitted himself with an ease,
propriety and vivacity, which gave me the most favourable im-

pression of his talents and accomplishments—talents, it is true,
which did not indicate the solid abilities his subsequent career
has unfolded, but which announced a brilliancy which might
adorn the most polished circles of society, and have fitted him
for the part of an Algarotti at the court of a Frederick.

> " Vous, que les graces et les ris
> Formerent pour flatter et plaire,"

to borrow the words of the king, in an address to this favourite:
Or in reference to his later conduct and matured capacity, where
shall we find one to whom the language of Tibullus to Messala,
would better apply!

> "Nam quis te majora gerit castrisve, forove ?"

> "Who the state's thunder, better form'd to wield,
> And shake alike the senate and the field !"*

---

* SULLIVAN, in his " Familiar Letters," already quoted, says, " The eloquence
of HAMILTON was persuasive and commanding; the more so as he had no guide
but the impulse of a great and rich mind, he having had little opportunity to be
trained at the bar, or in popular assemblies. Those who could speak of his manner from the best opportunities to observe him, in public and private, concurred
in pronouncing him to be a frank, amiable, high-minded, open-hearted gentleman.
He was capable of inspiring the most affectionate attachment; but he could make
those, whom he opposed, fear and hate him cordially."

HARRISON GRAY OTIS, of Boston, delivered there an eulogy upon HAMILTON,
and the following is a concluding paragraph of his eloquent performance : " The
universal sorrow, manifested in every part of the Union upon the melancholy
exit of this great man, is an unequivocal testimonial of his public worth. The
place of his residence is overspread with a gloom which bespeaks the pressure
of a public calamity ; and the prejudices of party are absorbed in the overflowing
tide of national grief."

The man, thus honoured and lamented, and whose reputation grows still
brighter with the lapse of time, was one of those towards whom MR. JEFFERSON,
as we learn from his own "Correspondence," cherished a degree of " envy, hatred
and malice," which it is difficult to believe even party rage and malevolence,
however violent and bitter, could have prompted and sustained. Yet this active,
energetic enmity, could not long operate injuriously to the character of such a
man as HAMILTON, while the "great Apostle of Democracy," in his own carefully
preserved and ostentatiously published " Writings," has greatly aided Posterity
in finding for him an appropriate niche in the temple of fame.

" In that remarkable chronicle of slander and second-hand abuse, the Ana
of Jefferson, HAMILTON," says the New York Review, " is assailed no less than
seventeen times; just one-fourth of all Mr. Jefferson's on dits are levelled against
the man whom he felt to be, of all others, his most dangerous competitor for the
highest honours of his country."—ED.

With Colonel Tilghman,* another of the General's aids, I was well acquainted, as he was a Philadelphian, and had been a Lieutenant of the light infantry company of Greens, already mentioned. By him and Colonel Hamilton, I was taken in the evening to drink tea with some of the ladies of the village, where were also those with whom we had dined.

I had been extremely anxious to see our army. Here it was, but I could see nothing which deserved the name. I was told, indeed, that it was much weakened by detachments ; and I was glad to find, there was some cause for the present paucity of soldiers. I could not doubt, however, that things were going well. The Commander-in-chief and all about him, were in excellent spirits ; and as to General Wayne, whom I waited upon at his quarters, he entertained the most sovereign contempt for the enemy. In his confident way, he affirmed, that the two armies had interchanged their original modes of warfare. That for our parts, we had thrown away the shovel, and the British had taken it up, as they dared not face us without the cover of an intrenchment. I made some allowance for the fervid manner of the General,† who, though unquestionably as brave a man as any in

---

* Colonel Tench Tilghman.—General Washington thus writes to General Sullivan in Congress, May, 1781: "This gentleman came out a captain of one of the light infantry companies of Philadelphia, and served in the flying camp in 1776. In August of the same year he joined my family, and has been in every action in which the main army was concerned. He has been a zealous servant and slave to the public, and a faithful assistant to me for nearly five years, a great part of which time he refused pay. Honour and gratitude interest me in his favour and make me solicitous to obtain his commission. His modesty and love of concord place the date of his expected commission at the 1st of April, 1777, because he would not take rank of Hamilton and Meade, who were declared Aids in order (which he did not choose to be) before that period, although he had joined my family and done all the duties of one, from the 1st of September preceding." Tilghman was despatched by Washington to Congress with intelligence of the surrender of Cornwallis, and "a horse properly caparisoned, and an elegant sword, were given to him." Colonel Tilghman died in Baltimore in April, 1786, in his 43d year. His death was deeply regretted by General Washington, and Robert Morris, in a letter to the General, said: "You have lost in him a most faithful and valuable friend. He was to me the same. I esteemed him very, very much, and I lamented his loss exceedingly."—Ed.

† In bravery, in heroic achievement, and in devotion to the cause of his country in all its phases, he was unsurpassed, and his abilities as a commander were

24

the army, was nevertheless, somewhat addicted to the vaunting style of Marshal Villars, a man who, like himself, could fight as well as brag. By the bye, I do not know whether this talent might not have been of use in our army: it certainly is, or at least is considered to be so, in a French one, since, of all the gasconaders in the world, the Gallic commanders must confessedly take the *pas*. It had been humourously stated in the English prints, that upon a gentleman, who had been in America and seen our troops, being asked, what was their uniform, he replied: "in general, it is blue and buff, but by this time it must be all buff!"· The period for this unity of colour, however, had not yet arrived; though from the motley, shabby covering of the men, it was to be inferred that it was rapidly approaching. Even in General Wayne himself, there was in this particular, a considerable falling off. His quondam regimental, as Colonel of the 4th battalion, was, I think, blue and white, in which he had been accustomed to appear with exemplary neatness ; whereas he was now dressed in character for M'Heath or Captain Gibbet, in a dingy red coat, with a black, rusty cravat, and tarnished laced hat. In short, from all I could see, I was by no means warranted in supposing that our affairs were in a very prosperous train, notwithstanding the cheerful appearance at Head Quarters : but I endeavoured to suspend my opinion until I should have longer and better means of forming a conclusion.

We hired a wagon at this place, to carry us to Mr. Vanhorne's at Bound-brook, where my mother expected to find her horse and chair, agreeably to the arrangement made with Major Pauli. This was a subject of much raillery on the road, particularly with Colonel Miles, who could not persuade himself that a Hessian could forego so fine a chance of plunder; and he took it for granted, that the Major had not only appropriated the equipage to himself, but sold it long since, and put the proceeds in his pocket. But, on the contrary, in the strutting phraseology of Burgoyne, he had been "conscious of the honour of soldiership,"

of a very high order. His life is a history of the war. He was at Ticonderoga, Brunswick, Brandywine, Germantown, White Marsh, Monmouth, Stony Point, and in several other engagements ;—always efficient, and always distinguished. He died in December, 1796, in the 52d year of his age.—ED.

and with good faith performed what he had promised. We had, in fact, met the poor beast in question, on the road to Morristown, but *quantum mutatus ab illo!* how changed from the sleek, well-fed animal, that had, about six weeks before, entered the town of Brunswick! A constant padding of the hoof for this space of time, first on the royal and then on the rebel side, with such casual supplies of forage as campaigning affords, had reduced him to the continental standard; and although it had been suggested to my mother as he passed with the chair, that they might be hers, she was unable to recognise either: the chair she could not claim, and as to the horse, she was sure he was not hers.

Whether there were any arrangements with Mr. Vanhorne, I do not know; but his hospitality ought certainly to have been recompensed, by an unlimited credit on the public stores.* His house, used as a hotel, seemed constantly full. It was at this time occupied by Colonel Bland,† of the Virginia cavalry, and the officers of his corps, to whom we were introduced; and among others, if my memory does not mislead me, to Captain Lee, afterwards so distinguished as a partisan, and now known as General Harry Lee.‡ Notwithstanding the number of guests that were to

---

* This Mr. VANHORNE, however, appears to have been a suspicious character, if it is of him that General WASHINGTON thus speaks in his letters to General REED. In the first, dated January 12th, 1777, he says:—

"I wish you had brought Vanhorne off with you, for, from his noted character, there is no dependence to be placed on his parole." In the other, of 19th January, of the same year, he says: "Would it not be best to order P. Vanhorne to Brunswick? These people, in my opinion, can do us less injury there than any where else." He kept his post notwithstanding, at Bound-Brook, where he alternately entertained the officers of both armies, being visited sometimes by the one, and sometimes by the other.

† COLONEL THEODORIC BLAND—of the first regiment of light dragoons, was appointed to superintend the march of the Convention troops to Charlottesville, Virginia, and was directed by WASHINGTON to take command there. He was the author of a Treatise on Military Tactics, which was approved and strongly recommended by the Commander-in-chief. General H. LEE speaks of him in his Memoirs, as "noble, sensible, honourable and amiable."—ED.

‡ This gallant and celebrated officer was a graduate of Princeton College, and during the whole war was actively and usefully employed. He commenced his brilliant public career as "a Captain of one of the six companies of cavalry, raised in Virginia, and in 1777, under Lieutenant-Colonel BLAND, he joined the main Provincial army." By his discipline and care of his men and horses, he

be provided for, there appeared no deficiency in accommodation; and we supped and lodged well. As the horse and chair were not expected back for a day or two, Major West, who was in no hurry, undertook to wait for it, and bring it on to Philadelphia; while the rest of us, who had objects, more or less attracting in view, pursued our way the next morning. No other incident on the road occurred, interesting enough to have left any trace in my memory, except the meeting with Mr. and Mrs. Coxe, at Neshaminy Ferry. Matters had been arranged for this interview with my mother on her way to New York; and they now met her in consequence of a notice from her, that she would be there at an appointed time. Their object was, to learn what she might know of their son, as well as son-in-law, Mr. Andrew Allen. They were deeply affected at the dispersed situation of their family, and feelingly alive to the unhappy effects of civil dissension. The old gentleman, I recollect, blamed the step which had been taken by Mr. Allen, and his son; alleging, that they had been precipi-

---

early attracted the attention of WASHINGTON, " who, at the battle of Germantown, selected him, with his company, to attend as his body-guard." In consequence of his cool and determined bravery in several exploits, which, for want of room, cannot be narrated here, he was promoted by Congress to the rank of Major, with the command of a separate corps of cavalry, consisting of three companies. In 1780 he was sent with his legion to the army of the South, under Gen. GREENE, having been previously raised to the rank of Lieutenant-Colonel. He served with great distinction throughout the war, and has left a well written, manly and authentic " History of the War in the Southern Department of the United States." In 1786 he was elected to Congress from Virginia, his native State. He was a member of the Convention of Virginia that ratified the present Federal Constitution, of which he was a strenuous advocate. He was three years Governor of the State. In 1799 he was again chosen a member of Congress, and was selected, while there, to pronounce a funeral eulogium upon WASHINGTON. He prepared the celebrated resolutions, moved by the late CHIEF JUSTICE MARSHALL in the House of Representatives, from which General LEE was accidentally absent at the time, expressive of the grief of Congress upon receiving intelligence of the decease of WASHINGTON, the last of which resolutions was as follows:—

"Resolved, that a Committee, in conjunction with one from the Senate, be appointed to consider on the most suitable manner of paying honour to the memory of the MAN, first in war, first in peace, and first in the hearts of his fellow-citizens."

Before the accession of Mr. JEFFERSON, General LEE, like many of the other Fathers of the Revolution, retired to private life. He died on the 25th of March, 1818, in his 63d year.—ED.

tated into it by Christian Huck, who had assured them, that measures were in agitation for their immediate arrest and confinement.

We reached Philadelphia in the evening, where, it will be enough for me to say, that my fondest anticipations were realized in a meeting with the object, which had caused the deepest sighs of my captivity. Were I dealing in fiction, or speaking of another, a more particular representation might be required, of so auspicious a winding up, of a more than twelve months' absence, incessantly galled by sickly hope and feverish uncertainty. But, in situations of tender interest, the fastidious delicacy, or, as the French might call it, the *mauvaise honte* of English manners, forbids a man to place himself. It is observable, that this highest seasoning of French memoir writing, is wholly omitted by Mr. Cumberland, who must have known the nation's taste. He gives us to understand, indeed, that he was married; and more than once, marshals his children before us; but he never ventures to disclose a single circumstance of his love, or to descant upon what ought to be considered, as the *sine qua non* of his two conditions of a husband and a father. Mr. Gibbon, it is true, touches upon his attachment to Mademoiselle Curchod, afterwards Madame Necker; but, evidently with a mortal fear of being laughed at, for only glancing at his "early love." Perhaps nothing is more characteristic of the manners of the two nations, than this very circumstance, which serves also among others, to justify Sterne, in his singular declaration, that the French are too serious.* An

* The Edinburgh Review, in descanting on the correspondence of Baron Grimm, observes, that it chronicles the deaths of half the Author's acquaintance, and makes jests upon them all; and is much more serious in discussing the merits of an opera-singer, than in considering the evidence for the being of a God, or the first foundations of morality. Grimm, though a German, was thoroughly *Frenchified* by his long residence in France. He was among Rousseau's most early acquaintances on his first going to Paris, and with some others, was once engaged with him to traverse all Italy on foot; but the project, of which the parties were at first highly enamoured, came to nothing. The pedestrian exploit lost its charms, as the time for undertaking it approached.

The review of the "*Correspondence, Littéraire, Philosophique et Critique. Par le Baron de Grimm, et par Diderot,*" is by Lord Jeffrey, and is included in the Philadelphia edition of Jeffrey's "*Contributions to the Edinburgh Review.*— Ed.

amour in their hands, be it their own or another's, is always an extremely grave affair; and thence derives an interest, which an English writer in his own case, would be sure to spoil, by a levity assumed from the apprehension of ridicule. But, to whatever cause this diversity of sentiment may be owing, it shows the superior decorum of English literature, as formed in the school of Addison, Steel, Johnson, &c. to that of the French, under the guidance of Voltaire, Rousseau, Raynal, &c.; the one, by its circumspection, cherishing religion, morals, and government; the other, by its licentiousness, undermining them all.

Having now brought myself back to Philadelphia, from whence I marched the preceding summer, it naturally puts an end to the narrative of my campaign and captivity; as, though yet a prisoner, I was at home. What I have farther to say, therefore, will have less the air of adventure; and I shall, consequently, be relieved, I hope, from so minute an attention to my own concerns.

One of the first things which struck us, on getting within our own territory, was the high price of wine and other liquors. We attributed this to their growing scarcity, though equally owing, probably, to the incipient depreciation of the paper currency, of which we had then no idea. We saw, to our great surprise, no military parade upon our journey, nor any indication of martial vigour on the part of the country. General WASHINGTON, with the little remnant of his army at Morristown, seemed left to scuffle for liberty, like another Cato at Utica.* Here and there, we saw a militia man with his contrasted coloured cape and facings; and we found besides, that Captains, Majors and Colonels had

---

* The wisdom of WASHINGTON'S proceedings was acknowledged and appreciated by those especially who were merely spectators of the great drama in which he was performing the most conspicuous part. WALPOLE, a cool and sagacious observer, writing to HORACE MANN, in December, 1776, says, "WASHINGTON has retired with his whole army to other heights about five miles off, *seeming to intend to protract the war, as was always thought would be their wisest way.*" Again March 5th, 1777, he writes: "The campaign in America has lost a great deal of its florid complexion, and General WASHINGTON is allowed by both sides not to be the worst General in the field." And again he writes, April 3, 1777: "WASHINGTON, THE DICTATOR, has shown himself both a Fabius and a Camillus. His march through our lines is allowed to have been a prodigy of generalship." WALPOLE here alludes to the passage of the Delaware, and the surprise and capture of the Hessians at Trenton.—ED.

become "good cheap" in the land. But, unfortunately, these war-functionaries were not found at the head of their men : They, more generally, figured as bar-keepers, condescendingly serving out small measures of liquor, to their less dignified customers. Still were they brimfull of patriotism, the prevailing feature of which was, to be no less ardent in their pursuit, than fervent in their hatred of Tories.*

During a stay of a few days in Philadelphia, my mother and myself, I recollect, dined at President Hancock's. He had been one of the opposers of her scheme of going into New York, but was sufficiently a man of the world, to put on an appearance of being pleased with its success. Yet, as he was among the most conspicuous on the American side, and deeply staked in the issue of the contest, it is not uncharitable to suppose, that he was not very cordially gratified by an event which might give to the adverse cause any colour of clemency. But I have no right to attribute his advice upon the occasion, to other than the most friendly motives; since mine, had I been consulted, would have been the same.

My mother, as already mentioned, having removed her residence to Reading, thither, in company with the lady so often adverted to, whose family was also established there, we proceeded in high spirits. Many other Philadelphians had recourse to this town, as a place of safety from a sudden incursion of the enemy; and, among a score or more of fugitive families, were those of General Mifflin and my uncle, as I have called Mr. Biddle, though only standing in that relation by marriage. It was also the station assigned to a number of prisoners, both British and German, as well as of the principal Scotch royalists, that had been subdued and taken in North Carolina. I soon discovered that a material change had taken place during my absence from Pennsylvania; and that the pulses of many, that at the time of my leaving it, had beaten high in the cause of Whigism and Liberty, were considerably lowered. Power, to use a language which had already ceased to be orthodox, and could, therefore,

* The generous exertions of the Philadelphia troop of cavalry, and other portions of the militia, in the preceding winter, are honourable exceptions to the general supineness.

only be whispered, had fallen into low hands: The better sort were disgusted and weary of the war. Congress, indeed, had given out that they had counted the cost of the contest; but it was but too apparent, that very many of their adherents, had made false calculations on the subject, having neither allowed enough for disasters in the field, nor domestic chagrins, the inevitable consequence of a dissolution of old power and the assumption of new.* It was, in fact, just beginning to be perceived, that the ardour of the inflamed multitude is not to be tempered; and that the instigators of revolutions are rarely those who are destined to conclude them, or profit by them. The great cause of schism among the Whigs, had been the Declaration of Independence. Its adoption had, of course, rendered numbers malcontent; and thence, by a very natural transition, consigned them to the Tory ranks. Unfortunately for me, this was the predicament in which I found my nearest and best friend, whose example had, no doubt, contributed to the formation of my political opinions, and whose advice, concurring with my own sense of duty, had placed me in the army. I now discovered, that we no longer thought or felt alike; and though no rupture took place, some coldness ensued, and I have to regret a few words of asperity which passed between us, on occasion of the French alliance. But this was but a momentary blast; as neither of us was infected with that hateful bigotry, which too generally actuated Whigs and Tories, and led to mutual persecution, as one or other had the ascendency. As to the Whigs, the very cause for which they contended was essentially that of freedom, and yet all the freedom it granted, was, at the peril of tar and feathers, to think and act like themselves, the extent, indeed, of all toleration proceeding from the multitude, whether advocating the divine right of a king; the divine sovereignty of the people; or of the idol it may be pleased to constitute its unerring plenipotentiary. Toleration is only to be looked for upon points in which men are indifferent; or where they are duly checked and restrained by a salutary authority.

---

* For some justifications of these remarks, which, I know, have been thought heterodox—see WILKINSON's Memoirs, vol. 1, pp. 201-2—particularly a cited letter from General SCHUYLER to General HEATH, dated Saratoga, July 28th, 1777.

Mr. Edward Biddle, then in a declining state of health, and no longer in Congress, apparently entertained sentiments not accordant with the measures pursuing; and in the fervid style of elocution, for which he was distinguished, he often exclaimed, that he really knew not what to wish for. "The subjugation of my country," he would say, " I deprecate as a most grievous calamity, and yet sicken at the idea of thirteen, unconnected, petty democracies: if we are to be independent, let us, in the name of GOD, at once have an empire, and place WASHINGTON at the head of it."* Fortunately for our existence as a nation, a great proportion of those, whose early exertions tended to that issue, were not aware of the price by which it was to be acquired; otherwise, my knowledge of the general feeling at this time, so far as my means of information extended, obliges me to say, that it would not have been achieved. Not that disgust and despondence were universal among the leading and best informed Whigs, but an equal proportion of disaffection to independence, in the early part of the year 1776, must have defeated the enterprize. Still, it may be observed, that as Whigism declined among the higher classes, it increased in the inferior; because they who composed them, thereby, obtained power and consequence. Uniforms and epaulets, with militia titles and paper money, making numbers of persons gentlemen who had never been so before, kept up every where throughout the country, the spirit of opposition; and if these were not real patriotism, they were very good substitutes for it. Could there, in fact, be any comparison between the condition of a daily drudge in agricultural or mechanic labour, and that of a spruce, militia-man, living without work, and, at the same time, having plenty of continental dollars in his pocket! How could he be otherwise than well affected to such a cause!

Shortly after the Declaration of Independence by Congress, a Constitution had been formed for the Commonwealth of Pennsylvania. This was understood to have been principally the work

* I have presumed to put in the wrong, those who were adverse to the Declaration of Independence; and the high ground on which we have since stood, fully justified me: but present appearances seem again to unsettle the question, in the minds of those at least who are heterodox enough to doubt the eligibility of a dependence on France.

of Mr. George Bryan, in conjunction with a Mr. Canon, a school-
master; and it was severely reprobated by those, who thought
checks and balances necessary to a legitimate distribution of the
powers of government.   Doctor Franklin was also implicated in
the production; and either his participation in it, or approbation
of it, was roundly asserted by its fautors.   The Doctor, perhaps a
sceptic in relation to forms of goverment, and ever cautious of
committing himself, had thrown out an equivoque about a wagon,
with horses, drawing in opposite directions; as, upon the adoption
of the federal constitution he told a pleasant story of a self-complacent French lady who always found herself in the right.   But
whether he meant by his rustic allusion, to show his approbation
of checks or otherwise, is an enigma that has never been solved;
nor is it worth the trouble of solution.   The constitutionalists,
however, claimed him; and whether he thought with them or not,
he was too prudent to disoblige them.   It is rather probable the philosopher was of opinion, that the ferment of the revolution should
be left to work itself off; that the effect could not be produced
by the exhibition of paper sedatives; and that, therefore, the form
of a constitution was scarcely worth quarrelling about.   His observations embraced moral, no less than natural subjects: and as
he had discovered that oil would smooth the ruffled surface of the
sea, so had he found it most effectual in assuaging the troubled
minds of his fellow men.   Hence, his demeanour to both parties
was so truly oily and accommodating, that it always remained
doubtful to which he really belonged; and while president of the
Executive Council, to which office he had been elected on his return from France, he sedulously avoided voting on questions,
which partook of the spirit of party.   No man had scanned the
world more critically than the Doctor; few have profited more by
a knowledge of it, or managed it more to their own advantage.
Old, and without an object to intrigue for, he seemed wholly devoted to his ease and amusement; and I have been told by a
gentleman who acted with him as Vice-President, that he not only
devolved upon him the whole business of the department, but
even declined the trouble of thinking.   As to the Constitution,
whose provisions it was sometimes necessary to consider, it did
not appear to him, that he had ever read it; or if he had, that he

deemed it worthy of remembering. In short, as to the political concerns of the State, he was apathy itself; and like King Lear it was obviously his "fast intent, to shake all cares and business from his age."*

With respect to Mr. Bryan, so conspicuous at this era in the home department, he was one of those, whose memory treasures up small things, with even more care than great ones. He was said to be a very diligent reader, and was certainly a never weary monotonous talker, who, in the discourses he held, seldom failed to give evidence of an acquaintance with the most minute, recondite, and out of the way facts; insomuch, that a bet was once offered, that he could name the town-cryer of Bergen-op-Zoom.† As Ireland had given him birth, he was probably like the bulk of his emigrating countrymen, in the antipodes at all points, to whatever was English; and a staunch patriot, of course. It was, moreover, his passion or his policy, to identify himself with the *people*, in opposition to those, who were termed the *well born*, a designation conceived in the genuine spirit of democracy, and which, as it

---

* Dr. Franklin was chosen President of the Convention to form a Constitution for the State of Pennsylvania, and while a member of this Convention, he was, also, a member of Congress where important duties required his occasional attendance. "He is reported," says Sparks, " to have been the author of the most remarkable feature in this Constitution, that is, a single Legislative Assembly, instead of two branches, which other Statesmen have considered preferable, and which have since been adopted by all the States of the Union, as well as in other countries where the experiment of popular forms has been tried. He disapproved of the distinctions of rank incident to two Assemblies, one being called the *Upper* and the other the *Lower* House, as having an aristocratical tendency, unfavourable to the liberty and equality, which are the essence of republican institutions." These distinctions, borrowed, as are too many other opinions and practices, from England, however significant and expressive *there*, are utterly meaningless *here*, yet are obstinately persevered in. It is time that this absurd imitation of Lords and Commons should be discontinued, and the *common-sense* of the country is appealed to in this behalf. At the period of the adoption of this Constitution, Franklin was in his 71st year; but he was, nevertheless, according to Sparks, actively attentive to his two-fold duties, the assertion of our author's informant, to the contrary notwithstanding.—Ed.

† This place was probably suggested to the mind of the bettor from the circumstance of its having been taken in the year 1747, by Marshal Count Lowendahl though deemed impregnable, and being, on that account, a common theme in conversation and newspapers.

may be supposed, did "yeoman's service" to her cause, now dispensing with its use from a just deference to its well born advocates from Virginia and her dependencies.   In other respects Mr. Bryan was well enough: let us say, a well meaning man, and even one, who, in the main, felt he was acting the patriot: for this part, it is well known, is played in very different styles. Should any reader require a proof of this, I might refer him to the modes of WASHINGTON and Jefferson.   Some only see danger, bless their optics! on the side of aristocracy; and, therefore, rivet themselves with all their might, in an anti-patrician spirit of perverseness to every thing candid, or noble, or honourable.   Nothing is republican with them, but as it is crawling, and mean, and candied over with a fulsome and hypocritical love for the people.   I do not say that Mr. Bryan was actuated by such motives, but merely, that his patriotism was of the humble character they are calculated to inspire.   Of his colleague Mr. Canon, it may not be uncharitable to presume, that having the little knowledge of man, and scholastic predilection for the antique in liberty, which generally falls to the lot of a pedagogue, he acted accordingly.*   But death quickly snatched him away; *ostendent terris hunc tantum fata*.   These constituted the duumvirate, which had the credit of framing the Constitution and thence laying, in Pennsylvania, the corner stone of that edifice, which, however retarded in its progress by aristocratical interferences, towers, like another Babel, to the skies, and will continue to tower, until finally arrested and dilapidated by an irremediable confusion of tongues: for anarchy ever closes the career of democracy.

---

* As to myself, who always find it impossible to separate from my idea of a good government, somewhat of ignoble fireside comfort and tranquillity, I must say, that I have but a poor opinion of old Roman felicity, notwithstanding the immense *amor patriæ* that attended it.

CHAPTER XII.

Philadelphia Threatened.—Washington Marches to meet the Enemy.—Review
of the Army.—Action at Brandywine.—Reflections on National Strength.—
Measures of Washington.—Character of his Operations.—Defeat of Burgoyne.—
Society at Reading.—Generals Mifflin, Gates, Conway, Lee.—Captain Speke.—
Prisoners.—British Officers on Parole.—Author Exchanged.—Married.—Re-
flections.—Occurrence of the War.—Charles Thomson.

GENERAL Howe had remained inactive during the summer,
and it was not until the latter part of August, that it became
manifest that Philadelphia was his object.   This rendered it expedient in the opinion of the active Whigs of that city, to put out
of the way of mischief, the most influential and zealous of the
disaffected; several of whom were accordingly, on authority of
Congress, apprehended, and deported to the western parts of
Virginia.   On their way thither, they passed through Reading;
and it being proposed by some of their old fellow citizens there
resident, to show them some attention in their misfortune, the proposition was generally approved, and I was among the number
of those who called on them, at the inn at which they stopped.
Here, we found some of the principal and most respectable
Quakers, Mr. James Pemberton, Mr. Myers Fisher, and several
others, whom I do not, with certainty, recollect.   Mr. Fisher
was the only one of this society, with whom I was personally
acquainted; and he, I remember, took occasion significantly to
observe, that "I did not look as if I had been starved by those
sad people the British."   But I found among them another acquaintance of a wholly different order.   This was no other than
my old friend Pike, the fencing master, who, although he had
dissembled so well at the outset of the business, as to render it
dubious whether he was for or against us, had, in the sequel it

25

seems, evinced himself a true-hearted Briton, to which circumstance, he owed the honour of his being in his present *very good company*, as he termed it. The red coat and laced hat of Pike, were, to be sure, very strikingly in contrast with the flat brims and plain drab-coloured garments of the rest of the assemblage: nevertheless, from an internal similarity, this seemingly discordant ingredient incorporated perfectly well with the mass; and friend Pike, as he was called, officiating in the capacity of a major domo or caterer at the inns they put up at, was a person, I found, of no small consideration with his party. The prisoners were not much dejected, probably looking upon themselves as martyrs to the cause of their country; and, in fact, though apparently well pleased with the civility we showed them, their manner rather indicated, that they considered us, as more objects of pity than themselves. How much is it to be lamented, that the public good should not always be so manifest as not to be mistaken! If this were the case, how many of the *fantastic tricks* we play off against each other, in its name, might be spared! But then, we should no longer be the self-important, " forked-animals," " the quintescence of dust," called man.

Having drawn together his forces, General WASHINGTON marched to meet the enemy, who, from the head of Elk, was directing his course to Philadelphia. As it had been given out by the disaffected, that we were much weaker than in truth we were, the General thought it best to show both Whigs and Tories the real strength he possessed; and in this view, took his route through the city, the *bellorum maxima merces*, or at least, the great object of the campaign, and the point, which if gained, would, in the opinion of Mr. Galloway, be decisive of the contest. I happened to be there at the time, and from the coffee-house corner, saw our army with the Commander-in-chief at its head, pass down Front street. The sight was highly interesting to persons of all descriptions; and among the many who, perhaps, equally disclaimed the epithet of Whig or of Tory, Mr. Chew, from an upper window in the house of Mr. Turner, appeared a very anxious spectator. By the bye, it might savour of bigotry, to impute guilt to this want of decision. In civil commotions, there is generally so much to disapprove on both sides, and the issue is so little answerable to the designs of the well-meaning men embarked in them, that neutrality, if it could be maintained, might often be the most eligible part. Atticus was perhaps as good, and probably a wiser man than either Cicero, or Pompey, or Cæsar. There are certainly times in which inaction becomes virtue, notwithstanding that active ardour may be more congenial to upright intention; and that it is in the glowing temperament of a Cato, disdaining that " his house should stand secure and flourish in a civil war," that the noblest feelings of an honest heart are to be looked for. And yet, this very Cato, under the guidance of the same poet, who puts this heroic sentiment into his mouth, is made to counsel his son to "live retired, and to content himself with being obscurely good."

The impression made by this review of the American army, it is to be presumed, was rather favourable than otherwise from the propensity of persons unaccustomed to the sight of large bodies of men, to augment them. But it was very disproportioned to the zeal for liberty, which had been manifested the year before. It amounted to but about eight or nine thousand men, according to Chief Justice Marshall; but these, though indifferently dressed, held well burnished arms, and carried them like soldiers, and looked, in short, as if they might have faced an equal number with a reasonable prospect of success.

The action which ensued at Brandywine, on the eleventh of September, is an instance, among many others furnished by history, both of the temptation to dispute the passage of a river by fronting the enemy on the opposite side, and of the inefficiency of such attempts. The difficulty and ineligibility of these undertakings, are noticed by most of the writers on the art of war, and particularly by the Marquis De Feuquiere.* To a person of any

---

* He says: " It is impossible to guard the shores of a river when the ground to be guarded is of a great extent, because the assailant, pointing his efforts to several places, for the purpose of separating the forces of his adversary, and to draw his attention to spots very distant from each other, at length determining to make his effort at the point where he finds the least ability to resist, always prevails over the labours and vigilance of his enemy; more especially when he employs the night for the execution of his enterprize, that being most favourable for concealing the place of his principal effort."

military experience, who reflects how easy it must be, to distract
the opposing army by fallacious demonstrations, in a situation at
once concealed from observation, and exempted from the peril
which results from movements in the face of an adversary, in a
state of profit by them, the little chance of succeeding in the
effort, on a merely defensive plan, must be apparent.   Where,
indeed, the defending General shall permit himself to become the
assailant, if occasion should offer, he, in some degree, balances
advantages; and the conception of General WASHINGTON, as
mentioned by Judge Marshall, of crossing at the lower ford to
attack the enemy's right under Knyphausen, was masterly; and
might, if rapidly put in execution, have handsomely turned the
tables.   It can hardly be doubted, however, that a position on
the enemy's flank to the westward, would have been more eligible
than that taken in front; and that the means of annoying and
possibly crippling him on his march, which was all that could
reasonably be looked for from an army so inferior as ours, might
have offered at this river or at Schuylkill.   This was probably, at
one time contemplated, under the recommendation, as it was said,
of General Greene.   But the public clamour demanded that a
battle should be risked for the city; and I well remember, that it
was given out at Reading, on the suggestion of General Mifflin,
that Greene, of whom he was no friend, was jealous of Southern
influence, and, therefore, indifferent to the fate of Philadelphia.
But if Greene really advised the measure attributed to him, thereby
securing the open country to our army in case of disaster, in preference to the plan adopted, and which, in addition to its other
faults, tended to place us in the nook formed by the course of the
Delaware, I cannot but say, that, whatever were his motives, and
we have no ground to presume them bad, he was right.   Yet, if
Congress required that the enemy should be fought, and we have
good authority that they did require it, the opportunity of bringing
him to action, in any other mode than that of placing ourselves
directly in his way, might have been lost.*

---

* "The expediency of fighting this battle," says SPARKS, in his Life of WASH-
INGTON, " with a force so much inferior, and under many disadvantages, has been
questioned by foreign writers.   If the subject be viewed in a military light only,
there may, perhaps, be just grounds for criticism.   But it should be differently

But why so much caution, it may be asked, against a foe in the very heart of the country? Why not rather turn out *en masse*, surround, and make a breakfast of Mr. Howe and his mercenaries? Could not a population of two millions of souls, have furnished fighting Whigs enough for the purpose? Where were the multitudes which used to appear in arms, in the commons of Philadelphia? Where the legions of New-England men that hemmed in Gage at Boston? Where, in short, the hundred and fifty thousand men in arms throughout the continent, spoken of by General Lee* and others, at the beginning of the contest? Where were the Pennsylvania riflemen, those formidable, unerring marksmen, each of whom, could venture to put a ball in a target, held by his brother? How came it, that that excellent jest of a British dragoon pursuing one of them round a tree, was not exemplified on this occasion? These things promised well; they were flattering in the extreme, and admirably calculated to buoy us up in a confidence of the martial superiority of freemen to slaves. Yet, on the day of trial, from whatever cause it proceeded, the fate of the country and its liberties, was always committed to a handful of mercenaries, the very things, which were the eternal theme of our scorn and derision. The fact must either be, that the effective strength of a nation does, after all, reside in regular, disciplined forces, or that appearances were lamentably deceitful; that all the patriotic ardour we had at first displayed, had already evaporated; and that the gallant affair of Bunker's hill, and others, were but the effects of mo-

regarded. General WASHINGTON knew the expectation of the country and of Congress; and he was persuaded, that a defeat would be less injurious in its effects on the public mind, than the permitting of the enemy to march to Philadelphia without opposition. He doubtless hoped to make a better resistance; which he would have done, if he had not been deceived by contradictory intelligence in the time of battle, against which no foresight could guard. Although some of his troops behaved ill, yet others, and the larger part, fought with signal bravery, and inspired him and themselves with a confidence, which could have been produced only by the trial." See Appendix K.—ED.

* Not less than a hundred and fifty thousand gentlemen, yeomen and farmers are in arms, determined to preserve their liberties or perish.—*Letter from General Lee to General Burgoyne.*

mentary excitement. America does not seem to be a soil for enthusiasm; and I am not at all disposed to dispute the assertion contained in a letter of General Du Portail, in the time of the war, that there was more of it in a single coffee-house in Paris, than on our whole continent put together. From these facts, and facts they assuredly are, let our theoretical men calculate the probable result of a formidable invasion of our country in our present state of preparation; and, if in the heroic epoch alluded to, when there had been really a promise of great things, so little was done, how much less, is rationally to be expected from the empty vapouring of demagogue valour. Would it have been credited in the year 1775, that a British army of eighteen thousand men could have marched in perfect security from the Chesapeake to Philadelphia? that a much smaller force could have penetrated through the Jerseys to the Delaware? and that mere partizan-bodies, could have traversed the southern states in utter contempt of the *long knife* of Virginia! All these things were done; and yet our babbling statesmen will talk, "Ye Gods! how they will talk," of the irresistable prowess of a nation of freemen! From the perseverance of Spain, when compared with the short-lived exertions of Austria and Prussia, some argue the superiority of a determined people to regular armies. But it is not certainly like Spain, that we would wish to have our country defended to be first over-run and destroyed! Neither can the glory we aspire to, be merely that of the boxer, who bears a great deal of beating, and solely depends on outwinding his adversary. I have lately seen sneers at what are called *technical* armies; but what are we to call those with which Napoleon has achieved his victories and attained his present fearful ascendancy! We can hardly say, they are not *technical*, because, in part, composed of conscripts; and, if by the term, is meant *disciplined*, who will deny them that qualification?

Previously to Sir William Howe's getting possession of Philadelphia, measures were taken by General WASHINGTON to give him battle a second time. The two armies were on the point of engaging, and the encounter was only prevented by a heavy fall of rain. The weather continued wet for a day or two; and by damaging our ammunition, rendered it inexpedient to seek the enemy.* While our army had been preparing for action, I have been informed by several discerning officers, that the General discovered unusual impetuosity ; and that as he rode along the line exhorting his men to do their duty, his manner evinced an extreme impatience of ill-fortune, and a determination to retrieve it, or perish in the attempt.

Although defeat had been the consequence of his unequal conflicts with the foe, and his country seemed lost to the generous ardour which had once inspired it, his manly mind was not subdued. Of this he gave an illustrious instance in his assault of the post at Germantown. That the British army was not destroyed on this occasion, and Philadelphia recovered, has been represented by certain malcontents, as a shameful dereliction of a victory already gained; and General C. Lee, sneeringly denominates it a stroke of the *bathos*. But what would he that we should have done? He would hardly have had us press on hap-hazard, without redressing the disorder which had taken place in our line; a disorder which might have ensued, had even General Lee himself commanded. Besides, the step would

* " After allowing his men one day for rest and refreshment, WASHINGTON returned across the Schuylkill, and took the Lancaster road, leading to the left of the British army, fully determined to offer battle. This bold step, taken before the enemy had left the field of action at the Brandywine, was a proof that the late repulse had in no degree unsettled his own resolution, or damped the ardour of his troops. The two armies met twenty-three miles from Philadelphia, and an engagement was actually begun between the advanced parties, when a heavy rain came on and rendered both armies totally unfit to pursue the contest. WASHINGTON retired to the Yellow Springs, but was not followed by the British; and he finally passed over the Schuylkill at Parker's Ford."

WASHINGTON gives the following account of his movements on this occasion :—

"When I last re-crossed the Schuylkill, it was with a firm intent of giving the enemy battle wherever I should meet them; and accordingly I advanced as far as the Warren Tavern upon the Lancaster road, near which place the two armies were upon the point of coming to a general engagement, but were prevented by a most violent flood of rain, which continued all the day and following night. When it held up, we had the mortification to find our ammunition, which had been completed to forty rounds a man, was entirely ruined; and in that situation we had nothing left for it, but to find out a strong piece of ground, which we could easily maintain, till we could get the arms put in order, and a recruit of ammunition."—*Sparks' Life of Washington.*—ED.

have been by no means congenial with his own conduct at
Monmouth; which was sufficiently circumspect and respectful
of an enemy, he here seems to consider as nothing.* But the
reputation of a commander ought not to depend upon a sarcasm;
and in order to have shown, wherein General WASHINGTON's
conduct had been defective, Mr. Lee should have fairly set before us, what *Duke* Ferdinand, whom he is pleased to bring into
contrast, would have done. Possibly, the Duke might have
duly respected the British grenadiers, and made comparisons not
altogether animating, between the respective numbers, equipments and discipline, of his own army, and that of his adversary.
But this, as a prudent General, he would, doubtless, have kept
to himself; since to proclaim the bravery of an enemy, to our
own men, on the field of action, is at best, but a doubtful mode
of encouraging them. It would, however, be no just disparagement of General WASHINGTON, to admit his inferiority to Prince
Ferdinand, in matters wherein the desultory Indian warfare, had
furnished no experience. We had no right to count upon him
as consummate in the science of tactics; or to hold him fully
competent to the nice arrangements required in the movements
of an army, should it even be disciplined. Indeed, it was observable, and confirmed by every instance which came under
my notice, that little benefit, with respect to the discipline of
parade, so essential to the effect of operations on the large scale,
was derived from any of the gentlemen who had been in the
provincial service. The fortitude which is acquired from a
familiarity with the perils and privations of war, was conspicuous
in many; but being too far advanced in life, readily to acquire
new habits, they were far from excelling in the business of
manœuvring, or in an aptitude of imparting to their men the air

---

* A partial advantage over the enemy, was, probably, all that was contemplated on this occasion, and it was certainly as much as we had a right to calculate upon with our very inferior army. This may account for the delay at Chew's
house, which has been so much censured by those, who have rashly asserted that
a complete victory was in our power.

I presume this is the first defence that has been made of the failure at Germantown, and I must confess my satisfaction to find that it agrees with General
WILKINSON's and General HENRY LEE's opinions of that affair.

and adroitness of regular soldiers.   In the situation of our army, necessarily deficient in discipline, something of that attention to minutiæ ; that acquaintance with the duties of the adjutant and drill sergeant with the occasional exercise of them, which have been ascribed to the King of Prussia ; that searching eye, which runs along the line, detecting at a glance, the remissness of every lounger, might have been desirable in its commander, possessing, in other respects, exterior qualifications for the station, in a degree not to be surpassed : a manner which at once inspired confidence and attachment ; a figure pre-eminently gentlemanly, dignified, commanding, equally removed from heaviness and flippancy, and blending the gravity of the sage, with the animation of the soldier. Had it belonged to Alexander, Hephæstion would have lost his compliment, as it must infallibly have prevented the mistake of the mother of Darius.

The success of General Howe ; the loss of Philadelphia ; as well as the ground given in the northern quarter by the retreat of General St. Clair ; were amply counterbalanced by the utter extinction of Burgoyne's army on the fifteenth of October.* As Reading lay in the route from Saratoga to York where Congress was now assembled, we received before that body, the particulars of this glorious event, from Major Wilkinson,† who was

* On the return of General BURGOYNE to England, on his parole, the King refused to see him, and he in vain solicited a Court-martial. Under these circumstances, he threw himself upon Parliament, and a motion was made in the House of Commons, for an inquiry into the Convention at Saratoga ; which was got rid of by the previous question." *Note by the Editor of Walpole's Letters.*—ED.

† Afterwards General JAMES WILKINSON. He was more distinguished for his ponderous " Memoirs " of doubtful authority, than for any very effective service in war at any period of his career, although, like another celebrated chieftain, he was a " *hero of two wars*," the Revolutionary and *Madisonian,* that is to say, he belonged to the army at both periods. He was no doubt a brave man. He was sent by GATES to Congress to communicate intelligence of BURGOYNE'S surrender. He was also charged with being concerned in the famous CONWAY CABAL. In return for the magnanimity of our author in his reference to this gentleman, it is but proper that the General's very favourable, but no doubt very just, impressions in regard to *him* should appear. In Vol. I. at p. 339, of the Memoirs of Wilkinson, we read as follows : " Besides Mr. BIDDLE, I had another acquaintance, a contemporary whose independence of sentiment and manly deportment, had attracted my attention and engaged my esteem during my residence in Philadelphia ; but exclusive of his personal merits, a congeniality of feeling and parity of

charged with the despatches of General Gates. But without
loading my Memoirs with obvious and trite reflections on this
memorable occurrence, I turn a moment to myself, to observe:
That were I a prey to the vulture of ill-starr'd ambition, the mention of a gentleman, with whom I commenced in the same rank,
my military career, and who is now in the chief command of the
American forces, might suggest somewhat unpleasantly, the im-
measurable distance he has left me behind; but the recollections
his name awakens with infinitely more interest, are of a nature
wholly different. They relate to pursuits and occupations of a
character more congenial to that season of life, when, as a student of physic, he attended medical lectures in Philadelphia, before either of us wore a uniform, and before a foundation was
laid for the many strifes which have since ensued. Thus much
without connecting him with any of them, I freely pay to the
remembrance of an early friendship, ever renewed when casualties have brought us together, maugre the estranging influence of
different party-associations.

The ensuing winter, at Reading, was gay and agreeable, notwithstanding that the enemy was in possession of the metropolis.
The society was sufficiently large and select; and a sense of common suffering in being driven from their homes, had the effect of
more closely uniting its members. Disasters of this kind, if duly
weighed, are not grievously to be deplored. The variety and
bustle they bring along with them, give a spring to the mind;
and when illumined by hope, as was now the case, they are,
when present, not painful, and when past, they are among the
incidents most pleasing in retrospection. Besides the families
established in this place, it was seldom without a number of visiters, gentlemen of the army and others. Hence the dissipation
of cards, sleighing-parties, balls, &c., was freely indulged.

predicament, as it regarded a passion which above all others most interests the
youthful heart, had produced a confidential intimacy, the recollection of which
at this distant day, awakens the sweetest sensibilities of my bosom; and I know
not whether I compliment the living or the dead, when I declare that I have
rarely met with a man of more refined honour, a more feeling heart, or more
polished manners, than ALEXANDER GRAYDON, Esq." The Memoirs of WILKINSON
were printed in 1816.—ED.

General Mifflin, at this era, was at home, a ˙chief out of war, complaining, though not ill, considerably malcontent, and apparently, not in high favour at Head Quarters. According to him, the ear of the Commander-in-chief, was exclusively possessed by Greene, who was represented to be neither the most wise, the most brave, nor most patriotic of counsellers.* In short, the campaign in this quarter, was stigmatized as a series of blunders; and the incapacity of those who had conducted it, unsparingly reprobated. The better fortune of the northern army, was ascribed to the superior talents of its leader; and it began to be whispered, that Gates was the man who should, of right, have the station so incompetently sustained by WASHINGTON. There was, to all appearance, a cabal forming for his deposition, in which, it is not improbable, that Gates, Mifflin and Conway were already engaged; and, in which, the congenial spirit of Lee, on his exchange, immediately took a share. The well known apostrophe of Conway to America, importing "that Heaven had passed a decree in her favour or her ruin, must long before have ensued, from the imbecility of her military counsels," was, at this time, familiar at Reading; and I heard him myself, when he was afterwards on a visit to that place, express himself to the

* A far abler, more sincere, and more " earnest man," as CARLYLE would express it, than General MIFFLIN, namely, GENERAL HENRY LEE, entertained and expressed a very different opinion. " No man," he says, " was more familiarized to dispassionate and minute research than General GREENE. He was patient in hearing every thing offered, never interrupting or slighting what was said; and, having possessed himself of the subject fully, he would enter into a critical comparison of the opposite arguments, convincing his hearers, as he proceeded, of the propriety of the decision he was about to pronounce." "His vivid plastic genius operated on the latent elements of martial capacity in his army, invigorated its weakness, turned its confusion into order, and its despondency into ardour. A wide sphere of intellectual resource enabled him to inspire confidence, to rekindle courage, to decide hesitation, and infuse a spirit of exalted patriotism in the citizens of the State. By his own example, he showed the incalculable value of obedience, of patience, of vigilance and temperance. Dispensing justice, with an even hand, to the citizen and soldier; benign in heart, and happy in manners; he acquired the durable attachment and esteem of all. He collected around his person, able and respectable officers; and selected, for the several departments, those who were best qualified to fill them. His operations were then commenced with a boldness of design, well calculated to raise the drooping hopes of his country, and to excite the respect of the enemy."—ED.

effect : " That no man was more a gentleman than General WASH-
INGTON, or appeared to more advantage at his table, or in the usual
intercourse of life; but as to his talents for the command of an
army, (with a French shrug) they were miserable indeed." Observations of this kind, continually repeated, could not fail to
make an impression within the sphere of their circulation ; and
it may be said, that the popularity of the Commander-in-chief,
was a good deal impaired at Reading. As to myself, however,
I can confidently aver, that I never was proselyted ; or gave into
the opinion for a moment, that any man in America, was worthy
to supplant the exalted character, that presided in her army.   I
might have been disposed, perhaps, to believe, that such talents
as were possessed by Lee, could they be brought to act subordi-
nately, might often be useful to him; but I ever thought it would
be a fatal error, to put any other in his place.   Nor was I the
only one, who forbore to become a partizan of Gates.*   Several
others thought they saw symptoms of selfishness in the business;
nor could the great *eclat* of the northern campaign, convince them,
that its hero was superior to WASHINGTON.   The duel which afterwards took place between Generals Conway† and Cadwalader,

---

* GENERAL HORATIO GATES was an Englishman, and had served in America
during the war of 1755.   Little is known of his early career.   He is said to have
been born in 1728, "and rose to the rank of major by the force of merit alone."
HORACE WALPOLE, in writing to HORACE MANN, speaks of the god-son of the latter, HORATIO GATES, and of his capture of BURGOYNE, at Saratoga.

He settled in Virginia, where, at the commencement of the war of the Revolution, he received from Congress the appointment of Adjutant-General, with the
rank of Brigadier to the army assembled before Boston in the first campaign.
After the capture of BURGOYNE, when the popularity of GATES, in consequence of
this good fortune, was at its height, " intrigues were commenced for elevating him
to the station occupied by WASHINGTON, which were as shameful as they were unsuccessful." How far he was engaged in them it is not now possible to determine.
In June, 1780, GATES received the Chief command of the Southern army, and
when about to leave Virginia for the south, "his old acquaintance, General
CHARLES LEE, waited on him to take leave, and pressing his hand, bade him bear
in mind, that the laurels of the North must not be exchanged for the willow of
the South." He was defeated by CORNWALLIS, at the battle of Camden, on the
16th of August. He died on the 10th of April, 1806, in the 78th year of his
age."—ED.

† GENERAL THOMAS CONWAY was born in Ireland. He received a military education in France, where, at the age six years, he accompanied his parents. He

though immediately proceeding from an unfavourable opinion expressed by the latter of the conduct of the former at Germantown, had perhaps a deeper origin, and some reference to this intrigue :* as I had the means of knowing, that General Cadwalader, suspecting Mifflin had instigated Conway to fight him, was extremely earnest to obtain data from a gentleman who lived in Reading, whereon to ground a serious explanation with Mifflin. So much for the manœuvring, which my location at one of its principal seats, brought me acquainted with ; and which, its authors were soon after desirous of burying in oblivion.

Among the persons, who, this winter, spent much time in

---

came to this country with strong recommendations, and, in 1777, received from Congress the appointment of Brigadier-General. He was, however, distinguished only by his ridiculous hostility to WASHINGTON, and by his absurd endeavour to place his friend General GATES, in the Chief command of the army. " In this he was supported by several members of Congress. He was appointed by that body Inspector-General of the Army, with the rank of Major-General, but, was soon obliged to resign his commission, on account of his unpopularity with the officers. In consequence of his calumnies against WASHINGTON, he was challenged by General Cadwalader, and wounded in the head. Supposing that he was mortally injured, he wrote a satisfactory letter of apology to WASHINGTON, for the injury he had endeavoured to inflict upon his character." He returned to France at the close of the year 1778.

The absurd aspirations of the English General, GATES, the weak and miserable intrigues of his countryman and partisan, CONWAY, the vanity and insubordination of their able but eccentric countryman, General CHARLES LEE, caused far more annoyance to the Commander-in-chief, than the inexperience of all the other officers together, who, suddenly summoned to the field from the ordinary avocations of life, were compelled to learn the art of war, amidst its perils and responsibilities.—ED.

* Not that General CADWALADER was induced from the intrigue to speak unfavourably of General CONWAY's behaviour at Germantown. That of itself, was a sufficient ground of censure. Conway, it seems, during the action, was found in a farm-house by Generals REED and CADWALADER. Upon their inquiring the cause, he replied, in great agitation, that his horse was wounded in the neck. Being urged to get another horse, and at any rate to join his brigade which was engaged, he declined it, repeating that his horse was wounded in the neck. Upon Conway's applying to Congress, some time after to be made a Major-General, and earnestly urging his suit, Cadwalader made known this conduct of his at Germantown ; and it was for so doing, that Conway gave the challenge, the issue of which was, his being dangerously wounded in the face from the pistol of General Cadwalader. He recovered, however, and some time time after went to France.

Reading, was one Luttiloe,* a foreigner, who was afterwards
arrested in London on suspicion of hostile designs; also Mr.
William Duer, who either was, or lately had been, a member of
Congress. His character is well known. He was of the dashing cast, a man of the world, confident and animated, with a
promptitude in displaying the wit and talents he possessed,
with very little regard to the decorum, which either time or
place imposed. Of this he gave an instance, one day, at Mr.
Edward Biddle's, which, had it been on a theatre, where the
royal cause was predominant, I should have relished : as it was,
it was unpleasant to me. Captain Speke† of the British army,
a prisoner, was present, with his eye on a newspaper, several
of which had lately come out of Philadelphia, when Duer,
taking up another began to read aloud, commenting with much
sarcasm on the paragraphs as he went along. Speke bore it a
good while, but at length Duer's remarks became so pinching
that he was roused to reply. To this he received a ready rejoinder, and a warm altercation was on the point of taking
place, when Captain Speke prudently took the resolution of relinquishing the field; and taking up his hat, abruptly retired.

---

* HENRY LUTTERLOH, Esq., a German. He is so called in the account, under the
head of Britain, in Dobson's Encyclopedia, and was concerned with De la Motte
who was executed for treason, whom, on being arrested, he informed against.
HENRY EMANUEL LUTTERLOH.—On the 14th of April, 1790, at the second session
of the first Congress, after the organization of the Government, a petition was
presented by this gentleman praying to be allowed the pay and emoluments of a
colonel, in consideration of military services rendered to the United States during
the war. This petition was referred to the Secretary of War, who reported on
the 20th May. His report was referred to a committee, and their report was
taken up on the 2d of August, and disagreed to, and the petitioner had leave
granted him to withdraw his petition. At the *third* session of this Congress, he
presented another petition praying that his memorial might be reconsidered—
and he was again rejected. At the first session of the second Congress, he again
petitioned. A committee reported, but there was no action on the report; but at
the next session, the House *resolved*—that the account of "Colonel Henry Emanuel Lutterloh, for his travelling and passage expenses incurred in coming to
America, and joining the army of the United States, in 1777, being seven hundred and forty-six dollars, be settled, and the amount thereof to be paid out of the
treasury of the United States." History of Congress during first term of WASH-
INGTON.—ED.

† CAPTAIN SPEKE was taken prisoner at the battle of Germantown.

As Speke, although a thorough Englishman, was a well-bred man, with whom I had become acquainted, and had exchanged some civilities, I was not a little hurt at this circumstance, as the company in general seemed to be. Duer for his part triumphed in his success, displaying a heart, which however bold on the safe side of the lines, might nevertheless have been sufficiently meek on the other; at least, such a conduct would but conform to the result of my observations on persons who play the bashaw in prosperity; and I believe it is pretty generally agreed, to be no mark of game to crow upon a dunghill. While upon the subject of Captain Speke, I will finish the little I have to say of him. He belonged, if my recollection does not fail me, to the same regiment with Mr. Becket; at least, he was well acquainted with him, and told me he had heard him speak of me. He was young and lively, with an addiction to that sly significance of remark, characteristic both of his profession and his nation; and which may be pardoned, when accompanied with good humour. Taking up my hat, one day, when at his quarters, to take coffee with him and one or two others of his fellow prisoners, he observed, that it was a very decent one, which is more, said he, than I can say of those generally worn by the officers of your army: they have precisely what we call in England, the *damn my eyes cock*. At another time, having called upon me at my mother's, I was led by some circumstance, to advert to the awkward form and low ceiling of the room; but " faith," said he, looking round, " you have made the most of it with furniture ;" which was true enough, as it was unmercifully overloaded with chairs, tables and family pictures. Such freedoms may fully justify me in scanning Mr. Speke, who, to say the truth, was, in point of information, far above the level which is allowed to the gentlemen of the British army, by Swift and other writers of their nation. As to " your *Noveds* and *Blutarks*, and *Omurs* and stuff," I know not if he was of the noble Captain's opinion, in Hannah's animated plea for turning Hamilton's bawn into a barrack; but he had read some of the English poets; and speaking of Prior and Pope, I remember his saying, that the former was much preferred to the latter, by people of taste in England. But grant what we may to the sprightliness and easy gaiety of Prior, this can hardly be

the award of sound criticism.   Being heartily tired of the condition of a captive, Mr. Speke was extremely anxious to get rid of
it, and to this effect suggested, that by mutual exertion, we might
be exchanged for each other.   He said, that if I could obtain
permission for him to go into Philadelphia on parole, he had no
doubt of having sufficient interest to effect it.   I accordingly
took the liberty to write to General WASHINGTON on the subject,
but was a long time in suspense as to the success of my application.   An additional inducement to the step, was, that both
Colonel Miles and Major West, had by requisition of General
Howe, repaired to Philadelphia ; and I every day expected a
similar summons.   It had been given out that these gentlemen
had not observed all the passiveness which had been enjoined
upon them by their parole ; and I well knew that I was charged
·with a like transgression.   I had spoken freely, it is true, of the
treatment of prisoners; and this was considered by the Tories and
some of the British officers in our hands, as very unpardonable
in one who had been favoured as I had been ; and I was aware
that I was threatened with a retraction of the indulgence.   I remained, however, unmolested.   The situation of Miles and West
in the neighbourhood of the army at White Marsh, was, perhaps,
the circumstance which gave colour to the accusation against
them ; but they were not long detained.

Besides, that it would have ill comported with the indulgence
I enjoyed, it was abhorrent to my feelings, to behave haughtily to
a prisoner.   There were two puppies, however, in that predicament, in whom I immediately recognised the insolent manner of
a genuine *scoundrel in red;* and these, I cautiously avoided.
They were subalterns ; one of whom, of the name of Wilson, was
base enough, under the false pretence of being related to the Captain Wilson, who he had some how learned had treated me with
civility, to borrow a few guineas of my mother, which it unluckily
slipped his memory to repay.   Had I been aware of the application, the loan would have been prevented ; but I never knew of
the circumstance until after his exchange.   With the exception of
these fellows, who, I had the mortification to hear, had found their
way to General WASHINGTON's table, at the time of their being

taken, all the prisoners in Reading behaved with much decency. Among them, were a number of German officers, who had really the appearance of being, what we call, down-right men. There was a Major Stine, a Captain Sobbe and a Captain Wetherholt of the Hessians, whom I sometimes fell in with. There were several others, with whom I was not acquainted, and whose names I do not remember. One old gentleman, a colonel, was a great professional reader, whom, on his application, I accommodated with such books of the kind, as I had. Another of them, a very portly personage, apparently replete with national phlegm, was, nevertheless, enthusiastically devoted to music, in which, he was so absorbed, as seldom to go abroad. I did not know this musical gentleman, except by sight; but I have understood from those who did, that call upon him at what time they would, and, like another Achilles in retirement,

Amus'd at ease, the godlike man they found.
Pleas'd with the solemn harp's harmonious sound:

for this was the obsolete instrument, from which he extracted the sounds that so much delighted him. But of all the prisoners, one Graff, a Brunswick officer taken by General Gates's army, was admitted to the greatest privileges. Under the patronage of Doctor Potts, who had been principal surgeon in the Northern Department, he had been introduced to our dancing parties; and being always afterwards invited, he never failed to attend. He was a young man of mild and pleasing manners, with urbanity enough to witness the little triumphs of party without being incited to ill humour by them. Over-hearing a dance called for, one evening, which we had named *Burgoyne's surrender*, he observed to his partner, that it was a very pretty dance, notwithstanding the name; and that General Burgoyne himself would be happy to dance it in such good company. There was also a Mr. Stutzoe, of the Brunswick dragoons, than whose, I have seldom seen a figure more martial; or a manner more indicative of that manly openness, which is supposed to belong to the character of a soldier. I had a slight acquaintance with him; and recollect with satisfac-

26*

tion, his calling on me at the time of his exchange, to make me
his acknowledgments, as he was pleased to say, for my civilities
to the prisoners.

Perhaps I may be excused for these trifling details, when it is
considered, that they serve to mark the temper of the times, and
to show, that they were not all fire and fury, as certain modern
pretenders to the spirit of *Seventy-Six*, have almost persuaded us
they were. It ought to be granted, indeed, that an equal degree
of toleration was not every where to be met with. It would
scarcely have been found in that description of persons, which
soon arrogated, and have since voted themselves the exclusive
possession of all the patriotism in the nation. Even that small
portion of the monopolists which resided at Reading, revolted at
a moderation they did not understand; and all who were less violent and bigoted than themselves, were branded as Tories. All
the families which had removed from Philadelphia were involved
in this reproach; and, in their avoidance of the enemy to the
manifest injury of their affairs, they were supposed to exhibit
proofs of disaffection. Nor was I much better off: my having
risked myself in the field was nothing: I should have staid at
home, talked big, been a militia-man and hunted Tories.

In confirmation of my remark, that toleration was not among
the virtues affected by those who were emphatically styled THE
PEOPLE, I will instance the case of a young Scotch officer of the
name of Dunlap, who was one day beset in the street by certain
persons overflowing with Whigism; and, for presuming to resent
the insults he received from them, was not only severely cudgeled,
but afterwards put to jail. This treatment might have fairly
squared with that of our officers from the royal side, in relation to
the fish sellers; though I will undertake to aver, that, generally
speaking, the prisoners in our hands, were treated both with lenity
and generosity. Some time after this affray, happening, at a table
in Philadelphia, to be placed by the side of Doctor Witherspoon,
then a member of Congress, I took occasion to mention it to him;
and to intercede for his good offices in regard to the liberation of
Dunlap, who was still in jail. I counted something upon the
national spirit, supposed to be so prevalent among North Britons;

and yet more, upon the circumstance of knowing from Dunlap and two other young Scotchmen, his fellow prisoners, that Doctor Witherspoon had been well acquainted with their families. I did not find, however, that the Doctor was much melted to compassion for the mishap of his countryman, as he contented himself with coldly observing, that if I could suggest any substantial ground for him to proceed upon, he would do what he could for the young man. It appeared to me, that enough had been suggested, by my simple relation of the facts ; and I had nothing more to offer. But whether or not my application was of any benefit to its object, my presentation of the *laddies* to the recollection of the Doctor, seemed to have something of national interest in it; and had the effect, to incite him to a shrewd remark, according to his manner. He told me he had seen the young men soon after they had been taken, and was suprised to find one of them, whose name I forget, so much of a cub. His father, said he, was a very sprightly fellow, when I knew him. This lad is the fruit of a second marriage ; and I immediately concluded, when I saw him, said the Doctor, that Jemmey, or Sawney something, mentioning the father's name, had taken some *clumsy girl* to wife for the sake of a fortune.*

---

* JOHN WITHERSPOON, D. D., L. L. D. He was born in Scotland, and was distinguished among the Scotch Clergy for talent and influence. He was twice invited to the Presidency of Princeton College, and finally arrived in New Jersey with his family, in 1768. The War of the Revolution dispersed the students, and President Witherspoon almost immediately entered upon political life. He was a member of the Convention which formed the Constitution of New Jersey, and in 1776 was appointed a member of Congress, and retained his seat during the War. His name is affixed to the Declaration of Independence, and the articles of Confederation. After the War, he returned to his duties at the College. He died in 1794, in the 73d year of his age.—*Ency. Amer.*

"On the morning of our national birth-day, the fourth of July, 1776, when the Declaration of American Independence was made—when the Committee, previously appointed to draft that instrument, made their report through their Chairman, THOMAS JEFFERSON—and by whom it was read, the House paused—hesitated, That instrument, they saw, cut them off even from the mercy of Great Britain. They saw with prophetic vision all the horrors of a sanguinary war— carnage and desolation passed in swift review before them. They saw the prospect of having riveted still more closely upon their already chafed and bleeding limbs the chains of slavery. The House seemed to waver—silence, deep and solemn silence, reigned throughout the hall of the spacious Capitol. Every

On looking back here, and adverting to the free observations I have from time to time made, both on revolutionary men and measures, I am aware, that I have no forgiveness to expect from many, for attempting to rub off the fine varnish which adheres to them. But I set out with the avowed design of declaring the truth; and to this, I have most sacredly and concientiously conformed, according to my persuasions, even as to the colouring of each particular I have touched upon. The same veracity shall direct my future delineations, well knowing, that, independently of my obligation to do justice, this alone must constitute the merit of my Memoirs. That we were not, and still are not without patriotism, in an equal degree, perhaps, with other nations, I have no inclination to question; but that a noble disinterestedness and willingness to sacrifice private interest to public good, should be the general disposition any where, my acquaintance with human nature, neither warrants me in asserting or believing. The prevalence of generous sentiment, of which, no doubt, there is a portion in all communities, depends very much upon those, who have the direction of their affairs. Under the guidance of WASHINGTON, both during the Revolution and his administration of the General Government, the honourable feelings being cherished and brought

countenance indicated that deep meditation was at work; and the solemn reso-- lutions were calling for double energy. At this fearful crisis, when the very destiny of the country seemed to be suspended upon the action of a moment, the silence, the painful silence was broken. An aged patriarch arose—a venerable and stately form, his head white with the frosts of many years.. He cast on the assembly a look of inexpressible interest and unconquerable determination; while on his visage the hue of age was lost as burning patriotism fired his cheek. 'There is,' said he, 'a tide in the affairs of men, a nick of time. We perceive it now before us. That noble instrument upon your table, which ensures immortality to its author, should be subscribed this very morning, by every pen in the house. He who will not respond to its accents and strain every nerve to carry into effect its provisions, is unworthy the name of a freeman. Although these gray hairs must descend into the sepulchre, I would infinitely rather they should descend thither by the hand of the public executioner, than desert at this crisis the sacred cause of my country.' The patriarch sat down, and forthwith the Declaration was signed by every member present. Who was that venerable patriarch? It was JOHN WITHERSPOON, of New Jersey, a distinguished Minister of the Presbyterian Church, a lineal descendant of JOHN KNOX, the great Scotch Reformer."—*Speech of the Rev. S. S. Templeton.*—ED.

into action, they had a temporary predominance over those, which were selfish and base.   But these, in their turn, having acquired the ascendency, we may sadly recognise with the poet, that

> " An empty form
> Is the weak virtue that amid the shade
> Lamenting lies, with future schemes amus'd,
> While wickedness and folly, *kindred powers*,
> Confound the world."

The liberty I have taken, in making the reader the confidant of the attachment I carried with me into the army, and brought home with me, unimpaired, on the extension of my parole, imposes it upon me as a sort of duty in point of poetical justice, to announce my marriage, which took place in the spring of 1778. But this was not until my exchange had been notified to me by Colonel Boudinot, the Commissary of prisoners; and having now little before me, but the vapid occurrences of retired life, I shall here hold myself absolved from farther attention to any matters merely of a personal or private nature.   Captain Speke had gone into Philadelphia, some time before; and it is not improbable, that we had been exchanged for each other; but, of this, I was not informed.   I was now at liberty to act, and was also liable to be called into Service; but, however willing I might have been to consider myself a soldier, or to obey orders, I had no regiment to join, or men to command.   The third battalion still existed in name, but with scarce a particle of its original materials.   It was entirely changed as to officers and men, with the exception, perhaps, of one or two of the former, that had escaped captivity by absence on account of sickness or otherwise.   The affair of Fort Washington, had an effect not unlike that of entering into a monastery in England, in days of yore: as, in the one case, a man was said to be *civilly* dead, so in the other he was *militarily* so; and although as much alive as ever to corporeal wants and necessities, yet was he dead as an antediluvian, as to all purposes of worldly advantage.   Nor was it the garrison alone, but the very event itself, that was offensive to remembrance; and it has grown into a sort of fashion among our annalists, to pass lightly over this inauspicious transaction, somewhat in the same spirit, that Rome, according to Lucan, was willing to forget the disastrous day of Pharsalia.

> " Tempora signavit leviorum Roma malorum
> Hunc voluit nescire diem."

The compiler of the article "America," in Mr. Dobson's Encyclopedia, does indeed inform us, that there was such a fortress, which, some how or other, fell into the hands of the British, who by the bye, did not catch a man of the garrison. Other chroniclers, of an humbler class, are equally concise upon the occasion; and even the very fanciful biographer, who gives to the boyhood of General WASHINGTON, certain prettinesses we should have little suspected it of, and to General Wayne, the manners of a rustic booby with the blundering facilities of a true Hibernian, finds, in it, no attractions for the strokes of his very popular pencil. These are but summaries, it is true, in which we ought not to look for full details; yet, as they are more generally read than ampler histories, and thence tend to fix the colours of the time, it is of consequence that they should exhibit some resemblance of the facts and characters they profess to treat of.*

---

* There is no allusion in these remarks to The Life of WATHINGTON, by Dr. Ramsay, which, in fact, I did not see until after they were written. Though brief on the transaction, as the nature of his work required, he touches it with a due regard to truth and the reputation of those concerned.

The false in manners and character is as reprehensible as the false in fact, but when the former is built upon the latter it is truly odious. Nor can the making of a *good* book, in the language of the Trade, justify the transferring a story from the infancy of Doctor BEATTIE to that of General WASHINGTON, nor from the cups of an old army contractor in the war of 1756, to those of General WAYNE in the war of the Revolution. In the one case, General WASHINGTON is represented as a pert jackanapes of a much later date, as the *bon repos* of General WAYNE sets him before our eyes as a man wholly unacquainted with the forms of good society. On the contrary, General WAYNE was a fashionable and dressy man, familiar with city manners, and the tone of good breeding in his day. How unworthy, then, of the biograpber, and still more of the clerical character, to vamp up and misapply old stories by way of seasoning to his kickshaws!*

---

* The present generation is more fortunate, if not wiser than the past. The press literally groans with elementary books, adapted to every capacity, and the business of education is becoming comparatively easy over the "*royal road,*" unknown to our plodding predecessors. In regard to Histories and Biographies,

But whatever may have been the common reluctance to advert to the unlucky occurrences of the war, and the propensity to dwell only on pleasing ones, nothing can be more fair, and free from misrepresentation, than were the official statements both of Congress and General WASHINGTON. Even the British officers, from an experience of their veracity, came to consider the name of Charles Thomson,* as a voucher, not to questioned; nor was

there is no end to them, and the silly and once popular inventions of WEEMS, who is above referred to, are seldom seen in the hands of judicious and well informed people. The streams of knowledge have been explored to their various sources, and the result is a flood of authentic and healthful information, invigorating and fertilizing every section of this broad land. Foremost among the ablest of these explorers is MR. JARED SPARKS, whose many and important contributions to historical and biographical lore entitle him to the gratitude of his country. The industry and research displayed, especially in his noble editions of the Life and Writings of WASHINGTON, and of FRANKLIN, can scarcely be conceived by the mere reader of History. The STUDENT only can properly appreciate the ability and labour of this indefatigable investigator and Author. These, with his " American Biographies," the work of various hands, and the numerous similar and equally authentic publications which every where abound, leave no excuse for ignorance in regard, especially, to the history of our country, and the lives and services of its distinguished men.—ED.

* CHARLES THOMSON—the " Man of Truth," as he was styled by the Indians. He was Secretary to the Congress of the Revolution—was a native of Ireland— and came to this country, indigent and friendless, at the age of eleven years. His " quiet memory" attracts but little notice in this bustling age, indifferent to every thing but gain, yet the simple story of his useful and virtuous life would be rich in impressive teachings. THOMSON was furnished by one of his brothers with the means to enter the school of Dr. ALLISON, before mentioned, at Thunder Hill, in Maryland. It is related,—so great was his thirst for knowledge, at a time when " books were so rare that a single lexicon served the whole school,— that one of the boys having brought from Philadelphia a volume of the Spectator, Thomson was so delighted with it, that upon his school-fellows' telling him that a whole set of the work was for sale at a Book-Store in that place, he set off the next day, without asking leave, walked the whole distance, and having possessed himself of the treasure, returned to school without farther delay." At this Seminary he made such proficiency in the Greek and Latin languages and Mathematics, as to enable him, while still very young, to keep the Friends' Academy in Philadelphia. He subsequently married and entered into business there. He was a strict republican in his principles, and has had the credit of having been first in opposition to the Stamp Act in Pennsylvania. He discharged the duties of the office of Secretary to Congress, from the period of its first assembling to the close of the war, with credit to himself and advantage to the public. His integrity was unimpeachable, and " procured implicit credit for every thing

less respect due to the communications of the Commander-in-chief, from which the annunciations of Congress were generally derived.   Such was the spirit and the policy of *Seventy-Six ;* and they were successful as they were honourable.   Why then, they should have been so lamentably departed from, and a *suppressio veri,* have become the primary maxim of our government, it is for the republicans of the Gallic school to explain.

published in his name."   He assisted in the organization of the new government, after the adoption of the Constitution, and was deputed to inform WASHINGTON of his nomination to the Presidency.   He soon after retired to private life, and employed himself upon a Translation of the Bible and a Synopsis of the New Testament.   He died in 1824, aged 95 years.—ED.

CHAPTER XIII.

Affeetation in Titles.—Escape of Prisoners.—Major Williams.—Mr. Forrest.—
General Exchange of Prisoners.—Supernumerary Officers.—Generals WASH-
INGTON and Charles Lee.—Character of Lee.—Drayton.—Laurens.—Military
Anecdotes.—Author enrolled in the Militia.—Wanton Oppression.—Mr. Parvin.
—Quaker Opinions of War.—Dr. Franklin.—Visiters at Reading.—Mrs.
Macaulay.—Popular Feeling.—Milton.—Constitutionalists and Republicans.—
Author obtains an appointment.—John Dickinson.—Political Consistency.—
Charles James Fox.

My hankerings after the business of the tented field, which,
dog's life as it is, I had become fond of, had led me to visit the
camps both of White Marsh and Valley Forge, at each of
which I spent a day or two. At the first, we had a better
army than I had yet seen. The post too, I thought a good one;
and it soon after appeared to be sufficiently respected by General
Howe, to induce him to decline attacking it, although he had
apparently drawn out his army for the purpose. At Valley
Forge, the aspect of affairs was different, the army being reduced and in a wretched state. Baron de Steuben was, however, here; and just beginning to infuse into it, that discipline
and regularity, in which it was still too deficient. On reaching
the camp, I shaped my course for the tent of Colonel Stewart,
who, I was informed, was at a barbecue on the banks of the
Schuylkill; and being directed to the place, I found him there,
together with the greater part of the principal officers of the
army. It is scarcely necessary to say, that the Commander in
Chief was not there, nor any of those more immediately attached
to his person. Neither was General Lee of the company. He
had been invited, but had drily replied, that "he did not like
barbecues." In fact, they are seldom a very attic entertainment; and it is probable that Lee's mind was not disposed to

27

hilarity. He had but lately been exchanged; and it is not uncharitable to suppose, that he was beginning to discover, that,
much as he hated the British court, he was not, as he had once
supposed, *Americanior ipsis Americanis*, more American than
the Americans themselves. It being late in the afternoon, the
party was joyous and pretty full of liquor; and I had the chagrin
to observe, that the drummer and fifer who made music for
them, and were deserters from the enemy, were sneering at
some of the gentlemen, who did not entirely preserve the dignity
of their stations; and were by much too liberal in the reciprocal
use of the term General, for that oblivion to self-consequence,
which is the most graceful attendant of condition, and so much
appreciated in the British army, as to introduce a species of
affectation in the other extreme, substituting Mr. for the title of
rank. Lee, for instance, says Mr. Howe and Mr. Wolf; and
it was not always a disrespect, when a British officer said Mr.
Washington. I am sensible, that it is against the laws of good
fellowship, for a sober man to make reflections upon a mellow
company into which he may chance to be introduced; but I
mention no names, and indeed my memory would hardly serve
me were I disposed to do it. Still, I have a perfect recollection of the circumstance; and cannot but recognise, that there
was no time, at which the question sometimes peevishly asked
by Conway, *Did Congress see you before they appointed you?*
might not have been applicable to some of the officers of our
army in every grade.

On the first day of December, 1777, my fellow-prisoners on
Long Island were, on account of a suspected descent upon that
place, put on board of a prison-ship, and there detained two
weeks. Their treatment, it seems, was not to be complained
of. It could hardly have been otherwise, says the officer from
whose information I give the statement, since, it would not have
been safe for any man or dozen of men to have treated us ill.
During their confinement, Major Jack Stewart, before noticed
in these memoirs, and one or two others, whom I do not remember, found means to make their escape. A boat, one evening, happened to be fastened to the vessel's side. The chance

of escaping in her was immediately suggested by Lieutenants Forrest and Woodside, the latter also of Shee's regiment, and they resolved to make the attempt: but, previously to engaging in it, they stepped between decks, either for some papers or articles of clothing that were in their trunks. In the mean time, Stewart and the others availed themselves of the opportunity, quietly let themselves down into the boat, cast her off, and let her drift astern of the ship. They were lucky enough to get clear of her unperceived; and at length to reach the Jersey shore in safety, notwithstanding that their elopement was soon discovered. But it being dark, pursuit was unavailing, as were also some random shots fired upon the occasion. The disappointment to Forrest and Woodside, when they found themselves supplanted, was extreme; and still more cruel when it appeared, that the adventurers had been successful.

Early in the Spring, I think, of 1778, I got a letter from Major Williams, acquainting me with his release, by exchange, if I am not mistaken.* It breathed the most extravagant joy; and the excessive friskiness he describes on touching our actual territory, put me in mind of that of Francis the First, upon finding himself once more at liberty, after his long detention at Madrid. Williams, it is true, was not restored to a throne; but he was restored to his country, to the right of proclaiming his sentiments and wishes, to the right of locomotion and action, and, above all, to the right of avenging his wrongs, and particularly a cruel confinement in the provost prison, from which his exchange had immediately delivered him. His motives, therefore, for exultation, were not less than those of the King of France.

In the summer following, I had also notice of the liberation of Mr. Forrest, which, from the singularity of its circumstances, requires some detail. It had been a settled opinion among us at Flatbush, that if the place, or we who were stationed there, by a military operation, should fall into the hands of our people, for

---

* He was exchanged for Major ACKLAND of BURGOYNE's army, of whose kindness and liberal treatment of Williams, see an interesting account in Wilkinson's Memoirs, v. i. pp. 376—77.—ED

ever so short a time, we were *ipso facto* released from the
obligation of remaining with the enemy, notwithstanding our
parole; and it was under this idea, combined with a lucky and
unexpected adventure, that Forrest found himself a freeman. I
know not how far this opinion of ours may be conformable to
the *jus belli* as established among nations, but it was our deduction from principles, which we held to be correct, and of general
and equal application. I think it is also recognised in the old
play of prison-base, from which, if the idea was not original, it
is more probable we derived it, than either from Grotius,
Puffendorf, or Vattel. One Mariner, a New Yorker, in revenge
for some real or supposed ill treatment from Matthews, the
mayor of that city, made a descent, with a small party, upon the
island, with the view of getting Matthews into his clutches, who,
as I have already mentioned, had a house at Flatbush, and
generally slept there. He had it also in view, to obtain the
release of a Captain Flahaven, who had been billetted in my
place, on Jacob Suydam. Disappointed in both objects, he
liberated Forrest by means of his magical power, and made
prisoners of Mr. Bache and Major Moncrief, the latter of whom
spent much of his time at Flatbush, where he had a daughter.
But I will give the relation in the words of Mr. Forrest, who,
on my application for the particulars of the event, has thus
communicated them in answer to certain queries proposed.
"Mariner was the man who took me from Long Island. He
was a shoemaker, and had been long confined and cruelly used,
as I understood, by Matthews, who, it seems, knew him personally. The name of the officer who lodged with me was
Flahaven, a captain, who had been in the provost with Mariner,
and whom he particularly wished to release; but, having
changed his quarters, he could not be got at. Mariner crossed
from the Jersey shore, and retreated to, and landed at the place
of his departure, or near it, a distance of two miles across. His
party consisted originally of twenty militia men, in two flat-
bottomed boats. At his landing on Long Island, he left his two
boats under the guard of five men, while he visited the interior;
but these five, hearing a firing, which was kept up upon us by

the Flatbush guard, while we were taking our prisoners, concluded that Mariner was defeated and taken; so, without further ceremony, they took one of the boats and made their escape. The other boat, as we reached the shore, was just going adrift: we were much crowded in her, but it fortunately was very calm, otherwise we could not have weathered it. Matthews was on the top of his house, at the time of the search for him. We got, from our place of landing, in wagons, to Princeton. Mr. Bache and Moncrief lodged there in the same house with me for two or three days. How they were disposed of afterwards, I do not know, as I was sent on with an explanatory letter from Governor Livingston to General Washington; but Bache I think was sent home shortly, and Moncrief also, (who was a good prize,) as a prisoner on parole. Mariner's party must have stayed at Flatbush nearly two hours, for they were there some time before the alarm was taken, and there was afterwards time to despatch an express to Brooklyn for assistance, and the reinforcement which came in consequence, was pretty close upon us, as we could see them on the shore, when we had left it about a quarter of an hour. This happened on the 15th of June, 1778, the very day two years, I had marched from Philadelphia."

From this episode it appears, that the moral of Æsop's fable, respecting the eagle at the top of the tree, that, by the law of power, had made free with the fox's whelps below, was very near being brought home to Mr. Matthews. Mr. Bache, as Forrest has told me, was overwhelmed with his disaster; and interceded with him, as, from his civility to us, he had a right to do, for his good offices with Governor Livingston, which, I have no doubt, were duly exerted for him. Major Moncrief, like an old soldier, submitted with a more equal mind to the fortune of war, reminding Bache, that he had often told him, they were not safe at Flatbush. But Bache had peculiar cause for dejection, on account of the consternation, into which his wife and children had been thrown by the attack of his house, and his being forcibly seized and borne away in the dead of the night. Upon delivering Governor Livingston's letter to General

Washington, Forrest stated the circumstances under which he had come out, and had conceived himself liberated, but added, that if the act did not meet his Excellency's entire approbation, he begged to be permitted to return immediately to New York. The General observed, that it was a nice case, on which, much might be said on both sides, but that, at any rate, a return to confinement was unnecessary; that he was at liberty to go home, and that, if upon consideration, he should be of opinion, that the mode of his release was not warranted by the rules and usages of war, a prisoner of equal rank should be exchanged for him. Not long after this enterprise of Mariner, a general exchange of prisoners took place, and all were put upon an equal footing. To beguile the tedious hours of captivity, Colonel Magaw had taken to himself a wife, as had one or two others.

A policy had arisen from the pressure of our affairs, to give every man a commission who was likely to pick up a few recruits. This, at least, was the case in Pennsylvania; hence, as to officers, all the regiments were not only complete, but overflowing; and upon the reorganization of the army, there were a great many supernumerary. Of this description, those who had been taken at Fort Washington, emphatically were. They were considered as extinct; and their places had been supplied by others. A show, indeed, was made in the fall of 1778, of doing justice to their claims, so far as it might be practicable. But it was evident, that a reinstatement in the rank to which they were entitled by the rule of seniority, was not to be effected without extreme embarrassment, and injury to the Service. A very few, who had been willing to engage in the scramble, had been retained; but none without the chagrin of seeing new men, and numbers who had originally ranked below them, now above them. Captain Tudor contrived to squeeze in, as did also Captain Biles; and I do not recollect another of our regiment, except Bitting, who was provided for. He was a second Lieutenant with us, and lost his life in the rank of a Captain, at the time of the mutiny in the Pennsylvania line. In Marshall's Life of Washington, he is erroneously called Billing. But on consideration, I rather think, that Bitting had not been a prisoner; and if so, he is no exception to the general exclusion, and his advance in rank is naturally accounted for. He was at liberty to attend to his interests. I never applied for reinstatement; but, had my country really wanted my services, and there had been an opening, in which I could have been provided for, without too much degradation, I do not hesitate to say, that I should have laid aside all private considerations, and embraced it. To show, that I do not exaggerate the difficulties which opposed a continuance in the army, I shall content myself with referring to two letters of General Washington upon the subject. In the first, dated the 10th of November, 1777, addressed to Congress, he says: "Among the various difficulties attending the army, the adjustment of rank is not the least. This, owing to the several modes, the several principles that have prevailed in granting commissions, is involved in great perplexity. The officers of the Pennsylvania troops are in much·confusion about it: in many instances, those who were junior in rank, from local and other circumstances, have obtained commissions older in date than those which were granted afterwards to officers their superiors before. This, with many other irregularities, has been, and is, the cause of great uneasiness; and though precedency of rank, so claimed, should not be supported in justice, or upon any principle, we find all, having the least pretence for the title, strenuous to support it, and willing to hold a superiority." In the second letter, dated August 21st, 1778, relating to the restoration of Colonel Rawlings, who had presented a memorial in behalf of himself and the officers of his corps, after doing ample justice to their bravery at Fort Washington, he says: "It seems hard that officers of their merit should be overlooked; and a loss to the service, that they should remain unemployed: but, the consequences that would attend their incorporation with any of the corps now existing, appear too disagreeable to try the experiment." A conviction of the existence of these obstacles, concurring with motives of a private nature, induced me to renounce the soldier's trade; but not without poignantly regretting my "occupation gone," as often as "the spirit-stirring drum," or other "circumstance of glorious war," reminded me of the deprivation.

The bitter animosity of General Lee* to the Commander in Chief after the affair of Monmouth, is well known. There were not wanting a good number, who thought he had been hardly dealt with; and, with these, added to many that had real or imaginary grounds for discontent, and the still greater number, who already saw in Washington a character and influence, which might give a check to the democratic career they had in contemplation, he was in hopes of being able to form a party. About this time, being in Philadelphia, I had the pleasure, one day, of meeting my old friend Edwards in the street. He was now the aide-de-camp of General Lee, with the rank of Major. He was lavish in the praise of his General, whom he spoke of as one with whose conversation, abounding with wit and instruction, I could not but be delighted; and proposed taking me to dine with him that very day. While we were yet upon his

---

* GENERAL CHARLES LEE was born in England, was a soldier of fortune, and a citizen of the world. He was the third major-general appointed by Congress. He was a man of ardent temperament, independent in thought and action, and very ambitious. He so far imposed upon the credulity of Mr. Thomas Rodney, of Delaware, as to induce him to believe that he was the author of the "Letters of Junius." Twenty years after the death of Lee, Mr. Rodney thus communicated this important confession to the public:

"General Lee said there was not a man in the world, no, not even Woodfall, the publisher, that knew who the author was; that the secret rested wholly with himself, and for ever would remain with him. Feeling in some degree surprised at this unexpected declaration, after pausing a little, I replied, ' No, General Lee, if you certainly know what you have affirmed, it can no longer remain solely with him; for certainly no one could know what you have affirmed but the author himself.' Recollecting himself, he replied, ' I have unguardedly committed myself, and it would be but folly to deny to you that I am the author; but I must request you will not reveal it during my life; for it never was, nor ever will be, revealed by me to any other.' He then proceeded to mention several circumstances to verify his being the author, and, among them, that of his going over to the Continent, and absenting himself from England the most of the time in which these letters were published in London. This he thought necessary, lest by some accident the author should become known, or at least suspected, which might have been his ruin." He died in Philadelphia, on the 2d of October, 1782, at the age of fifty-one. In his delirium, the last words he was heard to utter were, "Stand by me, my brave grenadiers!" He had previously expressed a wish "not to be buried within a mile of Presbyterian ground—as he would, otherwise, be too near very bad company!" He was buried in Christ Church Cemetery, in Second Street on the south side of the Church. See Appendix (L).—ED.

subject, the General appeared on the other side of the street, and, crossing over to us, I had the honour of being presented to him. He soon, however, marred Edwards's proposal of dining at his quarters, by asking where he dined, and giving him to understand, that he, the General, did not dine at home. Whether he was now in one of his saving moods, to which he was said to be occasionally addicted, and only meant this as a *ruse de guerre* to keep the war from his own territories, I know not, but certain it is, that Edwards had calculated upon a different arrangement, and fully expected to have owed his dinner of the day to the cook of his General. After a few minutes' conversation, I left him, but not before agreeing with Edwards upon a time and place of meeting next day.

The life of General Lee, as presented in the volume published by one of his friends, under the title of Memoirs, holds out very salutary instruction to factious and discontented spirits.* Though he commences his career among us, as an American and a democrat, he at length subsides in the Englishman and aristocrat. He finds out that he has kept very bad company in America; and that her independence, which he has been among the most ardent to promote, will be a curse rather than a blessing to her. Washington, to him, becomes another George the Third; and his 'earwigs,' courtiers as corrupt as those of any *sceptred calf, wolf, hog, or ass;* to use the language of his letter to Dr. Rush. It must be confessed, however, that if he acted to the best of his judgment at Monmouth, his treatment is to be lamented, as a hard and ungenerous return for the zeal he once manifested in our cause. But his conduct in this affair, to say the least of it, betrays a total want of American feeling. Having, in the latter part of his captivity, been treated with attention by the British officers, his old discontents appear to have been effaced by the greater poignancy of new ones; and if, as has been asserted, he ex-

* The LIFE OF LEE, by Mr. SPARKS, in the 8th volume of the new series of "The Library of American Biography," published in 1846, may also be strongly recommended. It is the most satisfactory account of this erratic genius that has yet appeared, and is exceedingly interesting and well written.—ED.

claimed in the hearing of his troops, that "the British grenadiers never run," it would almost seem a sufficient ground to
convict him of disaffection, if not treachery. I shall not, however, impute them to him; neither am I prepared to say, that
his conduct was unmilitary. I would rather suppose, if he
committed a fault, it was because he was too respectful of the
enemy; and that he was too scientific, too much of a reasoner
for a merely executive officer; "for action too refined," as
Pope says, or as Voltaire expresses it :

> Mais souvent il se trompe à force de prudence,
> Il est irresolu par trop de prevoyance,
> Moins agissant qu'habile.— *

As to his early republicanism, and fancied attachment to
liberty and the rights of man, there is no reason to think him
insincere. That he cordially detested, at least, the courtly arts,
for which he had not temper; and in whose career, if he ever
tried it, he had been far outstripped by more pliant competitors,
I have not the smallest doubt; but, if he supposed, by an exchange of the sovereign *one* for the sovereign *many*, he was to
restore the reign of manly candour and blunt honesty, how
much, how very much, alas, was he deceived!

With all his abilities and acquaintance with the polite world,
the General was certainly a very indiscreet man, with little
dignity of character: witness the frequent scrapes he got into,
and particularly the ridiculous one with Miss Franks, in which,
the most complete success of the *jeu d'esprit* could have added
nothing to the fame of the major-general.†

In my interview with Edwards the next day, he gave me a
number of military anecdotes, and let me into the state of parties in the army. As might be supposed, he was a warm partisan of Lee, though at the same time, expressing great respect
for the virtues of the Commander-in-chief. Among other things,
he gave me the details of Lee's quarrel with Mr. William Henry

* See Appendix M.—Ed.
† See Appendix N. for the particulars of this affair.—Ed.

Drayton,* repeating the words of the letter of defiance, of which he was the bearer, and in which Mr. Drayton is sarcastically represented as a mere Malvolio, &c.—also, of the duel with Colonel Laurens, in which he acted as the second or friend of Lee. Colonel Laurens and his attendant, Colonel Hamilton, were, it seems, rather late in coming to the ground. During the delay produced by this circumstance, Edwards took occasion to amuse his Principal, if amusement it might be called, with some metaphysical subtilties on predestination, free will, &c., a little in the style of the disquisition of the Brissotines on a future state, when on their way to the guillotine. From want of punctuality in the adversaries, he also suggested, that they might not come at all; but Lee replied, there was no danger of that, as Colonel Laurens was a man of unquestionable bravery; and the observation was immediately verified by his appearance.† The manner of fighting was somewhat new; and, if I am not mistaken, it was on Lee's suggestion it was adopted. Taking their ground and facing each other, it was agreed, that either should fire when he

* This eminent citizen was cut off in the midst of his useful and brilliant career, at an early stage of the Revolution. He died in Philadelphia, September, 1779, in his thirty-seventh year. WILLIAM HENRY DRAYTON, of South Carolina, was one of the earliest and most active defenders of the liberties of his country, in the first stages of the revolutionary movements. His writings contributed equally to enlighten the public mind, and enforce the claims of justice. A charge to the Grand Jury of Charleston, delivered by him as Chief Justice of South Carolina, on the 23d of April, 1776, is one of the most important historical documents of that period, whether considered in regard to the facts it contains, or the force of its arguments. He was an efficient member of Congress, and was conspicuous for the part he took in counteracting the objects of the British Commissioners, by several spirited and well-written essays in the newspapers.—*See Drayton's Memoirs, and Sparks' Writings of Washington*, vol. v. p. 439.

Mr. JEFFERSON was indebted almost as much to JUDGE DRAYTON's celebrated "Charge," as he was to the patriotic and spirited *citizens of Mecklenburgh*, for the sentiments and much of the language of the " Declaration of Independence," that enduring monument at once of patriotism, and of genius and skill in the art of *appropriation!*—ED.

† For another purpose the Editor has been kindly furnished by MR. GEORGE W. P. CUSTIS, with some interesting particulars in relation to this gallant officer, which, as they will bear repetition, he has placed in the Appendix, to which the reader is referred. See Appendix O.—ED.

thought proper. Accordingly they both advanced, and the effect was, that at the same instant, each presented and drew the trigger. Colonel Laurens' ball grazed the side of General Lee, carrying away some flesh and producing a considerable effusion of blood. The Principals proposed another shot, but the Seconds agreed that enough had been done; and so the affair ended, without the smallest bearing, however, on the point in controversy, to wit, whether General Lee was right or wrong in speaking reproachfully of the Commander-in-chief; and only establishing the fact, that the combatants could risk their lives with the gallantry and self-possession of soldiers and men of honour.*

Major Edwards further gave me the particulars of a similar affair, in which he himself had been concerned as principal in Carolina; and, in which, the small knowledge he had derived from me, in the noble science of fencing, had enabled him to triumph over an adversary, who thought to obtain an advantage of him by commuting the pistol, with which it had been at first agreed to fight, for the small sword. His skill in the weapon was not, indeed, brought to the test; but the readiness he evinced to put it to issue, induced his prevaricating opponent to succumb and make him concessions.

From his aptitude to take the tone of good company, and his

---

* Had not this "fact" been well "established" before? History informs us that it had; and if it were untrue, the hostile meeting here referred to, cannot fairly be cited in verification. Although brave men, as in this instance particularly, have resorted to this mode of adjusting their difficulties, many a poltroon has been forced, sadly against his own volition, into this position of " *honour.*" There can be nothing more *insanely absurd* than the condescension of men, especially those of unquestionable reputation for courage, to this savage and senseless mode of " *establishing the fact;*" and it is much to be regretted that *such* men, at least, should be deficient in the greater courage to resist and defy the customs and requisitions of society, when—as is too often the case—they are at variance with the solemn and imperative requisitions of the laws of GOD.

A clever anecdote has been related of General ADAIR. A young officer conceiving himself aggrieved, challenged the veteran, who took no notice of the matter. A second note was the consequence, in which ADAIR was informed, that if " satisfaction" were not accorded, he would " post" him as a coward! The General then replied, in substance, that he might proceed, but assuredly in so doing he would " post" himself a " *fool and a liar,*" as certainly no man would believe him.—ED.

close intimacy with Lee, whose manners and phraseology were
in the style of the highest military school, this gentleman, whose
first appearance had been so unpromising, had become a distinguished proficient in all the cavalier airs and "convenient
seeming" of a man of the sword ; of which the favour of Lee,
in selecting him for his second in his duels, may be considered
as a proof; as the devising to him a third part of his landed
estate in Virginia, may be taken as a voucher for his satisfaction with him, in the capacity of his aide-de-camp.

As soon as it was understood at Reading, that I was no
longer in the army, care was taken to have me enrolled in the
militia; and for declining to perform a tour of duty, which was
immediately imposed upon me, I found myself fined in a sum,
which I do not now recollect, but which, when reduced to
specie, was far from inconsiderable. I must confess, I considered this as very unfair treatment, and accordingly, submitted
my case in a memorial to President Reed, who shortly after
came to Reading, in consequence of a proclaimed intention to
visit the different parts of the State, for the purpose of hearing
and redressing grievances. I was not at home when he arrived,
but had left my memorial with a friend to be presented to him.
It was very favourably received, the gentleman who delivered
it, being instructed to inform me, that the President would have
been glad to have seen me at Reading : that he considered the
fine which had been imposed upon me, very improper, and that
he would do what he could to prevent its exaction. His interposition proved effectual; and I had no further molestation
from the militia-men.

During the high-handed game, that was at this time playing
by that description of patriots, who, from their close adherence
to their homes, might emphatically be said to be fighting *pro
focis*, a Mr. Thomas Parvin, of the Society of Friends, was an
object of much wanton oppression. He resided at Maiden
Creek, about six miles from Reading, and was nearly broken up
by the levies on his property for taxes and militia fines. A cow
or a horse, for instance, was often taken and sold for some trifling demand, and no surplus returned. Having sons grown up,
and enrolled in the militia, he was the more exposed to rapacity.
He frequently came to my mother's, to vend some product of

28

his farm, and talking with him one day, on the subject of his grievances, I was drawn into a discussion of the non-resisting principles of his sect; and urging their impracticability in the present state of the world, in a manner that discovered sympathy for his sufferings, he was not displeased, and proposed lending me a treatise in defence of their tenets, which he begged I would read and give him my opinion of. In a few days, he accordingly sent it, accompanied with a very long letter, so accurately written in all respects, as to convince me that Mr. Parvin was a well-educated man and no mean polemic. In compliance with his request, after reading his pamphlet, I gave him pretty fully my observations in writing; and here, I concluded the discussion would terminate. In a few weeks afterwards, however, I found it renewed in a letter from Anthony Benezet of Philadelphia.* This pious and truly benevolent man, thus explains in his first sentence, the cause of his addressing me :

" Esteemed Friend,

" My friend Thomas Parvin having communicated to me, thy remarks with respect to the sentiments many in our Society hold in the case of war, I found my mind drawn affectionately to salute thee, and take the liberty to enclose thee a collection of religious tracts, which, I have, at different times been instrumental in publishing." And he is further pleased to say—" I am persuaded, that to a man of thy generous turn of mind, many of the sentiments will not be disagreeable, particularly the extract from the writings of Soame Jenyns," &c.—This was an extract from his View of the Internal Evidence of the Christian Religion. There were several other tracts in the volume, one of which, A Letter from Elizabeth Webb to Anthony William Boehm, Mr. Benezet adds, " I think might prove agreeable to thy mother and aunt, whom I affectionately salute." As it is not my intention to lead the reader into the subject of this correspondence, it is enough to have barely stated it; and

* ANTHONY BENEZET was a native of France. His parents were Huguenots, and came to Philadelphia in 1731. His first employment was that of a teacher at Germantown. He was particularly distinguished for his general philanthropy, and ardent opposition to the slave trade. He became a Quaker, and died at Philadelphia in May 1784, at the age of 71 years.—ED.

it appears to me, that I should have been wanting to myself, had I suppressed an occurrence, which procured me the good opinion of these plain, but innoxious, intelligent, and pious men.

In the summer probably of 1782 or '83, or thereabouts, Mr. Ralph Izard, and Captain Gadsden, of South Carolina, being on a tour through Pennsylvania, brought me a letter of introduction from Colonel Magaw, at Carlisle. Being desirous to render them all the attention in my power, I had the pleasure of often being with them. Captain Gadsden was a young man, who had perhaps never been out of America; but Mr. Izard, who was advanced in years, had spent much of his time in Europe, and was very entertaining on the subject of his travels; giving me, among other things, a more satisfactory account of the awful wonders of Pompeii and Herculaneum, than I had yet received. His manner, though blunt, announced the style of the best company; and though one of those who deliver their opinions with freedom and decision, he seemed untinctured with asperity upon every subject but one; but this never failed to produce some excitement, and his tone ever derived animation from the name of Dr. Franklin.* When, therefore, the Doctor's daughter, Mrs. Bache, in speaking of the Carolinians, said, that " she hated them all from B to Z," the saying, I presume, must be taken inclusively; since, though I know nothing of the sentiments of Mr. Bee, I am enabled to pronounce those of Mr. Izard to have been anti-Franklinian in the extreme. What cause he had for this, I do not know, but he certainly lost no opportunity of inveighing against the philosopher, to whom, he said, he had once been warmly attached, and had

---

* MR. IZARD had been in France, and on his return " complained that Dr. Franklin neglected to make proper representations to the French Ministry." He deemed it necessary to alarm the French Government with the danger of the United States falling into the hands of England, unless she would contribute largely to the support of the Republican cause. Count de Vergennes upon hearing of these statements, declared that nothing could be more pernicious than to attempt to alarm the French Government with false and exaggerated accounts. And in his letter to LUZERNE the French Minister at Philadelphia, he writes, " I flatter myself, that these marks of regard will be understood by the patriots, and will destroy any prepossessions, which the ill-advised language of Mr. Izard and Mr. Arthur Lee may have produced."—*Sparks' Writings of Washington*, vol. vii.

ED.

attended as his friend, at the time he was so unmercifully bespattered by Wedderburne. I sat upon thorns, said Izard; and had it been me, that had been so grossly insulted, I should instantly have repelled the attack in defiance of every consequence, whereas, this old man sat cowering like a caitiff, without daring to utter a syllable.* But in repeating the words, I do not join in the reproach of the Doctor's forbearance. As he was not a ready public speaker, silence, was, perhaps, most prudent and dignified. The extreme wariness of his character, it is true, is not more congenial to my feelings than to those of Mr. Izard. Nevertheless, when I reflect, that he possessed qualities, which have not only enabled him to extend the limits of human knowledge, but have pre-eminently entitled him to the fame of a wise man; that, to solidity of understanding, he added the amenity of wit and good humour, and that his weight and influence, so far as I know, have never been lent to inhumanity, immorality, injustice, or oppression, I am entirely disposed to acquiesce in the award of the world, and to consider him as one, who has done honour to his country. He died before the volcanic explosion of the French Revolution; but, as he tells us in his life, he had an early and steady abhorrence of tyranny, we cannot, without giving the lie to this assertion, suppose, if he had lived, that he could in any event have been a jacobin or the fautor of a ferocious despotism.

Mr. George Lux, of Baltimore, who had married a daughter of Mr. Edward Biddle, was, at this time, at Reading, and by me, introduced to Mr. Izard and Mr. Gadsden. Mr. Lux was the greatest reader in a certain line, I have ever known. His historical knowledge was accurate to minuteness; and he seemed

---

* The forbearance and coolness of FRANKLIN on this memorable occasion, however offensive it may have been to MR. RALPH IZARD was well understood and appreciated by much wiser heads. The following letter quoted by Sparks in his Life of FRANKLIN, p. 370, from Dr. RUSH to Mr. ARTHUR LEE," will show the high estimation in which Dr. FRANKLIN was held by his countrymen." " There is a general union among the colonies which no artifices of a Ministry will be able to break. DR. FRANKLIN is a very popular character in every part of America. He will be received, and carried in triumph to his house, when he arrives among us. It is to be hoped he will not consent to hold any more offices under government. No step but this can prevent his being handed down to posterity among the first and greatest characters in the world."—ED.

intimately acquainted with the ramifications and affinities, not only of the great families in England, but also of those on every part of the continent of Europe. Of these, he spoke with a precision which astonished Mr. Izard, particularly when he learned that he had never been out of America. " To what purpose is it," said he, when afterwards speaking of Mr. Lux, " that I have been travelling all my life, when this gentleman, who has never left his armchair, knows more of the countries I have visited than I do; and what perplexes me most of all is, that he even knows better than myself, the public business I was employed in, and which was of a secret nature." But this latter knowledge was obtained by Lux's having officiated for his amusement, (having nothing better to do,) as secretary to the board of Congress, which had regulated Mr. Izard's affair. Yet with all this information, Mr. Lux appeared to me to possess but a very moderate share of judgment or discernment, and to be little more than a dry matter of fact man. He had a handsome paternal estate ; and at Chatsworth, his seat near Baltimore, was in the habit of entertaining all strangers of distinction, though so shamefully negligent of his person, which was naturally none of the best, as to seem not at all adapted to this function. Among his guests, he was once honoured with the company of Mrs. Macaulay, the historian, whom, at her request, as he informed me, he accompanied to Mount Vernon, on a visit to General Washington, where they stayed some days. While in conversation, one day after dinner, the lady, in a high republican strain, took occasion to expatiate on the vast advantages of rotation in office. This was in the manner of an appeal to her host, of whose approbation she seemed to be secure ; but as the General was rather a practical or accidental, than a republican by preference, I will not say a republican *malgre lui,**

---

* It may be safely averred, that a majority of our best whigs of 1776, were not republicans by predilection ; but still the best of practical republicans, as honest and virtuous men.

Nothing can be further from the truth than the idea propagated for party purposes, that the Declaration of Independence was an option made between the monarchical and democratical form of government. The measure was adopted with extreme reluctance, as the effect of dire necessity alone, as the only means of uniting and giving efficiency to the opposition, and of obtaining foreign aid if it should be

he could only carry his politeness so far as not absolutely to
dissent from the opinion; and there was, of course, no com-
mingled flow of soul upon the occasion.   But Mrs. Macaulay
was not the only person of her nation, who has found the republicanism of the new world, lagging shamefully behind that
of the old.   Experience is the best of schools; and, in the
philanthropic science of levelling, as in others, we may truly
say :

> Here, shallow draughts intoxicate the brain,
> And drinking largely sobers us again.

One of the strongest cases in point, and which has been strangely
overlooked, is that of the poet Milton, against whom the great
Samuel Johnson, is supposed to be even more than usually intolerant.   He certainly could not have been aware, nor Mr.
Boswell either, (or from his profusion we should have heard of
it) of the following passage in the Paradise Regained, the last
work, and therefore, to be presumed to contain the last and
most solemn opinion of its author.

necessary—in short, as the only alternative between subjugation and voluntary
submission.   The general sentiment in America, as the publications of the era will
testify, was an ardent attachment to the British Constitution, and a deep regret that
we were refused an equal participation in its benefits, in common with our fellow-
subjects on the other side of the ocean.   This was the constant language of the
day, both in public and private discourses, in official and in anonymous publications; and it was not until a separation was deemed unavoidable that any attempts
were made to set forth its advantages.   In the same spirit, after having become a
nation, and being invested with the right of governing ourselves, it was the policy
of our best and wisest men, alas, how fruitless ! to check the wildness of innovation, and to cling as much as might be, to the genius of the institutions under
which we had enjoyed our unexampled prosperity; and in the same view to obli-
terate, as soon as possible, the mutual animosities engendered by the unhappy
contest.   Such was the object of WASHINGTON, JAY, HAMILTON, and other virtuous
and enlightened statesmen; and we have it from Mr. Burke, that even DR. FRANKLIN
whose name is often used to sanction the vagaries of democracy, suffered not only
a sigh, but an expression of regret to escape him, on account of the happiness we
were about to lose by our separation from the mother country, (see his Appeal to
the Old Whigs); and yet our post-revolutionary and imported patriots, would make
us believe that the beginners of the Revolution were whigs after the fashion of
Thomas Paine and certain other European malecontents and reformers, and our
first Congresses composed of Jacobins, " as true as ever snuffed the scent of blood,"
or devised the expeditious mode of taking off the heads of aristocrats by the guillotine.

And what the people, but a herd confus'd,
A miscellaneous rabble, who extol
Things vulgar, and well weigh'd, scarce worth the praise:
They praise and they admire they know not what;
And know not whom, but as one leads the other;
And what delight to be by such extolled,
To live upon their tongues and be their talk,
Of whom to be despised, were no small praise.

It would be difficult to conceive sentiments more at variance with the republican maxim of *Vox populi vox Dei;* and yet, they are the sentiments of the sublime poet John Milton, the democrat, the regicide, the secretary and parasite of Oliver Cromwell. From this one man, we may learn the character of his sect, the immaculate, people-adoring republicans of the present hour. For the love of liberty, they will kill a king; yet fawn upon a usurper, clothed with a power infinitely less accountable, infinitely more oppressive and tremendous. The crime then, is not in "one proud man's lording it over the rest,"* but that he should lord it in opposition to our particular interests and prejudices. In the direction of these, he cannot be too high-handed.

Party spirit, in Pennsylvania, had by this time, taken a consistency, and the politicians were divided into *Constitutionalists* and *Republicans.* The first rallied round the constitution already formed, which was reprobated by the others, for its total deficiency in checks and counterbalancing powers, thence tending, as it was alleged, to rash, precipitate, and oppressive proceedings. The term republicans was embraced, as recognising the principles of the revolution, and as indicative perhaps of tenets, which admitted the utility of modifications and restraints, in a system resting on the broad base of general suffrage and popular sovereignty. The word *democrat* was not yet much in use, neither was the distinction established between a democrat and a republican, which appears to consist in the idea, that the former is for placing the whole governing power in the "multitude told by the head;" the latter, for giving it some checks, and infusing into it a leaven of what is termed by Mr. Burke, the natural aristocracy of a country. But to do

* ——Terres tot posse sub uno
Esse viro.—*Lucan.*

this, where the source of power has been diligently explored and discovered too, like that of the Nile, and universal suffrage with the right to pull down and build up again, thence recognised as a fundamental, may well puzzle the learned advocates for strong executives, and independent judiciaries, and in the end, perhaps, turn all their fine-spun theories into lumber, little better than nonsense.   However, like the rest of my countrymen,

> With sad civility, I read,
> With honest anguish and an aching head.

To counteract the constitutionalists, the disaffected to the revolution were invited to fall into the republican ranks; and there was an agreement, or at least an understanding, among the lawyers, who were generally on the republican side, neither to practise or accept of any office under the constitution, which, in that case, they would be bound, by an oath, to support.   But the constitutionalists had a Roland for their Oliver.   They had prothonotaryships, attorney-generalships, chief justiceships, and what not to dispose of.   Patriots have their price, 'tis said; and persons were found to accept of these, some of whom, indeed, had cautiously avoided committing themselves by the promulgation of rash anathemas. All, however, were not so fortunate, if fame is to be believed; and although the fruit was to them forbidden, they were tempted, and did eat.   But in this age of thrift and self-aggrandizement, I am not going to impute it to them as a crime.   Who would now reject the means of bettering his condition, through the childish fear of being charged with a dereliction of principle? It is not of such imbecility that the world is now " the friend, or the world's law."   Bonaparte would never have made himself a consul, much less an emperor, by such squeamishness.

Soon after the organization of the Republican Society, it was proposed to me by my friend Major Scull, then in Philadelphia, to join it; but after the recent agitations of the greater contest with the mother country, I felt no inclination to disturb myself with domestic broils.   My eyes, indeed, were open to the illiberality of the constitutionalists, and the extreme jealousy they already manifested against those who had been in the army; but on the other hand, so far as I can recall my feelings, I did not fully relish the policy of courting the disaffected, and those who had played a safe and calculating game. But they were rewarded for it: pelf, it appeared, was a better goal than liberty; and at no period in my recollection, was the worship of Mammon more widely spread, more sordid and disgusting. Those who had fought the battles of the country, at least in the humbler grades, had as yet earned nothing but poverty and contempt; while their wiser fellow-citizens who had attended to their interests, were the men of mark and consideration.* As to military rank, no man seemed to be without it, who had an inclination for it; and the title of major was the very lowest that a dasher of any figure would accept of. Nothing more was wanting for its attainment than to clap on a uniform and pair of epaulettes, and scamper about with some militia general for a day or two. And thus, the real soldier was superseded, even in the career of glory. Never having been good at a scramble, as already observed, whether honour or profit were the meed, I did not press into the field of pretension; and being in a state of apathy as to the political parties, I declined enlisting with either.

The agitations which now prevailed in the capital, led to the well-known outrage on Mr. Wilson, who, for the exercise of his professional duty as a lawyer, in behalf of certain persons who had been prosecuted for treason, had been proscribed by the mobility. The punishment decreed for his crime, was banishment to the enemy, yet in New York: and for the purpose of inflicting it, an attack, by men in arms, was made upon his house, into which a number of his friends had thrown themselves, with a determination to resist the assailants. A few lives were lost before the tumult was suppressed; but as my residence at Reading deprived me of the means of a personal knowledge of the transaction, it is enough for me to notice it as one of those which shows the toleration of the vulgar heart, and the

---

* These assertions are supported by sundry letters from General WASHINGTON to General REED, in which he reprobates, in strong language, the rage for " money-making speculations." In one dated December 12th, 1778, speaking of the officers in the army, he says, " resignations must cease to be wonderful, when it is a fact too notorious to be denied that officers cannot live in the army under present circumstances, whilst they see others enriching themselves in an infinity of ways. These are severe tests of public virtue, and should not in point of policy, be pushed too far."

idea it annexes, to what it is pleased to term the blessings of liberty.

The constitution kept its ground in defiance of its adversaries; and as it is sometimes easier to make a pun than to avoid it, it may be said, that *The confederates of Bar*, were completely foiled in their undertaking. They came over by degrees; and it at length appeared, that the cobweb ties, by which, they had vainly flattered themselves they could pinion the love of interest, had only benefited the least scrupulous of the confederates, who like the stronger flies, had burst their flimsy fetters, and thence, dashed at the treacle, unannoyed by competition.

All interdiction to practice being now removed, I found it necessary once more to open my law books. I obtained admittance as an attorney in the county of Berks; and was already employed to bring actions and defend them; but was soon drawn from this track by the following incident.

Among a number of newly introduced maxims of republicanism, it was a highly favoured one in Pennsylvania, to bring justice home to every man's door. In the spirit of this principle, several new counties had been erected; and in the year of 1785, I had the good fortune, through the warm exertions of an influential friend, to obtain an appointment to the Prothonotaryship of the county of Dauphin. By a combination of small circumstances working together for my advantage, I obtained, contrary to expectation, the suffrage of the Supreme Executive Council, of which Mr. Dickinson was then President. The Republican party possessed a majority in the Council; and Colonel Atlee, who belonged to it, was designated for the office. He was conspicuous as a party-man, and, if I mistake not, at the time, a member of the Legislature; and on the score of services and character, no one had better claims. But upon this occasion, the negative character of my politics, contrary to the usual course of things, probably gave me the advantage. To keep out Atlee, the constitutionalists were disposed to give their votes to any one of his competitors. Of course, I had all their strength; and by adding to it two or three republican votes, I acquired a greater number than any in nomination. As the mode was to vote for the candidates individually, there was no physical, or perhaps moral impediment, to each of them receiving the vote of every member. A promise to one, was not broken, by voting also for another, unless it was exclusively made. The President had, probably, given a promise to Colonel Atlee as well as to myself; and considering me, perhaps, as too weak to endanger his success, thought he might safely gratify my friend, who pinned him to the vote, which, on coming to the box, he seemed half inclined to withhold. Or, where was his crime, if he really thought our pretensions equal, and therefore determined not to decide between us? Such were the accidents which procured my unlooked-for appointment.

Mr. Dickinson, for his want of decision, as it was called, was bitterly inveighed against by his party; and the next day at the coffee-house, when receiving the congratulations of some of my acquaintances, Mr. Michael Morgan O'Brien, who chanced to be present, and to whom I was then introduced, asserted it as a fact, that the President had suffered his hand to be seized and crammed into the box with a ticket for me; "but no matter," said he, "you are a clever fellow, I am told, and I am glad that you have got the office." That this gentleman, who had been a short time among us, should have been so furious a partisan in our politics, can only be accounted for, from his being perfectly in the O'Flaherty style, and consequently a ready champion of the cause of those he was in the habit of associating with.

In the station of President, Mr. Dickinson added not much to his reputation, in the opinion of either of the parties. By endeavouring to stand well with both, he, unfortunately, pleased neither. He had been brought in by the republicans; and had soon after been virulently attacked by a writer under the signature of Valerius, who was no bad imitator of the manner of Junius. Against the charges that were urged against him, he made his own vindication, which, even by his political friends, was thought nerveless and whining. Upon the expiration of his term of service as President of Pennsylvania, he retired to Wilmington, in the State of Delaware, where he became a plain Quaker, in the principles of which sect, I think, he had been educated. But his Quakerism did not prevent his becoming President of this State, as he had before been of Pennsyl-

vania. Neither did it, in his old age, so far withdraw him
from worldly concerns, as to restrain his pen from again dipping
in politics, during the progress of the French Revolution, with
the sublime virtues and benign influences of which, he appears to
have been deeply and permanently smitten: insomuch as to be
rendered so acceptable to the Jeffersonians, as just before his
death, which happened in the year 1808, to be held up by them
as a candidate for a seat in the House of Representatives of
the United States. While residing in the State of Delaware,
he seems always to have been claimed by this class of politicians; and from his Fabius, which is a curious jumble of irre-
concilable, abstract contradiction, and philanthropic inconsist-
ency, he, probably, belonged to them. Like the rest of the sect,
he is for devolving the whole virus of the revolution on the
shoulders of Robespierre, and his immediate colleagues; and but
for a few unlucky *Ifs*, he is persuaded, all things would have gone
well. The unfortunate Louis, he loves with no less enthusiasm,
than he does the fanatic multitude, whose demoniac frenzy sent
him to the scaffold; and he apostrophizes the manes of the dead
monarch with as much solemnity and pathos, as if his blood
had been a banquet to the Federalists, who, it is true, are wholly
lost to the morality, which would, with Fabius, transfer the
gratitude which might have been due to the king, to those,
who, though not actually his murderers, do yet exultingly
trample upon his ashes.

Mr. Dickinson was very far from a consistent politician.
Though so little of a republican at the commencement of our
revolution as to boggle at independence, he became so outrageous a one in the sequel, as to be an amateur of French
liberty, and in respect to the parties in England, a Foxite* pro-

---

* Many, I am well aware, are partial to Mr. Fox as a statesman. His abilities
might have been very great, but he can hardly be called a candid, principled, and
virtuous citizen. If, when he became minister, he pursued the same policy that
Mr. Pitt had done, it is evident that his opposition to him proceeded from factious
and interested motives, under the influence of which, he acted the part of a wild
and disorganizing Jacobin. He is said to have been a pleasing companion, and
what is called a good-natured man, which is generally, by the by, an unprincipled
one. Refined virtue is indignant and somewhat austere. Estimating him, however, from his historical fragment of the reign of James the Second, one would
suppose him to have been a humane, just, and generous man.—(See Appendix P.)

fessed.* To account for this, for certainly there is a glow of sentiment in his writings which would promise better things, we must have recourse to some casualties in his public career.

* The successors of the MEN OF THE REVOLUTION must be grateful for what this distinguished gentleman did, and not indulge in feelings of dissatisfaction for what he omitted to do, especially as Mr. DICKINSON lived long enough, as may be inferred from his subsequent career, to regret the extreme moderation which characterized his proceedings at the period of the DECLARATION. He was like many men of whom we read, and who at all times abound, who are endowed with sufficient sagacity to discern the right, and with ample ability for its assertion or defence, but who, either from irresolution, or a desire to please all parties, are, at the final moment, unfaithful to themselves or to great public interests committed to their charge. It cannot be supposed that Mr. DICKINSON designedly erred, or that his motives, at any period, were either sordid or unpatriotic. He was a man of great elevation of character and purity of conduct; but it certainly is unfortunate for his reputation that he omitted the immortal act of affixing his signature to the DECLARATION OF INDEPENDENCE. That only was wanting to place him in the highest rank among the Revolutionary worthies to which, otherwise, his distinguished abilities would, unquestionably, have entitled him. With all his talents, however, he lacked the great qualifications essential to the perfection of the character of a real statesman,—the promptitude, decision, and boldness which nerved the heart and the pen of a HENRY and an ADAMS; and he was, moreover, not thoroughly weaned from habitual and hereditary attachment to England; or, perhaps, not sufficiently disinterested to stake his honour, and life, and fortune, upon an issue that it was, assuredly, his greatest misfortune ever to have considered doubtful, or uncalled for, by the suicidal policy of an infatuated Ministry;—a policy, the design and inevitable tendency of which was, the degradation of his country, and the consequent debasement of its citizens. The DECLARATION appears to have surprised Mr. DICKINSON into opposition before his mind could perceive that it was unavoidable, or necessary. With the best intentions, he was, of course, still under the guidance of human motives; and it will be no very violent exercise of charity to yield the largest allowance for the influence of early education, which inculcated endurance, and reverence, especially for the authority and institutions of the Father-land,—for constitutional timidity, from which even TULLY—glorious in other attributes,—was not exempt; or for a predilection for a cautious, temporizing policy which looked rather to a tardy and peaceful accomplishment of its end; than to a prompt redress of grave and acknowledged grievances, through violence and bloodshed. Whatever may have been the motives by which he shaped his course, he is, unquestionably, entitled to the enduring gratitude of his country,—gratitude that should not be withheld because he paused, irresolute, at that point of time and tide, which, "taken at the flood, leads on to fortune." He had, most ably and faithfully, served his country to that momentous and perilous period, and, if he then hesitated, or declined to take the leap, it should be remembered that the sacrifice was by no means essential to the cause of INDEPENDENCE; which, indeed, was neither injured nor retarded by his indecision: while the consequences flowing from such indecision affected his own reputation alone. There were, moreover,

29

In the first place, then, from his supposed want of energy while in the first Congress, Mr. John Adams had, in a letter intercepted and published by the British, styled him, "a piddling genius;" and Mr. Adams being afterwards President of the United States, and then thoroughly anti-Gallican, might, possibly, have contributed to place Mr. Dickinson in the opposite ranks. Probably, too, the once celebrated Pennsylvania farmer, and writer of Congressional addresses, was not altogether pleased at finding himself in the background, and eclipsed by statesmen of less standing than himself, the Hamiltons, the Ameses, &c. It is enough for those beneath the sphere of competition to exclaim:

> Let modest Forster, if he will, excel
> Ten metropolitans in preaching well.

In addition to this liberty was the stock, on which the farmer's celebrity was engrafted; and, lest the fine foliage might "grow into the yellow leaf," he was, perhaps, resolved to cherish, at all events, the vigour of the parent tree; and hence, liberty, even to jacobinism, was among the toys of his dotage. This is the best I can say, for a teacher of political ethics, who (with whatever good intentions) for wisdom, gives us folly; for virtue, "deeds to make heaven weep, all earth amazed," under the idea of modelling the world according to a pretty theory.

The post I was honoured with, fully satisfied my ambition; it was sufficiently respectable, and in a few years, wholly adequate to my wants. The duties it imposed, I was pretty well acquainted with; and I exerted myself to lay such a foundation in the office arrangements, as might support a regular superstructure. The trust committed to me, was conscientiously attended to, and I venture to say, not negligently executed. My cares for a future competency, which alone had disturbed me, were done away by my establishment; a new town was rising under my eyes on the magnificent banks of the Susquehanna; and though remote from the capital and obscure, I had little left to wish for;—a state too tranquil to be lasting.

other members of the same memorable Congress, equally irresolute, and without a tithe of his redeeming talents, who also suffered the "fair occasion" to pass "for ever by."—ED.

CHAPTER XIV.

Constitution of the United States.—Washington elected President.—Meeting of Convention.—The Senate.—Executive Power.—Regulation of the Press.—State of Parties.—Leading Characters in the Convention.—French Revolution.—Burke and Paine.—Washington's Administration.—Party Dissensions.—Mr· Jefferson.—State of Parties.

Being now about to enter upon political discussions, I deem it due to those enthusiastically *republican* readers, who think we can never sufficiently praise ourselves, to tell them to stop here ; if, from some unlucky notices I may have given, they have not already anticipated me. I am truly sorry that my convictions will not permit me to trace events in the usual strain of panegyric ; but I am compelled, in the style of a grumbler, to say, that the patriotism, which had been calculated upon to bear us out with little or no aid from authority, and, which, in the opinion of many, was still in full vigour, was, to the eyes of all sober men, wholly inadequate to the demands which were made upon it. It had the knack, indeed of evading the most important of them, by representing them as spurious ; and this was chiefly done, by restricting patriotic duties to the limits of a State· The country of a demagogue is the precise sphere of his influence ; and making common cause on this principle, they were every where deaf as adders to the claims of a general interest. The articles of Confederation, receiving cement from the sense of common danger, which prevailed during the war, had occasionally afforded faint marks of continental impression ; but as soon as the fear of subjugation was removed, they were no better than a rope of sand ; and the general sovereignty was a very unequal match for the thirteen individual ones. The voice of the United States, was, as it had been observed, but the drone of the bag-pipes. Its buz was heard, but it contributed not at all to the modulation of the music. It could recommend, but not enforce a measure; and hence, the imposition of certain internal taxes, and a duty of five *per centum* on imported articles, essential to the discharge of the public debt and the fulfilment of a stipulation in the treaty of peace, could never be accomplished. The refractory States were not to be moved by considerations of national justice or character; and they were equally regardless of the consequences of a dissolution of the Union.

To rescue the country from the impending anarchy and ruin, the influence of General Washington was called for, and again exerted for its salvation. Nothing less than the weight of his name could have induced the adoption of the new federal constitution, which had been framed under his auspices; and it had become very doubtful, whether the anxious struggle for independence had not been in vain, and the anticipated blessing of self-government, would not be frustrated in its very dawn. The interests opposed to an efficient union of the States, were truly formidable, as well from the conviction of the popular leaders that it would lessen, if not annihilate their importance, as from the too contracted notions of the people at large, and their inability to comprehend the necessity of a general controlling authority. The battle was hard fought on both sides. To the manly sense and patriotic eloquence of the one, was opposed the trite, but seductive cant of sedition and faction, The refined and irresistible reasoning of Publius, the signature to a series of essays chiefly written by Colonel Hamilton, was assailed by incessant volleys of words of dire import, such as monarchy, aristocracy, monopoly, and consolidation.* But the

---

* Whatever frantic and unscrupulous demagogues may choose to assert to the contrary, it is matter of history, which, however, it is not always convenient *or even possible* for them to consult,—that HAMILTON gave to the new Constitution, after its adoption, a cordial and manly support. That he had, previously, deliberately formed, and unreservedly expressed, opinions, which no man possessed of decent intelligence, or a spark of generosity, will deny were *honestly* entertained, —adverse to some of its provisions,—matters concerning which, wise and virtuous and patriotic men might well differ, and about which they unquestionably *did* differ,—is also true; and there were *then*, as there are *now*, few men living so well entitled, by deep study, and enlightened reflection, to hold, and to promulgate

last being the lucky hit, from which most immediate effect was anticipated, it was most unmercifully hackneyed in the service. The Constitution was represented to be a consolidation, not a

original views upon this or other grave national interests, as ALEXANDER HAMILTON; who, of all the statesmen of the period, or of later time, ranks next to WASHINGTON, and whose name and memory, second only to his, should be fondly cherished as a proud, national inheritance; for it has rarely happened that

> ———"to those mansions where the mighty rest
> Since their foundation came a nobler guest."

The Life of PATRICK HENRY, written by a disciple of THOMAS JEFFERSON, himself a *professed* admirer, at least, of the "Forest-born Demosthenes," and who furnished materials for his biography:—informs us that the celebrated orator, whose patriotism and wisdom the revilers of HAMILTON,—between whom and HENRY there was, on this subject, a perfect coincidence of opinion,—never think of questioning, opposed with all the power and influence of his surpassing eloquence, the adoption of this same Constitution. We learn also from unquestionable authority, that this Constitution as finally adopted in Convention, was the result of wise and patriotic conciliation and compromise on the part of all its members. WASHINGTON, as is well known, was President of this Convention, and even he has been charged with hostility to the work it accomplished. In the letter addressed by him in his official capacity, to the President of Congress, enclosing the result of the anxiously patriotic labours of the enlightened body over which he had presided,—this passage occurs, and should be deeply impressed on the hearts and memories of present and future statesmen and legislators:

"The Constitution which we now present, is the result of a spirit of amity, and of that mutual deference and concession which the peculiarity of our political situation rendered indispensable."

WASHINGTON'S opinion expressed on another occasion, as we learn from Sparks' Life, p. 403;—was, "Nor am I yet such an enthusiastic, partial, or indiscriminating admirer of it, as not to perceive that it is tinctured with some real though not radical defects."

FRANKLIN said, "I consent to the Constitution because I expect no better, and because I am sure it is not bad."

And MADISON, in the 57th number of the "FEDERALIST," a neglected volume which all honest "Democrats," not easily frightened by *a name*, would be wiser for perusing, says:—

"It was acceded to by a deep conviction of the necessity of sacrificing private opinion and partial interests to the public good, and by a despair of seeing this necessity diminished by delays or by new experiments."

The last number of the *Federalist*, written by HAMILTON, proves the coincidence of opinion between him and the illustrious men thus cited. He says—

"The system, though it may not be perfect in every part, is, upon the whole, a good one; is the best that the present views and circumstances will permit, and is such an one as promises every species of security, which a reasonable people can desire."—ED.

29*

confederation of the States; and under this shrewd idea, its adversaries very ingeniously endeavoured to ward off the imputation of anti-federalism, now becoming odious. They contended, that *they* were, in fact, the federalists, as the self-styled federalists, were consolidators, aristocrats, and monarchists. Luckily, at this time, there were no French imperialists, or promoters of universal despotism; or, without doubt, they would have been these too. But the tribunitial arts of the *soi disantes* federal men, were all in vain. Some dire infatuation, according to them, had seized upon the people; and to perdition they must go, since their best friends were no longer listened to. The grand processions of trades and occupations which were exhibited at Boston, New York, and Philadelphia; the hint of which, was, probably, taken from the shows of Tamerlane at Samarcand, * had completely federalized the populace of these capitals, and given an *eclat* to the business elsewhere, that could not be resisted. Under the " curses" therefore " not loud but deep," of its enemies, the measure was sullenly acquiesced in; and the Constitution gradually ratified by the States. By this event, the *constitutional party* of Pennsylvania, was laid at the feet of the *Republicans*, who now triumphing under the appellation of federalists, overwhelmed their adversaries with the short-lived odium of *anti-federalism.*

But the reputation of Washington which had carried the new system, was no less necessary to give efficacy to its operations, than it had been to originate it, and obtain its ratification; and as he could not but be aware of this, he consented from a sense of duty, but without a particle of that " sweet, reluctant, amorous delay" with which more ethereal patriots sometimes yield to the wishes of the people, to be a candidate for the presidency. As the disapprovers of the Constitution, knew that their opposition to his election would be unavailing, they gave none, but contented themselves with taunts and dismal forebodings. General Washington was then elected;† and I mention it as a

* " The public joy was testified by illuminations and masquerades ; the trades of Samarcand passed in review ; and every trade was emulous to execute some quaint device, some marvellous pageant, with the materials of their peculiar art."—*Gibbon's Decline and Fall, Harper's Edit.*, vol. iv. p. 283.—ED.

† He thus wrote in his Diary, on the day of his departure, two days after re-

proof of my decided conduct in the controversy, that my country did me the honour to appoint me one of his electors. Had not my persuasion of the pressing importance of the measure forbade my being passive, it would have been scarcely possible to have remained so. From an idea that those holding offices under the State, would feel it their interest to oppose a system which circumscribed the authority from which they derived them, and might, thence, disturb the enjoyment of them, or even render them nugatory, they were confidently appealed to by the anti-federalists, as the natural enemies of the constitution: while, on the other hand, persons who had been in the army, were counted upon by the federalists, as likely to promote a scheme, in which the late Commander-in-chief, had taken so warm a part. But I did not wait to be solicited by the parties; neither did I poise their relative strength, or listen, for a moment, to the narrow dictates of self-interest. I am happy in being able to say, that I was an early, undisguised, ardent, active, and, in my sphere, conspicuous partisan of the Constitution; of course, a mark for the vengeance of the professional wielders of the people, who felt the potency of their incantations most cruelly impaired by its adoption. The discomfiture being complete, they made a virtue of necessity; and not long after, yielded with a tolerably good grace, to the call of a convention for altering the constitution of the State, so as to render it more conformable to that of the United States. They considered this, and wisely, as a means of recovering their lost consequence; and exerting themselves at the elections for members of this convention, they contrived to take the field, with a force not very inferior to that of their adversaries.

This body has been considered respectable for abilities: and among the men of note who were delegated to it, may be found

ceiving from Congress, through its special messenger, CHARLES THOMSON, notification of his election:

"About ten o'clock I bade adieu to Mount Vernon, to private life, and to domestic felicity; and, with a mind oppressed with more anxious and painful sensations than I have words to express, set out for New York, in company with Mr. THOMSON and Colonel HUMPHREYS, with the best disposition to render service to my country in obedience to its call, but with less hope of answering its expectations."—ED.

the names of Mifflin, M'Kean, Wilson, Lewis, Ross, Addison, Sitgreaves, Pickering, Gallatin, Smilie, Findley, and Snyder. I had myself the equivocal honour of being a *yea* and *nay* member; but having been elected in the room of one who died, I did not take my seat, until some progress had been made in the business. The point which had excited most interest, and was thence the subject of the warmest controversy, was now upon the carpet. This was the construction of the senate, or upper house, (as it is sometimes called,) of the legislature. A committee, selected for the purpose, had reported an outline of the constitution; and that part of the report which recommended the choosing of senators through the medium of electors, was under discussion. Mr. Wilson took the lead in opposition to the report; Mr. Lewis in support of it. It was urged by the latter and his co-operators, that the senate should be so constituted as to form a check upon the house of representatives; and, as in the proposed mode of creating it through the alembic of electors, it would be purged of the impurities of an immediate election by the people, the *desideratum* would be obtained;— that being chosen by a selected few, it was presumable, it would be more wise, more respectable, and more composed of men of wealth, than if chosen by the multitude; and hence it was inferred that it would partake, in no inconsiderable degree, of the proper qualities of an upper house—of a house of lords, it might have been said if the idea had been endurable. As to Mr. Wilson's scheme, (for he had moved a substitute,) of choosing the senators in the same manner as the representatives, with the exception only of larger election districts, it was reprobated as doing away every purpose of a divided legislature— since that the persons composing the two houses, would be precisely of the same character, and too homogeneous to operate as correctives of each other; and that unless the elector-system should be adopted, the convention had been called in vain.

Wilson, in defence of his plan, was for resting the chance of the two bodies being sufficient checks upon each other, upon the circumstances of their different spheres of election; of their sitting in different chambers, which would produce, he contended, an *esprit du corps* in each; and their being chosen for different periods, the representatives for one year, the senators for four years. He moreover urged, that electors would open a door to unfair practice and intrigue; that the senators should be as much favourites of the people as the representatives, and be inspired with equal confidence, by equally feeling themselves their choice.

As the debate seemed to turn upon the idea, that this was a contest between the principles of democracy and aristocracy, and that great advantages would be gained to either that might prevail, a considerable degree of heat was engendered; and Wilson, hitherto deemed an aristocrat, a monarchist, and a despot, as all the federalists were, found his adherents on this occasion, with a few exceptions, on the democratic or anti-federal side of the house. In the list of exceptions, I was; but not so much from the arguments adduced, though appearing to me both ingenious and sound, as from my conviction of its being wholly immaterial, so far as a check was contemplated, whether the senate was brought together through the intervention of electors or not; and I was, of course, adverse to a measure, at once, circuitous, useless, and unpopular. As it was my practice to commit my thoughts to paper, upon questions which underwent discussion, I have the following note of this.

"The desire of choosing senators through the medium of electors, is certainly founded on a fallacious idea: for, admitting that a small number of dispassionate, sensible men, would make a better choice than the people at large, is it possible that the advocates for the measure can be so blinded by prejudice as not to see, that it is not the most dispassionate and intelligent men that will be sought for as electors, but the most devoted tools of party; and that the prevailing party, in the district, will always make the senator? To suppose the contrary, or that any one, when parties run high, (and when do they not?) would be voted for as an elector, merely from a reliance on his wisdom and integrity, without a knowledge of his sentiments, is to suppose a political miracle, and to forget that ever party spirit existed. Let it not be said that the object is to get a good man of whatever party. This is contrary to all party policy and practice, which, if it cannot succeed in procuring the election of its own

members, prefers the weakest and most contemptible of the
other side, as being less capable of doing mischief. The respectability of the Maryland Senate, which has been so often
instanced in the debate, proves nothing to the purpose. If it is
a respectable body, and of superior wisdom to the other house,
it is not because it is chosen by electors. It must be owing to
the more enlightened persons who compose it, reserving themselves for it, and having sufficient interest with the people to
secure their seats; which interest would be the same without
the intervention of electors; and if the State of Maryland shall
have a wiser and higher toned Senate than Pennsylvania, it
must be attributed to the more aristocratical state of society
there, which furnishes them with more suitable materials, and
gives the men of wealth and information a superior degree of
influence."

Thus far the note, the observations in which seem fully justified by events. Let us consider the objects which regulate the
choice of electors of a President and Vice-President, and then
say, whether the Senate would have been bettered by the elector
scheme. I myself was once chosen an elector, but it was because my voice was known to be for Washington, not personally on my own account.

As another mean to improve the upper house,* a proposition
was brought forward by the friends to the elector plan, to
apportion the senators by means of a ratio compounded of
wealth and numbers; the intention of which was, to give greater
security to property, by increasing the weight of the wealthy
districts, beyond what they would derive from population alone.
After reprobating the idea of introducing so invidious and
sordid a principle into the government, and remarking that it
could not answer its purpose, unless this increased representation was under the sole guidance of the rich, who are rarely
oppressed by the poor, my note goes on to say :—" Whatever
advantages may, for a time, be given to the poor, by a state of
turbulence and confusion, as soon as order is restored, the pre-

* A protest is again entered against the phrase. When will the good sense of
a republican people discard the senseless designation !—ED.

dominance of wealth immediately returns. It seems unnecessary to protect local wealth. It is not probable, that the local distinctions now prevailing will continue, but rather that wealthy individuals will make common cause." A scheme of the same kind as this compound ratio, was adopted by the National Assembly of France; speaking of which, I find Mr. Burke has this remark, with which part of mine exactly coincides. "If any favour," says he, "was meant to the rich, the privilege ought to have been conferred on the individual rich, or of some class formed of rich persons; because the contest between rich and poor, is not a struggle between corporation and corporation, but a contest between men and men; a competition, not between districts, but between descriptions."

I aim at no triumph by these remarks, and am not so uncandid as not to own, that before being led to examine it, I was as much seduced by the plausibility of the elector scheme as any one. I was at first induced to oppose it in the case of the Senate, in the view of applying it in the choice of a chief magistrate, under an idea, that it might at least have the wholesome effect of mitigating the fury of a general election in a matter of so great interest, by putting the object a little out of sight; but I now doubt whether it would be productive even of this good.

The animated discussions which had taken place in the Convention, on the formation of the Senate, had produced no inconsiderable degree of ill-humour among the members of that body, and more especially, as is usual, among the losers. For my own part, I was considered by them as an apostate from my principles; as a deserter of the federal standard; and at tables, where I occasionally fell in with my federal acquaintance, was treated by them with much unpleasant coldness and neglect. As, however, I had acted honestly, from the best lights my understanding afforded, I was not to be browbeaten into a retraction of the sentiments I had uttered; and was as confident in my opinions, as they could be in theirs; in which, I presume, I have been justified by events.

As to the executive power, the structure, as it now stands, appeared to have been reared before I became a member of the

Convention. It would seem, that it had been agreed upon, and reported by a committee of nine members, who had been selected for the purpose of framing and methodizing the outlines of the constitution. At any rate, no essential opposition was made to this article, which, in my opinion, is the most exceptionable of any in the instrument. The following note contains the chief ground of my objection to it, viz.: "When I consider the strong temptation to the courting of popular favour, held out by the governor's re-eligibility at the end of three years, I am induced to condemn the section, and to prefer electing him for a certain period, say four, five, six, seven, or so many years as might be deemed safe and expedient; at the end of which term, either a perpetual or very long exclusion to take place. An exclusion, long enough to wear out the influence acquired whilst in office, and to make a re-election a too remote and uncertain contingency, to be worth improper sacrifices and compliances.* The rotation founded on a short exclusion, appears to be inadequate to its object, and to have little other effect, than to compel us to part with a chief magistrate, however patriotic his conduct, or pressing the exigence. To it, I would prefer an uninterrupted re-eligibility." This idea I communicated to several of the leading members of the Convention, but do not recollect, that any of them seemed much impressed with its importance. Mr. Lewis, indeed, did not seem to think unfavourably of it; but had been so much hurt with losing the electors, that he seemed to despair of redeeming the loss, by the substitution of any other good, and therefore declined attempting any alteration in the article: and having too little confidence in myself to undertake a change in it, without able support, I suffered it to pass without publicly testifying my disapprobation of it. What made the general acquiescence in it more remarkable, was, that it was thought necessary to remedy the evil arising from the annual election of sheriffs, who, it was observed, were too intent on preserving the good will of their constituents, to do their duty to effect, until their

* I was not aware, until very lately, that General Lee uses precisely the same reasoning in a letter dated July 29th, 1776, to Patrick Henry, jun., Governor of Virginia.

ultimate term of service was secured. Perhaps it was deemed a kind of profanation of the high function of chief magistrate, to suppose that any considerations of this sort could warp the manly march of him, who might have the honour to be invested with it. But, whatever force there may be in the foregoing sentiments, candour compels me to own, that at this moment, I am much less tenacious of them than I have been. Were the Governor's the only station to be sought for, the reasoning might be conclusive; but there are so many other temptations to a man smitten with a love of the public coffers, of influence and power, that it amounts to much less than I once supposed. Indeed, the best, and perhaps only security, for a firm and upright administration, is to be found, in innate dignity of mind. And the more we contemplate the construction of a popular form of government, the more shall we be convinced, that no checks are competent to master corruption, or supply the want of integrity; and that after all the jargon about anti-republican tendencies, no tendency can be republican unless it be virtuous.

Next to the construction of the senate, the regulation of the press was the ground of most acrimony in the Convention. Whether or not the truth should be received as a justification, on prosecutions for libels, divided its law characters. I was among the simple voters who thought that it ought; and although now absolved from my sin, by federal opinion,* I was then subjected to the imputation of wild innovation and democracy. I could say a great deal more of what was done in this assembly, and produce a world of political reasoning, vastly edifying and profound; but enough, in all conscience, of the business of constitution making! Could we have made the people wise, moderate, disinterested, we should have laboured to some purpose; but, where they are under no dominion but that of their selfish passions, hurrying them on to a goal, regardless of conse-

---

* Declared in the Sedition Law, and in the defences to the prosecutions under the reign of JEFFERSON. It is also, if I am not mistaken, now the doctrine and law of libels in England, as introduced by Mr. Fox, and concurred in by Mr. PITT.

And HAMILTON's definition of the Liberty of the Press is,—" the right of publishing the truth with good motives, and to an useful end, whether it inculpates the government, the magistrates, or private individuals."

30

quences, of what use are all the constitutions that have been made by the friends to liberty, in America or France? They want an essential ingredient of all laws. They may be just in their sanctions, wise and honest in their injunctions; but where are their enforcing and prohibitory powers? As they are, I am sick of them. With all their seeming beauties, they contain a latent flaw; and I am almost tempted to reject the flattering theory of our institutions, as Bajazet does the Paradise of Mahomet.

> Prophet, take notice, I disclaim thy paradise,
> Thy fragrant bowers and everlasting shades;
> Thou hast placed woman there, and all thy joys are tainted.

If woman spoils the one, so does selfish man the other.

The sitting of this assembly for new-modelling the constitution, had the effect that had been anticipated by the anti-federalists. It enabled them to discharge a great portion of the odium with which they had been loaded by their recent discomfiture; and although they had been completely laid upon their backs, it was evident that from this position they had already turned upon their sides, and were in a fair way of being very soon on top of their antagonists. Such are the advantages of a steady, undeviating, profligate pursuit of power, over a regard for the public good, desultorily exerted without concert or system! A panic terror of the power of the union under the new constitution, prevailed in the Convention; and some, who were not infected with it, acted as if they were, for the purpose of mortifying Wilson, who had spoiled their favourite scheme. The bugbear of *consolidation* stalked hideously among us, to the dismay of many federalists, no less than of the anti-federalists; and, at no small expense of the cogitative powers, many ingenious devices were framed to resist his encroachments. A balance was anxiously sought where none could be obtained; for where two parties only fight, one must prove the strongest. By means of a third, indeed, the weaker adversary may be put upon a par with the stronger, as the House of Lords, in the British constitution, is supposed to hold the balance between the King and the Commons; or as either one of the three may do it between the other two. But with respect to any imagined hostility between the General Government and those of the particular States, if it exists, it must take its course; there seems to be no control. The former will be potent when administered by men who have no scruples in regard to means; but weak as the old confederation when in the hands of the principled and conscientious. The power of the country, under her existing establishments, will be wielded by the turbulent and most daring;* and if these, by any chance, should be thrown from the greater wheel, they will immediately avail themselves of inherent jealousies to get possession of the smaller ones, by an unprincipled use of which they will still find means to keep the ascendant. When the federalists held the helm of the General Government, there was an incessant jarring between that and the State authorities, then managed by their adversaries; and were the former as little restrained by a concern for the public good as the latter, they would have played the same game against Mr. Jefferson and his sect; instead of which, since their accession to national rule, they have been suffered to proceed without the smallest annoyance, in a part in which they were obviously most vulnerable; and in which, if their own malignant, Catilinarian spirit had prevailed among the federalists, they would most assuredly have been assailed. Nor let it be said, that they had not this in their power, after the actual war-measures of Governor Snyder against President Madison. If ever sincere men shall again acquire the stations they ought to possess, then again shall we be stunned by the brawlings of anti-federal discord. The edifying unity of democracy will no longer be marred by a division into schools, nor will the Binnses and Duanes turn their arms upon each other.

The Convention, it has been observed, was deemed respectable for ability; and upon a comparison with the materials of our State legislatures, it no doubt was. It had a good many

---

* The language here suggested by experience, is substantially the same as that quoted from the Cinna of Corneille, by Mr. Shepherd, in his Paris of 1802:

> Mais quand le peuple est maitre, on n'agit qu'on tumulte,
> La voix de la raison jamais ne se consulte;
> Les honneurs soul rendus aux plus ambitieux,
> L'autorité livree aux plus seditieux.

speakers in it; but, that an aptitude to prate is no conclusive evidence of sound judgment, is an observation as old, at least, as Sallust. The most able debaters in the body, were Wilson* and Lewis.† Ross,‡ Addison,§ Sitgreaves,‖ and Gal-

* The Honourable JAMES WILSON. He was born in Scotland, in 1742. He was educated at Glasgow, St. Andrews, and Edinburgh. He arrived in Philadelphia, in 1766, and found employment as a tutor in the college and academy, and early acquired a high reputation as a classical scholar. He commenced the study of law, in the office of JOHN DICKINSON, and commenced its practice at the expiration of two years, first at Reading, and then at Carlisle. In 1775 he was elected to Congress. He was a uniform advocate of the Declaration of Independence, which he signed. In 1787, he was a member of the Convention which framed the Federal Constitution. In 1789, he was appointed by WASHINGTON, a judge of the Supreme Court of the United States. He died in August, 1798, at the age of fifty-six years. His political and legal disquisitions are extant in three volumes, and much esteemed.—*Ency. Amer.*—ED.

† Mr. LEWIS became, subsequently, a prominent member of the Philadelphia Bar, distinguished alike for his talents and eccentricities.—ED.

‡ The Honourable JAMES ROSS. He still resides (1846) at Pittsburg, venerable for his years, his virtues, and public services. He acted a very conspicuous part in the politics of Pennsylvania, from the close of the Revolution until the year 1808. He was the candidate for the office of Governor in opposition to JUDGE McKEAN, in 1799, and in 1802; and was again a candidate, in opposition to SIMON SNYDER, in 1808. He was, for many years, the acknowledged head of the Bar in Allegheny county.—ED.

§ Judge ALEXANDER ADDISON. He was a man of strong and cultivated mind; a distinguished jurist, and an able theologian. He was the author of a volume of "Reports of Cases in the County Courts of the Fifth Circuit, and in the High Court of Errors and Appeals of the State of Pennsylvania."—ED.

‖ SAMUEL SITGREAVES was an eminent jurist, an upright and virtuous citizen. He was born in Philadelphia, on the 16th day of March, 1764, where he received an excellent education, and where, in 1784, under the auspices of the late respectable WILLIAM RAWLE, he was admitted to the Bar. In 1785, he removed to Easton, in Pennsylvania, where he entered upon the practice of his profession. In 1794, he was elected to Congress, where he served with usefulness and distinction. He also particularly distinguished himself as one of the Commissioners to England,—while the United States were worthily represented by the Honourable RUFUS KING,—for the settlement of claims under the Treaty of 1783. During his sojourn abroad, he visited the Continent, and was at Paris when NAPOLEON was invested with the office and honours of the First Consulship. Having accomplished the object of his mission, he returned from Europe in 1801, immediately after the inauguration of Mr. JEFFERSON; and from that event, may be dated the retirement of Mr. SITGREAVES from public life. It could hardly, indeed, be expected that the third President could find befitting employment for an ardent admirer of the first, for one who felt a pride in being known as a WASHINGTONIAN REPUBLICAN. On its organization, in 1814, Mr. SITGREAVES was elected President of the EASTON

latin,* were comparatively young statesmen; though each of the three first, acquitted himself handsomely; the last did not venture beyond an isolated observation. It was singular, by the bye, and honourable to the liberality of our country, to hear a French accent intermingling with our own, on a question for framing a Constitution for Pennsylvania. It was realizing the

BANK, in which office he continued to the time of his decease, in the sixty-fourth year of his age,—on the 4th day of April, 1827. Mr. SITGREAVES was much distinguished for his companionable qualities, for pungent wit, and keen repartee. He was a gentleman of the *old school*, of which few remain in advantageous contrast to the multitude of the *new*, and he well maintained the dignity of his order in the prominent social position to which his learning, abilities, and virtues eminently entitled him.—ED.

* ALBERT GALLATIN was born in Geneva, Switzerland, in 1761, and was educated at the University of that city. For many years he was a resident of Pennsylvania. He arrived at Boston, in 1780. He opposed the adoption of the Federal Constitution, a proceeding obnoxious to Democratic censure in the case of HAMILTON, but in that of GALLATIN, a venial offence. In 1793 Mr. GALLATIN was elected by the Legislature of Pennsylvania, to the Senate of the Union, "although," as it was said, "he entertained doubts of his own eligibility." When he took his seat, the question of citizenship was revived, and he lost it, "after an elaborate investigation and report, on the ground that he had not been nine years a legally naturalized citizen of the United States." He was, however, subsequently elected to Congress, where he continued for six years, distinguished for his financial abilities, and as one of the leaders of the Democratic party. In 1801 he received from Mr. JEFFERSON the appointment of Secretary of the Treasury, which office he filled, with distinguished ability, until the year 1813. He was one of the Commissioners at GHENT, and was subsequently appointed Minister to the Court of FRANCE, whence he returned in 1823. After a short interval spent in retirement at his residence, New-Geneva, he was, in 1826, appointed Minister to ENGLAND. On his return he retired to Baltimore, but soon removed to New York, where he still resides (1846). His last appearance in public life, was as a member of the Free Trade Convention, which assembled at Philadelphia, in 1831, and of which respectable and able body, it was intended to propose him for President; but, anticipating the movement, he rose and nominated for that office, Mr. P. P. BARBOUR of Virginia, who had, for a single session, occupied the post of Speaker of the House of National Representatives. Mr. BARBOUR was elected. In this Convention Mr. GALLATIN attracted much attention. His foreign accent, which was remarkable considering his long residence in the country, the character of his employments and associations,—rendered it extremely difficult to comprehend his speech, but, he was, nevertheless, considered an oracle by the members,—many of whom—their impracticable object to the contrary notwithstanding,—were men of high character and distinction in public life,—and when he rose to address the Convention, which was seldom, he was closely surrounded by an eager and attentive auditory.—ED.

30*

nihil humani alienum puto of Terence. May we never have
reason to repent our extreme complacency to *human race—
oratory*, whether declaiming on man's equality, or the freedom
of the seas! Wilson was truly great; but, enthusiastically
democratic. The symptoms of returning reason, evinced in
the adoption of the Federal Constitution, had, probably, put
him in good humour with the people, and made him more
than ever in love with "free and independent man." He drew,
to be sure, a picture of a free citizen, in the act of disposing of his
suffrage, little answerable to the sad realities, which are found
upon an election ground. Royalty, with its most splendid re-
galia, was made to hide its diminished head. Nevertheless, it
was a pretty fiction; and I will not deny, that I did not listen to
it, with, perhaps, somewhat more than a demi-conviction. *Ces
pauvres Savoyards sont si bonnes gens!* as Jean Jacques says.
And who could say less of the good souls of Pennsylvania?

There was something singular in Wilson's mode of arriving
at his goal. It was different at least from that which I should
have taken; and he appeared studious to avoid the beaten road.
Still, he never failed to throw the strongest lights on his subject, and thence, rather to flash than elicit conviction, syllogisti-
cally. It has been said, that he required preparation. At any
rate, he produced greater orations than any other man I have
heard; and I doubt much whether the ablest of those who
sneer at his occasional simplicities and "brilliant conceits,"
would not have found him a truly formidable antagonist.

Mr. Lewis furnishes an instance of what may be done by
fortitude and perseverance, in a pursuit to which the mind has
a bias. With nothing more than the common attainments of a
country school, he took the resolution to make himself a lawyer;
and quitting agricultural employments, he applied himself for a
year or two to the acquisition of Latin; after which, he commenced his jurisprudential studies in the office of Mr. Nicholas
Waln, then in the first practice in Philadelphia. His mind appeared to be wholly occupied by his business; and he gave
every difficulty which occurred a thorough investigation. In a
word, his success was complete; and from the first degree of
eminence at the Bar, he had been called upon to serve his coun-

try in the Legislature, and now in the Convention. He was not, however, with the sage of Monticello, for confining all virtue to the labouring orders ; though, from his early habits in life, probably well acquainted with them. Well knowing, that the morality of a gentleman, was at least upon a par with that of a tiller of the earth; that Don Quixote (supposed a natural character) had more honour, though less cunning than his squire, (a natural character too) ; and that city vices are amply matched by rustic rogueries; he seemed without a *chosen people ;* and, upon this occasion, was the advocate of what was called the aristocracy. But though keen and fertile in resources, he was, both from education and the bent of his studies, destitute of the comprehensive means possessed by Wilson, who was a Scotchman and a scholar, and had peculiarly devoted himself to the researches which afford materials for the construction of republican institutions; and which, in his hands would have been absolutely perfect, but for one unlucky thing, which seems to have eluded his calculations—this was, that political data do not admit of mathematical results.* Mr. Pickering was not an idle member.† His aims were honoura-

---

* MADAME DE STAEL is of a different opinion. She says, referring to M. de Condorcet's Essay on Probabilities, that the number of divorces, thefts, and murders, that will be committed in a country where the population and the religious and political situation remain the same, may be calculated with as much precision as the births and deaths; and hence, she infers, when the science of politics shall have arrived at her favoured *perfectibility*, it may be submitted to the evidence of mathematical conclusions.

† COLONEL TIMOTHY PICKERING.—He was sent by WASHINGTON, in 1787, as a Commissioner to organize the County of Luzerne, and to reconcile the minds of the Wyoming settlers to the new jurisdiction of Pennsylvania. He took up his abode in the valley, near Wilkesbarre, in the furtherance of these objects. He was born in Salem, Massachusetts, in 1745, and was graduated at Harvard College, in 1763; and, after the necessary preparation, was admitted to the practice of the law. He was in the public service from the commencement of the Revolution, almost to the close of his long and illustrious life, filling various elevated and responsible stations with great ability and unquestionable integrity. He was highly esteemed by General WASHINGTON, and heartily disliked by Mr. JEFFERSON, circumstances which entitle him, in advance, to the respect of his countrymen. He served faithfully and with distinction during the war, and was at the battles of Brandywine and Germantown. He succeeded General GREENE in the office of Quartermaster-General, in which he greatly "contributed to the surrender of CORNWALLIS at York-

ble and patriotic as those he has since pursued; and his suggestions were the emanations of right reason and experience. General MIFFLIN sometimes spoke to questions of order, but nothing more: and as to Chief Justice M'KEAN, I shall only say, that his conduct gave no token of the zeal he not long afterwards displayed in the democratic career. But, as it is the people who make governors, *Eh! que faire Mons. Peltier?*—what the deuce is an eager candidate to do? For least of all men, can he say with Fontaine, in his tale of Joconde:

> Ce n'est pas mon metier de cajoler personne.

As to those great occidental luminaries, Messrs. SMILIE* and FINDLAY,† their conduct upon this occasion, was truly in character; ever tremblingly alive to the *soveranity* of the people. Nor, have their labours in the good cause been less exemplary than their zeal; since, if we except a slight eclipse of a few digits through the obtrusion of Washington with his Federal Constitution and Federal exercises, they have been constantly glaring, full-orbed, in the political firmament; and we are certainly indebted for their uninterrupted public services, from the commencement of our independence to the present hour. Nor shall I risk lessening the merit of their perseverance, by inquiring how much of the public money they might have pocketed in all that time; or whether any other trade they could have

---

town." In 1791 he was made Postmaster General. In 1794, Secretary of War. In 1795, Secretary of State, from which office he was removed, in 1801, by President ADAMS, and he returned to Massachusetts. In 1803, he was chosen by the Legislature of that State, a Senator in Congress, for an unexpired term, and again in 1805. In 1811, he was chosen by the Legislature a member of the Executive Council of Massachusetts: and, during the Madisonian war, was a member of the Board of War for the defence of the State. In 1814, he was elected to Congress, where he continued until 1817, when he retired finally to private life. He died in January, 1829, in the eighty-fourth year of his age. "In private he was a model of republican simplicity—was mild, courteous, and unassuming. In public he was able, energetic, brave, and disinterested."—ED.

* JOHN SMILIE, subsequently a member of Congress; an active, energetic, and ardent politician of the Democratic school.—ED.

† The HON. WILLIAM FINDLAY, afterwards Senator in Congress, and three years Governor of Pennsylvania, from the year 1817. He was born at Mercersburg, and is still (1846) living in Philadelphia.—ED.

turned their hands to would have proved equally productive. Let it no longer be said that the people are ungrateful, or that virtue, in republics, goes unrewarded.

If Washington has no tomb, he must somehow have displeased the people. He fought their battles, it is true, but was he sufficiently tender of their pockets; sufficiently obsequious to their sovereignty? did he tell them, that he *loved them?* No: but he presumed to differ from them in opinion, and give them advice, and freemen choose to think for themselves: nor will they submit to admonition from the bench or the pulpit.*

During the sitting of the Convention, the direful revolution in France was in progress, and its proceedings sometimes appealed to, as guides for our conduct. Though hardly daring to blame, and less impressed than I ought to have been with the treatment of the clergy, I presume no one ever heard me praise: for there was folly enough to disgust, before the appearance of crime; and I thought the nation was about to throw away the most amiable part of its character. I remember, one day, at the table of General Mifflin, at this time President of the State, when the Parisian courtesans were applauded for contributing their patriotic gifts, I ventured to call in question the immense merit of the proceeding. I was stared at by a pious clergyman for the shocking heterodoxy of my sentiments; and should, probably,

* " The young American of the future, looking back on the history of his country in the days of his grandfathers, may, perchance, find books enough written in our own times, to teach him that what was called the old Federal party, with WASHINGTON at its head, and such men as JAY and HAMILTON in its ranks, was a vile nest of traitors, busily employed in the subversion of American freedom; that the *people*, alive to their machinations, and influenced only by strong intelligence and stern integrity, deposed these unworthy guardians of public freedom; and, selecting men who modestly shrank from notoriety, and whose patriotism was above suspicion, dragged them from their beloved retirement, and forced upon them office and honour; and that, under the auspices of THOMAS JEFFERSON and AARON BURR, placed in the highest stations as well-tried and honest friends of their country, the torrent of treason was checked. But, sometimes, it providentially happens that one who was an actor in the busy scenes of past history rises up and tells his story. He may inform us, for instance, how one of these high functionaries, of patriotism so pure, was afterward tried for treason to that country which he loved so well; and how the other, with the ferocity of a bloodhound, sought the life of his illustrious compeer, because he stood in the way of his ambition."—*New York Review*, vol. ii. p. 191.—ED.

have been drawn into an altercation, no less disagreeable than
indiscreet, had not the General in a friendly manner pacified the
parson by whispering him in the ear, that I was perfectly well
disposed, and only sporting an opinion.   So overwhelming was
the infatuation, so ominous the fanaticism, that even this godly
personage had quite forgotten that incontinence was a sin.   He
" could have hugged the *wicked sluts;* they pleased him."

Nearly about the time of this occurrence, I happened to be
at Reading, where Burke's Reflections on the French Revolution, with Paine's Rights of Man, both of which had just come
out, were the general topic of conversation.   I had seen neither;
and when they were given me to read, I was apprised of the
delight I should receive from the perusal of Paine's pamphlet.
As to Burke, I was told it was heavy and tedious, but that it
was necessary to condemn myself to a wading through it first,
for the sake of better understanding and relishing Paine's, which
was in answer to it.   I read them; but to my great misfortune,
and contrary to all expectation, I became so firm an adherent
to Burke, that his opponent made not the smallest impression.
I have already made confessions which cautious men may start
at.   But this is worse than all.   The stolen Ribbon of Rousseau
was nothing to it: nor, although events have proved me right,
is that of any consequence.   Many other things have turned out
right too; but that does not lessen the odium of their early
advocates.   It is the essence of sound civism to think with one's
fellow-citizens ; on no account to anticipate them; and I ought
to have thought wrong, because it was the fashion.   Republican
morality, like republican other things, being made by general
suffrage, will not always take the trouble to ferret truth from
her well; and as it is manufactured *pro re nata,* on the spur of
the occasion, it is liable, of course, to gentle fluctuations—but
infinitely safer, by the bye, in practice, than that of the old school.
I here speak from woful experience.

Under the administration of President Washington, the prosperity of the country was advanced with a rapidity which exceeded the most sanguine expectation of the friends to the new
system.   It afforded a cheering example of what a republic is
capable, whose councils are solely directed with a view to the

general good; and if ever a portion of the human race was in that auspicious predicament, it was that composing the population of these United States.*   But what is the general prosperity to hearts that are torn by the furies of disappointed ambition or avarice! It is but as paradise to the foe of mankind, engendering a more deadly venom in the tortured soul, soothing itself with the dire imagery of Claudian's Alecto.

> Siccine tranquillo produci sæcula cursu?
> Sic fortunatas patiemur viveres gentes? &c. &c.

Unfortunately there was no proportion between the offices to be disposed of, and the persons who had been in expectancy.   Nothing less than miraculous power could have so distributed the loaves and fishes as to fill the immense multitude that hungered for them; and the dissatisfied only repined at a success, which,

---

* All this is now historical and requires no illustration. Yet, in the year 1796, the "Sage of Monticello" thus wrote to Mazzei, an Italian who had resided in this country, and with whom the "Sage" had formed an intimacy:

"The aspect of our politics has wonderfully changed since you left us. In place of that noble love of liberty and republican government which carried us triumphantly through the war, an Anglican Monarchical and Aristocratical Party has sprung up, whose avowed object is to draw over us the substance, as they have already done the forms, of the British Government. The main body of our citizens, however, remain true to their republican principles; the whole landed interest is republican, and so is a great mass of the talents.   Against us are the Executive, the Judiciary, two out of the three branches of the legislature, all the officers of the government, all who want to be officers, all timid men who prefer the calm of despotism to the boisterous sea of liberty; British merchants, and Americans trading on British capitals, speculators and holders in the banks and public funds, a contrivance invented for the purposes of corruption, and for assimilating us in all things to the rotten, as well as the sound parts of the British model.   It would give you a fever, were I to name to you the apostates who have gone over to these heresies, men who were Samsons in the field, and Solomons in the council, but who have had their heads shorn by the harlot England."

The vanity of the Italian was not proof against the temptation to inform the world that he was in correspondence with this philosopher, and the letter found its way, much to the chagrin and annoyance of its writer, into the French newspapers. Mr. Jefferson attempted to explain, but it was an embarrassing business, and he could not, satisfactorily, dispose of it.   By "the Executive" he did *not* mean the President; and by "Samsons in the field," he *did* mean the Society of the Cincinnati, &c. &c.

> "Oh! what a tangled web we weave,
> When first we practice to deceive!"—Ed.

in giving happiness to the community, promised stability to the rulers whose labours had procured it, and, in so doing, seemed to ratify the blanks as well as prizes which had been drawn. In each of the States, there were, no doubt, numerous malecontents; but they probably most abounded in Virginia and Pennsylvania. In the former there was a number of aspirants for high office, who could illy brook, that while they, in their closets, remote from the din of arms and clangour of trumpets, had been qualifying themselves for the great affairs of the new empire coming out ready made to their hands, others, who had spent their youth in the unlettered business of the camp, should be preferred to employments they deemed exclusively due to their own superior attainments. Mr. Jefferson* and Mr. Randolph had indeed been gratified with places, but there were others equally ardent for them, unprovided for; and other motives concurring, the native State of the President was perhaps the most refractory in the Union. The chagrin in Pennsylvania did not proceed from precisely the same causes. The discontented here had hardly looked for the flattering notice of the General Government; but they felt, (I speak of them in the aggregate, with due latitude for honest exceptions,) that their intriguing parts would be miserably circumscribed by the operation of the new system; and that on a theatre, where talents and character were the sole recommendation to office and consequence, their chance of influence was a very sorry one. Far different was it in the State government, in which they had been accustomed to shine and to dictate. There a little learning would go a great way; and cunning was a quality of infinitely more advantage to the possessor than wisdom or true ability; and though the State authorities were still in force, they were no longer supreme, but subordinate. I am aware that this representation does not agree with the prevalent idea of our party dissensions. This recognises, with very little discrimination, a lofty tone and aristocratical tendency on the part of the federalists; while, on that of their opponents, it discovers an ardent concern for the

---

* Mr. JEFFERSON had been appointed Secretary of State; and EDMUND RANDOLPH, also of Virginia, Attorney-General.—ED.

people's rights, somewhat more jealous, perhaps, than necessary, and an enthusiastic attachment to liberty, excessive indeed, but even amiable in its extravagance. That this enthusiasm or fanaticism had once existed, may be granted; but to admit that it prevails to any degree at present, would require a determination to believe in defiance of the clearest evidence to the contrary, since they who are or were supposed to have it, are conspicuous for an overweening partiality for the most flagitious and desolating system of arbitrary rule that was ever established to an equal extent upon mankind, without even being disguised by a mollifying appellation. My hypothesis, therefore, must absolutely exclude the love of liberty and equal rights, as a general feeling, among the democrats of the day, not only now, but in time past. Whatever benevolent motives they might claim, it is perfectly fair to conclude, that they were actuated by a headlong instinct of self-love; a blind, infuriate impulse, prompting those possessed with it, to remove, at whatever price, every obstacle to the consummation of their unhallowed purpose, of rising upon the rubbish of widespread havoc and devastation. It is no objection to this supposition, that many of the democratical leaders had too much property themselves to favour such an object. They might not all have been aware of it; and those that were, no doubt entertained the idea that they could restrain their instruments when necessary; or even if they could not, they should, at all events, escape unhurt in virtue of their fellowship. This is the unction, which in these cases is always laid to the soul: nor can it be supposed, that the Duke of Orleans thought his head in the smallest danger from those he had kindly helped by his vote to the head of the king.

As to the great leader of the opposition, there is reason to believe, he was head, heart, and hand in the noble project of renovating, by first destroying, the world. *Tout detruire, oui tout detruire ; puisque tout est recreer*, says Mons. Robaud de St. Etienne. He had been in France, and drank deep of her literature and philosophy. His official doings and messages show his utter contempt for *un vrai trivial, un clartè trop familiaire ;* and that he was wholly of that school, which teaches, as Mr. Burke tells us, " that any good arising from religion or morality

31

may be better supplied by a *civic education*, founded in a knowledge of the physical wants of men, progressively carried to an
enlightened self-interest, which, when well understood, will identify with an interest more enlarged and public." Robespierre,
to be sure, gave an unlucky illustration of this fine doctrine in
France. His enlightened self-interest gave him clearly to perceive, that as he aspired to sovereign rule himself, so others did
the same; and that, therefore, unless he sent them to their *eternal sleep*, they would do as much for him. But in America, it
has turned out better; and the enlightened self-interest which
prompted Mr. Jefferson to cast an eye upon the presidency,* has
most edifyingly identified with the interests of the *mouth of labour;* if not the whole, at least a very essential part of the
public. This mouth of labour, by the bye, is one of the fine
figures of speech, by means of which this gentleman has been
enabled to triumph over the popularity even of Washington; although it is sacrilegiously thought by some to savour a little of
that jargon, which the same Mr. Burke somewhat harshly denominates, " the *patois* of fraud, the cant and gibberish of hypo-

---

* Of this "*enlightened* self-interest," and the enlightened tactics which enabled
Mr. JEFFERSON to triumph, there are extant very remarkable and satisfactory proofs.

DAVIS, in his Life of BURR, says, " It is a remarkable fact, that, previous to the
balloting in Congress, [for President,] all parties and sections of parties concurred
in the opinion that the election would finally be determined, as it was, by New
York, New Jersey, and Maryland. These three states would render the election
of Colonel BURR certain; *two* of them could elect Mr. JEFFERSON. The vote of New
York was to be decided by THEODORUS BAILY, of Duchess County, and EDWARD
LIVINGSTON, of the City of New York; the vote of New Jersey, by Mr. LINN; and
the vote of Maryland, by Mr. DENT, or Mr. BAER." The New York Review, in
commenting upon this passage, holds the following significant language:

" What was the future history of these gentlemen? Mr. BAILY was made Postmaster of the City of New York, Mr. LIVINGSTON was appointed United States
District Attorney for the district of New York, Mr. LINN became supervisor of
internal revenue for the State of New Jersey, and Mr. DENT was appointed United
States' Marshal for the Potomac District of Maryland. It is a marvellously striking coincidence that these gentlemen should thus all have been honoured with
appointments to offices in the President's gift. Doubtless the only inquiries, concerning each, were, is he honest—is he capable—is he faithful to the Constitution?
It is refreshing to turn away from the traitorous conspiracies of the wicked
Federalists, and dwell with lingering delight on such immaculate patriotism as
this."—ED.

crisy." But we, on this side of the water, ought to have more indulgence for a trade growing out of our institutions. As the people give power, and power promotes thrift, the people may certainly be complimented a little; and hence, intolerance towards demagogues, may fairly be ranked among the anti-republican tendencies. No censure, therefore, is aimed at one who is the quintessence of good republicanism, and too pure to take a stain, though fondling with imperialism. For my own part, I am elated with the opportunity of recording my veneration for a patriot who has so rapidly advanced the morals of this new world, and whose scrupulous observance of truth pre-eminently entitles him to the motto of *vitam impendere vero.*

The French revolution then, from the attachment now shown by the Jeffersonians to the absolute despotism that has been produced by it, it is fair to conclude, was less beloved by them for any philanthropic disposition it manifested, than from its being an engine wherewith to assail their adversaries in power; and it was so much the better adapted to this purpose, as it was in conflict with Britain, that accursed island, which, in the opinion of all sound Jacobins, ought long since to have been sunk in the sea. To declare a neutrality, therefore, with respect to the belligerents, as was done by the administration, what was it but a base dereliction of the cause of republicanism—a most enormous act of ingratitude to those liberty-loving men, who had benevolently taken off the head of Louis the Sixteenth, our late generous ally and " protector of the rights of man ?" and who, by so doing, had made themselves the undoubted heirs of the immense debt of gratitude we had contracted with the murdered monarch ? On the score of this gratitude transferred, can it ever be forgotten, what a racket was made with the citizen Genet ? The most enthusiastic homage was too cold to welcome his arrival; and his being the first minister of the infant republic, " fruit of her throes, and first born of her loves," was dwelt upon as a most endearing circumstance. What hugging and tugging ! What addressing and caressing ! What mountebanking and chanting ! with liberty-caps, and other wretched trumpery of *sans culotte* foolery !

" Give me an ounce of civet, good apothecary, to sweeten my imagination !"

In short, it was evident that the government was, if possible, to be forced from its neutrality; and that nothing less than a common cause with France, a war of extermination with England and the other monarchies of Europe, would satisfy the men who are now so outrageously pacific as to divest themselves of the means of annoyance and defence, and to place their glory in imitating the shrinking policy of a reptile.* Fortunately for the nation, Washington was at the head of it; or the rage for universal republicanism, combining with the plea of gratitude derived from Jacobin morality, would have riveted us in liege subjection to the imperial Napoleon.†

---

* "As events rolled on, one circumstance and another conspired to mark more distinctly the lines between the parties of the day, and at the period of the election of the third President of the United States, they were very clearly defined throughout the Union, under the names of Federalists and Democrats. In the first class were to be found WASHINGTON, HAMILTON, JAY, PICKERING, AMES, MARSHALL, and others like them; the last enrolled in its list JEFFERSON, BURR, GEORGE CLINTON, MADISON, and many more throughout the State."—*New York Rev.* ii. p. 192.—ED.

† By drawing themselves within the shell like a tortoise, and thence called the Terrapin system of policy.

CHAPTER XV.

Yellow Fever. — Marsh Effluvia.—Popular Feelings towards France.— Party Feelings.—A Threatened Insurrection suppressed by the President.—The Western Expedition.—Address to the President.—French Party.—Treaty with Great Britain Opposed. — Rochefoucault.— French Travellers. — M. Talon.— Genet.—Washington's Retirement.—Character of Washington.

Such was the state of parties in the summer of 1793, when the metropolis of Pennsylvania, then resounding with unhallowed orgies at the dismal butcheries in France, was visited with a calamity, which had much the appearance of one of those inflictions which Heaven sometimes sends to purify the heart. A disease that was soon recognised to be the pestilential yellow fever, carried off several persons early in the month of August; and gradually spreading in all directions, raged with the most fatal malignancy until the close of October. Those whose property enabled them to do it, fled with precipitation from the city, which was supposed to have been deserted by half its inhabitants; but enough remained behind to swell the mortality to several thousands. The dismay was, if possible, increased by the disagreement of the physicians as to the mode of treating the disorder; and numbers, who had exulted in the havoc of their kind, because belonging to a different class, feeling death to be a serious evil when brought home to themselves, shrunk appalled with abject terror, at the dangers which surrounded them.

> To each his suff'rings: all are men,
> Condemn'd alike to groan,
> The tender for another's pain,
> Th' unfeeling for his own.

A general gloom pervaded the country; for although the ravages

31*

of the disease were yet confined to Philadelphia, it was not supposed they would remain within these limits, notwithstanding
that every precaution which the most unfeeling vigilance could
suggest, was used, to prevent the spreading of the pestilence.
Measures were taken in almost every town and village to prohibit the entry of persons suspected of infection; and even fugitives from the seat of it, though in health, were regarded with a
jealous eye. Some of the people of Harrisburg were for following the example of their neighbours, though a malady not
less fatal than that in Philadelphia, was raging among themselves. But the difference was, that one was called a plague,
the other but a simple fever. It is somewhat remarkable, that if
the yellow fever is of foreign origin, as insisted upon by many,
that a disease of a similar type should make its appearance at
the same time on the banks of the Susquehanna, at the distance
of a hundred miles. Shall we say, that the state of the atmosphere which generated the one was favourable to the diffusion
of the other? This, I believe, is the doctrine of those who contend that the yellow fever is of exotic growth, and always
imported, when it appears among us. It would be highly presumptuous in me to undertake to decide, when "doctors dis-
agree;" but that a state of the air should be favourable and
adequate to the diffusion, but not to the origination of a contagion, is certainly refining somewhat nicely. I venture, however,
no opinion upon the subject. With respect to the mortality
produced by the two diseases, that at Harrisburg was, I believe,
in proportion to the population of the place, as great as that at
Philadelphia. I cannot take upon me minutely to describe the
symptoms of the Harrisburg disease, nor were they the same
in all that were sick, but a general one was, an affection of the
stomach, or nausea with violent retchings and a yellowness of
the skin. Some were ill a week, some longer, some died in two
or three days from the time of their being seized, and others,
who were walking about with symptoms only of the ague, suddenly took ill and expired. The black vomit, which has sometimes been supposed peculiar to the yellow fever, appeared in
some cases. I was attacked with a quartan ague about the

middle of September, but had none of the grievous symptoms of the malignant fever which prevailed.

Whatever may be the points of discrimination between the bilious and yellow fever, the origination of the one seems to depend on the same cause which spreads the other; and this appears to be a torrid sun acting upon a moist soil, or upon impure and stagnant water. The matter which produces agues, and which, according to Doctor Cullen, is miasmata alone, is, I take it, competent also to the generation of bilious fever in habits disposed to it; and if not to the generation, at least to the propagation or spreading of the yellow fever; wherefore, the vapours from low and marshy situations and waters, rendered baneful from certain adventitious circumstances, may be pronounced to be the support or aliment of all these diseases, more peculiarly of the latter perhaps, when the exhalations are rendered more than commonly noxious from the general state of the atmosphere. Egypt, Syria, and Turkey, are at once the seat of the plague, and of bilious and intermitting fevers.

But the deleterious effects of marsh effluvia in warm climates, have perhaps been known from the earliest time. They are at least recognised by Silius Italicus, who wrote in the reign of Nero. Speaking of a pestilence which raged in the Roman army in the second Punic war, he ascribes it to the fervid rays of the sun, acting upon the stagnant and widespread waters of the Cyane.

> Criniger astriferis Titan fervoribus auras
> Et patulam Cyanam, late palustribus undis
> Stagnantem, stygio Cocyti opplevit odore.

This cause existed at Harrisburg. A mill-dam had been erected the season before on the Paxton, rather a turbid and sluggish stream, within five or six hundred yards of the middle of the town, on its eastern side. The obstruction must have spread the water over a surface of from eight to ten acres; and this, co-operating with a state of the atmosphere unusually morbid this season in such situations, may fully account for the fever which prevailed. In the fall of the year 1792, there were some cases of it, and still more in that of 1794, equally malig-

nant; after which the mill-dam was removed. I have been the
more particular on this subject, though without being able to
offer any thing satisfactory, from knowing it to have been a
matter of some interest with the physicians of Philadelphia, to
ascertain the nature of the Harrisburg disease; thence to de-
duce data towards the solution of the question, whether the
yellow fever, as appearing in our cities, be, or not, a malady of
exclusively foreign origin.

The distress I saw around me; the dismal tidings from Phila-
ladelphia; and above all, the frightful mania which had taken
possession of a vast majority of my fellow-citizens, induced a
dejection of mind I had never before experienced. I had been
for some time labouring to stem the torrent of fanaticism among
my townsmen; but to no other purpose than that of increasing
their violence, and drawing down upon myself the denunciation
of being inimical to liberty and an unnatural partisan of England. It was in vain I urged that I was only treading in the
steps of the President, whom all pretended to revere; that he
had chosen for his country the path of neutrality,* and that it
was the duty of all good citizens to acquiesce in it, until it should
be abandoned by those who were legally constituted to say
what should be the state of the nation in relation to the powers
at war. The bringing of the name of Washington to my aid,
produced no sort of embarrassment among the maniacs for re-
generation, who, in the same breath, extolled him to the skies
and denounced perdition on those who supported his policy. In
fact, his name was constantly used to sanction the measures of
his opponents; and even in the contest for the presidency between Mr. Adams and Mr. Jefferson, it is a matter of notoriety,
that his dislike to the administration of the former was atro-
ciously asserted, in defiance of his letter announcing his accep-

* The cabinet of WASHINGTON decided, unanimously, that a proclamation should
be issued, " forbidding the citizens of the United States to take part in any hostilities on the seas, either with or against the belligerent powers, and warning them
against carrying to any such powers any of those articles deemed contraband according to the modern usages of nations, and enjoining them from all acts and
proceedings inconsistent with the duties of a friendly nation towards those at war."
—*Sparks' Life of Washington.*—ED.

tance of the command of the army, and unqualified approbation
of the steps which had been taken. It has been said, that hell
itself cannot be governed without some degree of truth; and if
so, for policy-sake at least, we ought not wholly to discard her.
My indignation at this base dereliction of every honourable and
moral principle, conspiring with my firm conviction that my
opinions were correct, made me an enthusiast in the cause I had
espoused; and the feeble efforts of my pen were employed in
vindicating the conduct of administration. In exposing the folly,
the frenzy, the duplicity and hideous wickedness of its adversaries, I derived an additional incentive to exertion, from the
consideration, that the civilized world was so singularly circumstanced, that good men of every nation and country had a
common cause to maintain; and, that in the threatened universal
wreck, conditions were so confounded, that even the private
American citizen might feel himself nearly on the same eminence
with those great and truly enlightened European statesmen, who
were labouring to avert the impending desolation: as in a
vessel in danger of foundering, the navigator's skill is, at the
moment, of no account; and the meanest hand on board, may
be engaged in stopping the leak and plying the pump, to as much
effect as the captain. But of what use are endeavours to fix
the charge of swindling on a political adversary? He denies
it, and retorts the accusation. Thus, with two-thirds of the
people, who are incapable of investigating the truth, did
they even think it worth their pains to do so, the parties as to
honesty, are left upon a level; and, hence, as the sovereign
has no objection to being deceived, he will be deceived, and
villany will be triumphant. Such has been, and will be, the
common effect of appeals to Mr. Jefferson's *Bar of Public
Reason*, which, if the phrase be not intended as a sarcasm upon
the tribunal, it must be meant as a cruel mockery of those who
are interested in just decisions from it.*

* The writer of these observations is not ignorant that writing in this strain of
remark, subjects him, in the eyes of your able politicians, to the imputation of extreme folly. Who, say they, but an *arrant oaf* could expect to succeed in a government of popular sovereignty, by reason and good faith? The people must be
deceived; and to be induced to be led by men of rank and intelligence, their proper

Among the abominations of this rage for French liberty and
fraternity, there has been all along an utter disregard of the
most obvious dictates of justice, humanity, and consistency.   In
the beginning, the Revolution must at all events go on : *ca ira*
was the word, and no matter by what monsters the business was
conducted.   Power, for this reason, was always the criterion
of right : and Robespierre, until his head was ascertained to be
off, was no less popi lar with us than the best of his predecessors.
And for what was this horrible sacrifice of every thing we had
heretofore been taught to consider as virtuous and honest ?   To
destroy kings and nobles, monarchy and aristocracy, and to
make a huge republic of the world, wherein all men were to be
equal; or if there should, peradventure, be a little temporary
inequality, it should alone be founded on the uninvidious pre-
eminence of intellectual acuteness in the acquisition of pelf, or
popular suffrage; sound titles, without question to superiority
among men !   Colonel Chartres,* for instance, among the first,

leaders, their prejudices must be humoured,—they must be flattered and cajoled.
But, *if it be really so*, for the interests of morality, and the safety and honour of
the community, he must say, in his turn, that it is matter of no very poignant regret how soon such form of government is exchanged for another, prosper who
may by the demagogue game.   The reader, nevertheless, will do him egregious
wrong, if he concludes, from the remarks of this kind scattered through his work,
that he is a friend to arbitrary rule,—or yet disposed to part with our present system, however much abused.   The remarks are the effect of an uncontrollable indignation at seeing the fair fabric of liberty we have reared, defaced by unhallowed
hands, and daily dilapidating under the sapping process of pretended patriots.
But so averse is man from giving himself a master, that though almost despairing
of the reappearance of the day when honest men shall emerge from their degradation, and the real friends of the people be again taken into favour, he would not yet
be among the last to oppose monarchical encroachments.   If we would look for the
persons most likely to favour these, we shall find them in that class, who consider
government as a source of selfish emolument, and always use it for that purpose,
whatever form it assume.   The demagogue and the court favourite, says Mr. Burke,
in a quotation from Aristotle, are not unfrequently the same identical men.

  * Damned to an eternal infamy of fame by Pope and Arbuthnot.   This wretch
was infamous for all manner of vices, and the point of the allusion will be better
understood by a quotation from Pope, and the celebrated character of him, in the
form of an epitaph, by Dr. Arbuthnot.   The former, speaking of *money*, and
doubting whether its invention has been more useful than injurious to mankind,
says,—

and names beginning with every letter of the alphabet among the latter. But since this great republic has not come, or since, at least, it has not come precisely in the form that was predicted, having clothed itself in imperial purple, instead of the plain homespun garb in which it was expected to appear; and, having, moreover, in the place of its former hosts of patriotic citizens and *citesses*, presented us with dukes and titled men innumerable, with its Abrantes, its Cadores, its Ponte Corvos and Beneventos, what is the ground of our attachment now to the great nation? To restore the freedom of the seas, and destroy that Pandora's box of human ills, Great Britain. Wisely answered again, and shrewd and patriotic must be the men who

> " And I, who think more highly of our kind,
> (And surely, Heav'n and I are of a mind,)
> Opine, that nature, as in duty bound,
> Deep hid the shining mischief under ground :
> But when by man's audacious labour won,
> Flam'd forth this rival to its sire, the sun,
> Then careful Heav'n supplied two sorts of men,
> To squander These, and Those to hide again.
> Like Doctors thus, when much dispute has past,
> We find our tenets just the same at last.
> Both fairly owning, Riches, in effect,
> No grace of Heav'n or token of the elect ;
> Giv'n to the fool, the mad, the vain, the evil,
> To Ward, to Waters, CHARTRES, and the Devil!"

The Epitaph is as follows; it conveys a moral, and no apology is offered for its insertion here :

" Here continueth to rot the body of *Francis Chartres*, who, with an *inflexible constancy* and *inimitable uniformity of life, persisted*, in spite of *age* and *infirmities*, in the *practice* of *every human vice*, excepting *prodigality* and *hypocrisy ;* his insatiable *avarice* exempted him from the first, his matchless *impudence* from the second. Nor was he more singular in the undeviating *pravity* of his *manners*, than successful in accumulating *wealth ;* for without *trade* or *profession*, without *trust* of *public money*, and without *bribe-worthy* service, he acquired, or more properly created, *a ministerial estate.* He was the only person of his time who could *cheat* without the mask of *honesty*, retain his primeval *meanness* when possessed of *ten thousand a year*, and having daily deserved the *gibbet* for what he DID, was at last condemned to it for what he *could* not *do.* Oh, indignant reader ! think not his life useless to mankind ! PROVIDENCE connived at his execrable designs, to give to after-ages a conspicuous *proof* and *example* of how small estimation is *exorbitant wealth* in the sight of GOD, by his bestowing it on the MOST UNWORTHY OF ALL MORTALS."—ED.

began and still maintain their claim to exclusive popularity and confidence by two such admirable and solid systems of policy and ethics; and shrewder still that goodly portion of the people, which shows itself capable of appreciating and rewarding such transcendent state ability! But I must not encroach on the province of the party editor.

As every circumstance was seized by the discontented to embarrass the administration, or, in the proverbial phrase, "to stop the wheels of government," a handle was made of the excise law. A duty being laid upon whiskey, that general and favourite beverage in Pennsylvania, it was found a potent theme for the purpose of sedition; and it was, accordingly, preached upon with so much unction, that an insurrection was the consequence. It began beyond the mountains in the summer of 1794, spreading from west to east with wonderful rapidity. Harrisburg was quickly infected; and a meeting had been called for the purpose of passing some inflammatory resolutions. By the persuasion, however, of a few of us, who were untouched by the contagion, these inconsiderate men were induced to desist; though less perhaps from a sense of their error, than from our assurance that a body of troops were on their march to the seat of insurrection; and that if they persisted in their undertaking, they would involve themselves in the guilt of a forcible opposition to the laws, and most surely have cause to repent of their temerity. It is difficult to say what might have been the issue of this commotion, had not the President taken immediate measures for its suppression, and called out a force so respectable as at once to overawe the seditious, and thereby prevent the effusion of blood. The insurgents, who had once assembled at Parkinson's ferry, had proposed another meeting at Braddock's field; a location, without doubt, adopted *in terrorem*, and by way of hint to the effeminate federalists, what a set of bloody-minded fellows they had to deal with. But the device, however well conceived, was wholly lost upon General Washington, who had seen all sorts of folks in his campaigning, and knew that men with moccasins, and leggings, and hunting shirts, and tomahawks, and rifles, were just about as brave as men with powdered heads and silk stockings, and no braver:

and that their standing on Braddock's field, (tremendous spot to be sure!) would not make them a jot more ready to leave their carcasses to bleach there among bones that had been whitening by a forty years' exposure. At any rate, these formidable circumstances did not prevent his putting himself in a posture to bring this lawless assemblage to reason; and what was equally unlucky for them, was, there being at his disposal a number of persons who had also seen Service, and therefore as little liable as himself to be dismayed by hideous grimaces. To cut a well-known story short, there was no fighting after all; it being thought best by the insurgents, on serious deliberation, to send ambassadors to sue for peace, one of whom, if I mistake not, was the veteran statesman Mr. Findlay, a man so minutely acquainted with the whole business, as to have been enabled to write a book upon it nearly as thick as a well-sized cheese; and in which, I am told, for I have never read it, he belabours General Hamilton most unmercifully.* Washington, as already observed, was still too popular for a direct attack. Whenever, therefore, he was spoken of, it was with the warmest professions of veneration for his virtues and good intentions—thus complimenting his heart at the expense of his head, and representing him as a good, easy simpleton, who, not very well aware of the tendency of his measures, was continually led into scrapes by the cunning rogues who surrounded him, the archest of whom, at this time, was Hamilton. How exhilarating to

---

* Ex-governor of Pennsylvania, to whom allusion has already been made. He was the father of the late JAMES FINDLAY, Secretary of the Commonwealth during a portion of the service of Governor PORTER ; and of the present respectable JUDGE FINDLAY, who is indebted for his position as President Judge of the District Court for the city and county of Philadelphia, to Governor SHUNK, son-in-law of ex-governor FINDLAY.

The " Cheese" referred to,—a mouldy affair,—contains a history of the Insurrection, which, as it was written by an ardent though able politician, may, perhaps, be consulted with some advantage by the curious reader, if he will, at the same time, peruse BRACKENRIDGE's " Incidents of the Western Insurrection," and also General HAMILTON's official Report in the American State Papers. Its censure of HAMILTON cannot be supposed to have operated very injuriously to that gentleman's reputation. What may be the view which posterity will take of the attempt,—or whether it will take any,—is solely the business of posterity, with which it would be presumptuous to intermeddle here.—ED.

32

wounded patriotism, thus by a stroke of the pen to sink into a fool and a knave, these two great champions of federalism!

The Western Expedition, as it was called, gave me an opportunity of seeing a number of my old friends from Philadelphia; and it afforded also a momentary triumph to the poor handful of Harrisburg Federalists, who were stated by their opponents to amount to only five. A French flag, which had been flying at the court-house then building, had been the cause of some squibbing in the newspaper; and this flag was peremptorily ordered to be taken down by the troops from the city. Had I been disposed for revenge, I might upon this occasion have been fully gratified, as I was repeatedly asked who had caused it to be put up, and impliedly censured for giving evasive answers to the questions; which, from their manner, evinced a disposition to treat the authors of it much more roughly than would have been agreeable to me.

Conspicuous among the crowd that rolled on from the eastward, was Governor Mifflin, who had been vibrating with much address between the parties; and had really the merit of keeping them in tolerable humour, within the sphere of his influence; that is, within the limits of the State.

> Such in the midst the parting isthmus lies,
> While swelling seas on either side arise.

He had a large suite, which, as it consisted of gentlemen of both parties, he was tugged a good deal in opposite directions; though, on this occasion, his leaning was decidedly Federal, and being so, he did me the honour to accept of a bed at my house, instead of one at General Hanna's, which he had in his offer. I have no doubt, however, that his head and heart were generally right, maugre a conduct often wrong; and though I am as little addicted as any one to compromise between my conscience and an opposing interest, and of course not at all disposed to apologize for his temporizing, I cannot but admit, that Mifflin was a pleasing man, and one to whom I was indebted for many acts of kindness. But popularity and the bustle of public life were hobby-horses he could not dispense with. He must mount them, therefore, though at something more than a risk of being spattered by the dirt which they raised.

On the day after his arrival he convened the people at the market-house, and gave them an animated harangue, in which there was nothing exceptionable save a monstrous suggestion, that the British had stirred up the discontents to the westward, and been the cause of the present opposition to government. I wonder if Mr. Smilie, Mr. Gallatin, and the rest of them, were aware that they were but the puppets of this abominable nation!

In a few days after the Governor, General Washington, accompanied by Colonel Hamilton, came on. After waiting on them, I prevailed upon the burgesses to present an address to the President, which I sketched out, and which, from the cordiality of the answer, appeared to have been well received. But as they have both been published, it is unnecessary to insert them here.*

As to myself, I could not partake of the glory of this expedition. An ague, which had hung about me ever since the preceding fall, had rendered me unfit for service. Nevertheless, I procured a substitute, in preference to claiming an exemption on account of my debility.

That this commotion, in its infancy, was highly pleasing to the opposition leaders, can hardly be doubted; and that it was cherished also by the French minister as a favourable circumstance towards the predominance of the Gallic interest, is fairly to be inferred from his notice of our " early decrepitude," and his intimation, that for some thousands of dollars he could have plunged us into a civil war. But, I think, he was mistaken here, as the intriguers were neither fighting men, nor disposed for absolute anarchy: yet, from his assertion, of what he might have done by means of cash, it is a matter of obvious deduction, unless Mr. Fouchet was a liar, that he had an understanding on the subject with the master-democrats, who, by way of apology, as I take it, for not driving on the insurrection with more spirit, had pleaded their want of pecuniary means.

---

* They will be found in Appendix Q. What the author hesitated to do, may not inappropriately be done by another.—Ed.

Some of them, indeed, might have been willing to touch the dollars, had the Frenchman been fool enough to bring them forth; but even in that case, he would have been overreached and got nothing for his money.

One more stand was made against the popularity of the President. The occasion was found in the treaty with Britain, negotiated by Mr. JAY. This was to have been expected; as a heavy clamour was raised at the time of his appointment to the mission, upon grounds it would be both tedious and unnecessary to go over. The treaty, after much deliberation, had been ratified in the constitutional mode; but as it depended on the House of Representatives to make the appropriations necessary for carrying it into effect, it was here attempted to be defeated by withholding them. Mr. Jay was as much vilified,* as if he had laid the entire interests of his country at the

---

* JOHN JAY was a native of New York, where he was born in December, 1745. He was a graduate of King's (now Columbia) College; and, in 1768, was admitted to the Bar. In 1774 he was a delegate to the first American Congress, which met at Philadelphia. In 1776 he was chosen President of Congress. In 1777 a member of the Convention which framed the Constitution of New York, and in the following year he was appointed Chief Justice of that State. In 1779 he was again in Congress, and presiding over the deliberations of that body. In the same year he was appointed Minister Plenipotentiary to Spain, for the purpose of obtaining from that government an acknowledgment of our independence, to form a treaty of alliance, and to procure pecuniary assistance. In 1782 he was appointed one of the Commissioners to negotiate a peace with England. In 1784 he returned to the United States. On his arrival he was placed at the head of the Department for Foreign Affairs; and on the adoption of the present Constitution, he was appointed Chief Justice of the United States. He was the author of several of the numbers of "The Federalist." In 1794 he concluded with Great Britain the treaty known as "Jay's." Before his return, in the year 1795, he had been elected Governor of New York. He resigned his office of Chief Justice, upon receiving information of this event, and continued in the office of Governor until 1801, when he retired to private life. He died, May 17, 1829.

His personal appearance is thus described by SULLIVAN :—

"His height was a little less than six feet; his person rather thin, but well formed. His complexion was without colour, his eyes black and penetrating, his nose aquiline, and his chin pointed. His hair came over his forehead, was tied behind, and lightly powdered. His dress black. The expression of his face was exceedingly amiable. When standing, he was a little inclined forward, as is not uncommon with students long accustomed to bend over a table. His manner was very gentle and unassuming. His deportment was tranquil; and one who

feet of a foreign power; for such things were then justly considered as crimes. But shall the treaty go into effect? This was the question in the House of Representatives, and it was debated for weeks upon every point but the one really in issue, namely, whether any treaty, whatever might be its stipulations or advantages, was admissible with Great Britain; and whether the anti-Federal party, should it relinquish the vital nourishment it derived from a deadly, implacable, and everlasting enmity to that accursed island, would be able to sustain itself, or have a chance of ever rising again. These were the merits of the case, though cautiously kept out of view. The treaty, however, stood its ground; and the sole consolation of the defeated faction, was to wait, with what patience it might, for the death or resignation (to borrow its own phraseology) of the "first and greatest of revolutionary patriots." Before dismissing the topic, it may be remarked, that the ground upon which the treaty was most strenuously assailed, was, that it imposed some slight restrictions upon our trade. Yes—this was a ground taken by the very candid and impartial men, who now advocate non-intercourse laws and perpetual embargoes, rather than expose themselves to a collision with the other belligerent nation.

In the spring or summer of 1795, a letter was delivered by a gentleman at my house, which gave me the opportunity of a transient acquaintance with the Duke de la ROCHEFOUCAULD LIANCOURT, who, being on a tour to see the country, was recommended to my attentions. My respect for the writer of the letter would have induced me to avail myself of the honour it offered me; but being indisposed and depressed by a domestic affliction, I did not go out, and thus escaped the scrutinizing

had met him, not knowing who he was, would not have been led to suppose that he was in the presence of one eminently gifted by nature with intellectual power, and who had sustained so many offices of high trust and honour. History will assign to JOHN JAY an elevated rank among the great; not only so, it will place him equally high among the pure and virtuous. Throughout his useful and honourable life, he was governed by the dictates of an enlightened Christian conscience. He thought and acted under the conviction, that there is an accountability far more serious than any which men can have to their fellow-men. The bravest soldiers, and the worthiest statesmen, have ever been those who believed in such accountability."—ED.

eye of an illustrious traveller.*   It is certainly a perilous thing,
to stand before a man about to make a book, and who gauges
and proves you with a view to making your quantities and
qualities a component part of the subject matter.   General
HANNA, it appears, had been in this predicament; and, all
things considered, he comes off very well.   His age, I must
say, was pretty accurately guessed at by the Duke, who is also
correct in his other observations, that the General preferred
chewing to smoking tobacco.   Were I about framing an hypothesis why Mr. Hanna makes a somewhat better figure in the
tour than the gentlemen of Reading, in spite of their acknowledged hospitality and " obliging answers to inquiries," I should
say, that he talked European politics with rather more understanding than they did, little, as the Duke tells us, they are at
best understood in America.   Those talked in Reading, probably, were not entirely to the taste of a good Frenchman, who,
if I understand the character that phrase would designate,
would cry *vive la nation et sa gloire*, not only in exile, but with
his neck under the guillotine.   Now, though the Reading gentlemen spoke with just abhorrence of the crimes of the Revolution and with due respect of the Marquis de la FAYETTE, they
might neither have testified a desire, that England should be
brought to the feet of France, nor that the destinies of the
world should be subjected to her control; things, which, from
his party-leanings, Mr. Hanna, might have countenanced.   All
this, however, is but conjecture; and as to the accuracy of
the noble tourist's facts, so far as I am acquainted with them, I
have nothing to object, except as to the havoc of names.

From this gentleman, I turn to others of his nation whom he
speaks of in his travels; and for whose acquaintance I was indebted to Major Adam Hoops, who, I should have mentioned

* This nobleman was a member of the Constituent Assembly in 1789, at the
dissolution of which he took the military command at Rouen, as Lieutenant-General.   He resided for eighteen months in England, previously to his tour through
the United States, which he completed in 1798.   After the restoration he was
created a Peer.   His life was published by his son in 1827.   The principal work
of ROCHEFOUCAULD is his *Voyage dans les États-Unis*, published at Paris in eight
vols. octavo.—ED.

before, did me the honour to attach himself to my company, in
the capacity of a volunteer, during part of the campaign of
1776. A letter from him about the year 1790 or '91, so far as
my recollection serves, introduced me to Mr. Talon, then engaged with the Viscount De Noailles, in establishing a settlement on the north branch of the Susquehanna, and to which
they gave the name of Asylum.* In the course of this business,
he several times passed through Harrisburgh, and never failed,
on these occasions, giving me an opportunity of seeing him.
Mr. Talon fully justified to my conception the favourable idea
that is given by Lord Chesterfield and others, of a Frenchman
of rank. I have seldom seen a gentleman with whose manners
I was more pleased. Though he spoke but little English, and
I less French, yet from the knowledge we respectively had of
each other's language, we contrived to make ourselves mutually
understood. On one of his visits to Harrisburgh, he was attended by not less than ten or a dozen gentlemen, all adventurers
in the new establishment, from which they had just returned on
their way to Philadelphia. Of these, I only recollect the names
of M. De Blacons, Captain Keating, and Captain Boileau. My
brother† and myself, who had waited on them at their inn, were

* The Duc DE LA ROCHEFOUCAULD, in his travels, has given a full account of this
place, as it appeared in 1795. " Messrs. TALONS and DE NOAILLES, came to this
country from France, intending to purchase, cultivate, and people, 200,000 acres
of land. They had interested in their project some planters of St. Domingo.
Messrs. MORRIS and NICHOLSON sold them the lands, and, in December, 1793, the
first tree was cut at Asylum. M. DE NOAILLES was to manage the concerns of
the colony at Philadelphia. M. TALON attended to the erection of log-houses, and
the preparation of land for the reception of the colonists. They were disappointed
in the receipt of a part of the funds upon which they had relied, and were obliged
to relinquish their purchase and improvements. They then became joint partners
in the business with Morris and Nicholson. The quantity of land was enlarged
to a million of acres, and TALON was to act as agent, with a salary of $3000 and
the use of a large house. Ignorance of the language, want of practice in business
of this nature, other avocations, and the embarrassments of the company, deprived
TALON of the happiness of opening a comfortable asylum for his unfortunate
countrymen, of aiding them in their settlement, and thus becoming the honoured
founder of a colony. He and M. De Noailles, sold out to Mr. Nicholson."—
Travels.—ED.

† The late highly respectable and estimable WILLIAM GRAYDON, Esq., of Harrisburgh, before mentioned. The same who was made prisoner, and concerning
whom the author, long in suspense, had suffered great anxiety.—ED.

kept to supper, and I have rarely passed a more agreeable evening. The refreshment of a good meal, coffee and wine, had put in motion the national vivacity; and the conversation, carried on in English, which many of the company spoke very well, was highly animated. Captain Keating was, in fact, an Irishman, and Captain Boileau had been among the troops which had served in this country. As to Mons. Blacons, he was but a novice in the language; yet hurried away by a high flow of spirits, he ventured so boldly in it, expatiating to me on a projected road from Asylum to Philadelphia, which, according to him, required nothing but the consent of the Legislature, to be completed out of hand, that Talon, astonished at his volubility, exclaimed *ce n'est pas lui c'est le vin que parle*, " that it certainly was not he, but the wine that was talking." The French Revolution being touched upon, it came into my head to ask Captain Boileau, how it happened, that he and the other gentlemen who had been in America, and must of course have been among the foremost in inculcating the doctrine of liberty in France, were now so entirely in the background? His answer was interrupted by a loud and general laugh; and Talon, who had probably been adverse to the revolution in all its stages and modifications, (as he was the person on account of whose courteous reception General Washington had been roundly taken to task by the citizen Genet,)* enjoyed the thing so much, that he thought it worthy of remembering, and put me in mind of it, in an interview with him a long time afterwards. This gentleman had apparently stood high in the confidence of the King, as, on once dining with him, at his lodgings, he, at the instance of a French lady, from St. Domingo, who was present and had observed that I was uninfected with the regicide mania,

---

* First Minister of the French Republic to the United States. He was the occasion of infinite trouble and embarrassment to President Washington. His conduct became at length so offensive, that the American Minister, Gouverneur Morris, was instructed to demand his recall of the French Government. Genet received letters of recall, although his mission would have terminated at the time if he had not been, as the party in France to which he had been indebted for his mission, was overthrown. M. Genet remained in the United States, and retired into the interior of the State of New York and devoted himself to agricultural pursuits. He married a sister of the late De Witt Clinton.—Ed.

showed me his picture on the lid of a box studded with diamonds, that had been presented to him by his Majesty, as the inscription imported.

The Duke de la Rochefoucauld gives some particulars of the Asylum settlement, humorously called by some of the settlers, *refugium peccatorum*, and enumerates the families which had established themselves there, many of whom from their names I remember to have seen; but I have understood, that the settlement is now entirely abandoned by the French, and I have been told by persons who have seen the tract, that one more rugged and mountainous, except the particular spot whereon the town stands, could hardly be found. In this, it agrees with Mr. Talon's account of it, who, upon my asking him as to its situation, said, the mountains were *trop rapproches*, thereby conveying the idea of a narrow strip of flat land along the river. The affairs of France were a subject not often touched upon by Mr. Talon; but it was impossible not sometimes to advert to them, and he testified much concern for the death of the murdered Malesherbes, who, if I mistake not, was one of the counsel for the king. He spoke of him as a noble, generous man—*un gallant homme*, was, I recollect, one of his expressions. Talon was understood to have been in the law-line himself, and to have been *Avocat-general* under the old regime. If this was the fact, the office was, apparently, through royal favour, hereditary in his family, as one of the same name in that office, is spoken of by Cardinal de Retz, in the following very honourable manner, and the more so from his being in the opposite party, and a foe to his seditious designs. " Talon, Advocate-general, made one of the finest speeches that was ever made on a like subject. I never heard or read any thing more eloquent. He mixed with his reasons whatever could serve to make them the more moving. He invoked the manes of Henry the Great, and kneeling down, he called upon St. Louis to protect the kingdom of France. You fancy, perhaps, that you had laughed at this spectacle; but it had moved you, as it did the whole company, upon whom it worked in such a manner, that the clamours of the inquests began, as I perceived, to decrease by it." Though this quotation may be thought a strange wandering from my purpose, inasmuch as it mingles the transactions of ages past with those of the present, I could not suppress it, since it places in so amiable a light the virtue of patriotism, and the irresistible eloquence which may flow from that source. We too have our sainted friend in Heaven, who, by a stretch of fiction, more warrantable, may be supposed to be watching over the destinies of this country; but much I question, whether an equally solemn invocation to his manes would find matter so soft as was found in the breast of this Catiline, and in the hearts of those who were set in motion by his machinations.

To return to our own affairs. Although no other specific ground of opposition than those already mentioned, was taken against the President, yet the whole tenor of his administration was bitterly and incessantly inveighed against as hostile to liberty. The logic of democracy was extremely compendious, and therefore the more satisfactory to superficial inquirers. On the one hand, it pointed to *republican* France; on the other, to a combination of despots—and this was enough. In so interesting a struggle, could any friend to his kind be neutral! And the inference was, that they who were not for France, were against her, and monarchists, tories, and tyrants of course. The name of England too, was well calculated to rouse old resentments; and the single circumstance of her being opposed to France, was quite sufficient to make all staunch, Bœotian whigs, allies of the latter. Was she not, it was asked, engaged in a cause exactly similar to our own—and shall we side with royalists against her. Shall we not rather, in the glowing language of Genet, march to combat under her banners, and repay her for the generous assistance she gave us in our contest? Such arguments struck the public sensory with force; and the impression they made, was not to be effaced by any reasoning more complex and refined. Besides, who listens to reasoning that runs counter to his passions, his prejudices, and his interests? One perhaps in a thousand. It now became evident that to be popular, or even tolerated, it was necessary to be a partisan of the French; as to doubt, merely, the holiness of their cause, was the certain road to odium and proscription. It is not at all to be wondered at, therefore, that the prudent, the timid, and the thrifty, all lent themselves to democracy, and helped to swell a tide, which seemed ready to rise above all mounds, and to bear down every thing before it, even to the weight and popularity of Washington. That good man now began to doubt whether the prize of independence, which had cost him so many anxious days and sleepless nights, were really worth the sacrifices which had been made for it;* and whether posterity might not have cause to question the value of his services, or even, under the smart of anarchy, to exclaim—"Curse on his virtues, they have undone his country!" Weary of the struggle "with vice and faction," he at length resolved, at the expiration of his second term of service, to retire from the presidency, and leave it to be scuffled for between Mr. Adams and Mr. Jefferson.

Never had the soul of Washington exhibited more illustrious proofs of true nobility than in that very part of his life which excited the most viperous malignity, and brought upon him the execrable charge of having legalized corruption. Though always great—though in his early manhood distinguished as the protector of his country from savage inroad and depredation— though the only man perhaps in America, who by a transcendently virtuous, prudent, dignified, and persevering deportment, could have kept us united, and carried us triumphantly through the Revolution—he never appeared to more advantage than during the arduous season of his eight years' presidency. Like the magnanimity displayed by Cato in his march through Syrtes and Libyan deserts, it might justly be preferred to the most brilliant military achievements.

> Hunc ego per Syrteis Libyesque extrema triumphum
> Ducere maluirim, quam ter Capitolia curru
> Scandere Pompeii, quam frangere colla Jugurthæ.

Contrasting the glorious height to which he carried the American name, with its present lamentable degradation; the prosperity to which he raised his country with its present wretched state of despondency and subserviency to a foreign and despotic power; are we not fully justified in applying to

---

* A very similar reflection is made by Judge Brackenridge in his Incidents of the Western Insurrection.

him the " fine rapture" of Lucan, in regard to the patriot of
Rome?

> Ecce parens verus patriœ, dignissimus aris
> Roma tuis!

> His country's father here, O Rome, behold,
> Worthy thy temples, priests, and shrines of gold !
> If e'er thou break thy lordly master's chain,
> If liberty be e'er restor'd again,
> Him shalt thou place in thy divine abodes,
> Swear by his holy name, and rank him with thy gods.*

---

* Next to a man's acts, it would seem that the best test of his feelings and dispositions was his private confidential sentiments to his friends ; and in a letter from
this virtuous citizen to Gen. REED, of November 27th, 1778, is the following passage :—" It is also most devoutly to be wished that faction was at an end, and that
those to whom every thing valuable was entrusted, would lay aside party views and
return to first principles. Happy, happy, thrice happy country, if such were the
government of it ! But, alas ! we are not to expect that the path will be strewed
with flowers. The great and good Being, who rules the universe, has disposed
matters otherwise, and for wise purposes, I am persuaded." Such were the emanations of his patriotism and piety !

CHAPTER XVI.

Election of John Adams to the Presidency.—His Administration.—Mission to France.—French Party in America.—Imposition of Taxes.—Singular Fabrication.—Another popular Insurrection.—Election of Jefferson to the Presidency. Popular Fanaticism.—Author's Political Principles.—Death of WASHINGTON. Character of Jefferson.—Concluding Reflections.—Conclusion.

In the contest for the Presidency, Mr. Adams prevailed by a very small majority. Hence, federalism was still ascendent in the national councils, though considerably depressed in those of some of the States, which were working by sap, while their myrmidons abroad, displayed as much ardour to storm the strong hold of aristocracy, as the Parisians had done to demolish the Bastile. The tone given by WASHINGTON was maintained by his successor. Equally federal, he spoke a language more lofty; and in his answers to the numerous addresses, which were presented to him on occasion of the insolence of the French Directory, he was thought egregiously heterodox; particularly in one, in which, he somewhat unnecessarily, indeed, takes occasion to speak of his having once had the honour to stand in the presence of the Majesty of Britain. Shocking sounds, to be sure, to the republican ears of the day! Though, now we can talk of the Imperial Majesty of France, without the smallest danger of setting our teeth on edge, or of being proscribed for incivism. Nay, we even permit a democratic editor to live, who not long since proposed to turn our republican President into a Monarch, and to invest his temples with a diadem.

But I must hasten through the stormy scene of Mr. Adams's Administration. The *Republicans*, as they now styled themselves, (for nothing is more conducive to a successful cajolery of the people, then a well chosen appellation,) having got rid of WASHINGTON, continued their efforts for the ascendency with increased

33

hopes and animation.   They were no longer the enemies, but the
friends and watchful guardians of that constitution they had so
lately deprecated as the greatest evil that could befal them; or,
to use the words of citizen Fouchet, they had " disembarrassed
themselves of the insignificant denomination of anti-federalists,
and taken that of patriots and republicans." This was, doubtless, an able *manœuvre*.   They got possession, by it, of a popular
name, and their next care was to show how well they deserved
it.   An occasion soon occurred for a display of their new patriotism and republicanism.   This was the arrogant and swindling
conduct of the Directory, already mentioned.   Their demand of
tribute, and threat, in case of non-compliance, to barter us away
as they had done Venice, being properly felt and resented by the
sound part of the community, addresses to the President were
poured in from every part of the Union, expressive of a sense of
the outrage received, and a determination to support the government in any measures of defence which the crisis might demand.
The Directory did, unquestionably, make a sad blunder here,
and might have ruined their cause, if any thing could have ruined
it.   Instead of playing to the hands of their partners on this side
the water, they forced them most unmercifully by leading a suit
they could not follow, but were absolutely obliged to ruff. Nevertheless, the awkward thrust was parried with admirable dexterity;
and joining a cry they could not silence, they came forward with
their addresses, too, breathing a most ardent zeal for the honour of
their country, and a vehement indignation at the affront which
had been offered it.   To take off a little, however, from the
odium incurred by the Directory, under whose auspices they
fought and machinated, they fell upon the extraordinary expedient
of sending an extraordinary envoy, on their own account, to
France, and the extraordinary personage selected for this service,
was Doctor Logan.   He was held out, at least, as the party's
messenger.   It appears to be in the essence of Jacobinism, as observed by Mr. Burke, to excite contempt and laughter no less
than horror and tears; in the words of a French writer, *on ne
peut s'empecher d'en pleurer, et d'en rire.*   In France, its *vis
comica* was illustrated in dubbing the ruthless Duke of Orleans,
Monsieur Egalite; and in America, it exemplified itself, in dub-

bing Doctor Logan an Ambassador of the people: and it was even attempted in abject apery of the fantastic tricks of the great *Alma mater* at Paris, to bring the Doctor's wife upon the stage in the manner of Roland's and Tallien's. It is perfectly in my recollection, that some of the democratic prints of the day, spoke of Logan and Deborah, in the style of Louvet and his Ladouiskie. The object of the Doctor's mission, or going, (if not sent,) was twofold;* first, to assure the Directory that they had yet a strong party in America, which, if properly cherished and co-operated with, would soon be predominant, and enabled to repay their assistance with interest; and second, to show the people of this

* In SULLIVAN's Letters there is a reference to this gentleman and his mission. He says "early in 1798, a certain DR. LOGAN departed from Philadelphia for Paris, charged with a *private* mission on *public* affairs to the Directory. By whom sent was no secret, the House addressed the President, two to one, on this serious subject; and a like address passed the Senate, with only five dissentients. In this address it is said, "We deplore that there are those who call themselves by the *American* name, who have daringly insulted our country, by an usurpation of powers not delegated to them, and by an obscure interference in our concerns." MR. JEFFERSON was said at the time, to have sent LOGAN to Paris. In one of his letters, he answers some inquiry on this subject; and says, that the accusation is groundless; that LOGAN was self-appointed, and that he (MR. JEFFERSON) did no more than give him some sort of passport." Whether this gentleman was self-appointed, or whether he was sent by MR. JEFFERSON and his party, to which MR. LOGAN was attached, is a matter of very little consequence *now*, whatever may have been the degree of irritation produced by his movements at the period of his alleged "obscure interference." He has been represented by his friends, as a respectable, benevolent, man, whose object in this affair, as in every other of a public nature, in which he engaged, was service to his country and his fellow-men. If he mistook his vocation and over estimated his abilities, and the sincerity and virtue of his associates, or employers, by whom he was flattered and caressed for purposes of their own, that was his misfortune, and without question, he lived long enough to discover it to be so! But, in regard to his truly estimable wife who, like himself, is now beyond the reach of censure or of praise, and who is here, somewhat rudely and abruptly exposed to public gaze, the Editor may be permitted to remark,—(while expressing surprise and regret that the Author should have permitted himself, even while under the influence of strong party resentment, to be betrayed into an otherwise unaccountable impropriety, inconsistent with his own elevation of character as a generous and accomplished gentleman,)—that none who knew her could, with truth, utter a word in disparagement of her fair claim to unlimited respect and regard, or could lay to her charge, aught that could derogate from the dignity and purity with which, meekly and beautifully, she invariably sustained, the proudest character to which woman may aspire— that of an enlightened, patriotic, unobtrusive, AMERICAN MATRON.—ED.

country, that the Directory had no quarrel with them, but merely with their rulers; and thence, holding out an inducement to change them. What a blessed picture of republicanism was here! and to give its figures full relief, the proper light to set them off, it should be observed, that the persons exhibiting it, had engrossed the commodity and possessed it exclusively. By the fundamental principles of the constitution, and indeed of all the elective systems, to certain persons is delegated the power to govern: if they misuse the trust, they are removable by the votes of the people, and others put in their places; but failing to accomplish this, the wheels of government were to be stopped, and its functions usurped by any that might choose to do it: Can a clearer definition be given of anarchy? What lover of state juggling but must be charmed with the series of able tricking, by which the virtuous Jeffersonians crawled into power? As Doctor Logan has lately been to England, with the same pacific views, (he tells us,) with which he went to France, I shall not contest his motives in either case. Still, the use that was made of his voyage to France, by the party devoted to her, is a circumstance too important to be omitted in a recognition of the devices of the faction.

It was to have been expected, that the unexampled profligacy and insolence of the ruling power in France, would have considerably depressed their Democratic adherents in America, and strengthened the Federalists in the same proportion; but the consequences were directly the reverse. Alarmed much more than necessary at the menace of the Directory, and relying more upon the addresses from the people, than a considerate attention to their sentiments would warrant; (as, although they all expressed a warm regard for the honour of the country, they, for the most part, drivelled about the unkindness of the *dear* Sister-Republic,) the administration and its friends in Congress, seemed to think, that they were assured of the public support, in any measures against France, however energetic they might be. In this persuasion, such as deemed a state of hostility preferable to a state of fraternity with her, probably thought the occasion too favourable to be suffered to pass away; and in this view, an attitude unequivocally hostile, was taken by the government. A provisional army was voted, volunteer corps invited, ships of war equipped, and as a part of the system of defence, against a foe, which was well known to have numerous partisans among us, the *alien* and *sedition* laws were enacted. But the most volcanic ground of all was yet to be trodden. Money was to be raised, and not a little would suffice. The ordinary revenues were insufficient; and the adherents of the foreign power, already exulted in the anticipated ruin of their adversaries, who vainly flattered themselves with a public confidence, which could not be shaken. With less ability, the intriguers had vastly more cunning than the federalists; and from their better acquaintance with the human heart in its selfishness and littlenesses, they well knew, that a direct and sensible application to the pocket, would be more likely to blow up the prevailing party than any thing else. It has been well said, that a disorderly people will suffer a *robbery* with more patience than an *impost*. Under this conviction, the patriots had long sickened at perceiving that the community was satisfied; and that the current expenses of government were so easily raised. This was truly provoking. They wished the people to feel, they said. It was not right that they should pay without knowing it; and hence, a furious and persevering clamour against indirect taxation. It was reprobated as hateful and anti-republican in the extreme; it was not to be endured; and, inasmuch as it aimed at deceiving the people (wicked thing!) by cheating them into contributions, which their love of country would always most cheerfully afford when necessary, it was represented to be unworthy of freemen; and to imply a suspicion both of the virtue and understanding of the community, which, about the same time was voted by the democratic part of congress, to be the most enlightened on the globe, France herself scarcely excepted. All this was vastly fine and highly pleasing, no doubt, to the galleries; a charming material too, for the *republican* editors to cook up a most savoury dish for their customers. The simple, well meaning federalists were, in their turn pleased also, at finding that their opponents were smoothing the way to a measure, that, in the present conjuncture, would be exceedingly eligible for them; and therefore, with no small degree of self-complacency for their supposed address, took the tricksters at their

33*

word, and passed a law for a direct tax. Its operation was on houses and lands; but still keeping in view, the policy of favouring the industrious and frugal at the expense of the luxurious, the farmer paid very little for his property in proportion to the idle gentleman or inhabitant of a city, who gratified himself in the enjoyment of a sumptuous house. In the same spirit, a tax had been laid upon carriages kept for comfort and pleasure; an article which, beyond all others, made manifest the discrimination in behalf of *the mouth of labour*. Nevertheless, it was the mouth that from the hollow, pretended solicitude of its parasites that it might not be "deprived of the bread that it earned," was brought to clamour the loudest against taxes which did not effect it, and had, in fact, a tendency to relieve it; another proof of the inconsiderateness of the multitude, and of the superior potency of words to things, and consequently, of the very little chance indeed of honesty and fair dealing in a contest with knavery and hypocrisy, before "the bar of public reason."

This tax on real property, was the fatal blow to federalism in Pennsylvania. The Stamp Act was, indeed, bad enough, because it was a Stamp Act that first excited our displeasure with the mother country: The very name of an excise was hateful to freemen:* The alien law, set at naught one of the inherent rights of man, that is, the right of *impatriation* and *expatriation*, of coming and going and saying and doing whatever the love of liberty prompted; and the sedition law was still more execrable, since, in permitting the truth to be given in evidence in exculpation of a libeller, it gagged the mouths alone of patriotic liars and calumniators, the only species of partisans whose labours could be efficient in a cause, emphatically that of falsehood. But, though all these sad doings had been carefully impressed upon the sensory of the great Germanic body of Pennsylvania, they had not fully wrought the desired effect. Their pockets had hitherto been spared, and wheat had borne a good price. But now their vulnerable part was touched, and they began to look about them.

---

* It is remarkable, that the Federalists seemed really to believe, what it was evident from the conduct of their opponents, they did not believe, viz. That the people were enlightened. They were persuaded, however, of the efficacy of flattery, and laid it on thickly.

Nor were there wanting "friends of the people" to sympathize in their oppression, and to put them in mind, that it was to avoid the payment of taxes we went to war with Great Britain; that the federalists, therefore, were as tyrannical as she had been, and that this tax upon farms, houses and *windows*, was but the beginning of a system, which would soon extend to every thing; and that we should have at length a tax upon horses, wagons and ploughs; or as it was expressed in a handbill, circulated in favour of the election of Thomas M'Kean, "a horse tax, a cart tax, a plough tax, &c. &c." The love of pelf was completely roused; and many an honest farmer came to the poll with a countenance of as much anxious determination, as if upon his vote the question was suspended, whether he was to remain the independent man he was, or to sink into a pennyless vassal. Nor is it to be wondered at, that he was thus " perplexed in the extreme," when it is considered, that although we never bribe, all offices were afloat, and depended for their re-settlement on the issue of the election and the will of the successful candidate.

The success of a good trick, is only a theme for mirth among those who have talents for the business of electioneering. Low cunning, indeed, such as is moulded into the buffoon characters, we see in novels and upon the stage, your Sancho Panzas, Tony Lumpkins, &c. passes current for extreme cleverness, among the bulk of our rural statesmen. These are of the class of Mr. Jefferson's chosen people, however; and though, when in their place, their petty rogueries are very harmless and diverting; yet, when agog for office, with the extensive means of mischief they possess, in their sovereign capacity, they may, nevertheless, be fully competent to the ruin of a nation.* The name of WASHINGTON, as

* This idea, a little dilated upon, will enable me to defend myself against a charge made against me, of portraying my countrymen in very dark colours. I do, however, believe that they are naturally as good, and from the influence of their habits and institutions, better as respects the more atrocious vices, than the people of most other countries, of Europe in particular. But, I am constrained to believe, also, that in a government so constituted as ours, when immoral men rule the corruption at the head, it will soon be diffused throughout every part of the the body politic. One thing tending to this is the desire of office very generally pervading the community, and still more so the wish of being on the strongest side and acting with the majority, which is even more prevalent. The ignorant

already observed, was always usurped by this species of good
republicans; and so deplorable was the stupidity of a certain portion of the most enlightened people upon earth, that the following
fabrication was not too monstrous for their intellectual gullets.
John Adams, it was stated, was about to unite his house to that
of his Majesty of Britain, either by marrying one of his sons to one
of the King's daughters, or one of his daughters to one of the
King's sons, (I forget which,) but the consequence was, that the
bridegroom was to be King of America:—That General WASH-
INGTON had heard of this, as well as of the other anti-republican
conduct of the President, at which, he was, of course, most
grievously displeased:—That, therefore, he went to talk to Mr.
Adams upon the subject, and by way of being more persuasive
by appearing gay, good-humoured and friendly, he dressed himself in a suit of white, and discoursed with him very mildly; but
neither his dress nor his arguments were of any avail.   Then he
waited upon him a second time, and in order to render his re-
monstrance more solemn and impressive, he put on a suit of black,
and set before Mr. Adams the heinousness of his proceedings; but
to as little purpose as before.   He, at length, paid him a third
and last visit, in which he appeared in full regimentals, when find-

and timid are entirely swayed by it, so are the cunning and interested, as well as
that lighter kind of stuff which yields to the puff of every fashion; descriptions
these, which comprehend by far the larger portion of all communities.   It requires
some strength of mind, as well as strong political impressions, and a dignified
sense of virtue, to resist a torrent of public opinion emanating from the source of
power, and carried by the force and influence of triumphant faction into private
dealings, consigning to odium and sometimes to proscription, every man whether
lofty or humble, who does not fall in.   Admitting this to be the case (and will
any candid man deny it when the public mind is in a state of high agitation?)
it is not to make the people more than ordinarily flagitious, to maintain that they
then become corrupt and instrumental to corruption.   Even their honest prejudices, no less than their vices may enlist them in a policy ruinous to their country.
Still I must say, that prejudices are as unamiable as they are mischievous.   No
political opinions should be taken up, and still less persisted in, without strict examination.   Want of candour is want of justice; and a tenet that will not bear
the test of that golden rule, of doing unto others, nothing that we would not choose
they should do unto us, ought, without hesitation, to be discarded.   Love of
country can no more justify us in doing wrong, than love of ourselves.   It is, in
fact, with most people, the same thing, however they may be pleased to dignify it
with the name of patriotism.

ing the President still deaf to good counsel, he drew his sword, declaring, he would never sheath it, until Mr. Adams had relinquished his wicked designs; and so left him a sworn enemy. During the circulation of this ingenious romance, not ill adapted to the capacities it was designed for, and having all the marks of veracity derivable from circumstantial minuteness; the letter from General WASHINGTON, announcing his acceptance of the command of the provisional army, and his approbation of the measures pursuing, was also circulating in the federal prints. But this signified nothing, as they never reached the persons to be deluded by the story; and even if they had reached them, the letter would immediately have been knocked down as a federal lie. Such, be it again observed, is *the bar of public reason.*

The consequence of these united efforts of patriotism and invention, was another insurrection. The sedition which began in the county of Northampton, ran in a vein through the counties of Berks and Dauphin, spreading the infection by means of liberty poles, successively rising in grand colonnade, from the banks of the Delaware to those of the Susquehanna. Mr. Adams had now to set to work, to quell this second effervescence of liberty; and it proved a matter of no great difficulty, when force was applied. Poor Fries,* like the whiskey insurgents, was, for a time, left in the lurch; but finally sent " a coloneling," by good Governor M'Kean. The object of the tumult, however, was perhaps fully obtained; and had Fries been hanged, it would have been deemed but a very small sacrifice. It enlisted the feelings and resentments of a populous district on the side of democracy; and by the spirit of turbulence and discontent it

* This was distinguished as *Fries's Insurrection.* It had its origin in an attempt of the Federal Government to collect a direct tax. The tax particularly objected to was the " house tax." It broke out at the close of the year 1798, and discords prevailed to an enormous extent, throughout a large portion of the counties of Bucks, Northampton and Montgomery; and great difficulties attended the Assessors in the execution of their duties. At the head of these hostile movements, was a certain *John Fries.* He was tried and found guilty of conspiracy, and was sentenced to one year's imprisonment, a fine of fifty dollars, and to give security for his good behaviour for a year. This interesting trial was published in Philadelphia, in the year 1800, and was reported in short hand by *Thomas Carpenter.*—ED.

scattered abroad in the State, it helped to prepare the way for
the coming in of Mr. M'Kean, as its Governor; and thence, by
the "momentum of Pennsylvania politics," (noticed by Mr.
Dallas,) to pave the way for the accession of Mr. Jefferson to
the Presidency. It gave occasion too, for a useful nickname on
the administration of Mr. Adams, which with a sardonic grin,
not unworthy the taunting malignity of demons, was by the recent shouters for the mountain party of Robespierre, denominated, a reign of terror, now become a truly odious thing.

Such a fund of republicanism, as was, by these means infused
into Pennsylvania, could not fail to operate favourably for the
republican candidate, Chief Justice M'Kean; and he was, consequently elected Governor in preference to Mr. Ross; and the
same causes, aided by Callender's Prospect before us, that *chef
d'œuvre* of civic piety, operating in the same direction throughout the Union, not long after, invested Mr. Jefferson with the
presidency. *Summoque ulul“arunt vertice nymphæ.** Ye who
have genius for the epic, employ your talents here! one entire
action of twelve years successfully terminated at last, not by
ruffians stained with blood, but by meek and gentle operators in
the " swindling arena."

Such a result was to have been looked for. The morbid state
of the public mind, was, I repeat it, to have been deduced from
the very addresses to the President, which have been considered
as indicative of a manly, patriotic vigour. They will on the contrary (at least it was the impression made upon me at the time
of their appearance) be too generally found to breathe a spirit of
bigotry; not a generous love of country, not an adequate horror
of vice, not a proper understanding of the subject, but rather a
whining lamentation, that the conduct of the Directory, so little
fraternal, had a tendency to impede and interrupt the glorious
career of illuminatism and kingly demolition. This was evidently perceived and felt by Mr. Adams; and was, doubtless
his inducement for complimenting the Harrisburgh address, whose
merit, if it had any, was, that it cut deeper and approached

---

* *Nymphæ*, by some of Virgil's commentators, are here understood to mean
furies, and may easily be extended to the *furies of Jacobinism ;* which, no doubt,
howled in exultation upon this occasion.

nearer to the source of the evil than the general tenor of the addresses had done.* Let us love our country, let us cherish our institutions, and check their tendency to corruption and abuse; but let us no more think of cutting the throats of those who may differ from us in their civil polity, than of those who differ from us in their religious creed. Should we not look with something more than pity on the fanatic, who should languish to kill the Pope, to exterminate the cardinals, and annihilate the Holy See? What then but an equally silly spirit of fanaticism, can induce us to sigh for the re-generation of Europe in the extinction of her kings and privileged orders! Does any one now suppose that it would meliorate the condition of mankind? But the symptoms of this most loathsome mental distemper, were never more manifest than shortly before the downfal of federalism, when the gallant Truxton, for an achievement that redounded to his country's glory, and for which he should have received her unqualified, warmest applause, was assailed with brutal rage, and called a ruffian and a murderer. Could any thing more clearly demonstrate, that love of country was swallowed up in a rage for political theory?

By this memorable victory of Pennsylvania democracy for the behoof of Virginia aristocracy, occasion is afforded for much serious reflection on the sad effects of party fury; and giving the reign to those vindictive passions, which arise from selfishness opposed. No man, perhaps, ever more fatally and intemperately rioted in their indulgence than Mr. M'Kean. But the affair is old, and I am little disposed to renew it. As keenly sensible to injury as any one, I have felt with poignancy, and given vent to my indignation; but it is neither for my reputation nor my repose, to cherish feelings which deform the outward man, and prey upon the breast which harbors them. I shall be cold, therefore, upon a subject, wherein warmth and even acrimony might be justified.

From the account I have given of my political opinions, it can scarcely be necessary to say, that my vote was on the federal side, and given for Mr. Ross; and that I was of course involved

---

* See the Address, with the answer of Mr. ADAMS, in Appendix R.—ED.

in the proscription that followed the defeat of my party. In a
word, I was one of those, who were loaded with reproach and
detruded from office, as men unworthy to partake of the honours,
or even to eat the bread of their country. The extent of my
offending, the reader is acquainted with. It was the crime of
my party in being prematurely right; in daring to be wiser than
the great body of the people. Why then did I not play the
dotard with my country? Why did I not sigh for fraternity with
France, unconscious of the peril that awaited it?

> " I swear 'tis better to be much abus'd,
> Than but to know't a little."

If I unfortunately thought differently from Mr. M'Kean on the
highly interesting subject of Gallic republicanism, and, in so
doing *apostatized* from my former Whigism, I can only say, I
could not help it. That I did not forego my opinion when I
found it repugnant to his, is not a matter of so easy extrication.
I was contumacious, I know I was. But my conscience is satisfied; and that I never shouted in the sanguinary triumphs of
the Jacobins, will, though it has made me poorer, bring consolation along with it, in the close of a life, which, in all other
respects I could wish, had been equally blameless. An early
enthusiast in a most unfashionable cause,

> Some sign to me unknown
> Dipp'd me in ink, my parent's or my own;

even before my sentiments could be relished by the generality
of the party to which I belonged; and while, from their novelty,
they were so shocking to others, as to draw into question the
sanity of my intellects. I had even ventured to shed a tear for
the fate of Louis and his family; I had presumed to doubt the
wisdom of Brissot, and to arraign the humanity of Robespierre,
long before the guillotine had granted toleration for these
opinions.

But independent of so much heterodoxy, my simple vote had
been sufficient for the punishment that ensued; since the possessions of the vanquished, were, in the true spirit of the feudal

system, to be parcelled out among the champions of the victorious leader.   This, without doubt, was a mutual preliminary to a part‑ nership in the war; and as among the holders of office, in the apologetic *naiveté* of Mr. Jefferson, "few died and none re‑ signed," what was left but to cashier them?   I forbear to reiterate here, the stale remark that the free, unbiassed suffrage of the citi‑ zens, is the basis of the republican form of government.   Maxims have their use, but must be wholly disregarded in extreme cases; as, in England, the Habeas Corpus act.   Republicanism herself, was here in danger.   Was not a band of conspirators, with WASHINGTON at their head, in the very act of establishing a mo‑ narchy under the insidious mask of federalism?*

A man desirous to know the world ought to place himself in every situation to which the vicissitudes of life may expose him.   Above all he should be acquainted with adversity, and that particular kind of it, which results from a sudden reverse of fortune.   But to see the heart of man, in that most unfavourable point of view, in which the milk of human kindness is turned to gall and bitterness, he should behold it when elate with a "republican triumph."   It has twice been my lot to smart under the hand of oppression.   I have been exposed to the fury both of royal and republican ven‑ geance; and unless I may be misled by the greater recency of the latter, I am compelled to say, that the first, though bad, was most mitigated by instances of generosity.   If it produced the enormities the reader has been made acquainted with, the other was ruthless enough to rejoice at the sight of helpless families, at once reduced to indigence, stripped of their subsistence, driven from their homes, and sent to seek their bread by toiling in a wilderness.   This is no exaggerated picture; I saw the reality and felt it too, in the case of a near connexion.   And for what crime was it the punishment?   For embracing the policy of WASHINGTON; for being true to the dictates of honesty; to the

---

* This apostacy to monarchy, was inferred from President WASHINGTON's not joining the French against England; but now, when Spain is contending for her rights and liberties, the Jeffersonians can make common cause with her perfidious oppressor without danger of any such deduction or imputation.   Their incorrupti‑ ble republicanism can even take the fraternal hug with an emperor without the smallest suspicion of contamination.

34

interests of their country, to the interests of humanity; for having larger hearts, and greater minds, and nobler souls than those, who, by the inscrutable will of Heaven, were permitted to be their chastisers.

The death of the great Father of his Country, which happened between the election and the inauguration of the Governor, afforded another instance of democratic versatility. He was publicly and pathetically lamented and extolled by the leaders of the party: By Mr. M'Kean, while in the very act of chastising his followers; and by Mr. Jefferson while contemplating a similar conduct. The latter, it is said, made a visit to his tomb, which he plenteously bedewed with tears, and groaned aloud with every gesture of the deepest woe.* Achilles himself was not more inconsolable for the loss of his Patroclus: and even in the sacrifice of twelve young Trojans to his manes, he was far outdone by this illustrious modern mourner, with the remarkable difference, however, that whereas the one made victims of the enemies, the other selected for immolation, the friends of the lamented dead.

Utcumque ferent ea facta minores;
Vincet amor patriæ, laudumque immensa cupido.

In the election of Mr. Jefferson the long and persevering efforts of democracy had obtained their *ultimatum;* the beginning of that millenium that had been so anxiously sighed for. With this propitious era, therefore, I close my narrative of political events and party machinations. I had, indeed, aimed at nothing more than

---

* The reader of Mr. JEFFERSON's "Memoirs and Correspondence" will turn away with loathing from this miserable exhibition of hypocrisy; particularly when he recalls to his recollection certain passages of the "ANA," in which the cloven foot is unskilfully concealed. WASHINGTON was fully advised of MR. JEFFERSON's duplicity as to himself, and placed a proper estimate upon his character and designs. In his letter to JOHN NICHOLAS, dated 8th March, 1798, WASHINGTON wrote: "Nothing short of the evidence you have adduced, corroborative of intimations which I had received long before through another channel, could have shaken my belief in the sincerity of a friendship which I had conceived was possessed for me by the person [Jefferson] to whom you allude. But attempts to injure those who are supposed to stand well in the estimation of the people, and are stumbling blocks in the way, by misrepresenting their political tenets, and thereby to destroy all confidence in them, are among the means by which the Government is to be assailed, and the Constitution destroyed."—ED.

a sketch of public affairs, in so far as my fortune was more peculiarly implicated in them. As to the conduct of Mr. Jefferson, in the management of his high trust, it would appear to have been his primary object, to discredit the republican form of government, by illustrating the abuses of which it is susceptible, and its proneness to become the prey of unprincipled intriguers. I should suppose him to be a monarchist of the true imperial cut; and that his administration was peculiarly calculated to surfeit us with liberty; to expose the nakedness of our systems, and the extreme fragility of those ties he once denominated Lilliputian. Upon this hypothesis, all is plain and consistent; on every other, inexplicable, unless we can admit the possibility of a philosopher being a fool, or, of a patriot being a man solely bent on filling his pocket. Methinks I see the mighty personage, like a sated Condor on the Andes, sublimely perched on Monticello, triumphantly deriding the clumsy labours of New England morality, and self-complacently counting the gains of his superior illumination. But whether the speculum through which I view him may magnify or diminish him, show him justly or distort him, it is too manifest a truth, that the lesson given by France, we are inculcating with all our might, and erecting America, also, into a beacon instead of a guide. To the sad example of former Republics, we are eagerly adding our own, and certifying in colossal characters to the world, the melancholy result of "this last and fairest experiment," in favour of free government.*

---

* The melancholy result alluded to, is, that a combination of selfish, unprincipled men, are able to pass themselves off for paragons of virtue and patriotism. But, such is our *vis medicatrix naturæ ;* our tendency to resist and recover from the impolicy of our rulers, that our country is still prosperous in defiance of all their sinister efforts for our ruin : and hence it is, that not only the mass of our own people are imposed upon, but the enlightened of other nations, who know nothing of our affairs in detail. "It is thus, in America," says Madame de Staël, "that a great number of political problems appear to be solved, because the citizens are happy and independent." Yes, several political problems are, indeed, solved, and one of them is, that demagogues are as omnipotent here as ever they were in the Republics of Greece, and that an Aristides among us is not a jot more secure from ostracism than he was at Athens. But still, it is true, we go on, and are getting rich, and have no tyranny or injustice that we do not inflict ourselves; and the great problem that yet remains to be solved, is, how long a Republic can flourish or subsist without good morals. A rigorous prosecution of

As to myself, I have obtained the reward which perhaps every man must look for, "who, upon the strength of innocence alone, shall dare openly to speak the truth, without first propping himself by cabals, without forming parties for his protection." I have not only been punished by my political enemies, but have seen the justice of the measure solemnly ratified by the suffrages of those whom I supposed to be my friends. For the sake of a paper constitution, whose threatened destruction has become the trick of the demagogue, seeking power, as its preservation becomes his device, so soon as he is invested with it, a host of officers, that had been prostrated by the pioneer of Mr. Jefferson, were coolly and remorselessly consigned to their fate by the federalists. The substance of justice was exchanged for its shadow, and the principle established, that virtue is a certain bar to the attainment of power, an encumbrance which the candidate cannot too soon shake off; and, that corruption and wrong mark the route to be pursued.* This, be it known, is the unanimous decree in Pennsylvania, the law of the land, *nemine contradicente*. A similar, but much less galling and extensively mischievous instance of ratified oppression, gave birth to the Social Contract of Rousseau. He had been borne down, unjustly, as he supposed, by the French ambassador to Venice, to whom he had been secretary, and with whom he had a dispute; and his oppressor, countenanced and supported by the community, first gave him, as he

the last war by Britain for two years more, would have thrown much light on the solution of the problem.

* They had soon, moreover, the mortification to find that he had no longer the ability to serve them. His influence with the democrats was at an end; and he was only potent while acting in their views, and hunting down with them in full cry, their political opponents. It might now be said of him as it was of Labienus, when he left Cæsar's standard for Pompey's:

Fortes in armis
Cæsaris Labienus erat nunc transfurga vilis.

The only result, then, of this grand political manœuvre was that the federalists exclusively fastened on themselves the odium of this man's tyrannical character by this their sanction of his violent and oppressive conduct. Strange that they should forget that their principles were essentially bottomed on morality and virtue; things much more sacred and radically important than the forms of a Constitution.

informs us, the idea of a comparative analysis of the government and society to whose justice he had appealed in vain. "Every body agreed," says he, "that I was insulted, injured and unfornate; that the ambassador was mad, cruel and iniquitous, and that the whole of the affair dishonoured him forever. But what of this? He was the ambassador, and I was nothing more than the secretary. The justice and inutility of my complaints, left in my mind seeds of indignation against our foolish civil institutions, by which the welfare of the public and real justice are always sacrificed, to I know not what appearance of order; and which does nothing more, than add the sanction of public authority to the oppression of the weak and iniquity of the powerful." It is scarcely necessary to mention, that these remarks refer to the ancient monarchy of France. Could the author of the Social Contract have supposed that they could ever be equally applicable to institutions expressly founded on the principles of liberty and justice, and which even aim at restoring the natural equality of mankind! But Rousseau was not aware, that the germ of the evil he complained of, was not in any particular form of goverment, but in the world, ever slavishly inclined to offer incense to power, with very little regard to the general justice of its exercise.

If the end of punishment be to reform, mine has been wholly lost upon me; though my example has no doubt been useful to others. I was too high-toned and indiscreet even in the opinion of many federalists; for many there were who saw no wisdom in martyrdom.* I am still, however, to speak the truth, a most

* Matters are now both better understood and better managed; and much toleration is granted to those ardent and aspiring spirits, who cannot endure to wait until virtue shall obtain her own reward. The process is too slow, the result too uncertain. Hence the short cut to distinction and office, bids fair to be all the mode; and, to the honour of democracy be it said, that she suffers apostacy to go unrewarded, having truly more joy, as it would seem, in the recognition of one repentant sinner, than in the contemplation of ninety just. All that appears exceptionable in the tergiversating business, is, that in the way it is now practiced, it looks too much like deserting and taking advantage of our duller and less ethereal political associates. But, if the federalists would one and all come into the measure; if, as a party they would renounce their opposition and their errors; if they would proclaim themselves converts, succumb to their victors, and taking their cue from the tamed shrew of Shakspeare, would say the sun was the moon, or the moon was the sun, in obedience to the whim of democratic dictation; why

incorrigible sinner, though somewhat cooled of my ardour; and so little amended by the chastisement I have received, as to behold, if possible, with increased contempt and execration, the procedures of those very great and good men, under whose auspices it has been administered. The possession of power has exhibited them in even blacker colours, than did the sink in which they "lay straining their low thought," to obtain it: and although unable to vie with our dear departed sister republic in deeds of martial emprize, we certainly " gall her kibes," in those of fraudulent achievement. In truth, we must by this time be nearly mature. Hypocrisy, we are told, is the consummation of vice; and the libertine hero of Moliere's Festin de Pierre, is not thought ripe for destruction until he receives this last polish of villany.

If there be any thing wrong in this language, it does not arise from its being applied to a point of which there is any doubt; but merely from its solemnity approximating it to bombast, by being employed on a matter, become trivial from extreme familiarity. However shocked at first, we now only laugh at the monstrosities of the era. After what we have seen in France, and are now witnessing at home, Caligula's making his horse consul is a thing of very easy belief; nor is any historical phenomenon more incredible than the mutual passion subsisting between enthusiastic republicanism on the one hand, and the most desolating and dismaying system of despotism, which the world has yet beheld, on the other.*

then "the doors of honour and confidence would be thrown open to all," and we should hear no more of faction and "anti-republican tendencies." But, how far this might improve our morals, and narrow the ground for European defamation, is another thing, but wholly immaterial to a community whose "own approbation of its own acts," to use the words of Burke, "has to them the appearance of a public judgment in their favour."

* "A perfect democracy," says the inspired Burke, "is the most shameless thing in the world. And as it is the most shameless it is also the most fearless. It is less under responsibility to one of the greatest controlling powers on earth, the sense of fame and estimation. The share of infamy that is likely to fall to the lot of each individual in public acts, is small indeed; the operation of opinion being in the inverse ratio to the number of those who abuse power. Their own approbation of their own acts, has to them the appearance of a public judgment in their favour." Who could not conclude, from the justness in every iota of

Though this picture may pass with some, for a hideous caricature, enough of truth, I trust will be found in it, to convince them that we are no longer in that full tide of successful experiment, that wafted Mr. Jefferson into office,* that, on the contrary, we felt the influence of "retiring ebb," and were therefore, needlessly vigilant in guarding against the inroads of British corruption. Neither have we shown that we are so entirely well adapted to our institutions as to render it a necessary ingredient in the education of our youth, to prepossess them with a bigoted aversion to every other mode of government, and thereby to render them the ready patrons of insurrection and anarchy in every quarter of the globe. The commentaries of Blackstone, we are told by a great law character and writer, should be studied with caution, since he is heterodox in some of his opinions, and does not trace power to its genuine source; that is, "through its small and pure streams up to the free and independent man." Mr. Burke too, comes under the lash of the American statesman, who, with a sneer, that had much better been spared, insinuates his want of integrity, and talks of his "new creed." But what did Mr. Wilson know of his old one? Was it ever confided to him? Did Mr. Burke ever tell him that he was not a monarchist, but a republican? For he certainly

these remarks, that their author had been an eye witness of the administration of JEFFERSON and MADISON, in every stage of their barefaced effrontery and duplicity! I almost pity these unhappy men, destined to wear out the wretched remnant of their days without one drop of the balm of self-approbation, absolutely cut off from the pleasure, no less than the profit of reading Burke, as in every page of his political morality, they would be sure of meeting a cutting satire on themselves. But, of demagogues and tyrants, the condemnation is the same.

> Magne pater divûm, sævos punire tyrannos
> Haud aliâ ratione velis, cum dira libido
> Moverit ingenium fervente tincta veneno
> Virtutem videant, intabescantque relictâ.
> *Pers. Sat.* 3d.

* This truly "successful experiment" is partially explained; and the means by which MR. JEFFERSON was "wafted into office," fully exposed, if biographers and historians always speak the truth, by a scrap of secret history for which, I believe, the world is indebted to Mr. DAVIS, the able and candid author of the Life of BURR. See Appendix S.—ED.

never told the world so.   Mr. Wilson was an able man, and his eloquence as a speaker, singularly forcible and commanding; but when he undertakes to raise trophies to himself from the dispraise of such men as Blackstone and Burke, he engages in a task which may justly be termed a bold one.   As to the fine allegory, under which the fountain of political power is represented to have been at length discovered, like the source of the Nile, what does it amount to?   It may be happily conceived, but it is little satis- factory.   "Men's rights," says Mr. Burke, "are their advan- tages."   This is coming to the point: and it is not a discovery of the source of power, that decides the question of human hap- piness, but how its streams can be best distributed for the attain- ment of that end.   After finding power to originate in the free and independent man, we have yet to inquire, Whether this free and independent man, will voluntarily submit to the restraints which the good of the community requires of him.   If he will, Mr. Wilson is both practically and theoretically right; and the question, as to forms of government, is at rest.   But his manner seems rather too dogmatical, considering that he is the advocate of a system, which, however plausible in theory, has experience against it: and when he compliments us Pennsylvanians, for our love " of liberty and *law*," he must certainly have adopted the maxim of *laudando admonere*, since neither in the attack of his own house, nor in our two more recent insurrections, is this dis- tinguished love of law to be recognised.   There appears to me, therefore, more propriety and wisdom in speaking of our institu- tions, as experiments, whose failure may be deemed the general misfortune of mankind, as is done by Mr. Hamilton, in his Fe- deralist, than in treating those with disrespect and asperity, who have laboured to support other principles of government,—prin- cipless too, which seem absolutely essential to order, in the na- tion of which they were subjects.   That we possess advantages, which are not to be found in the old world, I have no difficulty in believing; but in an estimate of our comparative superiority, it is but fair to abstract from our polity the benefits derived from our state of society and population.   Instead, then of engaging in scholastic disputations and wars of extermination about politi- cal modes of faith, let us be content with performing our duties.

to the system we have established for ourselves: and, in the writings of this very Mr. Burke, heretic and apostate though he be, a most excellent lesson may be found for our purpose. It is in his Appeal to the Old Whigs, page 82, of the New York edition. The passage struck me, as containing reasoning, at once new, moral and refined; but I have since found it to be merely a dilatation of the quatrain of Gui du Fur de Pibrac, in words, which are evidently the text of Mr. Burke's most beautiful commentary.

> Aime l'etat, tel que tu le vois etre :
> S'il royal aime la royaute;
> S'il ne l'est point, s'il est communaute
> Aime le aussi, quand dieu t'y a fait naître.*

Still if the sentiment be thought too indulgent to legitimate monarchy,† (and nothing royal is to be endured, it seems, unless proceeding from fraud, usurpation and violence) I say with Mr. Wilson, that democracy is the best of all possible governments—*if the people are not wanting to themselves.* But, that we have been latterly a good deal wanting to ourselves, I must be permitted to believe ; and also to think with Mr. Hillhouse, that in the present corrupted state of our morals, what has been absurdly termed a strong executive, and thought our best security, has become our greatest bane—that the splendour of chief-magistracy we must not look to have; but, in its stead, an unostentatious, ephemeral head, begotten by chance, and dying while yet in infancy—literally coming up and cut down like a flower. The attributes of royalty, neither become us, nor are good for us.

* It may thus be translated : Love the state to which you belong, such as you find it to be : if, of the royal kind, love and be loyal to it : if, on the contrary, it be a commonwealth, equally love and be faithful to it, since Heaven has made it the place of your nativity.

† This remark anticipated the great question, since made, between legitimacy and usurpation. A shape imparted to politics about the time of the battle of Waterloo, in 1815, and not adverted to in discussion, until after that event. Republicanism having been fairly renounced by the French Revolutionists, the only ground left for them, was the vindication of new monarchy in opposition to the old, of upstarts supported by human slaughter, termed glory, in opposition to the civil arts, of industry and commerce, fostered by the influences of religion and peace. A state of things vainly stigmatized as indicative of imbecility and national degradation.

They sink our great men into very little ones, or only, "aggrandize them into baseness." To give any chance therefore for the operations of patriotism, we must smother that obtrusive thing called *self*; and by taking away, or rendering power uncertain and fugitive, we must, with pious humility, endeavour to deliver ourselves from temptation.

I am aware of the offence which may be given by these observations; but I will not now begin to cajole, when I have foregone beyond redemption, what might once have been gained by it. Having spoken truth so long, I will persevere to the end; nor, though fully admitting that by a virtuous use of the government we possess, we may become the most happy people upon earth, am I at all disposed to conceal, that by the nefarious policy in fashion, we are in a fair way of rendering ourselves the most miserable. One of its fundamental maxims, and, to all appearance, its most favourite one, is, that Britian must be destroyed. A power which is evidently the world's last hope against the desolating scene of universal slavery.* A country too, which in the language of a native American, who tells us, he had entertained the common prejudices against her, presents "the most beautiful and perfect model of public and private prosperity, the most magnificent and at the same time, most solid fabric of social happiness and national grandeur. And yet all this is to be demolished, because some thirty years ago,† we were engaged with her in a contest, which, so far as independence is implicated, appears now to have been a truly 'unprofitable one.' But God forbid that the long-lived malice of Mr. Jefferson, should be gratified! And the deprecation is equally extended to his successor, should he unhappily harbour the same pitiable rancour. If these gentlemen, during the war, have had their nerves too rudely shocked by the invader, to be able to recover their propriety, or to adhere to the assurance given in

* If there is any thing degrading in this sentiment, we may thank ourselves for affording ground for it. For it is absurd to talk of fighting, where empty treasuries are preferred to full ones, where cowardice has been inculcated both by maxims, and devices, and where the people have been taught to believe, that taxation is oppression.

† It will be recollected that these Memoirs were first printed in the year 1811.—Ed.

the Declaration of Independence, of considering the English as "friends in peace, and only enemies in war," they ought to reflect, that it is not strictly patriotic, to risk the ruin of their country, to obtain revenge. Or, if they are only unluckily committed, through a prodigality of stipulation, for the sake of dear Louisiana—God send them a good deliverance, or at least their country a happy riddance, both of the vender and vendees.

That England has long been, and still is fighting the battle of the civilized world, I hold it to be an incontrovertible truth.* The observation I know to be trite, but I am not a servile follower in the use of it. So long ago as the year 1797, I was the author of the following sentiment in Mr. Fenno's Gazette. "As to Great Britian, with all her errors and vices, and little perhaps as America may owe her, considering the situation in which she has been fortuitously placed by the dreadful convulsions of Europe, so far from wishing her downfall, I consider her preservation as of real importance to mankind; and have long looked upon her as the barrier betwixt the world and anarchy."† The

---

* The reader must still bear in mind the period at which this was written. NAPOLEON, "the Conquerer of Nations," occupied the throne of France, and was waging his yet successful war against the dynasties of "out-worn Europe." England was *not* fighting the "battle of the civilized world;" she was fighting for its *mastery*. During all the early part of that contest down, at least, to the treaty of TILSIT, she was upholding the cause of despotism; and if she afterwards became involved in a struggle for self-preservation, it was owing in no inconsiderable degree to her own ambition. She has carried her encroachments into every quarter of the world; and, magnificent as is her now culminating power, and imposing the reputation and achievements of her statesmen, literati and warriors, the spectacle is marred by the consideration that injustice and outrage have contributed to place her on the lofty eminence which she occupies. Arrogance and oppression have every where marked her course. No barrier that force or genius could overthrow, has been permitted to stand between her interests, real or imaginary, and the rights and liberties of nations. In the East, province after province has been annexed to her possessions, and even the Celestial Empire has lately yielded to her aggressions. In her passion for aggrandizement and dominion, she has reared an empire upon which the sun never sets; and an AMERICAN may be pardoned some complacency in the reflection, that this nation, haughty, rapacious, and powerful as she is, received her first material check from the hands of the Fathers of this Republic.—ED.

† This passage is in an article in the Gazette of the United States of November 10th, 1797, signed "A Country Subscriber," and is the conclusion of a slight sparring with Mr. COBBETT, which gentleman, by the bye, has given a notable in-

sentiment was then in me an original conception, I had never
heard it before, if ever it had been uttered. It has unceasingly
been among my strongest convictions, with the modification,
that she is now our protection from despotism ; and it is therefore natural, that I should be gratified by the very able and
valuable pamphlet which Mr. Walsh has presented to his country.* It is to be wished it may be read as well as the other
writings he is submitting to us, with candour and a proper feeling for the general interest, not merely of this nation, but of
mankind. In contemplating the enormities of the time, it is remarkable, that we can only find matter for illustration, in the
poets who flourished amid the confusions which prevailed in the
decline of the Roman empire. Thus, Mr. Walsh has frequent
recourse to Claudian, whose poem in Rufinum very forcibly de-

---

stance of his candour in his *Selections from Porcupine's Gazette*, publishing
herein my attack and his answer to it, but wholly suppressing this rejoinder.

* "A Letter on the Genius and Dispositions of the French Government,'
published in 1810.

JEFFREY, in his review of MR. WALSH's "*Appeal from the Judgments of Great
Britain respecting the United States of America*," mentions this pamphlet in
cordial terms of praise,—he styles it "a work of great merit, which attracted
much notice, both in Great Britain and America." * * * "The author, in a
strain of great eloquence and powerful reasoning, exhorts his country to make
common cause with England in the great struggle in which she was then engaged with the giant power of BONAPARTE, and points out the many circumstances
in the character and condition of the two countries that invited them to a cordial
alliance." Within two years, however, after the publication of this eloquent
exhortation to an "*alliance*," the overweening insolence, and wanton outrages of
England upon the rights of American citizens, forced the country, all unprepared
as she was, into the MADISONIAN WAR ! That struggle taught our haughty and
hereditary foe, that she could not always expect to be invincible, and the recollection of its early disasters and subsequent triumphs will nerve the American heart
for future trials, if, unhappily, they should become necessary for the preservation
of the national integrity and honour; and for the advancement of the principles
which are identified with the American name. The question concerning OREGON
—prematurely agitated by the party President of the day, may yet, perchance,
afford cause for rupture, leaving still unsettled this absorbing question of the times,
and serving to revive the slumbering animosity which mutual interests have al-
layed but not eradicated. For the honour of human nature, and in deference to
the peaceful spirit and tendencies of the age, it is to be hoped that a resort to barbarous usage in the settlement of this great dispute, may be avoided; but the
pretensions of England are put forth with characteristic disregard of justice ;
and these pretensions it concerns the national honour strenuously to resist.—ED.

picts the dark atrocities of a ferocious and despotic usurpation, which, though acted on an infinitely smaller theatre than that of the present day, had those dismaying appearances which so over-power and confound the mind, as to perplex it, even with doubts of an overruling Providence.*

I have dipped deeper into politics than I intended, or conceived would be necessary at my outset: but without an obvious de-parture from the declarèd design of my work, and a dereliction of the sacred duty which every annalist owes to the world, the sub-ject, however trite and unpleasant, could not be avoided; and much as I dwell upon it, it yet forms but a very imperfect sketch of our public transactions. It has relieved me, however, from a detail of my own personal concerns, which being made up of the common occurrences of still life, chequered as usual with good and with evil, it would be highly arrogant in me to suppose could be in any degree worthy of the public attention. I shall only advert to them, therefore, for the single purpose of mentioning, that my mother, who has acted no inconsiderable part in my nar-rative, finished, under my roof, a long and well spent life, pro-tracted to her seventy-eighth year, on the 23d of January, 1807. Her excellent constitution sunk under the *republican* havoc on her family: her first symptom of decay followed close upon it; and she fell a martyr, in all probability, to the ever memorable triumph of what has been impiously called, The triumph of good princi-ples. Perhaps, however, she had lived long enough.

Of the part I have acted in this turbulent scene, the reader is truly informed. Whether it was wise or unwise, I will take upon me to say, it was conscientious and disinterested. Yet it certainly makes but a very sorry figure at an era so distinguished for rapid acquisitions of fortune and dignity. To have commanded a com-pany in the Continental army at the age of three and twenty, and not to have advanced an inch in the glorious career of personal aggrandizement, makes good, I think, my promise of negative instruction; and I must be as very a wretch in the eyes of the

---

* Thus expressed in the opening of the poem;

> Sæpe mihi dubiam traxit sententia mentem
> Curarent Superi terras, an nullus inesset
> Rector, et incerto fluerent mortalia casu.

aspiring, as was the unambitious Richard Cromwell in those of the Prince of Conti—Why even the imperial Napoleon himself had scarcely a fairer prospect, when making his *debut* as an artillerist before the walls of Toulon.

Then, " what a rogue and pleasant slave am I !"

Nevertheless, with respect to the glory acquired by what may be termed *civic accomplishments*, I have some ragged pride in making it known, that my insignificance, is not so much owing to an absolute ignorance of the game, as to a want of the nerve that is necessary for playing it to advantage. Though unambitious of *philosophic* fame, I have no desire to pass for a simpleton; and therefore wish it to be understood, that I am not to learn, that this revolution business and republicanism, with whatever purity begun, has nearly issued in a scramble, in which all morality and even decency being thrown aside, he is the cleverest fellow, that, by trick or violence can emerge the fullest handed. I regret that I am obliged to say so. I would much rather be the encomiast than the satirist of my country, which I have no doubt contains so ample a portion of manly sentiment, as, under better auspices, to entitle it to a lofty strain of panegyric.

But it will be said I am a party-man; and as all party-men are prejudiced, these censures must go for nothing. I am indeed a party-man, as I conceive there is a right and wrong in politics as in other things: I freely admit it too that I am prejudiced, to a great degree; but all my prejudices, I trust, are in favour of honesty and fair dealing, and where these appear, no one has more toleration for error. This is an indulgence I may have need of myself; but I reflect with satisfaction, that among my faults, I have no act of deceit, injustice or oppression, (for I have sometimes had a little power) to reproach myself with; and this I say without fear of contradiction. I have some reliance too that those who know me, even of the opposite political party, will give me credit for general good intention, and openness of character; and this granted, I ask no quarter for my sentiments. If they are erroneous and unfounded, let them be scouted and exposed; I shall be among the first to condemn them if persuaded of their falsity.

And I here recognise with suitable feelings, the liberal and unsought patronage to this undertaking, from many of my neighbours and townsmen, with whose political conduct and opinions, mine have generally been in collision. If I have been less accommodating to their sentiments, than I could have wished, they will read my apology in the tenor of my performance, which does not merely purport to speak with plainness, but manifests, I presume, that it has done so in reality, without respect to parties or to persons. I have occasionally, I am sensible, expressed myself with some asperity; with more, perhaps, than may be thought congenial to the nature of my work; but this must be attributed to my awful impression of the dangers which surround us, and a solemn apprehension, that all the advantages of our situation are about to be sacrificed to a profligate rage for place and party supremacy.

CONCLUSION.

THUS, uncalled for, have I ventured upon a pretty full account, both of my life, and my opinions.   Of the value of either, it is not for me to judge ; but as it was my lot to enter upon manhood just at the commencement of the Revolution, and to be a witness of its progress, its consummation, and its consequences, it appeared to me, that the period, if justly delineated, could not be altogether destitute of instruction : I have endeavoured to depict it truly ; and, I trust, I have done so, in regard at least to the phases presented to my vision.   The facts I have related, I have either witnessed myself, or received on such authority, as leaves with me little doubt of their correctness ; and my inferences, though sometimes harsh, are always the result of the most deliberate and candid reflection : Whatever therefore, may be the errors of my book, they are not those of wilful misrepresentation.

———

Ample* matter has occurred, since the publication of these MEMOIRS, not only to justify the free remarks therein made on the conduct and character of our democratic leaders, but to war· rant shafts of moral indignation against their subsequent acts, keen as were ever hurled from the pen of a Juvenal.   But, politics are at no time a pleasant topic, and their discussion must necessarily embrace newspaper common-places a hundred

* The observations that follow were found in the handwriting of the author upon the last page of his private copy of the " MEMOIRS."   It is proper that they should be added here, as they are explanatory of his motives, and, were no doubt, intended for the position in which they are now placed.—ED.

times repeated. For these reasons, and the additional one, that the registry of recent facts, is not the object of the writer, he spares himself the disagreeable task of tracing the undignified, pettifogging, mischievous course of the Madisonian policy. He cannot but felicitate himself, however, upon his good fortune in meeting with the letters of General WASHINGTON* serving as they do, to confirm many of his statements which were received with more than distrust,† perhaps, and thought to proceed either from a misanthropic temper, too hasty observation, or speculative notions of human virtue, graduated on too high a scale, and thence engendering a disposition to censure unnecessarily. As to his political opinions and remarks, he will only say in anticipation of comments, which may probably be made, that however shocking they may be to many honest, well-meaning, republicans, and however they may tinge with diabolical gall, the pancreatic juices of that other description of patriots, which no term can aptly designate but that of Jacobins, he feels pride no less than confidence in avowing them. Whatever may be their reception at the present day, he has not the smallest doubt of their entire orthodoxy in time to come, when the general interests of mankind, not those of a party, when history, not faction, shall decide.

"With respect to the freedom taken with private characters, it was at one time my intention, from knowing it to be the desire of some of my best friends, to expunge such passages as might, in any degree, give pain to the descendants or connexions of the persons mentioned. But, on reflecting that each of these friends would be as tenacious in retaining some, as in suppressing others of the passages; that by suppressing them all, I should reduce the work to a miserable piece of baldness and stupidity, and that by diminishing, I should, in regard to those who were suffered to remain, evince a premeditation that would afford new cause of offence,—that, moreover, as I have not presumed to meddle with what constitutes the real value of character, but, have merely glanced, at singularities and deficiencies of the

---

* Since included in the Writings of WASHINGTON, edited by Mr. SPARKS.—ED.
† In 1811, upon the first publication of the MEMOIRS.—ED.

lighter kind, neither inconsistent with uprightness nor benevolence, and that in these respects, I have made as free with my
own family as that of others, I have, at length, come to the
conclusion, that it will be best and most discreet, to abide by
my first indiscretion.

"It is unnecessary to pursue the topic; but a curious discussion of it may be found in a discourse of M. Boileau prefixed
to his satires, in which he undertakes to justify his own freedom
by the examples of the ancients, particularly of Horace and of
Persius; from whom, to be sure, he gives instances, that would,
by no means, comport with the correctness of modern manners.
It would appear, however, that somewhat of this questionable
license is essential to the relish of that description of composition, termed MEMOIRS. ' To entertain readers,' says Dr. Zimmerman, 'is, in my opinion, only to deliver freely in writing,
that which in the general intercourse of society, it is impossible
to say either with safety or politeness.' May it not be this,
which renders so agreeable, the apparently unimportant garru-
lity of Montaigne? Upon the whole, if he has sometimes been
querulous, it has been through the fear of trusting himself to the
vehemence of his feelings, which is apt to hurry him beyond
bounds, when he sees turpitude triumphant. He is not formed
for a miserable, passive, victim of injustice, however gilded by
high authority; and no man, however exalted his station, has yet
presumed, or ever shall presume, to treat him as such, without
feeling his resistance, and the keenest shafts of his resentment."

APPENDIX.

APPENDIX.

A.

PAGE 23.—Note.

ALEXANDER GRAYDON, ESQ.

The following is copied from papers filed in the office of the Secretary of the Commonwealth of Pennsylvania:

ALEXANDER GRAYDON RECOMMENDED TO BE A FIELD-OFFICER ON A LIST OF RECOMMENDATIONS.

ALEXANDER GRAYDON TO RICHARD PETERS.

April 30th, 1758.

DEAR SIR—

I yesterday received a letter from Richard Walker, Esq.* dated, the 27th inst. in which he informs me, that he has been prevailed on to enter his name in the list of officers, to command the new corps for this province, and that he has ventured to set my name down also, conjuring me at the same time, in a very friendly and affectionate manner, not to decline the service at this time. He farther desires I would communicate my answer to you without delay.

I have a very great esteem for Mr. Walker, and believe he will make an excellent officer. I am sure, that he will act upon principles that few soldiers do. I sincerely wish I could accompany him. I have employed the few hours between the receipt of his letter, and my present writing, in balancing the matter within my breast, and considering the position in which I find myself as to my affairs here, and the occasion so pressing,

---

* This Mr. Walker is marked on the list as having been recommended by Mr. Allen and Mr. Growdon.

it would be impossible to put my affairs in order, to accept such an employment. I have come, therefore, to the result, not to stand in the way of better men.

I was surprised never to have had the least intimation, from any of my friends, before Mr. Walker's letter, of there being any thoughts entertained of me. I have never been able to learn what officers are intended to be made; into what order the troops are to be disposed; or in short, any measures about this whole matter. Perhaps there was reason for keeping all secret. But I am of opinion, that had all the measures relative to raising these troops, been properly planned and published, as in some of our neighbouring provinces has been the case, the service would have been greatly forwarded. But I write to you as a friend, not a secretary. In short, there is little encouragement for any to enter into the service of this province, unless they can support themselves with the reflection, that virtue is its own reward.

I am, dear sir,

your affectionate friend, and

humble servant

ALEXANDER GRAYDON.

B.

PAGE 42.

DR. LAUCHLAN MACLEANE,

A name, which, from its subsequent association with the question of the authorship of JUNIUS, has acquired considerable posthumous, celebrity. PRIOR, in his excellent Life of GOLDSMITH, published in 1837, thus writes in reference to Dr. Macleane:

"A fellow student named Kennedy, under the plea of great distress and a pledge of the speedy arrival of his own remittances, persuaded Goldsmith to become answerable for a portion of his debts, which, however, failed to be discharged at the

specified time promised by the debtor. Goldsmith was, in consequence, called upon for payment, but being unable to raise
the amount, was, in turn, obliged to have recourse to the assistance of two fellow-students to escape a dilemma that threatened
his personal liberty. These were men of considerable attainments, and not undistinguished in their respective spheres of life.
One was Dr. Joseph Fenn Sleigh, an amiable and intelligent
Quaker, the school-fellow of Burke, at Ballitoro, the first friend of
Barry the painter, and who died prematurely in 1771, an eminent
physician in Cork. The other was Dr. Lauchlan Macleane, a
former associate in Trinity College, whose career seems to have
embraced many changes of scene, and who afterwards by the
public situations he held, the pamphlets he wrote, a challenge
sent to Wilkes and not accepted, and the party with which he
was connected, drew considerable notice in the political circles
of London between the years 1765 and 1776.

" The son of a gentleman of small fortune in the North of Ireland, and born about the year 1728, he was transferred, at the
age of eighteen, from a school near Belfast, to Trinity College,
Dublin. Here he became known to Burke and Goldsmith, and
proceeding to Edinburgh to study physic, his name appears in
the list of the Medical Society, January 4th, 1754, a year after
that of Goldsmith, by whom he was introduced. He afterwards
visited America—whether at first as a private practitioner, or
medical officer in the army, does not appear; probably, as was
then not unusual, officiating in both capacities. While in this
country he acquired great medical reputation; followed by its
common attendant, envy, from the less fortunate of his brethren;
and an anecdote is told of him at this time, which Almon quotes
in one of his publications, as an instance of what he terms ' true
magnanimity.' A rival practitioner, extremely jealous of his
success, and who had adopted every means, not excepting the
most unfair, of injuring his credit, was, at length, afflicted by the
dangerous illness of an only son; and as possessing the first character for professional skill, Dr. Macleane was solicited to attend.
His zeal proved unremitting; he sat up with the patient many
nights, and chiefly by his sagacity and indefatigable efforts succeeded beyond expectation in restoring the young man to health;

refusing all consideration for his labours, and saying to his friends, ' Now am I amply revenged.'

" In 1761, while surgeon of Otway's regiment, quartered at Philadelphia, a quarrel took place with the Governor, against whom Macleane, who was a man of superior talents, wrote a paper distinguished for ability and severity, which drew general attention. Colonel Barré, subsequently so well known in political life, then serving there with his regiment and who was probably involved in the quarrel, is said to have formed a regard for him in consequence of the part he took; but it is more likely that a previous acquaintance existed, as the Colonel had been likewise a member of Trinity College. Under the patronage of this officer he returned to England, renewed his acquaintance with Burke, and procured an office under government. While travelling on the continent, in 1766, he proved useful to Barry, then on his way to Italy, who became known to him through the introduction of his first patrons, Burke and Dr. Sleigh. Soon afterwards he became successively private Secretary to Lord Shelburne, and under Secretary of State for the Southern Department, retiring from office with his patron on the dissolution of the ministry drawn together by the Duke of Grafton. In May, 1771, Lord North gave him the situation of superintendent of lazarettos, with, as the newspapers of the day state, 'a salary of £1000 a year, and—two pounds per diem travelling expenses.' In January following, he received the collectorship of Philadelphia; this was soon exchanged for an appointment in India, where he subsequently became a kind of agent to Mr. Hastings. In that capacity he brought home the Governor General's conditional resignation of office; yet the latter, with that singularity which often influenced his proceedings in the government of India, took a speedy opportunity of disavowing both his agent and his act, although communicated to the Court of Directors in his own handwriting. In proceeding again to India, intending, it is said, to take strong measures for an explanation of behaviour that seemed to throw censure upon his honesty or honour, the ship, in which he embarked, foundered, and all on board perished, with papers seriously criminatory, according to report, of the administration of Mr. Hastings. Dr. Macleane enjoyed the credit of being quick, clear-headed, and well informed ; and by some was considered as possessing ' wonderful powers ;' an impediment in speech precluded him from being useful in Parliament, or shining in conversation. His private character for benevolence and several good qualities stood high in the opinion of his friends."

His claim to the credit of the authorship of JUNIUS is not treated with much respect by Mr. Prior, who proves, to his own satisfaction at least, that they have no real foundation; but his reasoning is far from conclusive. It is difficult, in this age of free and bold discussion, to appreciate either the depth of the excitement caused by the publication of these celebrated " Letters," 'or the danger to which discovery would have exposed their author, who was seldom free from apprehension. Every artifice, therefore, that would serve to divert attention from their real author would, naturally, be adopted by him, and the simple expedient of including himself in a general censure, or even the employment of the language of praise—would have been perfectly justifiable in view of the peculiar circumstances under which he wrote. Recent alleged discoveries have again connected Dr. Macleane's name with the authorship of Junius—a secret too long and mysteriously kept to admit a hope of its revelation.—ED.

C.

PAGE 75.

WARREN.

BATTLE OF BUNKER'S HILL.

The author, in a MS. note, says, " Hand it should be. I wrote from recollection not having the print before me. He has a sword, indeed, in one hand, but not in that employed in the humane act. But, if General Heath is correct, the whole per-

36

haps, is but a fiction of the painter. Heath says that Warren was killed merely as a spectator, at some distance from the combatants."

The scene, as represented by the picture of Trumbull, is undoubtedly a poetical license. No such occurrence as is there described really occurred. Neither is Heath correct in his statement of the circumstances of Warren's death. General Henry Lee, in his Memoirs, has also fallen into several errors in regard to the same event, although with a nearer approximation to truth than Heath or several others who have written upon the subject. He gives, it is true, just credit to the gallant Prescott. He says, " Warren who fell nobly supporting the action, was the favourite of the day, and has engrossed the fame due to Prescott. Bunker's Hill too has been considered as the field of battle, when it is well known that it was fought upon Breed's Hill, the nearest of the two hills to Boston." " No man," he continues, "reveres the character of Warren more than the writer; and he considers himself not only doing justice to Colonel Prescott, but performing an acceptable service to the memory of Warren, who, being a really great man, would disdain to wear laurels not his own."

The editor of this volume is fortunate in having in his possession, authentic and interesting *data* in relation to the " Battle of Bunker's Hill," and though the information may, by some, be deemed misplaced here, he will, nevertheless, risk the censure of the critics. The text affords an opportunity for its introduction—and TRUTH, wherever she may alight, should be welcomed and cherished.

To a MS. of his friend, the late estimable and Reverend Edward G. Prescott, a grandson of Colonel Prescott of Pepperell, Massachusetts, commander of the American forces, on the occasion of the memorable battle, the editor is indebted for the following particulars which he has abridged to the limits prescribed to a note, the interesting facts set forth rendering an apology for its length unnecessary.

On the 16th of June, 1775, Colonel William Prescott, of Pepperell, at his own especial request, received orders to march to Charlestown in the evening, having under his command his own regiment, that of Colonels Bridge and Frye, and one hundred and twenty men from the Connecticut regiment, together with Captain Gridley's company of artillery, and two field pieces. The object of this expedition which was to possess and fortify Bunker's Hill, was to be kept profoundly secret—one day's provision was distributed among the troops, and sufficient supplies, both of refreshments and men, were promised him, to be sent in the morning. The whole number of men under his command, amounted to about one thousand. Early on the evening of the memorable 16th of June, these few forces under the command of Prescott, assembled on the common at Cambridge, where a blessing upon their expedition was devoutly asked by the Reverend President Langdon, of Harvard College. At the conclusion of these services, Colonel Prescott led the way towards Charlestown neck, preceded by two sergeants having dark lanterns open only at the rear. He was accompanied by Colonel Gridley, the Chief Engineer, who was to lay out the ground—by the late Governor Brooks, who was, at that time, a Major in Bridge's regiment, and by Mr. Winthrop. Upon their arrival, great doubt arose as to which part of the heights it was expedient to fortify. It has often been asserted that Breed's Hill was selected through mistake—such was not the case. Both that and Bunker's Hill form a continuous chain, but, at that time, the name of *Bunker* was the *only one given to any part of the height.* The remainder of it might, therefore, properly enough, have been considered as included in the orders under that general title. At all events, according to the statements of Colonel Prescott, and of Governor Brooks, a council was called of the officers, and the subject discussed until very late in the night.

It was by them determined, that the hill *now* known as *Breed's,* but *then having no separate name,* was the most suitable for the purpose, and came within the orders given to Colonel Prescott. The reasons for this opinion, were sufficiently evident. Bunker's *height* was too far from the enemy to annoy their shipping, or to give our forces any advantage over their army, while the point selected, was admirably adapted for both purposes. Colonel Prescott, accompanied by Major Brooks twice went down to the sea shore to reconnoitre. They could not believe that they were at the very gates of the enemy's stronghold, and had not been perceived. It was, however, so. God had darkened their eyes, and they heard the British sentry on his rounds, uttering the deceitful hail, " all's well!" Morning, however, drew near. The English man of war, called the *Lively*, first discovered our little band, and opened upon them volley after volley. The enemy were taken by surprise. High above them, they saw our fortifications, commanding them in all their positions, and could scarcely credit their own senses, that so daring an exploit had been undertaken. General Gage summoned his officers to a council of war. All was commotion. The frigates, floating batteries,—the cannon and mortars on Copp's hill, were each aiming at our gallant countrymen—still they toiled on. There was but one moment of doubt, during the time they occupied that proud position. This was when the first man was killed. A private of the name of POLLARD from Billerica was the *first* martyr; he had ventured in front of the works, and was struck down by a cannon-shot. Our countrymen, unused to the sight of violent deaths, then hesitated. Colonel Prescott ordered his burial at once. The men, headed by the chaplain, demanded that prayers should be said over him. They were ordered by the Colonel to disperse to their work, and to bury him immediately—it was done, but some of the men left the hill, and did not again return to it. This circumstance depressed them at a time when all their energies were most needed. Their commander perceiving it, mounted the breast-works, and continued there in defiance of the shot of the enemy, giving the necessary directions, until again their usual spirits had returned to them.

Meanwhile the British were not idle. Gage, with his officers and others in whom he had confidence, went up to Beacon Hill to reconnoitre; after having looked through his telescope for some time, he handed it to a Mr. Willard, a mandamus counsellor, and describing the leader of the American troops as head and shoulders above the works, asked him who it was, and if the rebels would fight. Willard told him, that it was his brother-in-law, PRESCOTT; " as to his men," said he, " I cannot answer for them ; *but Colonel Prescott will fight you to the gates of Hell!*" The regiments were intrusted to Colonel Prescott, and the orders were transmitted to him alone. Upon him rested the responsibility; and that he had the chief command, was acknowledged on the field by General Warren, the President of the Provincial Congress of Massachusetts; who took a gun and cartouch box, and told him that he had " come to learn service under a soldier of experience." Alas! that the lesson should have been so short! Gallant, eloquent, patriotic Warren stepped but on the field of battle, to be gathered into the harvest of Death! Not obliged to be in the way of danger, he volunteered for the good of his country—and that country will never cease to repay him by a cherished recollection of his virtues, and an honest pride at the mention of his name!—ED.

D.

PAGE 77.

JOHN HANCOCK.

A few years later than the period referred to by our author, Hancock is thus described by SULLIVAN, in his interesting and instructive " Familiar Letters on Public Characters:"

" He will be considered in the history of our country, as one of the greatest men of his age. How true this may be, distant generations are not likely to know. He was the son of a clergyman in Braintree, and was educated at Harvard College, and inherited a very ample fortune from his childless uncle. Hancock left no child. He had a son who died at an early age from an unfortunate accident. Hancock was sent as a delegate to Congress in 1774; and in consequence of his personal deportment, and his fame as a patriot, he was elevated, in an assembly of eminent men, to the dignity of President, which office he held when the Declaration of Independence was signed, at which time he was only thirty-nine years of age.

" In June, 1782, Hancock had the appearance of advanced age, though only forty-five. He had been repeatedly and se-

verely afflicted with the gout, a disease much more common in
those days than it now is, while dyspepsia, if it existed at all,
was not known by that name. As recollected, at this time,
Mr. Hancock was nearly six feet in stature, and of slender
person, stooping a little, and apparently enfeebled by disease.
His manners were very gracious, of the old style of dignified
complaisance. His face had been very handsome. Dress was
adapted quite as much to be ornamental as useful. Gentlemen
wore wigs when abroad, and, commonly, caps, when at home.
At this time, (June, 1782,) about noon, Hancock was dressed in
a red velvet cap, within which was one of fine linen. The
latter was turned up over the lower edge of the velvet one,
two or three inches. He wore a blue damask gown, lined
with silk; a white stock, a white satin embroidered waistcoat,
black satin small-clothes, white silk stockings, and red morocco
slippers. It was a general practice in genteel families, to have
a tankard of punch made in the morning, and placed in a
cooler when the season required it. Visiters were invited to
partake of it. At this visit, Hancock took from the cooler,
standing on the hearth, a full tankard, and drank first himself,
and then offered it to those present. Hancock was hospitable.
There might have been seen at his table, all classes, from grave
and dignified clergymen, down to the gifted in song, narration,
anecdote, and wit, with whom 'noiseless falls the foot of Time,
that only treads on flowers.' There are more books, more
reading, more thinking, and more interchange of thoughts derived from books and conversation at present, than there were
fifty years ago. It is to be hoped that society is wiser and
happier than it was, from being better instructed. Some persons may be of opinion, that if social intercourse is on a better
footing now, than formerly, it is less interesting, less cordial
than heretofore. It is not improbable that increase of numbers
and of wealth, tend to make the members of society more selfish; and to stifle expansive and generous feelings. Modes of
life run into matters of show and ornament; and it becomes a
serious occupation, to be able to compare condition on advantageous terms.

"Though Hancock was very wealthy, he was too much oc-

cupied with public affairs to be advantageously attentive to his
private. The times in which he lived, and the distinguished
agency which fell to his lot, from his sincere and ardent devotion
to the patriot cause, engendered a strong self-regard. He was
said to be somewhat sensitive, easily offended, and very uneasy
in the absence of the high consideration which he claimed, rather
as a right, than a courtesy. He had strong personal friends,
and equally strong personal enemies. From such causes arose
some irritating difficulties. He had not only a commanding
deportment, which he could qualify with a most attractive
amenity, but a fine voice, and a highly graceful manner. These
were traits which distinguished him from most men, and qualified him to preside in popular assemblies, with great dignity.
He was not supposed to be a man of great intellectual force
by nature ; and his early engagements in political life, and as the
scenes in which he was conversant, called for the exercise of
his powers only in the public service, he was so placed as not
to have had occasion to display the force of his mind, in that
service, so as to enable those of the present day to judge of it,
excepting in his communications, as Governor of Massachusetts,
to the Legislature.

" If history has any proper concern with the individual
qualities of Hancock, it may be doubtful whether, in these respects, distant generations will know exactly what manner of
man he was. But, as a public man, his country is greatly indebted to him. He was most faithfully devoted to her cause, and
it is a high eulogy on his patriotism, that when the British
Government offered pardon to all the rebels, for all their
offences, Hancock and Samuel Adams were the only persons
to whom this grace was denied."—Ed.

E.

PAGE 99.

REVEREND JACOB DUCHÉ.

Extract from a letter from General Washington to the President of Congress, dated 16th October, 1777 :—

"I yesterday, through the hands of Mrs. Ferguson, of Graham Park, received a letter of a very curious and extraordinary nature from Mr. Duché, which I have thought proper to transmit to Congress. To this ridiculous, illiberal performance, I made a short reply, by desiring the bearer of it, if she should, hereafter, by any accident, meet with Mr. Duché, to tell him I should have returned it unopened, if I had had any idea of the contents; observing at the same time, that I highly disapproved the intercourse she seemed to have been carrying on, and expected it would be discontinued. Notwithstanding the author's assertion, I cannot but suspect that the measure did not originate with him; and that he was induced to it by the hope of establishing his interest and peace more effectually with the enemy."

" Mr. Duche had married a sister of Mr. Francis Hopkinson, one of the signers of the Declaration of Independence, who, when Duché's letter was written, was at Bordentown, as a member of the Continental Navy Board. A copy was forwarded to Mr. Hopkinson, and he wrote a letter to Mr. Duché on the subject, which he enclosed to General Washington, that it might be transmitted to him in Philadelphia through the regular conveyance of a flag."*

* Sparks' Life and Writings of Washington.—Ed.

The Editor of these Memoirs is indebted to a friend for a MS. copy of the celebrated letter of the Reverend Mr. Duché to General Washington, with corrections to conform to the copy revised and published by Mr. Duché himself, in the Pennsylvania Ledger of the 17th December, 1777. It is as follows:

MR. DUCHÉ TO GENERAL WASHINGTON.

"Philadelphia, October 8, 1777.

" SIR,

" If this letter should find you in council or in the field, before you read another sentence, I beg you to take the first opportunity of retiring, and weighing well its important contents.

" You are perfectly acquainted with the part I have taken in the present unhappy contest. I was indeed among the first to bear my public testimony against having any recourse to threats, or even indulging a thought of an armed opposition. The torrent soon became too strong for my feeble efforts to resist. I wished to follow my countrymen, as far only, as virtue and the righteousness of their cause would permit me. I was, however, prevailed upon, among the rest of my clerical brethren, to gratify the pressing desire of my fellow-citizens, by preaching a sermon to one of the city battalions. I was pressed to publish this sermon, and reluctantly consented. From a personal attachment of near twenty years' standing, and a high respect for your character, in private as well as in public life, I took the liberty of dedicating it to you. I had your affectionate thanks for my performance, in a letter wherein you express, in the most delicate and obliging terms, your regard for me, and your wishes of a continuance of my friendship and approbation of your conduct.

" Farther than this I intended not to proceed. My sermon speaks for itself, and utterly disclaims the idea of independency. My sentiments were well known to my friends. I communicated them without reserve, to many respectable members of Congress, who expressed a warm approbation of them. I persisted to the very last moment in using the Prayers for my Sovereign and Royal Family, though threatened with insult from the violence of a party.

"Upon the Declaration of Independency I called my vestry and solemnly put the question to them, whether they thought it best, for the peace and welfare of the congregations, to shut up the churches, or to continue the service without using the prayers for the royal family. This was the sad alternative. I concluded to abide by their decision, as I could not have time to consult my spiritual superiors in England. They determined it most expedient, under such critical circumstances, to keep open the churches, that the congregations might not be dispersed, which we had great reason to apprehend.

"A very few days after the fatal Declaration of Independence, I received a letter from Mr. Hancock, sent by express to Germantown, where my family were for the summer season, acquainting me that I was appointed Chaplain to the Congress, and desired to attend them at nine o'clock the next morning. Surprised and distressed by an event I was not prepared to expect—obliged to give an immediate answer, without the opportunity of consulting my friends, I rashly accepted the appointment. I could have but one motive for taking this step. I thought the churches in danger, and hoped by these means to have been instrumental in preventing those ills I had so much reason to apprehend. I can, however, with truth declare, that I then looked upon independency rather as an expedient, and a hazardous one indeed, thrown out in terrorem, in order to procure some favourable terms, than a measure that was to be seriously persisted in at all events. My sudden change of conduct will clearly evince this to have been my idea of the matter.

"Upon the return of the Committee of Congress, appointed to confer with Lord Howe, I soon discovered their real intentions. The different accounts which each member of the committee gave of this conference, the time they took to make up the matter for public view, and the amazing disagreement betwixt the newspaper accounts and the relation I myself had from the mouth of one of the committee, convinced me that there must have been some unfair and ungenerous procedure. Their determination to treat on no other ground than that of independency, which put it out of his lordship's power to mention any terms at all, was a sufficient proof to me that independency was the idol they had long wished to set up, and that rather than sacrifice this, they would deluge this country in blood.

"From this moment I determined upon my resignation, and in the beginning of October, 1776, sent it in form to Mr. Hancock, after having officiated only two months and three weeks; and from that time, as far as my safety would permit, I have been opposed to all their measures. This circumstantial account of my conduct, I think due to the friendship you were so obliging as to express for me, and I hope will be sufficient to justify any seeming inconsistencies in the part I have acted.

"And now, dear Sir, suffer me in the language of truth and real affection to address myself to you. All the world must be convinced that you are engaged in the service of your country from motives perfectly disinterested. You risked every thing that was dear to you. You abandoned all those sweets of domestic life of which your affluent fortune gave you the uninterrupted enjoyment. But had you? could you have had the least idea of matters being carried to such a dangerous extremity as they are now? Your most intimate friends at that time shuddered at the thoughts of a separation from the mother country; and I took it for granted that your sentiments coincided with theirs. What have been the consequences of this rash and violent measure? A degeneracy of representation—confusion of counsels—blunders without number. The most respectable characters have withdrawn themselves, and are succeeded by a great majority of illiberal and violent men.

"Take an impartial view of the present Congress, and what can you expect from them? Your feelings must be greatly hurt by the representation from your native province. You have no longer a Randolph, a Bland, or a Braxton; men whose names will ever be revered, whose demands never arose above the first ground on which they set out, and whose truly generous and virtuous sentiments I have frequently heard with rapture from their own lips. O my dear Sir, what a sad contrast! Characters now present themselves whose minds can never mingle with your own. Your Harrison alone remains, and he disgusted with his unworthy associates. As to those of my own province, some of them are so obscure that their very names never met my ears before, and others have only been distinguished for the weakness of their understandings and the violence of their tempers. One alone I except from the general charge. A man of virtue dragged reluctantly into their measures, and restrained by some false ideas of honour from retracting, after having gone too far. You cannot be at a loss to discover whose name answers to this character.

"From the New England Provinces can you find one that as a gentleman you could wish to associate with? unless the soft and mild address of Mr. Hancock can atone for his want of every other qualification necessary for the station he fills. Bankrupts, attorneys, and men of desperate fortunes are his colleagues.

"Maryland no longer sends a Tilghman and a Protestant Carroll. Carolina has lost its Lynch, and the elder Middleton has retired.

" Are the dregs of a Congress then still to influence a mind like yours? These are not the men you engaged to serve. These are not the men that America has chosen to represent her now. Most of them were elected by a little low faction, and the few gentlemen that are among them, now well known to be upon the balance, and looking up to your hand alone to move the beam. 'Tis you, Sir, and you alone that supports the present Congress. Of this you must be fully sensible. Long before they left Philadelphia, their dignity and consequence was gone. What must it be now, since their precipitate retreat? I write with freedom, but without invective. I know these things to be true. I write to one whose own observation must have convinced him that they are so.

" After this view of Congress, turn to your army. The whole world knows that its very existence depends upon you, that your death or captivity disperses it in a moment, and that there is not a man on that side of the question in America, capable of succeeding you. As to the army itself, what have you to expect from them? Have they not frequently abandoned even yourself in the hour of extremity? Have you, can you have, the least confidence in a set of undisciplined men and officers, many of whom have been taken from the lowest of the people, without principle and without courage. Take away those that surround your person, how few are there that you can ask to sit at your table?

"Turn to your little navy—of *that little,* what is *left?* Of the Delaware fleet, part are taken, the rest must soon surrender. Of those in the other Provinces, some taken, one or two at sea, and others lying unmanned and unrigged in their harbours.

"And now where are your resources? O, my dear Sir! how sadly have you been abused by a faction void of truth and void of tenderness to you and your country! They have amused you with hopes of a declaration of war on the part of France. Believe me from the best authority, it was a fiction from the first. Early in the year 1776, a French gentleman was introduced to me, with whom I became intimately acquainted. His business, to all appearance, was to speculate in the mercantile way. But I believe it will be known that in his own country he moved in a higher sphere. He saw your camp. He became acquainted with all your military preparations. He was introduced to Congress, and engaged with them in a mercantile contract. In the course of our intimacy he has frequently told me he hoped the Americans never would think of independency. He gave me his reasons: 'Independency,' said he, 'can never be supported unless France should declare war against England. I well know the state of her finances; years to come will not put them in a situation to venture upon a breach with England. At this moment there are two parties in the Court of Versailles, one enlisted under the Duc de Choiseul, the other under Count Maurepas. Choiseul has no chance of succeeding. He is violent for war. Maurepas must get the better. He is for economy and peace.' This was his information which I mentioned to several members of Congress. They treated it as a fable, depending entirely on Dr. FRANKLIN's intelligence. The truth of the matter is this: Dr. Franklin built upon the success of Choiseul. Upon his arrival in France, he found him out of place, his counsels reprobated, and his party dwindled to an insignificant faction. This you may depend upon to be the

37

true state of the Court of France. And further, by vast numbers of letters found on board prizes taken by the King's ships, it appears that all commerce with the merchants of France, through whom alone your supplies have been conveyed, will soon be at an end, the letters being full of complaints of no remittances from America, and many individuals having greatly suffered.

" From your friends in England, you have nothing to expect. Their numbers are diminished to a cipher. The spirit of the whole nation is in full activity against you. A few sounding names among the nobility, though perpetually rung in your ears, are said to be without character, without influence. Disappointed ambition, I am told, has made them desperate, and they only wish to make the deluded Americans instruments of their revenge. All orders and ranks of men in Great Britain, are now unanimous, and determined to risk their all on the contest. Trade and manufactures are found to flourish; and new channels are continually opening, that will, perhaps, more than supply the old. In a word, your harbours are blocked up, your cities fall one after another, fortress after fortress, battle after battle is lost. A British army, after having passed almost unmolested through a vast extent of country, have possessed themselves with ease of the Capital of America. How unequal the contest now! How fruitless the expense of blood!

"Under so many discouraging circumstances, can virtue, can honour, can the love of your country prompt you to persevere. Humanity itself (and sure I am humanity is no stranger to your breast) calls upon you to desist. Your army must perish for want of common necessaries, or thousands of innocent families must perish to support them. Wherever they encamp the country must be impoverished. Wherever they march the troops of Britain will pursue, and must complete the devastation which America herself has begun.

"Perhaps it may be said that ' it is better to die than to be slaves.' This, indeed, is a splendid maxim in theory; and, perhaps, in some instances, may be found experimentally true. But where there is the least probability of an happy accommodation, surely wisdom and humanity call for some sacrifices to

be made to prevent inevitable destruction. You well know
that there is but one invincible bar to such an accommodation;
could this be removed other obstacles might readily be overcome. 'Tis to you, and you alone, your bleeding country
looks, and calls aloud for this sacrifice. Your arm alone has
strength sufficient to remove this bar. May Heaven inspire
you with the glorious resolution of exerting this strength at so
interesting a crisis, and thus immortalizing yourself as friend
and guardian of your country.

" Your penetrating eye needs not more explicit language to
discern my meaning. With that prudence and delicacy, therefore, of which I know you to be possessed, represent to Congress the indispensable necessity of rescinding the hasty and
ill-advised Declaration of Independency. Recommend, and
you have an undoubted right to recommend, an immediate
cessation of hostilities. Let the controversy be taken up where
that Declaration left it, and where Lord Howe certainly expected to find it. Let men of clear and impartial characters,
in or out of Congress, liberal in their sentiments, heretofore
independent in their fortunes (and some such may surely be
found in America), be appointed to confer with His Majesty's
Commissioners. Let them, if they please, prepare some well-
digested constitutional plan, to lay before them as the commencement of a negotiation. When they have gone thus far,
I am confident that the most happy consequences will ensue.
Unanimity will immediately take place through the different
Provinces. Thousands who are now ardently wishing and
praying for such a measure, will step forth and declare themselves the zealous advocates of constitutional liberty, and millions will bless the Hero that left the field of war to decide this
most important contest with the weapons of wisdom and
humanity.

"O! Sir, let no false ideas of worldly honour deter you from
engaging in so glorious a task. Whatever censures may be
thrown out by mean and illiberal minds, your character will
rise in the estimation of the virtuous and noble; it will appear
with lustre in the annals of History, and form a glorious contrast to that of those who have sought to obtain conquests and

gratify their own ambition by the destruction of their species and the ruin of their country.

" Be assured, Sir, that I write not this under the eye of any British officer, or person connected with the British army or ministry. The sentiments I express are the real sentiments of my own heart; such as I have long held, and which I should have made known to you by letter before, had I not fully expected an opportunity of a private conference. When you passed through Philadelphia on your way to Wilmington, I was confined by a severe fit of the gravel to my chamber. I have since continued so much indisposed, and times have been so very distressing, that I had neither spirit to write a letter, nor opportunity to convey it when written. Nor do I yet know by what means I shall get these sheets to your hand.

" I would fain hope that I have said nothing by which your delicacy can be in the least hurt. If I have, I assure you, it has been without the least intention; and, therefore, your candour will lead you to forgive me. I have spoken freely of Congress and of the Army. But what I have said, is partly from my own knowledge, and partly from the information of some respectable members of the former, and some of the best officers in the latter. I would not offend the meanest person upon earth. What I say to you I say in confidence, and to answer what I cannot but deem a most valuable purpose. I love my country. I love you. But to the love of truth, the love of peace, and the love of God, I hope I should be enabled, if called to the trial, to sacrifice every other inferior love.

" If the arguments made use of in this letter, should have so much influence as to engage you in the glorious work which I have so warmly recommended, I shall ever deem my success as the highest temporal favour that Providence could grant me. Your interposition and advice I am confident would meet with a favourable reception from the authority under which you act. If it should not, you have an infallible resource still left. NEGOTIATE for AMERICA at the head of your ARMY.

" After all it may appear presumption in an individual to address himself to you on a subject of such magnitude, or to say what measures would best secure the interest and welfare of a whole continent. The friendly and favourable opinion you have always expressed for me, emboldened me to undertake it, and (which has greatly added to the weight of this motive) I have been strongly impressed with a sense of duty upon the occasion, which left my conscience uneasy and my heart afflicted till I had fully discharged it. I am no enthusiast. The case is new and singular to me. But I could not enjoy a moment's peace, till this letter was written. With the most ardent prayers for your spiritual as well as temporal welfare, I am,

Your most obedient and
Sincere friend and servant,
(Signed)   JACOB DUCHE.

His Excellency Gen. WASHINGTON.

GENERAL WASHINGTON TO FRANCIS HOPKINSON.*

"Head Quarters, 21 November, 1777.

" SIR,

" I am favoured with yours of the 14th instant, enclosing a letter for the Reverend Mr. Duché. I will endeavour to forward it to him, but I imagine it will never be permitted to reach his hands. I confess to you, that I was not more surprised than concerned at receiving so extraordinary a letter from Mr. Duché, of whom I had entertained the most favourable opinion, and I am still willing to suppose, that it was rather dictated by his fears than by his real sentiments; but I very much doubt whether the great numbers of respectable characters, in the State and Army, on whom he has bestowed the most unprovoked and unmerited abuse, will ever attribute it to the same cause, or forgive the man who has artfully endeavoured to engage me to sacrifice them to purchase my own safety.

" I never intended to make the letter more public, than by

---

* Sparks' Life and Writings of Washington.—ED.

laying it before Congress. I thought this a duty, which I owed to myself; for, had any accident happened to the army entrusted to my command, and had it ever afterwards appeared, that such a letter had been written to and received by me, might it not have been said, that I had betrayed my country? And would not such a correspondence, if kept a secret, have given good grounds for the suspicion? I thank you for the favourable sentiments which you are pleased to express of me, and I hope no act of mine will ever induce you to alter them. I am, &c.

" GEORGE WASHINGTON."

FRANCIS HOPKINSON TO JACOB DUCHE.*

" Bordentown, 14th November, 1777.

" DEAR BROTHER,

" A letter signed with your name, dated at Philadelphia, on the 8th of October, and addressed to his Excellency General Washington, is handed about the country. Many copies are taken, and I doubt not but it will soon get into the press, and become public throughout the continent. Words cannot express the grief and consternation that wounded my soul at the sight of this fatal performance. What infatuation could influence you to offer to his Excellency an address, filled with gross misrepresentation, illiberal abuse, and sentiments unworthy of a man of character? You have endeavoured to screen your own weaknesses by the most artful glosses, and to apologize to the General for the instability of your temper, in a manner that I am sure cannot be satisfactory to your own conscience.

" I could go through this extraordinary letter, and point out to you truth distorted in every leading part. But the world will doubtless do this with a severity that must be daggers to the sensibilities of your heart. Read that letter over again, and if possible divest yourself of the fears and influence, whatever they were, that induced you to pen it. Consider its contents with an impartial eye, and reflect on the ideas it will naturally

* Sparks' Life and Writings of Washington.—FD.

raise in the minds of the multitude. You will then find, that by
a vain and weak effort you have attempted the integrity of one
whose virtue is impregnable to the assaults of fear or flattery,
whose judgment needed not your information, and who, I am
sure, would have resigned his charge the moment he found it
likely to lead him out of the paths of virtue and honour. You
will find that you have drawn upon you the resentment of Congress, the resentment of the army, the resentment of many
worthy and noble characters in England, whom you know not,
and the resentment of your insulted country. You have ventured to assert many things at large of the affairs of England,
France, and America, which are far from being true, and
which, from your contracted knowledge in these matters, it is
impossible for you to be acquainted with. In the whole of your
letter, you have never once recommended yourself to those,
whose favour you seem desirous of obtaining, by expatiating on
the justice or humanity of their conduct, and at the same time
have said every thing that can render you odious to those, on
whom the happiness of your future life must depend.

" You presumptuously advise our worthy General, on whom
millions depend with implicit confidence, to abandon their dear-
est hopes, and with or without the consent of his constituents to
' *negotiate for America at the head of his army.*' Would not
the blood of the slain in battle rise against such perfidy ? And
with whom would you have him negotiate? Are they not
those, who, without the sanction of any civil, moral, or religious
right, have come three thousand miles to destroy our peace and
property, to lay waste *your* native country with fire and sword,
and cruelly murder its inhabitants? Look for their justice and
honour in their several proclamations, and look for their humanity in the jails of New York and Philadelphia, and in your
own Potter's Field. The whole force of the reasoning contained in your letter tends to this point: that virtue and honour
require us to stand by truth, as long as it can be done with
safety, but that her cause may be abandoned on the approach
of danger; or, in other words, that the justice of the American
cause ought to be squared by the success of her arms.

" On the whole, I find it impossible to reconcile the matter and style of this letter with your general conduct, or with the virtues of your heart. I would fain hope, notwithstanding your asser- tion to the contrary, that you wrote it with a bayonet held to your breast, by order of the unprincipled usurpers of your native city. But my chief motive for writing to you at this time is to assure you, that I firmly believe that our just defensive war will be crowned with success, and that we shall ere long return to our habitations in Philadelphia. I would, therefore, most earnestly warn you to evade the dismal consequences of your ill-judged address to our beloved General. Do all you can to wipe off, if possible, its unhappy effects. I tremble for you, for my good sister, and her little family. I tremble for your per- sonal safety. Be assured I write this from true brotherly love. Our intimacy has been of a long duration, even from our early youth ; long and uninterrupted, without even a rub in the way ; and so long have the sweetness of your manners, and the inte- grity of your heart, fixed my affections.

" I am perfectly disposed to attribute this unfortunate step to the timidity of your temper, the weakness of your nerves, and the undue influence of those about you. But will the world hold you so excused ? Will the individuals you have so freely censured and characterized with contempt have this tenderness for you? I fear not. They will only judge of your conduct by its rashness, and proportion their resentment to their sensibility of the wounds you have given. I pray God to inspire you with some means of extricating yourself from this embarrassing diffi- culty. For my own part, I have well considered the principles on which I took part with my country, and am determined to abide by them to the last extremity. I beg my love to my good mother, and my affectionate sisters. I often think of them with great pain and anxiety, lest they should suffer from the want of those necessary supplies, that are now cut off. May God pre- serve them and you in this time of trial. I am, &c.

" FRANCIS HOPKINSON."

JACOB DUCHE TO GENERAL WASHINGTON.*

"Asylum, Lambeth, 2 April, 1783.

" S<small>IR</small>,—

" Will your Excellency condescend to accept of a few lines from one, who ever was and wishes still to be your sincere friend, who never *intentionally* sought to give you a moment's pain, who entertains for you the highest personal respect, and would be happy to be assured under your own hand, that he does not labour under your displeasure, but that you freely forgive what a weak judgment, but a very affectionate heart, once presumed to advise? Many circumstances, at present unknown to you, conspired to make me deem it my duty to write to you. Ignorance and simplicity saw not the necessity of your divulging the letter. I am convinced, however, that you could not, in your public station, do otherwise. I cannot say a word in vindication of my conduct but this, that I had been for months before distressed with continual apprehensions for you and all my friends without the British lines. I looked upon all as gone; or that nothing could save you, but rescinding the Declaration of Independency. Upon this ground alone I presumed to speak; not to advise an act of base treachery, my soul would have recoiled from the thought; not to surrender your army, or betray the righteous cause of your country, but, at the head of that army, *supporting and supported by them*, to negotiate with Britain for our constitutional rights.

" Can you then join with my country in pardoning this error of judgment? Will you yet honour me with your great interest and influence, by recommending, at least expressing your approbation of the repeal of an act, that keeps me in a state of banishment from my native country, from the arms of a dear aged father, and the embraces of a numerous circle of valuable and long-loved friends? Your liberal, generous mind, I am persuaded, will never exclude me wholly from your regard for a mere political error; especially, as you must have heard, that, since the date of that letter, I have led a life of perfect retirement,

* Sparks' Life and Writings of Washington.—E<small>D</small>.

and since my arrival in England have devoted myself wholly to the duties of my profession, and confined my acquaintance to a happy circle of literary and religious friends.

"I have written to my father and to many of my friends largely on this subject, requesting them to make such application to the State of Pennsylvania in my behalf, as may be judged necessary and expedient. Should this application be honoured with success, I know of nothing that would more effectually satisfy my desires in a matter of such importance to myself and my family, as a line or two from your Excellency, expressive of your approbation of my return. Temporal emoluments are not wanting to induce me to remain for life on this side of the Atlantic. I have been most hospitably received and kindly treated by all ranks of people, and I should be ungrateful not to acknowledge in the strongest terms my obligations to those who have placed me in the easy and comfortable situation I now enjoy. It is not necessity, therefore, but unalterable affection to my native country, that urges me to seek a return. With every good wish and prayer for your best felicity, and my most hearty congratulations on the happy event of peace, I have the honour to be your Excellency's most obedient and humble servant,

"JACOB DUCHE."

GENERAL WASHINGTON TO JACOB DUCHE.

"Head Quarters, 10 August, 1783.

" SIR,

"I have received your letter of the 2d of April, and, reflecting on its contents, I cannot but say that I am heartily sorry for the occasion which has produced it. Personal enmity I bear none to any man. So far, therefore, as your return to this country depends on my private voice, it would be given in favour of it with cheerfulness. But, removed as I am from the people and policy of the State in which you formerly resided, and to whose determination your case must be submitted, it is my duty, whatever may be my inclination, to leave its decision to its constitutional judges. Should this be agreeable to your wishes, it cannot fail to meet my entire approbation. I am, &c.

" GEORGE WASHINGTON."

The laws of Pennsylvania, excluding the refugees from that State, were not repealed till after the adoption of the Constitution of the United States. Mr. Duché returned to Philadelphia in the year 1790, much broken in health, having suffered a paralytic affection. He died in 1794, being then about sixty years of age.*—ED.

F.

PAGE 117.

JOSEPH GALLOWAY.

The seventh volume of Sparks' edition of the works of Franklin contains, in a note, the following biographical notice of Mr. Galloway, from the pen of Mr. J. Francis Fisher, of Philadelphia:—

"Joseph Galloway, son of Peter Galloway, was born in the neighbourhood of West River, Anne Arundel County, Maryland, about the year 1730. As his family was respectable and of good fortune, his education was probably the best that could be obtained in the middle colonies. He came early in life to Philadelphia, where he commenced the practice of the law, in which he attained eminence. In the year 1757, he was elected to the Assembly for the County of Philadelphia, and immediately took a prominent stand in that body, being a member of most of the committees, and constantly employed in public duties, as we find, in the *votes*, by his compensation for extra services. The next year he was chairman of the committee on grievances, and managed the prosecution of Dr. Smith and Mr. Moore for a libel on the Assembly. In subsequent years he held the same place; and his Report, in 1764, on the state and grievances of the province, was the occasion of his well-known speech pub-

* Sparks' Life and Writings of Washington.—ED.

lished with Dr. Franklin's Preface, in answer to one of the celebrated John Dickinson.

" He sided with Dr. Franklin in opposition to the Proprietary interest, and urged the resumption of the Government by the Crown. And though, on this account in 1764 he lost his election in the county, he was, the next year, returned a member, and was chosen Speaker of the Assembly, to which office he was successively re-elected till the year 1774.

" In 1757 he was one of the agents of Pennsylvania at the treaty with the Indians at Easton. In the next year, as one of the commissioners under the act for granting one hundred thousand pounds, he entered into a controversy with the Governor, which may be seen at length in the *votes*, and Gordon's History. What were his powers as a speaker tradition does not say, but he led the popular party in all their attacks upon the Proprietary interest; and was so highly esteemed by them, that they delegated him as a member of the General Congress, which met at Philadelphia, in 1774. Whether he took an active part in their proceedings does not appear. His name is signed to the declarations and resolutions; but he seems to have soon abandoned the Revolutionary cause, under the influence of his loyal principles or his sordid fears.

" After the British troops had penetrated into New Jersey, in 1776, on their then intended march to Philadelphia, he was among those who joined the army, previous to the capture of the Hessians at Trenton. He afterwards accompanied them on their route by the way of Chesapeake Bay, and with them entered the city of Philadelphia, in the latter end of September, 1777. Here he was an active agent under Sir William Howe, the Commander-in-chief of the British forces in America. On the evacuation of Philadelphia, in June, 1778, he went to New York, where he remained some months, and thence sailed for England, accompanied by his only daughter, abandoning (according to his own account) an estate of the value of forty thousand pounds, which had been confiscated by the Government of Pennsylvania in pursuance of his proscription and attainder. But the larger part of this estate, which he held by courtesy, being the inheritance of his wife, the daughter of Lawrence Growdon of

Bucks County, (for a long time Speaker of the Provincial Assembly,) was restored to their daughter. It is called Trevose, and is still owned by his descendants, having continued in the family since the settlement of Pennsylvania.

"On his arrival in England, Galloway was examined before the House of Commons on the transactions in America, and his representations, which are in print, did not reflect much credit on the British Commanders. He published, in 1779, a pamphlet, entitled, Letters to a Nobleman on the conduct of the war in the Middle Colonies, in which, notwithstanding his attachments, he discloses and reprehends the conduct of the British troops, especially in New Jersey. He also published 'A Letter to Lord Howe,' 'A Reply to the Observations of General Howe,' 'Cool Thoughts on the Consequences of American Independence,' 'Candid Examination of the Claims of Great Britain and her Colonies,' 'Reflections on the American Rebellion in 1780,' and some other pamphlets. He was, it is believed, a pensioner of the British Government, and he resided in England till the time of his decease, in 1803."

During the controversy between the friends and opponents of the Proprietary interests, Galloway and Dickinson took each an active part. "Each published a speech which he had delivered in the Legislative Assembly; and it was remarkable that the introduction to each (one written by Dr. Franklin, who opposed the Proprietary interest, and the other by Dr. Smith the coadjutor of Dickinson,) were at the time more admired than the original compositions."—*Watson.*—ED.

G.

PAGE 119.

JOHN DICKINSON.

JOHN DICKINSON was a native of Maryland, where he was born in 1732. His parents soon afterwards removed to Delaware,

38

where they educated their son. He read law in Philadelphia,
and, in the farther prosecution of his legal studies, in the Temple
at London. Upon his return to Philadelphia, he commenced the
successful practice of his profession, and was early elected to the
Legislature of Pennsylvania, in which body his aptitude as a
speaker and general tact gave him considerable influence.

"The election of members of legislature, in the autumn of
1764, was," says Sparks, "sharply contested. It turned on the
question of a change of government. The proprietary party,
having much at stake, redoubled their efforts; and, in the city of
Philadelphia, and some of the counties, they were successful.
Franklin, after having been chosen fourteen years successively,
now lost his election, there being against him a majority of about
twenty-five votes in four thousand. But, after all, it was an
empty triumph. When the members convened, there were two
to one in favour of the measures of the last Assembly, and they
resolved to carry these measures into effect. Being determined
to pursue their object with all the force they could bring to bear
upon it, they appointed Dr. Franklin as a special agent to proceed to the Court of Great Britain, and there to take charge of
the petition for a change of government, and to manage the general affairs of the province. This appointment was a surprise
upon the proprietary party. They had imagined, that, by defeat-
ing his election, they had rid themselves of an active and troublesome opponent in the Assembly, and weakened his influence
abroad. When it was proposed, therefore, to raise him to a situation, in which he could more effectually than ever serve the same
cause, the agitation of the House, and the clamour out of doors
was extreme. His adversaries testified their chagrin by the means
they used to prevent his appointment. John Dickinson, while he
could not refrain from eulogizing him as a man, inveighed strenuously against his political principles and conduct; at the same
time exhibiting symptoms of alarm, that would seem almost ludicrous, if it were not known what power there is in the spirit of
party to distort truth and pervert the judgment. 'The gentleman
proposed,' he says, in a speech to the House, 'has been called
here, to-day, a great luminary of the learned world. Far be it
from me to detract from the merit I admire. Let him still shine,

but without wrapping his country in flames. Let him, from a private station, from a smaller sphere, diffuse, as, I think, he may, a beneficial light; but let him not be made to move and blaze like a comet, to terrify and distress.' When," continues Sparks, "the second Congress assembled, the relations between the Colonies and Great Britain had assumed a new character. The blood of American freemen had been shed on their own soil by a wanton exercise of military power. This rash act dissolved the charm, which had hitherto bound the affections of many a conscientious American to the British Crown, under the long revered name of loyalty. The hour of trial had come. After an animated debate, which continued for several days, it was declared that hostilities had commenced, on the part of Great Britain, with the design of enforcing 'the unconstitutional and oppressive acts of Parliament;' and it was then resolved, with great unanimity, that the Colonies should be immediately put in a state of defence. This was all that the most ardent friends of liberty desired; the more moderate party, at the head of which was Dickinson, urged that they never had anticipated resistance by force, but had always confided so much in the justice of the British government, as to believe that they would come to a reasonable compromise. Another opportunity ought to be offered, and they were strenuous for sending a petition to the king.' Its most zealous advocate was John Dickinson, by whom it was drafted. It has been said, indeed, that this token of humility was yielded mainly to gratify his wishes. The uprightness of his character, his singleness of heart, and the great services he had rendered to his country by his talents and his pen, claimed for him especial consideration. The tone and language of the petition were sufficiently submissive, and it stands in remarkable contrast in the Journals, with other papers, and the resolves for warlike preparations. Mr. Jefferson tells us, that Mr. Dickinson was so much pleased when it was adopted, that he could not forbear to express his satisfaction by saying: 'There is but one word, Mr. President, in the paper, which I disapprove, and that word is *Congress.*' Whereupon Mr. Harrison, of Virginia, rose and said : ' There is but one word in the paper, Mr. President, which I approve, and that word is *Congress.*' "

Mr. Dickinson's first publication against the English government appeared in 1765. In this year he was appointed a delegate to the Congress held at New York. In 1767, he issued, at Philadelphia, his celebrated "Farmer's Letters," a production "which had great influence in enlightening the minds of the American people, on the subject of their rights." They were written with his distinguished ability, against the revenue laws, and were widely popular with all classes of readers in this country, for their research, vigour and perspicuity of their style. At the time of their publication in the United States, Dr. Franklin, in the discharge of public duties, was in London, where he caused their re-publication, accompanied by a commendatory preface from his own pen. "Besides," says Sparks, "the patriotic motive for this re-publication, it afforded him an opportunity of showing that the extreme warmth with which Mr. Dickinson had opposed his appointment in the Pennsylvania Assembly had not produced, on his part, any diminution of personal regard." These " Letters " were translated into French and published at Paris.

At length, the great question of National Independence became the engrossing topic in "newspapers, pamphlets, at public meetings, as well as in private circles. It was evident that a large majority of the nation was prepared for that measure. Among the doubters was the virtuous, the patriotic, the able, but irresolute John Dickinson." His opposition to the Declaration rendering him unpopular, " he withdrew from the public councils, and did not recover his seat in Congress until about two years afterwards. He then returned earnest in the cause of Independence. He was subsequently President (Governor) of Pennsylvania and Delaware successively, and died at Wilmington, in February, 1808."

ED.

H.

PAGE 144.

GENERAL WASHINGTON TO PRESIDENT REED.

"Head Quarters, Passaic Falls, 18th October, 1780."

"DEAR SIR,

"By your favour of the 3d from Bethlehem, I perceive my letter of the 1st has not got to your hands; but I have the pleasure to find, that the business you were upon anticipated the purposes of it, and was in a fair way to answer the end.[*]

"Arnold's conduct is so villanously perfidious, that there are no terms which can describe the baseness of his heart. That overruling Providence, which has so often and so remarkably interposed in our favour, never manifested itself more conspicuously than in the timely discovery of his horrid design of surrendering the post and garrison of West Point into the hands of the enemy. I confine my remark to this single act of perfidy; for I am far from thinking he intended to hazard a defeat of this important object, by combining another with it, although there were circumstances which led to a contrary belief. The confidence and folly, which have marked the subsequent conduct of this man, are of a piece with his villany; and all three are perfect in their kind. The interest you take in my supposed escape, and the manner in which you speak of it, claim my thanks as much as if he had really intended to involve my fate with that of the garrison, and I consider it as a fresh instance of your affectionate regard for me.

"As I do not recollect ever to have had any very particular conversation with General Schuyler respecting Arnold, I should be glad to obtain a copy of the letter in which you say my 'opinion and confidence in him (Arnold) is conveyed in terms of affection and approbation.' Some time before or after Arnold's return from Connecticut (the conversation made so little

---

[*] General WASHINGTON had written, requesting President REED to cause to be sent forward as expeditiously as possible a supply of flour to the army.

impression on me, that I know not which,) General Schuyler informed me, that he had received a letter from Arnold, intimating his intention of joining the army, and rendering such services as his leg would permit, adding that he was incapable of active service, but could discharge the duties of a stationary command without much inconvenience or uneasiness to his leg. I answered, that, as we had a prospect of an active and vigorous campaign, I should be glad of General Arnold's aid and assistance, but saw little prospect of his obtaining such a command as appeared to be the object of his wishes, because it was my intention to draw my whole force into the field, when we were in circumstances to commence our operations against New York, leaving even West Point to the care of invalids, and a small garrison of militia; but if, after this previous declaration, the command of the post, for the reasons he assigned, would be more convenient and agreeable to him than a command in the field, I should readily indulge him, having had it hinted to me, by a very respectable character, a member of Congress* (not General Schuyler,) that a measure of this kind would not be unacceptable to the State most immediately interested in the welfare and safety of the post.

" This, to the best of my knowledge and recollection, is every syllable that ever passed between General Schuyler and me respecting Arnold, or any of his concerns. The manner and the matter appeared perfectly uninteresting to both of us at the time. He seemed to have no other view in communicating the thing, than because he was requested to do it, and my answer, dictated by circumstances, you already have; but how it was communicated, the letter will show.

" That General Schuyler possesses a share of my regard and confidence, I shall readily acknowledge. A pretty long acquaintance with him, an opinion of his abilities, his intimate knowledge of our circumstances, his candour as far as I have had opportunities of forming a judgment of it, added to personal civilities and proofs of a warm friendship, which I never had a doubt of, would leave me without excuse, were I to withhold these from him. What ascendency he may have over the army

* Robert R. Livingston.

is more than I can tell; but I should not be surprised if he stands in a favourable point of view with respect to their esteem. The means he took to acquire a true knowledge of their distress while he was with them, the representations he made to procure relief, and his evident endeavours to promote the object for which he was appointed, seem to have made this a natural consequence. I am, dear Sir, &c."—ED.

I.

PAGE 232.

CAPTURE OF GENERAL CHARLES LEE.

The capture of this eccentric officer occurred on the 13th of September, 1776, at Baskingridge, New Jersey. It was effected by a party of British cavalry under Colonel Harcourt. General Wilkinson in his "Memoirs" gives the following interesting account of the event:—

"General Lee wasted the morning in altercation with certain militia corps who were of his command, particularly the Connecticut Light Horse, several of whom appeared in large full-bottomed perukes, and were treated very irreverently. The call of the Adjutant-General for orders also occupied some of his time, and we did not sit down to breakfast before 10 o'clock. General Lee was engaged in answering a letter from General Gates, and I had risen from the table, and was looking out of an end window, down a lane about one hundred yards in length, which led to the house from the main road, when I discovered a party of British troops turn the corner of the avenue at full charge. Startled at this unexpected spectacle, I exclaimed, 'Here, sir, are the British cavalry!' 'Where?' exclaimed the General, who had signed the letter in the instant. 'Around the house;' for they had opened files and encompassed the building. General Lee appeared alarmed, yet collected, and his second observation marked his self-possession: 'Where is the guard?—d—n the guard, why

don't they fire?' and after a momentary pause, he turned to me
and said 'Do, sir, see what has become of the guard!' The
women of the house at this moment entered the room, and proposed to him to conceal himself in a bed, which he rejected with
evident disgust. I caught up the pistols which lay on the table,
thrust the letter he had been writing into my pocket, and passed
into a room at the opposite end of the house, where I had seen
the guard in the morning. Here I discovered their arms, but the
men were absent. I stepped out of the door, and perceived the
dragoons chasing them in different directions, and receiving a
very uncivil salutation, I returned into the house.

"Too inexperienced immediately to penetrate the motives of this
enterprise, I considered the *rencontre* accidental, and from the ter-
rific tales spread over the country, of the violence and barbarity
of the enemy, I believed it to be a wanton murdering party, and
determined not to die without company. I accordingly sought a
position where I could not be approached by more than one person at a time, and with a pistol in each hand, I awaited the expected search, resolved to shoot the first and the second person
who might appear, and then to appeal to my sword. I did not
long remain in this unpleasant situation, but was apprised of the
object of the incursion, by the very audible declaration, ' *If the
General does not surrender in five minutes, I will set fire to the
house;*' which, after a short pause, was repeated with a solemn
oath ; and within two minutes, I heard it proclaimed, ' *Here is
the General, he has surrendered.*' A general shout ensued, the
trumpet sounded the assembly, and the unfortunate Lee, mounted
on my horse, which stood ready at the door, was hurried off in
triumph, bareheaded, in his slippers and blanket-coat, his collar
open, and his shirt very much soiled from several day's use.

"What a lesson of caution is to be derived from this event, and
how important the admonition furnished by it ! What an evidence
of the caprice of fortune, of the fallibility of human projects, and
the inscrutable ways of Heaven ! The capture of General Lee,
was felt as a public calamity; it cast a gloom over the country,
and excited general sorrow. This sympathy was honourable to
the people, and due to the stranger who had embarked his fortune with them, and determined to share their fate, under cir-

cumstances of more than common peril. Although this misfortune deprived the country of its most experienced chief, I have ever considered the deprivation a public blessing, ministered by the hand of Providence; for if General Lee had not abandoned caution for convenience, and taken quarters two miles from his army, on his exposed flank, he would have been safe; if a domestic traitor, who passed his quarters the same morning on private business, had not casually fallen in with Colonel Harcourt, on a reconnoitring party, the General's quarters would not have been discovered; if my visit, and the controversy with the Connecticut Light Horse, had not spun out the morning unseasonably, the General would have been at his camp; if Colonel Harcourt, had arrived one hour sooner, he would have found the guard under arms, and would have been repulsed, or resisted until succour could have arrived; if he had arrived half an hour later the General would have been with his corps; if the guard had paid ordinary attention to their duty, and had not abandoned their arms, the General's quarters would have been defended; or if he had obeyed the peremptory and reiterated orders of General WASHINGTON, he would have been beyond the reach of the enemy. And shall we impute to blind chance, such a chain of rare incidents? I conscientiously answer in the negative; because the combination was too intricate and perplexed, for accidental causes, or the agencies of man. It must have been designed. So soon as Lieutenant Colonel Harcourt retreated with his prize, I repaired to the stable, mounted the first horse I could find, and rode full speed to General Sullivan, whom I found under march, towards Pluckamin."—ED.

J.

PAGE 238.

LETTER TO COLONEL REED, OR COLONEL JOHN CADWALADER, AT BRISTOL.

Camp above Trenton Falls, 23d December, 1776.

DEAR SIR,

The bearer is sent down to know whether your plan was attempted last night, and if not to inform you, that Christmas-day at night, one hour before day, is the time fixed upon for our attempt on Trenton. For Heaven's sake, keep this to yourself, as the discovery of it may prove fatal to us; our numbers, sorry am I to say, being less than I had any conception of; but necessity, dire necessity, will, nay must, justify an attack. Prepare, and, in concert with GRIFFIN, attack as many of their posts as you possibly can with a prospect of success; the more we can attack at the same instant, the more confusion we shall spread, and the greater good will result from it. If I had not been fully convinced before of the enemy's designs, I have now ample testimony of their intentions to attack Philadelphia, so soon as the ice will afford the means of conveyance.

As the colonels of the continental regiments might kick up some dust about command, unless CADWALADER is considered by them in the light of a brigadier, which I wish him to be, I desired General GATES, who is unwell, and applied for leave to go to Philadelphia, to endeavour, if his health would permit him, to call and stay two or three days at Bristol in his way. I shall not be particular; we could not ripen matters for an attack, before the time mentioned in the first part of this letter; so much out of sorts, and so much in want of every thing, are the troops under Sullivan. The letter herewith sent, forward on to Philadelphia; I could wish it to be in time for the southern post's departure, which will be, I believe, by eleven o'clock to-morrow.

I am, dear Sir, &c.

GO. WASHINGTON.

P. S. I have ordered our men to be provided with three days provisions ready cooked, with which, and their blankets, they are to march; for if we are successful, which Heaven grant, and the circumstances favour, we may push on. I shall direct every ferry and ford to be well guarded, and not a soul suffered to pass without an officer's going down with the permit. Do the same with you.—ED.

———

K.

PAGE 293.

WASHINGTON AT BRANDYWINE.

Bisset, in his continuation of Hume and Smollet, in his account of the battle of Brandywine, subjoins the following note of a private letter from Major Ferguson—son of the historian of Rome—to his father, from which, it is inferred, that the life of General WASHINGTON was, on that day, in imminent danger, and absolutely in the power of Major Ferguson.

While this officer lay with a party of his riflemen on a skirt of a wood in front of General Knyphausen's division, the circumstance happened of which the letter in question gives the following account:—

" We had not lain long when a rebel officer remarkable by a *Hussar dress*, passed towards our army within a hundred yards of my right flank, not perceiving us. He was followed by another dressed in dark green and blue, mounted on a good bay horse, with a remarkable large high cocked hat. I ordered three good shots to steal near them and fire at them; but the idea disgusted me and I recalled the order." The letter, after some farther particulars not necessary to repeat, states, that it was afterwards collected "from some wounded rebel officers, that General WASHINGTON was all that morning with the light troops, and only attended by a French officer in a Hussar dress, he himself dressed and mounted in every respect as above described."

In commenting on the above, Mr. Graydon, in a note appended to it, observes, "Whatever truth there may be in this relation, and whoever might have been the person in dark green and blue with the remarkable large high cocked hat, no one acquainted with the style of General WASHINGTON's costume during the war, or any other time, can suppose it to have been him, who was so generously dealt with by the Major. The General's uniform or military dress was blue and buff, which, it may be very safely averred he never varied, at least to an entire change of colours: neither was he ever seen in a hat of the description given in the letter. It is true, he wore a cocked hat, but, of a moderate size. It might, indeed, have been somewhat larger than those in fashion in America at the beginning of the war, but, it could by no means have answered to the colossal dimensions given by the Major. The General had too correct a taste in dress, to figure in the bully-like garb of a Bobadil or a Pistol; and there was no inducement to such a disguise, being as much in danger in green and blue with a large hat, as in blue and buff with a small one. Major Ferguson, therefore, might have spared himself the self-gratulation of 'not knowing at the time who it was,' since, if justly described, most assuredly it was not General WASHINGTON."—ED.

L.

PAGE 320.

THE BATTLE OF MONMOUTH.

The Editor is indebted to Mr. Sparks' edition of the "Life and Writings of Washington," for the following interesting particulars concerning General CHARLES LEE, and the Battle of Monmouth :—

"Soon after General Lee rejoined the army at Valley Forge, a curious incident occurred. By an order of Congress, General Washington was required to administer the oath of allegiance to the general officers. The Major-Generals stood around Washington, and took hold of a Bible together, according to the usual custom ; but, just as he began to administer the oath, Lee deliberately withdrew his hand twice. This movement was so singular, and was performed in so odd a manner, that the officers smiled, and Washington inquired the meaning of his hesitancy. Lee replied, 'As to King George, I am ready enough to absolve myself from all allegiance to him, but I have some scruples about the Prince of Wales.' The strangeness of this reply was such, that the officers burst into a broad laugh, and even Washington could not refrain from a smile. The ceremony was of course interrupted. It was renewed as soon as a composure was restored proper for the solemnity of the occasion, and Lee took the oath with the other officers. Connected with the subsequent conduct of General Lee, this incident was thought by some, who were acquainted with it, to have a deeper meaning than at first appeared, and to indicate a less ardent and fixed patriotism towards the United States, than was consistent with the rank and professions of the second officer in command of the American forces.

"The army having crossed the Delaware in pursuit of the

39

British retreating from Philadelphia, a council of war was held at Hopewell, June 24th, in which, after stating the relative strength and position of the two armies, the Commander-in-chief proposed the following questions.

"'Will it be advisable for us, of choice, to hazard a general action? If it is, should we do it by immediately making a general attack upon the enemy, by attempting a partial one, or by taking such a position, if it can be done, as may oblige them to attack us? If it is not, what measures can be taken, with safety to this army, to annoy the enemy in their march? In fine, what precise line of conduct will it be advisable for us to pursue?'

"Lee was strenuously opposed to a general action. Being the highest in rank, and an officer of great experience, the younger officers were much influenced by his arguments and opinions. The council finally decided that a general action was not advisable, but that 'a detachment of fifteen hundred men be immediately sent to act, as occasion may serve, on the enemy's left flank and rear, in conjunction with the other Continental troops and militia, who are already hanging about them, and that the main body preserve a relative position, so as to be able to act as circumstances may require.' This decision was signed by all the officers except Wayne. It appeared, however, that there was a wide difference of opinion as to the number of men, that ought to be sent against the enemy, although the council ultimately agreed on fifteen hundred. Lee, Stirling, Woodford, Scott, Knox, and Poor, were for this number; but Steuben, Duportail, Wayne, Patterson, Greene, and Lafayette were for twenty-five hundred, or at least two thousand. It was the idea of some of the officers, also, that the detachment ought to attack the enemy, though not to bring on a general action; while others believed, that nothing more should be done, than to skirmish with the out-guards, and thus harass the retreating enemy as circumstances would permit.

"After the council was dissolved, Greene, Lafayette, and Wayne, wrote separately to the Commander-in-chief, explaining more fully their views. They were not for pushing the enemy to a general action at all events; but they were decidedly of opinion, that a large detachment should be sent forward to attack their rear, and that the main army should be drawn into such a position as to commence an engagement, should the prospects be favourable. These views accorded with those of the Commander-in-chief, and he promptly determined to act in conformity with them.

From General Lee's rank the advanced detachment fell under his command, although he was totally opposed to the measure adopted. Lafayette went to Washington, reminded him of this embarrassment, and offered to take command of the attacking division. Washington said, that such an arrangement would be entirely agreeable to him, but that it could not be effected without the previous consent of General Lee. When Lafayette applied to Lee, he very readily assented, saying that he disapproved of the plans of the Commander-in-chief, that he was sure they would fail, and that he was willing to be relieved from any responsibility in carrying them into execution. Lafayette immediately took command of his division and marched towards the enemy. After reflecting upon the matter, Lee wrote to General Washington as follows.

GENERAL LEE TO GENERAL WASHINGTON.

"Camp at Kingston, 25th June, 1778.

"DEAR GENERAL,

"When I first assented to the Marquis de Lafayette's taking the command of the present detachment, I confess I viewed it in a very different light from that in which I view it at present. I considered it as a more proper business of a young, volunteering general, than of the second in command in the army; but I find it is considered in a different manner. They say that a corps consisting of six thousand men, the greater part chosen, is undoubtedly the most honourable command next to the Commander-in-chief; that my ceding it would of course have an odd appearance. I must entreat, therefore, after making a thousand apologies for the trouble my rash assent has occasioned you, that, if this detachment does march, I may have the command of it. So far personally; but, to speak as an officer, I do not think that this detachment ought to march at all, until at least the head of the enemy's right column has passed Cranberry; then, if it is necessary to march the whole army, I cannot see any impropriety in the Marquis's commanding this detachment, or a greater, as an advanced guard of the army; but if this detachment, with Maxwell's corps, Scott's, Morgan's, and Jackson's, is to be considered as a separate, chosen, active corps, and put under the Marquis's command until the enemy leave the Jerseys, both myself and Lord Stirling will be disgraced. I am, dear General, yours, &c.

" CHARLES LEE."

As Washington had already given the command to the Marquis, it could not with propriety be withdrawn without his consent. Lee applied to him for the purpose, but the Marquis said he could not without great reluctance give up the command; that it had been yielded to him freely, and he was particularly desirous of retaining it. This was on the second day before the battle, and there was a prospect that the enemy would be overtaken during the day. After Lee had urged the point, and appealed to the generosity and magnanimity of the Marquis, the latter at length agreed that if he did not come up with the enemy so as to make an attack that day, he would then resign the command. Lee had already been detached with a smaller division, but was instructed not to interfere with the Marquis, if he had concerted any definite plan of attacking the enemy. The day passed over without coming to an action, and late at night Lafayette wrote a note to Lee resigning the command. The result, in regard to General Lee, is well known. The battle took place the next day, in the midst of which Lee retreated, contrary to the expectations of the Commander-in-chief, and in such a manner as to threaten the most serious consequences to the army. He was met by Washington while retreating, and was addressed by him in a tone of reprimand and censure, which wounded the pride of Lee, and gave rise to the following correspondence.

GENERAL LEE TO GENERAL WASHINGTON.

"Camp, English Town, 1 July [29 June?], 1778.

" SIR,

"From the knowledge I have of your Excellency's character, I must conclude that nothing but the misinformation of some very stupid, or misrepresentation of some very wicked person, could have occasioned your making use of so very singular expressions as you did on my coming up to the ground where you had taken post. They implied that I was guilty either of disobedience of orders, want of conduct, or want of courage. Your Excellency will therefore infinitely oblige me, by letting me know on which of these three articles you ground your charge, that I may prepare for my justification, which I have the happiness to be confident I can do to the army, to the Congress, to America, and to the world in general. Your Excellency must give me leave to observe, that neither yourself, nor those about your person, could from your situation be in the least judges of the merits or demerits of our manœuvres; and, to speak with a becoming pride, I can assert that to these manœuvres the success of the day was entirely owing. I can boldly say, that had we remained on the first ground, or had we advanced, or had the retreat been conducted in a manner different from what it was, this whole army and the interests of America would have risked being sacrificed. I ever had, and hope ever shall have, the greatest respect and veneration for General Washington. I think him endowed with many great and good qualities; but in this instance I must pronounce, that he has been guilty of an act of cruel injustice towards a man, who certainly has some pretensions to the regard of every servant of this country. And I think, Sir, I have a right to demand some reparation for the injury committed; and, unless I can obtain it, I must, in justice to myself, when this campaign is closed, which I believe will close the war, retire from a service at the head of which is placed a man capable of offering such injuries. But at the same time, in justice to you, I must

repeat that I from my soul believe, that it was not a motion of
your own breast, but instigated by some of those dirty earwigs,
who will for ever insinuate themselves near persons in high
office; for I really am convinced, that when General Washington acts from himself, no man in his army will have reason to
complain of injustice or indecorum. I am, Sir, and hope I
ever shall have reason to continue, your most sincerely devoted
humble servant.

"Charles Lee."

GENERAL WASHINGTON TO GENERAL LEE.

"Head-Quarters, English Town, 30 June, 1778.

"Sir,

"I received your letter (dated through mistake the 1st of
July), expressed as I conceive in terms highly improper. I am
not conscious of having made use of any very singular expressions at the time of meeting you, as you intimate. What I recollect to have said was dictated by duty, and warranted by
the occasion. As soon as circumstances will permit, you shall
have an opportunity of justifying yourself to the army, to Congress, to America, and to the world in general, or of convincing
them that you were guilty of a breach of orders, and of misbehaviour before the enemy, on the 28th instant, in not attacking
them as you had been directed, and in making an unnecessary,
disorderly, and shameful retreat. I am, Sir, your most obedient
servant.

"George Washington."

GENERAL LEE TO GENERAL WASHINGTON.

"Camp 28 [30 ?] June, 1778.*

"Sir,

"I beg your Excellency's pardon for the inaccuracy in mis-

---

* This letter in the original is dated June 28th, which is evidently a mistake,
because that was the day of the battle; and moreover it must have been written
after the preceding one from General Washington to which it is an answer.
Hence both of General Lee's offensive letters were erroneously dated.

dating my letter. You cannot afford me greater pleasure, than in giving me the opportunity of showing to America the sufficiency of her respective servants. I trust that temporary power of office, and the tinsel dignity attending it, will not be able, by all the mists they can raise, to offuscate the bright rays of truth. In the mean time your Excellency can have no objection to my retiring from the army. I am, Sir, your most obedient humble servant.

"Charles Lee'.

GENERAL LEE TO GENERAL WASHINGTON.

"Camp, 30 June, 1778.

" Sir,

" Since I had the honour of addressing my letter by Colonel Fitzgerald to your Excellency, I have reflected on both your situation and mine, and beg leave to observe, that it will be for our mutual convenience that a court of inquiry should be immediately ordered; but I could wish that it might be a court-martial; for, if the affair is drawn into length, it may be difficult to collect the necessary evidences, and perhaps might bring on a paper war betwixt the adherents to both parties, which may occasion some disagreeable feuds on the continent; for all are not my friends, nor all your admirers. I must entreat therefore, from your love of justice, that you will immediately exhibit your charge, and that on the first halt I may be brought to a trial; and am, Sir, your most obedient humble servant.

"Charles Lee."

GENERAL WASHINGTON TO GENERAL LEE.

" Head-Quarters, English Town, 30 June, 1778.

" Sir,

" Your letter by Colonel Fitzgerald and also one of this date have been duly received. I have sent Colonel Scammell, the Adjutant-General, to put you in arrest, who will deliver you a copy of the charges on which you will be tried. I am, Sir, your most obedient servant.

"GEORGE WASHINGTON."

CHARGES AGAINST GENERAL LEE.

" *First;* Disobedience of orders in not attacking the enemy on the 28th of June, agreeably to repeated instructions.

" *Secondly;* Misbehaviour before the enemy on the same day, by making an unnecessary, disorderly, and shameful retreat.

" *Thirdly;* Disrespect to the Commander-in-chief, in two letters dated the 1st of July and the 28th of June."

The court-martial was convened on the 4th of July, consisting of one major-general, four brigadiers, and eight colonels. Lord Stirling was president. The court sat from time to time till the 12th of August, when they declared their opinion, that General Lee was guilty of all the charges, and sentenced him to be suspended from any command in the armies of the United States for the term of twelve months. The testimony of the trial was extremely full, and it exhibits a minute detail of the operations in the battle of Monmouth. Congress approved the sentence of the court-martial, by a vote of thirteen in the affirmative and seven in the negative, and ordered the *Proceedings* of the court to be published.—ED.

M.

PAGE 322.

WASHINGTON AND LEE.

The following letters and notes respecting the publications of General LEE, are taken from the 6th vol. of the "Life and Writings of Washington," edited by Mr. SPARKS:—

" General Lee's publication in Dunlap's Gazette of the 3d, and I have seen no other, puts me in a disagreeable situation.* I have neither the leisure nor inclination to enter the lists with him in a newspaper; and so far as his production points to personality, I can and do from my inmost soul despise it; but, when he has most barefacedly misrepresented facts in some places, and thrown out insinuations in others, that have not the smallest foundations in truth, not to attempt a refutation is a tacit acknowledgment of the justice of the assertions; for, though there are thousands who know how unsupported his piece is, there are yet tens of thousands that know nothing of the matter, and will be led naturally to believe, that bold and confident assertions uncontradicted must be founded in truth.

"It became a part of General Lee's plan, from the moment of his arrest, though it was an event solicited by himself, to have the world believe that he was a persecuted man, and party was at the bottom of it. But however convenient it may have been for his purposes to establish this belief, I defy him, or his most zealous partisans, to adduce a single instance in proof of it, unless bringing him to trial, at his own request, is considered in this light. I can do more; I will defy any person out of my own family, to say that I have ever mentioned his name, if it was to be avoided; and, when not, that I have not studiously declined expressing any sentiment of him or his behaviour. How far this conduct accords with his, let his own breast decide. If he conceives that I was opposed to him, because he found himself disposed to enter into a party against me; if he thought I stood in his road to preferment, and that it was therefore convenient to lessen me in the esteem of my countrymen, in order to pave the way for his own advancement, I have only to observe, that, as I never entertained any jealousy of him, so neither did I ever do more, than common civility and proper respect to his rank required, to conciliate his good opinion. His temper and plans were too versatile

---

* This was a long and elaborate article, signed by General LEE, and containing a free discussion of the affair at Monmouth, and of some points relating to his trial. Boastful and egotistic, it met with little favour from any party. It was reprinted in *Rivington's Gazette.*

and violent to attract my admiration; and that I have escaped the venom of his tongue and pen so long, is more to be wondered at than applauded; as it is a favour of which no officer, under whose immediate command he ever served, has the happiness, if happiness can thus be denominated, of boasting."

TO PRESIDENT REED.

"West Point, 29th July, 1779.

"DEAR SIR,

"I have a pleasure in acknowledging the receipt of your obliging favour of the 15th instant, and in finding by it, that the author of the *Queries Political and Military** has had no

* These *Queries* were written by General CHARLES LEE, and printed anonymously in the MARYLAND JOURNAL, a paper published by WILLIAM GODDARD, a friend of General LEE. The Queries were penned in a very malignant spirit, and were designed to injure General WASHINGTON, as far as it could be done by such an effusion of spleen and ill-temper. The following are specimens:

"Whether it is salutary or dangerous, consistent with or abhorrent from the spirit and principles of liberty and republicanism, to inculcate and encourage in the people an idea, that their welfare, safety, and glory depend on one man? Whether they really do depend on one man?

"Whether amongst the late warm, or rather loyal addresses of this city (Philadelphia) to his Excellency General WASHINGTON, there was a single mortal, one gentleman only excepted, who could possibly be acquainted with his merits?

"Whether the gentleman excepted does really think his Excellency a great man, or whether evidences could not be produced of his thinking quite the reverse?

"Whether the armies under GATES and ARNOLD, and the detachment under STARK to the northward, or that immediately under his Excellency in Pennsylvania, gave the decisive turn to the fortune of war?"

There were twenty-five queries of a similar tenor and bearing. The "gentleman" here referred to was President REED, who wrote to WASHINGTON, when he forwarded to him a copy of the Queries: "I should not have troubled you with the enclosed paper, if I did not know that you can look down with contempt on these feeble efforts of malevolence and resentment, and that I am introduced into it to bear false witness. I have addressed a piece to the printer, wherein I have made such remarks and taken such a notice of this attempt, as I thought a respect to my own character required. I have also the pleasure of assuring you, that the performance has met with the most general detestation and resentment, involving the printer and all concerned in a most disagreeable dilemma. This is so true a criterion of the sense of the public, that I cannot help congratulating you on this genuine mark of public affection."—*MS. Letter, July* 15th.

Much indignation was expressed against GODDARD when the *Queries* appeared

great cause to exult in the favourable reception of them by the public. Without a clue, I should have been at no great loss to trace the malevolent writer; but I have seen a history of the transaction, and felt a pleasure mingled with pain at the narration. To stand well in the estimation of one's country is a happiness that no rational creature can be insensible of. To be pursued, first under the mask of friendship, and, when disguise would suit no longer, as an open calumniator, with gross misrepresentation and *self-known* falsehoods, carries an alloy, which no mind can bear with perfect composure.

"The motives which actuated this gentleman, can better be accounted for by himself than by me. If he can produce a single instance, in which I have mentioned his name, after his trial commenced, where it was in my power to avoid it, and, when it was not, where I have done it with the smallest degree of acrimony or disrespect, I will consent that the world shall view my character in as disreputable a light, as he wishes to place it. What cause there is, then, for such a profusion of venom, as he is emitting upon all occasions, unless by an act of public duty, in bringing him to trial at his own solicitation, I have disappointed him and raised his ire; or he conceives that, in proportion as he can darken the shades of my character, he illuminates his own; whether these, I say, or motives still more hidden and dark, govern him, I shall not undertake to decide; nor have I time to inquire into them at present.

"If I had ever assumed the character of a military genius and an officer of experience; if, under these false colours, I had solicited the command I was honoured with; or if, after my appointment, I had presumptuously driven on, under the sole guidance of my own judgment and self-will, and misfortunes, the result of obstinacy and misconduct, not of necessity, had followed, I should have thought myself a proper subject

in his paper. A large number of the most respectable citizens of Baltimore withdrew their patronage from the *Maryland Journal*, publicly avowing as a reason, that they considered it subservient to the interests of the enemy. Mr. GODDARD published a recantation, in which he acknowledged, that "he had transgressed against truth, justice, and his duty as a good citizen," in giving currency to the *Queries*, and at the same time declared the author of them to be General LEE.

for the lash, not only of his, but of the pen of every other writer, and a fit object for public resentment. But when it is well known, that the command was in a manner forced upon me, that I accepted it with the utmost diffidence, from a consciousness that it required greater abilities and more experience than I possessed, to conduct a great military machine, embarrassed as I knew ours must be by a variety of complex circumstances, being as it were but little more than a mere chaos; and when nothing more was promised on my part, than has been most inviolably performed; it is rather grating to pass over in silence charges, which may impress the uninformed, though others know, that these charges have neither reason nor truth to support them, and that a plain and simple narrative of facts would defeat all his assertions, notwithstanding they are made with an effrontery, which few men do, and, for the honour of human nature, none ought to possess.

" If this gentleman is envious of my station, and thinks I stand in his way to preferment, I can assure him, in most solemn terms, that the first wish of my soul is to return to that peaceful retirement, and domestic ease and happiness, from whence I came. To this end all my labours have been directed, and for this purpose have I been more than four years a perfect slave, endeavouring under as many embarrassing circumstances as ever fell to one man's lot to encounter, and with as pure motives as ever man was influenced by, to promote the cause and service I had embarked in."—ED.

N.

PAGE 322.

MISS FRANKS AND GENERAL C. LEE.

Miss Franks, in throwing the pointed shafts of her wit, spared neither friend nor foe. At the Mischeanza, given at Philadelphia by the officers of the British army to Sir William Howe, previously to his relinquishment of command, Miss Franks appeared as one of the Princesses, in supporting whose claims to superior beauty and accomplishment, the assembled Knights were to contend at a tournament exhibited. The evacuation of the city immediately following, Miss Franks remained behind. Lieutenant-Colonel Jack Steward of Maryland, whose previous intimacy with her could alone justify the familiarity of his conduct, dressed out in a handsome suit of scarlet, taking an early occasion to pay his compliments, said to her in the true spirit of gallantry, " I have adopted your colours, my Princess, the better to secure a courteous reception—deign to smile on a true Knight." To this speech Miss Franks made no reply; but turning to the company who surrounded her, exclaimed—" How the ass glories in the lion's skin."

Nor was this the only rub experienced by the Lieutenant-Colonel. While the company were enjoying themselves in lively conversation, their mirth was interrupted by loud clamours from the street, which occasioned them to hasten to the windows, the better to ascertain the cause. High head-dresses were then the reigning fashion among the British belles. A female appeared on the street, surrounded by a crowd of idlers, ragged in her apparel, and barefoot, but adorned with a towering head-dress in the extreme of the mode. Miss Franks readily perceived the intent of this tumultuous visit; and on the Lieutenant-Colonel's observing, that the lady was equipped altogether in the English fashion, replied, " *Not altogether*, Colonel; for though the style of her head is British, her shoes and stockings are in the genuine *Continental fashion*."

During an interval of dancing, at a splendid ball given by the officers of the army, to the ladies of New York, Sir Henry Clinton, having previously engaged in conversation with Miss Franks, called out to the musicians, " Give us, 'Britons strike home.'" " The Commander-in-Chief has made a mistake," exclaimed Miss Franks, " he meant to say, Britons—*go home*."

There were very few men qualified to enter the lists with this intelligent lady—for her information was extensive, and she had wit at will. She did, however, on one occasion, meet a supe-

40

rior, and appeared bereft of her brilliancy of talent, by receiving with anger, what was only intended as a sally to excite merriment. I allude to her correspondence with General Charles Lee, whose letter is but little known, and certainly possesses a stamp of humour that renders it worthy to be preserved.

GENERAL LEE'S LETTER TO MISS FRANKS.

" MADAM,

" When an officer of the respectable rank I bear, is grossly traduced and calumniated, it is incumbent on him to clear up the affair to the world, with as little delay as possible. The spirit of defamation and calumny (I am sorry to say it) is grown to a prodigious and intolerable height on this Continent. If you had accused me of a design to procrastinate the war, or of holding treasonable correspondence with the enemy, I could have borne it : this I am used to ; and this happened to the great FABIUS MAXIMUS. If you had accused me of getting drunk, as often as I could get liquor, as two ALEXANDERS the Great have been charged with the vice, I should perhaps have sat patient under the imputation ; or even if you had given the plainest hints, that I had stolen the soldier's shirts, this I could have put up with, as the great Duke of MARLBOROUGH would have been an example : or if you had contented yourself with asserting that I was so abominable a sloven, as never to part with my shirt, until my shirt parted with me, the anecdotes of my illustrious namesake of Sweden* would have administered some comfort to me. But the calumny you have, in the fertility of your malicious wit, chosen to invent, is of so new, so unprecedented, and so hellish a kind, as would make Job himself swear like a Virginia Colonel.

" Is it possible that the celebrated Miss FRANKS,† a lady who has had every human and divine advantage, who has read, (or at least might have read) in the originals, the New and Old

* Charles XII.   † The young lady was a Jewess.

Testaments, (though I am afraid she too seldom looks even into
the translations) I say, is it possible that Miss FRANKS, with
every human and Divine advantage, who might, and ought to
have read these two good books, which (an old Welsh nurse,
whose uncle was reckoned the best preacher in Merionethshire,
assured me) enjoin charity, and denounce vengeance against
slander and evil-speaking; is it possible, I again repeat it, that
Miss FRANKS should, in the face of day, carry her malignity so
far, in the presence of three most respectable personages; (one
of the oldest religion in the world, one of the newest, for he is
a New-Light Man, and the other, most probably, of no religion
at all, as he is an English sailor) but I demand it again and
again, is it possible that Miss FRANKS should assert it, in the
presence of these respectable personages, 'that I wore green
breeches patched with leather?' To convict you, therefore, of
the falsehood of this most diabolical slander, to put you to eternal
silence, (if you are not past all grace) and to cover you with a
much larger patch of infamy than you have wantonly endeavoured to fix on my breeches, I have thought proper, by the
advice of three very grave friends, (lawyers and members of
Congress, of course excellent judges of delicate points of honour)
to send you the said breeches, and with the consciousness of
truth on my side, to submit them to the most severe inspection
and scrutiny of you, and all those who may have entered into
this wicked cabal, against my honour and reputation. I say I
dare you, and your whole junto, to your worst: turn them,
examine them inside and outside, and if you find them to be
green breeches patched with leather, and not actually legitimate
Sherry Vallies,* such as his Majesty of Poland wears, (who, let
me tell you, is a man who has made more fashions than all
your knights of the Mischeanza† put together, notwithstanding
their beauties) I repeat it, (though I am almost out of breath
with repetitions and parentheses) that if those are proved to be

---

* A kind of long breeches, reaching to the ankle, with a broad stripe of leather
on the inside of the thigh, for the conveniency of riding.

† An entertainment given to General Howe, just before his departure for Europe,
at which were introduced tilts and tournaments in honour of the ladies, of whom
Miss Franks was one.

patched green breeches, and not legitimate Sherry Vallies (which a man of the first *bon ton* might be proud of) I will submit in silence to all the scurrility which I have no doubt you and your abettors are prepared to pour out against me, in the public papers, on this important and interesting occasion. But Madam! Madam! reputation, (as ' Common Sense' very sensibly, though not very uncommonly, observes) is a very serious thing. You have already injured me in the tenderest part, and I demand satisfaction; and as you cannot be ignorant of the laws of duelling, having conversed with so many Irish officers, whose favourite topic it is, particularly in the company of ladies, I insist on the privilege of the injured party, which is to name his hour and weapons; and, as I intend it to be a very serious affair, will not admit of any seconds; as you may depend upon it, Miss FRANKS, that whatever may be your spirit on the occasion, the world shall never accuse General LEE of having turned his back upon you. In the mean time, I am yours,

C. L.

" P. S. I have communicated the affair only to my confidential friend, who has mentioned it to no more than seven members of Congress, and nineteen women, six of whom were old maids, so that there is no danger of its taking wind on my side, and I hope you will be equally guarded on your part." *Garden.*—ED.

O.

PAGE 323.

ARLINGTON HOUSE, *February,* 14, 1846.
Near Alexandria, D. C.

MY DEAR SIR,
   I send you a few sketches of Laurens. He was, indeed, the Bayard of his age, "*un chevalier, sans peur et sans reproche.*" Lieutenant-Colonel John Laurens was the son of Henry Lau-

rens, President of the Revolutionary Congress, and called Tower Henry, from the circumstance of his being confined in the Tower, (of which Earl Cornwallis was constable,) at the time that his gallant son, Lieutenant-Colonel Laurens, was negotiating at York Town, for the surrender of said constable, and his whole army. Colonel Laurens was educated in England, as were most of the young Carolinians of fortune and family in the olden time, and had married a Miss Manning, the daughter of the Lieutenant Governor of the Bank of England, when the troubles between the Mother Country, and the Colonies, commenced. Knowing the ardour of young Laurens in the cause of liberty and his native land, his English friends and connexions were very desirous of preventing his return to America, well knowing the part that he would take in the approaching contest. His father-in-law offered him a check for 10,000 guineas, if he would give his word of honour, not to leave the British shores. Laurens rejected the offer with disdain, and though closely watched, succeeded in concealing himself among the ballast of a ship bound to America, and safely reached his native land.

He immediatey took a decided and zealous part in behalf of his country, and though a very young soldier, soon acquired such distinction, that in the campaign of 1777, he was attached to the military family of the Commander-in-chief as Aid-de-camp, with the rank of Lieutenant-Colonel. Associated with Hamilton, the two youthful brothers in arms, and Aids-de-camp, were considered as the very elite of the Head Quarters. In the campaigns of 1777 and 1778, Laurens greatly distinguished himself. At the battle of Germantown, he rushed up to the door of Chew's House, which he forced partly open, and fighting with his sword with one hand, with the other he applied to the wood work a flaming brand, and what is very remarkable, retired from under the tremendous fire of the house, with but a very slight wound. At the battle of Monmouth, Laurens was again in the very thickest of the fight. Leading repeated charges on the enemy, rallying the broken, and every where displaying that chivalric courage, that extorted admiration from all, even from his enemies.

In 1781, he was sent on a special mission to France, to expe-

40*

dite the aid in money, stores, naval and military forces which
had been delayed, till the cause of American Independence began
to suffer grievously. Laurens, upon his arrival in France, proceeded directly in the object of his mission. He would not
listen to the arguments, apologies, &c., of ministers and courtiers; his demand was, " Show me the King," and would only,
in full court at Versailles, consent to deliver his despatches into
the king's own hand. His promptness, energy, and lofty bearing, brought the French court and ministry to their senses, his
demands were complied with, and Laurens sailed in triumph on
his return to America, laden with those essential aids that soon
after brought the War of the Revolution to a happy and glorious
end. The assistance obtained by the genius and force of character of Colonel Laurens, moved the armies to York Town, and
to the consummation of the contest. At York Town, Colonel
Laurens again assumed his station, as Aid-de-camp to the Commander-in-chief.

The 14th of October, 1781, when his beloved associate and
brother in arms, Hamilton, was about to lead the assault on the
redoubts, Laurens obtained a command of about eighty men, and
in the very height of the storming, the Lieutenant-Colonel was
seen gallantly leading his men, and the flank of the American
troops and leaping into the enemy's works, he made Major
Campbell, the British commanding officer, a prisoner with his
own hand. In 1782, Colonel Laurens had the command of a
body of troops in his native State, and while operating on the
Combahee, he encountered a British force sent out from Charleston. Laurens was at a lady's house, ill from fever, when informed that the enemy were approaching. He sprung from his
bed, and prepared for the combat, though scarcely able to sit on
his horse. As he moved from the house, he told the lady that
if she would look out from her portico, she would see a battle—
poor fellow it was his last. As the British troops landed from
their barges a spirited attack ensued, and Laurens was mortally
wounded at nearly the first fire. As he fell into the arms of Captain Beall, the Captain endeavoured to console him by expressing a hope that the wound would not prove mortal. Laurens
replied: " No, no my dear fellow, this is as it should be. I die

but you know I have often wished to die in battle; my country is free, and no longer needs my services. Farewell. I die content."

Such was the admiration felt for the personal character of Laurens in the British army, that Major B. who commanded the British detachment, on his return home after the war, was actually "sent to Coventry" by his brother officers, who said, "How could you kill that noble fellow, Colonel Laurens, and the war so nearly at an end," to which B. in justification, replied: "I went up the river rather on a trading, than a fighting expedition. We wanted bread, and proposed to give clothes and groceries in exchange, but to all our overtures, Laurens sternly answered: 'Blood for bread, with the enemies of my country. He attacked us on our landing, and I regret his fall, gentlemen, as much as you do."

Colonel Laurens lies buried in the garden of the house from which he marched to his last battle. The ancients would have erected an altar to "such a Roman;" the Americans are content that the rank grass should alone wave over the ashes of Him who was the pride of their chivalry. The purest of Patriots. The bravest of the brave of warriors. The most energetic and successful of diplomatists. "Do you remember Laurens?" said the author to the venerable General Philip Stuart, "who led the forlorn hope of Colonel William Washington's horse at the battle of Eutaws, and was desperately wounded." The gallant veteran replied, "After the action, our Hospital was in the most wretched state imaginable; the wounded were dressed with a kind of coarse osnaburgs, that rather irritated and increased, than assuaged the anguish of our wounds. At this time Laurens arrived. On beholding our destitute and suffering condition, he called to his servant, 'open my portmanteau, sir, take out the dozen cambric ruffled shirts that I brought from France, tear them up into bandages for the gentlemen's wounds.' It was done. Now, my dear sir," continued the maimed soldier of the Revolution, "you may well suppose that *I remember Laurens*."

I send you, my dear sir, these few sketches of the Life and Character of Colonel Laurens, from *The Recollections*. It is part of the plan of that work, to introduce brief Memoirs of those whom WASHINGTON loved, who were attached to his person, or employed by him in important services, during the War of Independence. I remain, dear sir,

Your obedient and

humble servant,

GEORGE W. P. CUSTIS.

JOHN S. LITTELL, ESQ.

P. S. The author of the "Recollections," knowing that La Fayette was the associate of Hamilton and Laurens, at the Head Quarters, in 1777, asked the good General as to the respective degrees of attachment felt toward the Chief, by the distinguished young Aids-de-camp. La Fayette replied: "The attachment of Hamilton was pure, generous, enthusiastic; that of Laurens—*devotional.*"

———

P.

Page 336.

CHARLES JAMES FOX.

The Philadelphia edition, published in 1846, of "CONTRIBUTIONS TO THE EDINBURGH REVIEW BY FRANCIS JEFFREY;"—a compilation that will find its way into every respectable library, contains an exceedingly able Review of Mr. Fox's "History of the early part of the Reign of James the Second." The glaring faults and the manly virtues,—no less than the transcendent genius and abilities of this illustrious statesman, have alike, arrested the attention of mankind; and Lord Jeffrey, within two years of his decease, and with the full development of his striking character, fresh before the world, has sketched it—its light and shade—with a master's hand; and while drawing

"His frailties from their dread abode,"

has done noble justice to a name that will ever adorn the period of England's annals, most illustrious for the number, talent and achievements of its statesmen, literati and heroes.

"To those," he says, "who know Mr. Fox only by the great outlines of his public history,—who know merely that he passed from the dissipations of too gay a youth, into the tumults and cabals of a political life,—and that his days were spent in contending about public measures, and in guiding or averting the tempests of faction,—the spirit of indulgent and tender feeling which pervades this book, must appear unaccountable. Those who live much in the world, even in a private station, commonly have their hearts a little hardened, and their moral sensibility a little impaired. But, statesmen and practical politicians, are, with justice, suspected of a still greater forgetfulness of mild impressions, and honourable scruples. Coming necessarily into contact with great vices and great sufferings, they must gradually lose some of their horror for the first, and much of their compassion for the last. Constantly engaged in contention, they cease pretty generally, to regard any human beings as objects of sympathy or disinterested attachment; and, mixing much with the most corrupt part of mankind, naturally come to regard the species itself with indifference, if not with contempt. All the softer feelings are apt to be worn off, in the rough conflicts of factious hostility; and all the finer moralities to be effaced, by the constant contemplation of expediency, and the necessities of occasional compliance.

"Such is the common conception which we form of men, who, have lived the life of Mr. Fox; and such, in spite of the testimony of partial friends, is the impression which most private persons would have retained of him, if this volume had not come to convey a truer, and a more engaging picture to the world at large, and to posterity.

" By far the most remarkable thing, then, in this book, is the tone of indulgence and unfeigned philanthrophy which prevails in every part of it;—a most amiable sensibility to all the kind and domestic affections, and a sort of soft-heartedness towards the sufferings of individuals, which seem hitherto to have been thought incompatible, with the stern dignity of history. It cannot but strike us with something still more pleasing than surprise, to meet with traits of almost feminine tenderness, in the sentiments of this veteran statesman; and a general character of charity towards all men, not only remote from the rancour of vulgar hostility, but purified in a great degree from the asperities of party contention. He expresses indeed, throughout, a high-minded contempt for what is base, and a thorough detestation for what is cruel: But yet is constantly led, by a sort of generous prejudice in favour of human nature, to admit all possible palliations for the conduct of the individual delinquent, and never attempts to shut him out from the benefit of those natural sympathies, of which, the bad as well as the good are occasionally the objects, from their fortune or situation. He has given a new character, we think, to history, by this soft and condescending concern for the feelings of individuals; and not only left a splendid record of the gentleness and affectionate simplicity of his own dispositions, but set an example, by which we hope that men of genius may be taught hereafter, to render their instructions more engaging and impressive. Nothing, we are persuaded, can be more gratifying to his friends, than the impression of his character, which this work will carry down to posterity; nor is it a matter of indifference to the country, that its most illustrious statesman should be yet more distinguished, for the amiableness of his private affections."—ED.

Q.

Page 375.

WASHINGTON AT HARRISBURGH.

[From the Oracle of Dauphin, of Monday, 6th October, 1794.]

" On Friday last, the President of the United States, arrived in this town. The pleasure excited in beholding, for the first time, our beloved chief, in this borough, is not easily described. The following address was delivered to him, by the burgesses, in behalf of the inhabitants of the town :—

" To his Excellency GEORGE WASHINGTON, Esquire, President of the United States of America :

" Sir, While we, the Burgesses and Citizens of Harrisburgh, rejoice in the opportunity of presenting our respects, to a character so justly revered and dear to Americans, we cannot but lament, that we should owe it to an interruption of the peace and prosperity of our country, those constant objects of your public cares. We trust, however, that the just indignation which fires the breasts of all virtuous citizens, at the unprovoked outrages committed by those lawless men, who are in opposition to one of the mildest and most equal governments, of which the condition of man is susceptible, will excite such exertions, as to crush the spirit of disaffection wherever it has appeared; and that our political horizon will shine brighter than ever, on a dispersion of the clouds, which now menace and obscure it.

" Though our sphere of action is too limited to produce any important effects, yet we beg leave to assure your Excellency, that, so far as it extends, our best endeavours shall not be wanting to support the happy constitution, and wise administration of our government.

" Signed in behalf of the Borough.

CONRAD BOMBACH, } Burgesses.
ALEXANDER BERRYHILL. }

" Harrisburgh, October 3d, 1794."

To which the President was pleased to return the following answer :—

" *To the Burgesses, and other Citizens of Harrisburgh:*

" Gentlemen—In declaring to you, the genuine satisfaction I derive from your very cordial address, I will not mingle any expression of the painful sensations, which I experience from the occasion that has drawn me hither. You will be at no loss to do justice to my feelings. But, relying on that kindness of Providence towards our country, which every adverse appearance hitherto has served to manifest; and counting upon the tried good sense, and patriotism of the great body of our fellow-citizens, I do not hesitate to indulge with you, the expectation of such an issue, as will serve to confirm the blessings we enjoy, under a constitution, that well deserves the confidence, attachment, and support of virtuous and enlightened men.

"To class the inhabitants of Harrisburgh among this number, is only to bear testimony to the zealous and efficient exertions, which they have made, towards the defence of the laws."

" Go: WASHINGTON."

"October 4th, 1794."

R.

Page 395.

PRESIDENT ADAMS.

The address of the inhabitants of the Borough of Harrisburgh, in the State of Pennsylvania, to the President of the United States:*

"Sir, at a time when the minds of men are so intoxicated with ideas of reform, and visionary schemes for meliorating the condition of humanity, as to be fatally inattentive to their own security, and regardless of considerations, which have hitherto been deemed the most sacred and obligatory, there may be propriety in the declaration of sentiments, which, in more settled times, might, at least, be thought superfluous. From the generality also of the practice of expressing approbation of the measures of government at the present crisis, motives might be attached to the omission of it, less honourable than a disinclination to intrude upon the managers of the public concerns, or a reluctance to suppose that, in the resistance of outrage and maintenance of national independence, they would not receive the support of the virtuous part of the community.

"Under these impressions, we, the subscribers, inhabitants of the Borough of Harrisburgh, beg leave to declare that we are too highly sensible of the prosperity we enjoy, to be willing to

---

* By ALEXANDER GRAYDON, Esq.—ED.

relinquish it without an effort for its preservation; and that, in our wishes for the happiness of others, we have not lost sight of our country and ourselves.—That in our opinion, the conduct and designs of the French Republic (scarcely aggravated or made more apparent by the profligacy of their avowal), are such as produce alarm and indignation, in every breast that feels for the honour and happiness of America, and to excite the apprehensions of every man, of whatever nation or country, who may place a sense of justice, morality and piety, among the ornaments of his nature and the blessings of society. That under this persuasion, we hold it wise to be prepared for every event, and shall, therefore, most cheerfully acquiesce in such measures of defence, as may be adopted by you, sir, and the other branches of the administration, at the present most momentous period. And as your past conduct has invariably commanded the respect and approbation of every ingenious mind, so we have the most perfect reliance that, in future, it will continue to be influenced by the purest motives, and clearest perceptions of the public good. We beg you to accept our cordial wishes for your personal welfare and happiness."

MR. ADAMS'S ANSWER.

" To the inhabitants of the Borough of Harrisburgh in the State of Pennsylvania:—

" Gentlemen—Your address has been presented to me by Mr. Hartley, Mr. Sitgreaves, and Mr. Hanna, three of your representatives in Congress.

" I know not which to admire most, the conciseness, the energy, the elegance or profound wisdom of this excellent address.

" Ideas of reformation, and schemes for meliorating the condition of humanity, should not be discouraged when proposed with reason, and pursued with moderation; but the rage for innovation, which destroys every thing because it is established, and introduces absurdities the most monstrous, merely, because they are new, was never carried to such a pitch of madness in any age of the world, as in the latter end of the boasted

41

eighteenth century, and never produced effects so horrible upon suffering humanity.

"Among all the appearances, portentous of evil, there is none more incomprehensible than the professions of republicanism, among those who place not a sense of justice, morality, or piety among the ornaments of their nature and the blessings of society. As nothing is more certain or demonstrable, than that free republicanism cannot exist without these ornaments and blessings, the tendency of the times is rapid towards a restoration of the petty military despotisms of the feudal anarchy, and by their means a return to the savage state of barbarous life.

"How can the press prevent this, when all the presses of a nation, and indeed of many nations at once, are subject to an *imprimatur*, by a veto upon pain of conflagration, banishment, or confiscation.

"That America may have the glory of arresting this torrent of error, vice, and imposture, is my fervent wish; and if sentiments as great as those from Harrisburgh, should be found universally to prevail, as I doubt not they will, my hopes will be as sanguine as my wishes."

"JOHN ADAMS."

"Philadelphia, 12th May, 1798."

COMMENTS BY MR. GRAYDON.

A comparison of this answer of Mr. Adams, with the preceding one of General WASHINGTON, tends to illustrate the different characters of the men. In the one, we find every sentiment restrained by the most prudent and judicious circumspection; it says no more "than just the thing it ought."—But, in that of President Adams, the address seems to have been seized on as a text, for a very bold and excursive commentary, in which have been indulged some flights of fancy, and a prophetic dictum, which, however it might be warranted by appearances at the time, has not yet been fulfilled, nor is likely to be. As to the admonitions scattered through the answers, generally to the numerous addresses presented, considering the temper of the time, and authority of Mr. Adams's character in point of political wisdom and sagacity, they are rather laudable than censurable; though in minds not duly impressed with the awfulness of the crisis, they might be liable to the imputation of a party spirit, not quite becoming in a chief magistrate. But, what is truly wonderful and deplorable, is, that the man who could utter such sentiments in the year 1798, should, in a very short time after, have fallen into the democratic ranks, and have advocated the pretensions of France, a war with England,—and in short, all the measures of that portion of the people, whose views and policy he had so poignantly reprobated.

     *   *   *   *   *   *

Whatever evasions may be employed to apologize for this change, as that the danger of democratic anarchy was removed, and the petty despotisms apprehended, were swallowed up in the grand, overwhelming empire of NAPOLEON, the character of revolutionary France, in some of its most menacing aspects, was the same. The same *imprimatur* on all the presses of one nation, and indeed of more nations than were subject to it in 1798, remained, the same torrent of vice and imposture, for the same flagitious purposes of arbitrary rule, and extended dominion. The same efforts, but with more alarming efficiency, were in operation for dangerous innovations, for Gallic predominance, and the flood of immorality inseparable from it. Yet lamentable to be reflected on, the patriotism of Mr. Adams, " with all these appearances portentous of evil," did ebb from the full tide of federalism, to the dead low water mark of democracy and jacobinism.

But Mr. Adams seems, unfortunately, to have exclusively chosen public life for his profession, as well as that of his sons. What then was to be done? Democracy was in the ascendant, and to be statesmen out of place, was as abhorrent to the genius of thrift, as to be lawyers without litigation, carpenters without houses to build, or shoemakers without leather. In this untoward predicament, the eldest son boldly determines " not to deliberate, but to act," and is rewarded accordingly. And the old gentleman, either for his own good, or of the rest of his family, seems equally bent on a course of activity. Well did General

Hamilton seem to comprehend his character, when he states him as capable, through the vexation of wounded vanity, of directly changing his political course. In the clashings of his cabinet, the federalists seemed to prefer the opinions of General Hamilton, to his own. Hence, he renounces at once both the party and the creed, and he takes himself to those of the jacobins, thus rendering himself a memorable example of the truth of Solon's aphorism,—that "no man can be pronounced happy, until he dies,—none secure from degeneracy until death has put its seal on his character."

S.

PAGE 403.

THOMAS JEFFERSON.

HIS ELECTION TO THE PRESIDENCY BY THE HOUSE OF REPRESENTATIVES.

"On the 11th of February the ballots were opened. During the performance of this ceremony, a most extraordinary incident occurred. As it is known to but few now living, and never been publicly spoken of, it has been deemed proper to record it here, as a part of the history of that exciting contest.

"The Aurora of the 16th of February, 1801, remarks, that 'the tellers declared that there was some informality in the votes of Georgia; but, believing them to be true votes, reported them as such.' No explanation of the nature of this informality was given; nor is it known that any has ever been given since. Had it been announced at the time, there can be no doubt it would have proved fatal to the election of Mr. Jefferson. Whether the interest of our country would or would not have been thereby promoted, is not a question for discussion here.

"By the Constitution of the United States at that time it was provided, art. 2, sect. 1, 'The electors shall meet in their respective States, and vote by ballot for two persons, of whom one at least shall not be an inhabitant of the same state with themselves. And they shall make a list of all the persons voted for, and of the number of votes for each, *which list they shall sign and certify*, and transmit, sealed, to the seat of Government of the United States, directed to the President of the Senate. The President of the Senate shall, in the presence of the Senate and House of Representatives open *all the certificates*, and the votes shall then be counted. The person having the greatest number of votes shall be the President, if such number be *a majority of the whole number of electors appointed*; and if there be more than one who have such majority, and have an equal number of votes, then the House of Representatives shall immediately choose, by ballot, one of them for President; and if no person have a majority, then from the *five highest* on the list the said House shall, in like manner, choose the President. But, in choosing the President, the votes shall be taken by States, and a majority of all the States shall be necessary to a choice.'

" From the above extract it will be seen that the Constitution is imperative as to the *form* and *manner* in which the electoral returns are to be made. The ceremony of opening was performed in the presence of the two Houses. The package of a State having been opened by the Vice-President, it was handed by him to the tellers. Mr. Jefferson was the presiding officer. On opening the package endorsed Georgia votes, it was discovered to be totally irregular. The statement now about to be given, is derived from an honourable gentleman, a member of Congress from the State of New York, during the administration of Mr. Jefferson, and yet living (1837) in this State. He says that Mr. Wells (a teller on the part of the Senate) informed him that the envelope was blank; that the return of the votes was not authenticated by the *signatures of the electors, or any of them, either on the outside or the inside of the envelope, or in any other manner;* that it merely stated in the inside that the votes of Georgia were, for Thomas Jefferson *four*, and for

41*

Aaron Burr *four*, without the *signature of any person* whatso-
ever.   Mr. Wells added, that he was very undecided as to the
proper course to be pursued by the tellers.   It was, however,
suggested by one of them that the paper should be handed to
the presiding officer, without any statement from the tellers,
except that the return was informal; that he consented to this
arrangement under the firm conviction that Mr. Jefferson would
announce the nature of the informality from the Chair; but, to
his utmost surprise, he (Mr. Jefferson) rapidly declared that the
votes of Georgia were *four* for Thomas Jefferson, and *four* for
Aaron Burr, without noticing their informality, and in a hurried
manner put them aside, and then broke the seals and handed to
the tellers the package from the next state.   Mr. Wells observed, that as soon as Mr. Jefferson looked at the paper purporting to contain a statement of the electoral vote of the State
of Georgia, his countenance changed, but that the decision and
promptitude with which he acted on that occasion, convinced
him of that which he (a Federalist,) and his party had always
doubted, that is to say, Mr. Jefferson's decision of character, at
least when his own interest was at hazard.   Mr. Wells further
stated, that if the votes of Georgia had not been thus counted,
as it would have brought all the candidates into the house, Mr.
Pinckney among the number, Mr. Jefferson could not have
been elected President.

  " The same honourable member of Congress further stated,
that some few years after receiving the above information from
Mr. Wells, he became intimately acquainted with JOHN NICHO-
LAS, who was one of the tellers referred to, and who had removed from Virginia, into the western part of the State of New
York.   Mr. Nicholas gave to the honourable member the same
statement in substance, not knowing that it had been previously
derived from Mr. Wells.   Mr. Nicholas was a warm personal
friend of Mr. Jefferson, and declared that he never felt so
astounded in his life, as when he discovered the irregularity.
He claimed some credit for the adroit manner in which he had
managed Mr. Rutledge, so far as to obtain his consent to hand
the paper to Mr. Jefferson without public explanation from the

tellers, and which was effected by a conciliatory appeal to the magnanimity of the member from South Carolina.

"The whole number of electoral votes given at the election in 1800, was *one hundred and thirty-eight :* necessary to a choice, *seventy.* Mr. Jefferson and Mr. Burr had each, according to the return made, *seventy-three.* Georgia gave *four* votes. If that number had been deducted from Jefferson and Burr, as illegally returned, of which there is no doubt, they would have had only *sixty-nine* votes each; consequently they would not have had, in the language of the Constitution, ' a majority of the whole number of electors appointed,' and the candidates out of which a choice of President must be made, would have been Mr. Jefferson, Mr. Burr, Mr. Adams, Mr. Pinckney. The Federal members would then have said to the Republicans, we will unite with you in the choice of either of the gentlemen presented to the House except Mr. Jefferson; and if the Government is to be brought to a termination by our failure to elect a President, the responsibility will be on you. And is it to be believed, that in such a case the *doubtful* members who were sighing for office, if any such there were, would have rejected the suggestion in toto?"—Davis' LIFE OF BURR, vol. ii. pp. 71–74.—ED.

INDEX.

THE END.